Using the C++ Standard Template Libraries

Ivor Horton

Apress®

Using the C++ Standard Template Libraries

ISBN-13 (pbk): 978-1-4842-0005-6

ISBN-13 (electronic): 978-1-4842-0004-9

Managing Director: Welmoed Spahr
Lead Editor: Steve Anglin
Technical Reviewer: Marc Gregoire
Editorial Board: Steve Anglin, Mark Beckner, Ewan Buckingham, Gary Cornell, Louise Corrigan, Morgan Ertel, Jonathan Gennick, Jonathan Hassell, Robert Hutchinson, Michelle Lowman, James Markham, Matthew Moodie, Jeff Olson, Jeffrey Pepper, Douglas Pundick, Ben Renow-Clarke, Dominic Shakeshaft, Gwenan Spearing, Matt Wade, Tom Welsh
Coordinating Editor: Mark Powers
Copy Editor: Karen Jameson
Compositor: SPi Global
Indexer: SPi Global
Artist: SPi Global
Cover Designer: Anna Ishchenko

Distributed to the book trade worldwide by Springer Science+Business Media New York, 233 Spring Street, 6th Floor, New York, NY 10013. Phone 1-800-SPRINGER, fax (201) 348-4505, e-mail orders-ny@springer-sbm.com, or visit www.springeronline.com. Apress Media, LLC is a California LLC and the sole member (owner) is Springer Science + Business Media Finance Inc (SSBM Finance Inc). SSBM Finance Inc is a Delaware corporation.

For information on translations, please e-mail rights@apress.com, or visit www.apress.com.

Apress and friends of ED books may be purchased in bulk for academic, corporate, or promotional use. eBook versions and licenses are also available for most titles. For more information, reference our Special Bulk Sales–eBook Licensing web page at www.apress.com/bulk-sales.

Any source code or other supplementary materials referenced by the author in this text is available to readers at www.apress.com. For detailed information about how to locate your book's source code, go to www.apress.com/source-code/.

This book is for my dear wife, Eve.

Contents at a Glance

Contents

About the Author

Ivor Horton graduated as a mathematician and was lured into information technology with promises of great rewards for very little work. In spite of the reality being a great deal of work for relatively modest rewards, he has continued to work with computers to the present day. He has been engaged at various times in programming, systems design, consultancy, and the management and implementation of projects of considerable complexity.

Ivor has many years of experience in designing and implementing systems for engineering design and manufacturing control. He has developed occasionally useful applications in a wide variety of programming languages, and has taught primarily scientists and engineers to do likewise. His currently published works include tutorials on C, C++, and Java. At the present time, when he is not writing programming books or providing advice to others, he spends his time fishing, traveling, and enjoying life in general.

About the Technical Reviewer

Marc Gregoire is a software engineer from Belgium. He graduated from the Catholic University of Leuven, Belgium, with a degree in "Burgerlijk ingenieur in de computer wetenschappen" (equivalent to master of science in engineering in computer science). The year after, he received the cum laude degree of master in artificial intelligence at the same university. After his studies, Marc started working for a software consultancy company called Ordina Belgium. As a consultant, he worked for Siemens and Nokia Siemens Networks on critical 2G and 3G software running on Solaris for telecom operators. This required working in international teams spanning from South America and the United States to Europe, the Middle East, Africa, and Asia. Now, Marc is working for Nikon Metrology on 3D laser scanning software.

His main expertise is C/C++, specifically Microsoft VC++ and the MFC framework. Next to C/C++, Marc also likes C# and uses PHP for creating web pages. In addition to his main interest of Windows development, he also has experience in developing C++ programs running 24/7 on Linux platforms (e.g., EIB home automation software).

Since April 2007, he has received the yearly Microsoft MVP (Most Valuable Professional) award for his Visual C++ expertise.

Marc is the founder of the Belgian C++ Users Group (`www.becpp.org`) and an active member on the CodeGuru forum (as Marc G). He also creates freeware and shareware programs that are distributed through his web site at `www.nuonsoft.com`, and maintains a blog on `www.nuonsoft.com/blog/`.

Acknowledgments

I'd like to thank Mark Powers and the rest of the Apress editorial and production teams for their help and support throughout. I would especially like to thank Marc Gregoire for his usual outstanding technical review. His many comments and suggestions have undoubtedly made the book much better that it otherwise would be.

Introduction

Welcome to *Using the C++ Standard Template Libraries*. This book is a tutorial on the class and function templates that are contained within a subset of the header files that make up the C++ Standard Library. These are generic programming tools that offer vast capability, are easy to use, and make many things simple to implement that would otherwise be difficult. The code they generate is usually more efficient and reliable than you could write yourself.

I'm usually unhappy with explanations of just what things *do*, without an elaboration of what things are *for*. It's often difficult to guess the latter from the former. My approach therefore, is not just to explain the functionality of the class and function templates, but as far as possible to show how you apply them in a practical context. This leads to some sizeable chunks of code at some points, but I believe you'll think that it's worth it.

The collection of header files from the C++ Standard Library that are the subject of this book have often been referred to in the past as the *Standard Template Library* or simply the *STL*. I'll use "the STL" in the book as a convenient shorthand to mean the set of headers containing templates that I discuss in the book. Of course, there's really no such thing as the STL - the C++ Language Standard doesn't mention it so formally it doesn't exist. In spite of the fact that it is undefined, most C++ programmers know roughly what is meant by the STL. It's been around in various guises for a long time.

The idea of generic programming that is embodied in the STL originated with Alexander Stepanov back in 1979 - long before there was a standard for the C++ language. The first implementation of the STL for C++ was originated by Stepanov and others around 1989 working at Hewlett Packard, and this STL implementation was complementary to the libraries that were provided with C++ compilers at that time. The capability offered by the STL was first considered for incorporation into the first proposed C++ language standard in the early 1990s, and the essentials of the STL made it into the first language standard for C++ that was published in 1998. Since then the generic programming facilities that the STL represents have been improved and extended, and templates are to be found in many header files that are not part of what could be called the STL. All the material in the book relates to the most recently approved language standard at the time of writing, which is C++ 14.

The STL is not a precise concept and this book doesn't cover all the templates in the C++ Standard Library. Overall, the book describes and demonstrates the templates from the Standard Library that I think should be a first choice for C++ programmers to understand, especially those who are relatively new to C++. The primary Standard Library header files that are discussed in depth include:

For data containers:	`<array>`, `<vector>`, `<deque>`, `<stack>`, `<queue>`, `<list>`, `<forward_list>`, `<set>`, `<unordered_set>`, `<map>`, `<unordered_map>`
For iterators:	`<iterator>`
For algorithms:	`<algorithm>`
For random numbers and statistics:	`<random>`
For processing numerical data:	`<valarray>`, `<numeric>`
For time and timing:	`<ratio>`, `<chrono>`
For complex numbers:	`<complex>`

Templates from other headers such as <pair>, <tuple>, <functional>, and <memory> also get dragged in to the book at various points. The templates for *data containers* are fundamental; these will be useful in the majority of applications. Iterators are a basic tool for working with containers so they are included also. *Algorithms* are function templates that operate on data stored in containers. These are powerful tools that you can also apply to arrays and they are described and illustrated with working examples. I have included a chapter that explains the templates that relate to random number generation and statistics. While some of these are quite specialized, many are widely applicable in simulations, modeling, and games programs. The templates for compute-intensive numerical data processing are discussed, and those relating to time and timing. Finally, there's a brief introduction to the class templates for working with complex numbers.

Prerequisites for Using the Book

To understand the contents of this book you need to have a basic working knowledge of the C++ language. This book complements my *Beginning* C++ book, so if you have worked through that successfully, you're in good shape to tackle this. A basic understanding of what class templates and function templates are, and how they work is essential, and I have included an overview of the basics of these in Chapter 1. If you are not used to using templates, the syntax can give the impression that they are lot more complicated than they really are. Once you get used to the notation, you'll find them relatively easy to work with. Lambda expressions are also used frequently with the STL so you need to be comfortable with those too.

You'll need a C++ 14-compliant compiler and of course a text editor suitable for working with program code. There has been quite a renaissance in C++ compiler development in recent years, and there are several excellent compilers out there that are largely in conformance with C++ 14, in spite of it being a recently approved standard. There are at least three available that you can use without charge:

- GCC is the GNU compiler collection that supports C++, C, and Fortran as well as other languages. GCC supports all the C++ 14 features used in this book. You can download GCC from gcc.gnu.org. The GCC compiler collection works with GNU and Linux, but there's a version for Microsoft Windows that you can download from www.mingw.org.

- The *ideaone* online compiler supports C++ 14 and is accessible through *ideaone.com*. The compiler it uses for C++ 14 is GCC 5.1 at the time of writing. *ideaone.com* also supports a wide range of other programming languages, including C, Fortran, and Java.

- The *Microsoft Visual Studio 2015 Community Edition* runs under the Microsoft Windows operating system. It supports C++ as well as several other programming languages and comes with a complete development environment.

Using the Book

For the most part, I have organized the material in this book to be read sequentially, so the best way to use the book is to start at the beginning and keep going until you reach the end. Generally, I try not to use capabilities before I have explained them. Once I have explained something, I plug it in to subsequent material whenever it makes sense to do so, which is why I recommend going through the chapters sequentially. There are a few topics that require some understanding of the underlying mathematics, and I have included the maths in these instances. If you are not comfortable with the maths, you can skip these without limiting your ability to understand what follows.

No one ever learned programming by just reading a book. You'll only learn how to use the STL by writing code. I strongly recommend that you key in all the examples – don't just copy them from the download files – and compile and execute the code that you've keyed in. This might seem tedious at times, but it's surprising how much just typing in program statements will help your understanding, especially when you may feel you're struggling with some of the ideas. It will help you remember stuff, too. If an example doesn't work, resist the temptation to go straight back to the book to see why. Try to figure out from your code what is wrong.

Throughout the chapters there are code fragments that are executable for the most part if the appropriate header files are included. Generally you can execute them and get some output if you put them in the main( ) function. I suggest you set up a program project for this purpose. You can copy the code into an empty definition for main( ) and just add further #include directives for the header files that are required as you go along. You'll need to delete previous code fragments most of the time to prevent name conflicts.

Making your own mistakes is a fundamental part of the learning process and the exercises should provide you with ample opportunity for that. The more mistakes that you make and that you are able to find and fix, the greater the insight you'll have into what can and does go wrong using the templates. Make sure you complete all the exercises that you can, and don't look at the solutions until you're sure that you can't work it out yourself. Many of these exercises just involve a direct application of what's covered in a chapter – they're just practice, in other words – but some also require a bit of thought or maybe even inspiration.

I wish you every success with the STL. Above all, enjoy it!

—Ivor Horton

CHAPTER 1

■ ■ ■

Introducing the Standard Template Library

This chapter explains the fundamental ideas behind the Standard Template Library (STL). This is to give you an overall grasp of how the various types of entities in the STL hang together. You'll see more in-depth examples and discussion of everything that I introduce in this chapter in the book. In this chapter you'll learn the following:

- What is in the STL

- How *templates* are defined and used

- What a *container* is

- What an *iterator* is and how it is used

- The importance of *smart pointers* and their use with containers

- What *algorithms* are and how you apply them

- What is provided by the *numerics* library

- What a *function object* is

- How *lambda expressions* are defined and used

Besides introducing the basic ideas behind the STL, this chapter provides brief reminders of some C++ language features that you need to be comfortable with because they will be used frequently in subsequent chapters. You can skip any of these sections if you are already familiar with the topic.

Basic Ideas

The STL is an extensive and powerful set of tools for organizing and processing data. These tools are all defined by *templates* so the data can be of any type that meets a few minimum requirements. I'm assuming that you are reasonably familiar with how class templates and function templates can be defined and how they are used, but I'll remind you of the essentials of these in the next section. The STL can be subdivided into four conceptual libraries:

- *The Containers Library* defines containers for storing and managing data. The templates for this library are defined within the following header files: array, vector, stack, queue, deque, list, forward_list, set, unordered_set, map, and unordered_map.

- *The Iterators Library* defines iterators, which are objects that behave like pointers and are used to reference sequences of objects in a container. The library is defined within a single header file, iterator.

- *The Algorithms Library* defines a wide range of algorithms that can be applied to a set of elements stored in a container. The templates for this library are defined in the algorithm header file.

- *The Numerics Library* defines a wide range of numerical functions, including numerical processing of sets of elements in a container. The library also includes advanced functions for random number generation. The templates for this library are defined in the headers complex, cmath, valarray, numeric, random, ratio, and cfenv. The cmath header has been around for a while, but it has been extended in the C++ 11 standard and is included here because it contains many mathematical functions.

Many complex and difficult tasks can be achieved very easily with remarkably few lines of code using the STL. For instance, without explanation, here's the code to read an arbitrary number of floating-point values from the standard input stream and calculate and output the average:

```
std::vector<double> values;
std::cout << "Enter values separated by one or more spaces. Enter Ctrl+Z to end:\n ";
values.insert(std::begin(values), std::istream_iterator<double>(std::cin),
                                   std::istream_iterator<double>());
std::cout << "The average is "
          << (std::accumulate(std::begin(values), std::end(values), 0.0)/values.size())
          << std::endl;
```

It requires only four statements! Long lines admittedly, but no loops are required; it's all taken care of by the STL. This code can be easily modified to do the same job with data from a file. Because of the power and wide applicability of the STL, it's a *must* for any C++ programmer's toolbox. All STL names are in the std namespace so I won't always qualify STL names explicitly with std in the text. Of course, in any code I will qualify names where necessary.

Templates

A *template* is a parametric specification of a set of functions or classes. The compiler can use a template to generate a specific function or class definition when necessary, which will be when you use the function template or class template type in your code. You can also define templates for parameterized type aliases. Thus a template is not executable code – it is a blueprint or recipe for creating code. A template that is never used in a program is ignored by the compiler so no code results from it. A template that is not used can contain programming errors, and the program that contains it will still compile and execute; errors in a template will not be identified until the template is used to create code that is then compiled.

A function or class definition that is generated from a template is an *instance* or an *instantiation* of the template. Template parameter values are usually data types, so a function or class definition can be generated for a parameter value of type int, for example, and another definition with a parameter value of type string. Parameter arguments are not necessarily types; a parameter specification can be an integer type that requires an integer argument. Here's an example of a very simple function template:

```
template <typename T> T& larger(T& a, T& b)
{
    return a > b ? a : b;
}
```

This is a template for functions that return the larger of the two arguments. The only limitation on the use of the template is that the type of the arguments must allow a > comparison to be executed. The type parameter T determines the specific instance of the template to be created. The compiler can deduce this from the arguments you supply when you use larger(), although you can supply it explicitly. For example:

```
std::string first {"To be or not to be"};
std::string second {"That is the question."};
std::cout << larger(first, second) << std::endl;
```

This code requires the string header to be included. The compiler will deduce the argument for T as type string. If you want to specify it, you would write larger<std::string>(first, second). You would need to specify the template type argument when the function arguments differ in type. If you wrote larger(2, 3.5), for example, the compiler cannot deduce T because it is ambiguous – it could be type int or type double. This usage will result in an error message. Writing larger<double>(2, 3.5) will fix the problem.

Here's an example of a class template:

```
template <typename T> class Array
{
private:
  T* elements;                                  // Array of type T
  size_t count;                                 // Number of array elements

public:
  explicit Array(size_t arraySize);             // Constructor
  Array(const Array& other);                    // Copy Constructor
  Array(Array&& other);                         // Move Constructor
  virtual ~Array();                             // Destructor
  T& operator[](size_t index);                  // Subscript operator
  const T& operator[](size_t index) const;      // Subscript operator-const arrays
  Array& operator=(const Array& rhs);           // Assignment operator
  Array& operator=(Array&& rhs);                // Move assignment operator
  size_t size() { return count; }               // Accessor for count
};
```

The size_t type alias is defined in the cstddef header and represents an unsigned integer type. This code defines a simple template for an array of elements of type T. Where Array appears in the template definition Array<T> is implied and you could write this if you wish. Outside the body of the template – in an external function member definition, you must write Array<T>. The assignment operator allows one Array<T> object to be assigned to another, which is something you can't do with ordinary arrays. If you wanted to inhibit this capability, you would still need to declare the operator=() function as a member of the template. If you don't, the compiler will create a public default assignment operator when necessary for a template instance. To prevent use of the assignment operator, you should specify it as deleted – like this:

```
Array& operator=(const Array& rhs)=delete;      // No assignment operator
```

In general, if you need to define any of a copy or move constructor, a copy or move assignment operator, or a destructor, you should define all five class members, or specify the ones you don't want as deleted.

■ **Note**   A class that implements a move constructor and a move assignment operator is said to have *move semantics*.

The size() member is implemented within the class template so it's inline by default and no external definition is necessary. External definitions for function members of a class template are themselves templates that you put in a header file – usually the same header file as the class template. This is true even if a function member has no dependence on the type parameter T, so size() would need a template definition if it was not defined inside the class template. The type parameter list for a template that defines a function member must be identical to that of the class template. Here's how the definition of the constructor might look:

```
template <typename T>                        // This is a function template with parameter T
Array<T>::Array(size_t arraySize) try : elements {new T[arraySize]}, count {arraySize}
{}
catch(const std::exception& e)
{
  st::cerr << "Memory allocation failure in Array constructor." << std::endl;
  rethrow e;
}
```

The memory allocation for elements could throw an exception so the constructor is a function try block. This allows the exception to be caught and responded to but the exception must be rethrown – if you don't rethrow the exception in the catch block, it will be rethrown anyway. The template type parameter is essential in the qualification of the constructor name because it ties the function template definition to the class template. Note that you *don't* use the typename keyword in the qualifier for the member name; it's only used in the template parameter list.

Of course, you can specify an external template for a function member of a class template as inline – for example, here's how the copy constructor for the Array template might be defined:

```
template <typename T>
inline Array<T>::Array(const Array& other)
try : elements {new T[other.count]}, count {other.count}
{
  for (size_t i {}; i < count; ++i)
    elements[i] = other.elements[i];
}
catch (std::bad_alloc&)
{
  std::cerr << "memory allocation failed for Array object copy." << std:: endl;
}
```

This assumes that the assignment operator works for type T. Without seeing the code for a template before you use it, you may not realize the dependency on the assignment operator. This demonstrates how important it is to *always* define the assignment operator along with the other members I mentioned earlier for classes that allocate memory dynamically.

■ **Note**   The class and typename keywords are interchangeable when specifying template parameters so you can write either template<typename T> or template<class T> when defining a template. Because T is not necessarily a class type, I prefer to use typename because I feel this is more expressive of the possibility that a template type argument can be a fundamental type as well as a class type.

The compiler instantiates a class template as a result of a definition of an object that has a type produced by the template. Here's an example:

```
Array<int> data {40};
```

An argument for each class template type parameter is always required, unless there is a default argument. When this statement is compiled, three things happen: the definition for the Array<int> class is created so that the type is identified, the constructor definition is generated because it must be called to create the object, and the destructor is created because it's needed to destroy the object. That's all the compiler needs to create and destroy the data object so this is the only code that it generates from the templates at this point. The class definition is generated by substituting int in place of T in the template definition, but there's one subtlety. The compiler *only* compiles the member functions that the program *uses*, so you don't necessarily get the entire class that would result from a simple substitution of the argument for the template parameter. On the basis of the definition for the data object, the class will be defined as:

```
class Array<int>
{
private:
  int* elements;
  size_t count;

public:
  explicit Array(size_t arraySize);
  virtual ~Array();
};
```

You can see that the only function members are the constructor and the destructor. The compiler won't create instances of anything that isn't required to create the object, and it won't include parts of the template that aren't needed in the program.

You can define templates for type aliases. This can be useful when you are working with the STL. Here's an example of a template for a type alias:

```
template<typename T> using ptr = std::shared_ptr<T>;
```

This template defines ptr<T> to be an alias for the smart pointer template type std::shared_ptr<T>. With this template in effect you can use ptr<std::string> in your code instead of std::shared_ptr<std::string>. It's clearly less verbose and easier to read. The following using directive will simplify it further:

```
using std::string;
```

Now you can use ptr<string> in your code instead of std::shared_ptr<std::string>. Templates for type aliases can make your code easier to understand and much easier to type.

The Containers

Containers are the bedrock of the STL capabilities because most of the rest of the STL relates to them. A container is an object that stores and organizes other objects in a particular way. When you use a container you'll inevitably be using *iterators* to access that data so you'll need a good understanding of those too. The STL provides several categories of container:

- *Sequence containers* store objects in a linear organization, similar to an array, but not necessarily in contiguous memory. You can access the objects in a sequence by calling a function member or through an iterator; in some cases you can also use the subscript operator with an index.

- *Associative containers* store objects together with associated keys. You retrieve an object from an associative container by supplying its associated key. You can also retrieve the objects in an associative container using an iterator.

- *Container adapters* are adapter class templates that provide alternative mechanisms for accessing data stored in an underlying sequence container, or associative container.

It's important to appreciate that unless the objects are rvalues – temporary objects – of a type that has move semantics, all the STL containers store *copies* of the objects that you store in them. The STL also requires that the move constructor and assignment operator must be specified as noexcept, which indicates they do not throw exceptions. If you add an object of a type that does not have move semantics to a container and modify the original, the original and the object in the container will be different. However, when you retrieve an object, you get a reference to the object in the container so you can modify stored objects. The copies that are stored are created using the copy constructor for the type of object. For some objects, copying can be a process that carries a lot of overhead. In this case, it will be better to either store pointers to the objects in the container, or to move objects into the container assuming that move semantics have been implemented for the type.

■ **Caution**   Don't store derived class objects in a container that stores elements of a base class type. This will cause slicing of the derived class objects. If you want to access derived class objects in a container with a view to obtaining polymorphic behavior, store pointers to the objects in a container that stores base class pointers – or better still – smart pointers to the base type.

Containers store the objects they hold on the heap and manage the space they occupy automatically. The allocation of space in a container storing objects of type T is managed by an *allocator*, and the type of the allocator is specified by a template parameter. The default type argument is std::allocator<T>, and an object of this type is an allocator that allocates heap memory for objects of type T. This provides the possibility for you to supply your own allocator. You might want to do this for performance reasons, but this is rarely necessary and most of the time the default allocator is fine. Defining an allocator is an advanced subject and

I won't be discussing it further in this book. I'll therefore omit the last template parameter for template types when it represents an allocator. The std::vector<typename T, typename Allocator> template has a default value for Allocator specified as std::allocator<T> so I'll write this as std::vector<typename T>. This explanation is just so you'll know the option to provide an allocator is there.

A type T must meet certain requirements if T objects are to be stored in a container, and these requirements ultimately depend on the operations you need to perform on the elements. A container will usually need to copy elements and may need to move and interchange elements. The bare minimum for type T objects to be stored in a container in this case looks like this:

```
class T
{
  public:
    T();                          // default constructor
    T(const T& t);                // Copy constructor
    ~T();                         // Destructor
    T& operator=(const T& t);     // Assignment operator
};
```

Considering that the compiler provides default implementations for all the members above in many circumstances, most class types should meet these requirements. Note that operator<() hasn't been included in the definition for T, but objects of a type without operator<() defined will not be usable as keys in any of the associative containers such as map and set, and the ordering algorithms such as sort() and merge() cannot be applied to sequences where the elements do not support the less-than operation.

■ **Note** If the type of your objects does not meet the requirements of a container that you are using, or you misuse the container template in some other way, you will often get compiler error messages relating to code that is deep in a Standard Library header file. When this occurs, don't rush to report errors in the Standard Library. Look for errors in your code that is using the STL!

Iterators

An *iterator* is an object of a class template type that behaves like a pointer. As long as an iterator, iter, points to a valid object you can dereference it to obtain a reference to the object by writing *iter. If iter points to a class object you can access a member, member, of the object by writing iter->member. Thus you use iterators just like pointers.

You use iterators to access the elements in a container when you are processing them in some way, and in particular when you are applying an STL algorithm. Thus iterators connect algorithms to the elements in a container regardless of the type of the container. Iterators decouple the algorithm from the data source; an algorithm has no knowledge of the container from which the data originates. Iterators are instances of template types that are defined in the iterator header, but this header is included by all of the headers that define containers.

You typically use a pair of iterators to define a *range* of elements; the elements can be objects in a container, elements in a standard array, characters in a string object, or elements in any other type of object that supports iterators. A *range* is a sequence of elements that is specified by a *begin iterator* that points to the first element in the range, and an *end iterator* that points to *one past the last* element. Even when the sequence is a subset of the elements in a container, the second iterator still points to *one past the last element* in the sequence – *not* the last element in the range. The end iterator for a range that represents all the elements in a container will not point to anything and therefore cannot be dereferenced. Iterators provide a standard mechanism for identifying a range of elements in the STL, and elsewhere. The specification of a range of elements is independent from where the elements originate so a given algorithm can be applied to a range of elements from *any* source as long as the iterators meet the requirements of the algorithm. I'll have more to say about the characteristics of different kinds of iterators later.

Once you understand how iterators work, it's easy to define your own template functions to process data sequences that are specified by iterators as arguments. Instances of your function templates can then be applied to data from any source that can be defined as a range; the code will work just as well with data from an array as it does with data from a vector container. You'll see examples of this in action later in the book.

Obtaining Iterators

You can obtain iterators from a container by calling the begin() and end() function members of the container object; these return iterators that point to the first element and one past the last element respectively. The iterator that the end() member of a container returns does not point to a valid element so you can't dereference it or increment it. The string classes such as std::string also have these function members so you can obtain iterators for these, too. You can obtain the same iterators as those returned by the begin() and end() function members of a container by calling the global functions std::begin() and std::end() with the container object as the argument; these are defined by templates in the iterator header. The global begin() and end() functions work with an ordinary array or a string object as the argument and therefore offer a uniform way of obtaining iterators.

Iterators allow you to step through the elements in a range by incrementing the begin iterator to move from one object to the next, as shown in Figure 1-1; 'container' in the figure implies a string object or an array, as well as an STL container. By comparing the incremented begin iterator with the end iterator you can determine when the last element has been reached. There are other operations you can apply to iterators, but this depends on the type of iterator, which in turn depends on the kind of container you are using. There are global cbegin() and cend() functions that return const iterators for array, containers, or string objects. Remember—a const iterator points to something that is constant and you can still modify the iterator itself. I'll introduce other global functions that return other kinds of iterators later in this section.

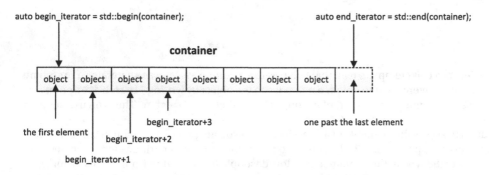

Figure 1-1. *Operation of iterators*

Iterator Categories

All iterator types must have a copy constructor, a copy assignment operator, and a destructor. The objects that an iterator point to must be *swappable*; I'll explain what this implies further in the next chapter. There are five *categories* of iterators that reflect different levels of capability. Different algorithms may require different levels of capability for the iterators that identify the range of elements they are to operate on. The categories are not new iterator template types; the category that an iterator type supports is identified by an argument value for a type parameter for the iterator template. I'll explain more about this a little later in this section.

The category of the iterators you get for a container depends on the type of the container. The categories enable an algorithm to determine the capabilities of the iterators that you pass to it. An algorithm can use the category of an iterator argument in two ways: first, it can establish that the minimum functional requirements for the operation are met; and second, if the minimum requirement for iterators is exceeded, the algorithm may use the extended capability to carry out the operation more efficiently. Of course, algorithms can only be applied to elements in containers that provide iterators with the required level of capability.

The iterator categories are as follows, ordered from the simplest to the most complex:

1. *Input iterators* have read access to objects. If iter is an input iterator, it must support the expression *iter to produce a reference to the value to which iter points. Input iterators are single use only, which means that once an iterator has been incremented, to access the previous element that it pointed to you need a new iterator. Each time you want to read a sequence, you must create a new iterator. The operations that you can apply to input iterators are: ++iter or iter++; iter1==iter2 and iter1!=iter2; and *iter Note the absence of the decrement operator. You can use the expression iter->member for input iterators.

2. *Output iterators* have write access to objects. If iter is an output iterator, it allows a new value to be assigned so *iter=new_value is supported. Output iterators are single use only. Each time you want to write a sequence, you must create a new iterator. The operations that you can apply to output iterators are: ++iter or iter++; and *iter Note the absence of the decrement operator. You only get write access with output iterators. You *cannot* use the expression iter->member for output iterators.

3. *Forward iterators* combine the capabilities of input and output iterators and add the capability to be used more than once. Therefore you can reuse a forward iterator to read or write an element as many times as necessary. The operation to be performed determines when forward iterators are required. The replace() algorithm that searches a range and replaces elements requires the capability of a forward iterator, for example, because the iterator that points to an element that is to be replaced is reused to overwrite it.

4. *Bidirectional iterators* provide the same capabilities as forward iterators but allow traversal through a sequence backward as well as forward. Therefore in addition to incrementing these iterators to move to the next element, you can apply the prefix and postfix decrement operators, --iter and iter--, to move to the previous element.

5.   *Random access iterators* provide the same capabilities as bidirectional iterators but
     also allow elements to be accessed at random. In addition to the operations permitted
     for bidirectional iterators, these support the following operations:

   •   Incrementing and decrementing by an integer: iter+n or iter-n and iter+=n
       or iter-=n

   •   Indexing by an integer: iter[n], which is equivalent to *(iter+n)

   •   The difference between two iterators: iter1-iter2, which results in an integer
       specifying the number of elements.

   •   Comparing iterators: iter1<iter2, iter1>iter2, iter1<=iter2, and
       iter1>=iter2.

     Sorting a range of elements will require the range to be specified by random
     access iterators.
     You can use the subscript operator with random access iterators. Given an iterator,
     first, the expression first[3] is equivalent to *(first+3) so it accesses the fourth
     element. In general, in the expression iter[n] with an iterator, iter, n is an offset
     and the expression returns a reference to the element at offset n from iter. Note that
     the index you use with the subscript operator applied to an iterator is not checked.
     There is nothing to prevent the use of index values outside the legal range.

Each iterator category is identified by an empty class called an *iterator tag class* that is used as a type
argument to the iterator template. The sole purpose of the iterator tag classes is to specify what a particular
iterator type can do so they are used as an iterator template type argument. The standard iterator tag
classes are:

```
input_iterator_tag
output_iterator_tag
forward_iterator_tag which is derived from input_iterator_tag
bidirectional_iterator_tag which is derived from forward_iterator_tag
random_access_iterator_tag which is derived from bidirectional_iterator_tag
```

The inheritance structure for these classes reflects the cumulative nature of the iterator categories.
When an iterator template instance is created, the first template type argument will be one of the iterator
tag classes, which will determine the capabilities of the iterator. In chapter 2 I'll explain how you can define
your own iterators and how you specify their category.

If an algorithm requires an iterator of a given category, then you can't use an inferior iterator; however
you can always use a superior iterator. The forward, bidirectional, and random access iterators can also
be *constant* or *mutable*, depending on whether dereferencing the iterator produces a reference, or a const
reference. Obviously you can't use the result of dereferencing a const iterator on the left of an assignment.

The characteristics of the iterators that you get for a container depend on the container type. For
example, vector and deque containers provide random access iterators; this reflects the fact that the
elements in these containers can be accessed randomly. On the other hand the list and map containers
always supply bidirectional iterators; these containers don't support random access to elements. Input
and output iterator and forward iterator types are typically used to specify parameters for algorithms to
reflect the minimum level of capability required by the algorithm. I'll be explaining iterators further with
working examples in the context of applying algorithms to the contents of containers later in the book – they

are much easier to understand in a practical context. In the meantime, here's a simple example showing iterators in action for an array:

```cpp
// Ex1_01.cpp
// Using iterators
#include <numeric>                         // For accumulate() - sums a range of elements
#include <iostream>                        // For standard streams
#include <iterator>                        // For iterators and begin() and end()

int main()
{
  double data[] {2.5, 4.5, 6.5, 5.5, 8.5};
  std::cout << "The array contains:\n";
  for (auto iter = std::begin(data); iter != std::end(data); ++iter)
    std::cout << *iter << " ";
  auto total = std::accumulate(std::begin(data), std::end(data), 0.0);
  std::cout << "\nThe sum of the array elements is " << total << std::endl;
}
```

You can see that the global begin() and end() functions return the iterators for the elements of the array that is the function argument. The iterators are used in the for loop that lists the element values. The expression *iter dereferences the iterator to access the value by reference. Of course you could increment iter in the for loop body, like this:

```cpp
for (auto iter = std::begin(data); iter != std::end(data);)
  std::cout << *iter++ << " ";
```

The directive to include the iterator header could be omitted because iterator is included by any header for containers and that includes the numeric header that defines the template for the accumulate() function. The accumulate() function returns the sum of the elements in the range defined by the first two arguments, which must be iterators specifying the first, and one past the last element in the range. The third argument is the initial value to be used for the sum. The accumulate() function works for any range of elements of a type that supports addition, so it also works with objects of any class type that defines operator+().

───

■ **Note**   As you'll see when we get to use accumulate() with containers, there's another version of the function template that allows you to specify a different binary operation to be applied between elements in place of the default, + .

───

Stream Iterators

You use *stream iterators* to transfer data in text mode between a stream and a source or destination that is accessible through iterators. Because the STL algorithms receive input as a range specified by a pair of iterators, you can apply algorithms to objects that are available from any source that is accessible through an input stream iterator. This means, for instance, that algorithms can be applied to objects from a stream as well as to objects from a container. Algorithms can also be applied in any other context in which you can provide an acceptable iterator; I'll explain later what makes an iterator acceptable. Equally, you can transfer a range of elements to an output stream by using an output stream iterator. Standard iterators have the iterator template type as a base class.

You create a stream iterator object that works with data of a specified type from a stream object; the type of data is the iterator template type parameter and the stream object is the constructor argument. An istream_iterator<T> is an *input iterator* that can read objects of type T from an istream, which could be a file stream or the standard input stream cin. Objects are read using the >> operator so the type of object that is to be read must support this. The no-arg constructor for istream_iterator<T> creates an end iterator object that will be matched when the end of a stream is reached. Obviously, a stream iterator is not the way to go when you want to transfer data of mixed types. By default, an istream_iterator object ignores whitespace; you can override this by applying the std::noskipws manipulator to the underlying input stream. You can only use an istream_iterator once. If you want to input objects from a stream a second time, you must create a new istream_iterator object.

An ostream_iterator complements istream_iterator in that it is an *output iterator* that provides a one-time output capability for objects to an ostream. Objects are written using the << operator. When you create an ostream_iterator object, you can optionally specify a delimiter string that is to be written following the output of each object.

Here's a working example that uses input stream iterators:

```
// Ex1_02.cpp
// Using stream iterators
#include <numeric>                          // For accumulate() - sums a range of elements
#include <iostream>                         // For standard streams
#include <iterator>                         // For istream_iterator

int main()
{
  std::cout << "Enter numeric values separated by spaces and enter Ctrl+Z to end:" << std::endl;

  std::cout << "\nThe sum of the values you entered is "
            << std::accumulate(std::istream_iterator<double>(std::cin),
               std::istream_iterator<double>(), 0.0)
            << std::endl;
}
```

This applies the accumulate() function to a range of values supplied by an input stream iterator for cin. An arbitrary number of values can be entered. The second argument is the end-of-stream iterator that will be matched by the iterator specified by the first argument when a read sets the end-of-stream condition (referred to as EOF for a file stream); entering Ctrl-Z from the keyboard will cause this.

Iterator Adaptors

Iterator adapters are class templates that provide specialized behavior for standard iterators so they are derived from the iterator template. There are three kinds of iterators that are defined by adapter class templates, *reverse iterators, insert iterators*, and *move iterators*. These are defined by the following template class types: reverse_iterator, insert_iterator, and move_iterator.

Reverse Iterators

Reverse iterators work in the opposite sense to the standard iterators. You can create reverse iterator versions of bidirectional or random access iterators. The rbegin() and rend() function members of a container return reverse iterators that point to the last element, and one before the first element respectively; the global functions with the same names do the same thing, as Figure 1-2 shows.

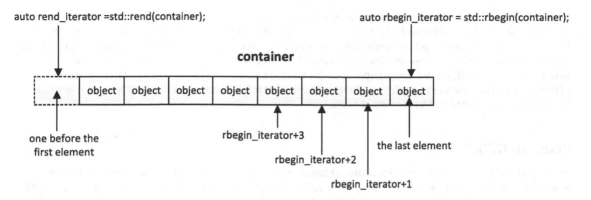

Figure 1-2. *Operations with reverse iterators*

Incrementing or decrementing a reverse iterator works in the opposite sense to standard iterators in relation to the order of the elements so incrementing a reverse begin iterator causes it to point to the preceding element – the one to the left – and decrementing it points to the next element – the one to the right. Figure 1-3 shows the increment direction for reverse iterators compared to standard iterators. The template for reverse iterator types is derived from the template for regular iterators and overloads the operator functions to implement the reversed operations. The string classes that are defined in the `string` header also make reverse iterators available so you can call the `rbegin()` member for a `string` object to get a reverse iterator pointing to the last character, and calling `rend()` for the string object will return a reverse iterator pointing to one before the first character. The global (and member) `crbegin()` and `crend()` functions return `const` reverse iterators.

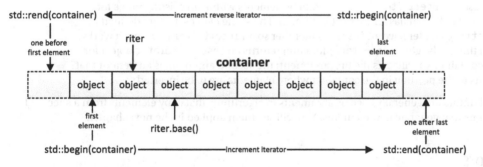

Figure 1-3. *How iterators and reverse iterators relate to a container*

You can use the subscript operator with reverse random access iterators, just like standard random access iterators, and that works in the opposite sense, too. For a standard iterator, `iter`, the expression `iter[n]` results in the element that is n positions after that pointed to by `iter`, so it's equivalent to `*(iter+n)`. For a reverse iterator, `riter`, the expression `riter[n]` is equivalent to `*(riter+n)`, so it returns the element that is n positions *before* the element pointed to by `riter`.

Figure 1-3 shows how reverse iterators and standard iterators for a container relate. You can see that the reverse iterators for the container elements are displaced one position left relative to normal iterators. Every reverse iterator contains a standard iterator inside it that is displaced similarly so it does *not* point to the same element. A `reverse_iterator` object has a `base()` function member that returns the underlying iterator, which, because it is a standard iterator, works in the opposite sense to the reverse iterator. The base iterator for a reverse iterator, riter, points to the next element toward the end of the range, as show in Figure 1-3. Some function members of a container won't accept reverse iterators. When you need to apply an algorithm where this is the case and the position has been found using reverse iterators, you can call base() to obtain the standard iterator corresponding to the reverse iterator. Obviously you need to take account of the fact that the base iterator will point to the element that follows that identified by the reverse iterator. You'll learn more about this in the next chapter.

Insert Iterators

Although insert iterators are based on standard iterators, there is a significant difference in what they do. Normal iterators can only access or change existing elements within a range. Insert iterators are used to add *new* elements anywhere in a container. Insert iterators cannot be applied to standard arrays or array<T,N> containers because the number of elements in these is fixed. There are three kinds of insert iterators:

- A back_insert_iterator adds new elements at the end of a container by calling the push_back() function member; vector, list, and deque containers have a push_back() member. If a container does not define push_back() then back_insert_iterator cannot be used. The global back_inserter() function returns a back_insert_iterator object for the container passed as the argument.

- A front_insert_iterator adds new elements at the beginning of a container by calling its push_front() member; list, forward_list and deque containers have a push_front() member. You cannot use front_insert_iterator with a container that does not have a push_front() member. The global front_inserter() function returns a front_inserter_iterator object for the container that is passed as the argument; obviously the container must be a list, a forward_list, or deque container.

- You use an insert_iterator to insert new elements within an existing range for any container that has an insert() member. The string classes that are defined in the string header have an insert() member so an insert_iterator object works with those. The global inserter() function returns an insert_iterator object for the container specified as the first argument; the second argument is an iterator that points to the position in the container where elements are to be inserted.

The insert iterators are generally used as arguments to algorithms that copy elements from a specified range or algorithms that generate new elements. You will see them applied in the next chapter.

Move Iterators

A *move iterator* is created from a regular iterator that points to an element in a range. You can use move iterators the move a range of class objects to a destination range, rather than copying them. A move iterator that you use as an input iterator converts the object to which it points to an rvalue, which allows the object to be moved rather than copied. Thus a move iterator will leave the original elements in the source range in an undefined state so you must not use them. You can obtain a move_iterator by passing a normal iterator, returned by begin() and end(), for example, to the make_move_iterator() function that is defined by a template in the iterator header. Thus you can create a pair of iterators defining a range of elements that are to be moved by passing the iterators returned by begin() and end() for a container to the make_move_iterator() function. You'll see examples that show how you use move iterators later in the book.

Operations on Iterators

The iterator header defines four function templates that implement operations on iterators:

- advance() increments the iterator you supply as the first argument the number of elements specified by the second argument. The first argument can be any iterator that has input iterator capability. The second argument can be negative to decrement the iterator if it is a bidirectional or random access iterator. There is no return value. For example:

```
int data[] {1, 2, 3, 4, 5, 6};
auto iter = std::begin(data);
std::advance(iter, 3);
std::cout << "Fourth element is " << *iter << std::endl;
```

- distance() returns the number of elements in a range specified by two iterator arguments. For example:

```
int data[] {1, 2, 3, 4, 5, 6};
std::cout << "The number of elements in data is "
          << std::distance(std::begin(data), std::end(data)) << std::endl;
```

- next() returns the iterator that results from incrementing the iterator you supply as the first argument by the number of elements specified by the second argument. The first argument must have forward iterator capability. The second argument has a default value of 1. For example:

```
int data[] {1, 2, 3, 4, 5, 6};
auto iter = std::begin(data);
auto fourth = std::next(iter, 3);
std::cout << "1st element is " << *iter << " and the 4th is " << *fourth <<
std::endl;
```

- prev() returns the iterator that results from decrementing the iterator you supply as the first argument by the number of elements you specify as the second argument, which has a default value of 1. The first argument must have bidirectional iterator capability. For example:

```
int data[] {1, 2, 3, 4, 5, 6};
auto iter = std::end(data);
std::cout << "Fourth element is " << *std::prev(iter, 3) <<  std::endl;
```

Obviously with random access iterators you can obtain the results that these functions produce using arithmetic operations, but with iterators in the less capable categories, you can't. These functions can simplify your code for operations on other than random access iterators. To produce the same effect as advance() on less capable iterators, for instance, you would need to code a loop.

Smart Pointers

The pointers that are part of the C++ language are referred to as *raw pointers* because variables of these types contain just an address; a raw pointer can contain the address of an automatic variable, a static variable, or a variable created on the heap. A *smart pointer* is an object of a template type that mimics a raw pointer in that it contains an address, and you can use it in the same way in some respects, but there are two major differences:

- Smart pointers are *only* used to store addresses of memory allocated in the free store - the heap.

- You *cannot* perform arithmetic operations such as increment or decrement on a smart pointer in the way that you can with raw pointers.

For objects created in the free store, it's usually much better to use smart pointers rather than raw pointers. The huge advantage of smart pointers is that you don't have to worry about using delete to free heap memory because memory allocated for an object pointed to by a smart pointer is released automatically when the object is no longer needed. This means that you eliminate the possibility of memory leaks.

You can store smart pointers in a container, which is particularly useful when you are working with objects of a class type. Storing pointers rather than objects allows you to retain polymorphic behavior – if you use a base class type as the template type argument for a smart pointer, you can use it to point to objects of a derived class type. The templates for smart pointer types are defined in the memory header so you must include this into your source file to use them. There are three types of smart pointers that are defined by the following templates in the std namespace:

- A unique_ptr<T> object behaves as a pointer to type T and is unique, which means there cannot be more than one unique_ptr<T> object containing the same address. A unique_ptr<T> object owns what it points to exclusively. You cannot assign or copy a unique_ptr<T> object. You can move the address stored by one unique_ptr<T> object to another using the std::move() function that is defined in the utility header. After the operation the original object will be invalid. You use unique_ptr<T> when you need to enforce single ownership of an object.

- A shared_ptr<T> object behaves as a pointer to type T, and in contrast with unique_ptr<T>, there can be any number of shared_ptr<T> objects containing the same address. Thus shared_ptr<T> objects allow shared ownership of an object in the free store. The number of shared_ptr<T> objects that contain a given address is recorded. The reference count for a shared_ptr<T> containing a given heap address is incremented each time a new shared_ptr<T> object is created containing that address; the reference count is decremented when a shared_ptr<T> object containing the address is destroyed or assigned to point to a different address. When there are no shared_ptr<T> objects containing a given address, the reference count will be zero and the heap memory for the object at that address will be released automatically. All shared_ptr<T> objects that point to the same address have access to the count of how many there are.

- A weak_ptr<T> is linked to and created from a shared_ptr<T> object and contains the same address. Creating a weak_ptr<T> does not increment the reference count of the linked shared_ptr<T> object so it does not prevent the object pointed to from being destroyed. Its memory will be released when the last shared_ptr<T> referencing is destroyed or reassigned to point to a different address, even though associated weak_ptr<T> objects may still exist.

The primary reason for having weak_ptr<T> objects is that it's possible to inadvertently create *reference cycles* with shared_ptr<T> objects. Conceptually, a reference cycle is where a shared_ptr<T> object, pA, points to another shared_ptr<T> object pB, and pB points to pA. With this situation, neither can be destroyed.

In practice this occurs in a way that is a lot more complicated. weak_ptr<T> objects are designed to avoid the problem of reference cycles. By using weak_ptr<T> objects to point to an object that a single shared_ptr<T> object points to, you avoid reference cycles; I'll explain how a little later. When the last shared_ptr<T> object is destroyed, the object pointed to is also destroyed. Any weak_ptr<T> objects associated with the shared_ptr<T> will then not point to a valid object.

Using unique_ptr<T> Pointers

A unique_ptr<T> object stores an address uniquely so the object to which it points is owned exclusively by the unique_ptr<T> object. When the unique_ptr<T> object is destroyed, the object to which it points is destroyed, too. This type of smart pointer applies when you don't need to have multiple smart pointers and you want to ensure a single point of ownership. When an object is owned by a unique_ptr<T>, you can provide access to the object by making a raw pointer available. Here's how you can create a unique_ptr<T> using a constructor:

```
std::unique_ptr<std::string> pname {new std::string {"Algernon"}};
```

The string object that is created on the heap is passed to the unique_ptr<string> constructor. The default constructor will create a unique_ptr<T> with nullptr as the internal raw pointer.

A much better way to create unique_ptr<T> objects is to use the make_unique<T>() function template that is defined in the memory header:

```
auto pname = std::make_unique<std::string>("Algernon");
```

The function create the string object on the heap by passing the argument to the class constructor and creates and returns the unique pointer to it. You supply as many arguments to the make_unique<T>() function as the T constructor requires. Here's an example:

```
auto pstr = std::make_unique<std::string>(6, '*');
```

There are two arguments that will be passed to the string constructor so the object that is created contains "******".

You can dereference the pointer to access the object, just like a raw pointer:

```
std::cout << *pname << std::endl;      // Outputs Algernon
```

You can create a unique_ptr<T> that points to an array. For example:

```
size_t len{10};
std::unique_ptr<int[]> pnumbers {new int[len]};th
```

This creates a unique_ptr object pointing to the array of len elements that is created in the free store. You could achieve the same result by calling make_unique<T>():

```
auto pnumbers = std::make_unique<int[]>(len);
```

This also creates a pointer to the array of len elements that is created on the heap. You can use an index with the unique_ptr variable to access the array elements. Here's how you can change the values:

```
for(size_t i{} ; i < len ; ++i)
  pnumbers[i] = i*i;
```

This sets the array elements to values that are the square of their index positions. Of course, you can use the subscript operator to output the values:

```
for(size_t i{} ; i < len ; ++i)
  std::cout << pnumbers[i] << std::endl;
```

You cannot pass a unique_ptr<T> object to a function by value because it cannot be copied. You must use a reference parameter in a function to allow a unique_ptr<T> object as an argument. You can return a unique_ptr<T> from a function because it will not be copied, but will be returned by an implicit move operation.

You can only store unique_ptr<T> objects in a container by moving them there or creating them in place because unique_ptr<T> objects cannot be copied. There can never be two unique_ptr<T> objects containing the same address. shared_ptr<T> objects don't have this characteristic, so you use these whenever you need multiple pointers to an object, or when you need to copy the contents of a container that stores smart pointers; otherwise use unique_ptr<T> objects. With a container that has unique_ptr<T> elements, you may need to make the raw pointer to an object available. Here's how you obtain a raw pointer from a unique_ptr<T>:

```
auto unique_p = std::make_unique<std::string>(6, '*');
std::string pstr {unique_p.get()};
```

The get() function member returns the raw pointer that the unique_ptr<T> contains. A typical circumstance when you would do this is to provide access to an object when the smart pointer to it is encapsulated in a class object. You can't return the unique_ptr<T> because it cannot be copied.

Resetting unique_ptr<T> Objects

The object to which a unique_ptr<T> object points is destroyed when the smart pointer is destroyed. Calling reset() for a unique_ptr<T> object with no argument destroys the object that is pointed to and replaces the raw pointer in the unique_ptr<T> object with nullptr; this enables you to destroy the object that is pointed to at any time. For example:

```
auto pname = std::make_unique<std::string>("Algernon");
...
pname.reset();                          // Release memory for string object
```

You can pass the address of a new T object in the free store to reset(), and the previous object that was pointed to will be destroyed and its address will be replaced by that of the new object:

```
pname.reset(new std::string{"Fred"});
```

This releases the memory for the original string that was pointed to by pname, creates a new string object "Fred" in the free store, and stores its address in pname.

■ **Caution** You must not pass the address of a free store object to `reset()` that is contained by a different `unique_ptr<T>` object, or create a new `unique_ptr<T>` using an address that is already contained in another `unique_ptr<T>`. Such code will probably compile, but your program will certainly crash. The destruction of the first `unique_ptr<T>` will release the memory for the object that it points to. The destruction of the second will result in an attempt to release the memory that has already been released.

You can release the object that a `unique_ptr<T>` points to by calling `release()` for the smart pointer. This sets the raw pointer contained in the `unique_ptr<T>` to `nullptr` without releasing the memory for the original object. For example:

```
auto up_name = std::make_unique<std::string>("Algernon");
std::unique_ptr<std::string> up_new_name{up_name.release()};
```

The `release()` member of up_name returns the original raw pointer to the string object containing "Algernon" so after executing the second statement, up_name will contain `nullptr`, and up_new_name will point to the original "Algernon" string object. The effect is to transfer ownership of the object in the free store from one unique pointer to another.

You can interchange the objects owned by two `unique_ptr<T>` pointers:

```
auto pn1 = std::make_unique<std::string>("Jack");
auto pn2 = std::make_unique<std::string>("Jill");
pn1.swap(pn2);
```

After executing the second statement here, pn1 will point to the string "Jill" and pn2 will point to "Jack."

Comparing and Checking unique_ptr<T> Objects

There are non-member function templates that define a full set of comparison operators that compare two `unique_ptr<T>` objects or compare a `unique_ptr<T>` object with `nullptr`. Comparing two `unique_ptr<T>` objects compares the addresses returned by their `get()` members. Comparing a `unique_ptr<T>` with `nullptr` compares the address returned by the `get()` member of the smart pointer with `nullptr`.

`unique_ptr<T>` objects are implicitly convertible to type `bool`. If the objects contains `nullptr` the result of the conversion is `false`; otherwise the result is `true`. This means you can use an `if` statement to check for a non-null `unique_ptr<T>` object:

```
auto up_name = std::make_unique<std::string>("Algernon");
std::unique_ptr<std::string> up_new{up_name.release()};
if(up_new)                                  // true if not nullptr
  std::cout << "The name is " << *up_new << std::endl;
if(!up_name)                                // true if nullptr
  std::cout << "The unique pointer is nullptr" << std::endl;
```

This kind of checking is desirable when you are calling `reset()` or `release()` for unique pointer objects because you need to be certain that a `unique_ptr<T>` is not `nullptr` before you dereference it.

Using shared_ptr<T> Pointers

You can define a shared_ptr<T> object like this:

```
std::shared_ptr<double> pdata {new double{999.0}};
```

You can also dereference a shared pointer to access what it points to or to change the value stored at the address:

```
*pdata = 8888.0;
std::cout << *pdata << std::endl;        // Outputs 8888.0
*pdata = 8889.0;
std::cout << *pdata << std::endl;        // Outputs 8889.0
```

The definition of pdata involves one allocation of heap memory for the double variable, and another allocation relating to the smart pointer object for the control block that it uses to record the number of copies of the smart pointer. Allocating heap memory is relatively expensive on time. You can make the process more efficient by using the make_shared<T>() function that is defined in the memory header to create a smart pointer of type shared_ptr<T>:

```
auto pdata = std::make_shared<double>(999.0);  // Points to a double variable
```

The type of variable to be created in the free store is specified between the angled brackets. The argument between the parentheses following the function name is used to initialize the double variable it creates. In general, there can be any number of arguments to the make_shared<T>() function, the actual number depending of the type of object being created. When you are using make_shared<T>() to create objects in the free store, there can be two or more arguments separated by commas if the T constructor requires them. The auto keyword causes the type for pdata to be deduced automatically from the object returned by make_shared<T>() so it will be shared_ptr<double>. Don't forget though – you should not use an initializer list when you specify a type as auto because the type will be deduced to be std::initializer_list.

You can initialize a shared_ptr<T> with another when you define it:

```
std::shared_ptr<double> pdata2 {pdata};
```

pdata2 points to the same variable as pdata, which will cause the reference count to be incremented. You can also assign one shared_ptr<T> to another:

```
std::shared_ptr<double> pdata{ new double{ 999.0 } };
std::shared_ptr<double> pdata2;         // Pointer contains nullptr
pdata2 = pdata;                         // Copy pointer - both point to the same variable
std::cout << *pdata << std::endl;       // Outputs 999.0
```

Of course, copying pdata increases the reference count. Both pointers have to be reset or destroyed for the memory occupied by the double variable to be released. You can't use a shared_ptr<T> to store the address of an array created in the free store by default. However, you can store the address of an array<T> or vector<T> container object that you create in the free store.

> ■ **Note**   It is possible to create a `shared_ptr<T>` object that points to an array. This involves supplying a definition for a *deleter function* that the smart pointer is to use to release the heap memory for the array. The details of how you do this are outside the scope of this book.

In a similar way to that for a `unique_ptr<T>`, you can get a raw pointer to the object to which a `shared_ptr<T>` object points by calling its `get()` member. For pdata as defined in the previous section, you could write:

```
auto pvalue = pdata.get();              // pvalue is type double* and points to 999.0
```

You only need to do this when it's essential to use the raw pointer.

> ■ **Caution**   Duplicates of a `shared_ptr<T>` object should only be created by the copy constructor or the copy assignment operator. Creating a `shared_ptr<T>` using the raw pointer returned by `get()` for a different pointer will result in undefined behavior, which in most cases means a program crash.

Resetting shared_ptr<T> Objects

If you assign `nullptr` to a `shared_ptr<T>` object the address stored will be replaced by `nullptr`, which has the effect of reducing the reference count for pointers to the object by 1. For example:

```
auto pname = std::make_shared<std::string>("Charles Dickens");  // Points to a string object
// ... lots of other stuff happening...
pname = nullptr;                                                 // Reset pname to nullptr
```

This creates a `string` object initialized with "Charles Dickens" in the free store and creates a shared pointer containing its address. Eventually, assigning `nullptr` to pname replaces the address stored with `nullptr`. Of course, any other `shared_ptr<T>` objects that hold the address of the `string` object will continue to exist – just the reference count will have been decremented.

You can obtain the same result by calling `reset()` for the `shared_ptr<T>` object with no argument value:

```
pname.reset();                                                  // Reset to nullptr
```

You can also pass a raw pointer to `reset()` to change what the shared pointer points to. For example:

```
pname.reset(new std::string{"Jane Austen"});                   // pname points to new string
```

The argument to `reset()` must be an address of the same type as was originally stored in the smart pointer, or must be implicitly convertible to that type.

Comparing and Checking shared_ptr<T> Objects

You can compare the address contained in one shared_ptr<T> object with another, or with nullptr using any of the comparison operators. The most useful are comparisons for equality or inequality, which tell you whether or not two pointers point to the same object. Given two shared_ptr<T> objects, pA and pB, that point to the same type, T, you can compare them like this:

```
if((pA == pB) && (pA != nullptr))
  std::cout << " Both pointers point to the same object.\n";
```

The pointers could both be nullptr and be equal so a simple comparison is not sufficient to establish that they both point to the same object. Like a unique_ptr<T>, a shared_ptr<T> object can be implicitly converted to type bool so you could write the statement as:

```
if(pA && (pA == pB))
  std::cout << " Both pointers point to the same object.\n";
```

You can also check whether a shared_ptr<T> object has any duplicates:

```
auto pname = std::make_shared<std::string>("Charles Dickens");
if(pname.unique())
  std::cout << there is only one..." << std::endl;
else
std::cout << there is more than one..." << std::endl;
```

The unique() function member returns true if the recorded number of instances of the object is 1, and false otherwise. You can also determine how many instances there are:

```
if(pname.unique())
  std::cout << there is only one..." << std::endl;
else
  std::cout << there are " << pname.use_count() << " instances." << std::endl;
```

The use_count() member return the number of instances of the object for which it was called. It returns 0 if the share_ptr<T> object contains nullptr.

weak_ptr<T> Pointers

A weak_ptr<T> object can only be created from a shared_ptr<T> object. weak_ptr<T> pointers are typically used as class members that store an address of another instance of the same class, when objects of the class are created in the free store. Using a shared_ptr<T> member to point to another object of the same type in such circumstances has the potential for creating a reference cycle, which would prevent objects of the class type from being deleted from the free store automatically. This is not a common situation, but it is possible, as Figure 1-4 shows.

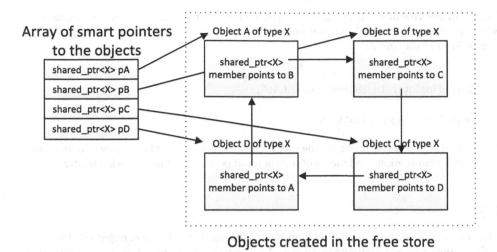

Figure 1-4. *How a reference cycle prevents objects from being deleted*

Deleting all the smart pointers in the array in Figure 1-4 or resetting them to nullptr does not delete the memory for the objects to which they point. There is still a shared_ptr<X> object containing the address of every object. There are no external pointers remaining that can access these objects so they cannot be deleted. The problem can be avoided if the objects used weak_ptr<X> members to refer to other objects. These would not prevent the objects from being destroyed when the external pointers in the array are destroyed or reset.

You can create a weak_ptr<T> object like this:

```
auto pData = std::make_shared<X>();       // Create a shared pointer to an object of type X
std::weak_ptr<X> pwData {pData};          // Create a weak pointer from shared pointer
std::weak_ptr<X> pwData2 {pwData};        // Create a weak pointer from another
```

Thus you can create a weak_ptr<T> from a shared_ptr<T> or from an existing weak_ptr<T>. You can't do very much with a weak pointer – you can't dereference it to access the object it points to, for example. You can do two things with a weak_ptr<T> object:

- You can test whether the object it points to still exists, which means there's a shared_ptr<T> still around that points to it.

- You can create a shared_ptr<T> object from a weak_ptr<T> object.

Here's how you can test for the existence of the object that a weak pointer references:

```
if(pwData.expired())
    std::cout << "Object no longer exists.\n";
```

The expired() function for the pwData object returns true if the object no longer exists. You can create a shared pointer from a weak pointer like this:

```
std::shared_ptr<X> pNew {pwData.lock()};
```

The lock() function locks the object if it exists by returning a new shared_ptr<X> object that initializes pNew. If the object does not exist, the lock() function will return a shared_ptr<X> object containing nullptr. You can test the result in an if statement:

```
if(pNew)
    std::cout << "Shared pointer to object created.\n";
else
    std::cout << "Object no longer exists.\n";
```

Working with weak_ptr<T> pointers is outside the scope of this book so I won't be delving into these any further. I'll be exploring the implications and merits of storing smart pointers in containers in chapter 3.

Algorithms

Algorithms provide computational and analysis functions that mainly apply to a range of objects that you specify by a pair of iterators – a begin iterator pointing at the first element and an end iterator pointing to one past the last element. Because they access data elements through iterators, an algorithm is not concerned with where the data is. You can apply algorithms to any sequence that can be accessed through iterators of the type required by the algorithm, so you can potentially apply algorithms to elements in containers, to the characters in a string object, to standard array elements, to streams, and to sequences stored in a container of a class type that you have defined as long as your class supports iterators.

The algorithms are the largest collection of tools in the STL. Many of these are relevant to a large number of applications, although some of them are quite specialized in their use. You can classify the algorithms by dividing them into three broad groups:

1. Non-mutating sequence operations don't change the sequence to which they are applied in any way. An algorithm that finds an element that matches a given value obvious doesn't change the original data. Numerical algorithms such as inner_product() and accumulate() that process a sequence or sequences without changing them to produce a result also fall into this category. Algorithms in this category include find(), count(), mismatch(), search(), and equal().

2. Mutating sequence operations do change the elements in a sequence. Algorithms in this category include swap(), copy(), transform(), replace(), remove(), reverse(), rotate(), fill(), and shuffle(). Heap operations also fall into this category.

3. Sorting, merging, and related operations in many instances will change the order of the sequences to which they are applied. Algorithms in this category include sort(), stable_sort(), binary_search(), merge(), min(),and max().

Of course, the examples of algorithm I have identified in these categories are by no means an exhaustive list of what is available; you'll learn about many more in subsequent chapters – and how to apply them. Some algorithms, such as transform(), need a function to be passed as an argument that is applied to the elements in a range. Others that reorder elements frequently provide the option to supply a predicate for comparing elements. Let's look at the possibilities for passing a function as an argument to another function next.

Passing a Function as an Argument

The signature of functions that are acceptable as argument to another function are determined by specification of the function parameter. The parameter specification depends on the nature of the function argument. There are three ways in which you can pass a function as an argument to another function:

- You can use a *function pointer*, where you use the function name as the argument value. I won't elaborate on this further because I'm assuming you are already familiar with function pointers and the next two possibilities are preferable.

- You can pass a *function object* as the argument.

- You can use a *lambda expression* as the argument.

You'll see quite of lot of examples that make use of the last two options in subsequent chapter so I'll remind you of the details of what's involved in these – just in case you're a little bit rusty on them.

Function Objects

Function objects – which are also referred to as *functors* – are objects of classes that overload the function call operator, operator()(); they offer a more efficient way to pass a function as an argument to another function than using a raw function pointer. Let's look at a simple example. Suppose I define a Volume class like this:

```
class Volume
{
public:
  double operator()(double x, double y, double z) {return x*y*z; }
};
```

I can create a Volume object that I can use like a function to calculate a volume:

```
Volume volume;                          // Create a functor
double room { volume(16, 12, 8.5) };    // Room volume in cubic feet
```

The value in the initializer list for room is the result of calling operator()() for the volume object so the expression is equivalent to volume.operator()(16, 12, 8.5). When a function receives a function object as an argument, it can be used just like a function. Of course you can define more than one version of the operator()() function in a class, which allows an object to be applied in various ways. Suppose that we have defined a Box class with members that define the length, width, and height of an object and accessor function members that return the values of these; we could extend the Volume class to accommodate Box objects like this:

```
class Volume
{
public:
  double operator()(double x, double y, double z) {return x*y*z; }

  double operator()(const Box& box)
  { return box.getLength()*box.getWidth()*box.getHeight(); }
};
```

Now a Volume object can be used to calculate the volume of a Box object:

```
Box box{1.0, 2.0, 3.0};
std::cout << "The volume of the box is " << volume(box) << std::endl;
```

To allow a Volume object to be passed as an argument to a function, you could just specify the function parameter as type Volume&. The STL algorithms typically use a more generalized specification for a parameter that requires an argument representing a function by having a function template parameter that identifies the type.

Lambda Expressions

A *lambda expression* defines an anonymous function. A function that you define by a lambda expression is different from a regular function in that it can capture variables that exist in the scope enclosing the lambda and access them. Lambda expressions are frequently used with STL algorithms. Let's take an example of a lambda expression. Suppose you want to pass the capability to calculate the cubes (x^3) of numerical values of type double to a function. Here's a lambda expression to do this:

```
[] (double value) { return value*value*value; }
```

The opening square brackets are called the *lambda introducer*. They mark the beginning of the lambda expression. There's more to the lambda introducer than there is here – the brackets are not always empty. The lambda introducer is followed by the *lambda parameter list* between parentheses. This is just like a regular function parameter list. In this case, there's just a single parameter, value, but there could be more, separated by commas. You can also specify default values for parameters in a lambda expression.

The *body* of the lambda expression appears between braces following the parameter list, again just like a normal function. The body for this lambda contains just one statement, a return statement that also calculates the value that is returned. In general the body of a lambda can contain any number of statements. Note that there's no return type specification in the example above. The return type defaults to that of the value returned. If nothing is returned, the return type is void. You can specify the return type using the trailing return type syntax. You could supply it for the lambda above like this:

```
[] (double value) -> double { return value*value*value; }
```

Naming a Lambda Expression

Although a lambda expression is an anonymous object, you can still store its address in a variable. You don't know what its type is, but the compiler does:

```
auto cube = [] (double value) { return value*value*value; };
```

The auto keyword tells the compiler to figure out the type that the variable cube should have from whatever appears on the right of the assignment, so it will have the type necessary to store the address of the lambda expression. You can always do this if there is nothing between the square brackets – the lambda introducer. Sometimes things between the square brackets will prevent you from using auto in this way. You can use cube just like a function pointer, for example:

```
double x{2.5};
std::cout << x << " cubed is " << cube(x) << std::endl;
```

The output statement produces the cube of 2.5.

Passing a Lambda Expression to a Function

In general, you don't know the type of a lambda expression. There's no generic "lambda expression type." I have said that you typically use a lambda expression to pass a function as an argument to another function, which immediately raises the question of how you specify the parameter type when the argument is to be a lambda expression. There's more than one possibility. A simple answer is to define a template for a function where the type parameter is the type of a lambda expression.

The compiler always knows the type of a lambda expression so it can instantiate a function template with a parameter that will accept a given lambda expression as an argument. It's easy to see how this works with an example. Suppose that you have a number of double values stored in a container that you want to be able to transform in arbitrary ways; sometimes you want to replace the values by their squares, or their square roots, or some more complex transformation that depends on whether or not the values lie within a particular range. You can define a template that allows the transformation of the elements to be specified by a lambda expression. Here's how the template looks:

```
template <typename ForwardIter, typename F>
void change(ForwardIter first, ForwardIter last, F fun)
{
  for(auto iter = first; iter != last; ++iter)    // For each element in the range...
    *iter = fun(*iter);                           // ...apply the function to the object
}
```

The fun parameter will accept any suitable lambda expression, as well as a function object or an ordinary function pointer. You may wonder how the compiler deals with this template, bearing in mind that there's no information as to what fun does. The answer is that the compiler doesn't deal with it. The compiler doesn't process a template in any way until it needs instantiating. In the case of the template above, all the information about the lambda is available to the compiler when you use it. Here's an example of using the template:

```
int data[] {1, 2, 3, 4};
change(std::begin(data), std::end(data), [] (int value){ return value*value; });
```

The second statement will replace the value of each element in the data array by the square of the original value.

The functional header in the Standard Library defines a template type, std::function<>, that is a wrapper for any kind of pointer to a function with a given set of return and parameter types; of course, this includes lambda expressions. The type argument for the std::function template is of the form Return_Type(Param_Types). Return_Type is the type of value returned by the lambda expression (or function pointed to). Param_Types is a list of the parameter types for the lambda expression (or function pointed to) separated by commas. The definition for a variable representing the lambda expression from the previous section could be specified as:

```
std::function<double(double)> op {  [] (double value) { return value*value*value; } };
```

The op variable can be passed as an argument to any function that accepts a function argument with the same signature. Of course, you can redefine op to mean something else, as long as the 'something else' has the same return type and number and type of parameters:

```
op = [] (double value) { return value*value; };
```

op now represents a function that returns the square of the argument. You can use the `std::function` type template to specify the type of anything callable, which includes any lambda expression or function object.

The Capture Clause

The lambda introducer, [ ], is not necessarily empty; it can contain a *capture* clause that specifies how variables in the enclosing scope can be accessed from within the body of the lambda. The body of a lambda expression with nothing between the square brackets can only work with the arguments and with variables that are defined locally within the lambda. A lambda with no capture clause is called a *stateless lambda expression* because it cannot access anything in its enclosing scope. Figure 1-5 shows the syntax for a lambda expression.

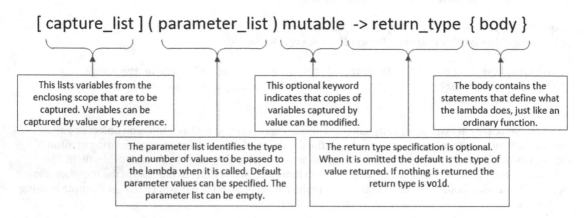

Figure 1-5. Components of a lambda expression

A *default capture* clause applies to all variables in the scope enclosing the definition of the lambda. If you put = between the square brackets, the body of the lambda can access all automatic variables in the enclosing scope by value – that is, the *values* of the variables are made available within the lambda expression, but the values stored in the original variables cannot be changed. You can modify the copy of a variable in the enclosing scope from within the lambda if you add the `mutable` keyword to the lambda definition following the parentheses enclosing the parameter list. A lambda remembers the local value of the copy of a variable captured by value from one execution of the lambda to the next, so the copy is effectively `static`.

If you put & between the square brackets, all variables in the enclosing scope are accessible by reference, so their values can be changed by the code in the body of the lambda. The `mutable` keyword is not necessary in this case. To be accessible, variables must be defined preceding the definition of the lambda expression.

You cannot use `auto` to specify the type of a variable to store the address of a lambda that accesses the variable containing its address. This implies you are trying to initialize the variable with an expression that uses the variable. You cannot use `auto` with any lambda that refers to the variable being defined – self-reference is not allowed with `auto`.

You can capture specific variables in the enclosing scope. To capture specific variables that you want to access by value, you just list their names in the capture clause. To capture specific variables by reference, you prefix each name with &. Two or more variables in the capture clause must be separated by commas.

You can include = in the capture clause along with specific variable names that are to be captured by reference. The capture clause [=, &factor] would allow access to factor by reference and any other variables in the enclosing scope by value. The capture clause [&, factor] would capture factor by value and all other variables by reference. You would also need to specify the mutable keyword to modify the copy of factor.

▓ **Warning**   Capturing *all* the variables in the enclosing scope by value in a lambda expression can add a lot of overhead because they will each have a copy created – whether or not you refer to them. It's much more sensible to capture only those that you need.

The transform() algorithm applies a function that you supply as an argument to a range of elements. The first two arguments to transform() are iterators specifying the range to which the function argument is to be applied; the third argument is an iterator specifying the start location where the results are to go; the fourth argument is the function to be applied to the input range. Here's an example demonstrating the use of functors, lambda expressions, and the std::function template type with the transform algorithm:

```cpp
// Ex1_03.cpp
// Passing functions to an algorithm
#include <iostream>                       // For standard streams
#include <algorithm>                      // For transform()
#include <iterator>                       // For iterators
#include <functional>                     // For function

class Root
{
public:
  double operator()(double x) { return std::sqrt(x); };
};

int main()
{
  double data[] { 1.5, 2.5, 3.5, 4.5, 5.5};

  // Passing a function object
  Root root;                              // Function object
  std::cout << "Square roots are:" << std::endl;
  std::transform(std::begin(data), std::end(data),
             std::ostream_iterator<double>(std::cout, " "), root);

  // Using an lambda expression as an argument
  std::cout << "\n\nCubes are:" << std::endl;
  std::transform(std::begin(data), std::end(data),
             std::ostream_iterator<double>(std::cout, " "), [](double x){return x*x*x; });

  // Using a variable of type std::function<> as argument
  std::function<double(double)> op {[](double x){ return x*x; }};
  std::cout << "\n\nSquares are:" << std::endl;
  std::transform(std::begin(data), std::end(data),
             std::ostream_iterator<double>(std::cout, " "), op);
```

```
// Using a lambda expression that calls another lambda expression as argument
std::cout << "\n\n4th powers are:" << std::endl;
std::transform(std::begin(data), std::end(data),
          std::ostream_iterator<double>(std::cout, " "), [&op](double x){return op(x)*op(x); });
std::cout << std::endl;
}
```

The output should be:

```
Square roots are:
1.22474 1.58114 1.87083 2.12132 2.34521

Cubes are:
3.375 15.625 42.875 91.125 166.375

Squares are:
3.375 15.625 42.875 91.125 166.375

4th powers are:

11.3906 244.141 1838.27 8303.77 27680.6
```

If you have understood the previous sections, you should not have too much trouble with this example. The input data that the transform() algorithm is to process is contained in the data array. The first two arguments to transform() in each call are the begin and end iterators for the array. The destination for the output is specified by an output stream iterator that writes the data to the standard output stream. The second argument to the ostream_iterator constructor is the separator to be written after each value.

The first transform() call passes a Root object as the last argument. The Root class defines the operator()() member to return the square root of the argument. The second transform() call shows that you can write a lambda expression as the argument which in this case computes the cubes of the input values. The third transform() call shows that the std::function type template also works here. The last call shows that a lambda can call another lambda. Thus you can apply any of these techniques when you need to pass a function as an argument to an algorithm.

Summary

This chapter introduced the basic ideas behind the STL. All the aspects of STL that I introduced in this chapter will be demonstrated and explained in more depth later in the book. This chapter also outlined some C++ capabilities that are important to understand because they are fundamental to applying the STL, and I'll be using them extensively in subsequent chapters. The most important points covered in this chapter are the following:

- The STL defines class templates that are *containers* for other objects.

- The STL defines *iterators*, which are objects that behave like pointers. A pair of iterators is used to define a contiguous range of elements; a begin iterator points to the first element in a range and an end iterator points to one past the last iterator in a range.

- A *reverse begin iterator* points to the last element in a range and a *reverse end iterator* points to one before the first element. Reverse iterators work in the opposite sense to normal iterators.

- The `iterator` header defines global functions that return iterators for containers, arrays, or any other kind of objects that supports iterator. The global functions `begin()`, `cbegin()`, `end()`, and `cend()` return normal iterators. The functions `rbegin()`, `crbegin()`, `rend()`, and `crend()` return reverse iterators. Function names in this set beginning with `'c'` return `const` iterators.

- You use *stream iterators* to transfer data of a given type to or from a stream.

- The STL defines function templates that define *algorithms* that are applied to a range of elements specified by iterators.

- *Smart pointers* are objects that behave like pointers and the addresses of objects created in the free store. Objects managed by smart pointers are deleted automatically when no smart pointers to them exist. Smart pointers cannot be incremented or decremented.

- A *lambda expression* defines an anonymous function. Lambda expressions are frequently used to pass a function as an argument to an STL algorithm.

- You can use the `std::function<>` template type that is defined in the `functional` header to specify the type for any kind of callable entity with a given signature.

EXERCISES

Here are a few exercises to test how well you remember the topics in this chapter. If you get stuck, look back over the chapter for help. If you're still stuck after that, you can download the solutions from the Apress website (`http://www.apress.com/9781484200056`), but this really should be a last resort.

1. Write a program that defines an array of `std::string` objects that is initialized with a set of words of your choice and lists the contents of the array, one to a line, using iterators.

2. Write a program that applies the `transform()` algorithm to the elements of the array in the previous exercise to replace all lowercase vowels in the words by `'*'` and write the results to the standard output stream one to a line. Define the function to replace vowels in a string as a lambda expression that uses iterators.

3. Write a program that applies the `transform()` algorithm to the array from the first exercise to convert the strings to uppercase and output the results. The function to convert the strings should be passed to `transform()` as a lambda expression that calls `transform()` to apply the `std::toupper()` library function to characters in a string.

CHAPTER 2

■ ■ ■

Using Sequence Containers

This chapter introduces the bread-and-butter containers that you are likely to use most often – sequence containers. And in it, you'll learn the following:

- The characteristics of a sequence container

- How you obtain and use iterators with sequence containers

- How you use an array container

- What the capabilities of a vector container are

- The characteristics and capabilities of a deque container and how it differs from a vector

- How a list container structures the data elements it contains and what its advantages and disadvantages are

- How a forward_list container differs from a list, and when you would use it

- How you can define your own iterators

The Sequence Containers

The sequence containers store elements in a linear sequence. There's no ordering imposed on the elements. The elements are in whatever order you store them. There are five standard sequence containers, each with different characteristics:

- An array<T,N> container is a sequence of a fixed length, N, of objects of type T. You cannot add or delete elements.

- A vector<T> container is a variable length sequence of objects of type T that grows automatically when necessary. You can only add or delete elements efficiently at the end of the sequence.

- A deque<T> container is a variable length sequence that grows automatically. You can add or delete elements efficiently at both ends of the sequence.

- A list<T> container is a variable length sequence of objects of type T organized as a doubly linked list. You can add or delete elements efficiently anywhere in the sequence. Accessing an arbitrary element that is interior to the sequence is relatively slow compared to the previous three containers because you must start with either the first element or the last element and move through the list until you arrive at the element that you want.

33

- A forward_list<T> is a variable length sequence of objects of type T organized as a singly linked list. This is faster and requires less memory than a list container, but elements interior to the sequence can only be accessed starting from the first element.

Figure 2-1 illustrates the sequence containers that are available and the differences between them.

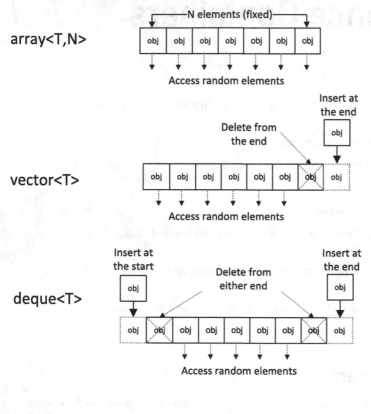

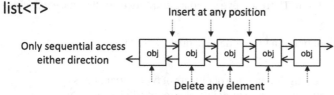

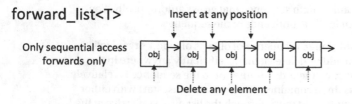

Figure 2-1. *The standard sequence containers*

The operations shown for each type of container in Figure 2-1 are those that can be carried out efficiently. Other operations are possible in some cases, as you will see, but these will be much slower.

Function Members That Are Common Between Containers

I'll be explaining in detail how you use each of the sequence containers in the rest of this chapter. The sequence containers have a number of function members in common and they behave the same in each. Rather than repeat detailed descriptions of what these members do for each type of container in which they occur, I'll describe each of them in the context of one container. Table 2-1 shows the function members of the array, vector, and deque containers and where two or more containers implement the same function member.

Table 2-1. *Function members of* array, vector, *and* deque *containers*

Function Member	array<T,N>	vector<T>	deque<T>
begin() – returns the begin iterator.	Yes	Yes	Yes
end() – returns the end iterator.	Yes	Yes	Yes
rbegin() – returns the reverse begin iterator.	Yes	Yes	Yes
rend() – returns the reverse end iterator.	Yes	Yes	Yes
cbegin() – returns the const begin iterator.	Yes	Yes	Yes
cend() – returns the const end iterator.	Yes	Yes	Yes
crbegin() – returns the const reverse begin iterator.	Yes	Yes	Yes
crend() – returns the const reverse end iterator.	Yes	Yes	Yes
assign() – replaces the contents with a new set of elements.	-	Yes	Yes
operator=() – replaces the elements with a copy of another container of the same type, or from an initializer list.	Yes	Yes	Yes
size() – returns the actual number of elements.	Yes	Yes	Yes
max_size() – returns the maximum number of elements.	Yes	Yes	Yes
capacity() – returns the number of elements for which memory is allocated.	-	Yes	-
empty() – returns true if there are no elements.	Yes	Yes	Yes
resize() – changes the actual number of elements.	-	Yes	Yes
shrink_to_fit() – reduces the memory to that required for the actual number of elements.	-	Yes	Yes
front() – returns a reference to the first element.	Yes	Yes	Yes
back() – returns a reference to the last element.	Yes	Yes	Yes
operator[]() – accesses the element at the index.	Yes	Yes	Yes
at() – accesses the element at the index argument with bounds checking.	Yes	Yes	Yes
push_back() – appends an element to the end of the sequence.	-	Yes	Yes
insert() – inserts an element or elements at a specified position.	-	Yes	Yes
emplace() – creates an element in place at a specified position.	-	Yes	Yes

(continued)

Table 2-1. (*continued*)

Function Member	array<T,N>	vector<T>	deque<T>
emplace_back() – creates an element in place at the end of the sequence.	-	Yes	Yes
pop_back() – removes the element at the end of the sequence.	-	Yes	Yes
erase() – removes an element or range of elements.	-	Yes	Yes
clear() – removes all the elements so the size is 0.	-	Yes	Yes
swap() – interchanges all the elements in two containers.	Yes	Yes	Yes
data() – returns a pointer to the internal array containing the elements.	Yes	Yes	-

The absence of 'Yes' in a column implies the function is not defined for that container. You don't need to remember this table. It's here just for reference. You'll know instinctively what many of the functions are that are not available for a given container when you learn more about how the containers structure the elements.

The containers that organize elements as a linked list are rather different in their internal organization from the containers in Table 2-1. The list and forward_list containers are very similar to each other though. A forward_list has most of the function members that a list container has. The ones missing from a forward_list are essentially those that require traversal of the sequence backwards, so there are no reverse iterators for example. For reference, Table 2-2 shows the function members of the list and forward_list containers.

Table 2-2. *Function members of* list *and* forward_list *containers*

Function Member	list<T>	forward_list<T>
begin() – returns the begin iterator.	Yes	Yes
end() – returns the end iterator.	Yes	Yes
rbegin() – returns the reverse begin iterator.	Yes	–
rend() – returns the reverse end iterator.	Yes	--
cbegin() – returns the const begin iterator.	Yes	Yes
before_begin() – returns an iterator pointing to before the first element.	–	Yes
cbefore_begin() – returns a const iterator pointing to before the first element.	-	Yes
cend() – returns the const end iterator.	Yes	Yes
crbegin() – returns the const reverse begin iterator.	Yes	-
crend() – returns the const reverse end iterator.	Yes	-
assign() – replaces the contents with a new set of elements.	Yes	Yes
operator=() – replaces the elements with a copy of another container of the same type, or from an initializer list.	Yes	Yes
size() – returns the actual number of elements.	Yes	-
max_size() – returns the maximum number of elements.	Yes	Yes

(*continued*)

Table 2-2. (*continued*)

Function Member	list<T>	forward_list<T>
resize() – changes the number of elements.	Yes	Yes
empty() – returns true if there are no elements.	Yes	Yes
front() – returns a reference to the first element.	Yes	Yes
back() – returns a reference to the last element.	Yes	–
push_back() – appends an element to the end of the sequence.	Yes	–
push_front() – inserts an element at the beginning of the sequence.	Yes	Yes
emplace() – creates an element in place before a specified position.	Yes	–
emplace_after() – creates an element in place following a specified position.	–	Yes
emplace_back() – creates an element in place at the end of the sequence.	Yes	–
emplace_front() – creates an element in place at the beginning of the sequence.	Yes	Yes
insert() – inserts one or more elements before a specified position.	Yes	–
insert_after() – inserts one or more elements following a specified position.	–	Yes
pop_back() – removes the element at the end of the sequence.	Yes	–
pop_front() – removes the element at beginning of the sequence.	Yes	Yes
reverse() – reverses the order of elements.	Yes	Yes
erase() – removes an element at a specified position or removes a range of elements.	Yes	–
erase_after() – removes an element following a specified position or removes a range of elements.	–	Yes
remove() - Removes elements matching the argument.	Yes	Yes
remove_if() – Removes elements for which the unary predicate argument returns true.	Yes	Yes
unique() – Removes consecutive duplicates.	Yes	Yes
clear() – removes all the elements so the size is 0.	Yes	Yes
swap() – interchanges all the elements in two containers.	Yes	Yes
sort() – sorts the elements.	Yes	Yes
merge() – Merges this container with another – both must be sorted.	Yes	Yes
splice() – Moves elements from another list of the same type before a specified position.	Yes	–
splice_after() – Moves elements from another list of the same type following a specified position.	–	Yes

The `max_size()` function member that all the sequence container have returns the maximum possible number of elements that can be stored; this is usually a very large number, typically $2^{32} - 1$, so the need to call this function is rare.

Using array<T,N> Containers

The `array<T,N>` template defines container types that are the equivalent of standard arrays. It's a fixed sequence of N elements of type T, so it's just like a regular array except that you specify the type and number of elements a little differently. Obviously you cannot add or delete elements. The elements in a template instance are stored internally in a standard array. `array` containers carry very little overhead compared to a standard array but offer two advantages: attempts to access elements with an index outside the legal range can be detected if you use `at()`, and a container knows how many elements it has, which means that an array container can be passed as an argument to a function without requiring the number of elements to be specified independently. You must include the `array` header in a source file to use the container type. It's very easy to use – here's how you create an `array<>` of 100 elements of type `double`:

```
std::array<double, 100> data;
```

When you define an `array` container without specifying initial values for the elements, the elements are not initialized, but you can initialize then to zero or its equivalent for the element type by default like this:

```
std::array<double, 100> data {};
```

With this statement all elements in the `data` container will be `0.0`. The specification for the parameter N must be a *constant expression* and the number of elements in the container cannot be changed. Of course, you can initialize the elements when you create an instance of an `array` container, just like a normal array:

```
std::array<double, 10> values {0.5, 1.0, 1.5, 2.0};    // 5th and subsequent elements are 0.0
```

The four values in the initializer list are used to initialize the first four elements; subsequent elements will be zero. This is illustrated in Figure 2-2.

std::array<double, 10> values { 0.5, 1.0, 1.5, 2.0 };

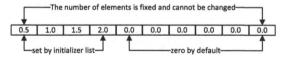

Figure 2-2. *Creating an* array<T,N> *container*

You can set all the elements to some given value by calling the `fill()` function member of the `array` object. For example:

```
values.fill(3.1415926);                                // Set all elements to pi
```

The `fill()` function sets all elements to the value you pass as the argument.

Accessing Elements

You can access and use elements from an `array` container in an expression using an index between square brackets in the same way as for a standard array, for example:

```
values[4] = values[3] + 2.0*values[1];
```

The fifth element is set to the value of the expression that is the right operand of the assignment. Using an index like this does *not* do bounds checking; using an out-of-range index value to access or store data will not be detected. To check for out-of-range index values, you use the `at()` function member:

```
values.at(4) = values.at(3) + 2.0*values.at(1);
```

This does the same as the previous statement except that if an argument to `at()` represents an out-of-range index value, an `std::out_of_range` exception will be thrown. Always use `at()` unless you're sure that an index out of range is not possible. The question obviously arises as to why the `operator[]()` implementation does not do bounds checking. The answer is performance; validating the index value each time you access an element carries overhead; you want to avoid the overhead when there's no possibility of an out-of-range index value.

The `size()` function for an `array` object returns the number of elements as type `size_t`, so you could sum the elements in the `values` array like this:

```
double total {};
for(size_t i {} ; i < values.size() ; ++i)
{
  total += values[i];
}
```

The presence of the `size()` function provides the advantage over a standard array that an `array` container knows how many elements it contains; a function receiving an array container as an argument can just call the `size()` member to get the number of elements. You don't have to call the `size()` member to decide whether an `array` container has no elements. The `empty()` member returns `true` if the container has no elements:

```
if(values.empty())
    std::cout << "The container has no elements.\n";
else
    std::cout << "The container has " << values.size() <<  " elements.\n";
```

However, it's hard to visualize how an `array` container would have no elements because the number of elements is fixed when you create it and cannot be changed. The only way to create an empty array container instance is to specify the argument for the second template parameter as zero – an unlikely occurrence. However, the same mechanism of calling `empty()` applies to other containers where the number of elements can vary and elements can be deleted so it provides a consistent operation.

You can use the range-based `for` loop with any container that makes iterators available so you can sum the elements in the `values` container more simply:

```
double total {};
for(auto&& value : values)
  total += value;
```

Of course, this can be done with a container that is passed as an argument to a function, too.

The front() and back() function members of an array container return references to the first and last elements respectively. There is also the data() function member that returns &front(), which is the address of the underlying standard array that stores the elements. You are unlikely to need this facility often.

There is a function template for a get<n>() helper function to access the nth element from an array container; the argument for the template parameter must be a constant expression that can be evaluated at compile time so it cannot be a loop variable, for example. The element that is accessed is the template parameter, which is checked at compile time. The get<n>() template provides a way to access elements with an assured index value without the runtime checking. Here's how you could use it:

```
std::array<std::string, 5> words {"one", "two", "three", "four", "five"};
std::cout << std::get<3>(words) << std::endl;  // Output words[3]
std::cout << std::get<6>(words) << std::endl;  // Compiler error message!
```

Here's an example that demonstrates array containers in action using some of what you've learned so far:

```cpp
// Ex2_01.cpp
/*
 Using array<T,N> to create a Body Mass Index (BMI) table
 BMI = weight/(height*height)
 weight is in kilograms, height is in meters
*/

#include <iostream>                         // For standard streams
#include <iomanip>                          // For stream manipulators
#include <array>                            // For array<T,N>

int main()
{
  const unsigned int min_wt {100U};         // Minimum weight in table in lbs
  const unsigned int max_wt {250U};         // Maximum weight in table in lbs
  const unsigned int wt_step {10U};         // Weight increment
  const size_t wt_count {1 + (max_wt - min_wt) / wt_step};

  const unsigned int min_ht {48U};          // Minimum height in table in inches
  const unsigned int max_ht {84U};          // Maximum height in table in inches
  const unsigned int ht_step {2U};          // Height increment
  const size_t ht_count { 1 + (max_ht - min_ht) / ht_step };

  const double lbs_per_kg {2.20462};        // Conversion factor lbs to kg
  const double ins_per_m {39.3701};         // Conversion factor ins to m

  std::array<unsigned int, wt_count> weight_lbs;
  std::array<unsigned int, ht_count> height_ins;

  // Create weights from 100lbs in steps of 10lbs
  for (size_t i{}, w{ min_wt } ; i < wt_count ; w += wt_step, ++i)
  {
    weight_lbs.at(i) = w;
  }
```

```cpp
// Create heights from 48 inches in steps of 2 inches
unsigned int h{ min_ht };
for(auto& height : height_ins)
{
  height = h;
  h += ht_step;
}

// Output table headings
std::cout << std::setw(7) << " |";
for (const auto& w : weight_lbs)
  std::cout << std::setw(5) << w << "  |";
std::cout << std::endl;

// Output line below headings
for (size_t i{1} ; i < wt_count ; ++i)
  std::cout << "---------";
std::cout << std::endl;

double bmi {};                              // Stores BMI
unsigned int feet {};                       // Whole feet for output
unsigned int inches {};                     // Whole inches for output
const unsigned int inches_per_foot {12U};
for (const auto& h : height_ins)
{
  feet = h / inches_per_foot;
  inches = h % inches_per_foot;
  std::cout <<  std::setw(2) << feet << "'" << std::setw(2) << inches << "\"" << "|";
  std::cout << std::fixed << std::setprecision(1);
  for (const auto& w : weight_lbs)
  {
    bmi = h / ins_per_m;
    bmi = (w / lbs_per_kg) / (bmi*bmi);
    std::cout << std::setw(2) << " " << bmi << " |";
  }
  std::cout << std::endl;
}
// Output line below table
for (size_t i {1} ; i < wt_count ; ++i)
  std::cout << "---------";
std::cout << "\nBMI from 18.5 to 24.9 is normal" << std::endl;
}
```

I haven't shown the output from the example in the book because it takes quite a lot of space. There are two sets of four const variables defined that relate to the range of weights and heights to be included in the BMI table. The weights and heights are stored in array containers that have elements of type unsigned int because all the weights and heights are integral and non-negative by definition. The containers are initialized with the appropriate values in for loops. The first loop demonstrates the at() function but you could safely use weight_lbs[i] here. The next two for loops output the table column headings and a line to separate the headings from the rest of the table. The table is created using nested range-based for loops. The outer loop iterates over the heights and outputs the height in the leftmost column in feet and inches. The inner loop iterates over the weights and outputs a row of BMI values for the current height.

Using Iterators with array Containers

The array template defines begin() and end() members that return *random access iterators* that point to
the first element and one past the last element respectively. As you saw in chapter 1, random access iterators
are the most capable so all operations are possible with these. You could use explicit iterators to code the
loop that sets up the values in the height_ins container:

```
unsigned int h {min_ht};
auto first = height_ins.begin();      // Iterator pointing to 1st element
auto last = height_ins.end();         // Iterator pointing to 1 past last element
while (first != last)
{
  *first++ = h;                       // Store h in current element and increment iterator
  h += ht_step;
}
```

The iterator objects are returned by the begin() and end() member functions of the array object. Using
auto saves having to worry about the actual type for the iterators – but in case you are wondering – in this
case they are of type std::array<unsigned int,19>::iterator, which implies that the iterator type is
defined within the array<T,N> type. You can see that you use an iterator object in the same way as a regular
pointer – the postfix ++ operator increments first after the value has been stored in the element. When
first is equal to end, all the elements have been set and the loop ends.

As I said in chapter 1, it's better to use the global begin() and end() functions to obtain iterators for a
container because they are applicable generally, so first and last could be defined like this:

```
auto first = std::begin(height_ins);   // Iterator pointing to 1st element
auto last = std::end(height_ins);      // Iterator pointing to 1 past last element
```

Keep in mind that while iterators point to specific elements in a container, they retain no information
about the container itself; there's no way to tell from an iterator whether it points to an element in an
array container or a vector. Having iterators identifying a range of elements in a container introduces the
possibility of applying algorithms to them, so are there any algorithms that could be used in Ex2_01.cpp?
The generate() function template that is defined in the algorithm header that provides a way to initialize
a range with values that are computed by a function object is one possibility. We could rewrite the previous
code fragment that initializes the height_ins container like this:

```
unsigned int height {};                // Stores the current height initializing value
std::generate(std::begin(height_ins), std::end(height_ins),
            [height, &min_ht, &ht_step]()mutable
                     { return height += height == 0 ? min_ht : ht_step; });
```

Setting the values for the container element is down to two statements now, and no explicit loops are
needed. The first statement defines a variable to hold the initializer for an element. The first two arguments
to the generate() function are the begin and end iterators that define the range whose values are to be
set by the function passed as the third argument. Here it is a lambda expression. The min_ht and ht_step
variables are captured by reference in the lambda and the mutable keyword enables the lambda to update
the value of the local copy of height, which is captured by value. In the return statement, the local height
copy is set to min_ht the first time the lambda executes and is incremented by ht_step in subsequent calls.
The value of a local copy of a variable that is captured by value in a lambda expression is retained from one
execution of the lambda to the next, which enables this mechanism to work as we want.

Suppose you wanted to initialize an array container with successively incremented values. There's the iota() function template for that – in the numeric header. Here's how it could be used:

```
std::array<double, 10> values;
std::iota(std::begin(values), std::end(values), 10.0);  // Set values elements to 10.0 to 19.0
```

The first two arguments are iterators defining the range of elements to be set. The third argument is the value for the first element in the range. Subsequent element values are generated by applying the increment operator. The iota() function is not limited to working with numeric values. The range of elements to be set can be of any type that supports operator++().

■ **Note**   Don't forget that algorithms are independent of the type of container. They work with elements from any container that has iterators of the required type. The generate() and iota() function templates only require forward iterators, so iterators defining a range from any container will work.

An array container defines cbegin() and cend() function members that return const iterators; you should use const iterators when you only want to access elements, and not modify them. As with non-const iterators, it's better to use the global cbegin() and cend() functions to obtain these. The rbegin() and rend() function – global and member – return reverse iterators that point to the last element and one before the first element respectively; the functions that return const reverse iterators are crbegin() and crend(). You use reverse iterators to process elements in reverse order. For example:

```
std::array<double, 5> these {1.0, 2.0, 3.0, 4.0, 5.0};
double sum {};
auto start = std::rbegin(these);
auto finish = std::rend(these);
while(start != finish)
  sum += *(start++);
std::cout << "The sum of elements in reverse order is " << sum << std::endl;
```

The elements are summed in the loop, starting with the last element. The finish iterator points to one before the first element, so the loop ends after the first element has been added to sum. Applying the increment operator to a reverse iterator moves what it points to in the opposite direction to a regular forward iterator. You could use a for loop here:

```
for(auto iter = std::rbegin(these); iter != std::rend(these); ++iter)
  sum += *iter;
```

Because an array container instance has a fixed number of elements, insert iterators don't apply; insert iterators are used to add new elements to a container.

Comparing array Containers

You can compare two entire `array<T,N>` containers using any of the comparison operators as long as the containers are of the same size and store elements of the same type and the type supports comparison operations. For example:

```
std::array<double,4> these {1.0, 2.0, 3.0, 4.0};
std::array<double,4> those {1.0, 2.0, 3.0, 4.0};
std::array<double,4> them  {1.0, 3.0, 3.0, 2.0};

if (these == those) std::cout << "these and those are equal."     << std::endl;
if (those != them)  std::cout << "those and them are not equal." << std::endl;
if (those < them)   std::cout << "those are less than them."      << std::endl;
if (them > those)   std::cout << "them are greater than those."  << std::endl;
```

Containers are compared element by element. For a `true` result for `==`, all pairs of corresponding elements must be equal. For inequality, at least one pair of corresponding elements must be different for a `true` result. For all the other comparisons, the first pair of elements that differ produces the result. This is essentially the way in which words in a dictionary are ordered where the first pair of corresponding letters that differ in two words determines their order. All the comparisons in the code fragment are `true`, so all four messages will be output when this executes.

Unlike standard arrays, you can assign one `array` container to another, as long as they both store the same number of elements of the same type. For example:

```
them = those;      // Copy all elements of those to them
```

The elements in the array container on the left of the assignment are overwritten with the elements from the container on the right of the assignment.

Using vector<T> Containers

The `vector<T>` container is a sequence container for elements of type `T`. It's like an `array<T,N>` container except that the size can grow automatically to accommodate any number of elements; hence the requirement for only the type parameter `T` – there's no need for the `N` template parameter with a `vector`. As soon as the current capacity of a `vector` is exceeded, additional space for more elements is allocated automatically. Elements can only be added or deleted efficiently at the end of the container. A `vector` container is a very useful and flexible alternative to an array. You can use a `vector` as a standard workhorse for storing a sequence instead of an array most of the time. As long as you are conscious of the overhead in extending the capacity of a `vector` or adding or deleting elements from the interior of the sequence, your code won't be appreciably slower in most instances. To use the `vector` container template you must include the `vector` header in your source file.

Creating vector<T> Containers

Here's an example of creating a `vector` container to store values of type `double`:

```
std::vector<double> values;
```

This has no elements and no space for elements allocated so memory will be allocated dynamically when you add the first data item. You can increase the capacity by calling reserve() for the container object:

```
values.reserve(20);                    // Memory for up to 20 elements
```

This sets the memory allocated in the container to accommodate at least 20 elements. If the current capacity is already greater than or equal to 20, this statement does nothing. Note that calling reserve() does not create any elements. The values container still has no elements at this point, but up to 20 elements can be added before more memory is allocated. Calling reserve() does not affect any existing elements. However, if the memory is increased by the call, any existing iterators, such as begin and end iterators, will be invalidated so you must recreate them. This is because elements are likely to be copied or moved to new memory locations as a result of increasing the capacity.

A further option for creating a vector is to use an initializer list to specify initial values as well as the number of elements:

```
std::vector<unsigned int> primes {2u, 3u, 5u, 7u, 11u, 13u, 17u, 19u};
```

The primes vector container will be created with eight elements with the initial values in the initializer list.

Allocating memory is relatively expensive in time so you don't want it to occur more often than necessary. A vector will increase capacity using an algorithm that depends on the implementation that is often logarithmic. This can result in several very small memory allocations early on, but with increments of an increasing amount as the vector is extended. You can create a vector with an initial number of elements defined, like this:

```
std::vector<double> values(20);    // Capacity is 20 double values and there are 20 elements
```

This container starts out with 20 elements created that are initialized with zero by default. It's a good idea to create a vector container with the number of elements that will minimize the number of times additional space needs to be allocated.

■ **Caution** The parentheses around 20, the number of elements, are essential in the statement above. You can't use braces here. If you write the following definition, the result is quite different:

```
std::vector<double> values {20};        // There is one element initialized to 20
```

This vector doesn't have 20 elements; it contains one element initialized to 20. Adding more elements will cause additional memory to be allocated.

If you don't like zero as the default value for elements, you can specify a value that will apply for all elements:

```
std::vector<long> numbers(20, 99L);    // Size is 20 long values - all initialized with 99
```

The second argument specifies the initial value for all elements so all 20 elements will be 99L. The first argument that specifies the number of elements in the vector does not need to be a constant expression. It could be the result of an expression executed at runtime or read in from the keyboard.

You can initialize a vector<T> container when you create it with elements of type T from another container. You specify the range of elements to be used as the initial values using a pair of iterators. Here's an example:

```
std::array<std::string, 5> words {"one", "two", "three", "four", "five"};
std::vector<std::string> words_copy {std::begin(words), std::end(words)};
```

The words_copy vector will be initialized with the elements from the words array container. If you were to use move iterators to specify the initializing range for words_copy, the elements would be moved from the words array. Here's how you could do that:

```
std::vector<std::string> words_copy {std::make_move_iterator(std::begin(words)),
                                     std::make_move_iterator(std::end(words))};
```

The words_copy vector would be initialized as before. Because the elements are moved rather than copied, the words array would now contain string objects representing the empty string, "".

The Capacity and Size of a Vector

The *capacity* of a vector is the number of elements that it can store without allocating more memory; these elements may or may not exist. The *size* of a vector is the number of elements it actually contains, which is the number of elements that have values stored. Figure 2-3 illustrates this.

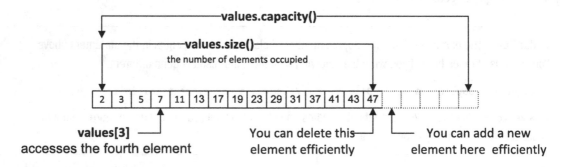

Figure 2-3. *The size and capacity of a vector*

Obviously the size of a vector container cannot exceed its capacity. When the size equals the capacity, adding an element will cause more memory to be allocated. You can obtain the size and capacity of a vector by calling the size() or capacity() function for the vector object. These values are returned as integers of an unsigned integral type that is defined by your implementation. For example:

```
std::vector<size_t> primes { 2, 3, 5, 7, 11, 13, 17, 19, 23, 29, 31, 37, 41 ,43 ,47 };
std::cout << "The size is " << primes.size() << std::endl;
std::cout << "The capacity is " << primes.capacity() << std::endl;
```

The output statements will present the value 14 for the size and the capacity, as determined by the initializer list. However, if you add an element using the push_back() function and output the size and capacity again, the size will be 15 and the capacity will be 28. The increment for increasing the capacity when the size is equal to the capacity is determined by an algorithm that is implementation dependent; some implementations double the existing capacity.

You might want to store the size or capacity of a vector in a variable. The type for the size or capacity for a vector<T> object is vector<T>::size_type, which implies that size_type is defined within the vector<T> class that the compiler generates from the class template. Thus for the primes vector the size value will be type vector<size_t>::size_type. You can avoid worrying about such details most of the time by using the auto keyword when you define the variable, for example:

```
auto nElements = primes.size();        // Store the number of elements
```

Remember, you must use = with auto – not an initializer list; otherwise the type will not be determined correctly. A common reason for storing the size is to iterate over the elements in a vector using an index. You can also use a range-based for loop with a vector:

```
for(auto& prime : primes)
  prime *= 2;                           // Double each element value
```

You saw earlier that you can call reserve() for a vector to increase its capacity; the number of elements is not changed. Calling the resize() function member changes the size of the vector, which may also increase the capacity. There are several varieties of resize(), for example:

```
std::vector<int> values {1,2,3};     // 1 2 3            : size is 3
values.resize(5);                    // 1 2 3 0 0        : size is 5
values.resize(7, 99);                // 1 2 3 0 0 99 99  : size is 7
values.resize(6);                    // 1 2 3 0 0 99     : size is 6
```

The first resize() call changes the size to the number of elements specified by the argument so it appends two elements initialized with the default value for the type. If adding the elements causes the current capacity to be exceeded, the capacity will be increased automatically. The second resize() call increases the size to the value specified by the first argument and initializes the new elements with the value specified by the second argument. The third call changes the size of the values container to 6, which is less than the current size. When the size needs to be reduced, excess elements are removed as if pop_back() for the container is called repeatedly, which I'll explain a little later in this chapter. Reducing the size of a vector does not affect its current capacity.

Accessing Elements

You can use an index between square brackets to set a value for an existing element or just to use its current value in an expression. For example:

```
std::vector<double> values(20);            // Container with 20 elements created
values[0] = 3.14159;                       // Pi
values[1] = 5.0;                           // Radius of a circle
values[2] = 2.0*values[0]*values[1];       // Circumference of a circle
```

Index values for a vector start from 0, just like a standard array. You can always reference existing elements using an index between square brackets but you cannot create new elements this way – you must use push_back(), insert(), emplace(), or emplace_back(). The index values are not checked when you index a vector like this. You can access memory outside the extent of the array and store values in such locations using an index between square brackets. The vector object provides the at() function that does bounds checking for the argument, just like an array container, so use the at() function to refer to elements whenever there is the potential for the index to be outside the legal range.

The front() and back() function members of a vector return references to the first and last elements in the sequence. For example:

```
std::cout << values.front() << std::endl;        // Outputs 3.14159
```

Because the front() and back() function members returns references, they can appear on the left of an assignment:

```
values.front() = 2.71828;                        // 1st element changed to 2.71828
```

The data() function member returns a pointer to the array that is used internally in a vector to store the elements. For example:

```
auto pData = values.data();
```

pData will be of type double*, and in general data() returns a value of type T* for a vector<T> container. You need to have a very good reason for using this capability.

Using Iterators with a vector Container

As you would expect, a vector container has a full complement of the function members that return iterators for its elements, including const and non-const iterators and reverse iterators. The iterators for a vector are *random access iterators*, and of course, you can use the global functions to obtain them too. A vector has a push_back() function member so you can use a back_insert_iterator to append new elements to it. You'll remember from chapter 1 that you can obtain a back insert iterator by calling the global back_inserter() function. A front_insert_iterator won't work with a vector container because it requires a push_front() function member, which a vector container doesn't define.

I can demonstrate how you can apply a back inserter iterator to a vector by showing how you use the copy() algorithm to add elements. The copy() algorithm copies elements from the range specified by the iterators supplied as the first two arguments to the destination specified by the iterator that is the third argument. The first two arguments only need to be input iterators so any category of iterators will be accepted; obviously the third argument must be an output iterator. Here's an example:

```
std::vector<double> data {32.5, 30.1, 36.3, 40.0, 39.2};
std::cout << "Enter additional data values separated by spaces or Ctrl+Z to end:"
          << std::endl;
std::copy(std::istream_iterator<double>(std::cin), std::istream_iterator<double>(),
                                       std::back_inserter(data));
std::copy(std::begin(data), std::end(data), std::ostream_iterator<double>(std::cout, " "));
```

The data container is created with elements set to the values in the initializer list. The first call of copy() has an istream_iterator object as the first argument that reads values of type double from the standard input stream. The second argument is effectively an end iterator for the stream iterator and the istream_iterator will have this value when the end of the stream is recognized; this occurs with cin when you enter Ctrl+Z from the keyboard. The third argument to copy() is the destination for the values read and this is a back_insert_iterator for data that is returned by the back_inserter() function. Thus the values that are read from cin are appended to the end of data as new elements. The last statement calls copy() to copy all the elements in data to cout; this is achieved by specifying the destination as an ostream_iterator object. Let's try a complete example using iterators with a vector container:

```cpp
// Ex2_02.cpp
// Sorting strings in a vector container
#include <iostream>                        // For standard streams
#include <string>                          // For string types
#include <algorithm>                       // For swap() and copy() functions
#include <vector>                          // For vector (and iterators)
using std::string;
using std::vector;

int main()
{
  vector<string> words;                    // Stores words to be sorted
  words.reserve(10);                       // Allocate some space for elements
  std::cout << "Enter words separated by spaces. Enter Ctrl+Z on a separate line to end:"
            << std::endl;
  std::copy(std::istream_iterator<string> {std::cin}, std::istream_iterator<string> {},
                                            std::back_inserter(words));

  std::cout << "Starting sort." << std::endl;
  bool out_of_order {false};               // true when values are not in order
  auto last = std::end(words);
  while (true)
  {
    for (auto first = std::begin(words) + 1; first != last; ++first)
    {
      if (*(first - 1) > *first)
      { // Out of order so swap them
        std::swap(*first, *(first - 1));
        out_of_order = true;
      }
    }
    if (!out_of_order)                     // If they are in order (no swaps necessary)...
      break;                               // ...we are done...
    out_of_order = false;                  // ...otherwise, go round again.
  }

  // Output the sorted vector
  std::cout << "your words in ascending sequence:" << std::endl;
  std::copy(std::begin(words), std::end(words),
            std::ostream_iterator<string> {std::cout, " "});
  std::cout << std::endl;

  // Create a new vector by moving elements from words vector
  vector<string> words_copy {std::make_move_iterator(std::begin(words)),
                             std::make_move_iterator(std::end(words)) };
```

```
std::cout << "\nAfter moving elements from words, words_copy contains:" << std::endl;
std::copy(std::begin(words_copy), std::end(words_copy),
          std::ostream_iterator<string> {std::cout, " "});
std::cout << std::endl;

// See what's happened to elements in words vector...
std::cout << "\nwords vector has " << words.size() << " elements\n";
if (words.front().empty())
  std::cout << "First element is empty string object." << std::endl;

  std::cout << "First element is \"" << words.front() <<  "\"" << std::endl;
}
```

Here's some sample output:

```
Enter words separated by spaces. Enter Ctrl+Z on a separate line to end:
one two three four five six seven eight
^Z
Starting sort.
your words in ascending sequence:
eight five four one seven six three two

After moving elements from words, words_copy contains:
eight five four one seven six three two

words vector has 8 elements
First element is empty string object.
First element is ""
```

This program reads words from the standard input stream as `string` objects into a `vector` container using a stream iterator. Any number of words can be entered. The container will expand automatically when necessary. Calling `reserve()` for the container allocates memory for 10 elements here. It's a good idea to always allocate roughly the memory or the number of elements that are likely be needed; this will minimize the overhead from allocating space in small increments. `back_inserter()` creates a `back_insert_iterator` that calls the `push_back()` member of the container to add each `string` object as a new element.

The first two arguments to the `copy()` algorithm are input stream iterators and the second of these is the end-of-stream iterator. The stream iterator will match this when `Ctrl+Z` is entered from the keyboard, which corresponds to end-of-file (EOF) for a file stream.

The code to sort the elements in the `vector` is there to demonstrate using iterators. You'll see later in the book that there's a `sort()` algorithm that would do the job in a single statement. The sort method here is a simple bubble sort that iterates over the elements to be sorted repeatedly. During each pass, adjacent elements are swapped if they are not in order. The `swap()` function that is defined by a template in the `algorithm` header will efficiently interchange elements of any type. If there is a complete pass through all the elements where no swaps are necessary, the elements are in ascending sequence. The outer loop is a `for` loop controlled by an iterator. The initial value for `first` is `begin(words)+1`, which is an iterator that points to the second element in the `vector`. Starting with the second element ensures that using `first-1` when comparing successive elements is always legal. Each pass ends when `first` is incremented to match the iterator corresponding to `end(words)`.

The sorted contents of the words vector are displayed by using the copy() algorithm to transfer the elements to an output stream iterator. The range to be transferred is specified by the iterators returned by begin() and end() so all the elements will be output. The arguments to the ostream_iterator constructor are the stream where the data is to go and the separator string that is to be written following each output value.

The last section of code in main() demonstrates using a move iterator and the effect on the source elements that are moved. You can see from the output that after the operation the elements in words end up as string objects that contain empty strings ; moving the elements has left behind objects that correspond to what the no-arg string constructor creates. In general though, moving an element that is a class object will leave the element in an indeterminate state, so it should not be used.

The code in main() that does the sorting is not really dependent on the container where the elements are stored. It only requires that the data to be sorted is specified by iterators that support the operations used by the sorting method. If I ignore for the moment that the STL has a sort() function template that is far better than anything I could come up with, I can define our very own function template for sorting elements of any type that meet the requirements for sorting them:

```
template<typename RandomIter>
void bubble_sort(RandomIter start, RandomIter last)
{
  std::cout << "Starting sort." << std::endl;
  bool out_of_order {false};                // true when values are not in order
  while (true)
  {
    for (auto first = start + 1; first != last; ++first)
    {
      if (*(first - 1) > *first)
      { // Out of order so swap them
        std::swap(*first, *(first - 1));
        out_of_order = true;
      }
    }
    if (!out_of_order)                       // If they are in order (no swaps necessary)...
      break;                                 // ...we are done...
    out_of_order = false;                    // ...otherwise, go round again.
  }
}
```

The template type parameter is the iterator type. The bubble_sort() algorithm needs random access iterators because of the arithmetic operations on the iterators in the for loop. This algorithm will sort the contents of *any* container that can supply random access iterators; this includes standard arrays and string objects. If you insert the code for the template preceding main() in the previous example, you can replace the code in main() that sorts the words vector by the following statement:

```
bubble_sort(std::begin(words), std::end(words));  // Sort the words array
```

Defining function templates for operations that can be implemented just using iterators makes their use very flexible. Any algorithm that you can define to operate on a range can be created similarly. The complete program using the bubble_sort() template is in the code download as Ex2_02A.

Adding New Elements to a vector Container

Keep in mind that the *only* way to add elements to a container is to call a function member. A non-member function can't add or delete elements without calling a function member for the container; this implies that the container object must be accessible in some way from the function to allow this—iterators are not sufficient.

Appending Elements

You can add an element to the end of a sequence using the push_back() function for the container object. For example:

```
std::vector<double> values;
values.push_back(3.1415926);              // Add an element to the end of the vector
```

The push_back() function adds a new element with the value you pass as the argument – 3.1415926 in this case – at the end of the existing elements. Since there are no existing elements here, this will be the first; if reserve() was not called for the container, this will cause memory to be allocated. There's a second version of push_back() with an rvalue reference parameter. This provides a move operation for adding elements. For example:

```
std::vector<std::string> words;
words.push_back(string("adiabatic"));  // Move string("adiabatic") into the vector
```

The argument to push_back() is a temporary object here so this will call the version with an rvalue reference parameter. Of course, you could write the operation as:

```
words.push_back("adiabatic");           // Move string("adiabatic") into the vector
```

The compiler will arrange for the string object argument to be created with "adiabatic" as the initial value and the object will be moved into the vector as before.

There's a better way to append a new element. The emplace_back() member does this more efficiently than push_back(). This fragment illustrates why:

```
std::vector<std::string> words;
words.push_back(std::string("facetious"));    // Calls string constructor & moves the
                                              //   string object
words.emplace_back("abstemious");             // Calls string constructor to create
                                              //   element in place
```

The arguments to the emplace_back() function are the arguments required by the constructor for the object to be appended to the container. The emplace_back() member creates the object in place in the container by calling the constructor for the object type using the argument or arguments you supply, thus eliminating the move operation for the object that push_back() would execute in this case. You can specify as many arguments in the emplace_back() member call as the constructor for the object requires. Here's an example with several arguments to emplace_back():

```
std::string str {"alleged"};
words.emplace_back(str, 2, 3);      // Create string object corresponding to "leg" in place
```

The emplace() function will call the string constructor that accepts the three arguments specified to create the object in place appended to the sequence in words. This constructor creates a string object that contains the three-character substring of str that begins with the character at index 2.

Inserting Elements

You can insert a new element in the interior of a vector sequence using the emplace() function member. The object is created in place rather than creating the object as a separate step, then passing it as the argument. The first argument to emplace() is an iterator that specifies the position where the object is to be created. The object will be inserted preceding the element specified by the iterator. The second and any subsequent arguments are passed to the constructor for the element to be inserted. For example:

```
std::vector<std::string> words {"first", "second"};
// Inserts string(5, 'A') as 2nd element
auto iter = words.emplace(++std::begin(words), 5, 'A');
// Inserts string("$$$$") as 3rd element
words.emplace(++iter, "$$$$");
```

After executing these statements, the vector elements will be the string objects for:

```
"first" "AAAAA" "$$$$" "second"
```

You can supply as many arguments to emplace() following the first as needed for the constructor call that creates the object to be inserted. The first call of the emplace() member in the code fragment above creates the string object that result from the string(5, 'A') constructor call. The emplace() function returns an iterator that points to the inserted element, and this is used in the following statement to insert another object following the previous object that was inserted.

The insert() function member can insert one or more elements in a vector. The first argument is always a const or non-const iterator that points to the insertion point. The element or elements are inserted immediately *before* the element pointed to by the first argument unless it is a reverse iterator, in which case elements are inserted immediately *after* the insertion point. You are spoiled for choice with the insert() member so I'll illustrate each of the possibilities with a separate statement. I'll first define a vector to which the list of insert() function calls that follow are applied successively:

```
std::vector<std::string> words {"one", "three", "eight"};          // Vector with 3 elements
```

The options you have available with the insert() members of words are:

1. Insert a single element that is specified by the second argument:

```
auto iter = words.insert(++std::begin(words), "two");
```

In this example the insertion point is specified by incrementing the iterator returned by begin(). This corresponds to the second element so the new element will be inserted before this as a new second element. The original elements from the second to the last will all be displaced one position to make room for the new element. There are two insert() overloads that insert a single object, one with the second parameter as type const T& and the other with the second parameter as type T&& – an rvalue reference. Because the second argument above is a temporary object, the second of these overloads will be called and the temporary object will be moved, rather than copied.

After executing the statement, the words vector contains string elements representing:

```
"one" "two" "three" "eight"
```

The iterator than is returned points to the element that was inserted, string("two"). Note that this insert() call is not as efficient as calling emplace() with the same arguments. With the insert() call, the constructor call string("two") is executed to create the object that is then passed as the second argument. With emplace() the second argument is used to construct the string object in place in the container.

2. Insert a sequence of elements that is specified by iterators that are the second and third arguments:

```
std::string more[] {"five", "six", "seven"};        // Array elements to be inserted
iter = words.insert(--std::end(words), std::begin(more), std::end(more));
```

The insertion point in the second statement is obtained by decrementing the iterator returned by end(). This corresponds to the last element, so the new elements will be inserted before this. After executing this statement, the words vector contains string object for:

"one" "two" "three" "five" "six" "seven" "eight"

The iterator than is returned points to the first element that was inserted, "five".

3. Insert an element at the end of the vector:

```
iter = words.insert(std::end(words), "ten");
```

The insertion point is one beyond the last element so the new element will be appended after the last element. After executing this statement, the words vector contains string objects for:

"one" "two" "three" "five" "six" "seven" "eight" "ten"

The iterator than is returned points to the element that was inserted, "ten". This is the same overload as point 1 above; this just illustrates that it works when the first argument is not pointing to an element, but one past the last element.

4. Insert multiples of a single element at the insertion point. The second argument is the number of times the object specified by the third argument is to be inserted:

```
iter = words.insert(std::cend(words)-1, 2, "nine");
```

The insertion point is the last element so two copies of the new element, string("nine"), will be inserted before the last element. After executing this statement, the words vector contains string objects for:

"one" "two" "three" "five" "six" "seven" "eight" "nine" "nine" "ten"

The iterator than is returned points to the first element that was inserted, "nine". Note that the first argument in the example is a const iterator, just to show that a const iterator works too.

5. Insert elements specified by an initializer list at the insertion point. The second argument is the initializer list of elements to be inserted:

```
iter = words.insert(std::end(words), {std::string {"twelve"},
                                       std::string {"thirteen"}});
```

The insertion point is one beyond the last element so the elements from the initializer list are appended. After executing this statement, the words vector contains string objects for:

"one" "two" "three" "five" "six" "seven" "eight" "nine" "nine" "ten" "twelve" "thirteen"

The iterator than is returned points to the first element that was inserted, "twelve." The values in the initializer list must match the type of the container elements. An initializer list of values of type T is of type std::initializer_list<T> so the list here is of type std::initializer_list<std::string>. Where a literal appears as an argument in previous insert() calls, the parameter type is std::string so the literal will be used as the value to initialize a string object that is passed to the function.

Keep in mind that all insertions other than at the end of a vector carry overhead. All the elements that follow the insertion point have to be shuffled along to make room for the new element or elements. Of course, if the number of elements after an insertion will be greater than the capacity, more memory will need to be allocated, which adds further overhead.

The insert() member of a vector expects you to use a standard iterator to specify the insertion point; a reverse iterator won't be accepted – it won't compile. The need to use reverse iterators could arise when you want to find the last occurrence of a given object in a sequence and insert a new element adjacent to it. The base() function member of a reverse iterator will help. Here's an example:

```
std::vector<std::string> str {"one", "two", "one", "three"};
auto riter = std::find(std::rbegin(str), std::rend(str), "one");
str.insert(riter.base(), "five");
```

The find() algorithm searches a range specified by the first two arguments for the first element that matches the third argument, so it's looking for string("one"). It returns an iterator of the type you use to specify the range. The result will be a reverse iterator pointing to the element that was found, or one before the first element, rend(str), if it was not found. Using reverse iterators means the search finds the last element that matches; using standard iterators would find the first occurrence, or return end(str) if it was not found. Calling the base() function member of riter returns the standard iterator corresponding to the position preceding iter in the reverse sense, that is, toward the end of the sequence. Since riter will point to the third element, which contains "one", riter.base() will point to the fourth element that contains "three". Using riter.base() as the first argument to insert() results in "five" being inserted *before* that position, which is *after* the element to which riter points. After executing these statements, str will contain these five string elements:

```
"one", "two", "one", "five", "three"
```

If you wanted the insertion to be *before* the position returned by find(), you would specify the first argument to insert() as iter.base()-1.

Deleting Elements

As I said, you can *only* delete elements from a container by calling a function member of the container object. You can remove all the elements from a vector object by calling its clear() member. For example:

```
std::vector<int> data(100, 99);        // Contains 100 elements initialized to 99
data.clear();                          // Remove all elements
```

The first statement creates a vector object with 100 elements of type int so the size is 100 and the capacity is 100; all the elements are initialized to 99. The second statement removes all the elements so the size will be 0; the capacity is unchanged by the operation so it will still be 100.

You can delete the last element from a vector object by calling its pop_back() function. For example:

```
std::vector<int> data(100, 99);        // Contains 100 elements initialized to 99
data.pop_back();                       // Remove the last element
```

The second statement removes the last element so the size of data will be 99 and the capacity left as 100.

As long as you don't care about the order of the elements, being able to delete the last element provides a way to remove any element without shuffling elements along. Suppose you want to delete the second element from the vector, data. Here's how you could do that:

```
std::swap(std::begin(data)+1, std::end(data)-1); // Interchange 2nd element with the last
data.pop_back();                                 // Remove the last element
```

The first statement calls the swap() template function that is defined in the algorithm header as well as in the utility header. This interchanges the second and last elements. Calling pop_back() then removes the last element, which was the second element, thus eliminating it from the container.

■ **Note**   A vector container has a swap() function member. This will swap the elements in the container for which the function is called with the elements of a vector container that is passed as the argument. Obviously, both vector containers must store elements of the same type. The global swap() function will also swap the elements of two vector containers passed as arguments.

If you don't need the excess capacity in a container – because you won't be adding further elements for example, you can eliminate it by calling the shrink_to_fit() member:

```
data.shrink_to_fit();                    // Reduce the capacity to that needed for elements
```

Whether this works depends on the implementation of your STL. If it does work, any iterators for the vector that are still around may be invalidated so it's best to obtain new iterators after this operation.

You can call the erase() function member of a vector to delete one or more elements. To remove a single element, you supply a single iterator argument, for example:

```
auto iter = data.erase(std::begin(data)+1);      // Delete the second element
```

The size of the vector will be reduced by 1 as a result of deleting the element; the capacity will be unchanged. The iterator that is returned points to the element following the element that was removed. Here the value will correspond to the expression std::begin(data)+1; if it was the last element that was removed, the iterator returned will be std::end(data).

To eliminate a sequence of elements, you supply two iterator arguments that define the range of elements to be erased. For example:

```
// Delete the 2nd and 3rd elements
auto iter = data.erase(std::begin(data)+1, std::begin(data)+3);
```

Don't forget – the second iterator in a range specification points to one after the last element in the range. This erases the elements at positions std::begin(data)+1 and std::begin(data)+2. The iterator that is returned points to the element following the deleted elements so it will be std::begin(data)+1 or std::end(data) if the last element was deleted.

The remove() algorithm that is produced by a template that is defined in the algorithm header removes elements from a range that match a specific value. Here's an example:

```
std::vector<std::string> words { "one", "none", "some", "all", "none", "most", "many"};
auto iter = std::remove(std::begin(words), std::end(words), "none");
```

The second statement removes all occurrences of the third argument to remove(), which will be string("none"), from the range specified by the first two arguments . Removing elements is a little misleading. remove() is a global function so it cannot *delete* elements from a container. The way remove() *removes* elements is similar to the process for eliminating spaces from a string – by copying elements from the right to *overwrite* the elements that match the third argument. Figure 2-4 illustrates how this works.

std::vector<std::string> words { "one", "none", "some", "all", "none", "most", "many"};

auto iter = std::remove(std::begin(words), std::end(words), "none");

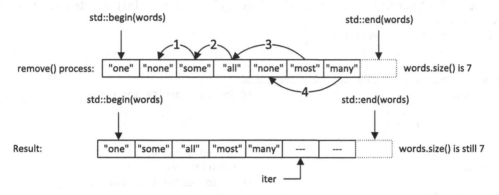

Figure 2-4. *How the remove() algorithm works*

If you output the elements in words after the remove() operation, only the first five elements would be displayed. However, the value returned by calling size() for the vector is still seven, so the last two elements are still there but have been replaced by empty string objects. To get rid of the surplus elements you must call the erase() member of the vector and the iterator that remove() returns can be used to do this:

```
words.erase(iter, std::end(words));                 // Remove surplus elements
```

This is called the *erase-remove idiom*. The iterator iter points to one past the last element after deletions so it identifies the first element in the range to be deleted. The end of the range to be deleted is given by std::end(words). Of course, you can remove the elements and then delete the unwanted elements at the end in a single statement:

```
words.erase(std::remove(std::begin(words), std::end(words), "none"), std::end(words));
```

The iterator that the remove() algorithm returns becomes the first argument to erase(); the second argument to erase() is the iterator pointing to one beyond the last element in the container.

Understanding how additional capacity is allocated for a vector container will give you an appreciation of how often you may incur the overhead, and the amount of memory that can get allocated. Here's an example that gives you an insight into this:

```
// Ex2_03.cpp
// Understanding how capacity is increased in a vector container
#include <iostream>                       // For standard streams
#include <vector>                         // For vector container
```

```cpp
int main()
{
  std::vector <size_t> sizes;               // Record numbers of elements
  std::vector <size_t> capacities;          // and corresponding capacities
  size_t el_incr {10};                      // Increment to initial element count
  size_t incr_count {4 * el_incr};          // Number of increments to element count

  for (size_t n_elements {}; n_elements < incr_count; n_elements += el_incr)
  {
    std::vector<int> values(n_elements);
    std::cout << "\nAppending to a vector with " << n_elements << " initial elements:\n";
    sizes.push_back(values.size());
    size_t space {values.capacity()};
    capacities.push_back(space);

    // Append elements to obtain capacity increases
    size_t count {};                        // Counts capacity increases
    size_t n_increases {10};
    while (count < n_increases)
    {
      values.push_back(22);                 // Append a new element
      if (space < values.capacity())        // Capacity increased...
      {                                     // ...so record size and capacity
        space = values.capacity();
        capacities.push_back(space);
        sizes.push_back(values.size());
        ++count;
      }
    }
    // Show sizes & capacities when increments occur
    std::cout << "Size/Capacity: ";
    for (size_t i {}; i < sizes.size(); ++i)
      std::cout << sizes.at(i) << "/" << capacities.at(i) << "  ";
    std::cout << std::endl;
    sizes.clear();                          // Remove all elements
    capacities.clear();                     // Remove all elements
  }
}
```

The operations in this example are straightforward. Elements are appended to a vector container until the capacity has to be increased, in which case the size and capacity at that point are recorded in the sizes and capacities containers. This is repeated for containers with different initial element counts. With my compiler, I got this output:

```
Appending to a vector with 0 initial elements:
Size/Capacity: 0/0  1/1  2/2  3/3  4/4  5/6  7/9  10/13  14/19  20/28  29/42

Appending to a vector with 10 initial elements:
Size/Capacity: 10/10  11/15  16/22  23/33  34/49  50/73  74/109  110/163  164/244  245/366
367/549
```

```
Appending to a vector with 20 initial elements:
Size/Capacity: 20/20   21/30   31/45   46/67   68/100   101/150   151/225   226/337   338/505
506/757   758/1135

Appending to a vector with 30 initial elements:
Size/Capacity: 30/30   31/45   46/67   68/100   101/150   151/225   226/337   338/505   506/757
758/1135   1136/1702
```

The output with your compiler may be different, depending on the algorithm used to increase vector capacity. You can see from the first set of output that the need to allocate more memory occurs very frequently when you start out with an empty vector because the capacity increments are small – memory for just one element to start with. The other groups of output show that the capacity increments are related to the size of the container. Each allocation is for an additional 50% of the current number of elements. This implies that some care is needed in choosing the initial size when you are able to do that.

Suppose that you create a vector with capacity for 1000 elements initially and in practice you store 1001 elements. You will have excess capacity for 499 elements. This won't matter if the elements are numerical values or objects that don't occupy much space. If the objects are large on the other hand 10 kilobytes each say—your program will have allocated almost 5 megabytes of memory that it doesn't use. Thus you can deduce that it's always better to overestimate the initial size of a vector a little, not underestimate it.

Of course it's possible to manage the allocation of additional memory yourself. If you compare the size and capacity, you can increase memory when necessary by an amount that you decide by calling reserve() for the container . For example:

```cpp
std::vector <size_t> junk {1, 2, 3};
for(size_t i {} ; i<1000 ; ++i)
{
  if(junk.size() == junk.capacity())        // When the size has reached the capacity...
    junk.reserve(junk.size()*13/10);        // ...increase the capacity
  junk.push_back(i);
}
```

The capacity increase here will be a maximum of 30%, instead of the default 50%. The capacity increment doesn't need to be a percentage of the current size. You can specify the argument to reserve() as junk. capacity()+10, for instance, to make the capacity increment 10 elements regardless of the current size. Don't forget that when reserve() increases the capacity, existing iterators for the container are no longer valid.

vector<bool> Containers

vector<bool> is a specialization of the vector<T> template that provides more efficient memory usage for elements of type bool. How it does this is implementation defined but usually bool elements are stored as single bits. Without the specialization, bool elements in a vector would typically occupy one byte each but it could be more – it's an implementation choice. The sequence of bool values won't necessarily be stored in contiguous memory locations so there is no data() function member. Some of the function members of the vector<bool> specialization operate slightly differently from a general template instance. bool values are not directly addressable when they are packed as bits in a word so the return values from the front() and back() are not bool& references but references to proxy objects that represent the first and last values in the sequence.

The bitset<N> class template that is defined in the bitset header is a better alternative to vector<bool> when you want to work with bool values and know how many you want to store. The template argument is the number of bits. This is not a container—there are no iterators for example, but a bitset instance provides a range of operations on bitsets that vector<bool> does not have. Because their applications tend to be rather specialized, I won't be discussing either vector<bool> or bitset<N> further.

Using deque<T> Containers

A deque<T> is a container template that is defined in the deque header that creates containers organized as a **d**ouble-ended **que**ue of elements of type T. It has the advantage over a vector container that you can add or delete objects efficiently at the beginning of the sequence as well as at the end so you choose this type of container when you need this capability. You would use a deque container whenever an application involves first-in first-out transaction processing. Applications such as processing database transactions or simulating checkout queues for a supermarket could make use of deque containers.

Creating deque Containers

If you create a deque container using the default constructor, the container has no elements so adding the first element will cause memory to be allocated:

```
std::deque<int> a_deque;        // A deque container with no elements
```

You create a deque container with a given number of elements in essentially the same way as a vector:

```
std::deque<int> my_deque(10);   // A deque container with 10 elements
```

A deque container with the name my_deque that stores elements of type int is illustrated in Figure 2-5; in this container, odd integers have been stored in the elements.

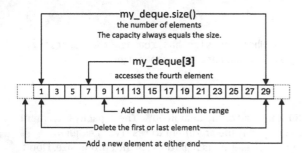

Figure 2-5. *An example of a deque container*

When you create a deque with a specified number of elements, each element will be the default value for the type stored, so the previous definition for my_deque will have all elements 0 initially. If you create a deque with a given number of string elements, each element will be initialized by calling the string() constructor.

You can also create a deque and initialize it using an initializer list:

```
std::deque<std::string> words { "one", "none", "some", "all", "none", "most", "many" };
```

This container will have seven string elements created using the literals in the initializer list. Of course, you could specify the objects in the initializer list as string("one"), string("none"), etc.

There's also a copy constructor for deque containers that creates a duplicate of an existing container:

```
std::deque<std::string> words_copy { words };        // Makes a copy of the words container
```

You can also use a range identified by two iterators to initialize a deque when you create it:

```
std::deque<std::string> words_part { std::begin(words), std::begin(words) + 5 };
```

This container will have five elements identical to the first five elements from the words container. Of course, the range of initial values could be from any kind of container – not necessarily a deque. A deque provides random access iterators, and you can obtain const and non-const iterators and reverse iterators for a deque container in the same way as for a vector.

Accessing Elements

You can access elements in a deque container using the subscript operator. This operation is similar to a vector so there's no bounds checking of the subscript. Elements in a deque container are a sequence but are stored internally in a different way from a vector. The way the elements are organized results in the size of a deque container always being equal to its capacity. For this reason there's no capacity() function member defined – a deque just has a size() member that returns the current size as an unsigned integer of the member type size_type. The slower operation compared to a vector is also the result of a deque container's different internal organization.

You can access elements using the subscript operator, but the index is not bounds checked. To access elements using an index that is bounds checked, you use the at() member function, just like a vector:

```
std::cout << words.at(2) << std::endl;          // Output the third element in words
```

The argument must be a value of type size_t and therefore cannot be less than 0. If the argument to at() is not within range, which will be when it is greater than words.size()-1, an std::out_of_range exception will be thrown.

The front() and back() function members also work in the same way as for a vector, however, there's no data() member function for a deque because the elements are not stored as an array. A deque container offers the same three variations of the resize() function member as a vector, and their operation is exactly the same.

Adding and Removing Elements

A deque container provides the same push_back() and pop_back() members that a vector has for adding and removing a single element at the end of the sequence and they work in the same way. A deque container also has push_front() and pop_front() functions members for analogous operations at the beginning of the sequence. For example:

```
std::deque<int> numbers {2, 3, 4};
numbers.push_front(11);          // numbers contains 11 2 3 4
numbers.push_back(12);           // numbers contains 11 2 3 4 12
numbers.pop_front();             // numbers contains 2 3 4 12
```

In addition to the emplace_back() member that a vector offers, a deque has an emplace_front() member for creating a new element in place at the beginning of the sequence. As with a vector, you can use emplace() or insert() to add or remove elements in the interior of a deque; the process is relatively slow because it always requires existing elements to be moved.

All the insert() function members that I described for a vector are also available for a deque container. Inserting elements anywhere in a deque invalidates all existing iterators for the deque so you must recreate them. The erase() member of a deque also works in the same way as for a vector. Calling clear() for a deque container removes all the elements.

Replacing the Contents of a deque Container

The assign() function member of a deque replaces all the existing elements. There are three versions; the new contents can be specified by an initializer list, the new contents can be a range specified by iterators, or the new contents can be multiple copies of a specified object. Here's how you replace the contents of a deque container with elements specified by an initializer list:

```
std::deque<std::string> words {"one", "two", "three", "four"};
auto init_list = {std::string{"seven"}, std::string{"eight"}, std::string{"nine"}};
words.assign(init_list);
```

The last statement replaces the elements in words by the string objects in init_list. Note that you cannot just put literals in the initializer list here. If you do, the type for init_list will be deduced to be initializer_list<const char*>, while assign() requires an argument of type initializer_list<string> so the code would not compile. Of course, you don't have to define init_list separately. You could call assign() and define the initializer list in the argument, like this:

```
words.assign({"seven", "eight", "nine"});
```

Because the assign() member of words expects an argument of type initializer_list<string>, the compiler will arrange to create an initializer list of this type using the literals. To assign a range of elements to a deque container, you supply two iterator arguments:

```
std::vector<std::string> wordset {"this", "that", "these", "those"};
words.assign(std::begin(wordset)+1, --std::end(wordset));  // Assigns "that" and "these"
```

The assign() function only needs input iterators so any category of iterator will do. The last possibility is to replace the contents by a repetition of an object:

```
words.assign(8, "eight");                        // Assign eight instances of string("eight")
```

The first argument is a count of the number of instances of the second argument that are to be used to replace the current contents of the container.

The vector container provides the same set of assign() function members so you can replace the elements in a vector by a new set.

You can also use the assignment operator to replace the contents of a deque container on the left of the assignment. The right operand of the assignment must be either a container of the same type, or an initializer list. This operation is supported by vector containers too. Here's an example that demonstrates assigning a new set of elements to a deque;

```
std::deque<std::string> words {"one", "two", "three", "four"};
std::deque<std::string> other_words;
other_words = words;                      // other_words same contents as words
words = {"seven", "eight", "nine"};       // words contents replaced
```

After executing these statements other_words will contain elements identical to the original sequence in words and words will contain string objects created from the literals in the initializer list. After an assignment, the size of the container will reflect the number of elements assigned. Assigning a new set of elements to a vector (from a vector of the same type or an initializer list) will result in the capacity of the vector being the same as the new size.

Here's a complete example that uses a deque container:

```
// Ex2_04.cpp
// Using a deque container
#include <iostream>                          // For standard streams
#include <algorithm>                         // For copy()
#include <deque>                             // For deque container
#include <string>                            // For string classes
#include <iterator>                          // For front_insert_iterator & stream
iterators

using std::string;

int main()
{
  std::deque<string> names;
  std::cout << "Enter first names separated by spaces. Enter Ctrl+Z on a new line to end:\n";
  std::copy(std::istream_iterator<string> {std::cin}, std::istream_iterator<string> {},
                                            std::front_inserter(names));
  std::cout << "\nIn reverse order, the names you entered are:\n";
  std::copy(std::begin(names), std::end(names), std::ostream_iterator<string>{std::cout, "  "});

  std::cout << std::endl;
}
```

Here is some sample output:

```
Enter first names separated by spaces. Enter Ctrl+Z on a new line to end:
Fred Jack Jim George Mary Zoe Rosie

^Z

In reverse order, the names you entered are:
Rosie  Zoe  Mary  George  Jim  Jack  Fred
```

This program reads a series of strings of any length and stores them in the names container. The copy() algorithm performs the input by copying the sequence obtained by the istream_iterator<string> iterator to the front_insert_iterator for the names container that the front_inserter() function returns. The first argument to copy() is the begin iterator for input and the second argument is the corresponding end iterator. The input iterator will correspond to the end iterator when you enter Ctrl+Z on the keyboard; if the data was being read from a file stream, the end iterator would result when EOF was reached. We can use a front_insert_iterator because a deque container has a push_front() member that adds an element to the beginning of the sequence; a front_insert_iterator works by calling push_front() for the container to add each element so it works for any container that has a push_front() member.

The output is also produced by calling the copy() algorithm. The first two arguments are iterators identifying the range of elements to be copied to the destination identified by the third argument. The first two arguments are the begin and end iterators for the deque container so all elements are copied. The destination is an ostream_iterator that accepts string objects and writes them to the standard output stream.

Using a list<T> Container

The list<T> container template that is defined in the list header implements a doubly linked list of objects of type T. This has the advantage over a vector or a deque container that you can insert or delete elements anywhere at a known position in the sequence in constant time. This advantage is the primary incentive for using a list container, rather than a vector or a deque. The disadvantage is that you can't access an element directly by its position in the sequence – in other words, there's no indexing of elements. To access an interior element in a list you must traverse the elements by stepping from one to the next, usually starting from the first or the last element. Figure 2-6 shows how the elements in a list container are conceptually structured.

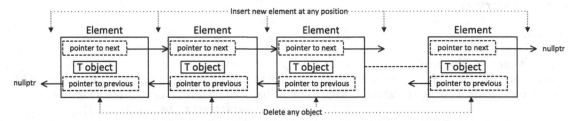

Figure 2-6. *Organization of elements in a list<T> container*

Each T object in a list<T> container is typically encapsulated in an internal node object that maintains pointers to the previous node and the next node in the list. These pointers tie the nodes together in a chain and allow traversal through the chain of elements in either direction from any position simply by following the pointers. The pointer to the previous element for the first element will be nullptr because there isn't one, and the next pointer for the last element will also be nullptr. These enable the ends of the chain to be detected. A list<T> instance records pointers to the first and last nodes. This enables the objects at either end to be accessed and allows the entire list of elements to be retrieved in sequence starting from either end.

You obtain iterators for a list container in the same way as for the other sequence containers. Because there's no random access to the elements in a list, the iterators that you get are *bidirectional iterators*. Calling begin() with a list argument returns an iterator pointing to the first element; by calling end() you get the iterator pointing to one past the last element so the entire range of elements is specified in exactly the same way as for other sequence containers. You can also obtain reverse iterators and const iterators by calling rbegin(), rend(), crbegin(), crend(), cbegin(), and cend() in the way you have seen with other containers.

Creating list Containers

The range of constructors for a list container is similar to that for a vector or a deque container. This statement creates an empty list:

```
std::list<std::string> words;
```

You can also create a list with a given number of default elements:

```
std::list<std::string> sayings {20};          // A list of 20 empty strings
```

The number of elements is specified by the argument to the constructor and each element is created by calling the default constructor for the type of element stored, so the elements are created by calling string() here.

Here's how you create a list containing a given number of identical elements:

```
std::list<double> values(50, 3.14149265);
```

This creates a list of 50 values of type double, each equal to the value of π. Note the parentheses here; you can't use an initializer list – if you use {50, 3.14159265}, the list will contain just two elements.

The list container has a copy constructor so you can create a duplicate of an existing list container:

```
std::list<double> save_values {values};          // Duplicate of values
```

You can also construct a list initialized with elements from another sequence that you specify in the usual way – by begin and end iterators:

```
std::list<double> samples {++cbegin(values), --cend(values)};
```

This creates a list from the contents of the values list, omitting the first and last elements. Because the iterators returned by the begin() and end() functions for a list are bidirectional, you can't add or subtract integer values. The only way to modify a bidirectional iterator is to use the increment or decrement operator. Of course, the iterators in the initializer list in the statement above could represent a range in any container, not just another list.

You can obtain the number of elements in a list container by calling its size() member. You can also change the number of elements by calling its resize() function. If the argument to resize() is less than the number of elements, elements will be deleted from the end; if the argument is greater, elements will be added using the default constructor for the type of elements stored.

Adding Elements

You add an element to the beginning of a list by calling its push_front() member. Calling push_back() for a list object adds an element to the end of the list. In both instances the argument is the object to be added. For example:

```
std::list<std::string> names {"Jane", "Jim", "Jules", "Janet"};
names.push_front("Ian");               // Add string("Ian") to the front of the list
names.push_back("Kitty");              // Append string("Kitty") to the end of the list
```

There are rvalue reference parameter versions of both functions that will move the argument rather than copying it to the new element. These are obviously going to be more efficient than the versions with an lvalue reference parameter. However, the emplace_front() and emplace_back() members do even better:

```
names.emplace_front("Ian");       // Create string("Ian") in place at the front of the list
names.emplace_back("Kitty");      // Create string("Kitty") in place at the end of the list
```

The arguments to these members are the arguments to the constructor that is to be called to create the element in place. These eliminate the need for a move operation that the rvalue versions of push_front() and push_back() have to execute.

You can add elements to the interior of a list using the insert() function member, which comes in three versions, just like the other sequence containers. The first version inserts a new element at a position specified by an iterator:

```
std::list<int> data(10, 55);                  // List of 10 elements with value 55
data.insert(++begin(data), 66);               // Insert 66 as the second element
```

The first argument to insert() is the iterator that specifies the insertion point, and the second argument is the element to be inserted. Incrementing the bidirectional iterator returned by begin() makes it point to the second element. After executing this, the list contents will be:

```
55 66 55 55 55 55 55 55 55 55 55
```

The list now contains 11 elements. Inserting the element doesn't necessitate moving any existing elements. After creating the new element, the process just requires 4 pointers to be set appropriately. The next pointer for the first element is changed to point to the new element; the previous pointer from the original second element is changed to point to the new element; the previous pointer for the new element will be set to point to the first element and its next pointer will point to the original element that was second in the sequence. This process is very fast compared to insertions in a vector or deque and will take the same time wherever the new element is inserted.

You can insert several copies of the same element at a given position:

```
auto iter = begin(data);
std::advance(iter, 9);                         // Increase iter by 9
data.insert(iter, 3, 88);                      // Insert 3 copies of 88 starting at the 10th
```

iter will be of type list<int>::iterator. The first argument to the insert() function is an iterator specifying the insertion position, the second is the number of elements to be inserted, and the third is the element to be inserted repeatedly. To get to the tenth element you increment the iterator by nine using the global advance() function that is defined in the iterator header. You can only increment or decrement a bidirectional iterator; you can't just add nine to it, so the advance() function will increment the iterator in a loop. After executing the previous fragment, the contents of the list will be:

```
55 66 55 55 55 55 55 55 55 88 88 88 55 55
```

Now the list contains 14 elements. Here's how you can insert a sequence of elements into the data list:

```
std::vector<int> numbers(10, 5);        // Vector of 10 elements with value 5
data.insert(--(--end(data)), cbegin(numbers), cend(numbers));
```

The first argument to insert() is an iterator pointing to the second to last element position in data. The sequence from numbers that is to be inserted is specified by the second and third arguments to the insert() function, so this will insert all the elements from the vector into the list, starting at the second to last element position in data. After executing this, data will contain:

```
55 66 55 55 55 55 55 55 55 88 88 88 5 5 5 5 5 5 5 5 5 5 55 55
```

The list now contains 24 elements. Inserting elements from numbers in the second-to-last element position displaces the last 2 elements in the list to the right. In spite of this, any iterators that point to the last two elements, or the end iterator, will not be invalidated. An iterator that points to an element within a list is only invalidated when you delete the element to which it points.

There are three functions that will construct an element in place in a `list` container: `emplace()` constructs an element at a position specified by an iterator; `emplace_front()` constructs an element at the beginning of the `list`, preceding the first element; and `emplace_back()` constructs an element at the end, following the last element. Here are some examples of their use:

```
std::list<std::string> names {"Jane", "Jim", "Jules", "Janet"};
names.emplace_back("Ann");
std::string name("Alan");
names.emplace_back(std::move(name));
names.emplace_front("Hugo");
names.emplace(++begin(names), "Hannah");
```

The fourth line of code uses the `std::move()` function to pass an rvalue reference to `name` to the `emplace_back()` function. After executing this operation, `name` will be empty because the contents will have been moved to the `list`. After executing these statements, `names` will contain the elements:

```
"Hugo" "Hannah" "Jane" "Jim" "Jules" "Janet" "Ann" "Alan"
```

Removing Elements

The `clear()` and `erase()` function members of a `list` container work in the same way and have the same effect as in the previous sequence container. The `remove()` member of a `list` container removes elements that match the argument. For example:

```
std::list<int> numbers { 2, 5, 2, 3, 6, 7, 8, 2, 9};
numbers.remove(2);                                    // List is now 5 3 6 7 8 9
```

The second statement removes all occurrences of the value 2 from `numbers`.

The `remove_if()` function member expects you to pass a *unary predicate* as the argument. A unary predicate accepts a single argument of the element type or `const` reference to the element type and returns a `bool` value. All elements for which the predicate returns `true` will be removed. For example:

```
numbers.remove_if([](int n){return n%2 == 0;});       // Remove even numbers. Result 5 3 7 9
```

The argument is a lambda expression here but it could be a function object.

The `unique()` function member is interesting. It removes consecutive duplicate elements, leaving just the first of two or more duplicates. For example:

```
std::list<std::string> words {"one", "two", "two", "two", "three", "four", "four"};
words.unique();                                       // Now contains "one" "two" "three" "four"
```

This version of `unique()` uses the `==` operator to compare successive elements. You could apply `unique()` after sorting the elements to ensure that *all* duplicates are removed from a sequence.

An overload of `unique()` accepts a binary predicate as the argument, and elements for which the predicate returns `true` are regarded as equal. This offers a very flexible notion of equality. You could treat strings that have the same length as equal, or maybe strings that have the same initial letter. The predicate can have parameters of different types as long as the result of dereferencing an iterator for the `list` is implicitly convertible to both types.

Sorting and Merging Elements

The sort() function template that is defined in the algorithm header requires random access iterators. A list container doesn't provide random access iterators, only bidirectional iterators, so you can't apply the sort() algorithm to the elements in a list. All is not lost however because the list template defines its own sort() function member. It comes in two versions: the sort() member with no parameters sorts list elements into ascending sequence, the second version accepts a function object or a lambda expression as an argument that defines a predicate for comparing two list elements. A predicate is just a function that accepts one or more arguments and returns a bool value. The sort() member of a list container that has a parameter requires a *binary predicate* as the argument, which means that the predicate has two parameters. Some algorithms expect a *unary predicate*, which has one parameter.

Here's an example of calling the sort() member of a list with a predicate as the argument:

```
names.sort(std::greater<std::string>());        // Names in descending sequence
```

This uses the greater<T> template that is defined in the functional header. The template defines a function object for comparing objects of type T; the operator()() function member returns true if the first argument is greater than the second. The functional header defines a wide range of templates that define predicates and you'll meet more of these later in the book. After executing the sort, the list elements would be:

```
"Jules" "Jim" "Janet" "Jane" "Hugo" "Hannah" "Ann" "Alan"
```

So the names in the list are now in descending order. There is a *transparent* version of the greater<T> predicate that you can use like this:

```
names.sort(std::greater<>());                   // Function object uses perfect forwarding
```

A *transparent function object* accepts arguments of any type and uses perfect forwarding to avoid unnecessary copying of them. Therefore it will be faster because the arguments to be compared will be moved, not copied.

Of course, you can pass your own function object to define the predicate for sorting a list when necessary. It's not always necessary for custom objects though. If you just define operator>() for your class then you can keep using std::greater<>. The need for a function object can arise when you want something other than a default comparison for a type. For instance, suppose you want to sort the elements in the names list but instead of the standard greater-than comparison for string objects, you want strings with the same initial character ordered by length. You could define this class for that:

```
// Order strings by length when the initial letters are the same
class my_greater
{
public:
  bool operator()(const std::string& s1, const std::string& s2)
  {
    if (s1[0] == s2[0])
      return s1.length() > s2.length();
    else
      return s1 > s2;
  }
};
```

You could use this to sort the original contents of the names container:

```
names.sort(my_greater());                    // Sort using my_greater
```

After executing this, the list would contain:

```
"Jules" "Janet" "Jane" "Jim" "Hannah" "Hugo" "Alan" "Ann"
```

This is significantly different from the result of using the standard comparison for string objects earlier. Names with the same initial letter now appear in descending order of length. Of course, if you don't need to reuse the my_greater predicate, you can use a lambda expression to obtain the same result. Here's the statement that does that:

```
names.sort([](const std::string& s1, const std::string& s2)
            { if (s1[0] == s2[0])
                return s1.length() > s2.length();
              else
                return s1 > s2;
            });
```

This does exactly the same as the previous statement.

The merge() function member of a list expects another list container as the argument that has elements of the same type. The elements in both containers must be in ascending sequence. The elements from the argument list are merged with those of the current list. For example:

```
std::list<int> my_values {2, 4, 6, 14};
std::list<int> your_values{ -2, 1, 7, 10};
my_values.merge(your_values);                // my_values contains: -2 1 2 4 6 7 10 14
your_values.empty();                         // Returns true
```

The elements are *transferred* from your_values to my_values, not *copied*, so your_values will contain no elements after the operation. The transfer of elements is achieved by changing the pointers for each node in the list that is the argument to link them to the elements in the current container at the appropriate position. The list nodes stay exactly where they are in memory; just their pointers that link them are changed. The elements in the two containers are compared using operator<() in the merge process. An overload of the merge() function has a second parameter for which you supply a comparison function that is to be used in the merge operation. For example:

```
std::list<std::string> my_words {"three", "six", "eight"};
std::list<std::string> your_words {"seven", "four", "nine"};
auto comp_str = [](const std::string& s1, const std::string& s2){ return s1[0]<s2[0]; };
my_words.sort(comp_str);                      // "eight" "six" "three"
your_words.sort(comp_str);                    // "four" "nine" "seven"
my_words.merge(your_words, comp_str);         // "eight" "four" "nine" "six" "seven" "three"
```

The comparison function for string objects here is defined by a lambda expression that only considers the first character. The effect is that in the merged list, "six" precedes "seven". If you called merge() with no argument in the code above, "seven" would precede "six", which is in the normal sort order.

The splice() member of a list container has several overloads. This function transfers elements from the argument list preceding a specific position in the current container. You can transfer a single element, a range of elements, or all the elements from the source container. Here's an example of how you splice a single element:

```
std::list<std::string> my_words {"three", "six", "eight"};
std::list<std::string> your_words {"seven", "four", "nine"};
my_words.splice(++std::begin(my_words), your_words, ++std::begin(your_words));
```

The first argument is an iterator pointing to a position in the destination container. The second argument is the source of elements, and the third argument is a pointer to the element in the source list that is to be spliced into the destination before the position indicated by the first argument. After executing this, the contents of the containers will be:

```
your_words: "seven," "nine"
my_words: "three," "four," "six," "eight"
```

When you want to splice a range from the source list, the third and fourth arguments define it. For example:

```
your_words.splice(++std::begin(your_words), my_words, ++std::begin(my_words),
                                             std::end(my_words));
```

This splices the elements from the second to the end from my_words preceding the second element in your_words. Given the state of the two lists is as above, the result will be:

```
your_words: "seven", "four", "six", "eight", "nine"
my_words: "three"
```

You could now splice all the elements from your_words into my_words with this statement:

```
my_words.splice(std::begin(my_words), your_words);
```

All the elements in your_words are transferred to my_words, preceding the first element, "three". After this, your_words will be empty(). Even though your_words is empty, you can still splice elements into it:

```
your_words.splice(std::end(your_words), my_words);
```

Now my_words is empty and your_words has all the elements. The first argument could be std::begin(your_words) because this also returns the end iterator when the container is empty.

Accessing Elements

The front() and back() function members of a list return a reference to the first or last element respectively; the effect of calling either of these for an empty list is undefined, so don't. To access elements that are interior to the list, you use an iterator and increment or decrement it to get to the element you want. As you've seen, begin() and end() return a bidirectional iterators that point to the first element, or one past the last element, respectively. The rbegin() and rend() functions return bidirectional iterators that allow you to step through the elements in reverse sequence. You can use a range-based for loop with a list so you don't have to use iterators when you want to process all the elements:

```cpp
std::list<std::string> names {"Jane", "Jim", "Jules", "Janet"};
names.emplace_back("Ann");
std::string name("Alan");
names.emplace_back(std::move(name));
names.emplace_front("Hugo");
names.emplace(++begin(names), "Hannah");
for(const auto& name : names)
    std::cout << name << std::endl;
```

The loop variable, name, is a reference that will reference each list element in turn so the loop will output the strings, each on a separate line.

Let's try out some of what we have seen in an example. This example reads proverbs from the keyboard and stores them in a list container:

```cpp
// Ex2_05.cpp
// Working with a list
#include <iostream>
#include <list>
#include <string>
#include <functional>

using std::list;
using std::string;

// List a range of elements
template<typename Iter>
void list_elements(Iter begin, Iter end)
{
  while (begin != end)
    std::cout << *begin++ << std::endl;
}

int main()
{
  std::list<string> proverbs;

  // Read the proverbs
  std::cout << "Enter a few proverbs and enter an empty line to end:" << std::endl;
  string proverb;
  while (getline(std::cin, proverb, '\n'), !proverb.empty())
    proverbs.push_front(proverb);

  std::cout << "Go on, just one more:" << std::endl;
  getline(std::cin, proverb, '\n');
  proverbs.emplace_back(proverb);
```

```
  std::cout << "The elements in the list in reverse order are:" << std::endl;
  list_elements(std::rbegin(proverbs), std::rend(proverbs));

  proverbs.sort();                              // Sort the proverbs in ascending sequence
  std::cout << "\nYour proverbs in ascending sequence are:" << std::endl;
  list_elements(std::begin(proverbs), std::end(proverbs));

  proverbs.sort(std::greater<>());              // Sort the proverbs in descending sequence
  std::cout << "\nYour proverbs in descending sequence:" << std::endl;
  list_elements(std::begin(proverbs), std::end(proverbs));
}
```

Here's an example of some output:

```
Enter a few proverbs and enter an empty line to end:
A nod is a good as a wink to a blind horse.
Many a mickle makes a muckle.
A wise man stands on the hole in his carpet.
Least said, soonest mended.

Go on, just one more:
A rolling stone gathers no moss.
The elements in the list in reverse order are:
A rolling stone gathers no moss.
A nod is a good as a wink to a blind horse.
Many a mickle makes a muckle.
A wise man stands on the hole in his carpet.
Least said, soonest mended.

Your proverbs in ascending sequence are:
A nod is a good as a wink to a blind horse.
A rolling stone gathers no moss.
A wise man stands on the hole in his carpet.
Least said, soonest mended.
Many a mickle makes a muckle.

Your proverbs in descending sequence:
Many a mickle makes a muckle.
Least said, soonest mended.
A wise man stands on the hole in his carpet.
A rolling stone gathers no moss.
A nod is a good as a wink to a blind horse.
```

The input is a series of proverbs that include whitespace so we use the getline() function for this. Each proverb is read as a single line and added as a new list element by calling push_front() for the proverbs container. The additional request for a proverb is just to exercise the emplace_back() member. Output is produced by the list_elements() function template that precedes the definition of main(). This template will output elements of any type that supports the insertion operator for a stream from any container that supports output iterators. The code shows the function template working with forward iterators and reverse iterators.

The first call of the sort() member of proverbs has no arguments so the elements are sorted in ascending sequence by default. The second sort() call passes the greater predicate as the argument; the template for this is defined in the functional header, along with several other standard predicates that you'll meet later in the book. The greater<>() expression defines a function object that compares objects using operator>() and deduces the template type argument. The effect is that the list elements are sorted in descending sequence. Other objects defining predicates that you might usefully use with sort() include greater_equal<>(), less<>(), and less_equal<>(); the names indicate what the comparisons are. The output from the example shows that everything works as expected.

Using forward_list<T> Containers

A forward_list container stores objects in a singly linked list. The template for forward_list is defined in the forward_list header. The principle difference between a forward_list and a list container is that you cannot traverse the elements in the former backwards; you can only go from the first to the last. There are other consequences implied by the singly linked nature of a forward_list. First, there are no reverse iterators available. You can only obtain const or non-const *forward iterators* for a forward_list, and these cannot be decremented – they can only be incremented. Second, there is no back() member to return a reference to the last element; there is just a front() member. Third, since the only way to arrive at the end of the sequence is to increment an iterator pointing to a previous element, the operations push_back(), pop_back(), and emplace_back() are not available. Given that you're happy with these restrictions in an application, a forward_list will be faster in operation than a list container, and requires less memory.

The range of constructors for a forward_list container is the same as for a list. The iterators for a forward_list are forward iterators. There's no size() member and you cannot subtract one forward iterator from another, but you can obtain the number of elements in a forward list using the distance() function that is defined in the iterator header. For example:

```
std::forward_list<std::string> my_words {"three", "six", "eight"};
auto count = std::distance(std::begin(my_words), std::end(my_words)); // Result is 3
```

The arguments to distance() specify a range so the first argument is a begin iterator and the second is an end iterator. The advance() function from the iterator header comes in useful when you need to increment a forward iterator by more than one. Here's an example:

```
std::forward_list<int> data {10, 21, 43, 87, 175, 351};
auto iter = std::begin(data);
size_t n {3};
std::advance(iter, n);
std::cout << "The " << n+1 << "th element is " << *iter << std::endl;   // Outputs 87
```

There's no magic here. The advance() function will just increment a forward iterator the number of times required. It's saving you the trouble of coding the loop to do it. You need to remember that the function increments the iterator that is the first argument but does not return it – the return type for advance() is void.

Because the links in a forward_list are only in a forward direction, inserting new elements and splicing elements from another container has to occur *after* an element, not as in a list container where these operations apply *before* an element. For this reason, a forward_list container has splice_after() and insert_after() members, in place of the splice() and insert() members of a list container; as the names suggest, the elements are spliced or inserted after a specified position in the list. These operations still have a problem when you need to insert or splice elements at the beginning of a forward_list; you can't insert or splice elements before any element and this applies to the first element. This difficulty is resolved by the availability of the cbefore_begin() and before_begin() function members that return const and non-const iterators that point to *one before* the first element. You use these iterators to insert or splice elements at the beginning – for example:

```
std::forward_list<std::string> my_words {"three", "six", "eight"};
std::forward_list<std::string> your_words {"seven", "four", "nine"};
my_words.splice_after(my_words.before_begin(), your_words, ++std::begin(your_words));
```

The effect of this operation is to splice the last element of your_words at the beginning of my_words so my_words will contain the string objects: "nine", "three", "six", "eight", and your_words will be left with two string element, "seven" and "four".

There's another version of splice_after() that will splice a range of elements from one forward_list<T> container to another:

```
my_words.splice_after(my_words.before_begin(), your_words,
                                   ++std::begin(your_words), std::end(your_words));
```

The last two arguments are iterators that specify a range of elements in the forward_list<T> container specified by the second argument. The elements in the range, *excluding the first*, are moved to the current container at the position specified by the first argument. Thus after this assuming the initial container states, my_words will contain "four", "nine", "three", "six", "eight", and your_words will contain just "seven".

Another version of splice_after() will splice all the elements from one forward_list<T> container to another:

```
my_words.splice_after(my_words.before_begin(), your_words);
```

This moves all the elements from your_words into my_words at the position specified by the first argument.

forward_list containers have sort() and merge() members the same as for a list. They also have remove(), remove_if() and unique() operations, all of which also work the same as for a list. We can try an example that demonstrates a forward_list container in action. This time the container will store objects of type Box that represent rectangular boxes. Here's the contents of the header file for the Box class:

```
// Box.h
// Defines the Box class for Ex2_06
#ifndef BOX_H
#define BOX_H
#include <iostream>                          // For standard streams
#include <utility>                           // For comparison operator templates
using namespace std::rel_ops;                // Comparison operator template namespace

class Box
{
private:
  size_t length {};
  size_t width {};
  size_t height {};
```

```
public:
  explicit Box(size_t l=1, size_t w=1, size_t h=1) : length {l}, width {w}, height {h} {}
  double volume() const { return length*width*height; }
  bool operator<(const Box& box) { return volume() < box.volume(); }
  bool operator==(const Box& box) { return length == box.length && width == box.width
                                           && height == box.height; }

  friend std::istream& operator>>(std::istream& in, Box& box);
  friend std::ostream& operator<<(std::ostream& out, const Box& box);
};

inline std::istream& operator>>(std::istream& in, Box& box)
{
  std::cout << "Enter box length, width, & height separated by spaces - Ctrl+Z to end: ";
  size_t value;
  in >> value;
  if (in.eof()) return in;

  box.length = value;
  in >> value;
  box.width = value;
  in >> value;
  box.height = value;
  return in;
}

inline std::ostream& operator<<(std::ostream& out, const Box& box)
{
  out << "Box(" << box.length << "," << box.width << "," << box.height << ")  ";
  return out;
}
#endif
```

The std::relops namespace in the utility header contain templates for comparison operators. If you define operator<() and operator==() for a class, the templates will create the rest when required. The Box class has three private members that define the integral box dimensions. The default values for the constructor arguments provide a no-arg constructor, which is necessary for storing Box objects in a container; elements that are not initialized are created by calling the default constructor for the type of element stored. The two inline friend functions overload the extraction and insertion operators for streams, which obviously include the standard I/O streams. The operator>>() function checks for EOF being reached by calling the eof() member of the stream object after reading the first of each group of three input values. EOF is set for the standard input stream when you enter Ctrl+Z, or by reading the end-of-file marker from a file input stream. When this occurs, input ends and the stream object is returned, the EOF state will remain set and therefore can be detected by a calling program.

Here's the program that stores Box objects in a forward_list container:

```
// Ex2_06.cpp
// Working with a forward list
#include <algorithm>                    // For copy()
#include <iostream>                     // For standard streams
#include <forward_list>                 // For forward_list container
```

```cpp
#include <iterator>                                 // For stream iterators
#include "Box.h"

// List a range of elements
template<typename Iter>
void list_elements(Iter begin, Iter end)
{
  size_t perline {6};                               // Maximum items per line
  size_t count {};                                  // Item count
  while (begin != end)
  {
    std::cout << *begin++;
    if (++count % perline == 0)
    {
      std::cout << "\n";
    }
  }
  std::cout << std::endl;
}

int main()
{
  std::forward_list<Box> boxes;
  std::copy(std::istream_iterator<Box>(std::cin), std::istream_iterator<Box>(),
                                                  std::front_inserter(boxes));

  boxes.sort();                                     // Sort the boxes
  std::cout << "\nAfter sorting the sequence is:\n";
  // Just to show that we can with Box objects - use an ostream iterator
  std::copy(std::begin(boxes), std::end(boxes), std::ostream_iterator<Box>(std::cout, " "));
  std::cout << std::endl;

  // Insert more boxes
  std::forward_list<Box> more_boxes {Box {3, 3, 3}, Box {5, 5, 5}, Box {4, 4, 4}, Box {2, 2, 2}};
  boxes.insert_after(boxes.before_begin(), std::begin(more_boxes), std::end(more_boxes));
  std::cout << "After inserting more boxes the sequence is:\n";
  list_elements(std::begin(boxes), std::end(boxes));

  boxes.sort();                                     // Sort the boxes
  std::cout << std::endl;
  std::cout << "The sorted sequence is now:\n";
  list_elements(std::begin(boxes), std::end(boxes));

  more_boxes.sort();
  boxes.merge(more_boxes);                          // Merge more_boxes
  std::cout << "After merging more_boxes the sequence is:\n";
  list_elements(std::begin(boxes), std::end(boxes));

  boxes.unique();
  std::cout << "After removing successive duplicates the sequence is:\n";
  list_elements(std::begin(boxes), std::end(boxes));
```

```
    // Eliminate the small ones
    const double max_v {30.0};
    boxes.remove_if([max_v](const Box& box){ return box.volume() < max_v; });
    std::cout << "After removing those with volume less than 30 the sorted sequence is:\n";
    list_elements(std::begin(boxes), std::end(boxes));
}
```

Here's an example of the output:

```
Enter box length, width, & height separated by spaces - Ctrl+Z to end: 4 4 5
Enter box length, width, & height separated by spaces - Ctrl+Z to end: 6 5 7
Enter box length, width, & height separated by spaces - Ctrl+Z to end: 2 2 3
Enter box length, width, & height separated by spaces - Ctrl+Z to end: 1 2 3
Enter box length, width, & height separated by spaces - Ctrl+Z to end: 3 3 4
Enter box length, width, & height separated by spaces - Ctrl+Z to end: 3 3 3
Enter box length, width, & height separated by spaces - Ctrl+Z to end: ^Z
After sorting the sequence is:
Box(1,2,3)   Box(2,2,3)   Box(3,3,3)   Box(3,3,4)   Box(4,4,5)   Box(6,5,7)
After inserting more boxes the sequence is:
Box(3,3,3)   Box(5,5,5)   Box(4,4,4)   Box(2,2,2)   Box(1,2,3)   Box(2,2,3)
Box(3,3,3)   Box(3,3,4)   Box(4,4,5)   Box(6,5,7)

The sorted sequence is now:
Box(1,2,3)   Box(2,2,2)   Box(2,2,3)   Box(3,3,3)   Box(3,3,3)   Box(3,3,4)
Box(4,4,4)   Box(4,4,5)   Box(5,5,5)   Box(6,5,7)
After merging more_boxes the sequence is:
Box(1,2,3)   Box(2,2,2)   Box(2,2,2)   Box(2,2,3)   Box(3,3,3)   Box(3,3,3)
Box(3,3,3)   Box(3,3,4)   Box(4,4,4)   Box(4,4,4)   Box(4,4,5)   Box(5,5,5)
Box(5,5,5)   Box(6,5,7)
After removing successive duplicates the sequence is:
Box(1,2,3)   Box(2,2,2)   Box(2,2,3)   Box(3,3,3)   Box(3,3,4)   Box(4,4,4)
Box(4,4,5)   Box(5,5,5)   Box(6,5,7)
After removing those with volume less than 30 the sorted sequence is:
Box(3,3,4)   Box(4,4,4)   Box(4,4,5)   Box(5,5,5)   Box(6,5,7)
```

The list_elements() function template outputs a range of objects specified by begin and end iterators six to a line. This is used in main() to output the contents of a forward_list. The first action in main() is to read the dimensions of a series of Box objects from cin. This is done by calling the copy() algorithm using an istream_iterator<Box> object as the data source and a front_inserter for the forward_list object as the destination for the data. The istream_iterator will call the operator>>() function that is defined in Box.h to read a Box object. A front_inserter calls the push_front() member of a container, so this works for a forward_list.

After sorting the elements in the boxes container, we output the Box objects using the copy() algorithm to transfer the elements to an ostream_iterator<Box> object, just to show that we can. This iterator will call the operator<<() function that is defined in Box.h. The limitation here is that we have no control over the number of outputs per line. In the rest of the code an instance of the list_elements() template is used for output.

Next the contents of the more_boxes container – which is another forward_list – is inserted at the beginning of the boxes container. This is achieved by calling the insert_after() member of boxes with the insertion position specified by the iterator returned by the before_begin() member.

The next operation is sort the boxes, then the contents of more_boxes is merged into boxes. Both containers have to be sorted prior to calling merge() because the operation only works when the contents of both containers are in ascending sequence. This will obviously result in duplicates of the elements from more_boxes being present in boxes because copies have already been inserted. Calling the unique() member of boxes eliminates successive duplicates of an element. The last operation is to call the remove_if() member of boxes to delete elements from the container. The elements to be deleted are determined by the unary predicate that is passed as the argument. Here it is a lambda expression that returns true for elements with a volume less than max_v; max_v is captured from the outer scope by value so different values could be set in the outer scope. The output shows that all operations are working as expected.

Defining Your Own Iterators

You don't need to understand this section for the rest of the book so don't get bogged down in it – if you find it heavy going, skip it and continue with chapter 3. However, this section will provide an insight into the architecture of STL iterators as well as an appreciation of the power of templates. Iterators are a powerful addition to any class type of your own that defines a sequence. They allow algorithms to be applied to the objects that an instance of your class contains. Circumstances can arise where none of the standard STL containers are quite what you need, in which case you'll be defining your own container type. Your container class is likely to need iterators. Developing an understanding of what makes a class that defines iterators acceptable to the STL will also give you an appreciation of what goes on under the covers in the STL.

STL Iterator Requirements

The STL places specific requirements on class types that define iterators. This is to ensure that all the algorithms that accept iterators will work as expected. The algorithms neither know nor care about what kind of container houses the data to be processed, but they do care about the characteristics of the iterators that are passed to them to identify the data to be processed. Different algorithms require iterators of different capabilities. You saw these iterator categories in chapter 1: input, output, forward, bidirectional, and random access iterators. You can always use a more capable iterator where a less capable one is required.

A template that defines an algorithm needs to determine the category of the iterator type that is passed to it to enable the algorithm to verify that the capability of the iterator is adequate. Knowing the category of its iterator arguments also provides the potential for the algorithm to take advantage of any functionality in excess of the minimum to make the operation more efficient. For this to be possible generally, the capability of an iterator has to be identified in a standardized way. The various iterator categories imply different sets of function members that an iterator class must define. You have seen that the iterator categories are cumulative in functionality, and this is obviously going to be reflected in the function member set for each category. Before we get to that, let's look at how a function template uses iterators.

A Problem with Using STL Iterators

A problem that arises with defining function templates that have parameters that are iterators is that you don't always know all the types that you need to use in a template definition. Consider the following template for a swap function with parameters that are iterators; the template type argument specifies the iterator type:

```
template <typename Iter> void my_swap(Iter a, Iter b)
{
  tmp = *a;                              // error -- variable tmp undeclared
  *a = *b;
  *b = tmp;
  }
```

Instances of this function template are intended to swap the objects to which the iterator arguments, a and b, point. What type should tmp be? You have no way of knowing – you know that it's the type of object to which the iterators point, but you have no idea what that is because it's not determined until an instance of the template is created. How do you define a variable when you don't know its type? Of course, you can use auto here but there are situations where you also want to know the value and difference types for the type of iterator.

There are additional mechanisms for determining the type of value pointed to by an iterator argument. One possibility would be to insist that every iterator type that is usable by my_swap() should include a public definition for a type alias, value_type say, for the type of object to which the iterator points. In this case you could use the value_type alias in the iterator class to specify the type for tmp in the my_swap() function template – like this:

```
template <typename Iter> void my_swap(Iter a, Iter b)
{
  typename Iter::value_type tmp = *a;        // Better - but has limitations...
  *a = *b;
  *b = tmp;
}
```

Since the value_type alias is defined within the Iter class, you can refer to it by qualifying value_type with the class name. This would work fine with iterators of class types that defined the value_type alias. However, the STL algorithms work with pointers as well as iterators; if Iter is an ordinary pointer type such as int*, or even Box* where Box is a class type – then this approach won't work. You can't write int*::value_type or Box*::value_type because pointer types are not classes that can contain type alias definitions. The STL solves this problem and other related problems very elegantly – using templates – what else!

The STL Approach

The iterator_traits template type is defined in the iterator header. This template defines a standard set of type aliases for the characteristics of an iterator type. This is the key to solving the difficulty outlined in the previous section and enables algorithms to work with iterators as well as ordinary pointers. The iterator_traits template definition looks like this:

```
template<class Iterator>
struct iterator_traits
{
typedef typename Iterator::difference_type   difference_type;
typedef typename Iterator::value_type        value_type;
typedef typename Iterator::pointer           pointer;
typedef typename Iterator::reference         reference;
typedef typename Iterator::iterator_category iterator_category;
};
```

I'm sure you remember that a struct is essentially the same as a class, except that its members are public by default. There are no data members or function members in this struct template. The body of the iterator_traits template only contains definitions for type aliases. These aliases are templates with Iterator as the type parameter. It defines a mapping between the type alias names in this template – difference_type, value_type, and so on – and the types used to create an iterator template instance – the type argument corresponding to Iterator. Thus for a concrete class, Boggle, the iterator_traits<Boggle> instance defines difference_type as an alias for Boggle::difference_type, value_type as an alias for Boggle::value_type, and so on.

So how is this helpful in solving the problem of not knowing what a type is in a template definition? Well, first, suppose that you define an iterator type, MyIterator, which includes definitions for the following type aliases names:

- difference_type – the type of the value that results from the difference between two iterators of type MyIterator.

- value_type – the type of value pointed to by an iterator of type MyIterator.

- pointer – the type of pointer that an iterator of type MyIterator represents.

- reference – the type of reference that results from *MyIterator.

- iterator_category – one of the iterator category tag class types you saw in chapter 1: that is, it must be one of the types input_iterator_tag, output_iterator_tag, forward_iterator_tag, bidirectional_iterator_tag, or random_access_iterator_tag.

An iterator class that conforms to the STL requirements must define all these type aliases, although for output iterators, all aliases except the iterator_category alias can be defined as void. This is because an output iterator points to a destination for an object, not an object. This set of aliases provides everything you are likely to want to know about an iterator.

When you define a function template with iterators as parameters, you can use the standard type alias names that the iterator_traits template defines as types in your template. Thus the type of *pointer* that an iterator of type MyIterator represents can always be referred to as std::iterator_traits<MyIterator>::pointer because it's equivalent to MyIterator::pointer. When you need to specify the type of value that a MyIterator iterator points to, you write std::iterator_traits<MyIterator>::value_type, which will map to MyIterator::value_type. We could apply the iterator_traits template type aliases in the my_swap() template to specify the type for tmp, like this:

```
template <typename Iter>
void my_swap(Iter a, Iter b)
{
  typename std::iterator_traits<Iter>::value_type tmp = *a;
  *a = *b;
  *b = tmp;
}
```

This specifies the type for tmp as the value_type alias from the iterator_traits template. When the my_swap() template is instantiated with the Iter template argument, the type for tmp will be the type to which the iterator points, Iter::value_type.

To clarify what is happening and exactly how this solves the problem, let's consider a specific situation of a my_swap() template instance. Suppose a program contains the following code:

```
std::vector<std::string> words {"one", "two", "three"};
my_swap(std::begin(words), std::begin(words)+1); // Swap first two elements
```

When the compiler encounters the my_swap() call, it creates an instance of the function template based on the arguments in the call. These are iterators of a template type – iterator<std::string> say. In the body of the template for my_swap() the compiler has to process the definition for tmp. The compiler knows that the type argument for the my_swap() template is iterator<std::string>, so after plugging this into the template, the definition for tmp will be:

```
typename std::iterator_traits< iterator<std::string> >::value_type tmp = *a;
```

The type for tmp is now a member of an instance of the iterator_traits template. To figure out what this really means, the compiler has to instantiate the iterator_traits template using the type argument that appears in the type specification for tmp in the my_swap() function. Here's the instance of the iterator_traits template that the compiler will create:

```
struct iterator_traits
{
typedef typename iterator<std::string>::difference_type   difference_type;
typedef typename iterator<std::string>::value_type        value_type;
typedef typename iterator<std::string>::pointer           pointer;
typedef typename iterator<std::string>::reference         reference;
typedef typename iterator<std::string>::iterator_category iterator_category;
};
```

From this the compiler determines that the type for tmp, which is iterator_traits<iterator<std::string>>::value_type, is yet *another* alias—an alias for iterator<std::string>::value_type. Just like all STL iterator types, the definition of the iterator<std::string> type that is created from the template for the iterator will include a definition for value_type, which will look like this:

```
typedef std::string    value_type;
```

The compiler now knows from the iterator_traits instance that iterator_traits<iterator<std::string>>::value_type is an alias for iterator<std::string>::value_type, and from the iterator<std::string> class definition it knows that iterator<std::string>::value_type is an alias for std::string. By working through the aliases to the actual type, the compiler will conclude that the definition for tmp in the my_swap() function is:

```
std::string tmp = *a;
```

Simple really, isn't it!

It's essential to keep reminding yourself that a template is not code – it's a recipe that the compiler uses to create code. The iterator_traits template only contains type aliases so no executable code can result from it. The compiler uses it in the process of creating the C++ code that ultimately will be compiled. The code that gets compiled will contain no trace of the iterator_traits template; its only use is in the process of creating the C++ code.

That still leaves the problem of pointers. How does the iterator_traits template fix the problem of allowing an algorithm to accept pointers as well as iterators? The iterator_traits template has specializations defined for types T* and const T*. For example, the specialization when the template type argument is a pointer type, T*, is defined as:

```
template<class T>
struct iterator_traits<T*>
{
typedef ptrdiff_t                   difference_type;
typedef T                           value_type;
typedef T*                          pointer;
typedef T&                          reference;
typedef random_access_iterator_tag iterator_category;
};
```

This defines the types corresponding to the alias names when the template type argument is a pointer type. For a pointer of type T* the value_type alias is always T; if you use a pointer of type Box* as an argument to my_swap(), the value_type alias is Box so tmp will be of that type. All the operations required for the random access iterator category apply to a pointer so the iterator_category alias is always equivalent to the type std::random_access_iterator_tag for a pointer. Therefore the way the iterators_traits template works depends on whether the template type argument is a pointer or an iterator class type. When the template type argument is a pointer, a specialization of the iterators_traits template for pointers will be selected; otherwise it will be the standard template definition.

Using the Iterator Template

The STL defines the iterator template to help you include the required type aliases in your own iterator classes. iterator is a template for a struct that defines the five type aliases from iterator_traits template:

```
template<class Category, class T, class Difference = ptrdiff_t, class Pointer = T*,
                                                     class Reference = T&>
struct iterator
{
typedef T          value_type;
typedef Difference difference_type;
typedef Pointer    pointer;
typedef Reference  reference;
typedef Category   iterator_category
};
```

This template defines all the types that the STL requires of an iterator. For example, if you have an unknown template parameter Iter, you can write Iter::pointer when you need to declare a pointer to the type that the iterator provides when it is dereferenced. The value of iterator_category must be one of the fixed set of category tag classes I introduced in chapter 1. When you are defining a class that represents an iterator, you can use an instance of the iterator template as a base class, and this will add the type aliases your class needs. For example:

```
class My_Iterator : public std::iterator<std::random_access_iterator_tag, int>
{
  // Members of the iterator class...
};
```

This takes care of defining all the types that are required by the STL for an iterator. The first argument to the template specifies the type of this iterator as a full random access iterator. The second argument is the type of object pointed to by an iterator. The last three template arguments for iterator will be the default values so the third argument is the type for a difference between two of the iterators, which will be ptrdiff_t. The fourth argument is the type of a pointer to an object so this will be int*. Finally the last template argument specifies the type for a reference, which will be int&. Of course, the iterator type doesn't do anything; all the members still need to be defined.

STL Iterator Member Function Requirements

The STL defines a set of function members that an iterator type must support, depending on its category. It helps if you collect them into groups. The first group is required for all iterators and includes some important functions that all iterator classes need to have: the *default constructor*, the *copy constructor*, and the *assignment operator*. As a rule of thumb, if you need to write any of these functions for an iterator class, then you should also write an explicit *destructor*. The full set of functions in this group for a type `Iterator` is:

```
Iterator();                               // Default constructor
Iterator(const Iterator& y);              // Copy constructor
~Iterator();                              // Destructor
Iterator& operator=(const Iterator& y);   // Assignment operator
```

The STL requires a full set of *equality* and *relational* operators for a random access iterator class. In fact, you can get away with defining just two by using some function templates provided by the `utility` standard library header:

```
bool operator==(const Iterator& y) const;
bool operator<(const Iterator& y)  const;
```

This assumes that you have an `#include` directive for the `utility` header and a `using` directive for the `std::relops` namespace:

```
#include <utility>
using namespace std::rel_ops;
```

If you define `operator==()` and `operator<()` for a class, then the `rel_ops` namespace that is declared within the `std` namespace contains function templates that use your operator functions to generate operator functions for `!=`, `>`, `>=`, and `<=` when necessary. So activating `std::rel_ops` with the `using` directive saves you the work of defining these four operators explicitly. If you define any of the operator functions that would be generated by the templates in the `std::rel_ops` namespace, your implementations take precedence over those that the templates in the namespace might create. The `operator<()` function is special. It is called the *ordering relation*. It is important in searching and comparison algorithms.

The `operator==()` function tests whether two containers or objects have identical contents. There's an interesting aspect to this. You might think that for any pair of operands, x and y, the expression (x<y || y<x || x==y) must always evaluate to `true` because exactly one of the three component expressions must be `true`. In fact, it doesn't necessarily have to work that way. It's clear that if x==y is `true`, then neither x<y nor y<x can be `true`. One thing you can be certain about is that equal elements can't be different. However, if x!=y you *must not* assume that one of x<y or y<x is true. When the expression (!(x<y))&&(!(y<x)) is true, the elements x and y are said to be *inequivalent*, which simply means that you don't have a preference when sorting. A common example of this occurs when you're sorting strings, but ignoring case. On a case-insensitive basis, the strings `"A123"` and `"a123"` are inequivalent (neither belongs first), but they're not the same, nor are they equal.

The other operations that an iterator class must define is determined by its category. You saw the operations specific to each category in chapter 1, and of course they are cumulative, with random access iterators supporting the complete set.

Let's look at a simple definition of an iterator type in a working example. We'll define a class template that represents a range of values of a numeric type and that can create begin and end iterators that specify the range. The iterator will also be of a template type and both templates will be defined in the same header file, Numeric_Range.h. Here's the definition for the Numeric_Range<T> template:

```
template <typename T> class Numeric_Iterator;   // Template type declaration

// Defines a numeric range
template<typename T>
class Numeric_Range
{
  static_assert(std::is_integral<T>::value || std::is_floating_point<T>::value,
                          "Numeric_Range type argument must be numeric.");

  friend class Numeric_Iterator <T>;

private:
  T start;                                // First value in the range
  T step;                                 // Increment between successive values
  size_t count;                           // Number of values in the range

public:
  explicit Numeric_Range(T first=0, T incr=1, size_t n=2) :
                                      start {first}, step {incr}, count {n}{}

  // Return the begin iterator for the range
  Numeric_Iterator<T> begin(){ return Numeric_Iterator<T>(*this); }

  // Return the end iterator for the range
  Numeric_Iterator<T> end()
  {
    Numeric_Iterator<T> end_iter(*this);
    end_iter.value = start + count*step;        // End iterator value is one step over the last
    return end_iter;
  }
};
```

The type argument for T is the type of the values in the range so this must be a numeric type. The static_assert() in the template body will produce a compile-time error message including the string that is the second argument if the first argument is false, which will be when T is not an integral or floating-point type. The predicate templates I used here are defined in the type_traits header, along with an extensive range of other predicates for compile-time type checking of template type arguments. The constructor has default values for the three parameters so it also serves as the default no-arg constructor. The parameters are the initial value, the increment from one value to the next, and the number of values in the range. Thus the defaults define a range with two values: 0 and 1. The compiler-supplied copy constructor will be adequate when this is required.

The two other function members create and return the begin and end iterators for the range. The value member for the end iterator is one increment more than the last value in the range. The end iterator is created by modifying the begin iterator to have the appropriate value for an end iterator. The declaration for the Numeric_Iterator<T> template type that precedes the template definition is necessary because the template for the iterator type has not yet been defined. The Numeric_Iterator<T> template is specified to be a friend of this template to allow instances of the iterator template to access the private members of Numeric_Range<T>. The Numeric_Range<T> template will also need to be a friend of the Numeric_Iterator<T> template because the end() member of the template defining a range accesses a private member of the iterator template,

The definition of the template type for the iterator is:

```
// Iterator class template - it's a forward iterator
template<typename T>
class Numeric_Iterator : public std::iterator <std::forward_iterator_tag, T>
{
  friend class Numeric_Range <T>;

private:
  Numeric_Range<T>& range;                        // Reference to the range for this iterator
  T value;                                        // Value pointed to

public:
  explicit Numeric_Iterator(Numeric_Range<T>& a_range) :
                                    range {a_range}, value {a_range.start} {}

  // Assignment operator
  Numeric_Iterator& operator=(const Numeric_Iterator& src)
  {
    range = src.range;
    value = src.value;
  }

  // Dereference an iterator
  T& operator*()
  {
    // When the value is one step more than the last, it's an end iterator
    if (value == static_cast<T>(range.start + range.count*range.step))
    {
      throw std::logic_error("Cannot dereference an end iterator.");
    }
    return value;
  }

  // Prefix increment operator
  Numeric_Iterator& operator++()
  {
    // When the value is one step more than the last, it's an end iterator
    if (value == static_cast<T>(range.start + range.count*range.step))
    {
      throw std::logic_error("Cannot increment an end iterator.");
    }
    value += range.step;                          // Increment the value by the range step
    return *this;
  }
```

```
// Postfix increment operator
Numeric_Iterator operator++(int)
{
  // When the value is one step more than the last, it's an end iterator
  if (value == static_cast<T>(range.start + range.count*range.step))
  {
    throw std::logic_error("Cannot increment an end iterator.");
  }
  auto temp = *this;
  value += range.step;                    // Increment the value by the range step
  return temp;                            // The iterator before it's incremented
}

// Comparisons
bool operator<(const Numeric_Iterator& iter) const { return value < iter.value; }
bool operator==(const Numeric_Iterator& iter) const { return value == iter.value; }
bool operator!=(const Numeric_Iterator& iter) const { return value != iter.value; }
bool operator>(const Numeric_Iterator& iter) const { return value > iter.value; }
bool operator<=(const Numeric_Iterator& iter) const { *this < iter || *this == iter; }
bool operator>=(const Numeric_Iterator& iter) const { *this > iter || *this == iter; }
};
```

It looks like a lot of code but it's quite straightforward. An iterator has a member that stores a reference to the Numeric_Range object to which it relates. It also stores the value in the range to which it points. The parameter to the constructor for an iterator is a reference to the range object. The constructor initializes the range reference member with the argument and sets the value member to be the start value for the range. The other members define the dereference operator, the prefix and postfix increment operators, and the set of comparison operators. It's illegal to dereference or increment the end iterator for a range so the increment operator function and the dereference operator function throw an exception if the operand is an end iterator; this is indicated by the value member being one increment more than the last value in the range. I chose to throw a standard exception object to keep things simple.

The complete contents of the Numeric_Range.h header will be:

```
// Numeric_Range.h for Ex2_07
// Defines class templates for a range and iterators for the range
#ifndef NUMERIC_RANGE_H
#define NUMERIC_RANGE_H
#include <exception>                        // For standard exception types
#include <iterator>                         // For iterator type
#include <type_traits>                      // For compile-time type checking

template <typename T> class Numeric_Iterator;   // Template type declaration

// Template to define a numeric range, as above...
// Template to define a numeric range iterator, as above...

#endif
```

The following program will try out the Numeric_Range template:

```
// Ex2_07.cpp
// Exercising the Numeric_Range template
#include <algorithm>                          // For copy()
#include <numeric>                            // For accumulate()
#include <iostream>                           // For standard streams
#include <vector>                             // For vector container
#include "Numeric_Range.h"                    // For Numeric_Range<T> & Numeric_Iterator<T>

int main()
{
  Numeric_Range<double> range {1.5, 0.5, 5};
  auto first = range.begin();
  auto last = range.end();
  std::copy(first, last, std::ostream_iterator<double>(std::cout, " "));
  std::cout << "\nSum = " << std::accumulate(std::begin(range), std::end(range), 0.0) << std::endl;

  // Initializing a container from a Numeric_Range
  Numeric_Range<long> numbers {15L, 4L, 10};
  std::vector<long> data {std::begin(numbers), std::end(numbers)};
  std::cout << "\nValues in vector are:\n";
  std::copy(std::begin(data), std::end(data), std::ostream_iterator<long>(std::cout, " "));
  std::cout << std::endl;

  // List the values in a range
  std::cout << "\nThe values in the numbers range are:\n";
  for (auto n : numbers)
    std::cout << n << " ";
  std::cout << std::endl;
}
```

The output from the example is:

```
1.5  2  2.5  3  3.5
Sum = 12.5

Values in vector are:
15  19  23  27  31  35  39  43  47  51

The values in the numbers range are:
15 19 23 27 31 35 39 43 47 51
```

This first creates a Numeric_Range instance that has five value of type double starting with 1.5 and incremented by 0.5. The iterators for the range are used in the copy() algorithm to copy the values to an ostream_iterator. This demonstrates that the iterators are acceptable to an algorithm. The second Numeric_Range instance has 10 values of type long. The begin and end iterators for this range are used in the initializer list for a vector container. The vector elements are then output using the copy() algorithm. Finally, to show that it works, the values in the range are output in a range-based for loop. The output confirms that the Numeric_Range template successfully creates integral and floating-point ranges and that we have indeed managed to define an iterator type that works with the STL.

Summary

This chapter has been about sequence containers, which you are likely to use most often because they are the most flexible. They impose no fundamental ordering on the data items they contain but allow you to order them in any way that you want. The more important points you learned about in this chapter include the following:

- An array<T,N> container stores a fixed number of elements, N, of type T. It can be used just like a regular array but offers the advantage over a regular array that an array container knows its size so it can be passed as an argument to a function without necessitating a second argument for the number of array elements. It also provides the possibility of checking an index used to access an element by calling its at() function member. Using an array container adds little overhead compared to a regular array.

- A vector<T> container stores an arbitrary number of elements of type T. A vector container grows automatically to accommodate as many elements as you want.

- You can add or delete elements efficiently at the end of a vector; adding or deleting elements in the interior of the sequence will be slower because elements will need to be moved.

- You can access any element in a vector container using an index, just like an array, or you can call its at() function member to check the index used. Although a vector carries a small overhead compared to a regular array, you won't notice this in the majority of situations.

- A deque<T> container stores an arbitrary number of elements of type T as a double ended queue. You can access elements in a deque container in the same way as a vector.

- You can add or delete elements efficiently to the front or the back of a deque container; adding or deleting elements in the interior of the sequence will be slow.

- The array, vector, and deque containers provide const and non-const random access iterators and reverse iterators.

- A list<T> container stores elements of type T as a double-linked list. Elements can be added or deleted efficiently anywhere in a list container.

- Elements in the interior of a list container can only be accessed by traversing the list starting from either the beginning or the end of the sequence.

- A list container provides bidirectional iterators.

- A forward_list<T> container stores elements of type T in a singly linked list that can only be traversed in the forward direction, starting with the first element. A forward_list container is faster and more compact than a list container.

- A forward_list container provides forward iterators.

- The copy() algorithm that is defined by a template in the algorithm header copies a range of elements to a destination specified by another iterator.

- You can use stream iterators with the copy() algorithm to read data from an input stream and copy it into a container, or write data from a container to an output stream.

- The sort() function template that is defined in the algorithm header sorts a range of elements specified by random access iterators. Elements can be sorted into ascending sequence by default, or into a sequence determined by a binary predicate that you supply as an argument to sort().

- The list and forward_list containers provide a sort() function member for sorting elements.

EXERCISES

Here are a few exercises to test how well you remember the topics in this chapter. If you get stuck, look back over the chapter for help. If you're still stuck after that, you can download the solutions from the Apress website (http://www.apress.com/9781484200056), but this really should be a last resort.

1. The Fibonacci series is the sequence of integers 0, 1, 1, 2, 3, 5, 8, 13, 21 ... where each integer after the first two is the sum of the two preceding integers. Write a program that uses a lambda expression to initialize an array<T,N> container with 50 values from the Fibonacci series. Use a global function in the program to output the elements in the container 8 to a line.

2. Write a program to read an arbitrary number of city names from the keyboard and store them as std::string objects in a vector<T> container. Sort the city names in ascending sequence and list them several to each line, each in a fixed field width that will accommodate the longest city name. Output the names grouped by their initial letter with each group separated from the next by an empty line..

3. Repeat the previous exercise using a list<T> container, and devise a way to use an input stream iterator to read the city names, even when they consist of two or more names such as "New York" and are stored as such. (Obviously, the input must use an alternative to a space character in a name.)

4. Extend the previous example to transfer the contents of the list container to a deque<T> container using a front inserter. Sort the contents of the deque container, and output the city names using an output stream iterator.

CHAPTER 3

■ ■ ■

Container Adapters

This chapter explains some variations on the containers you saw in the previous chapter that the STL provides. These define simpler interfaces to a sequence container that you use in particular circumstances. You'll also be seeing more about how you can store pointers in a container. In this chapter you'll learn:

- What a container adapter is.

- How you define a stack and when and how you use it.

- How you define and use a queue.

- How to create and use a priority queue and how it differs from a queue.

- What a heap is, how you create and use a heap, and how a heap relates to a priority queue.

- The benefits of storing pointers in a container, particularly smart pointers.

What Are Container Adapters?

A *container adapter* is a class template that wraps one of the sequence containers you learned about in the previous chapter to define another sequence container that provides a different capability. They are called *adapter* classes because they adapt the existing interface of a container to provide different functionality. There are three container adapters:

- A stack<T> container is an adapter class template that wraps a deque<T> container by default to implement a push-down stack, which is a last-in first-out (LIFO) storage mechanism. The stack<T> template is defined in the stack header.

- A queue<T> container is an adapter class template that wraps a deque<T> container by default to implement a queue, which is first-in first-out (FIFO) storage mechanism. You can specify an alternative underlying container provided it meets certain conditions. The queue<T> template is defined in the queue header.

- A priority_queue<T> container is an adapter class template that wraps a vector<T> container to implement a queue that orders the elements so that the largest element is always at the front. The priority_queue<T> template is also defined in the queue header.

The adapter classes implement their operations in terms of the operations on the underlying sequence container, which you could obviously do for yourself. The advantages they offer are the simplicity of their public interfaces and the readability of code that uses them. We'll explore what you can do with each of these container adapters in more detail.

Creating and Using a stack<T> Container Adapter

Data in a stack<T> container adapter is organized on a LIFO basis, similar to a sinking plate stack in a self-service cafeteria or a pile of books in a box; only the object at the top of a stack is accessible. Figure 3-1 shows a conceptual stack container and its basic operations. Only the top element is accessible; an element lower down in the stack can only be accessed by removing the elements above it.

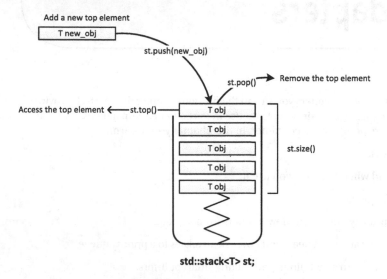

Figure 3-1. *Basic stack container operations*

There are a wide range of applications for stack containers. For example, the undo mechanism in your editor is likely to use a stack to record successive changes; the undo operation reverses the last action, which will be the action that is the top of the stack. Compilers use a stack for parsing arithmetic expressions, and, of course, compiled C++ code records function calls in a stack. Here's how you can define a stack container that stores string objects:

```
std::stack<std::string> words;
```

The template for the stack container adapter has two parameters. The first is the type of object stored and the second is the type of the underlying container. The underlying sequence container for a stack<T> is a deque<T> container by default so the template type is really stack<typename T, typename Container=deque<T>>. You can use any container type for the underling container that supports the operations back(), push_back(), pop_back(), empty(), and size(), by specifying the second template type argument. Here's how you define a stack that uses a list<T> container:

```
std::stack<std::string, std::list<std::string>> fruit;
```

You can't initialize a stack with objects in an initializer list when you create it, but you can create it so that it contains a copy of elements from another container, as long as the other container is the same type as the underlying container. For example:

```
std::list<double> values {1.414, 3.14159265, 2.71828};
std::stack<double, std::list<double>> my_stack (values);
```

The second statement creates my_stack so that it contains copies of the elements from values. You can't use an initializer list with the stack constructor here; you must use parentheses. If you didn't specify the underlying container type as a list in the second stack template type argument, it would be a deque so you would not be able to use the contents of a list to initialize the stack; only a deque would be accepted.

The stack<T> template defines a copy constructor so you can duplicate an existing stack container:

```
std::stack<double, std::list<double>> copy_stack {my_stack};
```

copy_stack will be a duplicate of my_stack. As you see, you *can* use an initializer list when you call the copy constructor; of course, you can also use parentheses.

Stack Operations

A stack is a simple storage mechanism that provides relatively few operations compared to other sequence containers. The following is a complete set of operations provided by a stack container:

- top() returns a reference of type T& to the element at the top of the stack. If the stack is empty, the value returned is undefined.

- push(const T& obj) pushes a copy of obj onto the top of the stack. This is done by calling the push_back() member of the underlying container.

- push(T&& obj) pushes obj onto the top of the stack by moving it. This is done by calling the push_back() member of the underlying container that has an rvalue reference parameter.

- pop() deletes the element at the top of the stack.

- size() returns the number of elements in the stack.

- empty() returns true if there are no elements in the stack.

- emplace() creates an object in the top of the stack<T> in place using the argument(s) you pass to emplace() to call a T constructor.

- swap(stack<T> & other_stack) swaps the elements of the current stack with those of the argument. The argument must contain elements of the same type as the current stack. There is also a specialization of the global swap() function template for stack objects that does the same thing.

The stack<T> template also defines copy and move versions of operator=() so you can assign a stack object to another. There are a full set of comparison operators for stack objects. Comparisons are executed by comparing corresponding elements of the underlying containers lexicographically. A lexicographical comparison is the kind of comparison used to sort words in a dictionary. Corresponding elements are compared until one element is not identical to the other. The result of comparing these first non-matching elements is the result of the lexicographical comparison. If one stack contains more elements than the other and the pairs of matching elements are equal, the stack with more elements is the greater one.

We can try out operations with stack containers in a program that implements a simple calculator. The program will support the basic operation, add, subtract, multiply, and divide, plus exponentiation; the corresponding operators are +, -, *, /, and ^. Exponentiation is provided by the pow() function that is defined in the cmath header. An expression will be read as a string on a single line that can include spaces. We'll eliminate spaces from the input expression using the remove() algorithm before analyzing the string and executing the operations it contains.

We'll define the following function to supply a value that represents the precedence of an operator:

```
inline size_t precedence(const char op)
{
  if (op == '+' || op == '-')
    return 1;
  if (op == '*' || op == '/')
    return 2;
  if (op == '^')
    return 3;
  throw std::runtime_error {string{"invalid operator: "} + op};
}
```

+ and - are the lowest precedence, followed by * and / as the next highest and ^ as the highest. The operator precedence will determine the sequence of execution in an expression involving two or more operators. If the argument is not one of the supported operators, a runtime_error exception object is thrown. The string argument to the constructor for the exception object can be retrieved in a catch block by calling what() for the object.

The program will analyze the input expression by scanning it from left to right and will store the operators in one stack container, operators, and the corresponding operands in another stack container, operands. All the operators require two operands so executing an operation will involve accessing the operator at the top of the operators stack and then retrieving the top two elements from the operands stack as its operands. Executing an operation will be carried out by the following function:

```
double execute(std::stack<char>& ops, std::stack<double>& operands)
{
  double result {};
  double rhs {operands.top()};                    // Get rhs...
  operands.pop();                                  // ...and delete from stack
  double lhs {operands.top()};                    // Get lhs...
  operands.pop();                                  // ...and delete from stack

  switch (ops.top())                               // Execute current op
  {
  case '+':
    result = lhs + rhs;
    break;
  case '-':
    result = lhs - rhs;
    break;
  case '*':
    result = lhs * rhs;
    break;
  case '/':
    result = lhs / rhs;
    break;
  case '^':
    result = std::pow(lhs, rhs);
    break;
```

```
    default:
      throw std::runtime_error {string{"invalid operator: "} + ops.top()};
  }
  ops.pop();                                  // Delete op just executed
  operands.push(result);
  return result;
}
```

The arguments are references to the two `stack` containers. The operands are obtained by calling `top()` for the operands container. The `top()` function just accesses the top element; to access the next element, you must call `pop()` to remove the top element. Note that the operand sequence is reversed in the `stack` so the first operand accessed is the right operand for the operation. The element from the top of the `operators` container is used in the `switch` that selects the operation. If none of the case statements apply, an exception is thrown to indicate that the operator is not valid.

Here's the code for the complete program:

```
// Ex3_01.cpp
// A simple calculator using stack containers

#include <cmath>                        // For pow() function
#include <iostream>                     // For standard streams
#include <stack>                        // For stack<T> container
#include <algorithm>                    // For remove()
#include <stdexcept>                    // For runtime_error exception
#include <string>                       // For string class
using std::string;

// Code for the precedence() function goes here...

// Code for the execute() function goes here...

int main()
{
  std::stack<double> operands;          // Push-down stack of operands
  std::stack<char> operators;           // Push-down stack of operators
  string exp;                           // Expression to be evaluated
  std::cout << " An arithmetic expression can include the operators +, -, *, /,"
            << " and ^ for exponentiation."
            << std::endl;
  try
  {
    while (true)
    {
      std::cout << "Enter an arithmetic expression and press Enter"
                << " - enter an empty line to end:"
                << std::endl;
      std::getline(std::cin, exp, '\n');
      if (exp.empty()) break;

      // Remove spaces
      exp.erase(std::remove(std::begin(exp), std::end(exp), ' '), std::end(exp));
```

```cpp
    size_t index {};                                  // Index to expression string

    // Every expression must start with a numerical operand
    operands.push(std::stod(exp, &index));            // Push the first (lhs) operand on the stack

    while (true)
    {
      operators.push(exp[index++]);                   // Push the operator on to the stack

      // Get rhs operand
      size_t i {};                                    // Index to substring
     operands.push(std::stod(exp.substr(index), &i)); // Push rhs operand
      index += i;                                     // Increment expression index

      if (index == exp.length())                      // If we are at end of exp...
      {
        while (!operators.empty())                    // ...execute outstanding ops
          execute(operators, operands);
        break;
      }

      // If we reach here, there's another op...
      // If there's a previous op of equal or higher precedence execute it
      while (!operators.empty() && precedence(exp[index]) <= precedence(operators.top()))
        execute(operators, operands);                 //  Execute previous op.
    }
    std::cout << "result = " << operands.top() << std::endl;
  }
}
catch (const std::exception& e)
{
  std::cerr << e.what() << std::endl;
}
std::cout << "Calculator ending..." << std::endl;
}
```

The while loop is in a try block to catch any exceptions that might be thrown. The catch block writes the string returned by the what() member of the exception object to the standard error stream. All of the action occurs in an indefinite while loop that is terminated by entering an empty string. Spaces are eliminated from a non-empty input string using the remove() algorithm. remove() doesn't remove elements because it can't; it just shuffled elements along to overwrite those to be removed. To get rid of the surplus elements that are left in the exp string, its erase() member is called with two iterators as arguments. The first is the iterator returned by remove(), which will point to the character following the last valid character in the string; the second iterator is the end iterator for the string in its original state. Elements in the range specified by these two iterators will be deleted.

Each operand is obtained as a floating-point value by calling the `stod()` function that is defined in the `string` header. This converts a sequence of characters from the `string` that is the first argument to a value of type double. The function takes the maximum length sequence of characters, starting at the first in the string, that represent a valid floating-point value. The second argument is a pointer to an integer variable in which `stod()` will store the index of the first character that is not part of the number in the string. The `string` header also defines `stof()`, which returns a `float` value, and `stold()`, which returns a `long double` value.

Because all the operators require two operands, a valid input string will always be of the form *operand op operand op operand* and so on, with an operand first and last in the sequence and an operator between each pair of operands. Since a valid input expression always starts with an operand, the first operand is extracted prior to executing the nested indefinite `while` loop analyzes the input. Within the loop, the operator that follows in the input string is pushed on to the `operators` stack. The second operand is then extracted from exp after verifying that the end of the string has not been reached. This time, the first argument to `stod()` is the substring of exp that starts at index, which corresponds to the character following the operator that was pushed on to the `operators` stack. The index of the first character not in the value string is stored in i. Because i is relative to index, we add its value to index to set index to point to the next operator following the operand (or one beyond the end of the string if the operand is the last in exp).

When the value of index is one beyond the last character in exp, any operators remaining in the `operators` container are executed. If the end of the string has not been reached and the `operators` container is not empty, we compare the precedence of the next operator in exp to the operator that is the top of the `operators` stack. If the operator that is the top of the stack is of higher or equal precedence to the next operator, the operator in the stack must be executed first. Otherwise, the operator currently at the top of the stack is not executed, and the next operator in the string is pushed on the stack at the beginning of the next loop iterator. By proceeding in this way, the expression is evaluated with proper regard to operator precedence.

Here's some sample output:

```
An arithmetic expression can include the operators +, -, *, /, and ^ for exponentiation.
Enter an arithmetic expression and press Enter - enter an empty line to end:
2^0.5
result = 1.41421
Enter an arithmetic expression and press Enter - enter an empty line to end:
2.5e2 + 1.5e1*4 - 1000
result = -690
Enter an arithmetic expression and press Enter - enter an empty line to end:
3*4*5 + 4*5*6 + 5*6*7
result = 390
Enter an arithmetic expression and press Enter - enter an empty line to end:
1/2 + 1/3 +1/4
result = 1.08333
Enter an arithmetic expression and press Enter - enter an empty line to end:

Calculator ending...
```

The output shows that the calculator works. It also shows that the `stod()` function can convert strings representing numbers in a variety of notations. Of course, it would be nice if the example supported expressions that included parentheses, but I'll leave that as an exercise for you to complete. You knew that was coming, didn't you?

Creating and Using a queue<T> Container Adapter

Only the first and last elements in a queue<T> container adapter are accessible. You can only add new elements at the back of a queue and you can only remove elements from the front. Many applications can use a queue. A queue container could be used to represent a queue at a supermarket checkout, or a sequence of database transactions waiting to be processed by a server. Any sequence that needs to be processed on a FIFO basis is a candidate for a queue container adapter. Figure 3-2 shows a queue and its basic operations.

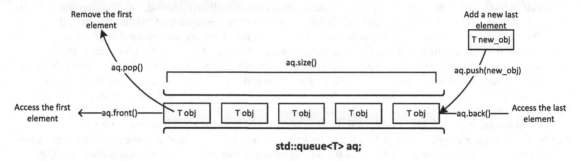

Figure 3-2. *A queue container*

The options for creating a queue are similar to those for a stack. Here's how you create a queue that stores string objects:

```
std::queue<std::string> words;
```

There's also a copy constructor:

```
std::queue<std::string> copy_words {words};       // A duplicate of words
```

Like a stack<T>, a queue<T> adapter class wraps a deque<T> container by default but you can specify another container as the second template type argument:

```
std::queue<std::string, std::list<std::string>> words;
```

The underlying container type must provide the operations front(), back(), push_back(), and pop_front(), empty(), and size().

Queue Operations

Some of the function members of a queue are similar to those for a stack but work a little differently in some cases:

- front() returns a reference to the first element in the queue. If the queue is const, a const reference is returned. If the queue is empty, the value returned is undefined.

- back() returns a reference to the last element in the queue. If the queue is const, a const reference is returned. The value returned is undefined if the queue is empty.

- push(const T& obj) appends a copy of obj to the end of the queue. This is done by calling the push_back() member of the underlying container.

- push(T&& obj) appends obj to the end of the queue by moving it. This is done by calling the push_back() member of the underlying container that has an rvalue reference parameter.

- pop() deletes the first element in the queue.

- size() returns the number of elements in the queue.

- empty() returns true if there are no elements in the queue.

- emplace() creates an object at the back of the queue in place using the argument(s) that you pass to emplace() in a call to a T constructor.

- swap(queue<T> &other_q) swaps the elements of the current queue with those of the argument. The argument must contain elements of the same type as the current queue. There is also a specialization of the global swap() function template for queue objects that does the same.

The queue<T> template defines copy and move versions of operator=(). There are a full set of comparison operators for queue objects that store elements of the same type and these work in the same way as those for stack objects.

Just as with a stack, there are no iterators for a queue. The only way to access the elements is to walk through the contents, removing the first element as you go. For example:

```
std::deque<double> values {1.5, 2.5, 3.5, 4.5};
std::queue<double> numbers(values);
while (!numbers.empty())                    // List the queue contents...
{
  std ::cout << numbers.front() << " ";     // Output the 1st element
  numbers.pop();                            // Delete the 1st element
}
std::cout << std::endl;
```

The loop to list the contents of numbers is necessarily controlled by the value returned by empty(). Calling empty() ensures that we don't call front() for an empty queue. As this code fragment shows, to access all the elements in a queue, you must delete them. If you need to keep the elements, you must copy them to another container. If this kind of operation is necessary, it's likely that you should be using something other than a queue.

A Practical Use of a Queue Container

Let's put together an example of using a queue container. This program will lean a little toward the practical application of a queue by simulating the operation of a supermarket. The length of the checkout queue is a critical element in the operation of a supermarket. It affects the number of customers that the store can handle – especially because long queues discourage customers. The same kind of queueing problem arises in lots of disparate situations – the number of beds available in a hospital can seriously affect the operation of the emergency treatment facility, for example. Our supermarket simulation will be a simple model, with limited flexibility.

We can define a class in a header, `Customer.h` that represents a customer sufficiently for the needs of the simulation:

```cpp
// Defines a customer by their time to checkout
#ifndef CUSTOMER_H
#define CUSTOMER_H
class Customer
{
private:
  size_t service_t {};                          // Time to checkout

public:
  explicit Customer(size_t st = 10) :service_t {st}{}

  // Decrement time remaining to checkout
  Customer& time_decrement()
  {
    if(service_t > 0)
      --service_t;
    return *this;
  }
  bool done() const { return service_t == 0; }
};
#endif
```

The only data member, `service_t`, records the time in minutes that is required to check out the customer's shopping. This will vary by customer. The `time_decrement()` function will be called whenever a minute has passed, so the function will decrement `service_t` value so that it reflects the time until the customer has been dealt with. The `done()` member returns `true` when the `service_t` value is zero.

Each supermarket checkout will hold a queue of customers waiting to be served. The class to define a checkout position in `Checkout.h` is:

```cpp
// Supermarket checkout - maintains and processes customers in a queue
#ifndef CHECKOUT_H
#define CHECKOUT_H
#include <queue>                                // For queue container
#include "Customer.h"

class Checkout
{
private:
  std::queue<Customer> customers;               // The queue waiting to checkout

public:
  void add(const Customer& customer) { customers.push(customer); }
  size_t qlength() const { return customers.size(); }

  // Increment the time by one minute
  void time_increment()
  { // There are customers waiting...
    if (!customers.empty())
```

```
  { // There are customers waiting...
    if (customers.front().time_decrement().done()) // If the customer is done...
      customers.pop();                             // ...remove from the queue
  }
};
```

```
  bool operator<(const Checkout& other) const { return qlength() < other.qlength(); }
  bool operator>(const Checkout& other) const { return qlength() > other.qlength(); }
};
#endif
```

This should be quite self-explanatory. The only member is the queue container for Customer objects waiting at this checkout. The add() member appends a new customer to the queue. Only the first queue element is processed. As each minute passes, the time_increment() member of the Checkout object will be called, which will call the time_decrement() member of the first Customer object to decrement the service time remaining and then call its done() member. If done() for the Customer object returns true, the customer has been dealt with and is therefore removed from the queue. The comparison operators for Checkout objects compare queue lengths.

We will need a random number generation capability for the simulation so I'm going to use a very simple facility from the random header without explaining it in detail; I'll go into the details of what the random header has to offer later in the book. The program will use instances of the uniform_int_distribution<> type. As the name implies, this defines a uniform distribution with integer values distributed uniformly between a minimum and maximum value. In a uniform distribution, all values within the range are equally likely. You can define such a distribution between 10 and 100 with this statement:

```
std::uniform_int_distribution<> d {10, 100};
```

This just defines a distribution object, d, which specifies how the values are to be distributed over the range. To obtain a random number within the range, we need a random number engine that we can pass to the function call operator for d, which will return the random integer. There are several random number engines defined in the random header. We will use the simplest here, which we can define like this:

```
std::random_device random_number_engine;
```

To produce a random value within the range defined by the distribution, d, we can write:

```
auto value = d(random_number_engine);        // Calls operator()() for d
```

The value stored in value will be an integer in the distribution defined by d.

The source file containing the complete program for the simulator looks like this:

```
// Ex3_02.cpp
// Simulating a supermarket with multiple checkouts
#include <iostream>                       // For standard streams
#include <iomanip>                        // For stream manipulators
#include <vector>                         // For vector container
#include <string>                         // For string class
#include <numeric>                        // For accumulate()
#include <algorithm>                      // For min_element & max_element
#include <random>                         // For random number generation
```

```cpp
#include "Customer.h"
#include "Checkout.h"

using std::string;
using distribution = std::uniform_int_distribution<>;

// Output histogram of service times
void histogram(const std::vector<int>& v, int min)
{
  string bar (60, '*');                          // Row of asterisks for bar
  for (size_t i {}; i < v.size(); ++i)
  {
    std::cout << std::setw(3) << i+min << " "    // Service time is index + min
      << std::setw(4) << v[i] << " "             // Output no. of occurrences
      << bar.substr(0, v[i])                     // ...and that no. of asterisks
      << (v[i] > static_cast<int>(bar.size()) ? "..." : "")
      << std::endl;
  }
}

int main()
{
  std::random_device random_n;

  // Setup minimum & maximum checkout periods - times in minutes
  int service_t_min {2}, service_t_max {15};
  distribution service_t_d {service_t_min, service_t_max};

  // Setup minimum & maximum number of customers at store opening
  int min_customers {15}, max_customers {20};
  distribution n_1st_customers_d {min_customers, max_customers};

  // Setup minimum & maximum intervals between customer arrivals
  int min_arr_interval {1}, max_arr_interval {5};
  distribution arrival_interval_d {min_arr_interval, max_arr_interval};

  size_t n_checkouts {};
  std::cout << "Enter the number of checkouts in the supermarket: ";
  std::cin >> n_checkouts;
  if(!n_checkouts)
  {
    std::cout << "Number of checkouts must be greater than 0. Setting to 1." << std::endl;
    n_checkouts = 1;
  }

  std::vector<Checkout> checkouts {n_checkouts};
  std::vector<int> service_times(service_t_max-service_t_min+1);

  // Add customers waiting when store opens
  int count {n_1st_customers_d(random_n)};
  std::cout << "Customers waiting at store opening: " << count << std::endl;
```

```cpp
int added {};
int service_t {};
while (added++ < count)
{
  service_t = service_t_d(random_n);
  std::min_element(std::begin(checkouts), std::end(checkouts))->add(Customer(service_t));
  ++service_times[service_t - service_t_min];
}

size_t time {};                              // Stores time elapsed
const size_t total_time {600};               // Duration of simulation - minutes
size_t longest_q {};                         // Stores longest checkout queue length

// Period until next customer arrives
int new_cust_interval {arrival_interval_d(random_n)};

// Run store simulation for period of total_time minutes
while (time < total_time)                    // Simulation loops over time
{
  ++time;                                    // Increment by 1 minute

  // New customer arrives when arrival interval is zero
  if (--new_cust_interval == 0)
  {
    service_t = service_t_d(random_n);           // Random customer service time
    std::min_element(std::begin(checkouts), std::end(checkouts))->add(Customer(service_t));
    ++service_times[service_t - service_t_min];  // Record service time

    // Update record of the longest queue occurring
    for (auto & checkout : checkouts)
      longest_q = std::max(longest_q, checkout.qlength());

    new_cust_interval = arrival_interval_d(random_n);
  }

  // Update the time in the checkouts - serving the 1st customer in each queue
  for (auto & checkout : checkouts)
    checkout.time_increment();
}

std::cout << "Maximum queue length = " << longest_q << std::endl;
std::cout << "\nHistogram of service times:\n";
histogram(service_times, service_t_min);

std::cout << "\nTotal number of customers today: "
          << std::accumulate(std::begin(service_times), std::end(service_times), 0)
          << std::endl;
}
```

The using directives are to save typing and simplify the code. The incidence of service times for customers are recorded in a vector container. The service time value is used to index the vector element to be incremented each time by subtracting the minimum value in the range of service times, which causes the number of occurrences for the lowest service time to be recorded in the first element of the vector. The histogram() function generates a histogram of the number of time each service time in the range occurs as a horizontal bar chart.

The only input is the number of checkouts. I chose 600 minutes for the duration of the simulation but you could arrange to input this, too, along with other parameters. The main() function creates distribution objects for the customer service time, the number of customers waiting at the door when the store opens, and the time interval between customers arriving. The implication is that customers arrive one at a time; you could easily extend the program to have a random number of customers within a range arriving each time.

Customers are always assigned to a checkout that has the shortest queue. The Checkout object with the shortest queue is found by calling the min_element() algorithm that returns the minimum element in a range. This uses the < operator to compare elements but another version of the algorithm has a third parameter to specify the comparison function. Before the time simulation begins, the initial sequence of customers waiting at the door when the store opens are added to the Checkout objects and the service time records are updated.

The simulation is all within a while loop. On each iteration, time is incremented by one minute. The time period for the arrival of the next customer, new_cust_interval, is decremented on each iteration and when it reaches zero, a new customer is created with a new random service time and appended to the Checkout object with the shortest queue. The longest_q variable is also updated at this time because a new longest queue can only occur as the result of adding a new customer.

Next the time_increment() function for each Checkout object is called to advance processing of the first customer in each queue. The loop continues until time reaches the value stored in total_time.

Here's some sample output:

```
Enter the number of checkouts in the supermarket: 3
Customers waiting at store opening: 18
Maximum queue length = 7

Histogram of service times:
  2    16 ****************
  3    20 ********************
  4    13 *************
  5    16 ****************
  6    16 ****************
  7    12 ************
  8    11 ***********
  9    14 **************
 10    10 **********
 11    20 ********************
 12    15 ***************
 13    15 ***************
 14    14 **************
 15    14 **************

Total number of customers today: 206
```

This is with three checkouts. When I ran it with two checkouts, the longest queue length increased to 42 – long enough to lose customers. There's a lot more you could do to make the simulation more realistic. Uniform distributions are not typical and customers often arrive in groups, for example. You could also add the effect of coffee breaks for the staff, or the effect of one member of staff coughing and sneezing with a cold, which might encourage a few customers to avoid this checkout.

Using a priority_queue<T> Container Adapter

Unsurprisingly, the priority_queue container adapter defines a queue in which the elements are ordered; the element with the highest priority – the largest element by default – will be at the front of the queue. Since it's a queue, only the first element is accessible, which implies that the element with the highest priority will always be processed first. How you define 'priority' is entirely up to you. If a priority_queue is recording patients arriving at the accident and emergency facility in a hospital, the seriousness of the patient condition will be the priority. If the elements are current account transactions in a bank, the debits are likely to take priority over credits.

The template for a priority_queue has three parameters, two of which have default arguments; the first is the type of object stored, the second is the underlying container used to store the elements, and the third is a function object type that defines a predicate that determine the ordering of the elements. The template type is therefore:

```
template
    <typename T, typename Container=std::vector<T>, typename Compare=std::less<T>>
    class priority_queue
```

As you see, a priority_queue instance wraps a vector container by default. The less<T> function object type that is defined in the functional header is the default ordering predicate, and this determines that the largest object in the container will be at the front. The functional header also defines greater<T>, which you can specify as the last template argument to order the elements such that the smallest element is at the front. Of course, if you specify the last template argument, you must provide the other two template type arguments.

The way the elements are shown in Figure 3-3 reflects the order in which they will be retrieved, which is not necessarily the way they are ordered in the vector, although it can be. I'll explain why this is so a little later when I discuss heaps.

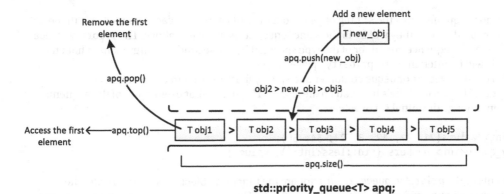

std::priority_queue<T> apq;

Figure 3-3. A priority_queue container

Creating a Priority Queue

You can create an empty priority queue like this:

```
std::priority_queue<std::string> words;
```

You can also initialize a priority queue with a range of objects of the appropriate type. For example:

```
std::string wrds[] {"one", "two", "three", "four"};
std::priority_queue<std::string> words {std::begin(wrds),
                                        std::end(wrds)}; // "two" "three" "one "four"
```

The range can be a sequence from any source and the elements do not need to be ordered. The elements in the range will be ordered appropriately in the priority queue.

The copy constructor creates a duplicate of an existing priority_queue object of the same type – specifically, an object with the same set of template type arguments. For example:

```
std::priority_queue<std::string> copy_words {words};            // copy of words
```

There's also a copy constructor with an rvalue reference parameter that will move the argument object.

When you want to order the contents in the opposite sense, with the smallest object at the front of the priority queue, you must supply all three template type arguments:

```
  std::string wrds[] {"one", "two", "three", "four"};
  std::priority_queue<std::string, std::vector<std::string>, std::greater<std::string>>
            words1 {std::begin(wrds), std::end(wrds)};        // "four" "one" "three "two"
```

This creates a priority queue using the operator>() function to compare the string objects in the range, so they are in the opposite sequence to those in the words priority queue above.

A priority queue can use any container to store the elements that has the function members front(), push_back(), pop_back(), size(), and empty(). This include a deque container so you can use that as an alternative:

```
std::string wrds[] {"one", "two", "three", "four"};
std::priority_queue<std::string, std::deque<std::string>> words {std::begin(wrds), std::end(wrds)};
```

The words priority queue stores the string objects from the wrds array in a deque container with the default comparison predicate so they will be in the same sequence as in words1 above. The priority_queue constructor will create a sequence container of the type specified by the second type argument to hold the elements, and this will be internal to the priority_queue object.

You can also create a vector or deque container and specify that as the source of elements for initializing the priority_queue. Here's how you create a priority_queue that uses copies of the elements from a vector container as the initial set of values:

```
std::vector<int> values{21, 22, 12, 3, 24, 54, 56};
std::priority_queue<int> numbers {std::less<int>(), values};
```

The arguments to the priority_queue constructor are the function object to be used to order the elements and the container providing the initial set of elements. The copies of the elements from the vector will be ordered in the priority queue using the function object. The elements in values will be in their original sequence, but the elements in the priority queue will be in the sequence: 56 54 24 22 21 12 3. The container used by a priority queue to store the elements remains private to the priority queue so the only way to interact with the contents is by calling function members of the priority_queue object. The type of the function object that is the first constructor argument must be the same as that specified as the Compare template type argument, which is less<T> by default. If you want to use a function object of a different type, you must specify all the template type arguments. For example:

```
std::priority_queue<int, std::vector<int>, std::greater<int>>
                                      numbers1 {std::greater<int>(), values};
```

The third type argument is the type for the comparison object. If you need to specify this, you must also specify the first two – the elements type and the type of the underlying container.

Operations for a Priority Queue

There's a limited range of operations needed to operate a priority_queue:

- push(const T& obj) pushes a copy of obj into the container at the appropriate place in the sequence, which will usually involve a sort operation.

- push(T&& obj) moves obj into the container at the appropriate place in the sequence, which will usually involve a sort operation.

- emplace(T constructor args...) constructs a T object in place at the appropriate place in the sequence by calling the constructor with the arguments passed. This will usually require a sort operation to maintain priority order.

- top() returns a reference to the first object in the priority queue.

- pop() removes the first element.

- size() returns the number of objects in the queue.

- empty() returns true if the queue is empty.

- swap(priority_queue<T>& other) interchanges the elements of this queue with those of the argument, which must contain objects of the same type.

The assignment operator is implemented for a priority_queue to assign the elements of the object that is the right operand to the object that is the left operand; copy and move versions of the assignment operator are defined. Note that there are no comparison operators defined for priority_queue containers. Clearly, adding a new element will often be quite slow because of the sorting that's likely to be necessary to maintain the order. I'll say a bit more about the internals of operations for a priority_queue later in the section on *heaps*.

Here's an illustration of how you might record data that is entered from the keyboard in a priority_queue:

```
std::priority_queue<std::string> words;
std::string word;
std::cout << "Enter words separated by spaces, enter Ctrl+Z on a separate line to end:\n";
while (true)
{
  if ((std::cin >> word).eof())
    break;
  words.push(word);
}
```

Entering Ctrl+Z sets the end of file state in an input stream so this is used to end the input loop. The operator>>() member of an istream object returns the object so we can call eof() to test the state of cin using the expression in the if condition. The words that are entered will be sequenced so that the largest word is at the front of the words queue – the input is sorted automatically.

There are no iterators for a priority_queue. If you want to access all the elements – to list or copy them, for example – you will empty the queue; a queue and a priority_queue have the same limitation. If you want to keep it after such an operation, you will need to copy it first, but if this is the case you should probably be using a different type of container. Here's how you might list the contents of the words priority queue above:

```
std::priority_queue<std::string> words_copy {words};  // A copy for output
while (!words_copy.empty())
{
  std::cout << words_copy.top() << " ";
  words_copy.pop();
}
std::cout << std::endl;
```

This first makes a copy of words because just outputting words would remove the contents. After outputting the element that top() returns, we remove it by calling pop() to make the next element accessible. Calling empty() in the loop condition ends the loop when all the elements have been removed. You could use the expression words_copy.size() to control when the loop ends because the value returned will be implicitly converted to bool, so when size() returns 0 the result is false.

If the input for words is:

```
one two three four five six seven
^Z
```

The output will be:

```
two three six seven one four five
```

Of course, if you need to output the contents of a priority_queue more than once, it would be better to do it in a function. You could make it a bit more general, like this:

```
template<typename T>
void list_pq(std::priority_queue<T> pq, size_t count = 5)
{
  size_t n{count};
  while (!pq.empty())
  {
    std::cout << pq.top() << " ";
    pq.pop();
    if (--n) continue;
    std::cout << std::endl;
    n = count;
  }
  std::cout << std::endl;
}
```

The arguments are passed by value so this processes a copy of the priority queue. It's a template that works with any type that has operator<<() implemented for output to an ostream object. The output values are five to a line by default if the second argument is omitted. Of course, you could define a similar function template to work with a queue container adapter object.

You could use the emplace() function member of a priority_queue like this:

```
words.emplace("nine");
```

The string literal that is the argument will be used as the argument in a call to the string class constructor to create the object in place in the container. This is much more efficient that this statement:

```
words.push("nine");
```

Here, the compiler will insert a string constructor call to create the argument to push() from the string literal and then call push() with this temporary string object as the argument. The push() function will then call the string class copy constructor to create the object that is added to the container.

We can put some of the code fragments together into a complete program:

```
// Ex3_03.cpp
// Exercising a priority queue container adapter
#include <iostream>                          // For standard streams
#include <queue>                             // For priority_queue<T>
#include <string>                            // For string class
using std::string;

// List contents of a priority queue
template<typename T>
void list_pq(std::priority_queue<T> pq, size_t count = 5)
{
  size_t n {count};
  while (!pq.empty())
  {
    std::cout << pq.top() << " ";
    pq.pop();
    if (--n) continue;
    std::cout << std::endl;
    n = count;
  }
  std::cout << std::endl;
}
int main()
{
  std::priority_queue<std::string> words;
  std::string word;
  std::cout << "Enter words separated by spaces, enter Ctrl+Z on a separate line to end:\n";
```

```
  while (true)
  {
    if ((std::cin >> word).eof())
      break;
    words.push(word);
  }
  std::cout << "You entered " << words.size() << " words." << std::endl;
  list_pq(words);
}
```

Here is some sample output:

```
Enter words separated by spaces, enter Ctrl+Z on a separate line to end:
one two three four five six seven eight nine ten eleven twelve
^Z
You entered 12 words:
two twelve three ten six
seven one nine four five
eleven eight
```

The output by the list_pq<T>() function template instance shows that the input was sequenced by the priority queue.

Heaps

A *heap* is not a container, but it is a particular organization of data. A heap is typically stored in a sequence container. Heaps are important because they turn up in many different computer processes. To understand what a heap is, you first need to have an idea of what a *tree* is, so I'll first explain what is meant by a tree data structure.

A *tree* is a hierarchical arrangement of *elements* or *nodes*. Each node has a *key*, which is the object stored in the node – just like a node in a linked list. A parent node is a node that has one or more subsidiary *child nodes*. In general a parent node can have any number of child nodes and the parent nodes in a tree do not have to have the same number of child nodes. A node that has no child nodes is called a *leaf node*. There is usually some relationship between the key of a parent node and the keys of its child nodes. A tree always has a *root node* that is the base of the tree and from which all subsidiary nodes can be reached.

Figure 3-4 shows a tree that presents the results final set of matches in the football World Cup competition in 2014. Germany won overall, so it's the root node; it beat Brazil in the final so its child nodes are itself and Brazil. A tree where each parent has up to two child nodes is called a binary tree. The tree in Figure 3-4 is a *complete binary tree* because *every* parent has two child nodes. The parent nodes in arbitrary trees need pointers to identify the child nodes. A complete binary tree can be stored as an array or other sequence such as a vector without requiring pointers to the child nodes because the number of nodes at each level is known. If you number each level in the tree as n, starting with the root node as level 0, each level contains 2^n nodes. Figure 3-4 shows how the nodes in the World Cup match tree could be stored in an array; the integers above each node are index values. The root node is stored as the first array element, followed by its two child nodes. The pairs of child nodes of those children appear next in sequence, and so on down to the leaf nodes. The index of the parent of a node stored at index n in an array is always the integral result of (n-1)/2. If the array elements are indexed from 1, the expression for the index of the parent of the node at index n is even simpler, the integer value of n/2.

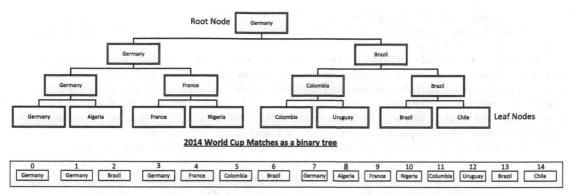

2014 World Cup Matches as a binary tree

Tree nodes stored in an array

Figure 3-4. *Example of a binary tree*

I can now define a heap: a heap is a *complete binary tree,* where each node is ordered relative to its child nodes. A parent node is either always greater than or equal to its children, in which case it is called *a max heap,* or always less than or equal to its children, which is described as a *min heap.* Note that the child nodes for a given parent are not necessarily ordered relative to each other in a heap.

Creating a Heap

The functions that you need to work with heaps are defined by templates in the algorithm header. The max_heap() function will rearrange the elements in a range that is defined by random access iterators so they form a heap. To do this it uses the < operator by default, which produces a max heap. Here's an example:

```
std::vector<double> numbers { 2.5, 10.0, 3.5, 6.5, 8.0, 12.0, 1.5, 6.0 };
std::make_heap(std::begin(numbers), std::end(numbers)); // Result: 12 10 3.5 6.5 8 2.5 1.5 6
```

After executing the make_heap() call, the elements in the vector will be as shown in the comment. This implies the structure shown in Figure 3-5.

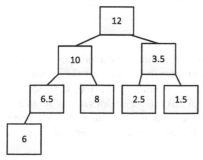

Figure 3-5. *The tree that a heap represents*

The root node is 12, with 10 and 3.5 as child nodes. The child nodes of the element with the value 10 are 6.5 and 8, and the child nodes of the element with the value 3.5 are 2.5 and 1.5. The element with the value 6.5 has a single leaf node as a child with the value 6.

A priority_queue is a heap! Under the covers, an instance of a priority_queue creates a heap. This is why Figure 3-3 does not reflect how the elements are arranged in the underlying container. In a heap it is not necessarily the case that the same comparison relationship applies between all successive pairs of elements. The first three elements in the heap shown in Figure 3-5 are in descending sequence but the fourth element is greater than the third. So why does the STL have facilities for both a priority_queue, which *is* a heap, *and* the ability to create a heap, especially since you can use a heap as a priority queue?

Well, a priority_queue provides an advantage over a heap; the element order is maintained automatically. You can't upset the ordered state of a priority_queue because you have no direct access to any element other than the first. This is a big plus if all you want is a priority queue.

On the other hand, a heap that you create using make_heap() offers some advantages over a priority_queue:

- You can access *any* element in a heap, not just the largest, because the elements are stored in a container such as a vector that you own. This does provide the potential for accidentally disrupting the order of the elements, but you can always restore it by calling make_heap().

- You can create a heap in any sequence container that has random access iterators. This includes ordinary arrays, string objects, or containers that you define. This means that you can arrange elements in such a sequence container as a heap whenever you need to, and repeatedly if necessary. You can even arrange for just a subset of the elements to be a heap.

- You can use a heap as a priority queue if you use the heap functions that maintain the heap order.

There's another version of make_heap() that has a third parameter for which you supply a comparison function that is the be used to order the heap. By specifying a function that defines the greater-than operator, you'll create a *min heap*. You can use a predicate from the functional header for this. For example:

```
std::vector<double> numbers {2.5, 10.0, 3.5, 6.5, 8.0, 12.0, 1.5, 6.0};
std::make_heap(std::begin(numbers), std::end(numbers),
                        std::greater<>()); // Result: 1.5 6 2.5 6.5 8 12 3.5 10
```

You can specify the template type argument for greater. The version here with the empty angled brackets deduces the type arguments and the return type. Having created a heap in a container using the make_heap() function, you have a bunch of operations you can apply to it so let's look into those next.

Heap Operations

Since a heap is not a container, but a particular organization of the elements within a container, you can only identify a heap as a range – by a begin iterator and an end iterator. This implies that you can make a heap of a subsequence of elements in a container. Having created a heap you are certainly going to want to add elements. The push_heap() template function in the algorithm does that but the way it does it may seem a little odd at first sight. To add an element to a heap you first append the element to the sequence by whatever method works for the sequence. You then call push_heap() to take care of inserting the last element – the element that you appended – at the correct position in the sequence to maintain heap arrangement. For example:

```
std::vector<double> numbers { 2.5, 10.0, 3.5, 6.5, 8.0, 12.0, 1.5, 6.0};
std::make_heap(std::begin(numbers), std::end(numbers)); // Result: 12 10 3.5 6.5 8 2.5 1.5 6
numbers.push_back(11);                                   // Result: 12 10 3.5 6.5 8 2.5 1.5 6 11
std::push_heap(std::begin(numbers), std::end(numbers)); // Result: 12 11 3.5 10 8 2.5 1.5 6 6.5
```

The comments show the effect of each operation on the elements in numbers. The process of adding an element to a heap has to work this way. You can only add a new element to a container by calling a function member – a function that receives a range specified by iterators has no mechanism for adding elements. It's push_back() that adds the element to the end of the sequence and push_heap() restores the heap order. By calling push_heap() you are signaling that you have appended an element to a heap that may have messed up the heap order. The push_heap() function therefore presumes that the last element is new, and rearranges the elements in the sequence to maintain the heap. You can see from the results that a significant rearrangement was necessary in this case. You'll also notice that while the sequence is a heap, the elements are not entirely in descending sequence. This shows clearly that while a priority queue is a heap, the ordering of elements in a heap is not necessarily the same as in a priority queue.

Of course, if you create the heap with your own comparison function, you *must* use the same comparison function with push_heap():

```
std::vector<double> numbers {2.5, 10.0, 3.5, 6.5, 8.0, 12.0, 1.5, 6.0};
std::make_heap(std::begin(numbers), std::end(numbers),
                            std::greater<>()); // Result: 1.5 6 2.5 6.5 8 12 3.5 10
numbers.push_back(1.2);                          // Result: 1.5 6 2.5 6.5 8 12 3.5 10 1.2
std::push_heap(std::begin(numbers), std::end(numbers),
                            std::greater<>()); // Result: 1.2 1.5 2.5 6 8 12 3.5 10 6.5
```

If you don't specify the third argument to push_heap() to be the same as the third argument to make_heap(), the code won't work correctly. The result shown in the comment looks a little strange with 6.5 last, but the heap tree shown in Figure 3-6 will clarify it.

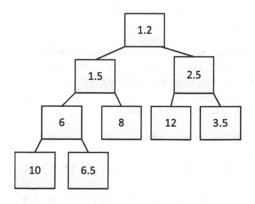

Figure 3-6. *A heap of floating-point values*

Now it's evident from the tree that 6.5 is a child of 6, not a child of 10, so the heap organization is as it should be.

Removing the largest element is a vaguely similar sort of process to adding an element to a heap, but things happen the other way round. You first call pop_heap() and then remove the largest element from the container, like this:

```
std::vector<double> numbers {2.5, 10.0, 3.5, 6.5, 8.0, 12.0, 1.5, 6.0};
std::make_heap(std::begin(numbers), std::end(numbers)); // Result: 12 10 3.5 6.5 8 2.5 1.5 6
std::pop_heap(std::begin(numbers), std::end(numbers));  // Result: 10 8 3.5 6.5 6 2.5 1.5 12
numbers.pop_back();                                     // Result: 10 8 3.5 6.5 6 2.5 1.5
```

The pop_heap() function puts the first element last, then makes sure the rest of the elements still represent a heap. You then call the pop_back() member of the vector to remove the last element.

If you created the heap using your own comparison function with make_heap(), you must also supply the function as the third argument to pop_heap():

```
std::vector<double> numbers {2.5, 10.0, 3.5, 6.5, 8.0, 12.0, 1.5, 6.0};
std::make_heap(std::begin(numbers), std::end(numbers),
                              std::greater<>()); // Result: 1.5 6 2.5 6.5 8 12 3.5 10
std::pop_heap(std::begin(numbers), std::end(numbers),
                              std::greater<>());  // Result: 2.5 6 3.5 6.5 8 12 10 1.5
numbers.pop_back();                              // Result: 2.5 6 3.5 6.5 8 12 10
```

The reason you need to supply the comparator to pop_heap() is evident from the results of the operation shown in the comment. The function doesn't just swap the first element with the last; it also reorders the elements in the range from begin(numbers) to end(numbers)-1 to maintain the heap order. To do this correctly, pop_heap() must use the same comparison function that make_heap() used.

Because you can do things to the container that stores a heap that can upset the heap, the STL provides a way to check whether a sequences is still a heap:

```
if (std::is_heap(std::begin(numbers), std::end(numbers)))
    std::cout << "Great! We still have a heap.\n";
else
    std::cout << "Oh bother! We messed up the heap.\n";
```

The is_heap() function returns true if the range is a heap. Of course, here this is checking the order using an instance of the default comparison predicate less<>. If the heap was created using an instance of greater<>, the result will be wrong. To get the correct result in this case you must use the expression std::is_heap(std::begin(numbers),std::end(numbers),std::greater<>()).

A further checking facility is to check a range that is only partly a heap. For example:

```
std::vector<double> numbers {2.5, 10.0, 3.5, 6.5, 8.0, 12.0, 1.5, 6.0};
std::make_heap(std::begin(numbers), std::end(numbers),
                              std::greater<>());  // Result: 1.5 6 2.5 6.5 8 12 3.5 10
std::pop_heap(std::begin(numbers),  std::end(numbers),
                              std::greater<>());  // Result: 2.5 6 3.5 6.5 8 12 10 1.5
auto iter = std::is_heap_until(std::begin(numbers), std::end(numbers), std::greater<>());
if(iter != std::end(numbers))
  std::cout << "numbers is a heap up to " << *iter << std::endl;
```

The is_heap_until() function returns an iterator that points to the first element in the range that is not in heap order. This fragment will output the value of the last element, 1.5, because this is not in heap sequence after the pop_heap() call. If the entire range is a heap, the function returns the end iterator, so the if statement is necessary to ensure you don't attempt to dereference the end iterator. You'll also get the end iterator returned if the range contains less than two elements. There's a second version of is_heap_until() with two parameters that will use the default predicate, less<>.

The last operation the STL provides is sort_heap(), which sorts a range that is assumed to be a heap. If it isn't a heap, you'll get a crash at runtime. The version of the function with two parameters that correspond to the iterators that define the range assumes the range is a max heap (i.e., arranged using an instance of less<>) and it sorts the elements into *ascending* order. The result won't be a max heap of course. Here's an example of using it:

```
std::vector<double> numbers {2.5, 10.0, 3.5, 6.5, 8.0, 12.0, 1.5, 6.0};
std::make_heap(std::begin(numbers), std::end(numbers));   // Result: 12 10 3.5 6.5 8 2.5 1.5 6
std::sort_heap(std::begin(numbers), std::end(numbers));   // Result: 1.5 2.5 3.5 6 6.5 8 10 12
```

The result of the sort operation obviously cannot be a max heap but it is a min heap, as the tree in Figure 3-7 shows. Although a heap does not have to be completely ordered, any sequence that is completely ordered is a heap.

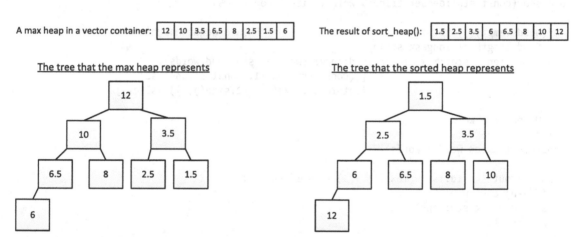

Figure 3-7. *A min heap resulting from sorting a max heap*

The second version of sort_heap() has a third parameter for which you supply the predicate that you used to create the heap. If the predicate you use to create the heap is greater<>, so it is a min heap, the result will be that the elements are sorted into *descending* order. The result cannot be a min heap. Here's a fragment illustrating this:

```
std::vector<double> numbers {2.5, 10.0, 3.5, 6.5, 8.0, 12.0, 1.5, 6.0};
std::make_heap(std::begin(numbers), std::end(numbers),
                              std::greater<>()); // Result: 1.5 6 2.5 6.5 8 12 3.5 10
std::sort_heap(std::begin(numbers), std::end(numbers),
                              std::greater<>()); // Result: 12 10 8 6.5 6 3.5 2.5 1.5
```

As the comment in the last line shows, the result of sort_heap() on a min heap is a max heap.

You know that the algorithm header defines a template for a sort() function that you could use to sort a heap, so why is there a sort_heap() function? The sort_heap() function uses a special sort algorithm that by an incredible coincidence is called *Heap Sort*. This first creates a heap, then sorts the data in a way that makes use of the fact the data is partially ordered; sort_heap() assumes the heap exists so it just does the second bit. Taking advantage of the partial ordering of a heap can potentially make the sort faster, although this may not always be the case.

We can use a heap as a priority queue in an example that's a variation on Ex3_03.cpp:

```cpp
// Ex3_04.cpp
// Using a heap as a priority queue
#include <iostream>                          // For standard streams
#include <iomanip>                           // For   stream manipulators
#include <algorithm>                         // For heap support functions
#include <string>                            // For string class
#include <deque>                             // For deque container
using std::string;

// List a deque of words
void show(const std::deque<string>& words, size_t count = 5)
{
  if(words.empty()) return;                  // Ensure deque has elements
  // Find length of longest string
  auto max_len = std::max_element(std::begin(words), std::end(words),
                          [](const string& s1, const string& s2)
                          {return s1.size() < s2.size(); })->size();

  // Output the words
  size_t n {count};
  for(const auto& word : words)
  {
    std::cout << std::setw(max_len + 1) << word << " ";
    if(--n) continue;
    std::cout << std::endl;
    n = count;
  }
  std::cout << std::endl;
}

int main()
{
  std::deque<string> words;
  std::string word;
  std::cout << "Enter words separated by spaces, enter Ctrl+Z on a separate line to end:\n";
  while (true)
  {
    if ((std::cin >> word).eof())
    {
      std::cin.clear();
      break;
    }
```

```
    words.push_back(word);
  }
  std::cout << "The words in the list are:" << std::endl;
  show(words);

  std::make_heap(std::begin(words), std::end(words));
  std::cout << "\nAfter making a heap, the words in the list are:" << std::endl;
  show(words);
  std::cout << "\nYou entered " << words.size() << " words. Enter some more:" << std::endl;
  while (true)
  {
    if ((std::cin >> word).eof())
    {
      std::cin.clear();
      break;
    }
    words.push_back(word);
    std::push_heap(std::begin(words), std::end(words));
  }
  std::cout << "\nThe words in the list are now:" << std::endl;
  show(words);
}
```

Here's some sample output:

```
Enter words separated by spaces, enter Ctrl+Z on a separate line to end:
one two three four five six seven
^Z
The words in the list are:
  one     two   three    four    five
  six    seven

After making a heap, the words in the list are:
  two     one   three    four    five
  six    seven

You entered 7 words. Enter some more:
eight nine ten twelve fifteen ninety forty fifty-three
^Z

The words in the list are now:
        two       twelve       three      nine         ten
        six       seven        eight      four         five
        one       fifteen      ninety     forty   fifty-three
```

The example creates a heap in a deque container, just to be different; a vector would be just as good. The show() function is a helper that lists the words in a deque<string> container. For neat output, the words are presented in a fixed field width that is one greater than the maximum word length. The statement that computes the maximum length uses an instance of the max_element() function template that is defined in the algorithm header. The function returns an iterator that points to the maximum element in a range that is

117

obtained using a comparison function that you supply. The first two arguments are the iterators that specify the range. The third argument is the comparison to be used, which in this instance is a lambda expression.

Note that the max_element() function requires a *less-than* operation to be defined to find the maximum element, not *greater-than*. The comparison function should be of the form:

```
bool comp(const T1& a, const T2& b);
```

In most cases the type of the first parameter will be the same as that for the second parameter but the types can be different in general. The only proviso is that elements in the range must be implicitly convertible to both types T1 and T2. The parameters need not be specified as const but it's a good idea to do so. In any event, the comparison function must not change the arguments that are passed to it.

The lambda expression just returns the result of comparing the values of the size() members of the string arguments. The iterator that max_element() returns will point to the longest string so it is used to call the size() member to record its length in max_len.

Words are read from cin in the manner you have seen before. Here, the clear() member of cin is called to clear the EOF state that is set when Ctrl+Z is entered. If you don't call clear(), the EOF state would remain set so you would not be able to obtain input from the standard input stream in the same way later in main().

After reading a sequence of words, the contents of the deque container is arranged as a heap by calling make_heap(). We then read some more words, but this time maintaining the heap order by calling push_heap() after each word is added to the container. push_heap() expects the new element to be added at the end of the container; if you were to use push_front(), the program would crash because the heap would not be valid. The output shows that it all works as expected.

Of course, you could use push_heap() after every input word, in which case you would not need to call make_heap(). The example illustrates how having the underlying container under your control enables you to access the entire sequence and retain it, without have to copy it as you would with a priority_queue container adapter.

Storing Pointers in a Container

More often than not it will be better to store pointers in a container, rather than objects, and most of the time *smart pointers* will be better than raw pointers. There are several reasons for this:

- Storing pointers in a containers means that the pointers are copied, not the objects to which they point. Copying a pointer is usually a *lot* faster than copying an object.

- You can get polymorphic behavior by storing pointers in a container. A container defined so that it stores pointers to elements of a base type can store pointers to objects of a derived type, too. This is a very useful capability when you need to process an arbitrary sequence of objects that have a common base class. A common example of where this applies is processing a sequence of objects such as lines, curves, and geometric shapes that are to be displayed.

- Sorting the contents of a container of pointers will be faster than sorting the objects; only the pointers need to be moved, not the objects.

- Storing smart pointers is safer that storing raw pointers because the objects in the free store are deleted automatically when they are no longer referenced. You have no need to worry about possible memory leaks. Smart pointers that don't point to anything are nullptr by default.

As you know, there are two primary types of smart pointers: unique_ptr<T> and shared_ptr<T>. A unique_ptr has exclusive ownership of whatever it points to whereas a shared_ptr allows multiple pointers to the same object to exist. There's also a weak_ptr<T> type, which is a smart pointer that is always created from a shared_ptr<T> and is used to avoid the problems caused by cyclic references that can occur with shared_ptrs. Pointers of type unique_ptr<T> can be stored in a container by moving them there. For example, this compiles OK:

```
std::vector<std::unique_ptr<std::string>> words;
words.push_back(std::make_unique<std::string>("one"));
words.push_back(std::make_unique<std::string>("two"));
```

The vector stores smart pointers of type unique_ptr<string>.The make_unique<T>() function creates both the object and the smart pointer, and returns the latter. Because the result is a temporary unique_ptr<string> object, the push_back() function with an rvalue reference parameter is called, so no copying is required. Another way to add a unique_ptr object is to create a local unique_ptr variable, and move it into the container using std::move(). However, any subsequent operation that requires copying an element of the container will fail. There can only ever be one. If you must be able to copy elements, shared_ptr objects are the ones to go for; otherwise use unique_ptr objects.

Storing Pointers in Sequence Containers

I'll explain the problems you can run into with raw pointers in a container first, and then move on to using smart pointers – which is the recommended approach. Here's a code fragment to read words from the standard input stream and to store pointers to string objects in the free store in a vector container:

```
std::vector<std::string*> words;
std::string word;
std::cout << "Enter words separated by spaces, enter Ctrl+Z on a separate line to end:\n";
while (true)
{
  if ((std::cin >> word).eof())
  {
    std::cin.clear();
    break;
  }
  words.push_back(new std::string {word});        // Create object and store its address
}
```

The expression that is the argument to push_back() creates a string object in the free store, so the argument to push_back() is the address of the object. Here's how you could list the contents of the words vector;

```
for (auto& w : words)
  std::cout << w << " ";
std::cout << std::endl;
```

If you want to use iterators to access the container elements, the code to output the strings looks like this:

```
for (auto iter = std::begin(words); iter != std::end(words); ++iter)
  std::cout << **iter << " ";
std::cout << std::endl;
```

iter is an iterator that you must dereference to access the element to which it points. The element is a pointer so you must dereference that to obtain the string object; hence the expression **iter.

You must take care when erasing elements that are pointers to release the free store memory first. If you don't, you will be unable to release the memory after the pointer has been deleted unless you have made a copy of the pointer. This is a common source of memory leaks with raw pointers in a container. Here's how it could happen with the words vector:

```
for (auto iter = std::begin(words); iter != std::end(words) ; )
{
  if (**iter == "one")
    words.erase(iter);                       // Memory leak!
  else
    ++iter;
}
```

This deletes a pointer but the memory to which it points remains. Whenever you delete an element that is a raw pointer, release the memory first:

```
for (auto iter = std::begin(words); iter != std::end(words) ; )
{
  if (**iter == "one")
  {
    delete *iter;                            // Release the memory...
    words.erase(iter);                       // ...then delete the pointer
  }
  else
    ++iter;
}
```

Before the vector goes out of scope, you must remember to delete the string objects from the free store. Here's one way to do this:

```
for (auto& w : words)
  delete w;                                  // Delete the string pointed to
words.clear();                               // Delete all the elements from the vector
```

Using an index accesses the pointer so you just use the delete operator to delete the string object. When the loop ends all the elements in the vector are invalid pointers so it's important not to leave the vector in this state. Calling clear() removes all the elements so calling size() for the vector will now return 0. Of course, you could use iterators, in which case the loop will be:

```
for (auto iter = std::begin(words); iter != std::end(words); ++iter)
  delete *iter;
```

If you store smart pointers, there's no need to worry about releasing memory in the free store. The smart pointers take care of that. Here's a code fragment to read strings and store shared_ptr<string> objects in the vector:

```
std::vector<std::shared_ptr<std::string>> words;
std::string word;
std::cout << "Enter words separated by spaces, enter Ctrl+Z on a separate line to end:\n";
```

```
while (true)
{
  if ((std::cin >> word).eof())
  {
    std::cin.clear();
    break;
  }
  words.push_back(std::make_shared<string>(word));      // Create smart pointer to string & store it
}
```

There's not a lot of difference between this and the raw pointer version. The type argument for the vector template is now std::shared_ptr<std::string> and the argument to push_back() calls make_shared(), which creates the string object in the free store and the smart pointer to it; the function then returns the smart pointer. Because the smart pointer is created by the argument expression, the version of push_back() with an rvalue reference parameter will be called, which will move the pointer into the container.

Template type arguments can get a little cumbersome but you can always simplify the appearance of the code with a using directive. For example:

```
using PString = std::shared_ptr<std::string>;
```

With this in effect you can define the vector container like this:

```
std::vector<PString> words;
```

Accessing the strings through elements that are smart pointers is exactly the same as with raw pointers. Both the earlier fragments to output the contents of words work just as well with smart pointers. Of course, there's no need to delete the string objects from the free store; the smart pointers take care of that. Executing words.clear() removes all the elements so the destructors for the smart pointers will be called; this will also release the memory allocated for the objects to which they point.

To prevent a vector container from allocating additional memory for elements too frequently, create the vector and then call reserve() to allocate an initial amount of memory. For example:

```
std::vector<std::shared_ptr<std::string>> words;
words.reserve(100);                              // Space for 100 smart pointers
```

This is better than creating the vector with a predefined number of elements because each element will be created by calling a shared_ptr<string> constructor when you do this. This is not a big deal but there's no point in incurring overhead unnecessarily, even if it is small. Usually, the space required for each smart pointer will be a lot less than the space required by the object to which it points, so you can afford to be generous with the space you allocate with reserve().

Storing shared_ptr<T> objects allows copies of the pointers to exist outside the container. If you don't need this capability, you should use unique_ptr<T> objects. Here's how that would work with the words vector:

```
std::vector<std::unique_ptr<std::string>> words;
std::string word;
std::cout << "Enter words separated by spaces, enter Ctrl+Z on a separate line to end:\n";
while (true)
{
  if ((std::cin >> word).eof())
  {
```

```
    std::cin.clear();
    break;
  }
  words.push_back(std::make_unique<string>(word));      // Create smart pointer to string & store it
}
```

It's essentially the same with 'unique' replacing 'shared' in the code.

We can see how using smart pointers could be used to implement the supermarket checkout simulation from earlier in this chapter, Ex3_02. The Customer class definition will be the same in this version but the definition of the Checkout class can use smart pointers, so that will change, and we can use them in main() too. There's not requirement for copies of the pointers so we can use unique_ptr<T> throughout. Here's the new contents for the Checkout.h header file:

```
// Supermarket checkout - using smart pointers to customers in a queue
#ifndef CHECKOUT_H
#define CHECKOUT_H
#include <queue>                                 // For queue container
#include <memory>                                // For smart pointers
#include "Customer.h"
using PCustomer = std::unique_ptr<Customer>;

class Checkout
{
private:
  std::queue<PCustomer> customers;               // The queue waiting to checkout

public:
  void add(PCustomer&& customer) { customers.push(std::move(customer)); }
  size_t qlength() const { return customers.size(); }

  // Increment the time by one minute
  void time_increment()
  {
    if (customers.front()->time_decrement().done())  // If the customer is done...
      customers.pop();                               // ...remove from the queue
  };

  bool operator<(const Checkout& other) const { return qlength() < other.qlength(); }
  bool operator>(const Checkout& other) const { return qlength() < other.qlength(); }
};
#endif
```

We need the directive to include the memory header to make the templates for smart pointer types available. The queue container that records the customers queueing at the checkout stores PCustomer elements. PCustomer is defined by a using directive to be an alias for std::unique_ptr<Customer>, which saves a lot of typing. PCustomer objects cannot be copied so the parameter for add() is an rvalue reference and when the function is called, the argument is moved into the container. With elements that are unique pointers, it has to be moves all the way; and, of course, the parameter cannot be const. No other changes are needed in the class definition so the changes necessary to use unique_ptr are quite modest.

Here's the main() program to implement the supermarket simulation using unique_ptr:

```cpp
// Ex3_05.cpp
// Using smart pointer to simulate supermarket checkouts
#include <iostream>                      // For standard streams
#include <iomanip>                       // For stream manipulators
#include <vector>                        // For vector container
#include <string>                        // For string class
#include <numeric>                       // For accumulate()
#include <algorithm>                     // For min_element & max_element
#include <random>                        // For random number generation
#include <memory>                        // For smart pointers
#include "Checkout.h"
#include "Customer.h"

using std::string;
using distribution = std::uniform_int_distribution<>;
using PCheckout = std::unique_ptr<Checkout>;

// Output histogram of service times
void histogram(const std::vector<int>& v, int min)
{
  string bar (60, '*');                  // Row of asterisks for bar
  for (size_t i {}; i < v.size(); ++i)
  {
    std::cout << std::setw(3) << i+min << " "    // Service time is index + min
      << std::setw(4) << v[i] << " "             // Output no. of occurrences
      << bar.substr(0, v[i])                     // ...and that no. of asterisks
      << (v[i] > static_cast<int>(bar.size()) ? "..." : "")
      << std::endl;
  }
}

int main()
{
  std::random_device random_n;

  // Setup minimum & maximum checkout periods - times in minutes
  int service_t_min {2}, service_t_max {15};
  std::uniform_int_distribution<> service_t_d {service_t_min, service_t_max};

  // Setup minimum & maximum number of customers at store opening
  int min_customers {15}, max_customers {20};
  distribution n_1st_customers_d {min_customers, max_customers};

  // Setup minimum & maximum intervals between customer arrivals
  int min_arr_interval {1}, max_arr_interval {5};
  distribution arrival_interval_d {min_arr_interval, max_arr_interval};
```

```cpp
size_t n_checkouts {};
std::cout << "Enter the number of checkouts in the supermarket: ";
std::cin >> n_checkouts;
if(!n_checkouts)
{
  std::cout << "Number of checkouts must be greater than 0. Setting to 1." << std::endl;
  n_checkouts = 1;
}

std::vector<PCheckout> checkouts;
checkouts.reserve(n_checkouts);                    // Reserve memory for pointers

// Create the checkouts
for (size_t i {}; i < n_checkouts; ++i)
  checkouts.push_back(std::make_unique<Checkout>());
std::vector<int> service_times(service_t_max-service_t_min+1);

// Add customers waiting when store opens
int count {n_1st_customers_d(random_n)};
std::cout << "Customers waiting at store opening: " << count << std::endl;
int added {};
int service_t {};

// Define comparison lambda for pointers to checkouts
auto comp = [](const PCheckout& pc1, const PCheckout& pc2){ return *pc1 < *pc2; };
while (added++ < count)
{
  service_t = service_t_d(random_n);
  auto iter = std::min_element(std::begin(checkouts), std::end(checkouts), comp);
  (*iter)->add(std::make_unique<Customer>(service_t));
  ++service_times[service_t - service_t_min];
}

size_t time {};                                    // Stores time elapsed
const size_t total_time {600};                     // Duration of simulation - minutes
size_t longest_q {};                               // Stores longest checkout queue length

// Period until next customer arrives
int new_cust_interval {arrival_interval_d(random_n)};

// Run store simulation for period of total_time minutes
while (time < total_time)                          // Simulation loops over time
{
  ++time;                                          // Increment by 1 minute

  // New customer arrives when arrival interval is zero
  if (--new_cust_interval == 0)
  {
    service_t = service_t_d(random_n);             // Random customer service time
    (*std::min_element(std::begin(checkouts),
             std::end(checkouts), comp))->add(std::make_unique<Customer>(service_t));
    ++service_times[service_t - service_t_min];    // Record service time
```

```
    // Update record of the longest queue length
    for (auto& pcheckout : checkouts)
      longest_q = std::max(longest_q, pcheckout->qlength());

    new_cust_interval = arrival_interval_d(random_n);
  }

  // Update the time in the checkouts - serving the 1st customer in each queue
  for (auto& pcheckout : checkouts)
    pcheckout->time_increment();
}

std::cout << "Maximum queue length = " << longest_q << std::endl;
std::cout << "\nHistogram of service times:\n";
histogram(service_times, service_t_min);

std::cout << "\nTotal number of customers today: "
          << std::accumulate(std::begin(service_times), std::end(service_times), 0)
          << std::endl;
}
```

The vector container now stores unique pointers to Checkout objects. An iterator for the vector points to a pointer to a Checkout object – a unique_ptr<Checkout> object – so to call a function member of a Checkout object that is identified by an iterator, you must dereference the iterator and then use the indirect member selection operator to call the function. You can see this in several of the statements that have been changed in main(). By default, the min_element() algorithm uses the < operator for the elements to which the iterators point to determine the result. The default would compare the smart pointers, which won't produce the correct result. We need to supply a third argument to min_element() to specify the comparison it should use. This is defined by a lambda expression that is named comp; it's named because we want to use it more than once. This lambda dereferences the smart pointer arguments to access the Checkout objects and then uses the operator<() member of the Checkout class to compare them. All the Checkout and Customer objects are created in the free store. The smart pointers take care of freeing the memory for them. The output of this version of the simulation program produces the same output as the original. You could use shared_ptr<T> in the example but it would be slower in execution. unique_ptr<T> objects carry minimal overhead over a raw pointer in terms of execution time and memory.

Storing Pointers in a Priority Queue

I'll now concentrate on smart pointers. Storing raw pointers is essentially the same, except that you are responsible for deleting the objects to which they point. When you create a priority_queue or a heap, an ordering relationship is necessary that determines the sequence of the elements. When raw pointers or smart pointers are stored, you'll *always* need to supply the comparison function that is to be used. If you don't, the pointers will be compared, not the objects they point to, which is almost certainly not what you want. Let's consider how you could define a priority_queue to store pointers to string object in the free store. I'll assume the following directives are in effect throughout subsequent sections to keep the length of statements in code fragments reasonable:

```
using std::string;
using std::shared_ptr;
using std::unique_ptr;
```

We need to define a function object that will compare objects pointed to by pointers of type shared_ptr<string>. I'll define the comparison like this:

```
auto comp = [](const shared_ptr<string>& wp1, const shared_ptr<string>& wp2)
                { return *wp1 < *wp2; };
```

This define comp to be a lambda expression that compares the elements that two smart pointers point to. The reason for naming the lambda is so we can specify its type as a type argument for the priority_queue template. Here's the priority queue definition:

```
std::priority_queue<shared_ptr<string>, std::vector<shared_ptr<string>>, decltype(comp)>
                                                          words1 {comp};
```

The first template type argument is the type of element stored, the second is the type of container to be used to store the elements, and the third is the type of function object used to compare elements. We have to specify the third template type argument because the type of the lambda expression will be different from the default comparison type, std::less<T>.

You can still specify an external container to initialize the priority_queue that contains pointers:

```
std::vector<shared_ptr<string>> init {std::make_shared<string>("one"),
                                      std::make_shared<string>("two"),
                                      std::make_shared<string>("three"),
                                      std::make_shared<string>("four")};
std::priority_queue<shared_ptr<string>, std::vector<shared_ptr<string>>, decltype(comp)>
                                                          words(comp, init);
```

The init vector has initial values that are created by calling make_shared<string>(). The arguments to the priority queue constructor are the object defining how elements are to be compared and the container that is the source of the initializing elements. The smart pointers in the vector are copied and used to initialize the words priority queue. Of course, initializing the priority queue with the elements from another container means that you cannot use unique_ptr<string> elements – they must be shared_ptr<string>.

If you don't need to keep the initial set of elements, you could call the emplace() member of the priority_queue object to create them in place in the container:

```
std::priority_queue<shared_ptr<string>, std::vector<shared_ptr<string>>, decltype(comp)>
                                                          words1 {comp};
words1.emplace(new string {"one"});
words1.emplace(new string {"two"});
words1.emplace(new string {"three"});
words1.emplace(new string {"five"});
```

The emplace() member of words1 will call the constructor for the type of object stored, which will be the shared_ptr<string> constructor. The argument to this constructor is the address of a string object that is created in the free store that is produced by the expression that is the argument to emplace(). This fragment will store four pointers to string objects in the priority queue that point to objects that contain "two," "three," "one," "five". The order of elements in the priority queue is determined by comp that was defined earlier in this section.

Of course, if you don't want to keep the initial set of elements, you could store unique_ptr<string> elements in the priority queue instead. For example:

```
auto ucomp = [](const std::unique_ptr<string>& wp1, const std::unique_ptr<string>& wp2)
            { return *wp1 < *wp2; };
std::priority_queue<std::unique_ptr<string>, std::vector<std::unique_ptr<string>>,
                                                decltype(ucomp)> words2 {ucomp};
```

The lambda expression that defines the comparison now accepts references to unique_ptr<string> objects. We must specify all three template type parameters for the priority queue because we need to specify the comparator type. The second template type argument could now be deque<string>, which is the default container type that is used. You can still add the elements to the priority queue using emplace():

```
words2.emplace(new string{"one"});
words2.emplace(new string {"two"});
words2.emplace(new string {"three"});
words2.emplace(new string {"five"});
```

Alternatively, you can use push():

```
words2.push(std::make_unique<string>("one"));
words2.push(std::make_unique<string>("two"));
words2.push(std::make_unique<string>("three"));
words2.push(std::make_unique<string>("five"));
```

The object returned by make_unique<string>() will be moved into the container because the version of push() with an rvalue reference parameter will be selected automatically.

Heaps of Pointers

You need to supply a function pointer that compares objects when you create a heap of pointers. Here's an example of how to do that:

```
std::vector<shared_ptr<string>> words
                    { std::make_shared<string>("one"), std::make_shared<string>("two"),
                      std::make_shared<string>("three"), std::make_shared<string>("four") };
std::make_heap(std::begin(words), std::end(words),
            [](const shared_ptr<string>& wp1, const shared_ptr<string>& wp2){ return *wp1 < *wp2; });
```

The third argument to make_heap() is a lambda expression defining the comparison function. It just compares the string objects by dereferencing the smart pointers. The template for the make_heap() function has a parameter for the function object type. Unlike the class template for the priority_queue container adapter, the template parameter has no default argument value so the compiler will deduce the type of the function object from the third argument in the function call. If the third type parameter to this function template had a default type specified, you would have to specify the type argument, as was necessary in the case of the priority queue template.

You must supply the *same* comparison function that you use with make_heap() as the last argument in any calls of the functions push_heap(), pop_heap(), is_heap() and is_heap_until(). Of course, you can use a named lambda expression to do this. You will also need to supply a comparison function if you call sort_heap().

Containers of Base Class Pointers

You can store pointers to derived class objects in any container or container adapter that is defined with elements of the base class type. This will enable you to obtain polymorphic behavior with the objects pointed to by the container elements. We will need a base class and a derived class to explore the possibilities, so let's start by resurrecting the Box class from Ex2_06 in the previous chapter and changing it a bit. Here's the class definition:

```
class Box
{
protected:
  size_t length {};
  size_t width {};
  size_t height {};

public:
  explicit Box(size_t l=1, size_t w=1, size_t h=1) : length {l}, width {w}, height {h} {}
  virtual ~Box() = default;

  virtual double volume() const;                 // Volume of a box

  // Comparison operators for Box object
  bool operator<(const Box& box) const;
  bool operator==(const Box& box) const;

  // Stream input and output
  virtual std::istream& read(std::istream& in);
  virtual std::ostream& write(std::ostream& out) const;
};
```

We will derive a Carton class from Box so the data members are protected and the destructor is specified as virtual. It's not essential here but it's a good habit to declare the destructor in a base class as virtual; it results in minimal overhead and you prevent the possibility of the wrong destructor being called for a derived class. The volume() member and the two members read() and write() that perform stream I/O are virtual so they can be overridden in a derived class when necessary.

The volume() function can be defined as inline in the Box.h file like this:

```
inline double Box::volume() const { return length*width*height; }
```

The comparison functions can also be inline:

```
// Less-than operator
inline bool Box::operator<(const Box& box) const
{ return volume() < box.volume(); }

//Equality comparion operator
inline bool Box::operator==(const Box& box) const
{
  return length == box.length && width == box.width && height == box.height;
}
```

The less-than operator function compares volumes of the operands while the equality operator function compares the values of the data members. We can also define overloads for the stream extraction and insertion operators for Box objects as inline in Box.h:

```cpp
// Stream extraction operator
inline std::istream& operator>>(std::istream& in, Box& box)
{
  return box.read(in);
}

// Stream insertion operator
inline std::ostream& operator<<(std::ostream& out, Box& box)
{
  return box.write(out);
}
```

These operator functions each call the appropriate function member, read() or write(), to perform the operation. The member functions are virtual, so if they are redefined in a derived class, either of these operator function will call the version of read() or write() that is for the object type that is passed as the second argument.

The complete contents of Box.h look like this:

```cpp
// Box.h
// Defines the Box class that will be a base for the Carton class
#ifndef BOX_H
#define BOX_H
#include <iostream>                        // For standard streams
#include <istream>                         // For stream classes
#include <utility>                         // For comparison operator templates
using namespace std::rel_ops;              // Comparison operator template namespace

// Definition for the Box class as above...

// Definitions for inline functions as above...
#endif
```

The read() and write() function members can go in a separate source file, Box.cpp, which will have the following contents:

```cpp
// Box.cpp
// Function members of the Box class
#include <iostream>
#include "Box.h"

// Read a Box object from a stream
std::istream& Box::read(std::istream& in)
{
  size_t value {};
  if ((in >> value).eof())
    return in;
  length = value;
```

```
  in >> width >> height;
  return in;
}

// Write a Box object to a stream
std::ostream& Box::write(std::ostream& out) const
{
  out << typeid(*this).name() << "(" << length << "," << width << "," << height << ")";
  return out;
}
```

They are defined in a straightforward way. Note that read() leaves the EOF indicator set in the istream object when an end of file is read; as you know, this results from reading Ctrl+Z from the keyboard (or EOF from a file) so you can use this to detect the end of input of sequences for Box object dimensions. The write() function writes the dimensions of the object between parentheses following the type name. The type name for the current object is obtained by calling the name() member of the type_info object that results from applying the typeid operator. Thus the specific type for each object that is written out will be identified in the output.

The definition of the derived class, Carton, will go in the Carton.h header file that will have the following contents:

```
// Carton.h
#ifndef CARTON_H
#define CARTON_H
#include "Box.h"

class  Carton :public Box
{
public:
  explicit Carton(size_t l = 1, size_t w = 1, size_t h = 1) : Box {l, w, h}{}
  double volume() const override {return 0.85*Box::volume(); }
};
#endif
```

There's not a lot to it. The only override is for the volume() member that returns 85 percent of the volume of a regular Box object. Clearly Carton has thicker sides or more interior packing, but most importantly its volume will be different from that of a Box with same dimensions so we will know when the override of the base class volume() member is called.

Here's a program to store pointers to objects of these types in a container:

```
// Ex3_06.cpp
// Storing derived class objects in a container of base pointers
#include <iostream>                          // For standard streams
#include <memory>                            // For smart pointers
#include <vector>                            // For the vector container
#include "Box.h"
#include "Carton.h"
using std::unique_ptr;
using std::make_unique;
```

```
int main()
{
  std::vector<unique_ptr<Box>> boxes;
  boxes.push_back(make_unique<Box>(1, 2, 3));
  boxes.push_back(make_unique<Carton>(1, 2, 3));
  boxes.push_back(make_unique<Carton>(4, 5, 6));
  boxes.push_back(make_unique<Box>(4, 5, 6));
  for(auto&& ptr : boxes)
    std::cout << *ptr << " volume is " << ptr->volume() << std::endl;
}
```

This doesn't need much explanation. The vector stores elements of type std::unique_ptr<Box> so we can store smart pointers to Box objects or smart pointers to objects of any type that has Box as a direct or indirect base class. The boxes container is populated with smart pointers to a mixture of Box and Carton objects by calling its push_back() member – the rvalue reference parameter version in this case. The using directives makes the code more readable. Details of each object pointed to by elements in the vector is output in the range-based for loop. The deduced type for ptr in the for loop will be an rvalue.

Here's the output:

```
class Box(1,2,3) volume is 6
class Carton(1,2,3) volume is 5.1
class Carton(4,5,6) volume is 102
class Box(4,5,6) volume is 120
```

The output shows that we get polymorphic calls of the volume() function member. The operator<<() function overload is displaying the correct class type so the write() function calls are also polymorphic. Clearly, smart pointers provide a lot of advantages when you need to work with elements of a variety of types in a hierarchy. By storing smart pointers to the base class in a container you get polymorphic behavior automatically. You also get automatic release of free store memory. This applies to any type of container or container adapter.

Applying Algorithms to a Range of Pointers

Algorithms process data that you specify by a range. When the range relates to a container that stores pointers, the iterators in the range point to pointers. Consequently, you must define a function object that an algorithm may require to take this into account. We have only seen a few algorithms so far, but let's look at the implications with some examples.

The accumulate() algorithm that is defined in the numeric header sums a range of elements using operator+() by default. A second version of accumulate() has four parameters—the first two parameters being the begin and end iterators for the range, and the second two being the initial value for the operation, and a function object that defines the binary operation to be applied between the running accumulation and each element in turn. You can use this version to provide an alternative to the default operation, and if the range contains pointers, then you *must* use this version to get a valid result. Here's how you could use accumulate() to concatenate string objects that are pointed to by shared_ptr<string> objects in a vector:

```
using word_ptr = std::shared_ptr<std::string>;
std::vector<word_ptr> words {std::make_shared<string>("one"), std::make_shared<string>("two"),
                   std::make_shared<string>("three"), std::make_shared<string>("four")};
auto str = std::accumulate(std::begin(words), std::end(words), string {""},
                  [](const string& s, const word_ptr& pw)->string
                    {return s + *pw + " "; });
```

The fourth argument to `accumulate()` is the binary operation to be applied and this is a lambda expression. The `accumulate()` function passes the third argument it receives as the first argument to your binary function. It passes the result of dereferencing an iterator in the range as the second argument to your function. Therefore the first parameter for the lambda has to be the type of the third argument and the second parameter must be the type of the element pointed to by the iterators in the range. The result that is stored in `str` will be the string `"one two three four"`.

You need to account for the elements being pointers with function members of a container that apply a predicate. The `remove_if()` function that the `list` and `forward_list` containers have is one example:

```
std::list<word_ptr> wrds {std::make_shared<string>("one"), std::make_shared<string>("two"),
                          std::make_shared<string>("three"), std::make_shared<string>("four")};
wrds.remove_if([](const word_ptr& pw){ return (*pw)[0] == 't'; });
```

The lambda expression that is passed to `remove_if()` will return `true` when the first character in a string is `'t'`. This will remove `"two"` and `"three"` from the list. The argument to the lambda will be a smart pointer to a `string` object so it's necessary to dereference this to access the string.

Summary

The container adapter templates provide specialized interfaces to the standard sequence containers; the containers that are used to store elements are only accessible through the interface provided by the adapter class. Choose one of these container adapters when you need the functionality they offer because the interfaces are simple, and they are easier to use than implementing the same functionality for yourself with a standard container. The ability to create a heap in a standard sequence using function templates from the `algorithm` header offers the same capability as a `priority_queue` container adapter, but with the added flexibility to access the container that stores the elements. The important points that were covered in this chapter include:

- The `stack<T>` container adapter template implements a *push-down stack*, which is a LIFO retrieval mechanism. A `stack<T>` instance can be defined so that it uses a `vector<T>`, a `deque<T>`, or a `list<T>` as the container that stores elements internally.

- The `queue<T>` container adapter template implements a *queue*, which provides a FIFO retrieval mechanism. A `queue<T>` instance can be defined so that it uses a `deque<T>` or a `list<T>` as the container that stores elements internally.

- The `priority_queue<T>` container adapter template implements a priority queue, where the element with the highest priority is always the one that can be retrieved next. You can define a `priority_queue<T>` instance so that it uses either a `vector<T>` or a `deque<T>` as the container that stores the elements.

- A *heap* is a binary tree where the nodes are partially ordered with the same ordering throughout; each parent node in a tree is either greater than or equal to its child nodes – a max heap, or less than or equal to its child nodes – a min heap.

- The `make_heap()` function template creates a heap of elements in a range specified by random access iterators. A max heap is created by default but you can supply a function object that defines a comparison for elements that will determine the heap ordering. Heap operations are supported by `push_heap()` and `pop_heap()` that maintain the heap order after adding an element or removing the first element from the range.

- You can store pointers in a container. Using smart pointers ensures proper deletion of objects from the free store when they are no longer required.

- You must provide function objects for comparisons or other operations required by algorithms for containers that store pointers where necessary.

EXERCISES

1. Write a program to store an arbitrary number of words entered from the keyboard in a deque<string> container. Copy the words to a list<string> container, sort the contents of the list in ascending sequence, and output the result.

2. Write a program that uses a stack<T> container adapter instance to reverse the sequence of letters in a sentence that is entered from the keyboard on a single line. The program should output the result and indicate whether or not the original sentence is a palindrome. (A palindrome is a sentence that can be read the same when reversed – if you ignore spaces and punctuation. For example: "Are we not drawn onward to a new era?").

3. Write a program to use a priority_queue container adapter instance to present an arbitrary number of words entered from the keyboard in descending alphabetical sequence.

4. Repeat Exercise 1 but with the words created in the free store and referenced by smart pointers in the containers.

5. Repeat Exercise 3 but with smart pointers to words stored in the priority_queue container adapter.

6. Write a program to output an arbitrary number of words entered from the keyboard in descending alphabetical sequence. The process should store smart pointers to the words in a vector container in which you create a heap.

CHAPTER 4

■ ■ ■

Map Containers

You retrieve an element from a sequence container by its position. You can access the first or last element of a deque, for example, or an element in a vector by its index position. Map containers work quite differently, as this chapter will explain. In this chapter you'll learn the following:

- What is meant by an *associative container*.

- What a map container is and how it is typically organized.

- The types of map containers that are available and their capabilities.

- The functions that map containers provide.

- What a pair is and what it is used for.

- What a tuple is and how you use it.

Introducing Map Containers

The sequence containers are a valuable tool for managing data, but for a vast number of applications they don't always provide a convenient data access mechanism. Working with names and addresses is a simple example of a situation where sequence containers may not do what you want. A typical operation would be to find an address for a given name. If the records are stored in a sequence container, you have to search. map containers provide a way of storing and accessing such data much more effectively.

Map containers are *associative containers*. In an associative container, each object is located based on the value of a *key* that is associated with the object. A key can be a value of a fundamental type or it can be an object of a class type. Strings are used very frequently as keys, and this is likely to apply when you want to store name and address records; a name is going to be one or more strings. How the location of an object within an associative container is determined from a key depends on the specific type of the container, and the internal organization for a particular container type can vary between different STL implementations.

There are four varieties of map containers that are each defined by a class template. All map container types store *key/value* pairs. The elements in a map are objects of type pair<const K,T> that encapsulate an object of type T and its associated key of type K. The key is const in a pair element in a container because allowing the key to be modified would disrupt the sequence of elements in the container. The class templates for map containers each have different characteristics:

- A map<K,T> container stores elements of type pair<const K,T> that encapsulate key/object pairs where the keys are of type K and the objects are of type T. Keys must be unique, so duplicate keys are not allowed. You can store duplicate objects as long as their keys are different. Elements are ordered and the order of elements in the container is determined by comparing the keys. Keys are compared using a less<K> object by default.

- A multimap<K,T> container is similar to a map<K,T> in that elements are ordered. Keys must be comparable and the order of elements is determine by comparing the keys. The difference is that duplicate keys *are* allowed. Thus a multimap can store more than one pair<const K,T> element with the same key value.

- An unordered_map<K,T> container is a map where the pair<const K,T> objects are not ordered directly by the key values. Elements are located using *hash values* that are produced from their keys. Hash values are integers that are generated by a process called *hashing* that I'll explain later in this chapter. Duplicate keys are not allowed.

- An unordered_multimap<K,T> container also locates objects using hash values produced from the keys but duplicate keys *are* allowed.

Templates for map and multimap are defined in the map header and templates for unordered_map, and unordered_multimap are defined in the unordered_map header. You can see that any prefixes to the map template type name identify the characteristics of the container:

- The multi prefix indicates that keys do not need to be unique; its absence indicates that keys *must* be unique.

- The unordered_ prefix indicates that the elements are positioned in the container using *hash values* that are generated from the keys rather than comparing key values. Its absence implies that elements are ordered by comparing keys.

Let's look into map containers first.

Using a map Container

The map<K,T> class template is defined in the map header, and it defines a map that stores objects of type T that each have an associated key of type K. The location of objects within the container is determined by comparing keys. You retrieve an object from a map container by supplying the appropriate key value. Figure 4-1 illustrates a map<K,T> container where the keys are names, and the objects are integer values representing age values.

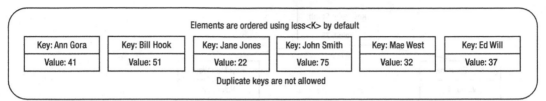

A map<K, T> Container

Figure 4-1. *A conceptual representation of a map<K,T> container*

The container represented in Figure 4-1 will be of type map<Name, size_t>, where the Name class could be defined like this:

```
class Name
{
private:
  std::string firstname{};
  std::string secondname{};
public:
  Name(std::string first, std::string second) : firstname{first}, secondname{second}{};
  Name()=default;

  bool operator<(const Name& name)
  { return secondname < name.secondname ||
                  ((secondname == name.secondname) && (firstname < name.firstname)); }
};
```

Objects stored in a container usually need a default constructor defined to allow default elements to be created when necessary. The operator<() function for Name objects compares the names with the secondname members determining the order when they are different. If the secondname members are equal, the firstname members determine the result of the comparison. The string class defines operator<() so the default less<string> comparison will work OK.

Don't be misled by the use of less<K> to order the elements in a map – the elements are not organized as a simple ordered sequence. There is no specific organization required for an STL map container, but typically elements are stored in a *balanced binary tree*. The elements in a balanced binary tree are organized so that the height of the tree – the number of levels between the root node and the leaf nodes – is minimized. A binary tree is said to be balanced if the height of the left sub-tree of each node never differs by more than one from the height of its right sub-tree. Figure 4-2 shows a possible balanced tree configuration for the map shown in Figure 4-1.

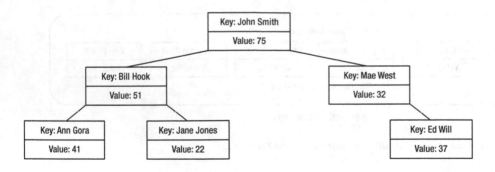

Figure 4-2. *Internal organization of a map container*

There are three levels in the tree in Figure 4-2 so any element can be found in a maximum of three steps from the root. The root node is chosen to minimize the tree height, and for each parent node, the key for the left child node is less than the key for the parent, and the key for the right child node is greater than that of the parent. Adding a new element can result in a different root node being necessary to maintain the balanced tree arrangement. Obviously there is going to be some overhead incurred in maintaining the balanced tree organization as elements are added to the container. The payoff is that retrieving elements will be faster compared to a sequential arrangement or an unbalanced tree, and the more elements there are in the container, the more effective the balanced tree organization is. The time to retrieve a random element from a balanced binary tree containing n elements is $O(\log_2 n)$; the time to retrieve elements from a sequence is $O(n)$.

■ **Note** The $O(n)$ notation in the context of computer operations characterizes how the time to execute an operation increases as a parameter increases. Think of the O as implying "the order of". $O(n)$ indicates that the execution time increases linearly with n. The time to execute an $O(\log_2 n)$ operation increases much more slowly than n increases – because it's proportional to $\log_2 n$.

Creating a map Container

The map class template has four type parameters, but normally you'll only need to specify values for the first two. The first is the type for the keys, and the second is the type for the objects to be stored. The third and fourth template parameters define the type of function object used to compare keys and the type of object used to allocate memory within the map, respectively. These last two have default values assigned. I'll show how you define a different type of function object for comparing keys a little later in this section, but I won't be going into defining alternative allocator types.

The default constructor for a map<> container class creates an empty map. For example, here's how you could create a map container that stores age values as type size_t with names of type string as the keys:

```
std::map<std::string, size_t> people;
```

The first template type argument specifies the type for the key as string, and the second template type argument specifies the type for the values as size_t. Of course, the template type parameters here can be of any types, the only requirement being that the keys must be comparable using less<K>, or an alternative function object type if you specify it.

Each element in a map<K,T> is an object of type pair<const K,T> that encapsulates both an object and its key, where const K implies that the keys cannot be modified. The template for the pair<T1,T2> class is defined in the utility header, which is included into the map header. Thus elements in the people container will be of type pair<const string, size_t>. The pair<T1,T2> template type is not exclusively for use in this context. You can use it yourself to package two objects of different types together as a single object when necessary. I'll have more to say about this later in this chapter.

You can use an initializer list to specify the initial values in a map but since the map contains pair<const K,T> elements, the values in the initializer list must be of this type. Here's how you could specify initial values for the people container:

```
std::map<std::string, size_t> people{ {"Ann", 25}, {"Bill", 46}, {"Jack", 32}, {"Jill", 32} };
```

The values in the initializer list are created by passing the two values between each nested brace pair to the pair constructor. Thus the list will contain four pair<const string, size_t> objects.

The utility header defines the make_pair<T1, T2>() function template, which provides a convenient way of combining objects of types T1 and T2. You could therefore create the pair objects to initialize a map like this:

```
std::map<std::string, size_t> people{ std::make_pair("Ann", 25), std::make_pair("Bill", 46),
                    std::make_pair("Jack", 32), std::make_pair("Jill", 32) };
```

The make_pair<T1, T2>() function template deduces the type parameter values from the function arguments so the objects returned by the make_pair<>() calls in the list will be of type pair<char const*, int>. Because these are initial values for the people map, these pair objects will be converted to the type for the elements in the map, which is pair<const string, size_t>. A pair<T1,T2> object has public members first and second that store the T1 and T2 objects, respectively. The template for the pair<T1,T2> constructor provides implicit conversion of a pair object as long as the first and second members of the original pair object can be implicitly converted to the types for the same members of the target pair object.

The map<K,T> template defines move and copy constructors so you can duplicate an existing container. For example:

```
std::map<std::string, size_t> personnel {people};   // Duplicate people map
```

The personnel map will contain copies of the pair elements in people.

You can create a map from a range of pair elements from another container. You specify the elements in the usual way by begin and end iterators. Obviously, the iterators must point to pair elements of a type that is compatible with the container. Here's an example:

```
std::map<std::string, size_t> personnel {std::begin(people), std::end(people)};
```

This creates personnel and initializes it with the elements identified by iterators for the people container. map containers produce bidirectional iterators so you can increment and decrement them. A map also offers reverse iterators so you can access the elements from the last to the first. The personnel map will contain elements identical to those in the people map. Of course, you can create a container with a subset of elements from another container:

```
std::map<std::string, size_t> personnel {++std::begin(people), std::end(people)};
```

Inserting Elements in a map

There are several versions of the insert() function member of a map<K,T> container that insert one or more pair<const K,T> objects in the map. Elements are only inserted if they are not already present in the map. Here's a code fragment illustrating how you could insert a single element:

```
std::map<std::string, size_t> people {std::make_pair("Ann", 25), std::make_pair("Bill", 46),
                                       std::make_pair("Jack", 32), std::make_pair("Jill", 32)};
auto pr = std::make_pair("Fred", 22);                    // Create a pair element...
auto ret_pr = people.insert(pr);                         // ..and insert it
std::cout << ret_pr.first->first << " " << ret_pr.first->second
          << " " << std::boolalpha << ret_pr.second << " \n";    // Fred 22 true
```

The first statement creates the map container and initializes it with the four values in the initializer list; these will be implicitly converted to the required type in this case. The second statement creates another pair object that is to be inserted. The pr object will be of type pair<const char*, int> because the type arguments for the make_pair<>() function template are deduced from the arguments types, but this object will be implicitly converted to the container element type in the insert() operation. Of course, if you don't want to rely on the implicit conversion, you can create the pair object of the required type:

```
auto pr = std::make_pair<std::string, size_t>(std::string {"Fred"}, 22);
```

The explicit template type arguments for the make_pair<>() template determine the type of the pair object that is returned. You could supply a string literal as the first argument and implicit conversion would be applied to create the string object that is required for the key. You can omit the template type arguments for make_pair<>() and let the compiler deduce them. Suppose that you write the statement as:

```
auto pr = std::make_pair("Fred", 22);                    // pair<const char*, int>
```

The pair object will be different from the type required. When you allow the compiler to deduce the template type arguments, the arguments to make_pair() determine the template type arguments for the pair exactly. The first argument is a literal of type const char* and the second argument is a literal of type int. Having said that, it doesn't matter much in this case because when you insert a new element, the pair object can be implicitly converted to the type required by the container. The time when you need to be cautious is when there are no implicit conversions from the types of the arguments to make_pair() to the types of the keys and objects in the container.

The insert() function member returns a pair<iterator, bool> object. The first member of the object is an iterator that points either to the element that was inserted, or to the element that prevented its insertion. The latter will be the case if an object has already been stored in the map with the same key. The second member of the object that is returned is a bool value that will be true if the insertion was successful, and false otherwise. As you see in the output statement, the expression to access the first member of the pair that was inserted is ret_pr.first->first; the first member of ret_pr is an iterator pointing to a pair object so you use the -> operator to access the first member of the object to which it points. The output shows that the element was inserted. You can verify this by executing this loop:

```
for(const auto& p : people)
  std::cout << std::setw(10) << std::left << p.first << " " << p.second << " \n";
```

The loop variable p will access each of the elements in the people map in turn by reference. The output will be:

```
Ann       25
Bill      46
Fred      22
Jack      32
Jill      32
```

The elements are in ascending order of the keys because the default less<string> function object is used to order them in the map.

You can see the effect of inserting an element that is already present by executing these two statements:

```
ret_pr = people.insert(std::make_pair("Bill", 48));
std::cout << ret_pr.first->first << " " << ret_pr.first->second
          << " " << std::boolalpha << ret_pr.second << "\n";       // Bill 46 false
```

The output that this produces is shown in the comment. The first member of the pair object returned by insert() points to the element that is already in the map with a matching key, and the second member is false to indicate that the insertion could not be made.

If you really want the age value for the key "Bill" to be altered to 48 when the element is present, you could use the pair object that insert() returns to do it, like this:

```
if(!ret_pr.second)                                     // If the element is there...
  ret_pr.first->second = 48;                           // ... change the age
```

The second member of ret_pr is false when the key already exists in the map so this code will assign the value 48 to the second member of the element in the map when it is present.

You can use the pair constructor to create the object to be inserted in the argument to insert():

```
ret_pr = people.insert(std::pair<const std::string, size_t> {"Bill", 48});
```

This will call a version of insert() that has an rvalue reference parameter so the element will be moved into the container, assuming it is not already present.

A further option allows you to provide a *hint* as to where the element should be inserted. The hint is in the form of an iterator that points to an existing element in the map, and the hint is used as the place to begin searching for where the new element is to be inserted. A good hint can speed up the insertion operation; a bad hint can do the opposite. For example:

```
auto ret_pr = people.insert(std::make_pair("Jim", 48));
people.insert(ret_pr.first, std::make_pair("Ian", 38));
```

The first statement inserts an element and returns a `pair` object as described earlier. The first member of this `pair` object is an iterator that points either to the element that was inserted, or an existing element with the same key as the element being inserted. The first argument in the next `insert()` call corresponds to the hint, so the hint here is the element just inserted. The new element is specified by the second argument to `insert()`, and this will be inserted prior to the element identified by the hint, and as close as possible to it. If the hint cannot be used in this way it will be ignored. Equally, if the element to be inserted is in the map, the operation fails. An `insert()` call with a hint returns an iterator that points to the inserted element, or to the element that prevented the insertion. Thus you can use the return value to determine whether or not the insertion was successful. It's therefore a good idea to only provide a hint for an insertion when you're sure the element is not present. If you are unsure, and still want to give a hint, the `count()` member of a map can help. It returns the number of elements in the map with a given key, and this can only be 0 or 1. You could therefore write:

```
if(!people.count("Ian"))
  people.insert(ret_pr.first, std::make_pair("Ian", 38));
```

The `insert()` call only occurs here when `count()` returns 0, indicating that the `"Ian"` key isn't in the map. Of course, you could make this check when you are inserting an element without a hint, but the return value from `insert()` would tell you anyway.

You can insert a range of elements from an external source into a `map`. The elements need not be from another map container but must be of the same type as the elements in the container into which they are being inserted. Here's some code demonstrating this:

```
std::map<std::string, size_t> crowd {{"May", 55}, {"Pat", 66}, {"Al", 22}, {"Ben", 44}};
auto iter = std::begin(people);
std::advance(iter, 4);                     // begin iterator+ 4
crowd.insert(++std::begin(people), iter);  // Insert 2nd, 3rd, and 4th elements from people
```

This creates a new map, `crowd`, with four elements initially. `iter` is initialized to the begin iterator for the `people` map. Iterators for a `map` container are bidirectional so you can increment or decrement them but you can't add or subtract values. An instance of the `advance()` function template you met in chapter 1 is used to increment `iter` by 4 so it will point to the fifth element, and this is used as the end iterator for the range specified in the arguments to the `insert()` call for `crowd` in the next line. The begin iterator for the range is the begin iterator for the `people` map incremented by 1, so the operation inserts three elements from `people` into `crowd`, beginning with the second.

There's a version of `insert()` that accept an initializer list as an argument:

```
crowd.insert({{"Bert", 44}, {"Ellen", 99}});
```

This inserts the two elements in the initializer list into the `crowd` map. The `initializer_list<>` object that is created by the argument expression will be of type `initializer_list<const string,size_t>` because the compiler knows that this is the type for the `insert()` function parameter. Of course, you could create the initializer list independently and pass it as the argument to `insert()`:

```
std::initializer_list<std::pair<const std::string, size_t>> init {{"Bert", 44}, {"Ellen", 99}};
crowd.insert(init);
```

CHAPTER 4 ■ MAP CONTAINERS

The first type parameter argument for the `initializer_list` template must be const. There is no implicit conversion from `initializer_list<string,size_t>` to `initializer_list<const string,size_t>` so an object of the former type would not be accepted as an argument to `insert()`.

We can see some of this working in a complete example. I'll use objects of a type that we will define to make it a little different. The `Name` type will represents a person's name and the header file contents for the class definition will be:

```
// Name.h for Ex4_01
// Defines a person's name
#ifndef NAME_H
#define NAME_H
#include <string>                          // For string class
#include <ostream>                         // For output streams
#include <istream>                         // For input streams

class Name
{
private:
  std::string first {};
  std::string second {};

public:
  Name(const std::string& name1, const std::string& name2) :
                                          first (name1), second (name2) {}
  Name() = default;

  // Less-than operator
  bool operator<(const Name& name) const
  {
    return second < name.second || (second == name.second && first < name.first);
  }

  friend std::istream& operator>>(std::istream& in, Name& name);
  friend std::ostream& operator<<(std::ostream& out, const Name& box);
};

// Extraction operator overload
inline std::istream& operator>>(std::istream& in, Name& name)
{
  in >> name.first >> name.second;
  return in;
}

// Insertion operator overload
inline std::ostream& operator<<(std::ostream& out, const Name& name)
{
  out << name.first + " " + name.second;
  return out;
}

#endif
```

The class is very simple with two private `string` members for the first and second names. There's a constructor that accepts either `string` arguments or string literals as arguments. We must define `operator<()` for the class to allow the objects to be used as keys in a map container. There is support for the extraction and insertion operators for streams to make input and output for Name objects easier.

The elements in the map will be of type `std::pair<const Name, size_t>`, but we can make the code a little less verbose with the follow alias definition:

```
using Entry = std::pair<const Name, size_t>;
```

Now we can just use `Entry` as the type for map elements when the container type is `map<Name,size_t>`. We can put this alias to good use in the definition of a function to help with map element input:

```
Entry get_entry()
{
  std::cout << "Enter first and second names followed by the age: ";
  Name name {};
  size_t age {};
  std::cin >> name >> age;
  return make_pair(name, age);
}
```

This reads a `Name` object followed by an age value from `cin` and creates a `pair` object from them. Reading input for `name` will invoke the `operator>>()` overload for `istream` objects that is defined in `Name.h`, and that supports reading a `Name` object.

A helper function to output the elements in a map will be useful:

```
void list_entries(const map<Name, size_t>& people)
{
  for(auto& entry : people)
  {
    std::cout << std::left << std::setw(30) << entry.first
              << std::right << std::setw(4) << entry.second << std::endl;
  }
}
```

This just uses a range-based for loop to iterate over the elements. The `entry` loop variable will reference each of the map elements in turn. Each element is a `pair` object where the `first` member is a Name object, and the `second` member is a `size_t` value for the age.

The source file containing `main()` will have the following contents:

```
// Ex4_01.cpp
// Storing names and ages
#include <iostream>          // For standard streams
#include <iomanip>           // For stream manipulators
#include <string>            // For string class
#include <map>               // For map container class
#include <utility>           // For pair<> & make_pair<>()
#include <cctype>            // For toupper()
#include "Name.h"
```

```cpp
using std::string;
using Entry = std::pair<const Name, size_t>;
using std::make_pair;
using std::map;

// Definition of get_entry() here...

// Definition of list_entries() here...

int main()
{
  map<Name, size_t> people { {{"Ann", "Dante"}, 25}, {{"Bill", "Hook"}, 46},
                             {{"Jim", "Jams"}, 32},  {{"Mark", "Time"}, 32} };

  std::cout << "\nThe initial contents of the map is:\n";
  list_entries(people);

  char answer {'Y'};
  std::cout << "\nEnter a Name and age entry.\n";
  while(std::toupper(answer) == 'Y')
  {
    Entry entry {get_entry()};
    auto pr = people.insert(entry);
    if(!pr.second)
    { // It's there already - check whether we should update
      std::cout << "Key \"" << pr.first->first
                << "\" already present. Do you want to update the age (Y or N)? ";
      std::cin >> answer;
      if(std::toupper(answer) == 'Y')
        pr.first->second = entry.second;
    }
    // Check whether there are more to be entered
    std::cout << "Do you want to enter another entry(Y or N)? ";
    std::cin >> answer;
  }

  std::cout << "\nThe map now contains the following entries:\n";
  list_entries(people);
}
```

There are some extra aliases defined to reduce the code verbosity further. You can use a using directive for the std namespace and completely eliminate the need for the std name qualification, but I prefer not to do this because all names in std are effectively imported so it nullifies the point of defining the namespace.

The definition of the map container has initial values for elements defined in an initializer list. This is just to illustrate how you use nested braces in this context. There's an initializer list between braces for the Name object in each initializer list that defines an element. Each element initializer is a Name object and an age value between braces, and all of the initial values for elements are enclosed in the outermost pair of braces.

The list_entries() helper function is called to show the initial state of the container. Further entries are read in the for loop. The loop is controlled by the value of answer, which is 'Y' at the outset so the loop executes at least once and at least one element must be entered from the keyboard. The entry object is of type Entry, the type for a container element. The object returned by the get_entry() helper function is used as the initial value. The entry element is inserted into the container by passing it as the argument to the insert() member. The pair object that is returned has a first member that points to the element in the container that has a key matching that of entry. This will be the original container element if it existed prior to the insertion operation. If this key was already in the container no insertion will be made and the second member of pr will be false. pr.first is an iterator pointing to the container element so pr.first->second accesses the object associated with the key and this is changed to the value in entry.second if the user confirms the update. The last action in the loop is to decide whether more entries are to be entered. The loop ends when no more entries are to be made and the final contents of the container are output by calling list_entries().

Here is some sample output from the example:

```
The initial contents of the map is:
Ann Dante                  25
Bill Hook                  46
Jim Jams                   32
Mark Time                  32
Enter a Name and age entry.
Enter first and second names followed by the age: Emma Nate 42
Do you want to enter another entry(Y or N)? y
Enter first and second names followed by the age: Emma Nate 43
Key "Emma Nate " already present. Do you want to update the age (Y or N)? Y
Do you want to enter another entry(Y or N)? y
Enter first and second names followed by the age: Eamonn Target 56
Do you want to enter another entry(Y or N)? N

The map now contains the following entries:
Ann Dante                  25
Bill Hook                  46
Jim Jams                   32
Emma Nate                  43
Eamonn Target              56
Mark Time                  32
```

The elements are output in ascending sequence by key because they are ordered in the container using a less<Name> object. The Name::operator<() member compares the last names first, and the first names are only compared when the last names are identical. This results in the normal sort order for the names.

Constructing map Elements in Place

A map container has an emplace() function member that constructs a new element in place, thus avoiding copy or move operations. The arguments are those necessary to construct an element, which is a pair<const K,T> object. The construction of the element will only occur if there is no existing element with the same key. Here's one example of how it can be used:

```
std::map<Name, size_t> people;
auto pr = people.emplace(Name{"Dan", "Druff"}, 77);
```

The map here contains keys of type Name, which is the class type defined in Ex4_01. The objects are type size_t so the map will contain elements of type pair<const Name,size_t>. The first argument to emplace() is the Name object that is the key, and the second argument is the size_t value and the function will use these in a call to the pair<const Name,size_t>constructor to create the element in place. If you construct the pair object in the argument to emplace(), the move constructor for the pair<const Name,size_t> class will be called.

The pair object that emplace() returns provides the same indication as that returned by the insert() function member. The first member of the pair is an iterator pointing to the element that was inserted, or the element preventing insertion, and the second member is a bool value that is true if the element was inserted.

The emplace_hint() member of a map creates an element in place in essentially the same way as emplace(), except that the iterator you supply as the first argument is used as the starting point in the search for the position to create the new element. For example:

```
std::map<Name, size_t> people;
auto pr = people.emplace(Name{"Dan", "Druff"}, 77);
auto iter = people.emplace_hint(pr.first, Name{"Cal", "Cutta"}, 62);
```

The emplace_hint() call uses the iterator from the pair that is returned by the preceding emplace() call as the hint. If the container takes the hint, the new element will be positioned preceding this position and as close as possible to it. The arguments following the hint are used to construct the new element. It's important to note that the value returned is quite different from that of the emplace() function member. The emplace_hint() member doesn't return a pair object – it returns an iterator that points to the new element if it was inserted, or the existing element that has the same key if it wasn't. You have no direct indication as to whether or not the element was created. However, all is not lost – one possibility is to use the size() member that returns the number of elements in the map to check for an increase in the element count. For example:

```
auto pr = people.emplace(Name{"Dan", "Druff"}, 77);
auto count = people.size();
auto iter = people.emplace_hint(pr.first, Name{"Cal", "Cutta"}, 62);
if(count < people.size()) std::cout << "Success!\n";
```

The message will only be displayed if the element count was increased by the call to emplace_hint().

Accessing Elements in a map

You already know that you can obtain begin and end iterators as well as reverse iterators that provide access to all the elements in a map container. The at() function member of a map returns the object associated with the key you supply as the function argument. If the key is not present, an out_of_range exception is thrown. Here is an example of how you might use it:

```
Name key;
try
{
  key = Name {"Dan", "Druff"};
  auto value = people.at(key);
  std::cout << key << " is aged " << value << std::endl;
  key = Name {"Don", "Druff"};
  value = people.at(key);
  std::cout << key << " is aged " << value << std::endl;
}
catch(const std::out_of_range& e)
{
  std::cerr << e.what() << '\n'
            << key << " was not found." << std::endl;
}
```

Statements that call at() for a map need to be in a try block – the program will be terminated if the exception is thrown and not caught. This fragment uses at() to obtain the objects associated with two Name keys in the people container. If the contents of the map are determined by executing the code fragments from the previous section, this will produce the output:

```
Dan Druff is aged 77
invalid map<K, T> key
Don Druff was not found.
```

The first at() call in the try block is successful and results in the first line of output. The second call fails and throws an out_of_range exception that is caught and result in the last two lines of output. The what() member of the exception object returns a string describing the cause of the exception. When the catch block code executes, all local variables in the try block have been destroyed and therefore cannot be accessed. The key variable is defined before the try block so this is still accessible from within the catch block.

The subscript operator is implemented by a map container to accept a key as an argument and return a reference to the associated object. Here's an example:

```
auto age = people[Name {"Dan", "Druff"}];
```

This retrieves the size_t value associated with the Name key. Note that using the subscript isn't simply a retrieval mechanism. If the key does not exist, a new element is created for the key with the associated object created using the default constructor for a class type, or the equivalent of zero if the associated object is of a fundamental type. For example:

```
auto value = people[Name {"Ned", "Kelly"}];    // Creates a new element if the key is not there
```

A new element will be created using the key because this key does not exist in the container. The associated value will be 0 and this value will be returned. You can use the subscript operator when you're updating elements in the map or inserting them if they aren't already present. The other major use for the subscript operator is on the left of an assignment to change an existing entry:

```
people[Name {"Ned", "Kelly"}]  =  39;        // Sets the value associated with the key to 39
```

Let's try a working example that uses a map in a somewhat different way from what you have seen up to now, and makes use of the subscript operator. You can use a map container to determine how often each word occurs in a text. Determining word frequency can be useful – it can help in classifying documents, for instance. Here's the code to count how often each word occurs in an arbitrary text sequence:

```cpp
// Ex4_02.cpp
// Determining word frequency
#include <iostream>                           // For standard streams
#include <iomanip>                            // For stream manipulators
#include <string>                             // For string class
#include <sstream>                            // For istringstream
#include <algorithm>                          // For replace_if() & for_each()
#include <map>                                // For map container
#include <cctype>                             // For isalpha()

using std::string;

int main()
{
  std::cout << "Enter some text and enter * to end:\n";
  string text_in {};
  std::getline(std::cin, text_in, '*');

  // Replace non-alphabetic characters by a space
  std::replace_if(std::begin(text_in), std::end(text_in),
                                    [](const char& ch){ return !isalpha(ch); }, ' ');

  std::istringstream text(text_in);           // Text input string as a stream
  std::istream_iterator<string> begin(text);  // Stream iterator
  std::istream_iterator<string> end;          // End stream iterator

  std::map<string, size_t> words;             // Map to store words & word counts
  size_t max_len {};                          // Maximum word length

  // Get the words, store in the map, and find maximum length
  std::for_each(begin, end, [&max_len, &words](const string& word)
                      { words[word]++;
                        max_len = std::max(max_len, word.length());
                      });
```

```
// Ouput the words and their counts
size_t per_line {4}, count {};
for(const auto& w : words)
{
  std::cout << std::left << std::setw(max_len + 1) << w.first
            << std::setw(3) << std::right << w.second << "   ";

  if(++count % per_line == 0)  std::cout << std::endl;
}
  std::cout << std::endl;
}
```

The text is read from the standard input stream into text_in using the getline() function for string objects. The replace_if() algorithm is used to replace non-alphabetic characters in the input by a space. The first two arguments to replace_if() are the iterators that define the range of elements, which are the characters in the input string in this case. The next argument is a function object that returns true when an element is to be replaced; here it's a lambda expression. The last argument is the replacement for the element – a space in this instance. The function will replace all punctuation so we end up with just the words separated by spaces.

We create an istringstream object, text, from text_in. An istringstream object allows stream input operations on the string that it encapsulates so it acts as a stream. This includes the ability to obtain stream iterators for text, which we can then use in the for_each() algorithm to extract individual words. The iterators for an input stream will point to each input entity in succession. Here the input is a succession of words, so the range specified by the begin and end iterators for text define all the words. The for_each() algorithm applies the function object that is the third argument to each element pointed to by the iterators in the range that is defined by the first two arguments – each word from text in this instance. The function object must have a reference to the type of object pointed to by the iterators as the parameter so here's it's const string&. The lambda expression captures the max_len variable and the map by reference so it can modify both. The body of the lambda stores each word as a key in the container by specifying it as the subscript and increments the value associated with the word. When the word is not present, this will create a new entry with the word as the key and the value as 1. If the word has been added to the container previously, the operation will just increment the value. Thus the value associated with each word is the accumulated number of occurrences in the text. The lambda expression also updates max_len so it records the length of the longest string; this value will be used subsequently in the output process.

Thus the call to the for_each() algorithm inserts all the words from the input into the map – however many there are – and accumulates the count of the number of occurrences of each word and figures out the maximum word length overall – not bad for a single statement! The rest of the code is to output words and their counts and I'm sure you can figure out how this works. Here is an example of the output from the program:

```
Enter some text and enter * to end:
How much wood would a wood chuck chuck,
If a woodchuck could chuck wood?
A woodchuck would chuck as much wood as a woodchuck could chuck
if a woodchuck could chuck wood.
*
A          1  How        1  If         1  a          4
as         2  chuck      6  could      3  if         1
much       2  wood       5  woodchuck  4  would      2
```

This example stores objects of an integer type in a map so we can apply the increment operator to the value returned by the subscript operator for the container. You can also use operators when the value returned by the subscript operator for a map returns an object of a class type as long as the operators have been implemented for the class. To illustrate the sort of thing I'm talking about, let's create another working example.

Suppose we want to store and retrieve quotations by people by name. Clearly some folks have a lot of well-known quotations to their name so we will need to allow for storing multiple quotations for a single key. We can't store duplicate keys in a map container but we can associate a key with an object that can encapsulate multiple quotations. We can use instances of the Name class from Ex4_01 as keys, and we can define a Quotations class to hold all the quotations for a given name.

We know that using the subscript operator with a key accesses the object associated with the key so we can extend the notation by implementing operator[]() in the Quotations class. We can also implement operator<<() in the class so that it will add a quotation to a Quotation object. We can store quotations conveniently in a vector container. Here's the contents of Quotations.h that defines the class:

```cpp
#ifndef QUOTATIONS_H
#define QUOTATIONS_H
#include <vector>                              // For vector container
#include <string>                              // For string class
#include <exception>                           // For out_of_range exception

class Quotations
{
private:
  std::vector<std::string> quotes;             // Container for the quotations

public:
  // Stores a new quotation that is created from a string literal
  Quotations& operator<<(const char* quote)
  {
    quotes.emplace_back(quote);
    return *this;
  }

  // Copies a new quotation in the vector from a string object
  Quotations& operator<<(const std::string& quote)
  {
    quotes.push_back(quote);
    return *this;
  }

  // Moves a quotation into the vector
  Quotations& operator<<(std::string&& quote)
  {
    quotes.push_back(std::move(quote));
    return *this;
  }
```

```
  // Returns a quotation for an index
  std::string& operator[](size_t index)
  {
    if(index < quotes.size())
      return quotes[index];
    else
      throw std::out_of_range {"Invalid index to quotations."};
  }

  size_t size() const {  return quotes.size();  }          // Returns the number of quotations

  // Returns the begin iterator for the quotations
  std::vector<std::string>::iterator begin()
  {
    return std::begin(quotes);
  }

  // Returns the const begin iterator for the quotations
  std::vector<std::string>::const_iterator begin() const
  {
    return std::begin(quotes);
  }

  // Returns the end iterator for the quotations
  std::vector<std::string>::iterator end()
  {
    return std::end(quotes);
  }

  // Returns the const end iterator for the quotations
  std::vector<std::string>::const_iterator end() const
  {
    return std::end(quotes);
  }
};
#endif
```

Using the << operator to add a quotation is reasonably consistent with its uses in other contexts such as stream input. You could use the += operator here instead. The class defines three versions of operator<<() that provide various ways of adding a new quotation. The first version accepts a string literal argument that is passed to the emplace_back() member of the vector, which will call the string constructor to create the element in place. The second version has a parameter that is a reference to a string so the argument is passed to the push_back() member of the vector. The third version has an rvalue reference parameter. When you access an rvalue reference parameter in the body of a function by name, it will be an lvalue, so you must use move() to pass the argument on to the push_back() member of the vector as an rvalue. This will enable the object to be moved all the way, with no copying.

The operator[]() member of the class accesses a vector element using an index. The function throws an exception in the event that the index is not within range; this should never occur, and if it does, it's a bug in the program.

The begin() and end() members return iterators for the quotations in the vector. Note how the return type is specified. Containers that supply iterators generally define an iterator member that is an alias for the type of iterator they support, so you don't need to know the detailed type specification. Objects of a class that defines iterators can be used in conjunction with a range-based for loop as long as the iterators are at least forward iterators.

There are also const versions of the begin() and end() members that return const iterators defined in the Quotations class. The return type is again an alias that is defined in the vector template. If the const version of begin() and end() were not defined, it would not be possible to use a range-based for loop with a const loop variable, like this:

```
for(const auto& pr : quotations)                // Requires const iterators
  ...
```

We can define a couple of inline helper functions for use in main(). The first reads a name from cin:

```
inline Name get_name()
{
  Name name {};
  std::cout << "Enter first name and second name: ";
  std::cin >> std::ws >> name;
  return name;
}
```

This reads a name as first and second names. The ws manipulator consumes whitespace and therefore skips any left behind by reading characters from cin.

The second helper just reads a quotation:

```
inline string get_quote(const Name& name)
{
  std::cout << "Enter the quotation for " << name
            << ". Enter * to end:\n";
  string quote;
  std::getline(std::cin >> std::ws, quote, '*');
  return quote;
}
```

Terminating the input using an asterisk allows multiple lines to be entered. The Ex4_03.cpp file to support storing quotations looks like this:

```
// Ex4_03.cpp
// Stores one or more quotations for a name in a map
#include <iostream>          // For standard streams
#include <cctype>            // For toupper()
#include <map>               // For map containers
#include <string>            // For string class
#include "Quotations.h"
#include "Name.h"
```

```cpp
using std::string;

// get_name() definition goes here...

// get_quote() definition goes here...

int main()
{
  std::map<Name, Quotations> quotations;            // Container for name/quotes pairs

  std::cout << "Enter 'A' to add a quote."
              "\nEnter 'L' to list all quotes."
              "\nEnter 'G' to get a quote."
              "\nEnter 'Q' to end.\n";
  Name name {};                                     // Stores a name
  string quote {};                                  // Stores a quotation
  char  command {};                                 // Stores a command

  while(command != 'Q')
  {
    std::cout << "\nEnter command: ";
    std::cin >> command;
    command = static_cast<char>(std::toupper(command));
    switch(command)
    {
    case 'Q':
      break;                                        // Quit operations

    case 'A':
      name = get_name();
      quote = get_quote(name);
      quotations[name] << quote;
      break;

    case 'G':
    {
      name = get_name();
      const auto& quotes = quotations[name];
      size_t count = quotes.size();
      if(!count)
      {
        std::cout << "There are no quotes recorded for "
                  << name << std::endl;
        continue;
      }
      size_t index {};
      if(count > 1)
```

```
      {
        std::cout << "There are " << count << " quotes for " << name << ".\n"
                  << "Enter an index from 0 to " << count - 1 << ": ";
        std::cin >> index;
      }
      std::cout << quotations[name][index] << std::endl;
    }
    break;
    case 'L':
      if(quotations.empty())                              // Test for no pairs
      {
        std::cout << "\nNo quotations recorded for anyone." << std::endl;
      }
      // List all quotations
      for(const auto& pr : quotations)                    // Iterate over pairs
      {
        std::cout << '\n' << pr.first << std::endl;
        for(const auto& quote : pr.second)               // Iterate over quotations
        {
          std::cout << "  " << quote << std::endl;
        }
      }
      break;

    default:
      std::cout << " Command must be 'A', 'G', 'L', or 'Q'. Try again.\n";
      continue;
      break;
    }
  }
}
```

The quotations container stores objects of type pair<const Name, Quotations>. An expression such as quotations[name] results in a reference to the object associated with the Name object, name. If there is no existing pair in the map that corresponds to the name key, one will be created with a default Quotations object associated with it that will be empty. The statement to store a new quotation, quote, for a given name is:

```
quotations[name] << quote;
```

The left operand for << is equivalent to quotations.operator[](name) that returns the Quotations object associated with name. Thus the statement is equivalent to:

```
quotations.operator[](name).operator<<(quote);
```

You can see in main() that we can access a quotation for a name at a given index with the expression quotations[name][index], which corresponds to quotations.operator[](name).operator[](index). I think you should now be able to figure how the rest of the code in main() works. Here's some sample output:

```
Enter 'A' to add a quote.
Enter 'L' to list all quotes.
Enter 'G' to get a quote.
Enter 'Q' to end.

Enter command: a
Enter first name and second name: Winston Churchill
Enter the quotation for Winston Churchill . Enter * to end:
There are a terrible lot of lies going around the world, and the worst of it is half of them
are true.*

Enter command: a
Enter first name and second name: Dorothy Parker
Enter the quotation for Dorothy Parker . Enter * to end:
Beauty is only skin deep, but ugly goes clean to the bone.*

Enter command: a
Enter first name and second name: Winston Churchill
Enter the quotation for Winston Churchill . Enter * to end:
Never in the field of human conflict was so much owed by so many to so few.*

Enter command: a
Enter first name and second name: Winston Churchill
Enter the quotation for Winston Churchill . Enter * to end:
Courage is what it takes to stand up and speak, Courage is also what it takes to sit down
and listen.*
Enter command: a
Enter first name and second name: Dorothy Parker
Enter the quotation for Dorothy Parker . Enter * to end:
Money cannot buy health, but I'd settle for a diamond-studded wheelchair.*

Enter command: g
Enter first name and second name: Winston Churchill
There are 3 quotes for Winston Churchill .
Enter an index from 0 to 2: 1
Never in the field of human conflict was so much owed by so many to so few.

Enter command: L

Winston Churchill
  There are a terrible lot of lies going around the world, and the worst of it is half of
them are true.
  Never in the field of human conflict was so much owed by so many to so few.
  Courage is what it takes to stand up and speak, Courage is also what it takes to sit down
and listen.

Dorothy Parker
  Beauty is only skin deep, but ugly goes clean to the bone.
  Money cannot buy health, but I'd settle for a diamond-studded wheelchair.

Enter command: q
```

Clearly this program could do with more error recovery capability and maybe provide for comparing keys regardless of case, but you get the idea.

A map container has the `find()` function member that returns an iterator that points to the element with the key that matches the argument. For example:

```
std::map<std::string, size_t>  people {{"Fred", 45}, {"Joan", 33}, {"Jill", 22}};
std::string name{"Joan"};
auto iter = people.find(name);
if(iter == std::end(people))
  std::cout <<"Not found.\n";
else
  std:: cout << name << " is " << iter->second << std::endl;
```

If no match for the argument is found, `find()` returns the end iterator for the container so you must check for this before attempting to use the iterator.

For compatibility with a `multimap`, a map container includes the `equal_range()`, `upper_bound()` and `lower_bound()` function members but since the purpose of these is to find multiple elements with the same key, I'll discuss these later in the chapter in the context of `multimap` containers.

Deleting Elements

The `erase()` function member of a map will remove the element that has a key matching the argument and returns the number of elements that were removed. For example:

```
std::map<std::string, size_t>  people {{"Fred", 45}, {"Joan", 33}, {"Jill", 22}};
std::string name{"Joan"};
if(people.erase(name))
  std::cout << name << " was removed." << std::endl;
else
  std::cout << name << " was not found." << std::endl;
```

Obviously the return value can only be 0 or 1 with a map container, and 0 will indicate that the element was not found. You can also pass an iterator that points the element to be removed as the argument to `erase()`. In this case an iterator is returned that points to the element following the one that was removed. The argument must be a valid iterator for the container and must not be the end iterator. If the iterator argument points to the last element in the container, the end iterator will be returned. For example:

```
auto iter = people.erase(std::begin(people));
if(iter == std::end(people))
  std::cout << "The last element was removed." << std::endl;
else
  std::cout << "The element preceding " << iter->first << " was removed." << std::endl;
```

This fragment will output a message when the last element is removed or output the key of the element that follows the element that was removed.

There's a further version of `erase()` that accepts two iterator arguments defining a range of elements to be removed. For example:

```
auto iter = people.erase(++std::begin(people), --std::end(people));  // Erase all except 1st & last
```

The iterator that is returned points to the element following the last element in the range that was removed. When you want to remove all the elements from a map, you can call the clear() member.

Using pair<> and tuple<> Objects

You have seen how a pair<const K,T> object encapsulates a key and an associated object and represents an element in a map. In general, the objects that a pair encapsulates can be of any type and you can create pair<T1,T2> objects for any purpose that you want – you could create an array or a vector of pair<T1,T2> objects, for example, or a pair encapsulating two sequence containers or two pointers to sequence containers. The pair<T1,T2> template is defined in the utility header, and you'll need to include this when you want to use pair objects independently from a map.

The tuple<> template is a generalization of the pair template and permits the definition of tuple template instances that encapsulate any number of objects of different types. Thus a tuple instance can have an arbitrary number of template type arguments. The tuple template is defined in the tuple header, believe it or not. The term tuple is also used in many other environments such as the database environment where a *tuple* is a record consisting of a number of different data items of varying types so the concept is similar. You'll find you have many uses for tuple objects. A tuple type is very useful for passing multiple objects to a function as a single object or returning multiple objects. Clearly the capability to define container elements that are composed of several objects will also come in handy. I'll go into the details of the pair<T1,T2> template first, then we'll look at creating and using tuple objects.

Operations with a pair

Considering it's a relatively simple template type with just two public data members, first and second, there's a surprising variety of constructors for a pair<T1, T2>. You have already seen how you can create an object using values for first and second. There are versions with reference parameters as well as rvalue reference parameters. and there are versions with rvalue reference parameters that allow arguments to be implicitly converted to the required type. For example, here are four ways to define the same pair object:

```
std::string s1 {"test"}, s2{"that"};
std::pair<std::string, std::string> my_pair{s1, s2};
std::pair<std::string, std::string> your_pair{std::string {"test"}, std::string {"that"}};
std::pair<std::string, std::string> his_pair{"test", std::string {"that"}};
std::pair<std::string, std::string> her_pair{"test", "that"};
```

The first pair constructor call copies the argument values, the second moves the argument values, the third forwards the first argument to the string constructor for the implicit conversion, and the last constructor call implicitly converts both arguments to string objects and these are moved to the first and second members of the pair. Because of the provision of rvalue reference versions of the constructor, either or both pair template type arguments can be a unique_ptr<T>.

The make_pair<T1, T2>() function template is a helper function that creates and returns a pair<T1,T2> object. You could create the pair objects that the previous block of code produces like this:

```
auto my_pair = std::make_pair(s1, s2);
auto your_pair = std::make_pair(std::string {"test"}, std::string {"that"});
auto his_pair = std::make_pair<std::string, std::string>("test", std::string {"that"});
auto her_pair = std::make_pair<std::string, std::string>("test", "that");
```

In the first two statements the type argument for the function template are deduced by the compiler. In the last two statements they are explicit. If the template type arguments were omitted in the last two statements, the objects would be of types pair<const char*, string> and pair<const char*, const char*>.

A pair object is also copy or move constructible as long as its members are. For example:

```
std::pair<std::string, std::string> new_pair{my_pair};        // Copy constructor
std::pair<std::string, std::string> old_pair{std::make_pair(std::string{"his"}, std::string{"hers"})};
```

old_pair is created by the pair<string,string> class move constructor.

There's another pair constructor that uses a mechanism that was introduced in C++11 that allows a pair<T1, T2> object to be constructed by creating the first and second members in place. The arguments to the T1 and T2 constructors are passed as tuple<> arguments to the pair constructor; I'll explain what you can do with tuple objects in detail in the next section. Here's an example of using this pair constructor:

```
std::pair<Name, Name> couple{std::piecewise_construct,
            std::forward_as_tuple("Jack", "Jones"), std::forward_as_tuple("Jill", "Smith")};
```

The first argument to the pair constructor here is an instance of the piecewise_construct_t type that is defined in the utility header. This is an empty type that is used as a tag or marker. The only purpose for the piecewise_construct argument is to differentiate between this constructor call, and a constructor call where the two tuple arguments are to be used as values for the first and second members of the pair. Here, the second and third arguments to the constructor specify the sets of arguments for the construction of the first and second objects. forward_as_tuple() is a function template defined in the tuple header; here, it creates a tuple of references to its arguments that can then be forwarded on. You are not likely to need this pair constructor often, but it provides the unique ability to create a pair<T1, T2> object where the types T1 and T2 do not support copy or move operations – they can only be created in place.

Note that forward_as_tuple() will create a tuple of rvalue references if the arguments are temporary objects. For example:

```
int a {1}, b {2};
const auto& c = std::forward_as_tuple(a,b);
```

Here, the type for c is tuple<int&, int&>, so the members are references. However, suppose that you write this statement:

```
const auto& c = std::forward_as_tuple(1,2);
```

Here c is tuple<int&&, int&&>, with the members as rvalue references.

Copy and move assignment is supported for pair objects if the members can be copied or moved. For example:

```
std::pair<std::string, std::string> old_pair;                    // Default constructor
std::pair<std::string, std::string> new_pair{std::string{"his"}, std::string{"hers"}};
old_pair = new_pair;                                             // Copy assignment
new_pair = pair<std::string, std::string>
                {std::string{"these"}, std::string{"those"}};  // Move assignment
```

old_pair will be created by the default pair constructor with members that are empty string objects. The third statement copies new_pair to old_pair, member by member. The fourth statement moves the members of the pair object that is the right operand of the assignment to new_pair.

You can also assign one pair to another when the pair objects contain members of different types, as long as the types of the members of the pair that is the right operand are implicitly convertible to the types of the members of the pair that is the left operand. Here's an example:

```
auto pr1 = std::make_pair("these", "those");    // Type pair<const char*, const char*>
std::pair<std::string, std::string> pr2;        // Type pair<string, string>
pr2 = pr1;                                       // OK in this case
```

The first and second members of pr1 are of type const char*. This type is implicitly convertible to type string, which is the type of the members of pr2, so the assignment works. If the types are not implicitly convertible, the assignment will not compile.

You have the full set of comparison operators for pair objects, ==, !=, <, <=, >, and >=. For these to work, the pair objects that are the operands must be of the same type and their members must be comparable in the same way. The equality operator returns true if the corresponding members of the left and right operand are equal:

```
std::pair<std::string, std::string> new_pair;
new_pair.first = "his";
new_pair.second = "hers";
if(new_pair == std::pair<std::string, std::string> {"his", "hers"})  std::cout << "Equality!\n";
```

The assignments for the first and second members of new_pair set their values to string objects that contain the string that is the right operand. The if statement will output the message because the pair objects are equal. A != comparison will result in true if either or both of the members of the pair objects are not equal.

For less-than or greater-than comparisons, the members of the pair objects are compared lexicographically. The expression new_pair < old_pair will be true if new_pair.first is less than old_pair.first. It will also be true if the first members are equal and new_pair.second is less than old_pair.second. Here's an illustration:

```
std::pair<int, int> p1 {10, 9};
std::pair<int, int> p2 {10, 11};
std::pair<int, int> p3 {11, 9};
std::cout << std::boolalpha << (p1 < p2) << " "      // Outputs "true"
                            << (p1 > p3) << " "      // Outputs "false"
                            << (p3 > p2) << std::endl;   // Outputs "true"
```

The first comparison is true because the first member of p1 is equal to the first member of p2 and the second member of p1 is less than that of p2. The second comparison is false because the first member of p1 is not greater than that of p3. The third comparison is true because the first member of p3 is greater than that of p2.

The swap() member of a pair object swaps its first and second members with those of the pair that is passed as the argument. Clearly, the argument must be of the same type. Here's an example:

```
std::pair<int, int> p1 {10, 11};
std::pair<int, int> p2 {11, 9};
p1.swap(p2);                                         // p1={11,9} p2={10,11}
```

If you execute the same swap() call twice, you'll be back where you started.

Operations with a tuple

The easiest way to create a tuple object is to use the make_tuple() helper function that is defined in the tuple header. The function accepts an arbitrary number of arguments of any types, and the type of the tuple that it returns is determined by the types of the arguments. For example:

```
auto my_tuple = std::make_tuple(Name{"Peter", "Piper"}, 42, std::string{"914 626 7890"});
```

The my_tuple object will be of type tuple<Name, int, string> because the template type arguments are deduced to be those of the arguments to make_tuple(). If you supplied just a string literal as the third argument to make_tuple(), the type of my_tuple would be tuple<Name, int, const char*>, which is different.

The constructors for tuple objects offer just about every option you are likely to need. Here are some examples:

```
std::tuple<std::string, size_t> my_t1;                        // Default initialization
std::tuple<Name, std::string> my_t2{Name{"Andy", "Capp"}, std::string{"Programmer"}};
std::tuple<Name, std::string> copy_my_t2{my_t2};             // Copy constructor
std::tuple<std::string, std::string> my_t3{"this", "that"};  // Implicit conversion
```

The default constructor initializes the objects in the tuple with default values. The constructor call for my_t2 moves the arguments into the elements in the tuple. The next statement call the copy constructor to create the tuple and in the last constructor call, the tuple elements are created by implicit conversion of the arguments to type string.

You can construct a tuple from a pair, where the pair can be an lvalue or an rvalue. Obviously, the tuple can only have two elements. Here are a couple of examples:

```
auto the_pair = std::make_pair("these", "those");
std::tuple<std::string, std::string> my_t4 {the_pair};
std::tuple<std::string, std::string> my_t5 {std::pair <std::string, std::string > {"this", "that"}};
```

The second statement creates a tuple from the_pair, which is an lvalue. The first and second members of the_pair will be implicitly converted to the types of the elements in the tuple here. The last statement creates the tuple from a pair object that is an rvalue.

You can compare tuple objects of the same type using any of the comparison operators. The elements in the tuple objects that are compared are compared lexicographically. Here's an example:

```
std:: cout << std::boolalpha << (my_t4 < my_t5) << std::endl;  // true
```

The elements in the tuple objects are compared successively and the first that differ determines the result in this instance. The first element in my_t4 is less that the first element in my_t5 so the result is true. If the comparison is for equality, any pair of corresponding elements that are different produces a false result.

The swap() function member of a tuple object interchanges its elements with that of the argument. The argument must be a tuple object of the same type. For example:

```
my_t4.swap(my_t5);
```

Elements are exchanged by calling the swap() member for each element in my_t4 with the corresponding element in my_t5. Clearly, all the element types in the tuple must be swappable, The tuple header defines a global swap() function that will swap the elements in two tuple objects in the same way.

Because a tuple is a generalization of a pair, it has to work differently. The number of objects in a pair is fixed, so they have member names. There can be any number of objects in a tuple so the mechanism for accessing them has to accommodate this. The get<>() template function returns an element from a tuple. The first template type argument can be a value of type size_t that is an index to the elements in the tuple that is the argument, so 0 selects the first tuple element, 1 selects the second, and so on. The remaining type arguments for the get<>() template are deduced to be the same as those for the tuple that is the argument. Here's an example of using get<>() with an index value to select an element:

```
auto my_tuple = std::make_tuple(Name{"Peter", "Piper"}, 42, std::string{"914 626 7890"});
std::cout << std::get<0>(my_tuple)
         << " age = " << std::get<1>(my_tuple)
         << " tel: "  << std::get<2>(my_tuple) << std::endl;
```

The first call to get<>() in the output statement returns a reference to the first element in my_tuple, which is a Name object. The second get<>() call returns a reference to the next element, which is an integer; and the third call returns a reference to the third element, which is a string object. The output would therefore be:

```
Peter Piper  age = 42 tel: 914 626 7890
```

You can also obtain an element from a tuple using get<>() based on the type, as long as there is only one element of that type. For example:

```
auto my_tuple = std::make_tuple(Name{"Peter", "Piper"}, 42, std::string{"914 626 7890"});
std::cout << std::get<Name>(my_tuple)
         << " age = " << std::get<int>(my_tuple)
         << " tel: "  << std::get<std::string>(my_tuple) << std::endl;
```

If the tuple contains more than one element with the type argument value for get<>(), the code won't compile. Here, all three members of the tuple are of different types, so it works.

The global tie<>() function template that is defined in the tuple header provides another way to access the elements in a tuple. This function can transfer the values of the elements in a tuple to a set of lvalues that are tied together by tie<>(). The template type arguments for tie<>() are deduced from the function arguments. Here's an example:

```
auto my_tuple = std::make_tuple(Name{"Peter", "Piper"}, 42, std::string{"914 626 7890"});
Name name{};
size_t age{};
std::string phone{};
std::tie(name, age, phone) = my_tuple;
```

The `std::tie(name,age,phone)` expression that is the left operand of the assignment in the last statement returns a tuple of references to the arguments. Thus the left and right operands of the assignment are tuple objects. The variables that are the arguments to `tie()` will be assigned the values of the elements from `my_tuple`. It may be that you don't want to store the value of every element. Here's how you could store just the name and phone elements from `my_tuple`:

```
std::tie(name, std::ignore, phone) = my_tuple;
```

`ignore` is defined in the `tuple` header and is used to mark a value in a `tie()` function call that is to be ignored. The value of the `tuple` element that corresponds to `ignore` will not be recorded. In the example it enables just the first and third elements of `my_tuple` to be copied.

You can also use the `tie()` function to implement a lexicographical comparison of the data members of a class. For example, you could implement `operator<()` in the `Name` class from `Ex4_01` as:

```
bool Name::operator<(const Name& name) const
{
  return std::tie(second, first) < std::tie(name.second, name.first);
}
```

The elements in the `tuple` objects that result from the `tie()` calls in the body of the function are compared in sequence. Successive corresponding pairs of elements are compared using the < operator. The first pair that is different determines the result; the result is the result of the comparison of the different elements. If all the elements are equal or equivalent, the result is `false`.

tuples and pairs in Action

Let's put together a working example that exercises `tuples` and `pairs`; it won't necessarily reflect the best way of doing what it does, but the objective is to try out operations with `tuple` and `pair` objects. The example will make use of a `map` container that has a `pair` object as a key and a `tuple` as the object associated with the key. Each `map` element will record data about a person. The key will be a name and the associated `tuple` object will contain the date-of-birth, the height, and the occupation of the person as elements. The date-of-birth will also be a tuple, so we will create a `tuple` that has a `tuple` as an element. The example will use a bunch of type aliases to make the code less verbose:

```
using std::string;
using Name = std::pair<string, string>;                 // Defines a name
using DOB = std::tuple<size_t, size_t, size_t>;         // Month, day, year
using Details = std::tuple< DOB, size_t, string> ;      // DOB, height(inches), occupation
using Element_type = std::map<Name, Details>::value_type; // Type of map element
```

`Name` is an alias for a pair type that encapsulates two string objects. `DOB` is an alias for a tuple type that has three elements of `size_t` that are the month, day, and year values. `Details` is the type alias for an object that is associated with a key, and is a `tuple` of three elements of type `DOB`, `size_t` for the age value, and

163

string for the occupation. The type of element in the map is a pair<const K,T> object, which is quite a messy type in this case. We can define the Element_type alias for it quite easily though as the type specified by the value_type member of the map container. If you make the substitutions you'll see that the full explicit type name for a map element is:

```
std::pair<std::pair<std::string, std::string>,
                    std::tuple<std::tuple<size_t, size_t, size_t>, size_t, std::string>>
```

This demonstrates how helpful type aliases can be.

We can define the container using these aliases like this:

```
std::map<Name, Details> people;                          // Records of the people
```

The keys are type Name and the associated objects are type Details – simple really with the alias definitions. We could go further and define an alias for the container type:

```
using People = std::map<Name, Details>;
```

Now we can define the container just as:

```
People people;                                           // Records of the people
```

We can package the input process for the map elements in a function:

```
void get_people(Peoples& people)
{
  string first {}, second {};                            // Stores name inputs
  size_t month {}, day {}, year {};                      // Stores DOB input
  size_t height {};                                      // Stores height input
  string occupation {};                                  // Stores occupation input
  char answer {'Y'};

  while(std::toupper(answer) == 'Y')
  {
    std::cout << "Enter a first name and a second name: ";
    std::cin >> std::ws >> first >> second;

    std::cout << "Enter date of birth as month day year (integers): ";
    std::cin >> month >> day >> year;
    DOB dob {month, day, year};                          // Create DOB tuple

    std::cout << "Enter height in inches: ";
    std::cin >> height;

    std::cout << "Enter occupation: ";
    std::getline(std::cin >> std::ws, occupation, '\n');
```

```
    // Create the map element in place- a pair containing a Name pair and a tuple object
    people.emplace(std::make_pair(Name {first, second}, std::make_tuple(dob, height, occupation)));

    std::cout << "Do you want to enter another(Y or N): ";
    std::cin >> answer;
  }
}
```

Most of this is straightforward stream input. The occupation is read using getline() to allow multiple word descriptions to be entered. The first argument to getline() eliminates whitespace that may be left in the input buffer by a previous input operation, as will be the case here. If there's a newline in the buffer, an empty line would be read by getline(). The tuple that holds the date-of-birth values is created from the input using the DOB alias for the tuple type. The element pair object is created in place in the map by calling the emplace() member. The first member of the element pair is a pair<string,string> object that is created using the Name alias, so the constructor is called. The second member of the element pair is a tuple that contains the DOB tuple, the height, and the occupation. This is created by calling the make_tuple() helper function.

After reading the input data for the map, the program will list the people in name order together with their occupations. Another function will do this:

```
void list_DOB_Job(const People& people)
{
  DOB dob;
  string occupation {};
  std::cout << '\n';
  for(auto iter = std::begin(people); iter != std::end(people); ++iter)
  {
    std::tie(dob, std::ignore, occupation) = iter->second;
    std::cout << std::setw(20) << std::left << (iter->first.first + " " + iter->first.second)
              << "DOB: " << std::right
              << std::setw(2) << std::get<0>(dob) << "-"
              << std::setw(2) << std::setfill('0') << std::get<1>(dob) << "-"
              << std::setw(4) << std::get<2>(dob) << std::setfill(' ')
              << "  Occupation: " << occupation << std::endl;
  }
}
```

The for loop that produces the output uses iterators – just to show that we can. It would be simpler to use a range-based for loop, but the next function will demonstrate that. The first statement in the loop is an assignment. The left operand is a tie() function call that creates a tuple with the function arguments as lvalue members. The right operand of the assignment is the second member of the pair object to which iter points, which is a tuple of type Details. The assignment copies the members of the tuple that is the right operand to the members of the tuple that is the left operand. Because the second argument to tie() is ignore, only the first and third members of the tuple on the right of the assignment are stored – in the variables dob, which is itself a tuple, and occupation.

The second statement in the loop body outputs the name, the date-of-birth and the occupation. The first and second names of a person are recorded in the first and second members of the pair element: that is, the key. iter points to the pair element so iter->first references the key object; thus iter->first.first accesses the first member of the pair that is the key, and iter->first.second accesses the second member. The members of the DOB tuple are accessed using the get<>() function template. The get<>() template parameter argument selects the tuple member.

We can also include a function to output all the details of each person. It would be nice to have the option of ordering the records in the output by any of the fields in a record. One way to do this would be to allow a function object to be passed as an argument that compares one of the members of the Details object that is associated with a key. Here's the code to do that:

```
template<typename Compare>
void list_sorted_people(const People& people, Compare comp)
{
  std::vector< Element_type*> folks;
  for(const auto& pr : people)
    folks.push_back(&pr);

  // Lambda to compare elements via pointers
  auto ptr_comp =
      [&comp](const Element_type* pr1, const Element_type* pr2)->bool
            { return comp(*pr1, *pr2);  };

  std::sort(std::begin(folks), std::end(folks), ptr_comp); // Sort the pointers to elements

  // Output the sorted elements
  DOB dob {};
  size_t height {};
  string occupation {};
  std::cout << '\n';

  for(const auto& p : folks)
  {
    std::tie(dob, height, occupation) = p->second;
    std::cout << std::setw(20) << std::left << (p->first.first + " " + p->first.second)
            << "DOB: " << std::right << std::setw(2) << std::get<0>(dob) << "-"
            << std::setw(2) << std::setfill('0') << std::get<1>(dob) << "-"
            << std::setw(4) << std::get<2>(dob) << std::setfill(' ')
            << "  Height: " << height
            << "  Occupation: " << occupation << std::endl;
  }
}
```

This is a function template that enables the type of the function object that determines the order of the output to be deduced in a function call. The order of elements in the map is determined by the order of the keys, so clearly the reordering has to occur outside the map container. We could copy all the elements to another container but a better and more efficient approach is to store *pointers* to the elements in another container and sort the pointers using the function object passed as the second argument.

The pointers that are stored in the vector container are raw pointers of type const Element_type*. It's not a good idea to use unique_ptr objects here because a unique_ptr<T> owns the T object to which it points. If the vector contained unique_ptr<Element_type> elements, copies would be made of the map elements thus defeating the purpose of using pointers. There's no downside to using raw pointer in this case because vector and its elements are local to the function and just act as observers of the map elements.

The vector elements are just the addresses of the pair objects in the map and these are created and stored in the for loop that iterates over the elements in the map. The caller won't necessarily be aware that sorting is done using pointers so the list_sorted_people() function template assumes that the function object passed to it implements a comparison of two map elements. The lambda expression, ptr_comp, that is defined in the function body uses comp for the comparison by using it with the result of dereferencing the pointers to map elements as arguments. The ptr_comp lambda expression is therefore used in the sort() function call that sorts the pointers in the vector. Finally, the output is produced in the range-based for loop that iterates over the pointers in the vector. The tie() function is used to extract all the elements from a Details tuple into local variables. The name and the elements from the associated Details tuple are then output.

The contents of the source file containing main() to exercise these functions are:

```
// Ex4_04.cpp
// Using tuples and pairs
#include <iostream>                                  // For standard streams
#include <iomanip>                                   // For stream manipulators
#include <string>                                    // For string class
#include <cctype>                                    // For toupper()
#include <map>                                       // For map container
#include <vector>                                    // For vector container
#include <tuple>                                     // For tuple template
#include <algorithm>                                 // For sort() template

using std::string;
using Name = std::pair <string, string>;             // Defines a name pair
using DOB = std::tuple <size_t, size_t, size_t>;     // Month, day, year tuple
using Details = std::tuple < DOB, size_t, string > ; // DOB, height(inches), occupation
using Element_type = std::map<Name, Details>::value_type; // Type of map element
using People = std::map<Name, Details>;              // Type of people container

// Code  for get_people() function goes here...

// Code  for list_DOB_Job() function goes here...

// Code  for list_sorted_people() function template goes here...

int main()
{
  std::map<Name, Details> people;                    // Records of the people
  get_people(people);                                // Read all the people

  std::cout << "\nThe DOB & jobs are: \n";
  list_DOB_Job(people);                              // List names, DOB & job

  // Define height comparison for people
  auto comp = [](const Element_type& pr1, const Element_type& pr2)
  {
    return std::get<1>(pr1.second) < std::get<1>(pr2.second);
  };

  std::cout << "\nThe people in height order are : \n";
  list_sorted_people(people, comp);
}
```

There's an impressive list of #include directives for standard library headers followed by the definitions for the type aliases you saw earlier. The code in main() is relatively simple – essentially three function calls. The comparator for map elements is defined by a lambda expression, although it could be a function object. In this case it compares the second element in the Details objects, which is the height of a person. The height value is extracted using get<>() in the way you have seen. The list_sorted_people() template will work just as well with a comparator for any of the characteristics of a map element. Here's some sample output:

```
Enter a first name and a second name: Dan Druff
Enter date of birth as month day year (integers): 2 3 1978
Enter height in inches: 74
Enter occupation: Trichologist
Do you want to enter another(Y or N): y
Enter a first name and a second name: Jane Brudit
Enter date of birth as month day year (integers): 13 11 1990
Enter height in inches: 63
Enter occupation: Barista
Do you want to enter another(Y or N): y
Enter a first name and a second name: Will Derness
Enter date of birth as month day year (integers): 5 5 1981
Enter height in inches: 76
Enter occupation: Explorer
Do you want to enter another(Y or N): N
The DOB & jobs are:

Dan Druff          DOB:  2-03-1978  Occupation: Trichologist
Jane Brudit        DOB: 13-11-1990  Occupation: Barista
Will Derness       DOB:  5-05-1981  Occupation: Explorer

The people in height order are :
Jane Brudit        DOB: 13-11-1990  Height: 63  Occupation: Barista
Dan Druff          DOB:  2-03-1978  Height: 74  Occupation: Trichologist
Will Derness       DOB:  5-05-1981  Height: 76  Occupation: Explorer
```

Using a multimap Container

A multimap container is ordered and stores key/value pairs, just like a map, but it allows duplicate keys. Elements with the same key will appear in a multimap in the sequence in which they were added to the container. You have the same range of constructors for a multimap as you have for a map and the default function object for comparing keys is less<K>(). Most of the function members of a multimap work in the same way as those for a map. The differences arise because of the potential for duplicate keys in the container. I'll just describe the function members of a multimap that differ from those for a map.

The insert() member of a multimap container inserts one or more elements and always succeeds. This function comes in a variety of versions to insert() a single element, all of which return an iterator that points to the element that was inserted. Here are some examples that assume a using declaration for std::string:

```
std::multimap<string, string> pets;                    // Element is pair{pet_type, pet_name}
auto iter = pets.insert(std::pair<string, string>{string{"dog"}, string{"Fang"}});
iter = pets.insert(iter, std::make_pair("dog", "Spot"));   // Insert Spot before Fang
pets.insert(std::make_pair("dog", "Rover"));               // Inserts Rover after Fang
pets.insert(std::make_pair("cat", "Korky"));               // Inserts Korky before all dogs
pets.insert({{"rat", "Roland"}, {"pig", "Pinky"}, {"pig", "Perky"}}); // Inserts list elements
```

The first argument in the third statement is an iterator that is a hint as to where the element should be placed. The element is inserted immediately before the element pointed to by iter, so this allows you to override the default insertion position, which would be following the previous element that was inserted with a key equivalent to "dog". Elements are inserted in ascending sequence of keys with the default comparison. Elements with the same key will be in the order in which you insert them, unless you supply a hint that changes this. The last statement inserts elements from an initializer list. There's a further version of insert() that accepts two iterator arguments that identify a range of elements to be inserted.

The emplace() member of a multimap constructs a new element in place in the container in the same way as for a map. You also have emplace_hint() available with a multimap where you can supply a hint in the form of an iterator to control where the element is created in relation to elements with the same key:

```
auto iter = pets.emplace("rabbit", "Flopsy");
iter = pets.emplace_hint(iter, "rabbit", "Mopsy");          // Create preceding Flopsy
```

Both functions return an iterator that points to the element that was inserted. The emplace_hint() function creates the new element preceding the position pointed to by the first argument and as near as possible to it. Just using emplace() to insert "Mopsy" would position it immediately following all existing elements with the "rabbit" key.

The subscript operator is not supported by a multimap because a key does not necessarily identify a unique element. Similarly the at() function you have for a map container is not available with a multimap. The find() function member of a multimap returns an iterator that points to an element with a key that is equivalent to the argument. For example:

```
std::multimap<std::string, size_t> people{ {"Ann", 25}, {"Bill", 46}, {"Jack", 77},
                                            {"Jack", 32}, {"Jill", 32}, {"Ann", 35} };
std::string name {"Bill"};
auto iter = people.find(name);
if(iter != std::end(people))  std::cout << name << " is " << iter->second << std::endl;
iter = people.find("Ann");
if(iter != std::end(people))  std::cout << iter->first << " is " << iter->second << std::endl;
```

If the key is not found, the end iterator for the container is returned so you should always check for this. The first find() call has a key object as an argument and the output statement will execute because the key exists. The second find() call has a string literal as an argument, which demonstrates that the argument does not have to be the same type as the key. You can pass any value or object as the argument that can be compared to the key using the function object that is in effect for the container. The last output statement executes because there is a key equivalent to "Ann." In fact there are two keys equivalent to "Ann" and on my system the output corresponds to the 25-year-old Ann. You will probably get the same output – that for the first Ann – but this is not guaranteed.

If you are using a multimap container, it almost certainly will contain elements with duplicate keys; otherwise you would be using a map. So typically, you will want to access all the elements corresponding to a given key. The equal_range() function member does this. The range of elements with keys equivalent to the argument is returned as a pair of iterators encapsulated in a pair object – what else! For example:

```
auto pr = people.equal_range("Ann");
if(pr.first != std::end(people))
{
  for(auto iter = pr.first ; iter != pr.second; ++iter)
    std::cout << iter->first << " is " << iter->second << std::endl;
}
```

The argument to equal_range() can be an object of the same type as the keys, or an object of a different type that can be compared to a key. The first member of the pair object that is returned is an iterator pointing to the first element that has a key that is not less than the argument; this will be the first element with an equivalent key if it is present. If the key is not found, the first member of the pair will be the end iterator for the container so you should always check for this possibility. The second member of the pair is an iterator pointing to the first element that has a key greater than the argument; this will be the end iterator if there is no such element. The code fragment outputs information from the container elements with keys that are equivalent to "Ann."

The lower_bound() function member of a multimap returns an iterator that either points to the first element with a key that is equal to or greater than the argument to the function, or the end iterator for the container. The upper_bound() member returns an iterator that points to the first element with a key that is greater than the function argument, or the end iterator if there is no such element. Thus when one or more equivalent keys are present, these functions return the begin and end iterators for the range of elements in the container that match the key, which are the same iterators as those returned by equal_range(). You could rewrite the previous fragment in terms of these:

```
auto iter1 = people.lower_bound("Ann");
auto iter2 = people.lower_bound("Ann");
if(iter1 != std::end(people))
{
  for(auto iter = iter1 ; iter != iter2; ++iter)
    std::cout << iter->first << " is " << iter->second << std::endl;
}
```

This produces exactly the same output as the preceding code fragment. You can discover how many elements there are with keys that are equivalent to a given key by calling the count() function member of a multimap:

```
auto n = people.count("Jack");                    // Returns 2
```

You can use this in various ways. One possibility is to choose between find() or equal_range() to access elements. If you stored students in a multimap using classes as the keys, you could use the count() member to obtain the class size. Of course, you can also obtain the number of elements equivalent to a given key by applying the distance() function template that you met back in chapter 1 to the iterators returned by the equal_range() function member or those returned by lower_bound() and upper_bound():

```cpp
std::string key{"Jack"};
auto n = std::distance(people.lower_bound(key),
                       people.upper_bound(key));        // No. of elements matching key
```

■ **Note**   There are global equal_range(), lower_bound(), and upper_bound() function templates that work slightly differently to identically named function members of the associative containers. You'll learn about these later in the book.

There are three versions of the erase() member of a multimap. One version accepts an iterator pointing to an element as an argument to delete that element; nothing is returned by the function. A second version accepts a key as the argument and deletes all the elements that have that key; it returns the number of elements removed from the container. The third version accepts two iterators that define a range of elements within the container as arguments. All elements in the range are deleted, and the function returns an iterator that points to the element that follows the last element removed.

Let's try out some multimap operations in a working example:

```cpp
// Ex4_05.cpp
// Using a multimap
#include <iostream>                              // For standard streams
#include <string>                               // For string class
#include <map>                                  // For multimap container
#include <cctype>                               // For toupper()

using std::string;
using Pet_type = string;
using Pet_name = string;

int main()
{
  std::multimap<Pet_type, Pet_name> pets;
  Pet_type type {};
  Pet_name name {};
  char more {'Y'};
  while(std::toupper(more) == 'Y')
  {
    std::cout << "Enter the type of your pet and its name: ";
    std::cin >> std::ws >> type >> name;
```

```
    // Add element - duplicates will be LIFO
    auto iter = pets.lower_bound(type);
    if(iter != std::end(pets))
      pets.emplace_hint(iter, type, name);
    else
      pets.emplace(type, name);

    std::cout << "Do you want to enter another(Y or N)? ";
    std::cin >> more;
  }

  // Output all the pets
  std::cout << "\nPet list by type:\n";
  auto iter = std::begin(pets);
  while(iter != std::end(pets))
  {
    auto pr = pets.equal_range(iter->first);
    std::cout << "\nPets of type " << iter->first << " are:\n";
    for(auto p = pr.first; start != pr.second; ++p)
      std::cout << "   " << p->second;
    std::cout << std::endl;
    iter = pr.second;
  }
}
```

There are type aliases to make the types in the code relate to what they represent. The pets container stores pair<string,string> objects that contain the type of pet as the key and the pet's name as the object. The code in the first loop arranges for the second and subsequent elements with a given key to be inserted at the beginning of the sequence with that key. This uses emplace_hint() to insert the element. If it's the first element of a given type, the element is created in place by calling emplace(). Elements are output grouped by pet type in the second while loop. This is done by finding the type of the first pet entry pointed to by iter and listing the entire sequence for that pet type using the iterators returned by equal_range(). iter is then set to the end iterator for the sequence, which will either be the iterator pointing to the first element of the next pet type, or the end iterator for the container. The latter ends the loop. Here's some sample output:

```
 Enter the type of your pet  and their name: rabbit Flopsy
Do you want to enter another(Y or N)? y
Enter the type of your pet  and their name: rabbit Mopsy
Do you want to enter another(Y or N)? y
Enter the type of your pet  and their name: rabbit Cottontail
Do you want to enter another(Y or N)? y
Enter the type of your pet  and their name: dog Rover
Do you want to enter another(Y or N)? y
Enter the type of your pet  and their name: dog Spot
Do you want to enter another(Y or N)? y
Enter the type of your pet  and their name: snake Slither
Do you want to enter another(Y or N)? y
Enter the type of your pet  and their name: snake Sammy
Do you want to enter another(Y or N)? y
```

```
Enter the type of your pet  and their name: cat Max
Do you want to enter another(Y or N)? n

Pet list by type:

Pets of type cat are:
  Max

Pets of type dog are:
  Spot   Rover

Pets of type rabbit are:
  Cottontail  Mopsy  Flopsy

Pets of type snake are:
  Sammy   Slither
```

The output shows that the elements are ordered in ascending sequence of the keys, and that the elements with the same key are ordered in the opposite sequence to that in which they were entered.

Changing the Comparison Function

There are a couple of reasons why you may need to change the comparison function for a map or a multimap: you may want the elements ordered in descending sequence instead of the default ascending sequence; or your keys may need a comparison function that is different from a direct less-than or greater-than operation, which will apply if the keys are pointers, for example. Before I get into examples of how you specify an alternative comparison, I'll first emphasize a *very* important requirement on any function object you define for comparing keys:

■ **Caution**   A comparison function for a map container *must not* return true for equality.

In other words, you *must not* use <= or >= comparisons. So why is this? A map or multimap container uses *equivalence* to determine when keys are equal. Two keys, key1 and key2, are *equivalent* and therefore considered to be equal if the expressions key1 < key2 and key2 < key1 both result in false. To put it another way, equivalence implies that the expression !(key1 < key2) && !(key2 < key1) evaluates to true. Consider what happens if your function object implements <=. When key1 is equal to key2, both key1 <= key2 and key2 <= key1 evaluate to true so the expression !(key1 <= key2)&&!(key2 <= key1) evaluates to false; this means that from the container's perspective the keys are not equal after all. Indeed, there is *no* circumstance where keys will be determined as equal. This means the container cannot operate correctly. Let's look at how you supply an alternative comparison function so that the container does operate correctly.

Using a greater<T> Object

Let's suppose that we implement operator>() for the Name class we used earlier in this chapter. Within the class definition, the code for the operator>() member will be:

```
bool operator>(const Name& name) const
{
  return second > name.second || (second == name.second && first > name.first);
}
```

Of course, you could put the definition of the member outside the class:

```
inline Name::bool operator>(const Name& name) const
{
  return second > name.second || (second == name.second && first > name.first);
}
```

Now we can define a map with Name objects as keys and have the pair objects in the container ordered in descending sequence:

```
std::map<Name, size_t, std::greater<Name>> people
        { {Name{"Al", "Bedo"}, 53}, {Name{"Woody", "Leave"}, 33}, {Name{"Noah", "Lot"}, 43} };
```

The type for the function object that compares keys is specified by the third template type argument. A greater<Name> object will use the > operator to compare Name objects and this works because the Name class implements operator>(). The three elements will now be ordered in descending sequence. This will be apparent if you list the elements, which you could do like this:

```
for( const auto& p : people)
  std::cout << p.first << " " << p.second << " \n";
```

The range-based for loop iterates over the elements in the people container and the output would be:

```
Noah Lot   43
Woody Leave   33
Al Bedo   53
```

Defining Your Own Function Object for Comparing Elements

If the keys in a map or multimap are pointers, then you'll need to define a function that compares what they point to, otherwise the addresses that the pointers represent will be compared, and this is rarely what you want. If the keys are of a type that does not support less-than or greater-than comparison directly, you must define a function object that enables keys to be compared appropriately to use them in a map or a multimap. You deal with both situations in essentially the same way.

Suppose we want to use pointers to objects that we create on the heap as keys in a map container. I'll use smart pointers to string objects to illustrate this. The keys can be of type unique_ptr<string>, in which case we need a comparison function that will have two unique_ptr<string> parameters, and will compare the string objects pointed to. You can define this by a functor – a function object – I'll assume a using directive for std::string:

```
// Compares keys that are unique_ptr<string> objects
class Key_compare
{
public:
  bool operator()(const std::unique_ptr<string>& p1, const std::unique_ptr<string>& p2) const
  {
    return *p1 < *p2;
  }
};
```

We can use the Key_compare type as the type of function object a map should use to compare keys:

```
std::map<std::unique_ptr<string>, std::string, Key_compare> phonebook;
```

The third map template parameter specifies the type for the function object that provides the element comparison. Because this type parameter has a default value specified of less<T>, you must specify the type of your function object. The elements in the map are pair objects encapsulating a smart pointer to a name stored as a string, and a phone number that is also stored as a string. We can't use an initializer list with this map because an initializer list involves copying, and unique_ptr objects cannot be copied. We have at least a couple of ways to add elements to the container:

```
phonebook.emplace(std::make_unique<string>("Fred"), "914 626 7897");
phonebook.insert(std::make_pair(std::make_unique<string>("Lily"), "212 896 4337"));
```

The first statement created the pair object that is the element in place. There's a pair constructor that can move the arguments that are specified here, so there's no requirement to copy them. The second statement calls the insert() member of the container, and this will also move the element that is the argument into the container.

You could list the elements in the phonebook container like this:

```
for(const auto& p: phonebook)
  std::cout << *p.first << " " << p.second << std::endl;
```

The range-based for loop iterates over the elements in the map, which are pair objects. The first member of each pair object is a unique pointer, so this has to be dereferenced to access the string to which it points. If you use iterators to access the elements, the syntax is a little different:

```
for(auto iter = std::begin(phonebook); iter != std::end(phonebook); ++iter)
  std::cout << *iter->first << " " << iter->second << std::endl;
```

This produces the same output as the previous loop, but using iterators. The -> operator has to be used to access the members of the pair object. Because of the way the Key_compare functor is defined, the elements in the container will be in ascending sequence.

Hashing

If you store objects and their associated keys in a container and the key/object pairs are not ordered by the keys, there has to be a scheme for locating the elements in memory using the key value in some way. The problem with keys that are objects such as strings, for instance, is that the number of possible variations is enormous. The number of possible values for a 10-character alphabetic string, for example, is 26^{10}, which is 2.6×10^{10} – 260 billion in other words. This is not a useful index range. What you need is a mechanism for reducing such a range to be within more sensible limits; and ideally, the mechanism should produce a unique value for each key. This is one of the things that *hashing* does.

Hashing is a process that generates an integer value within a given range from a data item of a fundamental type, or from an object such as a string. The values that result from hashing are called *hash values* or *hash codes*, and these are typically used in a container to locate an object within a table. As I said, the ideal is that hashing should result in unique values in every case, but this is impossible in general. "You can't put a quart into a pint pot" as the saying goes, which is obvious because when the number of different key values is greater than the number of possible hash values, you *must* get duplicates sooner or later. Duplicate hash values are referred to as *collisions*. The containers that locate elements using hashing make provision for dealing with duplicate hash values arising from different keys, and I'll explain more about how they do this in the context of the unordered map containers.

Hashing is not only used for storing objects in a container. It has many other applications such as in cryptography and security systems for converting data to a form that is not readily understood. Password recognition sometimes involves hashing, for example. Storing passwords to a system in their original form is a major security risk. Storing the hash values for passwords rather than the original password strings provides some security against hacking. A hacker gaining access to the hash values needs to be able to convert the hash values back to the original passwords for them to be useful – a difficult if not impossible task. Thus the capabilities that the STL provides for hashing data of various types are not only for use with associative containers; they can also be used in a wider context.

It's not essential to understand how hashing works to work with the containers that use it, but it's useful and interesting to have a basic understanding of some of the ways in which it can be done. There are many algorithms for hashing but there is no universally appropriate method. Determining a suitable hashing method for a particular context is not always easy. Calculating remainders after division is often involved. Perhaps the simplest hashing algorithm is to treat the key – whatever it is – as a numerical value, k say, and just calculate the remainder after dividing by a given number, m say, and use that as the hash value. Thus a hash value will be the result of the expression k%m. Obviously, this method allows a maximum of m different hash values, and the values can be from 0 to m-1. It's easy to see where some duplicate hash values will arise. The hash value for a given k will be duplicated for key values of k+m, k+2*m, and so on where these values can occur. The choice of value for m is critical in minimizing the likelihood of duplicate hash values being generated and ensuring the values are distributed evenly. If m is a power of 2, 2^n say, the hash value is just the least significant n bits of k. This is not a very good result because the most significant bits of k have no effect on the hash value; ideally, all the bits in a key should affect the result of hashing. m is often chosen to be a prime number because this makes it more likely that the hash values are distributed evenly across the range.

Another and better method for computing hash values is to multiply the key value, k, by a carefully selected constant, a, calculate the remainder after dividing a*k by an integer, m, and then select a bit sequence of a given length, n, from the middle of the result of (a*k)%m to be the hash value. Clearly the choices for a and m are important. For computers with 32-bit integers, m is usually chosen to be 2^{32}. The multiplier a is then chosen to be a value that is relatively prime to m – which means that a and m have no common factors greater than 1. Also, the binary representation of a should not have leading or trailing zeroes, otherwise there will be collisions resulting from key values that have leading and/or trailing zeroes. This method is described as the *multiplication method* of hashing for obvious reasons.

There are specialized algorithms to hash strings. One approach is to treat a string as a number of words, compute the hash value for the first word using a method such as the multiplication method, add the next word to that and hash the result, and continue in the same way for all the words to produce the final hash value for the string. Fortunately, the STL provides quite a lot of help with hashing, so that's the next topic.

Functions That Generate Hash Values

The functional header defines specializations of a hash<K> template for use by the unordered associative containers. The hash<K> template defines types for function objects that create hash values from objects of type K. The operator()() member of a hash<K> instance accepts a single argument of type K and returns the hash value as type size_t. There are specializations of the hash<K> template for all of the fundamental types, and for pointer types.

The algorithms that the hash<K> template specializations use depend on the implementation, but they must meet some specific requirements if they are to conform to the C++14 standard. These include:

- They must not throw exceptions.

- They must produce equal hash values for keys that are equal.

- The probability of collisions for unequal keys must be very small – approaching the reciprocal of the maximum value of size_t.

Note that the requirement to generate the same hash values for equal keys only applies within a single execution. It is specifically allowed that hashing a given key may produce different hash values on different occasions. This allows random data to be used in the hashing algorithm, which is desirable when hashing is applied in cryptography – when hashing passwords, for instance. Note further that the conditions for C++14 conformance does not exclude the possibility that hash values for a given type of key may be identical to the key. This may be the case with hash functions that are used for hashing integer keys in unordered associative containers.

Here's an example of using hash<K> to generate hash values from integers:

```
std::hash<int> hash_int;                              // Function object to hash int
std::vector<int> n {-5, -2, 2, 5, 10};
std::transform(std::begin(n), std::end(n), std::ostream_iterator<size_t>(std::cout, " "), hash_int);
```

This uses the transform() algorithm to hash the values of the elements in the vector. The arguments to transform() are the iterators defining the range to be operated on, an iterator defining the destination for the result, which is an ostream iterator here, and finally the function to be applied to the values in the range – the hash<int> object. On my system, the output is:

```
554121069 2388331168 3958272823 3132668352 1833987007
```

With your C++ compiler and library, the hash values may well be different, and this applies to all hash values. Here's an example of hashing floating-point values:

```
std::hash<double> hash_double;
std::vector<double> x {3.14, -2.71828, 99.0, 1.61803399, 6.62606957E-34};
std::transform(std::begin(x), std::end(x),
               std::ostream_iterator<size_t>(std::cout, " "), hash_double);
```

The output on my system is:

4023697370 332724328 2014146765 3488612130 3968187275

Hashing pointers is just as easy:

```
std::hash<Box*> hash_box;                              // Box class as in Chapter 2
Box box{1, 2, 3};
std::cout << "Hash value = " << hash_box(&box)
          << std::endl;                                // Hash value = 2916986638 for me
```

You can use the same function object to hash smart pointers:

```
std::hash<Box*> hash_box;                              // Box class as in Chapter 2
auto upbox = std::make_unique<Box>(1, 2, 3);
std::cout << "Hash value = " << hash_box(upbox.get())
          << std::endl;                                // Hash value = 1143026886 for me
```

This just calls the get() member of the unique_ptr<Box> object to obtain the raw pointer that will be an address in the free store, and this is passed to the hash function. There is also a specialization of the hash<K> template for unique_ptr<T> and shared_ptr<T> objects. For example, you could hash the unique_ptr<Box> object rather that the raw pointer it contains:

```
std::hash<std::unique_ptr<Box>> hash_box;              // Box class as in Chapter 2
auto upbox = std::make_unique<Box>(1, 2, 3);
std::cout << "Hash value = " << hash_box(upbox)
          << std::endl;                                // Hash value = 4291053140 for me
```

The hash values for the raw pointer and the unique_ptr will be the same. Don't be misled by this into thinking that the ability to hash pointers is appropriate when keys are of a type for which there is no specific hashing function. You are hashing an *address*, not the object itself. Whatever the pointer points to is irrelevant. Consider what would happen if you were to store objects in an unordered container using *pointers* to keys, rather than the keys. The hash value for a pointer to a key will be quite different from the hash value for the original key because the addresses are different, so it's useless for retrieving the object. There needs to be a way to generate a hash value for whatever type of key you are using. If the keys are of a type that you have defined, one option is to use the hash functions that the STL provides to generate a hash value from the data members of your class.

There are specializations for the hash<K> template defined in the string header. These generate function objects that will compute hash values from objects that represent strings. There are four specializations, corresponding to the string types, string, wstring, u16string, and u32string. A string of type wstring contains wide characters of type wchar_t; type u16string contains char16_t characters, which are Unicode characters in UTF-16 encoding. A type u32string contains char32_t characters, which are Unicode characters in UTF-32 encoding. Of course, the character types char, wchar_t, char16_t, and char32_t are all fundamental types in C++ 14. Here's an example of hashing a string object:

```
std::hash<std::string> hash_str;
std::string food {"corned beef"};
std::cout << "corned beef hash is " << hash_str(food) << std::endl;
```

This creates a function object to hash `string` objects in the same way as in the previous examples in the section. My output from this code is:

```
corned beef hash is 3803755380
```

There is no specific provision for hashing C-style strings. Using the `hash<T>` template with type `const char*` will use the specialization for pointers. If you want to obtain a hash value for a C-style string as a hash of the character sequence, you can create a `string` object from it and use a `hash<string>` function object.

The hash values produced by the code fragments I have shown are all huge numbers that don't look incredibly useful for deciding where to store an object in an unordered container. There are various ways in which hash values can be used to locate objects in a container. A common method is to use a subsequence of bits from the hash value as an index to identify where an object is in a table or a tree.

Using an unordered_map Container

An `unordered_map` container stores elements that are key/value pairs with unique keys. Elements are not ordered in the container. An element is located using the hash value for the key so there must be a hash function for the type of the keys that you use. If you are using objects of a class type that you have defined as keys, you need to define a function object that implements a hash function for it. If your keys are objects of a type supported in the STL by a specialization of `hash<T>`, the container can use that to generate the hash value for a key. Because a key allows an object in an unordered map to be accessed without searching, elements can be retrieved faster that in an ordered map container. Iterating over a range of elements in an unordered map will generally be slower that in an ordered map, so the choice of container in any particular application is down to how you want to access the elements.

Elements in an `unordered_map` container are organized quite differently from those in a `map` and the specific way elements are organized internally depends on your C++ implementation. Typically, elements are stored in a *hash table* where entries in the table are referred to as *buckets* and a bucket can hold several elements. A given hash value selects a specific bucket and because the number of possible hash values is almost certainly greater than the number of buckets, two different hash values may map to the same bucket. Thus there can be collisions due to two different keys resulting in the same hash value, and there can also be collisions due to two different hash values selecting the same bucket.

There are a number of parameters that affect how the storage for elements is managed:

- The *number of buckets* in the container. There will be a default for the number of buckets but you can also specify the initial number.

- The *load factor*, which is the average number of elements per bucket. This is the number of elements stored in the container divided by the number of buckets.

- The *maximum for the load factor*, which is 1.0 by default, but you can change this, as you'll see. This is an upper limit for the load factor. When this maximum for the load factor is reached, the container will allocate space for more buckets, which will usually involve rehashing the elements in the container.

Don't confuse the maximum number of elements in a bucket at any given moment with the maximum load factor. Suppose you have a container with eight buckets Suppose further that there are 3 elements in each of the first two buckets and the remaining buckets are empty. The load factor in this case is 6/8, which is 0.75 – less than the default maximum load factor of 1.0 so this is OK.

The basic organization of an `unordered_map` is illustrated in Figure 4-3.

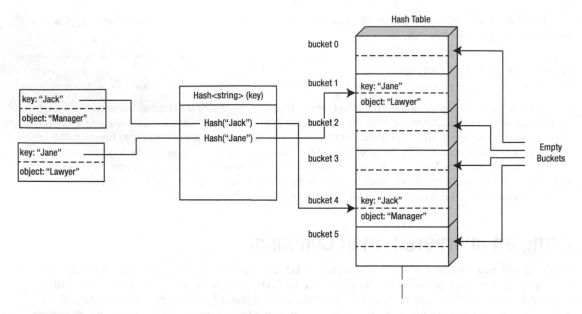

Figure 4-3. *Data in an unordered_map*

Figure 4-4 shows only one element per bucket for simplicity. Buckets can be accessed using an index starting from 0.

There are various approaches to how buckets are organized. One possibility is simply to define a bucket as a sequence such as a vector, and store the address of the sequence in the hash table. Another approach is to define a bucket as a linked list and store the root node in the hash table. The specific method used depends on your implementation.

An unordered_map has to be able to compare keys for equality. This is necessary to identify the specific element to be retrieved from a bucket that contains more than one element and to decide when the same key is already in the container. By default the container will use an instance of the equal_to<K> template that is defined in the functional header. This will use the == operator to compare keys so the container is determining that keys are the same when they are *equal*, which is different from a map container that uses *equivalence*. If the keys you are using are of a class type that does not implement operator==(), you will need to supply a function object that will compare your keys.

Creating and Managing unordered_map Containers

You can create an unordered_map container as simply as you can create a map, as long as the key type, K, can be hashed using a hash<K> instance and keys can be compared using the == operator. For example, here's how you can define and initialize an unordered_map:

```
std::unordered_map<std::string, size_t> people {{"Jan", 44}, {"Jim", 33}, {"Joe", 99}}; // Name,age
```

This creates the container to contain pair<string, size_t> elements and initializes it from the initializer list. The container will have a default number of buckets and use an equal_to<string>() object to compare keys for equality. It will use an instance of the hash<string> specialization of the hash<K> template that the string header defines to hash the keys. If you don't supply initial values, the default constructor creates an empty container with the default number of buckets.

When you have a good idea of the number of elements you will want to store in the container, you can specify the number of buckets that the constructor should allocate:

```
std::unordered_map<std::string, size_t> people {{{"Jan", 44}, {"Jim", 33}, {"Joe", 99}}, 10};
```

There are two arguments to this constructor: the initializer list and the number of buckets to be allocated.

You can also create a container with the contents of a range of pair objects that is defined by iterators. Clearly, as long as the range contains pair object of the required type, any source of the objects is acceptable. For example:

```
std::vector<std::pair<string, size_t>> folks {{"Jan", 44}, {"Jim", 33}, {"Joe", 99},
                                               {"Dan", 22}, {"Ann", 55}, {"Don", 77}};
std::unordered_map<string, size_t> neighbors {std::begin(folks), std::end(folks), 500};
```

The neighbors container is populated with the pair<string,size_t> elements from the folks vector. This also allocates 500 buckets for neighbors, but you could omit this argument and get the default bucket count.

You can specify a function object that defines a hash function with either of the previous two constructors; the function object is the third argument for the initializer list constructor and the fourth argument for the range constructor so you must also specify a bucket count when you do this. I'll illustrate how you do this with the constructor that accepts an initializer list.

Suppose that we wanted to use Name objects as keys, with the Name class defined as in Ex4_01. We must define a hash function for the class, as well as the equality operator so the class definition will need to be extended like this:

```
class Name
{
  // Private and public members and friends as in Ex4_01...

public:
  size_t hash() const { return std::hash<std::string>()(first+second); }

  bool operator==(const Name& name) const { return first == name.first && second== name.second; }
};
```

The default operator==() function member that the compiler can supply is satisfactory in this case, but I put the definition in anyway. The hash() member uses a hash<string>() function object to hash the concatenation of the first and second members of a Name object. The hash function that an unordered_map container requires must accept a single argument of the same type as the key, and return the hash value as type size_t. We can define a function object type that will call the hash() member of a Name object to meet the requirements:

```
class Hash_Name
{
public:
  size_t operator()(const Name& name) const { return name.hash(); }
};
```

We can use a Hash_Name object to specify the hash function that an unordered_map container should use when we create it:

```
std::unordered_map<Name, size_t, Hash_Name> people
         {{{{"Ann", "Ounce"}, 25}, {{"Bill", "Bao"}, 46}, {{"Jack", "Sprat"}, 77}},
         500,                                       // Bucket count
         Hash_Name()};                              // Hash function for keys
```

The elements will be pair<Name, size_t> objects. The initializer list that is the first argument to the constructor for the container defines three such objects. Note how the braces are nested. The innermost braces enclose the arguments to the Name constructor. The next level braces enclose the arguments to the pair<Name,size_t> constructor. The second argument to the unordered_map constructor is the bucket count – we must specify this because we want to specify the third argument, which is the function object for hashing the keys. The type for the function object is to specify as the third template type argument for the container as Hash_Name. This is necessary because the template type parameter has a default value, which will be different from the type of our function object. With the constructor that creates a unordered_map initialized with a range, the first two arguments are the iterators and the third and fourth arguments are the bucket count and the hash function respectively.

When you need to specify a function object to compare key objects for equality, you must also specify the bucket count, and the function object that will generate hash values from keys. If we ignore the operator==() member of the Name class, and assume we have defined a Name_Equal class type that defines function objects, you could specify a Name_Equal function object to the constructor like this:

```
std::unordered_map<Name, size_t, Hash_Name, Name_Equal> people
         {{{{"Ann", "Ounce"}, 25}, {{"Bill", "Bao"}, 46}, {{"Jack", "Sprat"}, 77}},
         500,                                       // Bucket count
         Hash_Name(),                               // Hash function for keys
         Name_Equal()};                             // Equality comparison for keys
```

There's one extra template type argument and one extra constructor argument. The template type argument is necessary because the parameter has a default value. Specifying the function object for key equality comparisons would be essentially the same using the constructor that accepts a range of elements as initializers.

You have move and copy constructors for an unordered_map. Obviously you are going to create a duplicate container with the same bucket count and hash function as the argument container has.

Adjusting the Bucket Count

If you insert more elements into a container than the number of buckets can accommodate while maintaining the current load factor, the container will have to increase the number of buckets. This will cause elements to be rehashed to reallocate them in the new set of buckets. This will invalidate any existing iterators from the container. You can change the number of buckets at any time by calling the rehash() function member:

```
people.rehash(15);                                 // Make bucket count 15
```

The argument to rehash() can be more or fewer buckets that currently. This statement will change the bucket count to 15 as long as is does not result in the maximum load factor being exceeded. The entire contents will be rehashed to reallocate elements across the new set of buckets, which will invalidate any iterators that are around. If the maximum load factor would be exceeded with the bucket count specified, the bucket will be increased so the maximum will not be exceeded.

If you want to be sure that you will increase the bucket count, you can use the value that
bucket_count() returns:

```
people.rehash((5*people.bucket_count())/4);                    // Increase bucket count by 25%
```

Another possibility is to increase the maximum load factor, thus allowing the average number of
elements per bucket to increase:

```
people.max_load_factor(1.2*people.max_load_factor());          // Increse max load factor by 20%
```

To change the maximum load factor, you call max_load_factor() for the container with the new value
as the argument; if you call the member without an argument, it returns the current maximum, which you
can use as in this statement to specify a new value.

You can discover the current load factor by calling load_factor() for the unordered_map object with
the value returned is type float:

```
float lf = people.load_factor();
```

You also have the option of setting the number of buckets so that they will accommodate a given
number of elements while maintaining the load factor within the maximum:

```
size_t max_element_count {100};
people.reserve(max_element_count);
```

This sets the bucket count so that it will accommodate 100 elements without exceeding the current
load factor limit. This will cause the contents of the container to be rehashed and thus will invalidate any
existing iterators. Of course, you can create and use unordered_map containers without worrying about
bucket counts or load factors. It will all be taken care of by the container. It's worth thinking about for real-
world application where performance is important and the container is a significant factor in that. The
fastest access will be obtained when there is no more than one element per bucket, but this is not realistic in
practice because it would require a lot of memory because inevitably there would be a lot of empty buckets.
Increasing the maximum load factor allows more elements per bucket and therefore fewer buckets in total,
so this is more efficient on memory usage. However, more elements per bucket will result in slower access
to elements so performance will be poorer. It's a judgment in each application context, where you set the
conditions. Perhaps the most important thing you can do is avoid rehashing the contents repeatedly. If you
can make a good guess at the number of elements that will be stored, you can set the number of buckets
and/or the load factor at the right level to minimize the likelihood of rehashing.

Inserting Elements

The insert() member of an unordered_map container offers the same range of capabilities as it does in a
map. You can insert a single element by copying or moving it, with or without a hint as to where it should go.
You can also insert several elements identified in an initializer list, or identified by two iterators that define a
range. Let's look at some examples – here's the first:

```
std::unordered_map<std::string, size_t> people { {"Jim", 33}, {"Joe", 99}};        // Name,age
std::cout << "people container has " << people.bucket_count() << " buckets.\n";  // 8 buckets for me
auto pr = people.insert(std::pair<string,size_t> {"Jan", 44});                    // Move insert
std::cout << "Element " << (pr.second ? "was" : "was not") << " inserted." << std::endl;
```

The first statement creates a container with two initial elements and a default bucket count. The next statement calls the bucket_count() member of people to obtain the bucket count; executing this code on my system returns the value shown in the comment but your system may well be different. The insert() call will be the version with an rvalue reference parameter so the pair object will be moved into the container. This function returns a pair object where the first member is an iterator that points either to the new element, or if it was not inserted, the element that prevented its insertion. The second member of the pair is a bool value that is true if the object was inserted.

Look at these statements:

```
std::pair<std::string, size_t> Jim {"Jim", 47};
pr = people.insert(Jim);
std::cout << "\nElement " << (pr.second ? "was" : "was not") << " inserted." << std::endl;
std::cout << pr.first->first << " is " << pr.first->second << std::endl;          // 33
```

Because the argument is an lvalue, the insert() version with a const reference parameter is called, which will copy the argument if the insertion is successful. This insertion will fail because there is already an element with the key value string("Jim"), so the last statement will report the age as 33.

Here's how you insert an element with a hint as to where it should go:

```
auto count = people.size();
std::pair<std::string, size_t> person {"Joan", 33};
auto iter = people.insert(pr.first, person);
std::cout << "\nElement " << (people.size() > count ? "was" : "was not") << " inserted." << std::endl;
```

The first argument to insert() here is the iterator that is the first member of the pair returned by the previous insert() call above, and this is a hint as to where the element should be placed; the container may or may not abide by the hint. The second argument to insert() is the element to be inserted. This version of the insert() function doesn't return a pair object; it returns just an iterator that points either to the element that was inserted, or to the element that prevented its insertion. The code fragment uses the count of elements in the container that is returned by its size() member to determine whether or not the insertion was successful.

You can also insert the contents of an initializer list:

```
people.insert({{"Bill", 21}, {"Ben", 22}});              // Inserts the two elements in the list
```

This version of insert() does not return a value and neither does the version that inserts a range of elements:

```
std::unordered_map<std::string, size_t> folks;         // Empty container
folks.insert(std::begin(people), std::end(people));  // Insert copies of all people elements
```

The range that these iterators define contains elements from a container of the same type as folks, but it could be from any type container as long as the elements are of the type required by folks.

You can create elements in place in an unordered_map container by calling its emplace() or emplace_hint() members. For example:

```
auto pr = people.emplace("Sue", 64);                    // returns pair<iterator, bool>
auto iter = people.emplace_hint(pr.first, "Sid", 67);   // Returns iterator
people.emplace_hint(iter, std::make_pair("Sam", 59));   // Uses converting pair<string, size_t>
```

The emplace() member creates the object in place in the container from the arguments you supply. It returns a pair containing an iterator and a bool value with the same significance as with insert(). The first argument to emplace_hint() is the iterator that is the hint, followed by the arguments to be used to create the element. It returns just an iterator that points to the inserted element or the element that prevented its insertion.

An unordered_map container implements the assignment operator to replace the contents of the container by the contents of the unordered_map object that is the argument;

```
folks = people;                          // Replace folks elements by people elements
```

Obviously, the argument must contain elements of the same type as the current container.

Accessing Elements

You can use the subscript operator with a key to obtain a reference to the corresponding object in an unordered_map. For example:

```
people["Jim"] = 22;                      // Set Jim's age to 22;
people["May"] = people["Jim"];           // Set May's age to Jim's
++people["Joe"];                         // Increment Joe's age
people["Kit"] = people["Joe"];           // Set Kit's age to Joe's
```

This works the same as in a map container. Using a key that does not exist with the subscript operator for an element will cause an element with that key to be created with a default value for the associated object. The last statement will create the element with "Kit" as the key and the age as 0 if there is no "Kit" in the container; the object associated with "Joe" will then be copied to "Kit."

The at() member returns a reference to the object associated with the argument that is a key but throws an out_of_range exception if the key is not present. Thus you use at() rather than the subscript operator when you don't want elements to be created with a default object. You also have find() and equal_range() members that work in the same way as I described for a map.

Iterators are available for an unordered_map so you can access the elements in a range-based for loop, for example:

```
for(const auto& person : people)
  std::cout << person.first << " is " << person.second << std::endl;
```

This lists all the elements in the people container.

Removing Elements

You can remove an element from an unordered_map by calling its erase() member. The argument can be a key that identifies the element or an iterator that points to it. When the argument is a key, the erase() member returns an integer that is the number of elements that were removed, so a 0 return indicates it wasn't found. When the argument is an iterator, an iterator is returned that points to the element that followed the element that was removed. Here are some examples of its use:

```
auto n = people.erase("Jim");              // Returns 0 if key not found
auto iter = people.find("May");            // Returns end iterator if key not found
if(iter != people.end())
  iter = people.erase(iter);               // Returns iterator for element after "May"
```

You can also remove a sequence of elements that are identified by a range. For example:

```
// Remove all except 1st and last
auto iter = people.erase(++std::begin(people), --std::end(people));
```

This returns an iterator that points to the element following the last that was removed.

The clear() function member removes all elements and the empty() member returns true when there are no elements in the container.

Accessing Buckets

You can access an individual bucket in an unordered_map and the elements it contains. You do this using overloads of the begin() and end() members of the container that return iterators for the elements in the container. The buckets are indexed from 0, and you can obtain an iterator that points to the first element in a bucket as a given index position by passing its index to the begin() member of the container. For example:

```
auto iter = people.begin(1);                    // Returns an iterator for the 2nd bucket
```

Passing an index to the cbegin() member of the container returns a const iterator that points to the first element in the bucket at that index position. The end() and cend() members of the container also come in versions that accept an index and these return an iterator and a const iterator respectively that point to one past the last element in the bucket at the specified index position. Thus you can output the elements in a particular bucket – a bucket list, in other words – with a loop such as this:

```
size_t index{1};
std::cout << "The elements in bucket[" << index << "] are:\n";
for(auto iter = people.begin(index); iter != people.end(index); ++iter)
  std::cout << iter->first << " is " << iter->second << std::endl;
```

You have already seen that the bucket_count() member of an unordered_map returns the number of buckets. The bucket_size() member returns the number of elements in the bucket selected by the index that is the argument. The bucket() function member returns an index to the bucket that contain the element with the key you pass as the argument. You can use these in combination in various ways. For example:

```
string key {"May"};
if(people.find(key) != std::end(people))
   std:: cout << "The number of elements in the bucket containing " << key << " is "
           << people.bucket_size(people.bucket(key)) << std::endl;
```

The argument to bucket_size() is the index that is returned by bucket(). This fragment executes the output statement when key is in the container. The output records the number of elements in the bucket that contains key.

Here's an example that will give you some insight as to how an unordered_map container behaves on your system as you add elements:

```
// Ex4_06.cpp
// Analyzing how and when the number of buckets in an unordered_map container increases
#include <iostream>                        // For standard streams
#include <iomanip>                         // For stream manipulators
#include <string>                          // For string class
#include <unordered_map>                   // For unordered_map container
#include <vector>                          // For vector container
#include <algorithm>                       // For max_element() algorithm

using std::string;
using std::unordered_map;

// Outputs number of elements in each bucket
void list_bucket_counts(const std::vector<size_t>& counts)
{
  for(size_t i {}; i < counts.size(); ++i)
  {
    std::cout << "bucket[" << std::setw(2) << i << "] = " << counts[i] << "   ";
    if((i + 1) % 6 == 0) std::cout << '\n';
  }
  std::cout << std::endl;
}
int main()
{
  unordered_map<string, size_t> people;
  float mlf {people.max_load_factor()};      // Current maximum load factor
  size_t n_buckets {people.bucket_count()};  // Number of buckets in container

  std::vector<size_t> bucket_counts (n_buckets);  // Records number of elements per bucket
  string name {"Name"};                      // Key - with value appended
  size_t value {};                           // Element value
  size_t max_count {8192};                   // Maximum number of elements to insert
  auto lf = people.load_factor();            // Current load factor
  bool rehash {false};                       // Records when rehash occurs
```

```cpp
while(mlf <= 1.5f)                                      // Loop until max load factor is 1.5
{
  std::cout << "\n\n*************New Container**************"
            << "\nNumber of buckets: " << n_buckets
            << "  Maximum load factor: " << mlf << std::endl;

  // Insert max elements in container
  for(size_t n_elements {}; n_elements < max_count; ++n_elements)
  {
    lf = people.load_factor();                          // Record load factor before insert
    people.emplace("name" + std::to_string(++value), value);
    auto new_count = people.bucket_count();             // Current bucket count
    if(new_count > n_buckets)                           // If bucket count increases...
    {                                                   // Output info
      std::cout << "\nBucket count increased to " << new_count
                << ". Load factor was " << lf << " and is now " << people.load_factor()
                << "\nMaximum elements in a bucket was "
                << *std::max_element(std::begin(bucket_counts), std::end(bucket_counts))
                << std::endl;
      if(n_buckets <= 64)
      {
        std::cout << "Bucket counts before increase were: " << std::endl;
        list_bucket_counts(bucket_counts);
      }

      n_buckets = new_count;                            // Update bucket count
      bucket_counts = std::vector < size_t > (n_buckets); // New vector for counts
      rehash = true;                                    // Record rehash occurred
    }

    // Record current bucket counts
    for(size_t i {}; i < n_buckets; ++i)
      bucket_counts[i] = people.bucket_size(i);

    if(rehash)                                          // If the container was rehashed...
    {                                                   // ...output info
      rehash = false;                                   // Reset rehash indicator

      std::cout << "\nRehashed container. Bucket count is " << n_buckets
                << ". Element count is " << people.size()
                << "\nMaximum element count in a bucket is now "
                << *std::max_element(std::begin(bucket_counts), std::end(bucket_counts))
                << std::endl;

      if(n_buckets <= 64)                               // If no more than 64 buckets...
      {
        std::cout << "\nBucket counts after rehash are:\n";
        list_bucket_counts(bucket_counts);
      }
    }
```

```
  }
  std::cout << "Final state for this container is:\n"
            << "Bucket count: " << people.bucket_count()
            << "  Element count: " << people.size()
            << "  Maximum element count in a bucket: "
            << *std::max_element(std::begin(bucket_counts), std::end(bucket_counts))
            << std::endl;
  value = 1;                                        // Reset key suffix
  people = unordered_map<string, size_t>();         // New empty container
  n_buckets = people.bucket_count();
  bucket_counts = std::vector < size_t >(n_buckets);  // New vector for bucket counts
  mlf += 0.25f;                                     // Increase max load factor...
  people.max_load_factor(mlf);                      // ...and set for container
  }
}
```

The idea of this program is the track the load factor and the number of buckets as the number of elements in a container increases. This will provide insight into how the container increments the bucket count and under what conditions. You need to be patient because it takes quite a long time to execute. If it's taking too long, reduce the value of the max variable.

The example starts out with an empty unordered_map container and inserts new elements up to a limit specified by max. Unique keys are manufactured by appending the string that to_string() returns with the result of incrementing value as the argument to "name." The to_string() function that is defined in the string header converts any type of numerical value to a string object.

The number of elements in each bucket is recorded in a vector container. The outer while loop continues as long as the maximum load factor is less than or equal to 1.5. The nested for loop inserts max_count elements in the unordered_map container. Whenever the number of buckets changes, The list_bucket_counts() helper function is called to output the number of elements in each bucket. To prevent the already voluminous output from becoming unmanageable, the bucket counts are only listed for 64 or less buckets. When max_count elements have been inserted, a new unordered_map is created with a greater maximum load factor, and the inner loop is repeated with the new container. This is to show how the maximum load factor affects the level at which the number of buckets is increased, thus causing the elements to be rehashed.

I won't reproduce the output from my system because it would fill too much space, but I'll outline what happens. The initial default bucket count is 8. After adding 8 elements, the bucket count increases from 8 to 64, which is a very substantial change. This occurs when the maximum number of elements in any bucket is 2 and all but one of the buckets contains elements; the total number of elements is 9. The output shows that the increase in bucket was triggered by the load factor reaching 1.0. The next increase in bucket count on my system is again by a factor of 8, from 64 to 512. The factor by which the bucket count is increased slows after that to 2, so the sequence of bucket counts is, 8, 64, 512, 1024, 2048, 4096, and 8192. It's interesting to see how the number of empty buckets increases with the number of buckets. The maximum number of elements in any bucket overall on my system was 8 and unsurprisingly this was with the highest maximum load factor. I did get 7 elements in a bucket with a load factor maximum of 1.5. Each increase in the number of buckets causes all elements in the container to be rehashed and assigned to new bucket locations. You could tweak the program easily to output how specific elements are moved by outputting them before and after a bucket count increase. This involves considerable overhead so getting the bucket count right to start with becomes more important as the number of elements to be stored increases.

The output from my system gives a bit more insight into how the container is mapping the raw hash values to a bucket index. The number of buckets is always a power of 2. This allows the index to a bucket to be a fixed length bit sequence from the raw hash value – 3 bits for 8 buckets, 6 bits for 64 buckets, 9 bits for 512 buckets, and so on. This makes obtaining the bucket index simple – and fast. This explains why elements need to be rehashed after the bucket count increases. Taking 6 bits from a given hash value is almost certainly going to represent a different index value than 3 bits from the same value, so a given raw hash value is likely to map to a different bucket.

Using an unordered_multimap Container

An unordered_multimap container is an unordered map that allows duplicate keys. Thus, the operations it supports are essentially the same as for an unordered_map container except for the changes and additions necessary to deal with multiple keys that are identical. I'll just discuss the differences. Creating an unordered_multimap is via the same range of constructor options as an unordered_map. Here's an example:

```
std::unordered_multimap<std::string, size_t> people {{"Jim", 33}, {"Joe", 99}};
```

Adding new elements using insert(), emplace() or emplace_hint() always works with an unordered_multimap, as long as the argument(s) are consistent with the type of elements in the container. Each of these function members returns an iterator that points to the new element in the container; this is different from an unordered_map in the cases of insert() and emplace() where a pair object is returned to provide an indication of success or otherwise as well as an iterator. Here are some examples:

```
auto iter = people.emplace("Jan", 45);
people.insert({"Jan", 44});
people.emplace_hint(iter, "Jan", 46);
```

The third statement uses the iterator that the first statement returns as a hint for placing the element. The hint may be ignored at the whim of the container – or your implementation.

The at() and operator[]() members that an unordered_map supports are not available for an unordered_multimap because of the potential for duplicate keys. The only options you have for accessing elements are the find() and equal_range() members. The find() member always returns an iterator to the first element it finds, or the end iterator if it doesn't find the key. You can call count() with a key argument to discover the number of elements in a container with a given key. Here's an illustration of these in action:

```
std::string key{"Jan"};
auto n = people.count(key);                      // Number of elements stored with key
  if(n == 1)
    std::cout << key << " is " << people.find(key)->second << std::endl;
  else if(n > 1)
  {
    auto pr = people.equal_range(key);           // pair of begin & end iterators returned
    while(pr.first != pr.second)
    {
      std::cout << key << " is " << pr.first->second << std::endl;
      ++pr.first;                                // Increment begin iterator
    }
  }
```

This uses find() to access the element if there is only one with key, and equal_range() to access the range if there are more than one. Of course, you could just use equal_range() in either case.

Let's look at a working example of an unordered_multimap. This example will also show some of the ways in which you can define function templates to work with containers. The program will implement a phone book that allows the look up of phone numbers for a name or names. I'll use a pair object to encapsulate a first and second name and a tuple to record the area code, exchange, and number as string objects. I'll use the following directives to simplify the appearance of the code:

```
using std::string;
using std::unordered_multimap;
using Name = std::pair<string, string>;
using Phone = std::tuple<string, string, string>;
```

A phone number could be represented as three integers but the components are more like codes than numbers. Each element in a number has a fixed number of digits and certain combinations of digits are not permitted. Using string objects makes checking for the correct number of digits or validating the area code very simple if you wanted to add that capability. I did not include it because the code gets too voluminous for the book.

Overloading the extraction operator for reading a phone number from an istream object will help with input operations in the example. The function looks like this:

```
inline std::istream& operator>>(std::istream& in, Phone& phone)
{
  string area_code {}, exchange {}, number {};
  in >> std::ws >> area_code >> exchange >> number;
  phone = std::make_tuple(area_code, exchange, number);
  return in;
}
```

Phone is a tuple template type. This uses make_tuple() to create the phone object from the values of the local variables that are read from in.

We can do the same sort of thing for Name objects:

```
inline std::istream& operator>>(std::istream& in, Name& name)
{
  in >> std::ws >> name.first >> name.second;
  return in;
}
```

This just discards any leading whitespace and reads the two name strings that are member of the pair object, name, from in.

Of course, we'll need output capability too. Here's the operator<<() function definition to provide output for a Phone object:

```
inline std::ostream& operator<<(std::ostream& out, const Phone& phone)
{
  std::string area_code {}, exchange {}, number {};
  std::tie(area_code, exchange, number) = phone;
  out << area_code << " " << exchange << " " << number;
  return out;
}
```

This uses the `tie<>()` function template to create a `tuple` of references to three local variables. Assigning phone to the `tuple` produced by `tie<>()` stores the values of the members of phone in the local variables, which are then written to out. Alternatively, you could use the `get<>()` function template to access the values of the members of phone. This would be a better approach because it would avoid the copying of string objects that occurs in the implementation above, but the idea is to show the `tie<>()` function in action.

Overloading `<<` for a Name object is trivial:

```cpp
inline std::ostream& operator<<(std::ostream& out, const Name& name)
{
  out << name.first << " " << name.second;
  return out;
}
```

All these I/O functions are `inline` so I put them in a header file with the name `Record_IO.h`. The `#include` and `using` directives at the beginning of the file are:

```cpp
#include <string>                          // For string class
#include <istream>                         // For istream class
#include <ostream>                         // For ostream class
#include <utility>                         // For pair type
#include <tuple>                           // For tuple type

using Name = std::pair <std::string, std::string>;
using Phone = std::tuple <std::string, std::string, std::string>;
```

The program will use two associative containers – one with names as keys and the other with phone numbers as keys, so they both contains the same basic information but accessible in different ways. There are other, more efficient ways of achieving the same thing, but the idea is to try out `unordered_multimap` containers. The containers will be defined in `main()` like this:

```cpp
unordered_multimap<Name, Phone, NameHash> by_name {8, NameHash()};
unordered_multimap<Phone, Name, PhoneHash> by_number {8, PhoneHash()};
```

There's no default hashing capability provided for `pair` or `tuple` objects so we have to define them. Here they are function objects of types `NameHash` and `PhoneHash`. The constructor parameter for the hash function object is preceded by the parameter for the bucket count so this has to be specified. I just made it the default value for my system.

I put the definition for both hash function types in the same header file, which I called `Hash_Function_Objects.h` with the following directives at the beginning:

```cpp
#include <string>                          // For string class
#include <utility>                         // For pair type
#include <tuple>                           // For tuple type

using Name = std::pair<std::string, std::string>;
using Phone = std::tuple < std::string, std::string, std::string>;
```

I defined the PhoneHash type like this:

```
class PhoneHash
{
public:
  size_t operator()(const Phone& phone) const
  {
    return std::hash<std::string>()(std::get<0>(phone)+std::get<1>(phone)+std::get<2>(phone));
  }
};
```

The hash value is produced by applying the hash<string>() template specialization that is defined in the string header to the result of concatenating the three elements in a phone number. I defined the HashName type in a similar way:

```
class NameHash
{
public:
  size_t operator()(const Name& name) const
  {
    return std::hash<std::string>()(name.first + name.second);
  }
};
```

I packaged the output that displays the operations that are supported in a separate function:

```
void show_operations()
{
  std::cout << "Operations:\n"
            << "A: Add an element.\n"
            << "D: Delete elements.\n"
            << "F: Find elements.\n"
            << "L: List all elements.\n"
            << "Q: Quit the progr.\n\n";
}
```

The operation to list all elements will allow output by name or by number. We could define a function template to deal with both possibilities:

```
template<typename Container>
void list_elements(const Container& container)
{
  for(const auto& element : container)
    std::cout << element.first << "  " << element.second << std::endl;
}
```

The template will deduce the container type from the argument used when the function is called. The elements in both container are pair objects. For the by_name container the elements are pair<Name, Phone> objects and for the by_number container they are pair<Phone, Name> objects. Because we have overloaded operator<<() for the Name and Phone types, the body of the loop will automatically select the appropriate function for output from the types of the members of the pair element. I'll put this function template and the templates that follow in the My_Templates.h header file in the complete example.

The process for finding elements by name or by number is essentially the same, so we can define a function template for that, too:

```
template<typename Container>
auto find_elements(const Container& container) ->
        std::pair<typename Container::const_iterator, typename Container::const_iterator>
{
  typename Container::key_type key {};
  std::cin >> key;
  auto pr = container.equal_range(key);
  return pr;
}
```

This code for the template corresponds to the C++ 11 standard. The return type is a pair<> template type that depends on the container type. This is because the types of the iterators encapsulated by the pair that is returned are specific to the container type. This means that the compiler cannot process a return type specification preceding the function name, because the container type is determined from the function argument, which comes later. To enable a C++ 11 compiler to determine the return type you must use the trailing return type syntax. This allows the compiler to process the return type *after* it has processed the function argument. Note that the typename keyword is essential in the specification of the pair template type arguments. It is also essential in the specification of the type of the local variable, key. The type of the key in a container is specified by the key_type member of the container class, so the type specification for key automatically selects the correct type for the container. If you need the type of object associated with a key, it is specified by the Container::mapped_type member, and the type of element for a container is given by Container::value_type.

The C++ 14 standard introduced the ability for the compiler to deduce the return type for a function, so the function template can be written like this:

```
template<typename Container>
auto find_elements(const Container& container)
{
  typename Container::key_type key {};
  std::cin >> key;
  auto pr = container.equal_range(key);
  return pr;
}
```

No trailing return type is necessary because the compiler can deduce the return type to be that of the value returned, namely that of pr.

The operation to find elements will allow searching by name or number and in each case the result can be a `pair` object containing iterators that define a range of elements of one type or the other. We can define another function template to output such a range of elements:

```
template<typename T>
void list_range(const T& pr)
{
  if(pr.first != pr.second)
  {
    for(auto iter = pr.first; iter != pr.second; ++iter)
      std::cout << "  " << iter->first << "  " << iter->second << std::endl;
  }
  else
    std::cout << "No records found.\n";
}
```

If the members of the `pair` object that is the argument are the same, the range is empty, in which case we just output a message. The functions that implement the insertion operator for the Name and Phone types enable this template to work. The actual types of the `pair` members will automatically select the required `operator<<()` function. Note that these templates do not reduce the code in the compiled program. They just provide a convenient mechanism for generating the functions that are used, and provide a couple of simple illustrations of how you can use templates.

The `main()` function will be in `Ex4_07.cpp` in the code download, and it contains the following statements:

```
// Ex4_07.cpp
#include <iostream>                        // For standard streams
#include <cctype>                          // For toupper()
#include <string>                          // For string class
#include <unordered_map>                   // For unordered_map container

#include "Record_IO.h"
#include "My_Templates.h"
#include "Hash_Function_Objects.h"

using std::string;
using std::unordered_multimap;
using Name = std::pair<string, string>;
using Phone = std::tuple<string, string, string>;

// show_operations() definition goes here...

int main()
{
  unordered_multimap<Name, Phone, NameHash> by_name {8, NameHash()};
  unordered_multimap<Phone, Name, PhoneHash> by_number {8, PhoneHash()};

  show_operations();
```

```cpp
char choice {};                                          // Operation selection
Phone number {};                                         // Records a number
Name name {};                                            // Records a name

while(std::toupper(choice) != 'Q')                       // Go until you quit...
{
  std::cout << "Enter a command: ";
  std::cin >> choice;

  switch(std::toupper(choice))
  {
  case 'A':                                              // Add a record
    std::cout << "Enter first & second names, area code, exchange, "
              << "and number separated by spaces:\n";
    std::cin >> name >> number;
    by_name.emplace(name, number);                       // Create in place...
    by_number.emplace(number, name);                     // ...in both containers
    break;
  case 'D':                                              // Delete records
  {
    std::cout << "Enter a name: ";                       // Only find by name
    auto pr = find_elements(by_name);
    auto count = std::distance(pr.first, pr.second);     // Number of elements
    if(count == 1)
    {                                                    // If there's just the one...
      by_number.erase(pr.first->second);                 // ...delete from numbers container
      by_name.erase(pr.first);                           // ...delete from names container
    }
    else if(count > 1)
    {                                                    // There's more than one
      std::cout << "There are " << count << " records for "
                << pr.first->first << ". Delete all(Y or N)? ";
      std::cin >> choice;

      if(std::toupper(choice) == 'Y')
      {
        // Erase records from by_number container first
        for(auto iter = pr.first; iter != pr.second; ++iter)
        {
          by_number.erase(iter->second);
        }
        by_name.erase(pr.first, pr.second);              // Now delete from by_name
      }
    }
  }
  break;

  case 'F':                                              // Find a record
    std::cout << "Find by name(Y or N)? ";
    std::cin >> choice;
```

```
      if(std::toupper(choice) == 'Y')
      {
        std::cout << "Enter first name and second name: ";
        list_range(find_elements(by_name));
      }
      else
      {
        std::cout << "Enter area code, exchange, and number separated by spaces: ";
        list_range(find_elements(by_number));
      }
      break;
    case 'L':                                    // List all records
      std::cout << "List by name(Y or N)? ";
      std::cin >> choice;
      if(std::toupper(choice) == 'Y')
        list_elements(by_name);
      else
        list_elements(by_number);
      break;
    case 'Q':
      break;

    default:
      std::cout << "Invalid command - try again.\n";
    }
  }
}
```

I don't think you'll find this difficult to follow. After outputting the possible operations, everything happens in the while loop until 'q' or 'Q' is entered. The body of the loop is just one big `switch` statement that selects the required operation.

Adding an element just involves creating an element in place in each container with the key/object values used with the by_name container switched for the by_number container.

Deleting elements uses the `find_elements()` function template with the by_name container. It's essential to delete the elements from the by_number container first to keep the contents of the containers synchronized. To remove several elements from the by_name container, its `erase()` function is called with the iterators that define the range as arguments. All the elements have the same key, so you could pass the key of the first element in the range to `erase()` to delete them, like this:

```
by_name.erase(pr.first->first);              // Delete elements with the specified key
```

For the find operation, the `pair` returned by an instance of the `find_elements()` template is passed directly to an instance of the `list_range()` template instance. The compiler automatically ensures the right calls are made. Finally, to list the elements, an instance of the `list_elements()` template is called to output elements by the specified key.

Here's an example of some output:

```
Operations:
A: Add an element.
D: Delete elements.
F: Find elements.
L: List all elements.
Q: Quit the program.

Enter a command: a
Enter first & second names, area code, exchange, and number separated by spaces:
Bill Bloggs 112 234 4545
Enter a command: a
Enter first & second names, area code, exchange, and number separated by spaces:
Nell Bloggs
112 234 4545
Enter a command: a
Enter first & second names, area code, exchange, and number separated by spaces:
Bill Bloggs 914 626 7890
Enter a command: a
Enter first & second names, area code, exchange, and number separated by spaces:
Al Capone 312 334 4566
Enter a command: l
List by name(Y or N)? y
Nell Bloggs   112 234 4545
Bill Bloggs   112 234 4545
Bill Bloggs   914 626 7890
Al Capone   312 334 4566
Enter a command: l
List by name(Y or N)? n
112 234 4545  Bill Bloggs
112 234 4545  Nell Bloggs
914 626 7890  Bill Bloggs
312 334 4566  Al Capone
Enter a command: f
Find by name(Y or N)? y
Enter first name and second name: Bill Blogs
No records found.
Enter a command: f
Find by name(Y or N)? y
Enter first name and second name: Bill Bloggs
  Bill Bloggs  112 234 4545
  Bill Bloggs  914 626 7890
Enter a command: f
Find by name(Y or N)? n
Enter area code, exchange, and number separated by spaces: 112 234 4545
  112 234 4545  Bill Bloggs
  112 234 4545  Nell Bloggs
Enter a command: q
```

Summary

The associative containers you have learned about in this chapter are powerful tools for accessing data using keys rather than index values. This particularly applies in applications that involve related data items – names and phone numbers, for instance: people and addresses, assemblies and subassemblies; or subassemblies and parts. The unordered map containers usually provide faster access to objects that the ordered map containers, but this depends on the keys having hash functions that generate unique hash values most of the time. A poor hashing function will slow element retrieval because the need to search a bucket for a matching key will occur more often. If you have doubts about the hashing of your keys, you may be better off using an ordered map container.

While the map containers offer a great deal of convenience and ease of programming, it's always worth considering whether sequence containers storing pair objects represent a reasonable alternative, particularly when you can sort the container by key. This can occasionally offer a better solution than an associative container.

The significant things you learned about in this chapter include:

- A pair<T1,T2> object encapsulates two objects of any type.

- An instance of the tuple<> template type can encapsulate any number of objects of different types.

- All map containers store elements that are key/object pairs as pair<const K,T> objects.

- A map<K,T> container stores elements with unique keys that are ordered by key using the less-than operator by default so the key type must support the < operator unless you specify an alternative comparison function.

- The elements in a multimap<K,T> container are ordered in the same way as a map but duplicate keys are permitted.

- Ordered associative containers use equivalence to determine when two keys are the same. A consequence of this is that the comparison for keys can only be less-than or greater-than. A comparison function that returns true when keys are equal will prevent the container from working correctly.

- Hashing is a process for generating relatively unique integers called hash values from objects. Hashing is used to decide where elements are stored in unordered associative containers. Hashing is also important in cryptography.

- Elements are stored in an unordered_map<K,T> container using hash values that are generated from the keys. A hash value selects a specific bucket and each bucket can contain several elements. Keys in an unordered_map<K,T> must be unique.

- An unordered_multimap container is like an unordered_map but allows duplicate keys.

- Keys are compared for equality in unordered map containers using equal_to<K> by default so the key type must support == comparison and hashing of key objects.

EXERCISES

1. Implement a program that uses a map<K,T> container to store the names of the students in each of an arbitrary number of classes. The program should support adding and deleting classes and listing all classes. The list of students in a class should be retrieved and displayed by supplying the class name such as "Biology."

2. Implement a program that uses a multimap<K,T> container to store the classes that are attended by each student where there may be more than one student with the same name. The elements should be in descending order. Provide for adding and deleting students, listing all students and their classes, and retrieving and displaying the class for a given student name.

3. Write a program that simulates a supermarket with a number of checkouts entered from the keyboard. Each checkout should be represented by an element in a map container where the key is the checkout ID, and the queue at that checkout is the associated object. Customers should arrive at random intervals with random checkout occupancy times when they are served. The program should report average and maximum queue lengths for each checkout after a given period that is also entered from the keyboard.

4. Define a class for Person objects that store a name, an address, and a phone number. Use an unordered_multimap container to store Person object with names as keys. Provide for retrieving an address, or a phone number for a name, as well as listing all Person objects in ascending sequence of names. Define a main() program to demonstrate all the functions offered.

CHAPTER 5

■ ■ ■

Working with Sets

This chapter is about working with *sets*. A set is a simple mathematical concept that is intuitive in its meaning – a collection of things with some common characteristic. There are two notions of a set in the STL, both of which relate to the mathematical idea of a set. A set can be a sequence of objects within a range that is defined by two iterators. A set is also a type of container with particular characteristics. *Set containers* are associative containers in which the objects are their own keys. In this chapter, you'll learn the following:

- What set containers are provided by the STL.

- The functions available with set containers of different types.

- The operations you can apply to set containers.

- How you create and use set containers.

- The operations you can apply to sets of objects that are defined by ranges.

Understanding Set Containers

Apart from not having separate keys, the set containers are very similar to the map containers. There are four templates that define sets, two of which store elements ordered by less<T> by default, and another two that store elements using their hash values. The templates for ordered sets are defined in the set header, and the templates for unordered sets are defined in the unordered_set header. Thus, objects stored in ordered set containers must support comparison, and those in unordered sets must be of types that can be hashed.

The templates that define set containers are:

- set<T> containers store objects of type T and objects must be unique. Elements in the container are ordered and are compared using a less<T> object by default. Equivalence, not equality, is used to determine when objects are the same.

- multiset<T> containers store objects of type T in the same way as a set<T> container but duplicate objects can be stored.

- unorderd_set<T> containers store objects of type T and objects must be unique in the container. The elements are located in the container using the hash values generated from the objects. Elements are compared for equality using an equal_to<T> object by default.

- unordered_multiset<T> containers store objects of type T in the same way as an unordered_set<T> container, but duplicate objects can be stored.

There's a difference between the kinds of iterators you can obtain for ordered and unordered associative containers. You can get both forward and reverse iterators for ordered containers, but only forward iterators are available with unordered containers.

If you haven't come across set containers before, you may be wondering what on earth the use of a container is where to retrieve an object, you supply the same object. If you have the object already, why would you need to retrieve it? Perhaps surprisingly, there are many uses for set containers.

Sets are candidates for storing data in applications that involve sets of things, where determining membership of a particular set is of interest. An application working with classes in an academic institution is one example. Each class can be represented by a separate set container that stores students. A set container might be suitable because there cannot be duplicate students in a class; obviously, two students could have a common name, but the objects representing them should be unique. You can easily discover whether a particular student has registered for a given class. You can also determine all the classes for which a given student has registered.

Generally an unordered set will be faster in operation that an ordered set when there are a large number of elements stored and when there are random insertion and retrieval operations. Retrieving elements from an ordered set of n elements is proportional to $\log n$. Retrieving elements from an unordered set is constant on average, and independent of the number of elements, although the actual performance can be adversely affected by the effectiveness of the hashing operation and internal organization of the elements.

Where an object is stored depends on the comparison function for an ordered set and on the hash function for an unordered set. You have the possibility to use different comparison functions or different hash functions for different sets that store the same objects. A simple example is to consider a Person class type that represents an employee with the class encapsulating many different aspects of an individual. The class could include the personnel ID, the department, the name, the age, the address, the gender, the phone number, the pay grade, and so on. You could then create several sets for categorizing individuals in various ways. You could choose to compare or hash work departments in one set and compare or hash the pay grade in another. This would allow you to access employees with a given pay grade, or employees in a given department. These sets would not necessarily need to store duplicates of the Person objects. You could create the Person objects in the free store and store smart pointers in the containers. You'll see some working examples that do this later in this chapter. I'll assume a using directive for std::string in this chapter to minimize line spills in statements.

Using set<T> Containers

The internal organization of the elements in a set<T> container is typically the same as that of a map<K,T> container – a balanced binary tree. Consider this set container definition that creates the container with its contents specified by an initializer list:

```
std::set<int> numbers {8, 7, 6, 5, 4, 3, 2, 1};
```

Because the default comparison will be less<int>, the elements will be in ascending order in the container. The internal binary tree will be similar to that shown in Figure 5-1. You can see that the elements are in ascending sequence by executing the following statement:

```
std::copy(std::begin(numbers), std::end(numbers), std::ostream_iterator<int>
        {std::cout, " "});
```

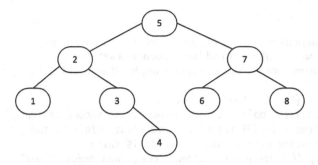

Figure 5-1. *Balanced binary tree of integers ordered by less<int>*

The copy() algorithm copies the range specified by the first two arguments to the destination specified by the third argument, which in this case is an output stream iterator. The statement will output the integers from 1 to 8 in ascending sequence.

Of course, you can supply a different comparison function object for the elements:

```
std::set<std::string, std::greater<string>> words
                      {"one", "two", "three", "four", "five", "six", "seven", "eight"};
```

The elements in this container will be ordered in descending sequence so the tree in the container will be similar to Figure 5-2.

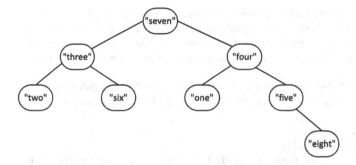

Figure 5-2. *Balanced binary tree of strings ordered by greater<string>*

You can create a set container with the elements from a range and optionally specify the comparison:

```
std::set<string> words2 {std::begin(words), std::end(words)};
std::set<string, std::greater<string>> words3 {++std::begin(words2), std::end(words2)};
```

The first statement defines words2 to contain copies the elements from the words container ordered by the default comparison – a less<string> instance. The second statement defines words3 to contain copies of all the elements from words2 except the first. This container is ordered using a greater<string> instance.

The set<T> template also defines copy and move constructors. The provision of the move constructor is important because it allows a locally defined set container in a function to be returned efficiently – without copying. The compiler can recognize when you return a local set container that is to be destroyed when the function ends, and will use the move constructor to return it. You'll see an example of using this later in this chapter.

Adding and Removing Elements

There is no at() member or operator[]() implementation for a set, but apart from that the operations that set containers provide largely mirror those of map containers. To add an element to a set, you have insert(), emplace(), and emplace_hint() function members. Here are some examples of using insert():

```
std::set<string, std::greater<string>> words {"one", "two", "three"};
auto pr1 = words.insert("four");        // pr1.first points to new element. pr1.second is true
auto pr2 = words.insert("two");         // Element is NOT inserted - pr2.first points to the
                                        // existing element and pr.second is false
auto iter3 = words.insert(pr.first, "seven"); // iter3 points to new element just before "four"
words.insert({"five", "six"});              // Insert list of elements - no return value
string wrds[] {"eight", "nine", "ten"};
words.insert(std::begin(wrds), std::end(wrds)); // Inserts range - no return value
```

Inserting a single element returns a pair<iterator,bool> object, and inserting a single element with a hint just returns an iterator. Inserting multiple elements in a range or an initializer list returns nothing. In the statement where the argument to insert() is an initializer list, the values in the list are string literals that will be used to create objects of type string.

Here are a couple of examples of creating elements in place in a set:

```
std::set<std::pair<string,string>> names;
auto pr = names.emplace("Lisa", "Carr");   // pr.first points to new element. pr.second is true
auto iter = names.emplace_hint(pr.first, "Joe", "King");
```

It's the same as you've seen with a map. The emplace() member returns a pair<iterator,bool> object, and the emplace_hint() member returns just an iterator. The arguments to the former are passed directly to the constructor for the element to create it in place. The first argument to emplace_hint() is the iterator that is the hint for where the element might be located, and the subsequent arguments are passed to the element constructor.

The clear() function member deletes all elements from a set. The erase() member can delete an element from the position specified by an iterator or an element that matches an object. For example:

```
std::set<int> numbers {2, 4, 6, 8, 10, 12, 14};
auto iter = numbers.erase(++std::begin(numbers));
                                    // Removes the 2nd element - 4. iter points to 6
auto n = numbers.erase(12);                    // Returns no. of elements removed - 1
n = numbers.erase(13);                         // Returns no. of elements removed - 0
numbers.clear();                               // Removes all elements
```

The erase() member can also delete a range of elements:

```
std::set<int> numbers {2, 4, 6, 8, 10, 12, 14};
auto iter1 = std::begin(numbers);                        // iter1 points to 1st element
advance(iter1, 5);                                       // Points to 6th element - 12
auto iter = numbers.erase(++std::begin(numbers), iter1);
                                     // Remove 2nd to 5th inclusive. iter points to 12
```

The empty() member returns true if a set contains no elements, and the size() member returns the number of elements it contains. If you are worried about not be able to store as many objects as you like in a set, you can call the max_size() member that returns the maximum possible number of elements, which is typically a lot.

Accessing Elements

The find() member of a set container returns an iterator that points to the element that matches the argument when it's present; if the object is not in the set, the end iterator is returned. For example:

```
std::set<string> words {"one", "two", "three", "four", "five"};
auto iter = words.find("one");                  // iter points to "one"
iter = words.find(string{"two"});               // iter points to "two"
iter = words.find("six");                       // iter is std::end(words)
```

Calling the count() member of a set returns the number of elements with a given key, which can only be 0 or 1 since elements must be unique in a set container. The set container template also defines the equal_range(), lower_bound(), and upper_bound() members, largely for consistency with a multiset container where they are more useful.

Working with sets

It's time to see set containers in action. We can put together an example that will combine using vector, set, and map containers and introduce another useful algorithm. The example will distribute a group of students across a number of course subjects. Each student will have to study a specified minimum number of subjects. The students for a particular subject can be stored in a set container since a student cannot appear more than once in a given course. The example won't be very efficient. There will be a lot of copying of students that won't matter in the example but would matter if the object that represent students were very large, and there were a great many of them. You'll learn how you could eliminate the copying of objects later in this chapter. The basic concepts of how the example will work are illustrated in Figure 5-3.

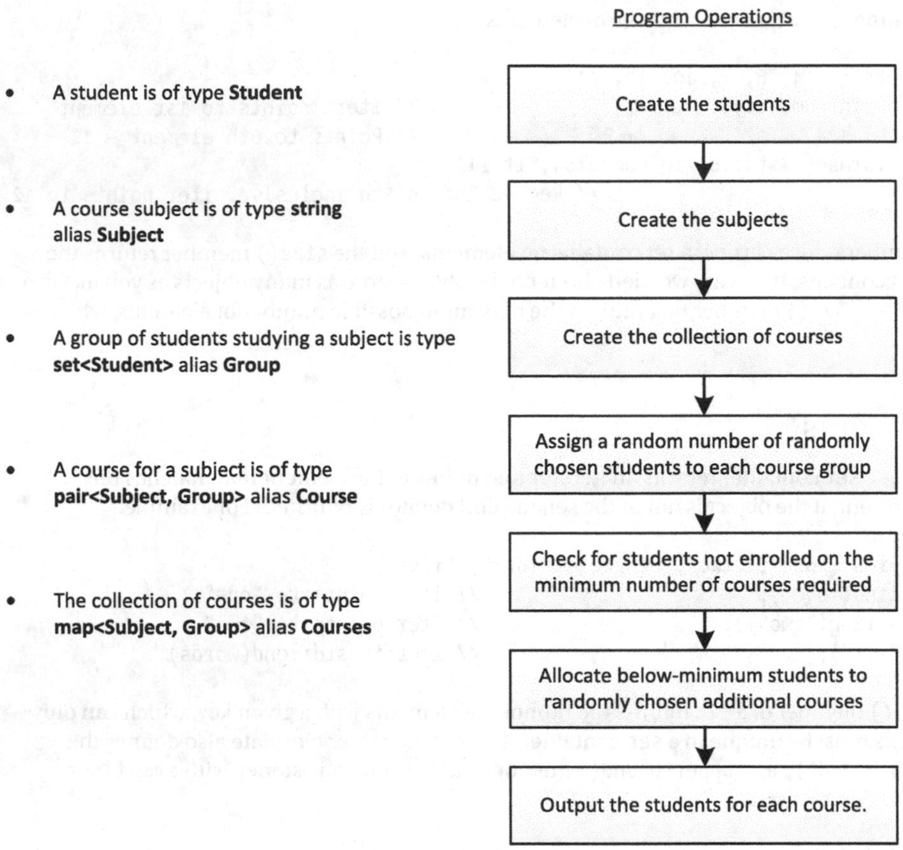

Program Operations

- A student is of type **Student**

  | Create the students |

- A course subject is of type **string** alias **Subject**

  | Create the subjects |

- A group of students studying a subject is type **set<Student>** alias **Group**

  | Create the collection of courses |

  | Assign a random number of randomly chosen students to each course group |

- A course for a subject is of type **pair<Subject, Group>** alias **Course**

  | Check for students not enrolled on the minimum number of courses required |

- The collection of courses is of type **map<Subject, Group>** alias **Courses**

  | Allocate below-minimum students to randomly chosen additional courses |

  | Output the students for each course. |

Figure 5-3. *Operations in the example using set containers to represent course groups*

The using directives to define the type aliases in the example:

```
using std::string;
using Distribution = std::uniform_int_distribution<size_t>;
using Subject = string;                           // A course subject
using Subjects = std::vector<Subject>;            // A vector of subjects
using Group = std::set<Student> ;                 // A student group for a subject
using Students = std::vector<Student>;            // All the students
using Course = std::pair<Subject, Group>;         // A pair representing a course
using Courses = std::map<Subject, Group>;         // The container for courses
```

These aliases are not essential but they make the code less cluttered. The Distribution alias is for a type that you met in Chapter 4. This type defines a normal statistical distribution and will be used for generating random numbers.

First we can define a class that represents a student. Students are simple souls, so we can define the class in a Student.h header in a simple way, like this:

```cpp
#ifndef STUDENT_H
#define STUDENT_H
#include <string>                                          // For string class
#include <ostream>                                         // For output streams

class Student
{
private:
  std::string first {};
  std::string second {};

public:
  Student(const std::string& name1, const std::string& name2) : first (name1), second (name2){}

  // Move constructor
  Student(Student&& student) : first(std::move(student.first)),
                               second(std::move(student.second)){}

  Student(const Student& student) :
                    first(student.first), second(student.second){}    // Copy constructor
  Student() {}                                                        // Default constructor

  // Less-than operator
  bool operator<(const Student& student) const
  {
    return second < student.second || (second == student.second && first < student.first);
  }

  friend std::ostream& operator<<(std::ostream& out, const Student& student);
};

// Insertion operator overload
inline std::ostream& operator<<(std::ostream& out, const Student& student)
{
  out << student.first + " " + student.second;
  return out;
}
#endif
```

There are just two data members that store a student's first and second names. Student objects will be stored initially in a vector container so the default constructor is defined. There's a copy constructor and a move constructor, the latter to avoid copying objects when this is appropriate. The less-than operator is defined because students will be stored in set containers representing courses on different subjects. There's also a friend function that overloads the stream insertion operator to help with output.

Creating the Students

The program will need a reasonable number of students to work with so to avoid having to enter them laboriously from the keyboard, we will synthesize a vector of Student objects by creating all combinations of first and second names:

```
Students create_students()
{
  Students students;
  string first_names[] {"Ann", "Jim", "Eve", "Dan", "Ted"};
  string second_names[] {"Smith", "Jones", "Howe", "Watt", "Beck"};

  for(const auto& first : first_names)
  {
    for(const auto& second : second_names)
    {
      students.emplace_back(first, second);
    }
  }
  return students;
}
```

There's a using directive that defines Students as an alias for a vector of Student objects. The function creates Student objects in place in the local students container using all possible combinations of names from the two arrays. The outer loop iterates over first names, and the inner loop appends each second name to a given first name. Thus we will end up with twenty-five different students. We can call the function to create the students like this:

```
Students students = create_students();
```

A vector container has a move constructor so the compiler will arrange to move the local students object that is returned, rather than copying it. The statement above will call the move assignment operator for vector<Student> to move the value returned by create_students() so no copying of the vector or its elements will occur. The type for students is explicit here, but you could use auto to have the compiler deduce it from the return type for create_students().

Creating a set of Students for a Subject

The example will select students at random and pick courses for them at random so a random number engine will be needed. To make it available throughout the program we can create it at global scope:

```
static std::default_random_engine gen_value;
```

The default_random_engine type is defined in the random header, along with the uniform_int_distribution type. A distribution object is a function object, and to generate a random number with that distribution, you pass a random engine object to the operator()() member of the distribution object. We can make use of this in a function that will create a group of random students for a given subject:

```
Group make_group(const Students& students, size_t group_size,
                                           const Distribution& choose_student)
{
  Group group;                                    // The group of students for a subject
```

```
// Select students for the subject group

// Insert a random student into the group until there are group_size students in it
while(group.size() < group_size)
{
  group.insert(students[choose_student(gen_value)]);
}
return group;
}
```

The first parameter is the vector of Student objects, the second is the number of students that are required in the group, and the last parameter is the distribution of index values that is to be used to select students at random. group is a set container of Student objects. The function inserts randomly selected students from the vector passed as the first argument into the local set container, group, by calling its insert() member. There's no need to check whether an insertion is successful. The insert() member will not insert a new object if it already exists in the container. Random choices from the students container may select a student that has already been stored in the group container, but the loop will just continue with the next iteration to try another random choice until group_size students have been added. When the function ends, the local group object that is returned will be moved rather than copied, as in the previous function.

Creating the Subjects and the Courses

The course subjects will be defined like this:

```
Subjects subjects {"Biology", "Physics",  "Chemistry",  "Mathematics", "Astronomy",
                  "Drama",   "Politics", "Philosophy", "Economics"};
```

Subjects is an alias for vector<Subject> and Subject is an alias for type string so subjects is a vector of string objects. We will be storing courses in a map<Subject,Group> container so the key for each course will be a unique Subject object from the subjects container. The map<Subject,Group> type has the alias Courses defined so we can define the container for all the courses like this:

```
Courses courses;                                    // All the courses with subject keys
```

The minimum number of subjects each student is required to study needs to be defined. We'll also put some initial constraints on the group size for a subject when we generate the set of students studying the subject:

```
size_t min_subjects {4};                           // Minimum number of Subjects per student
size_t min_group {min_subjects};                   // Minimum no. of students per course
size_t max_group {(students.size()*min_subjects)/subjects.size()};
                                                   // Max initial students per course
```

I chose an arbitrary value of 4 for the minimum number of subjects to be studied and I made the minimum student count in a group the same. The maximum size of a subject group is also set arbitrarily to be the average number in a group if all students studied the minimum number of subjects and the students were distributed equally among the groups. You can play with these parameters to see how they affect the allocation of students to subject groups.

We will need function objects that define distributions for choosing a random value for the number of students allocated to a subject group, and for selecting students at random:

```
Distribution group_size {min_group, max_group};        // Distribution for students per course
Distribution choose_student {0, students.size() - 1}; // Random student selector
```

The group_size object will generate numbers from min_group to max_group inclusive. Similarly, the choose_student distribution will generate valid index values for selecting from the vector of students.

We will want to select courses at random for a student to attend so we will need a Distribution object for that too:

```
Distribution choose_course {0, subjects.size() - 1};  // Random course selector
```

This will generate random index values to select courses from the subjects container.

Enrolling Students on Courses

The code in main() to populate the courses container with elements representing the courses will be just a for loop with a single statement as the loop body:

```
for(const auto& subject : subjects)
    courses.emplace(subject, make_group(students, group_size(gen_value), choose_student));
```

Admittedly, the statement that is the loop body does quite a lot. Calling emplace() for the courses container creates an element in place. Each element must be a pair<Subject, Group> object so the arguments to emplace() must be a Subject object and a Group object that the emplace() function will pass to the pair constructor. The first argument is provided by the loop variable, subject, because the loop iterates over all the subjects. The second argument is the Group object that is returned by the make_group() function you saw earlier. The first argument to make_group() is the vector of students; the second is a random value for the size of the group that is produced by passing the gen_value engine to the group_size function object; the third argument is the distribution to be used for selecting a student.

Checking the Students' Courses

When the loop above has created all the courses, we must check to see whether any students have not fulfilled their obligation to enroll in a minimum number of courses. The following loop will do that, and sign them up for additional courses if they have failed in their duty:

```
for(const auto& student : students)
{ // Verify the minimum number of Subjects has been met

  // Count how many Subjects the student is on
  size_t course_count = std::count_if(std::begin(courses), std::end(courses),
        [&student](const Course& course) { return course.second.count(student); });
  if(course_count >= min_subjects) continue;         // On to the next student
```

```
// Minimum no. of Subjects not signed up for
size_t additional {min_subjects - course_count};        // Additional no. of Subjects needed
if(!course_count)                                        // If none have been chosen...
  std::cout << student << " is work-shy, having signed up for NO Subjects!\n";
else                                                    // Some have - but E for effort
  std::cout << student << " is only signed up for " << course_count << " Subjects!\n";

std::cout << "Registering " << student << " for " << additional
          << " more course" << (additional > 1 ? "s" : "") << ".\n\n";

// Register for additional Subjects up to the minimum
while(course_count < min_subjects)
  if((courses.find(subjects[choose_course(gen_value)])->second.insert(student)).second)
    ++course_count;
}
```

The outer loop iterates over the Student objects in the vector. The count_if() algorithm is used to determine the number of courses each student has enrolled in. This algorithm counts the number of elements in the range specified by the first two arguments for which the function passed as the third argument returns true. The first two argument here specify the range of elements in the courses container, so the iterators point to pair<Subject,Group> objects. The third argument to count_if() must be a unary function that returns a bool value, or a value that can be implicitly converted to type bool. The parameter must be of the type that results from dereferencing the iterators in the range. Here it's a lambda expression that returns the value of the expression course.second.count(student). course is an object of type pair<Subject,Group> so the expression first selects the second member of the course object. The second member is a Group object, which is type set<Student>, so the expression calls the count() member of the set container that holds the students. Since duplicate elements are not permitted in a set container, the count() member can only return 1 if student is present, and 0 if it is not. Luckily, these values are implicitly convertible to true and false respectively so count_if() will increase the count whenever student is in the current course.

We output a suitable message for any student not signing up for the required number of subjects and execute the nested while loop that registers the student for new courses until the minimum requirement is met. This is another loop with a single statement body that does a lot of work. Essentially, this statement is an if statement that increments course_count each time the current student succeeds in signing on to a course. A course is selected from the courses container by calling its find() member that returns an iterator that points to the element that corresponds to the key that is the argument, or the end iterator if the key is not found. We created courses using all possible Subject keys so the latter situation should not arise – if it does, we'll know because the program will crash. A new course is selected using a random key from subjects using an index value produced by the choose_course distribution. The second member of the pair element that find() returns is the Group containing the students on the course, so calling its insert() member with the student argument will add the student to the group if they are not already in the set. It's always possible that the student is already on the chosen course, in which case the second member of the pair object that insert() returns will be false, and in this case course_count will not be incremented and the loop will continue to try another course selected at random. The loop ends when the number of courses for the current student reached the minimum, min_subjects.

Outputting the Courses

To allow the use of another STL algorithm for outputting the courses, we will define the following function object type in a `List_Course.h` header file:

```cpp
// List_Course.h
// Function object to output the students in a group for Ex5_01
#ifndef LIST_COURSE_H
#define LIST_COURSE_H
#include <iostream>                        // For standard streams
#include <string>                          // For string class
#include <set>                             // For set container
#include <algorithm>                       // For copy()
#include <iterator>                        // For ostream_iterator
#include "Student.h"

using Subject = std::string;              // A course subject
using Group = std::set<Student>;          // A student group for a subject
using Course = std::pair<Subject, Group>; // A pair representing a course

class List_Course
{
public:
  void operator()(const Course& course)
  {
    std::cout << "\n\n" << course.first << "  " << course.second.size() << " students:\n  ";
    std::copy(std::begin(course.second), std::end(course.second),
            std::ostream_iterator<Student>(std::cout, "  "));
  }
};
#endif
```

The parameter for the `operator()()` member of the `List_Course` class is a reference to a Course object, which is type `pair<string,set<Student>>`. The function outputs the course subject, which of course is the `first` member of `course`, and the number of students for this course, which is obtained by calling the `size()` member for the `second` member of the `pair`. The students in the course are listed by the `copy()` algorithm. The first two arguments are the begin and end iterators for the `set<Student>` container that is identified by the `second` member of `course`, of course. The range of Student objects are copied to the destination specified by the third argument to `copy()`, which is an `ostream_iterator<Student>` object. This object will call the `operator<<()` member of each Student object in the range to output the student to cout, followed by a couple of spaces.

We can use an instance of `List_Course` in `main()` to output all the courses in a single statement, like this:

```cpp
std::for_each(std::begin(courses), std::end(courses), List_Course());
```

The `for_each()` algorithm applies the function object specified by the third argument to each of the elements in the range that is specified by the first two arguments. The first two arguments define the range that corresponds to all the courses, so `List_Courses()()` will be called with successive courses as the argument. The result will be that all the students in each course will be written to cout.

Of course, it's not essential to define the List_Course function object type. You could use a lambda expression as the third argument to the for_each() algorithm instead:

```
std::for_each(std::begin(courses), std::end(courses),
[](const Course& course){
std::cout << "\n\n" << course.first << "   " << course.second.size() << " students:\n   ";
std::copy(std::begin(course.second), std::end(course.second),
                               std::ostream_iterator<Student>(std::cout, "  "));
});
```

I defined the List_Course type for this example just to show how, but unless the function object is needed more than once in a program, it's simpler and easier to use a lambda expression.

The Complete Program

The contents of the source file containing main() will be:

```
// Ex5_01.cpp
// Registering students on Subjects
#include <iostream>                          // For standard streams
#include <string>                            // For string class
#include <map>                               // For map container
#include <set>                               // For set container
#include <vector>                            // For vector container
#include <random>                            // For random number generation
#include <algorithm>                         // For for_each(), count_if()
#include "Student.h"
#include "List_Course.h"

using std::string;
using Distribution = std::uniform_int_distribution<size_t>;
using Subject = string;                      // A course subject
using Subjects = std::vector<Subject>;       // A vector of subjects
using Group = std::set<Student>;             // A student group for a subject
using Students = std::vector<Student>;       // All the students
using Course = std::pair<Subject, Group>;    // A pair representing a course
using Courses = std::map<Subject, Group>;    // The container for courses

static std::default_random_engine gen_value;

// create_students() helper function definition goes here...

// make_group () helper function definition goes here...

int main()
{
  Students students = create_students();
  Subjects subjects {"Biology", "Physics", "Chemistry", "Mathematics", "Astronomy",
                     "Drama", "Politics", "Philosophy", "Economics"};
  Courses courses;                                    // All the courses with subject keys
```

```cpp
  size_t min_subjects {4};                             // Minimum number of Subjects per student
  size_t min_group {min_subjects};                     // Minimum no. of students per course

  // Maximum initial students  per course
  size_t max_group {(students.size()*min_subjects)/subjects.size()};

  // Create groups of students for each subject
  Distribution group_size {min_group, max_group};      // Distribution for students per course
  Distribution choose_student {0, students.size() - 1}; // Random student selector
  for(const auto& subject : subjects)
    courses.emplace(subject, make_group(students, group_size(gen_value), choose_student));

  Distribution choose_course {0, subjects.size() - 1};  // Random course selector

  // Every student must attend a minimum number of Subjects...
  // ...but students being students we must check...
  for(const auto& student : students)
  { // Verify the minimum number of Subjects has been met

    // Count how many Subjects the student is on
    size_t course_count = std::count_if(std::begin(courses), std::end(courses),
                          [&student](const Course& course)
                                      {  return course.second.count(student); });
    if(course_count >= min_subjects) continue;         // On to the next student

    // Minimum no. of Subjects not signed up for
    size_t additional {min_subjects - course_count};   // Additional no. of Subjects needed
    if(!course_count)                                  // If none have been chosen...
      std::cout << student << " is work-shy, having signed up for NO Subjects!\n";
    else                                               // Some have - but E for effort
      std::cout << student << "  is only signed up for " << course_count << " Subjects!\n";

    std::cout << "Registering " << student << " for " << additional
              << " more course" << (additional > 1 ? "s" : "") << ".\n\n";

    // Register for additional Subjects up to the minimum
    while(course_count < min_subjects)
      if((courses.find(subjects[choose_course(gen_value)])->second.insert(student)).second)
      ++course_count;
  }

  // Output the students attending each course
  std::for_each(std::begin(courses), std::end(courses), List_Course());
  std::cout << std::endl;
}
```

I won't list all the output in the book because it's quite voluminous, but here are some segments of the output that I got:

```
Ann Smith is only signed up for 1 Subjects!
Registering Ann Smith for 3 more courses.

Ann Watt is only signed up for 2 Subjects!
Registering Ann Watt for 2 more courses.

Ann Beck is only signed up for 3 Subjects!
Registering Ann Beck for 1 more course.

Jim Smith is work-shy, having signed up for NO Subjects!
Registering Jim Smith for 4 more courses.
...
Ted Beck is work-shy, having signed up for NO Subjects!
Registering Ted Beck for 4 more courses.

Astronomy  9 students:
  Dan Beck  Ted Beck  Eve Howe  Ann Jones  Dan Jones  Eve Jones  Ted Smith  Ann Watt  Dan Watt

Biology  14 students:
  Ann Beck  Dan Beck  Jim Beck  Ann Howe  Dan Howe  Jim Howe  Dan Jones  Ted Jones  Dan
Smith  Eve Smith
  Ann Watt  Eve Watt  Jim Watt  Ted Watt

Chemistry  10 students:
  Eve Beck  Dan Howe  Ann Jones  Eve Jones  Ted Jones  Dan Smith  Jim Smith  Ann Watt  Dan
Watt  Jim Watt
...
Physics  15 students:
  Ann Beck  Dan Beck  Eve Beck  Jim Beck  Eve Howe  Ted Howe  Ann Jones  Jim Jones  Ann
Smith  Eve Smith
  Ted Smith  Dan Watt  Eve Watt  Jim Watt  Ted Watt

Politics  12 students:
  Eve Beck  Jim Howe  Ted Howe  Dan Jones  Eve Jones  Jim Jones  Ann Smith  Dan Smith  Eve
Smith  Jim Smith
  Dan Watt  Ted Watt
```

Set Iterators

The iterators that members of a set<T> container can return are bidirectional iterators. The types of these iterators are defined by alias definitions within the set<T> template. The aliases for the types of iterators you can get from a set are iterator, reverse_iterator, const_iterator, and const_reverse_iterator, where the names indicate what they are. For example, the begin() and end() members return iterators of type iterator. A set container also has rbegin() and rend() members that return iterators of type reverse_iterator and cbegin() and cend() members that return iterators of type const_iterator. Lastly, the crbegin() and crend() members return iterators of type const_reverse_iterator.

However, the alias names for iterator types for a set container are somewhat misleading. *All* iterators returned by function members of a set<T> container point to a const T element. Thus an iterator iterator points to a const element, as does a reverse_iterator iterator as well as the other types. This means that you *cannot modify* an element. If you want to change an element in a set container, you must first delete it and then insert the modified version.

If you think about it, this is not unreasonable. The objects in a set are their own keys, and the locations of objects in the container are determined by comparing them. If you were to modify an element, you could invalidate the order of the elements, thus disrupting subsequent access operations. When you *must* be able to modify objects, and still group them in one or more set containers, there's still a way to do it. You store pointers to the objects in a set container – preferably smart pointers. When you are using set containers, you'll typically store shared_ptr<T> or weak_ptr<T> objects. Storing unique_ptr<T> objects in a set container doesn't make much sense. You could never retrieve an element directly since an independent key to match a unique_ptr<T> object in the container cannot exist.

Storing Pointers in a set Container

If the changes you want to make to objects could potentially alter the order of pointers to those objects that you have stored in a set, the comparison function for the pointers *must not depend on the objects*. Most of the time, you won't care about the specific order of elements in a set, only whether or not a given element is in the container. In this case you can use a comparison function object that applies to the pointers without considering the objects to which they point. The recommended option for comparing smart pointers in a container is to use an instance of the owner_less<T> function object type that is defined in the memory header.

The owner_less<T> template defines function object types for a less-than comparison for shared_ptr and/or weak_ptr objects; in other words it allows weak_ptr objects to be compared with shared_ptr objects and vice versa, as well as allowing two weak_ptr or shared_ptr objects to be compared. An owner_less<T> instance implements a comparison by calling an owner_before() function member of the smart pointer to T, which provide a less-than comparison with another smart pointer. Both the shared_ptr<T> and weak_ptr<T> templates define this member function. An owner_before<T>() instance returns true when this smart pointer is less-than the smart pointer that is the argument, or false otherwise. The comparison is based on the addresses of the objects that are *owned* by the pointers and allows equivalence to be determined when two pointers point to same object.

The prototypes for the function templates that define owner_before() instances in the shared_ptr<T> class template look like this:

- `template<typename X> bool owner_before(const std::shared_ptr<X>& other) const;`

- `template<typename X> bool owner_before(const std::weak_ptr<X>& other) const;`

The weak_ptr<T> class template defines the members similarly. Note that the template type parameter is not the same as the type parameter for the class template. This means that as well as comparing pointers to the same type of object, you can compare pointers that point to different types of object; in other words, a shared_ptr<T1> object can be compared to a shared_ptr<T2> object or a weak_ptr<T2> object. This implies that what a pointer *points to* can be different from what it *owns*.

The ownership aspect can be important with shared_ptr<T> objects. This topic is a little advanced for this book, but let's live dangerously. A shared_ptr<T> can share the ownership of one object but *point to* a different object that it does not own; in other words, the address the shared pointer contains is not the address of the object it owns. One use for this kind of shared_ptr is to point to a member of the object that it owns. This is illustrated in Figure 5-4.

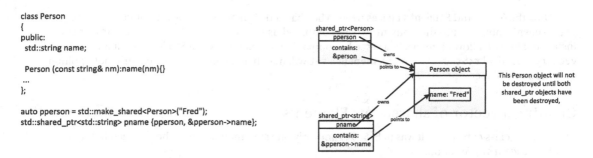

```
class Person
{
public:
  std::string name;

  Person (const string& nm):name(nm){}
  ...
};

auto pperson = std::make_shared<Person>("Fred");
std::shared_ptr<std::string> pname {pperson, &pperson->name};
```

Figure 5-4. *A shared pointer that points to a different object from the object it owns*

The constructor that is used to create pname in Figure 5-4 is called an *alias constructor*. The first argument is another shared_ptr object that owns the object that pname will also own. The second argument is a raw pointer and this pointer will be stored in pname. The object *pointed to* by the second argument is not owned or managed by pname. However, pname can be used to access this object, which happens to be a data member of the Person object. The object the pname *owns* in this example is the Person object. It *points to* a member of that object.

Destroying the pperson pointer in Figure 5-4 will not result in the Person object that it owns being destroyed because it is still owned by the pname pointer. The pointer pname has been created to provide access to the name member of the Person object. *pperson refers to the Person object because pperson contains the address of the object it has shared ownership of. *pname refers to the name member of the Person object because pname contains the address of that member, and it also has shared ownership of the Person object. This enables you to continue to use pname even though there are no shared_ptr<Person> pointers that contain the address of the Person object still around. The Person object will only be destroyed when all the shared_ptr objects that share ownership of it have been destroyed. Without the capability provided by the alias constructor, there would be no guarantee of the validity of the pointer stored in pname.

An Example Storing Smart Pointers in a set Container

To show how storing smart pointers in a set container might work, I'll reconstruct Ex5_01 as Ex5_02. The elements in the students vector and those in the set containers that represent groups of students for the various subjects will be smart pointers. I could use shared_ptr<Student> objects in the set containers, but I'll only use shared_ptr<Student> elements for the vector of students and use weak_ptr<Student> objects in the set containers to show you what that involves. Note that when you store weak_ptr<T> objects, you need to be sure that the shared_ptr<T> objects on which they depend continue to exist as long as you are making use of the weak_ptr<T> objects. Of course, you can always detect whether the shared_ptr<T> object associated with a weak_ptr<T> still exists by calling the expired() member of the weak_ptr<T> object; this returns true when the shared_ptr<T> object has been deleted.

The first thing I must do is to redefine the type aliases used in Ex5_02.cpp to accommodate smart pointers:

```
using std::string;
using Distribution = std::uniform_int_distribution<size_t>;
using Subject = string; ·                                      // A course subject
using Subjects = std::vector<Subject>;                         // A vector of subjects
using Group =                                                  // Group for a subject
  std::set<std::weak_ptr<Student>, std::owner_less<std::weak_ptr<Student>>>;
using Students = std::vector<std::shared_ptr<Student>>;        // All the students
using Course = std::pair<Subject, Group>;                      // Represents a course
using Courses = std::map<Subject, Group>;                      // The courses
```

217

Only the Group and Students aliases need to be changed. A Group is now a set containing weak_ptr<Student> objects, and the elements will be compared using an owner_less<weak_ptr<Student>> instance. This will allow elements in a set to be compared with elements in a Students container of type vector<shared_ptr<Student>>. An element in a set will match an element in the vector if both pointers own the same object.

Creating a vector of shared_ptr Elements

The Student class can stay as it was in Ex5_01, and only one statement needs to be changed in the create_students() function:

```
Students create_students()
{
  Students students;
  string first_names[] {"Ann", "Jim", "Eve", "Dan", "Ted"};
  string second_names[] {"Smith", "Jones", "Howe", "Watt", "Beck"};

  for(const auto& first : first_names)
    for(const auto& second : second_names)
    {
      students.emplace_back(std::make_shared<Student>(first, second));
    }

  return students;
}
```

Now the argument to emplace_back() is a shared_ptr<Student> object that is returned by make_shared<Student>(). Because it is temporary, this pointer will be forwarded by emplace_back() to the shared_ptr<Student> move constructor to create the element in place in the vector.

Amazingly, the make_group() function doesn't need to be changed at all. All the changes necessary are taken care of by the type aliases.

Outputting Objects Referenced by weak_ptr

The List_Course function object type does need changing though:

```
using Subject = std::string;                            // A course subject
using Group =                                           // A group for a subject
    std::set<std::weak_ptr<Student>, std::owner_less<std::weak_ptr<Student>>>;
using Course = std::pair<Subject, Group>;               // A pair representing a course

class List_Course
{
public:
  void operator()(const Course& course)
  {
    std::cout << "\n\n" << course.first << "  " << course.second.size() << " students:\n  ";
    std::copy(std::begin(course.second), std::end(course.second),
            std::ostream_iterator<std::weak_ptr<Student>>(std::cout, "  "));
  }
};
```

```
inline std::ostream& operator<<(std::ostream& out, const std::weak_ptr<Student>& wss)
{
  out << *wss.lock();
  return out;
}
```

The change to the definition of the Group alias in Ex5_02.cpp has to be replicated in the header file. The first change is in the definition of the function call operator function. The ostream_iterator template type argument must be changed to be weak_ptr<Student>. This requires an overload of the insertion operator for weak_ptr<Student> objects. To write a Student object to the stream, the pointer needs to be dereferenced. You *can't* dereference a weak_ptr<T>; you must first obtain a shared_ptr<T> that owns the same object, and then dereference that. Calling lock() for the weak_ptr<Student> object returns a shared_ptr<Student> object that owns the object that the weak_ptr references, and that *can* be dereferenced. In the example, we are reasonable certain that the Student object will still exist, but in general this may not be the case. If the object referenced by a weak_ptr has been destroyed because all the owning shared_ptr objects have been destroyed, calling lock() for the weak_ptr will return a shared_ptr that contains nullptr. Where this might occur, you must check for nullptr to avoid a crash.

The type aliases have taken care of most of the changes needed in main(), but you also need to dereference the student variable to output it in the loop that iterates over the Student objects in the students container, thus:

```
if(!course_count)                                      // If none have been chosen...
  std::cout << *student << " is work-shy, having signed up for NO Subjects!\n";
else                                                   // Some have - but E for effort
  std::cout << *student << " is only signed up for " << course_count << " Subjects!\n";

  std::cout << "Registering " << *student << " for " << additional
            << " more course" << (additional > 1 ? "s" : "") << ".\n\n";
```

The complete program is in the code download in the Ex5_02 folder for Chapter 5. If you run this program, you should get similar output to Ex5_01.

Using Smart Pointers as Keys in a map Container

There's another aspect of Ex5_02 that could be changed – the keys in the map container for all the courses are copies of the string objects from the subjects vector currently. How would the code need to change if the keys were smart pointers?

The Subject alias would need to change, and for convenience I added a using declaration for std::make_shared. The definition of the Courses alias will also be different:

```
using std::make_shared;
using Subject = std::shared_ptr<string>;                        // A course subject
using Courses = std::map<Subject, Group, std::owner_less<Subject>>; // The container for courses
```

The keys are now shared_ptr<string> pointers so the function object type to be used to compare keys is now owner_less<shared_ptr<string>>. Obviously, the definition of the vector of subjects in main() is going to change, too:

```
Subjects subjects { make_shared<string>("Biology"),   make_shared<string>("Physics"),
                    make_shared<string>("Chemistry"), make_shared<string>("Mathematics"),
                    make_shared<string>("Astronomy"), make_shared<string>("Drama"),
                    make_shared<string>("Politics"),  make_shared<string>("Philosophy"),
                    make_shared<string>("Economics") };
```

The elements in the vector are now smart pointers.

The definition for the operator()() member of List_Course must take account of the fact that the key for a course in the map is now a pointer:

```
void operator()(const Course& course)
{
  std::cout << "\n\n" << *course.first << "  " << course.second.size() << " students:\n  ";
  std::copy(std::begin(course.second), std::end(course.second),
          std::ostream_iterator<std::weak_ptr<Student>>(std::cout, "  "));
}
```

The only change is the * to dereference the first member of course, which is the key. No more changes to main() are necessary – it works as it is and produces similar output to previous versions, but there's something that is subtly different. I can bring it to light by extending the functionality a little.

The Trouble with Comparing Smart Pointers

Suppose that instead of outputting all the courses at the end of main(), we provide the capability for entering a subject from the keyboard, then displaying the students that are studying that topic. First, we could provide a prompt for the course subjects, just to make sure the right course is entered:

```
std::cout << "Course subjects are:\n  ";
for(const auto& p : subjects)
  std::cout  << *p << "  ";
std::cout << "\n\n";
```

Now we can define a loop to read a subject from the keyboard and itemize the students on a given course:

```
 // Code that doesn't work!
char answer {'Y'};
string subject {};
while(std::toupper(answer) == 'Y')
{
  std::cout << "Enter a course subject to get the list of students: ";
  std::cin >> subject;
  auto iter = courses.find(make_shared<string>(subject));
  if(iter == std::end(courses))
    std::cout << subject << " not found!\n";
```

```
else
{
  List_Course()(*iter);
  std::cout << std::endl;
}
std::cout << "Do you want to see another subject(Y or N)? ";
std::cin >> answer;
}
```

Superficially this looks reasonable. We create a shared_ptr<string> object from the input and use that to search for the key. However, this code fails to find a single subject. The program can list all the courses but can't find a course for any subject that is entered. Why not?

The answer lies in the owner_less<T> comparison function object for the keys in the map that stores the courses. Two pointers match *only* when both *own the same object*; two pointers that point to identical objects is not the same thing at all and will *never* be equivalent. The only way to retrieve a course based on a subject is to access the original smart pointer to the subject, or a clone of it. Here's how the code can be modified to accommodate that:

```
char answer {'Y'};
string subject {};
while(std::toupper(answer) == 'Y')
{
  std::cout << "Enter a course subject to get the list of students: ";
  std::cin >> subject;
  auto iter = std::find_if(std::begin(subjects),
                           std::end(subjects),  // Find the pointer in subjects
                                [&subject](const Subject& psubj){ return subject == *psubj; });
  if(iter == std::end(subjects))
    std::cout << subject << " not found!\n";
  else
  {
    List_Course()(*courses.find(*iter));
    std::cout << std::endl;
  }
  std::cout << "Do you want to see another subject(Y or N)? ";
  std::cin >> answer;
}
```

The find_if() algorithm returns an iterator that points to the first element in the range specified by the first two arguments for which the function object that is the last argument returns true. If there are none, the last iterator you specify for the range is returned. Here the range includes all the elements in the subjects vector, and the last argument is a lambda expression that returns true when the result of dereferencing an element in the range matches subject. If the iterator is not the end iterator for subjects, it points to a shared_ptr<Subject> in the vector. Dereferencing the iterator accesses the element in subjects and this is passed to the find() member of the courses container. This returns an iterator that points to the Course object with that key so the Course object that results from dereferencing the iterator that find() returns is passed to the function call operator for a List_Course instance to output the students on the course. This version of the program is in the code download as Ex5_03.

Using multiset<T> Containers

A multiset<T> container is just like a set<T>, but you can store duplicate elements. This means you can always insert an element – as long as it's an acceptable type of course. Elements are compared using less<T> by default, but you can specify a different comparator that must not return true for equality. For example:

```
std::multiset<string, std::greater<string>> words{ {"dog", "cat", "mouse"},
                                                    std::greater<string>()};
```

This statement defines a multiset of string elements that are compared using a greater<string> instance that is the second argument to the constructor. The container has three initial elements that are specified by the initializer list that is the first constructor argument. Just as with a set, two elements match if they are equivalent – in a multiset with a comparison operator comp, elements a and b are equivalent if the expression !(a comp b)&&!(b comp a) evaluates to true. A multiset container has the same function members as a set, but some of them behave differently as a consequence of the potential for duplicate elements. The function members that operate a little differently from those in a set container are:

- insert() always succeeds. When a single element is inserted, the iterator that is returned points to the elements that was inserted. When you insert a range of elements, the iterator points to the last element that was inserted.

- emplace() and emplace_hint() always succeed and both return an iterator that points to the new element.

- find() returns an iterator that points to the first element that matched the argument, or the end iterator for the container if there are none that match.

- equal_range() returns a pair object containing iterators that define the range of elements that match the argument. If there are no elements matching the argument, the first member of the pair will be the end iterator for the container; the second member in this case will be the first element that is greater than the argument, or the end iterator for the container if there are none.

- lower_bound() returns an iterator that points to the first member that matches the argument, or the end iterator for the container if there are none. The iterator is the same as the first member of the pair that equal_range() returns.

- upper_bound() returns the same iterator as the second member of the pair that equal_range() returns.

- count() returns the number of elements that match the argument.

We could implement word frequency analysis in text that you saw in the example Ex4_02 using a multiset container instead of a map:

```cpp
// Ex5_04.cpp
// Determining word frequency
#include <iostream>              // For standard streams
#include <iomanip>               // For stream manipulators
#include <string>                // For string class
#include <sstream>               // For istringstream
#include <algorithm>             // For replace_if() & for_each()
#include <set>                   // For set container
#include <iterator>              // For advance()
#include <cctype>                // For isalpha()
```

```cpp
using std::string;

int main()
{
  std::cout << "Enter some text and enter * to end:\n";
  string text_in {};
  std::getline(std::cin, text_in, '*');

  // Replace non-alphabetic characters by a space
  std::replace_if(std::begin(text_in), std::end(text_in),
                                  [](const char& ch){ return !isalpha(ch); }, ' ');

  std::istringstream text(text_in);            // Text input string as a stream
  std::istream_iterator<string> begin(text);   // Stream iterator
  std::istream_iterator<string> end;           // End stream iterator

  std::multiset<string> words;                 // Container to store words
  size_t max_len {};                           // Maximum word length

  // Get the words, store in the container, and find maximum length
  std::for_each(begin, end, [&max_len, &words](const string& word)
                      {  words.emplace(word);
                         max_len = std::max(max_len, word.length());
                      });

  size_t per_line {4},                         // Outputs per line
         count {};                             // No. of words output

  for(auto iter = std::begin(words); iter != std::end(words);
  iter = words.upper_bound(*iter))
  {
    std::cout << std::left << std::setw(max_len + 1) << *iter
              << std::setw(3) << std::right << words.count(*iter) << "  ";
    if(++count % per_line == 0)  std::cout << std::endl;
  }
  std::cout << std::endl;
}
```

The input process and removing non-alphabetic characters from the input is the same as in Ex4_02. Words are extracted from the text in the istringstream object by the for_each() function and passed to the lambda expression that is the last argument to for_each(), which creates the elements in place in the multiset container. Every word from the text will be stored as a separate element so typically there will be duplicates in the container. The for loop iterates over the iterators for the multiset container, words, starting with the begin iterator that points to the first element. The elements are ordered in the container so all equivalent elements will be in successive locations. The number of identical elements is obtained by calling the count() member of the container with the element to which iter points as the argument. At the end of each loop iteration, iter is set to the iterator returned by upper_bound(), which will be the iterator for the element that is different from the current element. If there are none, upper_bound() will return the end iterator for the container, so the loop will end.

Because the elements are ordered in a `multiset`, you could use the identical word count to increment the iterator in the for loop, like this:

```
size_t word_count {};                           // Number of identical words
for(auto iter = std::begin(words); iter != std::end(words);)
{
  word_count = words.count(*iter);
  std::cout << std::left << std::setw(max_len + 1) << *iter
            << std::setw(3) << std::right << word_count << "   ";
  if(++count % per_line == 0)  std::cout << std::endl;
  std::advance(iter, word_count);
}
```

This works but the original loop is better. How the loop ends is less obvious is this version. The Ex4_02 solution is more elegant than the `multiset` version in my view. Here's an example of some output:

```
Enter some text and enter * to end:
He was saying godnight to his horse.
He was saying goodnight to his horse,
And as he was saying goodnight to his horse, he was saying goodnight to his horse.
"Goodnight horse, goodnight horse", he was saying goodnight to his horse.*
And       1  Goodnight  1  He    2  as    1
godnight  1  goodnight  5  he    3  his   5
horse     7  saying     5  to    5  was   5
```

Storing Pointers to Derived Class Objects

You may want to store pointers to derived class objects in a `set` or `multiset` container, and you can do this by specifying the element type as a pointer to a base class type. The main thing to worry about is the comparison function – it must be able to compare base class pointers that point to objects of different derived class types. You can usually arrange for this without difficulty, and how you do it depends on whether you have any special requirements for the order of the elements. If you don't care about the way the elements are sequenced, you can use an `owner_less<T>` instance, but remember that retrieving an element requires that you use a pointer to the *same* object, *not* an equivalent object. Let's consider an example. I'll use a `multiset` even though there won't be duplicate elements stored. However, there will be elements of different types.

Suppose that we want to store pets owned by a person in a container, where the type of pet is defined by a class type that is derived from a base class Pet. This class will be defined in the Pet_Classes.h header in the code download like this:

```
ussing std::string;

class Pet
{
protected:
  string name {};

public:
  virtual ~Pet(){}                              // Virtual destructor for base class
  const string& get_name() const { return name;  }
```

```
   virtual bool operator<(const Pet& pet) const
   {
     auto result = std::strcmp(typeid(*this).name(), typeid(pet).name());
     return (result < 0) || ((result == 0) && (name < pet.name));
   }
   friend std::ostream& operator<<(std::ostream& out, const Pet& pet);
};
```

There are some points to note about the definition of the operator<() member of the Pet class. It's specified as virtual to get polymorphic behavior with derived class objects. It uses the typeid operator, which produces a type_info object that encapsulates the type of its operand. Using typeid requires the typeinfo header to be included. Calling the name() member of the type_info object returns a C-style string, which will be an implementation-defined representation of the type name. On my system class type names are prefixed with "class " so the name() member returns "class My_Type" for an object of type My_Type. It may be different on your system.

The type name strings are compared using strcmp() that is defined in the cstring header. This function returns a negative integer if the first argument is less than the second, 0 if the arguments are equal, or a positive integer otherwise. The operator<() function returns the result of two expressions ORed together. The function will always return true if the first expression is true. This will be when the type name for the current object is less than the type name for the object that is the argument. Thus objects are ordered primarily by type. When the first expression is false, the result of the comparison will be the result of the second expression. This will only return true when the type name strings are equal, AND the name member of the left operand of the comparison is less than the name member of the right operand.

The comparison for equal type names in the return expression is *very* important. The comparison you specify for a set container (or a map) must impose a *strict weak ordering*. Among other conditions, this requires that if a < b is true, then b < a must be false. Without comparing the type names for equality, this condition would not be met by the expression for the return value. This can cause the program to crash when storing derived class objects in a container. It's easy to see how this can arise. Suppose you compare a Cat object, cat, which has the name "Tiddles" with a Dog object, dog, named "Rover." The expression cat < dog is true because of the type names. The expression dog < cat is also true because of the pet names! Two objects where simultaneously either is less than the other is definitely going to be a problem...

Of course instead of using strcmp(), you could convert the null-terminated strings that the name() member of type_info returns to type string, then use the < operator to compare them.

The insertion operator for an output stream will be defined in the Pet_Classes.h header, like this:

```
inline std::ostream& operator<<(std::ostream& out, const Pet& pet)
{
  return out << "A " <<
    string {typeid(pet).name()}.erase(0,6) << " called " << pet.name;
}
```

This writes the type name and the pet name to the output stream. The expression for the type name string first converts the C-style string to type string, then removes the first six characters, "class," from the front of the string. You'll need to modify this if your system uses a different type name representation.

To keep things simple, I'll just define three classes derived from Pet: Cat, Dog, and Mouse. Apart from the types, their definitions will be essentially the same. Here's the Dog class as an example:

```
class Dog : public Pet
{
public:
  Dog() = default;
```

```
  Dog(const string& dog_name)
  {
    name = dog_name;
  }
};
```

This just initializes the inherited name member in the constructor. All the derived classes will be in the same header as Pet.

Defining the Containers

The multiset container will store shared_ptr<Pet> objects. I'll specify two using declarations to define type aliases for this:

```
using Pet_ptr = std::shared_ptr<Pet>;          // A smart pointer to a pet
using Pets = std::multiset<Pet_ptr>;           // A set of smart pointers to pets
```

The Pet_ptr alias simplifies the definition of the multiset container type and the Pets alias will simplify the definition of the type of map container that will store multiset containers with people's names as keys. A Pets container can store pointers to Pet objects, as well as pointers to Cat, Dog, or Mouse objects.

The multiset container of Pet_ptr objects will need a less-than comparison operator defined:

```
inline bool operator<(const Pet_ptr& p1, const Pet_ptr& p2)
{
  return *p1 < *p2;
}
```

This dereferences the pointers that are passed as the arguments and passes the objects that result to the virtual operator<() function member that the derived classes inherit from Pet. This function will be called by the default less<Pet_ptr> function object that will apply for a multiset container in the example.

There are two further using declarations that will be helpful:

```
using std::string;
using Name = string;
```

The Name alias will just make it clearer what the key type is in the map container. I'll define the map in main() like this:

```
std::map<Name, Pets> peoples_pets;
```

The elements in the container are pair<Name, Pets> objects, which in full is the type pair<string, multiset<shared_ptr<Pet>>>. The latter is much less informative of what an element represents.

Defining main() for the Example

Reading people's names and their pets from the standard input stream will be done by a helper function:

```
Pets get_pets(const Name& person)
{
  Pets pets;
  std::cout << "Enter " << person << "'s pets:\n";
```

```
char ch {};
Name name {};
while(true)
{
  std::cin >> ch;
  if(toupper(ch) == 'Q') break;
  std::cin >> name;
  switch(std::toupper(ch))
  {
  case 'C':
    pets.insert(std::make_shared<Cat>(name));
    break;
  case 'D':
    pets.insert(std::make_shared<Dog>(name));
    break;
  case 'M':
    pets.insert(std::make_shared<Mouse>(name));
    break;
  default:
    std::cout << "Invalid pet ID - try again.\n";
  }
}
return pets;
}
```

It's looks like quite a lot of code but it's very simple. A local multiset container of type Pets is created first. The person's name is passed as the argument to the function for use in the prompt and that person's pets are read in the indefinite while loop. A pet type is identified by the initial letter – 'C' for cat, 'D' for dog, and so on. A prompt for this will be generated in main(). The type character is followed by the pet's name and entering 'Q' will end input for the current person. A shared_ptr<T> object of the appropriate type is created in the switch statement and stored in the pets container. When input is complete, the local pets object is returned, and this will be returned by a move operation.

The program will output pets in a Pets container so implementing a stream insertion operator will be useful:

```
inline std::ostream& operator<<(std::ostream& out, const Pet_ptr& pet_ptr)
{
  return out << " " << *pet_ptr;
}
```

This dereferences the smart pointer and uses the insertion operator to write the object to the output stream, out. Thus this will call the operator<<() function that is a friend of the Pet class. I'll use this function in the definition of another function to output an element from the map container:

```
void list_pets(const std::pair<Name, Pets>& pr)
{
  std::cout << "\n" << pr.first << ":\n";
  std::copy(std::begin(pr.second), std::end(pr.second),
                        std::ostream_iterator<Pet_ptr>(std::cout, "\n"));
}
```

An element is a pair object where the first member is the person's name and the second member is the multiset container containing pointers to their pets. After writing the first member of the pair to the standard output stream, the elements in the container that is the second member are output by the copy() algorithm. The first two arguments to copy() are iterators that define the range of objects to be copied. The destination of the copy operation is specified by the third argument, which is an ostream_iterator<Pet_ptr> object. This will call the operator<<() function with Pet_ptr as the type of the second parameter, and this will call the operator<<() function that is a friend of the Pet class.

The code for the main() function will be in Ex5_05.cpp in the download. Here's the file contents:

```cpp
// Ex5_05.cpp
// Storing pointers to derived class objects in a multiset container
#include <iostream>                        // For standard streams
#include <string>                          // For string class
#include <algorithm>                       // For copy() algorithm
#include <iterator>                        // For ostream_iterator
#include <map>                             // For map container
#include <set>                             // For multiset container
#include <memory>                          // For smart pointers
#include <cctype>                          // For toupper()
#include "Pet_Classes.h"

using std::string;
using Name = string;
using Pet_ptr = std::shared_ptr<Pet>;      // A smart pointer to a pet
using Pets = std::multiset <Pet_ptr>;      // A set of smart pointers to pets

// operator<() function to compare shared pointers to pets goes here...

// Stream insertion operator for pointers to pets goes here...

// get_pets() function to read in all the pets for a person goes here...

// list_pets() function to list the pets in a Pets container goes here...

int main()
{
  std::map<Name, Pets> peoples_pets;                // The people and their pets
  char answer {'Y'};
  string name {};
  std::cout << "You'll enter a person's name followed by their pets.\n"
            << "Pets can be identified by C for cat, D for dog, or M for mouse.\n"
            << "Enter the character to identify each pet type followed by the pet's name.\n"
            << "Enter Q to end pet input for a person.\n";
  while(std::toupper(answer) == 'Y')
  {
    std::cout << "Enter a name: ";
    std::cin >> name;
    peoples_pets.emplace(name, get_pets(name));
    std::cout << "Another person(Y or N)? ";
    std::cin >> answer;
  }
```

```
  // Output the pets for everyone
  std::cout << "\nThe people and their pets are:\n";
  for(const auto& pr : peoples_pets)
    list_pets(pr);
}
```

After defining the map container for people and their pets in main(), there's a prompt explaining the input process. All the input is managed by the while loop. Elements are added to the people_pets container by calling its emplace() member, which creates an element in place. The first argument is the name and the second argument is the multiset container that get_pets() returns. When input is complete, people and their pets are output by the range-based for loop that iterates over the elements in the map. The output for each person is produce by calling the list_pets() helper function with the current pair element from the map container as the argument.

Here's an example of some output:

```
You'll enter a person's name followed by their pets.
Pets can be identified by C for cat, D for dog, or M for mouse.
Enter the character to identify each pet type followed by the pet's name.
Enter Q to end pet input for a person.
Enter a name: Jack
Enter Jack's pets:
d Rover c Tom d Fang m Minnie m Jerry c Tiddles q
Another person(Y or N)? y
Enter a name: Jill
Enter Jill's pets:
m Mickey d Lassie c Korky d Gnasher q
Another person(Y or N)? n

The people and their pets are:

Jack:
 A Cat called Tiddles
 A Cat called Tom
 A Dog called Fang
 A Dog called Rover
 A Mouse called Jerry
 A Mouse called Minnie

Jill:
 A Cat called Korky
 A Dog called Gnasher
 A Dog called Lassie
 A Mouse called Mickey
```

The pets are listed in ascending name order within pet type order, which is exactly what we were hoping for. The output also shows that we were successful in storing smart pointers to a variety of derived class objects in a container with elements that are of type 'smart pointer to base.'

unordered_set<T> Containers

The template for the unordered_set<T> container type is defined in the unordered_set header. The capabilities provided by an unordered_set<T> container parallels that of an unordered_map<T>, but with the objects that you store acting as their own keys. Objects of type T are located in the container using their *hash values* so a Hash<T>() function must exist. You cannot store duplicates objects in the container. Elements must be of a type that can be compared for equality because this is necessary to determine when elements are identical. Like an unordered_map, elements are stored in *buckets* within a hash table; the bucket in which an element is stored, is selected based on its hash value. The conceptual organization of an unordered_set container is illustrated in Figure 5-5.

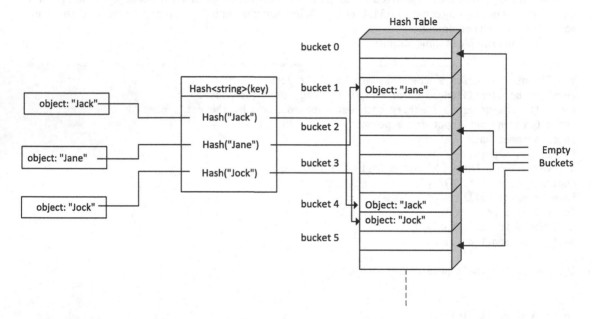

Figure 5-5. *Conceptual data organization in an unordered_set container*

Figure 5-5 illustrates a situation where the hash values for two different objects, "Jack" and "Jock," might select the same bucket. There's a default number of buckets but you can change that when you create a container. Remember that, as you saw with an unordered_map, buckets counts are typically powers of two because that makes it easier to select a buckets from a number of bits in a hash value. The range of options for creating an unordered_set is similar to what you saw for an unordered_map. Here are some examples:

```
std::unordered_set<string> things {16};                                    // 16 buckets
std::unordered_set<string> words {"one", "two", "three", "four"};          // Initializer list
std::unordered_set<string> some_words {++std::begin(words), std::end(words)};  // Range
std::unordered_set<string> copy_wrds {words};                              // Copy constructor
```

There's a default type argument for the template parameter that indicates the hash function type. When you are storing objects for which you must supply a hash function, you need to specify the template type argument for this as well as the function argument in the constructor. To store objects of the type Name that I introduced for Ex4_01, the unordered_set<Name> container could be defined like this:

```
std::unordered_set<Name, Hash_Name> names {8, Hash_Name()};      // 8 buckets & hash function
```

The second template type argument is the function object type that hashes Name objects. The second constructor argument is an instance of the function object. You have to specify a bucket count when you need to specify a hashing function, because it's the first constructor argument. If you omit the second argument to this constructor, the container will use a default instance of the type you specify as the second template type argument. If Hash_Name is a function object type, there's no need to specify the second constructor argument.

You can increase the bucket count for an existing container by calling its reserve() member. This may take some time because it will cause the existing elements to be rehashed to allocate them among the new set of buckets.

The maximum load factor is the maximum allowed for the average number of elements per bucket. By default the maximum load factor is 1.0, just like an unordered_map container, but again like the map, you can change this by passing a new load factor to the max_load_factor() member. For example:

```
names.max_load_factor(8.0);                        // Max average no. of elements per bucket
```

By increasing the maximum load factor you can decrease the number of buckets used, but this will adversely affect the time to access elements because you increase the probability that accessing an element will involve searching a bucket.

There's no at() function member of an unordered_set container and the subscript operator is not defined. Other than that, the range of function members is the same as for an unordered_map.

Adding Elements

The insert() function member can insert a single element that you pass as an argument. In this case it returns a pair object containing an iterator, plus a bool value indicating whether or not the insertion was successful. If the element was inserted, the iterator points to the new element, and if it wasn't, it points to the element that prevented the insertion. You can supply an iterator as the first argument to insert() as a hint as to where the insertion of the second argument should be. In this case just an iterator is returned; the hint may be ignored. Yet another version of the insert() member can insert elements from an initializer list, in which case nothing is returned. Here are some illustrative statements:

```
auto pr = words.insert("ninety");          // Returns a pair - an iterator & a bool value
auto iter = words.insert(pr.first, "nine"); // 1st arg is a hint. Returns an iterator
words.insert({"ten", "seven", "six"});     // Inserting an initializer list
```

Nothing is returned when you call insert() to insert a range of elements:

```
std::vector<string> more {"twenty", "thirty", "forty"};
words.insert(std::begin(more), std::end(more)); // Insert elements from the vector
```

The emplace() and emplace_hint() function members of an unordered_set enable you to create elements in place. As you have seen with other set containers, the arguments to emplace() are the arguments that are to be passed to the constructor to create the element, and the arguments to emplace_hint() are the iterator that is the hint, followed by the constructor arguments to create the element. For example:

```
std::unordered_set<std::pair<string, string>, Hash_pair> names;
auto pr = names.emplace("Jack", "Jones");              // Returns pair<iterator, bool>
auto iter = names.emplace_hint(pr.first, "John", "Smith"); // Returns an iterator
```

The elements in the container are pair objects representing names, where each name consists of two string objects representing a person's first and second names. The default hash function for an unordered_set<T> element is an instance of the hash<T> class template. This template has specializations defined for fundamental types, pointers, and string objects. Because there's no hash<pair<string,string>> template specialization defined, it's necessary to define a function object that will hash the elements, and specify its type - Hash_pair here – as the second template type argument for the container. The call to emplace() has first and second names as arguments that will be passed to the pair constructor. The emplace_hint() call has the iterator that points to the previously inserted element as a hint, which may be ignored. The subsequent arguments are for the pair constructor. The function object type, Hash_pair, to hash the pair objects that are stored in the names container could be defined as:

```
class Hash_pair
{
public:
  size_t operator()(const std::pair<string, string>& pr)
  {
    return std::hash<string>()(pr.first + pr.second);
  }
};
```

This just uses an instance of the hash<string> function object that is defined in the string header. It hashes the string that results from concatenating the first and second members of a pair object and returns that as the hash value for a pair element.

Retrieving Elements

Calling find() for an unordered_set() returns an iterator. This iterator points to the element that has a hash value that matches that of the argument, or the end iterator for the container if the element is not present. For example:

```
std::pair<string, string> person {"John", "Smith"};
if(names.find(person) != std::end(names))
  std::cout << "We found " << person.first << " " << person.second << std::endl;
else
  std::cout << "There's no " << person.first << " " << person.second << std::endl;
```

Given the container from the code in the previous section, this code fragment will report that John Smith is present. If he wasn't, the find() function would return the end iterator for the container and the second output statement would execute.

The elements in an unordered_set container are not ordered, so there's no upper_bound() or lower_bound() function members. The equal_range() member returns a pair object with iterators as members that define a range containing all elements that match the argument; there can only be one with an unordered_set. If there are none, both iterators will be the end iterator for the container. Calling the count() member returns the number of occurrences of the argument in the container. This can only be 0 or 1 with an unordered_set. When you need to know how many elements there are in total in a container, you can call its size() member. The empty() member will return true if there are no elements in the container.

Deleting Elements

Calling the clear() function member of an unordered_set container will delete all its elements. The erase() function member can delete an element that hashes to the same value as the argument. Another version of erase() can delete the element to which an iterator argument points. For example, here's an unnecessarily long-winded way of deleting an element when it is present:

```
std::pair<string, string> person {"John", "Smith"};
auto iter = names.find(person);
if(iter != std::end(names))
  names.erase(iter);
```

An iterator argument to erase() must be a valid and dereferenceable iterator that points to an element in the container, so it's essential to ensure it is not the end iterator for the container. This version of erase() returns an iterator that points to the element following the one that was deleted, which will be the end iterator if the last element was removed.

The easy and sensible way to delete the person object if it's there, is to write this:

```
auto n = names.erase(person);
```

This version of erase() returns the number of elements that were deleted as size_t. This can only be 0 or 1 in this case, but for an unordered_multiset container it can be greater than 1. Obviously, if 0 is returned, the element wasn't there.

In spite of my initial example that was not useful, calling erase() to delete an element that an iterator points to can be very useful – when you want to remove elements that have particular characteristics for instance. Suppose that you need to remove all elements in the names container that have a second name beginning with 'S'. This loop would do it:

```
while(true)
{
  auto iter = std::find_if(std::begin(names), std::end(names),
                  [](const std::pair<string, string>& pr ){ return pr.second[0] == 'S';});
  if(iter == std::end(names))
    break;
  names.erase(iter);
}
```

The find_if() algorithm returns an iterator that points to the first element in the range that is defined by the first two arguments for which the predicate that is the third argument returns true. The parameter for the predicate must be an object of the type that results from dereferencing an iterator from the range. The range here is all the elements in the names container, which are pair<string,string> objects, and the predicate is a lambda expression that returns true when the second member of the pair has 'S' as the initial character. The algorithm will return the end iterator for the range when no element results in a true return from the lambda.

There's another version of erase() that removes a range of elements. The following statement will remove all elements from names except the first and the last:

```
auto iter = names.erase(++std::begin(names), --std::end(names));
```

The arguments are the iterators that define the range of elements to be deleted. The function returns an iterator that points to the element that followed the last deleted element.

Producing a Bucket List

You have access to the buckets in an unordered_set container using the same functions that you saw for an unordered_map container. You can access the elements stored in a particular bucket through iterators. A particular bucket is selected using a *bucket index* that you pass to the begin() and end() members of the container; this returns begin and end iterators for the range of elements that the bucket contains. When you want const iterators, you pass the bucket index to the cbegin() and cend() members of the container. The bucket_count() member returns the number of buckets so you can use this to control a loop that iterates over all the buckets in a container. Here's how you could list the elements in each bucket in the names container:

```
for(size_t bucket_index {}; bucket_index < names.bucket_count(); ++bucket_index)
{
  std::cout << "Bucket " << bucket_index << ":\n";
  for(auto iter = names.begin(bucket_index); iter != names.end(bucket_index); ++iter)
  {
    std::cout << "  " << iter->first << " " << iter->second;
  }
  std::cout << std::endl;
}
```

The outer loop iterates over the bucket index values. The inner loop iterates over the range of elements in the current bucket, and writes the first and second members of the pair objects to the standard output stream.

The bucket_size() member will return the number of elements in a bucket that you identify by the index argument. You can obtain the index for the bucket that contains a particular object by passing the object as the argument to the bucket() member of the container. If the object you pass to bucket() is not in the container, the function will return the index of the bucket in which it would be stored if you added it to the container. Thus the bucket() member provides you with no insight into whether the object is actually there. Here's how you could list the elements from the names container along with their bucket numbers:

```
for(const auto& pr : names)
  std::cout << pr.first << " " << pr.second << " is in bucket " << names.bucket(pr) << std::endl;
```

Calling bucket() returns the bucket number for the argument.

■ **Note**   Of course, calling the begin(), cbegin(), end(), and cend() members with no arguments returns the corresponding begin and end iterators for the container elements.

Using unordered_multiset<T> Containers

An unordered_multiset<T> container is essentially similar to an unordered_set<T>, except that you can store duplicate T objects in the container. All the function members I have described for an unordered_set container are available for an unordered_multiset and work in the same way, except where duplicate elements affect the outcome. The count() member can return a value greater than one, for example, and calling the erase() function member with an object as the argument will delete *all* elements that hash to the same value as the hash value for the argument, not just a single element. Let's see a working example that shows an unordered_multiset in action.

The example, Ex5_06, will store instances of a variation on the Name class that I defined for Ex4_01 in an unordered_multiset container. The container will represent a record of all the friends I have, so I know who to send cards to on holiday occasions. Because of the cost of stamps these days, the list has to be as short as possible in the interests of economy. Here's the contents of the Name.h header for this example:

```cpp
// Name.h for Ex5_06
// Defines a person's name
#ifndef NAME_H
#define NAME_H
#include <string>                              // For string class
#include <ostream>                             // For output streams
#include <istream>                             // For input streams
using std::string;

class Name
{
private:
  string first {};
  string second {};

public:
  Name(const string& name1, const string& name2) : first (name1), second (name2) {}
  Name() = default;

  const string& get_first() const  { return first; }
  const string& get_second() const { return second; }

  size_t get_length() const { return first.length() + second.length() + 1; }

  // Less-than operator
  bool operator<(const Name& name) const
  {
    return second < name.second || (second == name.second && first < name.first);
  }

  // Equality operator
  bool operator==(const Name& name) const
  {
    return (second == name.second) && (first == name.first);
  }

  size_t hash() const { return std::hash<std::string>()(first+second); }

  friend std::istream& operator>>(std::istream& in, Name& name);
  friend std::ostream& operator<<(std::ostream& out, const Name& name);
};

// Extraction operator overload
inline std::istream& operator>>(std::istream& in, Name& name)
{
  in >> name.first >> name.second;
  return in;
}
```

```
// Insertion operator overload
inline std::ostream& operator<<(std::ostream& out, const Name& name)
{
  out << name.first + " " + name.second;
  return out;
}
#endif
```

The additions to the Name class over the Ex4_01 version are accessor function members for the data members, a member to return the total length of a name, the operator==() member that allows objects to be compared for equality, and the hash() member that return a hash value for an object as the hash value of the concatenation of the two member names. The comparison for equality is required by the container type. The get_length() member is just an enabler for aligning output nicely. The length() member returns the sum of the lengths of the two names plus one, the 'plus one' takes account of the space between the names on output. In the operator<<() definition, the names are concatenated for output to allows names to be aligned in the output by setting an output field width. Using multiple << operators would make the output more efficient, but it would prevent the names from being aligned in the output.

The container type will need the type of the hash function object that hashes the objects to be stored to be specified as a template type argument. This function object type will be defined in the Hash_Name.h header like this:

```
// Hash_Name.h
// Function object type to hash Name objects for Ex5_06
#ifndef HASH_NAME_H
#define HASH_NAME_H
#include "Name.h"

class Hash_Name
{
public:
  size_t operator()(const Name& name) {  return name.hash();  }
};
#endif
```

The function call operator function just calls the hash() member of the Name objects that is passed to it.

I'll synthesize the Name objects to be stored in the container from sequences of first and second names that will be stored in vector containers. It will be convenient to populate the unordered_multiset container in another helper function that will assume the following type alias definition is in effect:

```
using Names = std::unordered_multiset<Name, Hash_Name>;
```

The first unordered_multiset template type parameter is the element type, and the second is the function object type to hash elements. Here's the helper function that will create the elements in the container:

```
void make_friends(Names& names)
{
  // Names are duplicated to get duplicate elements
  std::vector<string> first_names {"John", "John", "John", "Joan", "Joan", "Jim", "Jim", "Jean"};
  std::vector<string> second_names {"Smith", "Jones", "Jones", "Hackenbush", "Szczygiel"};
```

```
  for(const auto& name1 : first_names)
    for(const auto& name2:second_names)
      names.emplace(name1,name2);
}
```

Name objects are created in place in the names container in the nested loops. This will create objects using all possible combinations of first and second names. Some first and second names are duplicated to ensure that we create and store some identical elements.

The program will list the contents of the buckets in the container to show which friends share a bucket, and another helper function will help:

```
void list_buckets(const Names& names)
{
  for(size_t n_bucket {} ; n_bucket < names.bucket_count(); ++n_bucket)
  {
    std::cout << "Bucket " << n_bucket << ":\n";
    std::copy(names.begin(n_bucket), names.end(n_bucket), std::ostream_
              iterator<Name>(std::cout, " "));
    std::cout << std::endl;
  }
}
```

The for loop iterates over the bucket index values. On each loop iteration, a header line that identifies the bucket is written out, then all the elements in the bucket are written out by the copy() algorithm. The copy() algorithm copies the Name element to which each iterator points to the ostream_iterator, which writes the object to cout. The overload of the operator<<() function for writing a Name object to an ostream object that is defined in the Name.h header allows this operation to work.

The source file that includes main() will contain the following code:

```
// Ex5_06.cpp
// Using an unordered_multiset container
#include <iostream>                          // For standard streams
#include <iomanip>                           // For stream manipulators
#include <string>                            // For string class
#include <unordered_set>                     // For unordered_multiset containers
#include <algorithm>                         // For copy(), max(), find_if(), for_each()
#include "Name.h"
#include "Hash_Name.h"

using std::string;
using Names = std::unordered_multiset<Name, Hash_Name>;

// Code for make_friends(Names& names) goes here...

// Code for list_buckets() goes here...

int main()
{
  Names pals {8};                            // 8 buckets
  pals.max_load_factor(8.0);                 // Average no. of elements per bucket max
  make_friends(pals);                        // Load up the container with Name objects
  list_buckets(pals);                        // List the contents by bucket
```

```cpp
// Report the number of John Smith's that are pals
Name js {"John", "Smith"};
std::cout << "\nThere are " << pals.count(js) << " " << js << "'s.\n" << std::endl;

// Remove all the John Jones's - we just don't get on...
pals.erase(Name {"John", "Jones"});

// Get rid of the Hackenbushes - they never invite us...
while(true)
{
  auto iter = std::find_if(std::begin(pals), std::end(pals),
                      [](const Name& name){ return name.get_second() == "Hackenbush"; });
  if(iter == std::end(pals))
    break;
  pals.erase(iter);
}

// List the friends we still have...
size_t max_length {};                      // Stores the maximum name length
std::for_each(std::begin(pals), std::end(pals),  // Find the maximum name length...
  [&max_length](const Name name){ max_length = std::max(max_length, name.get_length()); });

size_t count {};                           // No. of names written out
size_t perline {6};                        // No. of names per line
for(const auto& pal : pals)
{
  std::cout << std::setw(max_length+2) << std::left << pal;
  if((++count % perline) == 0) std::cout << "\n";
}
std::cout << std::endl;
}
```

The container is constructed so it has 8 buckets initially. The number of buckets in a container will be increased automatically if the maximum load factor is exceeded, so the maximum load factor is set to 8.0 by the max_load_factor() call to reduce the likelihood of this. Apart from showing this function in action, the idea of increasing the maximum load factor in this example is to minimize the number of lines of output when listing the buckets. With the default maximum load factor of 1.0, the number of buckets goes up to 64 on my system – which results in a lot of output. In practice, increasing the maximum load factor like this would slow operations significantly, because it would increase the number of occasions when searching a bucket becomes necessary. This would tend to nullify the advantage an unordered_multiset has over a multiset.

Calling make_friends() uses all combination of the first and second names to create Name elements in place in the container. Calling list_buckets() outputs the elements in each bucket. The program then outputs the number of friends called "John Smith" by calling the count() function member of the container.

In a fit of pique, I then delete all friends with the name "John Jones" by passing the Name object corresponding to that to the erase() member of the container. Remembering that none of the Hackenbushes have invited me for even a cup of coffee, I decide that they are for the chop too. This is a little trickier because we have to find the elements in the container with that second name. The find_if() algorithm comes to the rescue by returning the iterator that points to the first element for which the lambda expression that is the third argument returns true. The iterator that find_if() returns is stored in iter, which is defined using auto in the loop so the type is deduced. If you needed to reference iter outside the loop, you could define it as type Name::iterator. iterator is a type alias for iterators for elements in the unordered_multiset<Name> container that is defined within the template. The loop continues until find_if() returns the end iterator for the container, indicating that none of the elements are Hackenbushes. Finally, we output all the friends we have left by iterating over the elements in the container using a range-based for loop. The value to use as the field width to line the output up in columns is determined by the for_each() algorithm. The algorithm dereferences each iterator in the range specified by the first two arguments and passes the result to the lambda expression. This will eventually store the maximum name length in max_length, which is captured by reference in the lambda.

You could output the elements using the copy() algorithm:

```
std::copy(std::begin(pals), std::end(pals), std::ostream_iterator<Name>{std::cout, "\n"});
```

This outputs the elements one per line, which is a lot of lines. The only other alternative is to output them all on a single line, which is also not very satisfactory when writing to cout. Using copy() for output tends to be more useful for writing files.

Here's the output from the example on my system:

```
Bucket 0:
Joan Jones   Joan Jones   Joan Jones   Joan Jones
Bucket 1:
Joan Szczygiel   Joan Szczygiel
Bucket 2:
Jean Jones   Jean Jones   Jean Smith
Bucket 3:
Jim Szczygiel   Jim Szczygiel   Jim Hackenbush   Jim Hackenbush   John Jones   John Jones   John
Jones   John Jones   John Jones   John Jones
Bucket 4:
Joan Smith   Joan Smith   John Hackenbush   John Hackenbush   John Hackenbush
Bucket 5:
Joan Hackenbush   Joan Hackenbush
Bucket 6:
Jim Jones   Jim Jones   Jim Jones   Jim Jones   Jim Smith   Jim Smith   John Szczygiel   John
Szczygiel   John Szczygiel
Bucket 7:
Jean Szczygiel   Jean Hackenbush   John Smith   John Smith   John Smith


There are 3 John Smith's.
Jean Szczygiel   John Smith     John Smith     John Smith     Jim Szczygiel   Jim Szczygiel
Joan Smith       Joan Smith     Jim Jones      Jim Jones      Jim Jones       Jim Jones
Jim Smith        Jim Smith      John Szczygiel John Szczygiel John Szczygiel  Joan Jones
Joan Jones       Joan Jones     Joan Jones     Joan Szczygiel Joan Szczygiel  Jean Jones
Jean Jones       Jean Smith
```

The way the names are distributed between the buckets may be different on your system. It depends on how the bits from a hash value that select a bucket are chosen. Every bucket contains some elements and bucket 3 contains 10. The number of buckets won't increase until the *average* per bucket exceeds 8. Of course, all the friends that have the same name end up in the same bucket because they have identical hash values.

Operations on Sets

The mathematical concept of a set is very like that of a set container – it's a collection of things that are alike in some way. There are binary operations on sets defined that combine the contents of two sets in various ways to produce another set. Figure 5-6 illustrates these, and shows the following:

- Two examples of sets A and B that contain integers.

- The *union* of the sets A and B is the set of elements that belongs to either or both sets.

- The *intersection* of the sets A and B is the set of elements that are common to both.

- The *difference* between the sets A and B is the set that results when you remove the elements from A that are common to A and B.

- The *set symmetric difference* between the sets A and B is the set of elements from either set that are not in both.

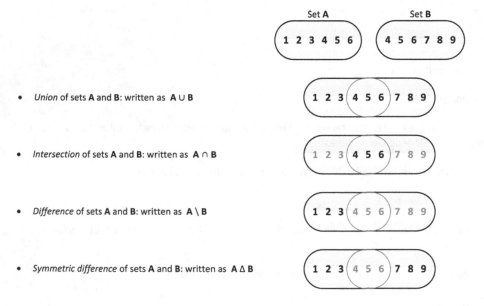

Figure 5-6. Set operations

The elements that result from the operations in Figure 5-6 are shown in bold font. If you have not met these operations before, they may seem somewhat abstract but they are extremely useful. In Ex5_01 we were allocating students to courses where the student in each course were stored in a set. The college staff might be interested in finding out which students had elected to study physics without signing up for the mathematics course. A difference operation applied to the two courses will provide the answer immediately, and you'll see how this works later, in an example.

The STL offers several algorithms that implement operations on sets of objects, including the four binary operations in Figure 5-6. They are defined by templates in the algorithm header. These functions do not necessarily involve set containers, although they can. A set of objects is passed to these algorithms as a range – specified by two iterators in other words. The elements in a range that represents a set must be sorted. Ascending sequence is assumed by default, but you can change this when necessary. This is partly because the execution performance of the operations is linear when the objects are sorted. Sorting is not included within the operations because it would involve sorts that are not necessary in many instances. Obviously, this would be the case for ranges of elements from container types such as set and map that are ordered anyway. All the algorithms for set operations require that both sets are sorted in the same sense, ascending or descending. The set of objects that results from any of the STL algorithms that implement these operations will be copies of the objects from the original ranges.

The set algorithms cannot be applied to elements in associative containers that are unordered because elements in unordered containers cannot be sorted. Sorting requires random access iterators to the elements, which are not available from unordered associative containers. However, you could copy the elements to another type of container, such as a vector, sort the vector elements and apply the set operations to that. I'll explain each of the STL algorithms for set operations and then show some of them working in an example.

The set_union() Algorithm

The first version of the set_union() function template that implements the set union operation requires five arguments: two iterators that specify the range for the set that is the left operand, two iterators that specify the range for the set that is the right operand, and an iterator that specifies the destination for the set of results. Here's an example:

```
std::vector<int> set1 {1, 2, 3, 4, 5, 6};
std::vector<int> set2 {4, 5, 6, 7, 8, 9};
std::vector<int> result;
std::set_union(std::begin(set1), std::end(set1), // Range for set that is left operand
               std::begin(set2), std::end(set2), // Range for set that is right operand
               std::back_inserter(result)); // Destination for the result: 1 2 3 4 5 6 7 8 9
```

The initial values in set1 and set2 are in ascending sequence. If they were not, it would be necessary to sort the vector containers before applying the set_union() algorithm. You saw in Chapter 1 that the back_inserter() function template that is defined in the iterator header returns a back_inserter_iterator object that calls push_back() for the container that is passed as the argument. Thus the elements that result from the union of the elements in set1 and set2 will be stored in the result vector. The set of elements that result from the union operation will be copies of the elements from the container, so the original contents of the containers are not affected by the operation.

Of course, you don't need to store the results; you could use a stream iterator to write the elements out:

```
std::set_union(std::begin(set1), std::end(set1), std::begin(set2), std::end(set2),
               std::ostream_iterator<int> {std::cout, " "});
```

Here, the destination is an ostream_iterator that transfers the results to the standard output stream.

The second version of the set_union() function template accepts a sixth argument that is a function object to be used for comparing the elements in the sets. Here's an example of using that possibility:

```
std::set<int, std::greater<int>> set1 {1, 2, 3, 4, 5, 6}; // Contains 6 5 4 3 2 1
std::set<int, std::greater<int>> set2 {4, 5, 6, 7, 8, 9}; // Contains 9 8 7 6 5 4
std::set<int, std::greater<int>> result;                  // Elements in descending sequence
std::set_union(std::begin(set1), std::end(set1),std::begin(set2), std::end(set2),
std::inserter(result, std::begin(result)),       // Result destination: 9 8 7 6 5 4 3 2 1
               std::greater<int>());             // Function object for comparing elements
```

This time the sets are elements in set containers. The elements are ordered using a function object of type greater<int> so they will be in descending sequence. The last argument to set_union() is an instance of the greater<int> type that the function will use to compare set elements. The destination for the result is an inserter_iterator for the result container that will call the insert() member to add an element. You can't use a back_insert_iterator with a set container because it has no push_back() function member. The result of the union operation will be copies of elements from both sets in descending sequence.

Both versions of set_union() return an iterator that points to one past the end of the range of elements that are copied to the destination. This can be useful if the destination is a container that contains elements prior to the operation. For example, if the destination is a vector container, the iterator that is returned by set_union() will point to the first of the original elements if the new elements are inserted by set_union() using a front_insert_iterator, or the end iterator for the container if you use a back_inserter_iterator.

The set_intersection( ) Algorithm

Apart from producing the intersection of two sets, rather than the union, the set_intersection() algorithm works the same as the set_union() algorithm. It comes in two versions that have the same sets of arguments as set_union(). Here are some statements illustrating its use:

```
std::set<string> words1 {"one", "two", "three", "four", "five", "six"};
std::set<string> words2 {"four", "five", "six", "seven", "eight", "nine"};
std::set<string> result;
std::set_intersection(std::begin(words1), std::end(words1),
                      std::begin(words2), std::end(words2),
                      std::inserter(result, std::begin(result)));
                                              // Result: "five" "four" "six"
```

The set containers store string objects that are ordered using a less<string> instance by default. The intersection of the elements from the two containers will be those elements common to both, and these are stored in the result container. Of course, these will be in ascending string sequence. The set_intersection() algorithm returns an iterator that points to one beyond the last element in the range that was inserted in the destination.

The set_difference() Algorithm

The set_difference() algorithm that produces the difference of two sets also has two version with the same set of parameters as set_union(). Here's an example applied to elements from set containers that are in descending sequence:

```
std::set<string, std::greater<string>> words1 {"one", "two", "three", "four", "five", "six"};
std::set<string, std::greater<string>> words2 {"four", "five", "six", "seven", "eight", "nine"};
std::set<string, std::greater<string>> result;
std::set_difference(std::begin(words1), std::end(words1),
                    std::begin(words2), std::end(words2),
                    std::inserter(result, std::begin(result)),  // Result: "two" "three" "one"
                    std::greater<string>());            // Function object to compare elements
```

This calls the version of the algorithm with a sixth parameter for the function object to be used to compare elements because the ranges from the set containers are ordered using this. The difference is obtained by removing the elements common to words1 and words2 from the first set, which consists of the elements from words1. The elements that result are the first three elements from words1, in descending sequence. This algorithm also returns an iterator pointing to one beyond the last element in the range that was inserted in the destination.

The set_symmetric_difference() Algorithm

The set_symmetric_difference() algorithm follows the same pattern as the previous set algorithm. Here's some statements showing it working:

```
std::set<string> words1 {"one", "two", "three", "four", "five", "six"};
std::set<string> words2 {"four", "five", "six", "seven", "eight", "nine"};
std::set_symmetric_difference(std::begin(words1), std::end(words1),
                              std::begin(words2), std::end(words2),
                              std::ostream_iterator<string> {std::cout, " "});
```

The elements in the ranges are in the default ascending sequence. The set symmetric difference produces the elements from the two sets excluding those that are in both. The last function argument that defines the destination for the resultant set is an ostream_iterator, so the elements will be written to cout and the output will look like this:

```
eight nine one seven three two
```

Naturally these are in the sequence that results from applying the < operator to the string objects because the default comparison object will be of type less<string>.

The includes( ) Algorithm

The includes() algorithm compares two sets of elements and returns true if the first set contains *all* the elements from the second set. It also returns true if the second set is empty. Here are some examples:

```
std::set<string> words1 {"one", "two", "three", "four", "five", "six"};
std::set<string> words2 {"four", "two", "seven"};
std::multiset<string> words3;
std::cout << std::boolalpha
          << std::includes(std::begin(words1), std::end(words1),
                           std::begin(words2), std::end(words2))
          << std::endl;                       // Output: false

std::cout << std::boolalpha
          << std::includes(std::begin(words1), std::end(words1),
                           std::begin(words2), std::begin(words2))
          << std::endl;                       // Output: true

std::set_union(std::begin(words1), std::end(words1), std::begin(words2), std::end(words2),
               std::inserter(words3, std::begin(words3)));
std::cout << std::boolalpha
          << std::includes(std::begin(words3), std::end(words3),
                           std::begin(words2), std::end(words2))
          << std::endl;                       // Output: true
```

There are two set containers of string elements, words1 and words2, initialized with the strings from the initializer lists. The first output statement displays false because words1 does not contain a string("seven") element that occurs in words2. The second output statement displays true because the range specifying the second operand is empty - the begin iterator for the range is the same and the end iterator. The set_union() function call copies the union of the sets from words1 and words2 to words3 using an inserter_iterator. The result in words3 will contain all the elements that are in words2 so the third output statement will display true.

It's easy to get confused about what happens with the union operation when the containers are multisets. Although words3 is a multiset that allows duplicate elements, the elements common to words1 and words2 *will not* be duplicated in words3. This statement will output the words3 elements:

```
std::copy(std::begin(words3), std::end(words3),
                        std::ostream_iterator<string> {std::cout, " "});
```

The output will be:

```
five four one seven seven six three two
```

This is because the union operation will only include one copy of each element that is duplicated. Of course, if words1 and words2 were multiset containers each with duplicate words, then the result may include duplicate elements:

```
std::multiset<string> words1 {"one", "two", "nine", "nine", "one", "three", "four", "five", "six"};
std::multiset<string> words2 {"four", "two", "seven", "seven", "nine", "nine"};
std::multiset<string> words3;
```

"one" is duplicated in words1 and "seven" is duplicated in words2. "nine" is duplicated in both containers. You can now execute the same set_union() call:

```
std::set_union(std::begin(words1), std::end(words1),
              std::begin(words2), std::end(words2),
              std::inserter(words3, std::begin(words3)));
```

Outputting the contents of words3 will produce the following:

```
five four nine nine one one seven seven six three two
```

The duplicate elements that are unique to one container or the other are duplicated in the result of the union, but the union operation does not duplicate the elements that appear singly in both. Of course, when duplicates appear in both, they are duplicated in the result.

Set Operations in Action

We can see the set operations applied in an extension of Ex5_01 that will be Ex5_07 in the code download. The new code will be appended to the end of the body of main() in Ex5_01 so I'll just show the additional code here. Here's the code to discover which students have taken up physics, but will struggle because they are not studying maths:

```
auto physics = courses.find("Physics");
auto maths = courses.find("Mathematics");
if(physics == std::end(courses) || maths == std::end(courses))
  throw std::invalid_argument {"Invalid course name."};
```

```
std::cout << "\nStudents studying physics but not maths are:\n";
std::set_difference(std::begin(physics->second), std::end(physics->second),
                    std::begin(maths->second), std::end(maths->second),
                              std::ostream_iterator < Student > {std::cout, "  "});
  std::cout << std::endl;
```

Calling the find() member of the courses container returns an iterator that points to the element with the key matching the argument. The function returns the end iterator for the container if there is no matching key so it's a good idea to check. Here, we *know* the keys are present but a spelling error in the argument would cause the code to fail. If this occurs, a standard exception is thrown, which will end the program. The set_difference() algorithm produces the result we are looking for, and in this case the Student objects are written to cout by an ostream_iterator object. Of course, you can store the resultant set in another container, as the next code will show.

The following code identifies the students that are doing the right thing – studying both maths and physics:

```
std::vector<Student> phys_and_math;
std::cout << "\nStudents studying physics and maths are:\n";
std::set_intersection(std::begin(physics->second), std::end(physics->second),
                    std::begin(maths->second), std::end(maths->second),
                    std::back_inserter(phys_and_math));
std::copy(std::begin(phys_and_math), std::end(phys_and_math),
                              std::ostream_iterator <Student> {std::cout, "  "});
  std::cout << std::endl;
```

The set_intersection() algorithm returns the set of elements common to both original sets, which is what we want. The elements that result are inserted into a vector container by the back_insert_iterator that the back_inserter() function returns for the phys_and_math container. You could use a front_insert_iterator with a vector container. The contents of the vector are output by the copy() algorithm.

You can also further combine the set that results from a set operation, as long as you store the result somewhere. Here's how you can determine the set of students signed up for physics, maths, and astronomy:

```
auto astronomy = courses.find("Astronomy");
if(astronomy == std::end(courses)) throw std::invalid_argument{"Invalid course name."};
std::cout << "\nStudents studying physics, maths, and astronomy are:\n";
std::set_intersection(std::begin(astronomy->second), std::end(astronomy->second),
                    std::begin(phys_and_math), std::end(phys_and_math),
                              std::ostream_iterator<Student>{std::cout, "  "});
  std::cout << std::endl;
```

This intersects the set from the previous operation with the set of students that represents the astronomy course. This turned out to be just a single student on my system.

Next we can find the students studying either drama or philosophy, but not both:

```
auto drama = courses.find("Drama");
auto philosophy = courses.find("Philosophy");
if(drama == std::end(courses) || philosophy == std::end(courses))
  throw std::invalid_argument{"Invalid course name."};

Group act_or_think;                            // set container for result
std::cout << "\nStudents studying either drama or philosophy are:\n";
```

```
std::set_symmetric_difference(std::begin(drama->second), std::end(drama->second),
                              std::begin(philosophy->second), std::end(philosophy->second),
                              std::inserter(act_or_think, std::begin(act_or_think)));
std::copy(std::begin(act_or_think), std::end(act_or_think),
                              std::ostream_iterator<Student>{std::cout, "  "});
  std::cout << std::endl;
```

The container for the result is defined using the Group alias, which corresponds to the set<Student> type. The results of a set operation can go anywhere that can be accessed to insert elements through an iterator. The set_symmetric_difference() algorithm does what is required here. Because the destination for the result is a set container, we can't use the back_insert_iterator or a front_insert_iterator. What we need here is an insert_iterator, which is created by calling the inserter() function. The arguments to inserter() are the container object and an iterator that points to the position for inserting elements.

The last addition to the code in Ex5_01 outputs students studying either drama or philosophy, or both:

```
act_or_think.clear();                          // Empty the container to reuse it
std::cout << "\nStudents studying drama and/or philosophy are:\n";
std::set_union(std::begin(drama->second), std::end(drama->second),
               std::begin(philosophy->second), std::end(philosophy->second),
               std::inserter(act_or_think, std::begin(act_or_think)));
std::copy(std::begin(act_or_think), std::end(act_or_think),
               std::ostream_iterator<Student>{std::cout, "  "});
  std::cout << std::endl;
```

This reuses the act_or_think container to store the results of this operation so its clear() member is called to remove the existing elements. The set_union() algorithm generates the set of elements that occur in either of the original sets. The output is produced by the copy() algorithm in the usual way.

Summary

The set containers have similar operations to the corresponding map containers, but generally they are used quite differently. You use map containers for storing and retrieving objects that are associated with a key. Finding an address or a phone number for a name is a typical example. The set containers apply when you are working with collections of objects where the membership of a given collection is important. You can use a set when you need to know if a particular person is in a given class, or whether someone plays in both the football and basketball teams, or whether someone is an inmate of San Quentin, for instance.

The important points you learned in this chapter include:

- The set containers store objects using the objects themselves as keys.

- A set<T> container stores unique objects of type T in order. Objects are ordered using less<T> by default.

- A multiset<T> container stores objects in the same way as a set, but objects do not have to be unique.

- Two objects are determined to be the same in a set or multiset container if they are *equivalent*. Objects a and b are equivalent if a<b is false and b<a is false.

- An unordered_set<T> container stores unique objects of type T that are located using the hash values for the objects.

- Objects in an `unordered_multiset<T>` container are also located using the hash values for the objects but the objects do not need to be unique.

- The unordered set containers determine two objects to be the same by comparing them using the `==` operator so type T must support this operation.

- Objects in unordered set containers are typically stored in *buckets* in a *hash table*. A bucket is usually selected for an object using a specific sequence of bits from its hash value.

- The *load factor* for an unordered set container is the average number of elements per bucket.

- An unordered set container allocates an initial number of buckets. The number of buckets will be automatically increased when the *maximum load factor* for the container is exceeded.

- The STL defines algorithms that implement *set operations*. The binary set operations are *union, intersection, difference, symmetric difference,* and *inclusion.* The sets of elements to which these apply are defined by ranges.

EXERCISES

1. Define a Card class to represent playing cards in a standard deck. Create a vector of Card objects that represents a complete deck of fifty-two cards. Deal the cards randomly into four set containers so that each represents a hand of thirteen cards in a game. Output the cards in the four set containers under the headings "North," "South," "East," and "West". (These are the usual denotations of hands at Bridge.) The output should be in the usual suit and value order – in card value order within suit sequence Clubs, Diamonds, Hearts, Spades.

2. Use an unordered_multiset container to store words from an arbitrary paragraph of text entered from the keyboard. Output the words and the frequency with which they occur within the text with six words on each output line.

3. Simulate throwing a pair of dice (with each face value from 1 to 6) and record the sum of the two dice in a multiset container for 1,000 throws of the pair. Obviously, the sum can be from 2 to 12. Output the number of times each of the possible results occurs.

4. Define a vector container initialized with ten book titles of your choice. Create a multimap container where the keys are names and the objects are set containers with elements that are book titles. Allocate a random selection of four to six books to each person in the multimap. List the people in name order along with the books each has. Determine and record the pairs of names that have two books in common, three books in common, and so on, up to the unlikely six books in common. Output the pairs of names that have two or more books the same, along with the books each pair has in common. This output should be in ascending sequence of the number of shared books.

CHAPTER 6

■ ■ ■

Sorting, Merging, Searching, and Partitioning

This chapter describes algorithms that are loosely related to sorting and merging ranges. Two groups of these specifically provide sorting and merging capabilities. Another group provides mechanisms for partitioning a range relative to a given element value. Two further groups provide ways of finding one or more elements in a range. In this chapter you'll learn about:

- How to sort a range defined by random access iterators into ascending or descending sequence.

- How to prevent equal elements from being resequenced in a sort operation.

- How to merge ordered ranges.

- How you can search an unordered range to find one or more given elements.

- What partitioning a range means and how to use the partitioning algorithms the STL provides.

- How to use the binary search algorithms.

Sorting a Range

Sorting is essential in many applications, and many STL algorithms will only work with ranges of objects that are in order. The sort<Iter>() function template that is defined in the algorithm header sorts a range of elements into ascending order by default, which means that the < operator is assumed to be supported for the type of objects to be sorted. The objects must also be *swappable*, which just means that it must be possible to interchange two objects using the swap() function template that is defined in the utility header. This further implies that the type of the objects must implement a move constructor and a move assignment operator. The sort() function template type parameter, Iter, is the type of iterators in the range and they must be *random access iterators*. This implies that only elements in the containers that offer random access iterators can be sorted by the sort() algorithm, which means that only elements in array, vector, or deque containers are acceptable, or elements in a standard array. You saw back in Chapter 2 that the list and forward_list containers have sort() function members; these special members for sorting are necessary because list provides only bidirectional iterators and forward_list only forward iterators.

The template type argument for sort() will be deduced from the function call arguments, which will be the iterators that define the range of objects to be sorted. Of course, the iterator type implicitly defines the type of the objects in the range. Here's an example of using the sort() algorithm:

```
std::vector<int> numbers {99, 77, 33, 66, 22, 11, 44, 88};
std::sort(std::begin(numbers), std::end(numbers));
std::copy(std::begin(numbers), std::end(numbers),
          std::ostream_iterator<int> {std::cout, " "});    // Output: 11 22 33 44 66 77 88 99
```

The sort() call sorts all the elements in the numbers container into ascending sequence and the copy() algorithm outputs the result. You don't have to sort the entire contents of a container. This statement sorts the elements in numbers excluding the first and the last:

```
std::sort(++std::begin(numbers), --std::end(numbers));
```

To sort into descending sequence, you supply the function object that is to be used for comparing elements as the third argument to sort():

```
std::sort(std::begin(numbers), std::end(numbers), std::greater<>());
```

The comparison function must return a bool value and have two parameters that are either of the type resulting from dereferencing the iterators, or of a type to which the dereferenced iterators can be implicitly converted. The parameters can be of different types. As long as the comparison function meets the requirements, it can be anything you like, including a lambda expression. For example:

```
std::deque<string> words {"one", "two", "nine", "nine", "one", "three", "four", "five", "six"};
std::sort(std::begin(words), std::end(words),
                    [](const string& s1, const string& s2){ return s1.back() > s2.back(); });
std::copy(std::begin(words), std::end(words),
  std::ostream_iterator<string> {std::cout, " "}); // six four two one nine nine one three five
```

This sequence of statements sorts the string elements in the deque container, words, and outputs the result. The comparison function here is a lambda expression that compares the last letter in each word to determine the sort order. The result is the elements in descending sequence of their last letters.

Let's see sort() in action with a simple working example that will read Name objects from the keyboard, sort them in ascending sequence, then output the result. The Name class will be defined in the Name.h header, which will contain the following code:

```
#ifndef NAME_H
#define NAME_H
#include <string>                                    // For string class

class Name
{
private:
 std::string first{};
 std::string second{};
```

```cpp
public:
  Name(const std::string& name1, const std::string& name2) : first(name1), second(name2){}
  Name()=default;
  std::string get_first() const {return first;}
  std::string get_second() const { return second; }

  friend std::istream& operator>>(std::istream& in, Name& name);
  friend std::ostream& operator<<(std::ostream& out, const Name& name);
};

// Stream input for Name objects
inline std::istream& operator>>(std::istream& in, Name& name)
{
  return in >> name.first >> name.second;
}

// Stream output for Name objects
inline std::ostream& operator<<(std::ostream& out, const Name& name)
{
  return out << name.first << " " << name.second;
}
#endif
```

The stream insertion and extraction operators are defined for Name objects as friend functions. You could define operator<() as a class member, but I omitted it to show specifying the comparison as an argument to sort(). Here's the program:

```cpp
// Ex6_01.cpp
// Sorting class objects
#include <iostream>                          // For standard streams
#include <string>                            // For string class
#include <vector>                            // For vector container
#include <iterator>                          // For stream and back insert iterators
#include <algorithm>                         // For sort() algorithm
#include "Name.h"

int main()
{
  std::vector<Name> names;
  std::cout << "Enter names as first name followed by second name. Enter Ctrl+Z to end:";
  std::copy(std::istream_iterator<Name>(std::cin), std::istream_iterator<Name>(),
                            std::back_insert_iterator<std::vector<Name>>(names));

  std::cout << names.size() << " names read. Sorting in ascending sequence...\n";
  std::sort(std::begin(names), std::end(names), [](const Name& name1, const Name& name2)
                            {return name1.get_second() < name2.get_second(); });

  std::cout << "\nThe names in ascending sequence are:\n";
  std::copy(std::begin(names), std::end(names), std::ostream_iterator<Name>(std::cout, "\n"));
}
```

Pretty much everything in `main()` is done using STL templates. The `names` container will store the names that are read from `cin`. Input is executed by the `copy()` algorithm, which reads Name object using an `istream_iterator<Name>` instance. The default constructor for `istream_iterator<Name>` creates the end iterator for the stream. The `copy()` function copies each input object to `names` using a `back_inserter<Name>` iterator that is created by the `back_insert_iterator<Name>()` function. Overloading the stream operators for the Name class allows stream iterators to be used for input and output of Name objects.

The comparison function for Name objects is defined by the lambda expression that is the third argument to the `sort()` algorithm. If you were to define `operator<()` as a member of the Name class you could omit this argument. The sorted names are written to the standard output stream by the `copy()` algorithm, which copies the range of elements specified by the first two arguments to the `ostream_iterator<Name>` object that is the third argument.

Here's some sample output:

```
Enter names as first name followed by second name. Enter Ctrl+Z to end:
Jim Jones
Bill Jones
Jane Smith
John Doe
Janet Jones
Willy Schaferknaker
^Z
6 names read. Sorting in ascending sequence...

The names in ascending sequence are:
John Doe
Jim Jones
Bill Jones
Janet Jones
Willy Schaferknaker
Jane Smith
```

The names are sorted only taking the second names into account. You could extend the lambda expression to compare first names when the second names are identical.

You may wonder why I didn't use `pair<string,string>` objects to represent names in this example; it would be simpler than defining a new class. Obviously it is possible to do this but it would be much less clear.

Sorting and the Order of Equal Elements

The `sort()` algorithm may change the order of elements that are equal, which is sometimes not what you want. Suppose you have a container that stores transactions of some kind, perhaps for bank accounts. Suppose further that you want to sort the transactions by account number before processing them so that the accounts can be updated in sequence. If the order in which equal elements appear reflects the time sequence in which they were added to the container, you will need to preserve the order. Allowing the transactions for a given account to be rearranged could result in an account appearing to have been overdrawn, when this was not the case.

The `stable_sort()` algorithm provides what you need in this instance. It sorts the elements in a range and ensures that equal elements remain in their original sequence. There are two versions; one accepts two iterator arguments that specify the range to be sorted, and the other that accepts an additional argument for the comparison. You could modify the statement that sorts the names container in Ex6_01.cpp to see stable_sort() working:

```
std::stable_sort(std::begin(names), std::end(names),
        [](const Name& name1, const Name& name2) { return name1.get_second() < name2.get_second(); });
```

Of course, the output I showed for Ex6_01 that uses sort() did not disturb the order of equal elements so using stable_sort() does not change the output for the same input. The difference is that with stable_sort() it is *guaranteed* that the order of equal elements will not be changed, which is not the case with the sort() algorithm. When you want to be certain that the order of equal elements will remain the same, use stable_sort().

Partial Sorting

It's easiest to understand what is meant by partial sorting through an example. Suppose that you have a container in which you have collected a few million values, but you are only interested in the lowest 100 of these. You could sort the entire contents of the container and select the first 100, but this could be somewhat time consuming. What you need is a *partial sort*, where only the lowest n of a larger number of values in a range are placed in order. There's a special algorithm for this, the partial_sort() algorithm, which expects three arguments that are random access iterators. If the function parameters are first, second, and last, the algorithm is applied to elements in the range [first,last). After executing the algorithm, the range [first,second) will contain the lowest second-first elements from the range [first,last) in ascending sequence.

■ **Note** In case you have not met it before, the notation, [first,last), that I use to represent a range originates in mathematics where it defines an *interval*, which defines a range of numbers. The two values are called *end points*. In this notation, a square bracket indicates that the adjacent end point is included in the range and a parenthesis indicates that the adjacent end point is not included. For example, if (2,5) is an interval of integers, the 2 and the 5 are excluded so it represents just the integers 3,4; this is called an *open interval* because neither end point is included. The interval [2,5) includes 2 but excludes 5 so it represents 2,3,4. (2,5] represent 3,4,5. [2,5] represents 2,3,4,5 and is called a *closed interval* because both end points are included. Of course, first and last are iterators and [first,last) indicates that what first points to is included and what last points to is not – so it expresses exactly a range in C++.

Here's some code that shows how the partial_sort() algorithm works:

```
size_t count {5};                               // Number of elements to be sorted
std::vector<int> numbers {22, 7, 93, 45, 19, 56, 88, 12, 8, 7, 15, 10};
std::partial_sort(std::begin(numbers), std::begin(numbers) + count, std::end(numbers));
```

The effect of executing partial_sort() above is shown in Figure 6-1.

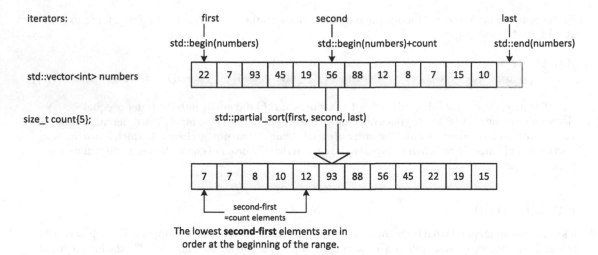

Figure 6-1. *Operation of the* partial_sort() *algorithm*

The lowest count elements are in order. In the range [first,second), the element that second points to is not included because second is the one-past-the-end iterator. Figure 6-1 shows the results from executing the statements on my system; it may be different on your system. Note that the original order of the elements that are not sorted is not maintained. The sequence of these elements after the execution of partial_sort() is unspecified and depends on your implementation.

If you want the partial_sort() algorithm to use a comparison that is different from the < operator, you can supply a function object as an additional argument. For example:

```
std::partial_sort(std::begin(numbers), std::begin(numbers) + count, std::end(numbers),
                                                          std::greater<>());
```

Now the *largest* count elements from numbers will be in *descending* sequence at the beginning of the container. On my system the result of executing this statement is:

---

93 88 56 45 22 7 19 12 8 7 15 10

Again, the original order of the elements in numbers that are not sorted is not preserved.

The partial_sort_copy() algorithm does essentially the same as partial_sort() except that the sorted elements are copied to a different range – in another container. The first two arguments are the iterators specifying the range to which the partial sort is to be applied; the third and fourth arguments are the iterators identifying the range where the result is to be stored. The number of elements in the destination range determines the number of elements from the input range that will be sorted. Here's an example:

```
std::vector<int> numbers {22, 7, 93, 45, 19, 56, 88, 12, 8, 7, 15, 10};
size_t count {5};                        // Number of elements to be sorted
std::vector<int> result(count);          // Destination for the results - count elements
std::partial_sort_copy(std::begin(numbers), std::end(numbers), std::begin(result),
                                                          std::end(result));
std::copy(std::begin(numbers), std::end(numbers), std::ostream_iterator<int> {std::cout, " "});
std::cout << std::endl;
```

```
std::copy(std::begin(result), std::end(result), std::ostream_iterator<int> {std::cout, " "});
std::cout << std::endl;
```

These statements implement a partial sort of the numbers container. The idea is to place the lowest count elements from numbers in order and store them in the result container. The range you specify as the destination must exist so there must be at least count elements in the destination container, result, and in this instance we allocate exactly the number necessary. The output from executing these statements is:

```
22 7 93 45 19 56 88 12 8 7 15 10
7 7 8 10 12
```

You can see that the sequence of elements in numbers is undisturbed, and result contains copies of the lowest count elements from numbers in ascending sequence.

Of course, you can specify a different comparison function by an extra argument:

```
std::partial_sort_copy(std::begin(numbers), std::end(numbers), std::begin(result), std::end(result),
                                                    std::greater<>());
```

Specifying an instance of greater<> as the function object will cause the *largest* count elements to be copied to result in *descending* sequence. If this statement is followed by the output statements from the previous code fragment, the output will be:

```
22 7 93 45 19 56 88 12 8 7 15 10
93 88 56 45 22
```

As before, the order of elements in the original container is undisturbed.

The nth_element() algorithm is different from partial_sort(). The range to which it applies is defined by the first and third arguments to the function, and the second argument is an iterator pointing to the nth element. Executing nth_element() will result in the nth element being set to the element that would be there if the range was fully sorted. All the elements that precede the nth element in the range will be less than the nth element, and all the elements that follow it will be greater. By default the algorithm uses the < operator to produce the result. Here's some code to exercise nth_element():

```
std::vector<int> numbers {22, 7, 93, 45, 19, 56, 88, 12, 8, 7, 15, 10};
size_t count {5};                              // Index of nth element
std::nth_element(std::begin(numbers), std::begin(numbers) + count, std::end(numbers));
```

The nth element is the 6th in the numbers container, which corresponds to numbers[5]. Figure 6-2 illustrates how this works.

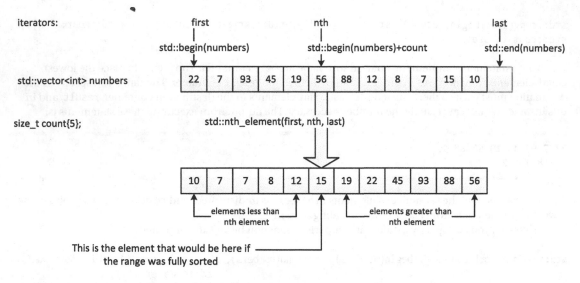

Figure 6-2. *Operation of the* nth_element() *algorithm*

The elements preceding the nth element will be less than the nth element, but will not necessarily be in order. Similarly, the elements that follow the nth element will be greater than it, but not necessarily ordered. If the second argument is the same as the third argument – the end of the range, the algorithm has no effect.

As with the previous algorithms in this chapter, you can supply a function object that defines the comparison as a fourth argument:

```
std::nth_element(std::begin(numbers), std::begin(numbers) + count, std::end(numbers),
                                                            std::greater<>());
```

This uses the > operator to compare elements so the nth element will be what it should be if the elements are in descending sequence. Elements preceding the nth element will be greater, and elements following will be less. With the initial values in the numbers container as previously, the result will be:

---

45 56 93 88 22 19 10 12 15 7 8 7

The order of the elements either side of the nth element may be different on your system, but those on the left should be greater than it and the ones to the right should be smaller.

Testing for Sorted Ranges

Sorting is time consuming, particularly so when you have a large number of elements. Testing whether or not a range is already ordered can avoid unnecessary sort operations. The is_sorted() function template returns true if the elements in the range specified by the two iterator arguments are in ascending sequence. The iterators must be at least forward iterators to allow the elements to be processed sequentially. Just to remind you – forward iterators supports prefix and postfix increment operations. Here's an example of using is_sorted():

```
std::vector<int> numbers {22, 7, 93, 45, 19};
std::vector<double> data {1.5, 2.5, 3.5, 4.5};
```

```
std::cout << "numbers is "
          << (std::is_sorted(std::begin(numbers), std::end(numbers)) ? "": "not ")
          << "in ascending sequence.\n";
std::cout << "data is "
          << (std::is_sorted(std::begin(data), std::end(data)) ? "": "not ")
          << "in ascending sequence." << std::endl;
```

The default comparison used is the < operator. The output will show that numbers is not in ascending sequence whereas data is. There's a version that allows you to supply a function object to compare elements:

```
std::cout << "data reversed is "
          << (std::is_sorted(std::rbegin(data), std::rend(data), std::greater<>()) ? "": "not ")
          << "in descending sequence." << std::endl;
```

The output from this statement will indicate that the elements in data in reverse order are in descending sequence.

You can also determine the elements in a range that are ordered using the is_sorted_until() function template. The arguments are iterators that define the range to be tested. This function returns an iterator that is the upper bound of elements from the range that are in ascending sequence. Here's an example:

```
std::vector<string> pets {"cat", "chicken", "dog", "pig", "llama", "coati", "goat"};
std::cout << "The pets in ascending sequence are:\n";
std::copy(std::begin(pets), std::is_sorted_until(std::begin(pets), std::end(pets)),
                                      std::ostream_iterator<string>{std::cout, " "});
```

The first two arguments to the copy() algorithm are the begin iterator for the pets container and the iterator that is_sorted_until() returns when it is applied to all the elements in pets. The is_sorted_until() algorithm will return the upper bound of the elements in pets that are in ascending sequence – which will be an iterator pointing to the first element that is less than its predecessor or the end iterator of the sequence if it sorted. The output from this code will be:

```
The pets in ascending sequence are:
cat chicken dog pig
```

"llama" is the first element that is less than its predecessor so "pig" is the last of the elements that are in ascending sequence.

You have the option of supplying a function object to be used to compare elements:

```
std::vector<string> pets {"dog", "coati", "cat", "chicken", "pig", "llama", "goat"};
std::cout << "The pets in descending sequence are:\n";
std::copy(std::begin(pets),
          std::is_sorted_until(std::begin(pets), std::end(pets), std::greater<>()),
                                      std::ostream_iterator<string>{std::cout, " "});
```

This time we are looking for a descending sequence of elements because the operator>() member of the string class will be used to compare elements. The output will be:

```
The pets in descending sequence are:
dog coati cat
```

"chicken" is the first element that is greater than its predecessor so the iterator returned by is_sorted_until() will point to this element. Thus "cat" is the last of the elements that are in descending sequence.

Merging Ranges

A *merge* operation combines elements from two ranges that are ordered in the same sense – either both in ascending sequence or both descending. The result is a range containing copies of the elements from both input ranges with the result ordered in the same way as the original ranges. Figure 6-3 illustrates how this works.

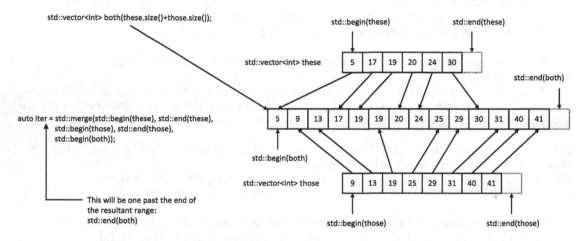

Figure 6-3. *Merging elements from two* vector *containers*

The merge() algorithm merges two ranges and stores the result in a third range. It uses the < operator to compare elements. Figure 6-3 shows a merge operation applied to the contents of the these and those containers, where the resultant range is stored in the both container. The merge() algorithm expects five arguments. The first two are iterators that specify the first input range – these in this case, the second two are iterators identifying the second input range – those in this example, and the last argument is an iterator identifying where the first of the merged range of elements should go – the both container. The iterators that identify the ranges to be merged only need to be input iterators as a minimum, and the iterator for the destination range to hold the result only needs to be an output iterator.

The merge() algorithm has no information about the container for the merged range of elements so it cannot create elements – it can only store elements using the iterator you supply as the fifth argument. Therefore the elements in the destination range in the example must already exist. This is ensured in Figure 6-3 by creating the both container with the number of elements specified as the sum of the element count for each of the input containers. The destination range can be anywhere, even in one of the source range containers, but the source and destination ranges *must not* overlap; if they do, the consequences are undefined but you can be sure the effect will not be good. Of course, if you specify the destination by an insert iterator, elements will be created automatically.

The merge() algorithm returns an iterator that points to one past the last element in the merged range, so you can identify the merged range by the fifth iterator argument you used in the function call plus the iterator that the function returns.

When the comparison needs to be other than the < operator, you can supply a function object as a sixth argument. For example:

```
std::vector<int> these {2, 15, 4, 11, 6, 7};              // 1st input to merge
std::vector<int> those {5, 2, 3, 2, 14, 11, 6};           // 2nd input to merge
std::stable_sort(std::begin(these), std::end(these),      // Sort 1st range in...
                 std::greater<>());                       // ...descending sequence
std::stable_sort(std::begin(those), std::end(those),      // Sort 2nd range
                 std::greater<>());
std::vector<int> result(these.size() + those.size() + 10); // Plenty of room for results

auto end_iter = std::merge(std::begin(these), std::end(these),    // Merge 1st range...
                    std::begin(those), std::end(those),           // ...and 2nd range...
                    std::begin(result), std::greater<>()); // ...into result
std::copy(std::begin(result), end_iter, std::ostream_iterator<int>{std::cout, " "});
```

This sequence of statements first sorts the contents of the two vector containers into descending sequence using stable_sort(), which guarantees that the original order of equal elements will be maintained. The merge operation merges the contents of the two container into a third container, result, which has 10 more elements created than are necessary – just to demonstrate the use of the iterator that merge() returns. The copy() algorithm copies the range specified by the begin iterator for result and the end_iter iterator that merge() returns to the output stream iterator. The output will be:

---

15 14 11 11 7 6 6 5 4 3 2 2 2

The inplace_merge() algorithm merges two consecutive sorted sequences of elements in the same range in place. There are three parameters, first, second, and last that are bidirectional iterators. The range that is the first input sequence is [first,second) and the range that is the second input sequence is [second,last) so the element pointed to by second is in the second input range. The result will be the range [first,last). Figure 6-4 shows this operation.

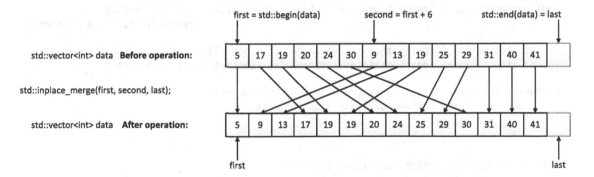

Figure 6-4. inplace_merge() operation

The data container in Figure 6-4 contains two ranges, both in ascending sequence. The inplace_merge() operation combines these to produce a range in ascending sequence in the same container.

We can merge several of the algorithms you have seen in this chapter into a single working example. This somewhat contrived example will process credit and debit transactions that are entered from the keyboard and apply them to a set of accounts that are created as necessary. We'll always create accounts with zero balances. A transaction will be an object containing the account number, the amount, and whether the amount is a credit or a debit. Processing a transaction for a nonexistent account will cause the account to be created. An account object will contain members that identify the unique account number, the owner's name, and the current balance. The name of an account holder will be a pair object containing a first name and a second name. An account number will be an unsigned integer. A credit will be indicated as a bool value, and account balances and amounts to be debited or credited will be of type double.

The Transaction type will be defined in the Transaction.h header file like this:

```cpp
#ifndef TRANSACTION_H
#define TRANSACTION_H
#include <iostream>                           // For stream class
#include <iomanip>                            // For stream manipulators
#include "Account.h"

class Transaction
{
private:
  size_t account_number {};                  // The account number
  double amount {};                          // The amount
  bool credit {true};                        // credit = true debit=false

public:
  Transaction()=default;
  Transaction(size_t number, double amnt, bool cr) : account_number {number}, amount {amnt},
                                                    credit {cr}{}

  size_t get_acc_number() const { return account_number; }

  // Less-than operator - compares account numbers
  bool operator<(const Transaction& transaction) const { return account_number <
                                            transaction.account_number; }

  // Greater-than operator - compares account numbers
  bool operator>(const Transaction& transaction) const { return account_number >
                                            transaction.account_number; }

  friend std::ostream& operator<<(std::ostream& out, const Transaction& transaction);
  friend std::istream& operator>>(std::istream& in, Transaction& transaction);

  // Making the Account class a friend allows Account objects
  // to access private members of Transaction objects
  friend class Account;

};
// Stream insertion operator for Transaction objects
std::ostream& operator<<(std::ostream& out, const Transaction& transaction)
{
  return out << std::right << std::setfill('0') << std::setw(5)
             << transaction.account_number
             << std::setfill(' ') << std::setw(8) << std::fixed << std::setprecision(2)
             << transaction.amount
             << (transaction.credit ? " CR" : " DR");
}
```

```
// Stream extraction operator for Transaction objects
std::istream& operator>>(std::istream& in, Transaction& tr)
{
  if((in >> std::skipws >> tr.account_number).eof())
    return in;
  return in >> tr.amount >> std::boolalpha >> tr.credit;
}
#endif
```

The default constructor is typically required to allow default elements to be created in a container. Including both the < and > operators in the class allows the possibility to order Transaction objects in ascending or descending sequence, although the example won't make use of both options. The Account class, which we will get to next, is a friend of the Transaction class, so a function member of the Account class can access the private data members of a Transaction object that is passed to it. With the overloaded stream input and output operators defined, we will be able to use the copy() algorithm in conjunction with the stream iterators that the STL provides to read and write Transaction objects.

The Account class will be defined in the Account.h header:

```
#ifndef ACCCOUNT_H
#define ACCCOUNT_H
#include <iostream>                               // For stream class
#include <iomanip>                                // For stream manipulators
#include <string>                                 // For string class
#include <utility>                                // For pair template type
#include "Transaction.h"

using first_name = std::string;
using second_name = std::string;
using Name = std::pair<first_name, second_name>;

class Account
{
private:
  size_t account_number {};                       // 5-digit account number
  Name name {"", ""};                             // A pair containing 1st & 2nd names
  double balance {};                              // The account balance - negative when
overdrawn

public:
  Account()=default;
  Account(size_t number, const Name& nm) : account_number {number}, name {nm}{}

  double get_balance() const { return balance; }
  void set_balance(double bal) { balance = bal; }

  size_t get_acc_number() const {return account_number;}
  const Name& get_name() const { return name; }

  // Apply a transaction to the account
  bool apply_transaction(const Transaction& transaction)
```

```
  {
    if(transaction.credit)                          // For a credit...
      balance += transaction.amount;                // ...add the mount
    else                                            // For a debit...
      balance -= transaction.amount;                // ...subtract the amount
    return balance < 0.0;                           // Return true when overdrawn
  }

  // Less-than operator - compares by account number
  bool operator<(const Account& acc) const { return account_number < acc.account_number; }

  friend std::ostream& operator<<(std::ostream& out, const Account& account);
};

// Stream insertion operator for Account objects
std::ostream& operator<<(std::ostream& out, const Account& acc)
{
  return out << std::left << std::setw(20) << acc.name.first + " " + acc.name.second
    << std::right << std::setfill('0') << std::setw(5) << acc.account_number
    << std::setfill(' ') << std::setw(8) << std::fixed << std::setprecision(2) << acc.balance;
}
#endif
```

In addition to the account number, the class has a Name member to identify the owner of the account. A Name is just an alias for the pair<string,string> type, and the first_name and second_name aliases are solely to identify the significance of each of the pair members. Type aliases are often useful for imparting application-specific meaning to general types.

Overloading the stream insertion operator for Account objects allows the object to be written to an output stream using <<. The operator<() member definition allows Account objects to be ordered by account number when sorting or storing in an ordered container. If you want Account objects to be ordered in a different way – by name for instance, you can define a function object that provides the comparison function. The example will sort Account objects by name and the function object to enable this will be defined in Compare_Names.h, like this:

```
#ifndef COMPARE_NAMES_H
#define COMPARE_NAMES_H
#include "Account.h"

// Order Account objects in ascending sequence by Name
class Compare_Names
{
public:
  bool operator()(const Account& acc1, const Account& acc2)
  {
    const auto& name1 = acc1.get_name();
    const auto& name2 = acc2.get_name();
    return (name1.second < name2.second) ||
                        ((name1.second == name2.second) && (name1.first < name2.first));
  }
};
#endif
```

You should have no trouble understanding how this works. The function call operator definition compares the Name members of two Account objects, primarily by second name, and secondarily by first name.

The main() program to make use of the classes we have defined will be in Ex6_02.cpp:

```cpp
// Ex6_02.cpp
// Sorting and inplace merging
#include <iostream>                          // For standard streams
#include <string>                            // For string class
#include <algorithm>                         // For sort(), inplace_merge()
#include <functional>                        // For greater<T>
#include <vector>                            // For vector container
#include <utility>                           // For pair template type
#include <map>                               // For map container
#include <iterator>                          // For stream and back insert iterators
#include "Account.h"
#include "Transaction.h"
#include "Compare_Names.h"

using std::string;
using first_name = string;
using second_name = string;
using Name = std::pair<first_name, second_name>;
using Account_Number = size_t;

// Read the name of an account holder
Name get_holder_name(Account_Number number)
{
  std::cout << "Enter the holder's first and second names for account number " << number << ": ";
  string first {};
  string second {};
  std::cin >> first  >> second;
  return std::make_pair(first, second);
}

int main()
{
  std::vector<Transaction> transactions;

  std::cout << "Enter each transaction as:\n"
            << "   5 digit account number   amount   credit(true or false).\n"
            << "Enter Ctrl+Z to end.\n";

  // Read 1st set of transactions
  std::copy(std::istream_iterator<Transaction> {std::cin}, std::istream_iterator<Transaction> {},
                                           std::back_inserter(transactions));
  std::cin.clear();                          // Clear the EOF flag for the stream

  // Sort 1st set in  descending account sequence
  std::stable_sort(std::begin(transactions), std::end(transactions), std::greater<>());
```

```
// List the transactions
std::cout << "First set of transactions after sorting...\n";
std::copy(std::begin(transactions), std::end(transactions),
                           std::ostream_iterator<Transaction>{std::cout, "\n"});

// Read 2nd set of transactions
std::cout << "\nEnter more transactions:\n";
std::copy(std::istream_iterator<Transaction> {std::cin}, std::istream_iterator<Transaction> {},
                           std::back_inserter(transactions));
std::cin.clear();                              // Clear the EOF flag for the stream

// List the transactions
std::cout << "\nSorted first set of transactions with second set appended...\n";
std::copy(std::begin(transactions), std::end(transactions),
                           std::ostream_iterator<Transaction>{std::cout, "\n"});

// Sort second set into descending account sequence
auto iter = std::is_sorted_until(std::begin(transactions), std::end(transactions),
                                            std::greater<>());
std::stable_sort(iter, std::end(transactions), std::greater<>());

// List the transactions
std::cout << "\nSorted first set of transactions with sorted second set appended...\n";
std::copy(std::begin(transactions), std::end(transactions),
                           std::ostream_iterator<Transaction>{std::cout, "\n"});

// Merge transactions in place
std::inplace_merge(std::begin(transactions), iter, std::end(transactions), std::greater<>());

// List the transactions
std::cout << "\nMerged sets of transactions...\n";
std::copy(std::begin(transactions), std::end(transactions),
                           std::ostream_iterator<Transaction>{std::cout, "\n"});

// Process transactions creating Account objects when necessary
std::map<Account_Number, Account> accounts;
for(const auto& tr : transactions)
{
  Account_Number number = tr.get_acc_number();
  auto iter = accounts.find(number);
  if(iter == std::end(accounts))
    iter = accounts.emplace(number, Account {number, get_holder_name(number)}).first;

  if(iter->second.apply_transaction(tr))
  {
    auto name = iter->second.get_name();
    std::cout << "\nAccount number " << number
              << " for " << name.first << " " <<name.second << " is overdrawn!\n"
              << "The concept is that you bank with us - not the other way round, so fix it!\n"
              << std::endl;
  }
}
```

```
  // Copy accounts to a vector container
  std::vector<Account> accs;
  for(const auto& pr :accounts)
    accs.push_back(pr.second);

  // List accounts after sorting in name sequence
  std::stable_sort(std::begin(accs), std::end(accs), Compare_Names());
  std::copy(std::begin(accs), std::end(accs), std::ostream_iterator < Account > {std::cout, "\n"});
}
```

The get_holder_name() is a helper function that reads a name from cin for a given account number. This is for use when a transaction is processed for a given account number and there is no Account object. The Name object that is returned will be used in the creation of the Account object.

Transactions are read and stored as Transaction objects in a vector<Transaction> container, transactions. The code reads one sequence of transactions that are sorted into descending sequence using stable_sort(). A second sequence of transactions is then read into the same container and sorted in the same way. By contriving to create a vector that contains two sorted sequences of transactions, we are then able to make use of inplace_merge() to create an ordered combination of the two sequences.

Here's an example of output resulting from seven transactions against five accounts. I chose the transaction amounts to demonstrate the way the sort and merge operations behave.

```
Enter each transaction as:
  5 digit account number    amount    credit(true or false).
Enter Ctrl+Z to end.
12345 40 true
12344 50 true
12346 75.5 true
^Z
First set of transactions after sorting...
12346    75.50 CR
12345    40.00 CR
12344    50.00 CR

Enter more transactions:
12344 25.25 true
12345 75 false
12345 100 true
12346 100 true
^Z

Sorted first set of transactions with second set appended...
12346    75.50 CR
12345    40.00 CR
12344    50.00 CR
12344    25.25 CR
12345    75.00 DR
12345   100.00 CR
12346   100.00 CR
```

```
Sorted first set of transactions with sorted second set appended...
12346    75.50 CR
12345    40.00 CR
12344    50.00 CR
12344    25.25 CR
12346   100.00 CR
12345    75.00 DR
12345   100.00 CR

Merged sets of transactions...
12346    75.50 CR
12346   100.00 CR
12345    40.00 CR
12345    75.00 DR
12345   100.00 CR
12344    50.00 CR
12344    25.25 CR
Enter the holder's first and second names for account number 12346: Stan Dupp
Enter the holder's first and second names for account number 12345: Ann Ounce

Account number 12345 for Ann Ounce is overdrawn!
The concept is that you bank with us - not the other way round, so fix it!

Enter the holder's first and second names for account number 12344: Dan Druff
Dan Druff        12344    75.25
Stan Dupp        12346   175.50
Ann Ounce        12345    65.00
```

The sequence of Transaction objects are listed at each stage so you can see that the stable_sort() and inplace_merge() algorithms work as I described. In particular, the order of equivalent transactions is maintained, so the debits and credits are applied in the sequence in which they originate. Finally, the accounts are listed in name order to show that the transactions have been applied correctly. This is done by copying the Account objects from the map container to a vector<Account> container and applying the stable_sort() algorithm to the elements in the vector with a Compare_Names function object providing the comparison. You could copy the Account objects to a set<Account, Compare_Names> container instead of a vector<Account> to have the objects ordered automatically, but then you would miss the opportunity to use stable_sort().

Searching a Range

The STL offers a diversity of algorithms for searching a range of objects in various ways. Most of these work with unordered sequences. but some, which I'll get to later, require the sequences to be sorted.

Finding an Element in a Range

There are three algorithms for finding a single object in a range that you define by two input iterators.

- The find() algorithm finds the first object in the range specified by the first two arguments that is equal to the third argument.

- The find_if() algorithm finds the first object in the range specified by the first two arguments for which the predicate specified by the third argument returns true. The predicate must not modify the object that is passed to it.

- The find_if_not() algorithm finds the first object in the range specified by the first two arguments for which the predicate specified by the third argument returns false. The predicate must not modify the object that is passed to it.

Each algorithm returns an iterator that points to the object that was found, or the end iterator of the range if the object was not found. Here's an illustration of how you can use find():

```
std::vector<int> numbers {5, 46, -5, -6, 23, 17, 5, 9, 6, 5};
int value {23};
auto iter = std::find(std::begin(numbers), std::end(numbers), value);
if(iter != std::end(numbers)) std::cout << value << " was found.\n";
```

This code fragment will output the message that 23 is indeed found in the numbers vector. Of course, you can use find() repeatedly to find all occurrences of a given element in a range:

```
size_t count {};
int five {5};
auto start_iter = std::begin(numbers);
auto end_iter = std::end(numbers);
while((start_iter = std::find(start_iter, end_iter, five)) != end_iter)
{
  ++count;
  ++start_iter;
}
std::cout << five << " was found " << count << " times." << std::endl;    // 3 times
```

The count variable that is incremented in the while loop counts the number of times five is found in the numbers vector. The loop expression calls find() to find five within the range defined by start_iter and end_iter. The iterator that find() returns is stored in start_iter, overwriting the previous value of the variable. Initially, the range that is searched is all the elements in numbers so find() will return an iterator that points to the first occurrence of five. Each time five is found, start_iter is incremented in the loop so it will point to the element that follows the element that was found. Thus the next iteration will search from that point to the end of the sequence. When five is no longer found, find() will return end_iter so the loop will end.

You could use find_if() to find the first element in numbers that is greater than value like this:

```
int value {5};
auto iter1 = std::find_if(std::begin(numbers), std::end(numbers),
                                     [value](int n) { return n > value; });
if(iter1 != std::end(numbers)) std::cout << *iter1 << " was found greater than " << value << ".\n";
```

The third argument to find_if() is a predicate defined by a lambda expression. The lambda expression captures value by value and returns true when the argument to the lambda is greater than value. This fragment will find the element with the value 46. You could use find_if() in a loop to find all occurrences of numbers greater than value in the same way as the previous code fragment.

You could use the find_if_not() algorithm to find elements for which a predicate is false like this:

```
size_t count {};
int five {5};
auto start_iter = std::begin(numbers);
auto end_iter = std::end(numbers);
while((start_iter = std::find_if_not(start_iter, end_iter,
                              [five](int n) {return n > five; })) != end_iter)
{
  ++count;
  ++start_iter;
}
std::cout << count << " elements were found that are not greater than "<< five << std::endl;
```

The predicate that is the third argument to find_if_not() is a lambda expression that is similar to what I used earlier with the find_if() algorithm. This returns true only when an element is greater than five. An element is found when the predicate returns false so the operation is effectively finding elements that are less than or equal to five. Five elements will be found with this fragment corresponding to the values 5, -5, -6, 5, and 5 in the range.

Finding any of a Range of Elements in a Range

The find_first_of() algorithm searches a range for the first occurrence of any element from a second range. The range to be searched can be specified by just input iterators, but the range identifying what is being sought must be at least forward iterators. Elements from the two ranges are compared using the == operator, so if the ranges specify objects of a class type, the class must implement operator==(). Here's an example of using find_first_of():

```
string text {"The world of searching"};
string vowels {"aeiou"};
auto iter = std::find_first_of(std::begin(text), std::end(text), std::begin(vowels),
                                          std::end(vowels));
if(iter != std::end(text)) std::cout << "We found '" << *iter << "'." << std::endl; // We found 'e'.
```

This code searches text for the first occurrence of any of the characters in vowels. An iterator pointing to the third letter in "The" is returned in this instance. You could use a loop to find all occurrences in text of any character from vowels:

```
string found {};                                // Records characters that are found
for(auto iter = std::begin(text);
    (iter = std::find_first_of(
             iter, std::end(text), std::begin(vowels), std::end(vowels))) != std::end(text);   )
  found += *(iter++);

std::cout << "The characters \"" << found << "\" were found in text." << std::endl;
```

This uses a for loop - just to show that you can. The first loop control expression defines iter with its initial value as the begin iterator for text. The second control expression calls find_first_of() to search the range [iter, std::end(text)) for the first occurrence of any character from vowels. The iterator that find_first_of() returns is stored in iter, which is then compared with the end iterator for text. If iter is now the end iterator for text, the loop ends. If iter is not the end iterator for text, the body of the loop executes to append the character to which iter points to the found string, and increments iter to point to the next character. This character will be used as the start position for the range in the next search. The output that this fragment produces will be:

```
The characters "eooeai" were found in text.
```

Another version of find_first_of() enables you to search a range for the first occurrence of any element from a second range where the binary predicate specified by the fifth argument returns true. The elements in the ranges do not need to be of the same type. You can use this version of the algorithm to define a comparison for equality when the == operator is not supported for the elements to be compared, but you can use it in other ways too. For example:

```
std::vector<long> numbers {64L, 46L, -65L, -128L, 121L, 17L, 35L, 9L, 91L, 5L};
int factors[] {7, 11, 13};
auto iter = std::find_first_of(std::begin(numbers),
                               std::end(numbers),              // The range to be searched
                    std::begin(factors), std::end(factors),   // Elements sought
                    [](long v, long d) { return v % d == 0;}); // Predicate - true for a match
  if(iter != std::end(numbers)) std::cout << *iter << " was found." << std::endl;
```

The predicate is a lambda expression that returns true when the first argument is exactly divisible by the second argument. Thus this code fragment finds -65 because this is the first element in numbers that is exactly divisible by one of the elements in the factors array, 13 in this case. The types of the parameters in the predicate can be different from the types of the elements in the ranges as long as the elements in each range can be implicitly converted to the corresponding parameter type. Here, the elements in the factors array are being implicitly converted to type long.

Of course, you can use a loop to find all elements for which the predicate returns true:

```
std::vector<long> numbers {64L, 46L, -65L, -128L, 121L, 17L, 35L, 9L, 91L, 5L};
int factors[] {7, 11, 13};
std::vector<long> results;                            // Stores elements found

  auto iter = std::begin(numbers);
  while((iter = std::find_first_of(iter, std::end(numbers),          // Range searched
                          std::begin(factors), std::end(factors),    // Elements sought
                      [](long v, long d) { return v % d == 0; }))    // Predicate
                                              != std::end(numbers))
    results.push_back(*iter++);

std::cout << results.size() << " values were found:\n";
std::copy(std::begin(results), std::end(results), std::ostream_iterator < long > {std::cout, " " });
std::cout << std::endl;
```

This code fragment finds all the elements in numbers that have an element from factors as a factor. The while loop continues as long as the iterator that find_first_of() returns is not the end iterators for numbers. The iter variable starts out pointing to the first element in numbers and the iterator that points to the element found is stored in iter, overwriting the previous value. In the loop body, the element to which iter points is stored in the results container, and iter is then incremented to point to the element that follows. When the loop ends, results contains all the element that were found and these are output using the copy() algorithm.

Finding Multiple Elements from a Range

The `adjacent_find()` algorithm searches for two successive elements in a range that are identical. Successive pairs of elements are compared using the == operator and an iterator that points to the first of the first two equal elements is returned. The algorithm returns the end iterator for the range if no pairs of elements are equal. For example:

```
string saying {"Children should be seen and not heard."};
auto iter = std::adjacent_find(std::begin(saying), std::end(saying));
if(iter != std::end(saying))
    std::cout << "In the following text:\n\"" << saying << "\"\n'"
              << *iter << "' is repeated starting at index position "
              << std::distance(std::begin(saying), iter) << std::endl;
```

This searches the saying string for the first two successive characters that are identical so the code will produce the output:

```
In the following text:
"Children should be seen and not heard."
'e' is repeated starting at index position 20
```

A second version of the `adjacent_find()` algorithm allows you to supply a predicate that is applied to successive elements. Here's how you could use this to find the first pair of successive integers in a range that are both odd:

```
std::vector<long> numbers {64L, 46L, -65L, -128L, 121L, 17L, 35L, 9L, 91L, 5L};
auto iter = std::adjacent_find(std::begin(numbers), std::end(numbers),
                                 [](long n1, long n2){ return n1 % 2 && n2 % 2; });
if(iter != std::end(numbers))
  std::cout << "The first pair of odd numbers is "
            << *iter << " and " << *(iter+1) << std::endl;
```

The lambda expression returns true when both arguments are not multiples of 2 so this code fragment will find the numbers 121 and 17.

The find_end() Algorithm

The `find_end()` algorithm finds the last occurrence in a range of a second range of elements. You can visualize this as finding the last occurrence of a subsequence in a sequence of elements of any type. The algorithm returns an iterator that points to the first element in the last occurrence of the subsequence, or the end iterator for the range being searched. Here's an example of using this:

```
string text  {"Smith, where Jones had had \"had\", had had \"had had\"."
              " \"Had had\" had had the examiners\' approval."};
std::cout << text << std::endl;
  string phrase {"had had"};
  auto iter = std::find_end(std::begin(text), std::end(text), std::begin(phrase), std::end(phrase));
  if(iter != std::end(text))
    std::cout << "The last \"" << phrase
              << "\" was found at index " << std::distance(std::begin(text), iter) << std::endl;
```

This searches text for the last occurrence of "had had" and produces the following output:

Smith, where Jones had had "had", had had "had had". "Had had" had had the examiners' approval.
The last "had had" was found at index 63

You could search for all occurrences of phrase in text. This example simply counts the number of occurrences:

```
size_t count {};
auto iter = std::end(text);
auto end_iter = iter;
while((iter = std::find_end(std::begin(text), end_iter, std::begin(phrase),
                                                    std::end(phrase))) != end_iter)
{
  ++count;
  end_iter = iter;
}
std::cout << "\n\""<< phrase << "\" was found " << count << " times." << std::endl;
```

The while loop expression does the searching. The loop expression searches the range
[std::begin(text), end_iter) for phrase, and the first range that is searched is all the elements in text.
To help clarify what is happening here, the process is illustrated in Figure 6-5.

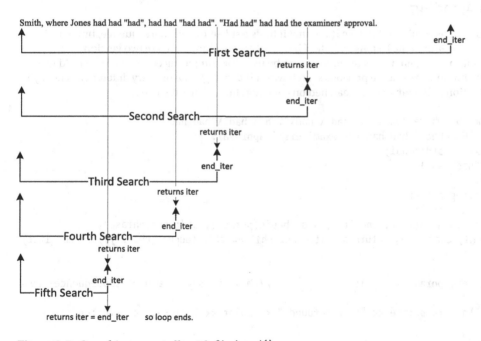

Figure 6-5. *Searching repeatedly with find_end()*

The iterator that is returned by find_end() is stored in iter, and when this is equal to end_iter – the previous value of iter – the loop ends. Because find_end() finds the *last* occurrence of a subsequence, the end iterator for the range to be searched next time (end_iter) must be changed to the iterator that the algorithm returns. This points to the first character of the sequence that was found so the next search will be from the beginning of text up to this point, omitting the sequence that was found. After incrementing count within the loop body, end_iter is set to iter. This is necessary because the next search will return this iterator if phrase is not found.

A second version of find_end() accepts a binary predicate as a fifth argument that is used to compare elements. You could use this to repeat the previous search ignoring case:

```
size_t count {};
auto iter = std::end(text);
auto end_iter = iter;
while((iter = std::find_end(std::begin(text), end_iter, std::begin(phrase), std::end(phrase),
    [](char ch1, char ch2){ return std::toupper(ch1) == std::toupper(ch2); })) != end_iter)
  {
    ++count;
    end_iter = iter;
  }
```

Now pairs of characters from the two ranges will be compared after converting them to upper case. Five instances of phrase will be found in text because "Had had" will be found to be equal to phrase.

The search() Algorithm

The search() algorithm is similar to find_end() in that it finds a subsequence in a sequence, but it finds the first occurrence rather than the last. As with the find_end() algorithm, there are two versions – the second accepting a fifth argument that is the predicate to be used for comparing elements. You could use the search() algorithm to carry out the previous search with find_end(). The primary difference is how you change the specification of the range to be searched on each iteration. Here's the code:

```
string text {"Smith, where Jones had had \"had\", had had \"had had\"."
             " \"Had had\" had had the examiners\' approval."};
std::cout << text << std::endl;
string phrase {"had had"};
size_t count {};
auto iter = std::begin(text);
auto end_iter = end(text);
while((iter = std::search(iter, end_iter, std::begin(phrase), std::end(phrase),
      [](char ch1, char ch2){ return std::toupper(ch1) == std::toupper(ch2); })) != end_iter)
{
  ++count;
  std::advance(iter, phrase.size());                // Move to beyond end of subsequence found
}
    std::cout << "\n\"" << phrase << "\" was found " << count << " times." << std::endl;
```

Executing this code will produce the following output:

```
Smith, where Jones had had "had", had had "had had". "Had had" had had the examiners' approval.

"had had" was found 5 times.
```

We are still searching for "had had" ignoring case, but in the forward direction to find the first occurrence. The iterator that the search() algorithm returns points to the first element in the subsequence that was found, so to search for the next instance of phrase, iter must be incremented by the number of elements in phrase to make it point to the first element that follows the subsequence that was found.

The search_n() Algorithm

The search_n() algorithm searches a range for a given number of successive occurrences of an element. The first two arguments are forward iterators defining the range to be searched, the third argument is the number of successive occurrences of the element that is the fourth argument that you want to find. Here's an example:

```cpp
std::vector<double> values {2.7, 2.7, 2.7, 3.14, 3.14, 3.14, 2.7, 2.7};
double value {3.14};
int times {3};
auto iter = std::search_n(std::begin(values), std::end(values), times, value);
if(iter != std::end(values))
    std::cout << times << " successive instances of " << value
              << " found starting index " << std::distance(std::begin(values), iter)
              << std::endl;
```

This code searches for the first occurrence of a sequence of times instances of value in the values container. It finds the sequence at index position 3. Note that the third argument that specifies the count must not be an unsigned integer type; if it is, the code won't compile without at least a warning.

Elements are compared using ==, but you can provide an extra argument that specifies a predicate that is to be used instead. Of course, this need not necessarily define a comparison for equality. Here's a complete working example that does something different:

```cpp
// Ex6_03.cpp
// Searching using search_n() to find freezing months
#include <iostream>                    // For standard streams
#include <vector>                      // For vector container
#include <algorithm>                   // For search_n()
#include <string>                      // For string class
using std::string;
```

```
int main()
{
std::vector<int> temperatures {65, 75, 56, 48, 31, 28, 32, 29, 40, 41, 44, 50};
int max_temp {32};
int times {3};
auto iter = std::search_n(std::begin(temperatures), std::end(temperatures), times, max_temp,
                                [](double v, double max){return v <= max; } );
std::vector<string> months {"January", "February", "March", "April", "May", "June",
                      "July", "August", "September", "October", "November", "December"};
if(iter != std::end(temperatures))
  std::cout << "It was " << max_temp << " degrees or below for " << times
            << " months starting in " << months[std::distance(std::begin(temperatures), iter)]
            << std::endl;
}
```

The temperatures container stores average temperatures for each month in a year. The predicate that is the last argument to search_n() is a lambda expression that will return true when an element is less than or equal to max_temp. The months container stores the names of the months. The expression std::distance (std::begin(temperatures), iter) produces the index of the element in temperatures that is the first of a sequence of times elements for which the predicate returns true. This value is used to index the months vector to select the name of the month. Thus this code will produce the following output:

```
It was 32 degrees or below for 3 months starting in May
```

Partitioning a Range

Partitioning the elements in a range rearranges the elements such that all the elements for which a given predicate returns true precede all the elements for which the predicate returns false. The partition() algorithm does this. The first two arguments are forward iterators that identify the range that is to be partitioned and the third argument is the predicate. Here's how you could use the partition() algorithm to rearrange a sequence of values so that all those less than the average preceded all those greater than the average:

```
std::vector<double> temperatures {65, 75, 56, 48, 31, 28, 32, 29, 40, 41, 44, 50};
std::copy(std::begin(temperatures), std::end(temperatures),      // List the values
                          std::ostream_iterator<double>{std::cout, " "});
std::cout << std::endl;

auto average = std::accumulate(std::begin(temperatures),         // Compute the average value
                      std::end(temperatures), 0.0)/ temperatures.size();
std::cout << "Average temperature: " << average << std::endl;

std::partition(std::begin(temperatures), std::end(temperatures), // Partition the values
                          [average](double t) { return t < average; });
std::copy(std::begin(temperatures), std::end(temperatures),   // List the values after   partitioning
                          std::ostream_iterator<double>{std::cout, " "});
std::cout << std::endl;
```

These statements produce the following output:

```
65 75 56 48 31 28 32 29 40 41 44 50
Average temperature: 44.9167
44 41 40 29 31 28 32 48 56 75 65 50
```

The average of the values in the `temperatures` container is produced using the `accumulate()` algorithm to generate the sum of the elements, and dividing that by the number of elements. You have seen the `accumulate()` algorithm before, so you'll recall that the third argument is the initial value for the sum. You can see that after executing the `partition()` algorithm, all temperature values less than `average` precede those that are greater than `average`.

The predicate doesn't have to be an ordering relationship – it can be anything you like. For example, you could partition a sequence of `Person` objects that represent individuals so that all the females precede the males, or all those with university degrees precede those without. Here's an example partitioning a range of tuple objects that represent people and identifies their gender:

```
using gender = char;
using first = string;
using second= string;
using Name = std::tuple<first, second, gender>;
std::vector<Name> names {std::make_tuple("Dan", "Old", 'm'), std::make_tuple("Ann", "Old", 'f'),
                          std::make_tuple("Ed", "Old", 'm'),  std::make_tuple("Jan", "Old", 'f'),
                                                     std::make_tuple("Edna", "Old", 'f')};
std::partition(std::begin(names), std::end(names),          // Partition the names
                          [](const Name& name) { return std::get<2>(name) == 'f'; });
for(const auto& name : names)
  std::cout << std::get<0>(name) << " " << std::get<1>(name) << std::endl;
```

The `using` declarations are there to explain the significance of the members of the `tuple` objects. The predicate returns true when the last member of the tuple is `'f'`, so the output will present Edna, Ann, and Jan before Ed and Dan. You could use the expression `std::get<gender>(name)` to reference the third member of the `tuple` in the predicate. This is possible because the type of the third member is unique, which allows the member to be identified by its type.

The `partition()` algorithm does not guarantee that the relative order of the original elements in the range will be maintained. In the example of using it above, the elements 44 and 41 follow 40 in the original range but after the operation that is no longer the case. To maintain the relative order of elements, you use the `stable_partition()` algorithm. The arguments are the same as for `partition()`. You could replace the statement that calls `partition()` in the previous code that partitioned temperatures with this statement:

```
std::stable_partition(std::begin(temperatures), std::end(temperatures),
                                           [average](double t) { return t < average; });
```

With this change, the output will be:

```
65 75 56 48 31 28 32 29 40 41 44 50
Average temperature: 44.9167
31 28 32 29 40 41 44 65 75 56 48 50
```

You can see that the relative order of the elements has been preserved when reordering is not necessary to partition the range. All the elements less than the average are in their original order, as are all the elements that are not less than the average.

The partition_copy() Algorithm

The partition_copy() algorithm partitions a range in the same way as stable_partition(), but the elements for which the predicate return true are copied to a separate range, and elements for which the predicate returns false are copied to the third range. The operation leaves the original range unchanged. The source range is identified by the first two arguments, which must be input iterators. The beginning of the destination range for elements for which the predicate returns true is identified by the third argument, and the beginning of the destination for elements for which the predicate is false is the fourth argument; both must be output iterators. The fifth argument is the predicate that is to be used for partitioning the elements. Here's a complete program showing partition_copy() in action:

```cpp
// Ex6_04.cpp
// Using partition_copy() to find values above average and below average
#include <iostream>                          // For standard streams
#include <vector>                            // For vector container
#include <algorithm>                         // For partition_copy(), copy()
#include <numeric>                           // For accumulate()
#include <iterator>                          // For back_inserter, ostream_iterator

int main()
{
  std::vector<double> temperatures {65, 75, 56, 48, 31, 28, 32, 29, 40, 41, 44, 50};
  std::vector<double> low_t;                 // Stores below average temperatures
  std::vector<double> high_t;                // Stores average or above temperatures

  auto average = std::accumulate(std::begin(temperatures),std::end(temperatures), 0.0) /
                                                         temperatures.size();
  std::partition_copy(std::begin(temperatures), std::end(temperatures),
                  std::back_inserter(low_t), std::back_inserter(high_t),
                         [average](double t) { return t < average; });

  // Output below average temperatures
  std::copy(std::begin(low_t), std::end(low_t), std::ostream_iterator<double>{std::cout, " "});
  std::cout << std::endl;

  // Output average or above temperatures
  std::copy(std::begin(high_t), std::end(high_t), std::ostream_iterator<double>{std::cout, " "});
  std::cout << std::endl;
}
```

This code does the same as the stable_partition() operation you saw earlier but with the below-average elements in temperatures copied to the low_t container, and the elements that are average or above copied to high_t. The output statements verify that this works as I described since they produce the following output:

```
31 28 32 29 40 41 44
65 75 56 48 50
```

Note that the code in main() uses back_insert_iterator objects that are created using the back_inserter() helper function as the iterators for both destination containers in the partition_copy() call. A back_insert_iterator calls push_back() to add a new element to a container so using this approach avoids the necessity to know in advance how many elements are to be stored. If you use a begin iterator for a destination range, sufficient elements must already exist in the destination prior to the operation to accommodate however many will be copied. Note that the algorithm will not work correctly if the input range overlaps either of the output ranges.

The partition_point() Algorithm

You use the partition_point() algorithm to obtain the end iterator for the first partition in a partitioned range. The first two arguments are forward iterators defining the range to be examined, and the last argument is the predicate that was used to partition the range. You will not typically know how many elements there are in each partition so this algorithm enables you to extract or access the elements in either partition. For example:

```
std::vector<double> temperatures {65, 75, 56, 48, 31, 28, 32, 29, 40, 41, 44, 50};
auto average = std::accumulate(std::begin(temperatures),          // Compute the average value
                         std::end(temperatures), 0.0)/ temperatures.size();
auto predicate = [average](double t) { return t < average; };
std::stable_partition(std::begin(temperatures), std::end(temperatures), predicate);
auto iter = std::partition_point(std::begin(temperatures), std::end(temperatures), predicate);

std::cout << "Elements in the first partition:  ";
std::copy(std::begin(temperatures), iter, std::ostream_iterator<double>{std::cout, " "});
std::cout << "\nElements in the second partition: ";
std::copy(iter, std::end(temperatures), std::ostream_iterator<double>{std::cout, " "});
std::cout << std::endl;
```

This code partitions the elements in the temperatures container relative to the average temperature and finds the partition point by calling partition_point() for the range. This is the end iterator for the first partition and is stored in iter. Thus the range [std::begin(temperatures), iter) corresponds to the elements in the first partition, and the range [iter, std::end(temperatures)) contains the elements in the second partition. The two applications of the copy() algorithm output the partitions, and the output will be:

```
Elements in the first partition:  31 28 32 29 40 41 44
Elements in the second partition: 65 75 56 48 50
```

Before applying partition_point() you need to be sure that the range has been partitioned. When there is doubt about this you can call is_partitioned() to determine whether or not it is the case. The arguments are input iterators specifying the range and the predicate that should have been used to partition the range. This algorithm returns true if the range is partitioned and false otherwise. You could use it to verify that the temperatures range is partitioned before applying the partition_point() algorithm to it:

```
if(std::is_partitioned(std::begin(temperatures), std::end(temperatures),
                                       [average](double t) { return t < average; }))
{
  auto iter = std::partition_point(std::begin(temperatures), std::end(temperatures),
                                       [average](double t) { return t < average; });
  std::cout << "Elements in the first partition:  ";
  std::copy(std::begin(temperatures), iter, std::ostream_iterator<double>{std::cout, " "});
  std::cout << "\nElements in the second partition: ";
  std::copy(iter, std::end(temperatures), std::ostream_iterator<double>{std::cout, " "});
  std::cout << std::endl;
}
else
  std::cout << "Range is not partitioned." << std::endl;
```

This code only executes the call to partition_point() when is_partitioned() returns true. The iter variable that points to the partition point is local to the if block for a true result. If you wanted iter to be available subsequently you could define it before the if statement like this:

```
std::vector<double>::iterator iter;
```

The iterator type alias is defined within all container type templates that make iterators available, and it corresponds to the type of iterator that the begin() and end() members of the container type return.

Binary Search Algorithms

The search algorithms you have seen so far in this chapter search a range sequentially and place no prior ordering requirements on the elements. The *binary search* algorithms are typically faster than a sequential search, but require that the elements in the range to which they are applied are sorted. This is because of the way a binary search works. This is illustrated in Figure 6-6.

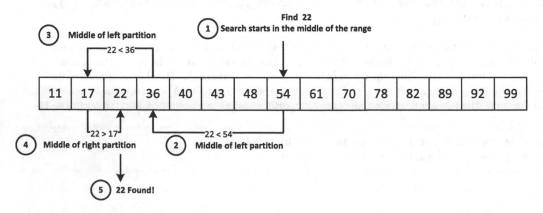

Figure 6-6. *A binary search*

278

Figure 6-6 shows the sequence of events for a binary search for 22 from a range of values that are in ascending sequence. Because the elements are in ascending sequence, the search mechanism uses the less-than operator to find the element. A search of a range in descending sequence would use the greater-than operator to compare elements. A binary search always starts by choosing the element in the middle of the range and comparing that with the value sought. An element that is *equivalent* to the element to be found is considered to be a match so a value, n, will match a value, x, when !(x < n) && !(n < x). If the element being checked is not a match, the search continues with the middle element of the left partition if x < n, or the middle element of the right partition otherwise. The search ends when an equivalent element is found, or when the partition being checked contains only a single element. If that is not a match, the element is not present in the range.

The binary_search() Algorithm

As you will undoubtedly guess, the binary_search() algorithm implements a binary search. It searches the range specified by the first two arguments for an element that is equivalent to the third argument. The iterators specifying the range must be forward iterators and elements are compared using the < operator. The elements in the range must be sorted in ascending sequence or at least partitioned relative to the value you want to find. This algorithm returns a bool value that is true if the third argument is found, or false otherwise, so it just tells you whether or not the element is present, but not where it is when it is. Of course, if you must know where it is, you can use one of the find algorithms you have already seen, or lower_bound(), upper_bound() or equal_range(). Here's an example of using binary_search():

```
std::list<int> values {17, 11, 40, 36, 22, 54, 48, 70, 61, 82, 78, 89, 99, 92, 43};
values.sort();                                  // Sort into ascending sequence
int wanted {22};                                // What we are looking for
if(std::binary_search(std::begin(values), std::end(values), wanted))
  std::cout << wanted << " is definitely in there - somewhere..." << std::endl;
else
  std::cout << wanted << " cannot be found - maybe you got it wrong..." << std::endl;
```

I used a list to store a set of arbitrary values in arbitrary order – just to remind you about this container. The code uses the binary_search() algorithm to search for the value of wanted. Since binary_search() only works with a sorted range we must first make sure the elements in the list are ordered. The sort() algorithm can't be applied to a range of elements in a list container because it requires random access iterators and a list container offers only bidirectional iterators. For this reason, the list container defines a sort() member that sorts all the elements in ascending sequence so this is used to sort the values container. The message confirming that wanted is in values will be output when this code executes.

A second version of binary_search() accepts an additional argument that is a function object to be used for the search; obviously, this must be effectively the same comparison as that was used to order the range being searched. Here's how you could order values in descending sequence and then search for wanted:

```
std::list<int> values {17, 11, 40, 36, 22, 54, 48, 70, 61, 82, 78, 89, 99, 92, 43};
auto predicate = [](int a, int b){ return a > b; };
values.sort(predicate);                                    // Sort into descending sequence
int wanted {22};
if(std::binary_search(std::begin(values), std::end(values), wanted, predicate))
  std::cout << wanted << " is definitely in there - somewhere..." << std::endl;
else
  std::cout << wanted << " cannot be found - maybe you got it wrong..." << std::endl;
```

This uses the sort() member of the list container that accepts a function object that defines the comparison. Here, it's defined by a lambda expression. The same lambda expression is used as the fourth argument to binary_search(). Of course, the result will be the same as the previous code.

The lower_bound() Algorithm

The lower_bound() algorithm finds the element in the range specified by the first two arguments that is not less than the third argument – in other words, the first element that is greater than or equal to the third argument. The first two arguments must be forward iterators. The upper_bound() algorithm finds the first element in the range defined by its first two arguments that is greater than the third argument. For both algorithms, the ranges must be ordered, and they are assumed to be ordered using the less-than operator. Here's an example:

```
std::list<int> values {17, 11, 40, 36, 22, 54, 48, 70, 61, 82, 78, 89, 99, 92, 43};
values.sort();                              // Sort into ascending sequence
int wanted {22};                            // What we are looking for
std::cout << "The lower bound for " << wanted
          << " is " << *std::lower_bound(std::begin(values), std::end(values), wanted)
          << std::endl;
std::cout << "The upper bound for " << wanted
          << " is " << *std::upper_bound(std::begin(values), std::end(values), wanted)
          << std::endl;
```

This produces the output:

```
The lower bound for 22 is 22
The upper bound for 22 is 36
```

You can see from the integers in the list container that the algorithms are working as described. There are additional versions of both algorithms that accept a function object as the fourth argument that specifies the comparison that was used for ordering the range.

The equal_range() algorithm

The equal_range() algorithm finds all elements in a sorted range that are equivalent to a given element. The first two arguments are forward iterators specifying the range and the third argument is the element that is wanted. The algorithm returns a pair object with members that are forward iterators, the first of which points to the element that is not less than the third argument and the second points to the element that is greater than the third argument. Thus you get the result of calling lower_bound() and upper_bound() in a single call. Thus you could replace the two output statements in the previous code fragment by these statements:

```
auto pr = std::equal_range(std::begin(values), std::end(values), wanted);
std::cout << "the lower bound for " << wanted << " is " << *pr.first << std::endl;
std::cout << "the upper bound for " << wanted << " is " << *pr.second << std::endl;
```

The output will be exactly the same as from the previous code. As with previous binary search algorithms, there's a version of equal_range() with an extra parameter that provides for ranges ordered with a comparison other than the less-than operator.

I have said that the algorithms in this section require that the elements in the range to which they are applied are sorted, but that is not the whole story. All the binary search algorithms will also work with ranges that are *partitioned* in a particular way. For a given wanted value, the elements in the range must be partitioned with respect to (element < wanted), and partitioned with respect to !(wanted < element). I can show that this works using the equal_range() binary search algorithm. Before executing equal_range() for the elements in the values container, we can partition it like this:

```
std::list<int> values {17, 11, 40, 36, 22, 54, 48, 70, 61, 82, 78, 89, 99, 92, 43};

// Output the elements in original order
std::copy(std::begin(values), std::end(values), std::ostream_iterator<int> {std::cout, " "});
std::cout << std::endl;

int wanted {22};                                        // What we are looking for

std::partition(std::begin(values), std::end(values),    // Partition the values wrt value < wanted
          [wanted](double value) { return value < wanted; });
std::partition(std::begin(values), std::end(values), // Partition the values wrt !(wanted < value)
          [wanted](double value) { return !(wanted < value); });

// Output the elements after partitioning
std::copy(std::begin(values), std::end(values), std::ostream_iterator<int> {std::cout, " "});
std::cout << std::endl;
```

The output from this will be:

```
17 11 40 36 22 54 48 70 61 82 78 89 99 92 43
17 11 22 36 40 54 48 70 61 82 78 89 99 92 43
```

The first line contains the elements in their original sequence and the second line shows the sequence after partitioning. The order has been changed by the two partitioning operations but not that much. We can now apply equal_range() to the elements in values using the value of wanted:

```
auto pr = std::equal_range(std::begin(values), std::end(values), wanted);
std::cout << "the lower bound for " << wanted << " is " << *pr.first << std::endl;
std::cout << "the upper bound for " << wanted << " is " << *pr.second << std::endl;
```

The output from this will be the same as for the previous code fragment where the elements were fully ordered using the sort() member of the container object. All the algorithms in this section work with ranges partitioned in this way. Obviously, if the partitioning uses >, you must supply a function object to the search algorithm consistent with this.

The previous code fragment applies equal_range() to a range that contains only a single instance of wanted. If the range contained several instances, pr.first would point to the first occurrence of wanted so the range [pr.first, pr.second) will contain all instances. Here's a working program to show that this is so:

```cpp
// Ex 6_05.cpp
// Using partition() and equal_range() to find duplicates of a value in a range
#include <iostream>                           // For standard streams
#include <list>                               // For list container
#include <algorithm>                          // For copy(), partition()
#include <iterator>                           // For ostream_iterator

int main()
{
  std::list<int> values {17, 11, 40, 13, 22, 54, 48, 70, 22, 61, 82, 78, 22, 89, 99, 92, 43};

  // Output the elements in their original order
  std::cout << "The elements in the original sequence are:\n";
  std::copy(std::begin(values), std::end(values), std::ostream_iterator<int> {std::cout, " "});
  std::cout << std::endl;

  int wanted {22};                                      // What we are looking for

  std::partition(std::begin(values), std::end(values),    // Partition the values with (value < wanted)
              [wanted](double value) { return value < wanted; });
  std::partition(std::begin(values), std::end(values),  // Partition the values with !(wanted < value)
              [wanted](double value) { return !(wanted < value); });

  // Output the elements after partitioning
  std::cout << "The elements after partitioning are:\n";
  std::copy(std::begin(values), std::end(values), std::ostream_iterator<int> {std::cout, " "});
  std::cout << std::endl;

  auto pr = std::equal_range(std::begin(values), std::end(values), wanted);
  std::cout << "The lower bound for " << wanted << " is " << *pr.first << std::endl;
  std::cout << "The upper bound for " << wanted << " is " << *pr.second << std::endl;

  std::cout << "\nThe elements found by equal_range() are:\n";
  std::copy(pr.first, pr.second, std::ostream_iterator<int> {std::cout, " "});
  std::cout << std::endl;
}
```

The output will be:

```
The elements in the original sequence are:
17 11 40 13 22 54 48 70 22 61 82 78 22 89 99 92 43
The elements after partitioning are:
17 11 13 22 22 22 48 70 54 61 82 78 40 89 99 92 43
The lower bound for 22 is 22
The upper bound for 22 is 48

The elements found by equal_range() are:
22 22 22
```

The values container here has several elements with the value 22, which is the value of wanted. All three instances of wanted are in the range that equal_range() returns. The range has only been partitioned, not fully sorted, so this will obviously work when the range is fully sorted.

So why does equal_range() return all occurrences of wanted, when the range is just partitioned as in Ex6_05, and not fully sorted? To appreciate this you need to understand the effect of the two partition() calls:

- The first partition operation ensures that all elements that are strictly *less than* wanted are in the left partition; these elements are not necessarily in order. This operation also ensures that all elements that are *not less than* wanted – so elements that are greater than *or equal to* wanted – are in the right partition, so they follow it in sequence, and are also not necessarily in order. All occurrences of wanted will be in the right partition, but mixed up with the elements that are greater than wanted. After the first partition() call in the previous fragment, the elements in values are:

---

17 11 13 40 22 54 48 70 22 61 82 78 22 89 99 92 43

17, 11, and 13 are the only values less than wanted and these are clearly in the left partition. Partitioning does not locate the values corresponding to wanted in any particular way. All instances of 22 are in arbitrary positions among the elements in the right partition.

- The second partition operation is applied to the result of the first. The expression !(wanted < value) is equivalent to (value <= wanted). Thus all elements that are less than or equal to wanted will be in the left partition as a result of this, and all elements strictly greater that wanted will be in the right partition. The effect of this is to move all instances of wanted into the left partition so they are together as a sequence as the last elements in the left partition. After the second partition() call, values contains:

---

17 11 13 22 22 22 48 70 54 61 82 78 40 89 99 92 43

Thus the lower bound found by equal_range() points to the first occurrence of 22 and the upper bound points to the element following the last occurrence of 22 - which is the element with the value 48.

Summary

If you use STL containers, you will want to be comfortable with the algorithms I have discussed in this chapter. Sorting is a very common requirement, especially in applications that process transactions. When you need to sort data, you usually need to merge data, too. Ensuring that transactions are in the same order as the records to which they apply will usually make the update process faster. Of course, the ordered set and map containers and the priority_queue container adapter provide ordering of the elements they contain by default, which obviates the needs for explicit sort operations. However, when you need to work with the same data in different sequences at different times, you need sort operations to rearrange objects when required. The power of the STL sort() algorithms are in their flexibility on the one hand – you can sort anything you can compare, and in their efficiency on the other hand – the implementation is almost certainly better than a sort algorithm that you implement yourself. That's not to say the STL algorithms are always the best choice. There are many specialized data sorting methods that are not implemented in the C++ Standard Library but when you are using STL containers to manage data and just want a general sort capability, the STL offers an instant solution.

The STL *find* algorithms apply even more widely than the sort and merge algorithms. They place no requirements on the range to be searched, other than the ability to compare elements. Equally, the functionality required for the iterators that define the range to be searched are minimal. The algorithms that implement binary search complement the find algorithms when the ranges are ordered. Finally, the partition algorithm provide a halfway house between unordered and ordered ranges. As you've seen, you can apply the binary search algorithms to partitioned ranges and allow a sequence of identical elements to be found without applying a full sort.

EXERCISES

1. Define a `Card` class to represent playing cards in a standard deck. Create a `vector` of `Card` objects that represents a complete deck of fifty-two cards. Deal the cards randomly into four `vector` containers so that each represents a hand of thirteen cards in a game. Output the cards in the four vector containers under the headings "North," "South," "East," and "West" after sorting each hand using the sort() algorithm. The cards should be sorted into the usual suit and value order - so in card value order from 2 through to 10, then Jack, Queen, King, Ace within the suit sequence Clubs, Diamonds, Hearts, Spades.

2. Add code to your solution to Exercise 1 to merge the four hands and output the result.

3. Define a `Person` class that identifies a person by at least their name and hair color. The class should implement `operator<<()` for output streams and function members to compare hair color. Create a `vector` that contains `Person` objects in no particular order, including some that have blond, gray, brown, and black hair. Use the `partition()` algorithm to arrange the objects in the container so that they are ordered by hair color with those that have black hair first, then those that are gray, followed by brown, and blond last. Output the `Person` objects in hair color groups using the `copy()` algorithm.

4. Add function members for comparing names to the `Person` class type in Exercise 3, and extend your solution to this exercise to use the `sort()` algorithm to order the `Person` objects with a given hair color in ascending sequence of their names before outputting them.

Elections for public office often randomize the sequence in which candidates' names appear on the ballot paper to avoid bias against candidates with names such as Joe Yodel and Bob Zippo that occur later in alphabetic sequence. Define a `Name` class that orders names using the following letter sequence:

R W Q O J M V A H B S G Z X N T C I E K U P D Y F L

So names beginning with R come first and names beginning with L come last. Create a variety of `Name` objects in a vector container and order them in ascending sequence according to the letter sequence above using the `stable_sort()` algorithm.

CHAPTER 7

■ ■ ■

More Algorithms

This chapter describes more of the algorithms the STL offers. Algorithms are commonly divided into two groups: *mutating algorithms* that change the range to which they are applied, and *non-mutating algorithms*. I'll discuss the algorithms in this chapter subdivided into groups by what you can do with them, not by whether or not they change things. If you know what an algorithm does, it will be obvious whether or not it changes the data to which it's applied. In this chapter you will learn about:

- Algorithms that test the properties of the elements in a range
- Algorithms that count the number of elements in a range with a given property
- Algorithms that compare two ranges of elements
- Algorithms for copying or moving a range
- Algorithms that set or change the elements in a range

Testing Element Properties

There are three algorithms defined in the `algorithm` header that test for when a given predicate returns true when applied to a range of elements. The first two arguments to these algorithms are input iterators that define the range to which the predicate is to be applied; the third argument specifies the predicate. Testing elements to see whether a predicate returns true may seem simplistic, but it's a powerful facility nonetheless. For instance, you could test whether any or all students passed all their exams, or if it's true that all students attended classes, or whether there is no `Person` object with green eyes, or even whether every `Dog` object has had its day. The predicate can be as simple - or as complex - as you like. The three algorithms for testing element properties are:

- The `all_of()` algorithm returns true if the predicate returns true for *all* the elements in the range.

- The `any_of()` algorithm returns true if the predicate returns true for *any of* the elements in the range.

- The `none_of()` algorithm returns true if the predicate returns true for *none of* the elements in the range.

It's not difficult to imagine how these work. Here's some code to illustrate how the none_of() algorithm might be used:

```
std::vector<int> ages {22, 19, 46, 75, 54, 19, 27, 66, 61, 33, 22, 19};
int min_age{18};
std::cout << "There are "
         << (std::none_of(std::begin(ages), std::end(ages),
                             [min_age](int age) { return age < min_age; }) ? "no": "some")
         << " people under " << min_age << std::endl;
```

The predicate is a lambda expression that compares an element in ages that is passed as the argument with the value of min_age. The bool value returned by none_of() is used to select either "no" or "some" to be included in the output message. The none_of() algorithm returns true when there are no elements in ages less than min_age so "no" is selected in this case. Of course, you could use any_of() to produce the same result:

```
std::cout << "There are "
         << (std::any_of(std::begin(ages), std::end(ages),
                             [min_age](int age) { return age < min_age; }) ? "some": "no")
         << " people under " << min_age << std::endl;
```

The any_of() algorithm only returns true when one or more elements are less than min_age. There are no elements less than min_age so "no" is selected here, too.

Here's a code fragment showing the use of all_of() to test elements in the ages container:

```
int good_age{100};
std::cout << (std::all_of(std::begin(ages), std::end(ages),
                             [good_age](int age) { return age < good_age; }) ? "None": "Some")
         << " of the people are centenarians." << std::endl;
```

The lambda expression compares an element in ages with the value of good_age, which is 100. All the elements are less than 100 so all_of() will return true, and the output message will correctly report that there are no centenarians recorded.

The count() and count_if() algorithms tell you how many elements in a range specified by the first two arguments meet some condition that you specify with the third argument. The count() algorithm returns the number of elements that equal the third argument. The count_if() algorithm returns the number of elements for which the predicate that is the third argument returns true. Here's some code showing these applied to the ages container:

```
std::vector<int> ages {22, 19, 46, 75, 54, 19, 27, 66, 61, 33, 22, 19};
int the_age{19};
std::cout << "There are "
         << std::count(std::begin(ages), std::end(ages), the_age)
         << " people aged " << the_age << std::endl;

int max_age{60};
std::cout << "There are "
         << std::count_if(std::begin(ages), std::end(ages),
                             [max_age](int age) { return age > max_age; })
         << " people aged over " << max_age << std::endl;
```

The first output statement uses the count() algorithm to determine the number of elements in ages that are equal to the_age. The second output statement uses count_if() to report the number of elements that exceed the value of max_age.

All the algorithms in this section are for use when you want information about the general characteristics of a range of elements - when you just want to know whether or not a characteristic applies, or how many meet a criterion. When you want to know the specifics - which elements in a range match - you can use the *find* algorithms that you met in Chapter 6.

Comparing Ranges

You can compare two ranges in a similar way to comparing strings. The equal() algorithm returns true if two ranges are the same length and pairs of corresponding elements are equal. There are four versions of the equal() algorithm, two of which compare elements using the == operator, and two that compare elements using a function object that you supply as an argument. All iterators that specify ranges must be at least input iterators.

One version that compares two ranges using the == operator expects three arguments that are input iterators. The first two arguments are begin and end iterators for the first range. The third argument is the begin iterator for the second range. If the second range contains fewer elements than the first range, the result is undefined. The second version that uses the == operator expects four arguments: the begin and end iterators for the first range and the begin and end iterators for the second range. If the lengths of the two ranges differ, then the result is always false. I'll demonstrate both versions, but I recommend that you always use the version of equal() that accepts four arguments because it cannot result in undefined behavior. Here's a working example showing how these could be applied:

```
// Ex7_01.cpp
// Using the equal() algorithm
#include <iostream>                              // For standard streams
#include <vector>                                // For vector container
#include <algorithm>                             // For equal() algorithm
#include <iterator>                              // For stream iterators
#include <string>                                // For string class
using std::string;

int main()
{
  std::vector<string> words1 {"one", "two", "three", "four", "five", "six", "seven", "eight", "nine"};
  std::vector<string> words2 {"two", "three", "four", "five", "six", "seven", "eight", "nine", "ten"};
  auto iter1 = std::begin(words1);
  auto end_iter1 = std::end(words1);
  auto iter2 = std::begin(words2);
  auto end_iter2 = std::end(words2);

  std::cout << "Container - words1:  ";
  std::copy(iter1, end_iter1, std::ostream_iterator<string>{std::cout, " "});
  std::cout << "\nContainer - words2:  ";
  std::copy(iter2, end_iter2, std::ostream_iterator<string>{std::cout, " "});
  std::cout << std::endl;

  std::cout << "\n1. Compare from words1[1] to end with words2:                 ";
  std::cout << std::boolalpha << std::equal(iter1 + 1, end_iter1, iter2) << std::endl;
```

```
    std::cout << "2. Compare from words2[0] to second-to-last with words1:              ";
    std::cout << std::boolalpha << std::equal(iter2, end_iter2 - 1, iter1) << std::endl;

    std::cout << "3. Compare from words1[1] to words1[5] with words2:                   ";
    std::cout << std::boolalpha << std::equal(iter1 + 1, iter1 + 6, iter2) << std::endl;

    std::cout << "4. Compare first 6 from words1 with first 6 in words2:                ";
    std::cout << std::boolalpha << std::equal(iter1, iter1 + 6, iter2, iter2 + 6) << std::endl;

    std::cout << "5. Compare all words1 with words2:                                    ";
    std::cout << std::boolalpha << std::equal(iter1, end_iter1, iter2) << std::endl;

    std::cout << "6. Compare all of words1 with all of words2:                          ";
    std::cout << std::boolalpha << std::equal(iter1, end_iter1, iter2, end_iter2) << std::endl;

    std::cout << "7. Compare from words1[1] to end with words2 from first to second-to-last: ";
    std::cout << std::boolalpha
              << std::equal(iter1 + 1, end_iter1, iter2, end_iter2 - 1) << std::endl;
}
```

The output will be:

```
Container - words1:  one two three four five six seven eight nine
Container - words2:  two three four five six seven eight nine ten

1. Compare from words1[1] to end with words2:                          true
2. Compare from words2[0] to second-to-last with words1:               false
3. Compare from words1[1] to words1[5] with words2:                    true
4. Compare first 6 from words1 with first 6 in words2:                 false
5. Compare all words1 with words2:                                     false
6. Compare all of words1 with all of words2:                           false
7. Compare from words1[1] to end with words2 from first to second-to-last: true
```

The example compares various sequences of elements from the words1 and words2 containers. The reasons for the output that results from the equal() calls are:

- The first output produces true, because words1 elements from the second to the end match the elements from words2 starting with the first. The number of elements in the second range is one more than the number in the first range but the number of elements in the first range determine how many corresponding elements are compared.

- The second output produces false because there is an immediate mismatch; the first elements in words2 and words1 are different.

- The third statement displays true because the five elements from words1, starting with the second, are identical to the first five elements from words2.

- In the fourth statement, the range for elements from words2 is specified by begin and end iterators. The ranges have the same lengths but the first elements are different so the result is false.

- In the fifth statement the first elements in the two ranges are an immediate mismatch so the result is `false`.

- The sixth statement produces `false` because the ranges are different. This statement is different from the previous `equal()` call because an end iterator is specified for the second range.

- The seventh statement compares elements from `words1` starting with the second, with the same number of elements from `words2` starting with the first, so the output is `true`.

When the second range is identified to `equal()` by just a begin iterator, the number of elements from the second range that are compared to the first is determined by the length of the first range. The second range could have more elements than the first and `equal()` can still return `true`. When you supply begin and end iterators for both ranges, the ranges must be the same length to get a `true` result.

Although you can use `equal()` to compare the entire contents of two containers of the same type, it's better to use the `operator==()` member of a container to do this. The sixth output statement in the example could be written as:

```
std::cout << std::boolalpha << (words1 == words2) << " ";                    // false
```

The two versions of `equal()` that accept a predicate as an additional argument work in the same way. The predicate defines the comparison for equality between elements. Here's a code fragment that illustrates their use:

```
std::vector<string> r1 {"three", "two", "ten"};
std::vector<string> r2 {"twelve", "ten", "twenty"};
std::cout << std::boolalpha
          << std::equal(std::begin(r1), std::end(r1), std::begin(r2),
             [](const string& s1, const string& s2) { return s1[0] == s2[0]; })
          << std::endl;                                         // true
std::cout << std::boolalpha
          << std::equal(std::begin(r1), std::end(r1), std::begin(r2), std::end(r2),
             [](const string& s1, const string& s2) { return s1[0] == s2[0]; })
          << std::endl;                                         // true
```

The first use of `equal()` specifies the second range by just the begin iterator. The predicate is a lambda expression that returns `true` when the first character in the `string` arguments are equal. The last statement shows the `equal()` algorithm with both ranges fully specified and uses the same predicate.

You should not use `equal()` to compare ranges of elements from unordered `map` or `set` containers. The order of a given set of elements in one unordered container may well be different from an identical set of elements stored in another unordered container because the allocation of elements to buckets can vary between containers.

Finding Where Ranges Differ

The `equal()` algorithm tells you whether or not two ranges match. The `mismatch()` algorithm tells you whether or not two ranges match and where they differ if they don't match. The four versions of `mismatch()` have the same parameters as the four versions of `equal()` - with and without an end iterator for the second range, and each of these versions with and without and extra parameter for a function object to define the comparison. The `mismatch()` algorithm returns a `pair` object containing two iterators. The `first` member is an iterator from the range specified by the first two arguments, and the `second` member is an iterator from the second range. When the ranges don't match, the pair contains iterators that point to the first pair of elements that do not match; thus the object will be pair<iter1 + n, iter2 + n> where the elements at index n in the ranges are the first elements that do not match.

When the ranges match, the pair members depend on which version of mismatch() you use, and the circumstances. With iter1 and end_iter1 representing iterators that define the first range and iter2 and end_iter2 representing the begin and end iterators for the second range, the contents of the pair that is returned for matching ranges is as follows:

For mismatch(iter1, end_iter1, iter2):

- pair<end_iter1, (iter2 + (end_iter1 - iter1))> is returned, so the second member is iter2 plus the length of the first range. If the second range is shorter than the first range, the behavior is undefined.

For mismatch(iter1, end_iter1, iter2, end_iter2):

- When the first range is longer than the second range pair<end_iter1, (iter2 + (end_iter1 - iter1))> is returned, so the second member is iter2 plus the length of the first range.

- When the second range is longer than the first range pair<(iter1 + (end_iter2 - iter2)), end_iter2> is returned, so the first member is iter1 plus the length of the second range.

- When the ranges are the same length pair<end_iter1, end_iter2> is returned.

The same applies whether or not you add an argument that defines a function object for the comparison. Here's a working example showing mismatch() being used with the default comparison for equality:

```
// Ex7_02.cpp
// Using the mismatch() algorithm
#include <iostream>                          // For standard streams
#include <vector>                            // For vector container
#include <algorithm>                         // For equal() algorithm
#include <string>                            // For string class
#include <iterator>                          // For stream iterators

using std::string;
using word_iter = std::vector<string>::iterator;

int main()
{
  std::vector<string> words1 {"one", "two", "three", "four",
                              "five", "six", "seven", "eight", "nine"};
  std::vector<string> words2 {"two", "three", "four", "five",
                              "six", "eleven", "eight", "nine", "ten"};
  auto iter1 = std::begin(words1);
  auto end_iter1 = std::end(words1);
  auto iter2 = std::begin(words2);
  auto end_iter2 = std::end(words2);
```

```
// Lambda expression to output mismatch() result
auto print_match = [](const std::pair<word_iter, word_iter>& pr, const word_iter& end_iter)
                   {
                     if(pr.first != end_iter)
                       std::cout << "\nFirst pair of words that differ are "
                                 << *pr.first << " and " << *pr.second << std::endl;
                     else
                       std::cout << "\nRanges are identical." << std::endl;
                   };

std::cout << "Container - words1:  ";
std::copy(iter1, end_iter1, std::ostream_iterator<string>{std::cout, " "});
std::cout << "\nContainer - words2:  ";
std::copy(iter2, end_iter2, std::ostream_iterator<string>{std::cout, " "});
std::cout << std::endl;

std::cout << "\nCompare from words1[1] to end with words2:";
print_match(std::mismatch(iter1 + 1, end_iter1, iter2), end_iter1);

std::cout << "\nCompare from words2[0] to second-to-last with words1:";
print_match(std::mismatch(iter2, end_iter2 - 1, iter1), end_iter2 - 1);

std::cout << "\nCompare from words1[1] to words1[5] with words2:";
print_match(std::mismatch(iter1 + 1, iter1 + 6, iter2), iter1 + 6);

std::cout << "\nCompare first 6 from words1 with first 6 in words2:";
print_match(std::mismatch(iter1, iter1 + 6, iter2, iter2 + 6), iter1 + 6);

std::cout << "\nCompare all words1 with words2:";
print_match(std::mismatch(iter1, end_iter1, iter2), end_iter1);

std::cout << "\nCompare all of words2 with all of words1:";
print_match(std::mismatch(iter2, end_iter2, iter1, end_iter1), end_iter2);

std::cout << "\nCompare from words1[1] to end with words2[0] to second-to-last:";
print_match(std::mismatch(iter1 + 1, end_iter1, iter2, end_iter2 - 1), end_iter1);
}
```

Note that the content of words2 is slightly different from the previous example. The result of each application of mismatch() is generated by a lambda expression that is defined as print_match. The parameters are a pair object and an iterator for a vector<string> container. The using directive for the word_iter alias makes the definition of the lambda simpler. The code in main() applies variations on mismatch() using versions that do not include a parameter for a comparison function object. When the second range is identified by just a begin iterator, it is only necessary that it has at least as many elements as the first range for a match but it can be longer. When the second range is completely specified, the shortest range determines how many elements are compared.

Here's the output:

```
Container - words1:  one two three four five six seven eight nine
Container - words2:  two three four five six eleven eight nine ten

Compare from words1[1] to end with words2:
First pair of words that differ are seven and eleven

Compare from words2[0] to second-to-last with words1:
First pair of words that differ are two and one

Compare from words1[1] to words1[5] with words2:
Ranges are identical.

Compare first 6 from words1 with first 6 in words2:
First pair of words that differ are one and two

Compare all words1 with words2:
First pair of words that differ are one and two

Compare all of words2 with all of words1:
First pair of words that differ are two and one

Compare from words1[1] to end with words2[0] to second-to-last:
First pair of words that differ are seven and eleven
```

The output shows the result of each application of mismatch().

When you supply your own comparison object, you have complete flexibility as to how you define equality. For example:

```
std::vector<string> range1 {"one", "three", "five", "ten"};
std::vector<string> range2 {"nine", "five", "eighteen", "seven"};
auto pr = std::mismatch(std::begin(range1), std::end(range1),
                        std::begin(range2), std::end(range2),
                                    [](const string& s1, const string& s2)
                                    { return s1.back() == s2.back(); });
if(pr.first == std::end(range1) || pr.second == std::end(range2))
  std::cout << "The ranges are identical." << std::endl;
else
  std::cout << *pr.first << " is not equal to " << *pr.second << std::endl;
```

The comparison returns true when the last letters in two strings are equal so the output from executing this code will be:

```
five is not equal to eighteen
```

Of course, this is correct - and according to the comparison function, "one" is equal to "nine" and "three" is equal to "five".

Lexicographical Range Comparisons

The alphabetical ordering of two strings is obtained by comparing corresponding pairs of characters, starting with the first. The first pair of corresponding characters that are different determines which string comes first. The order of the strings will be the order of the differing characters. If the strings are of the same length and all characters are equal, the strings are equal. If the strings differ in length and the sequence of characters in the shorter string is the same as the initial sequence in the longer string, the shorter string is less than the longer string. Thus "age" comes before "beauty" and "a lull" comes before "a storm." It's also obvious that "the chicken" comes first, not "the egg."

Lexicographical ordering is a generalization of the idea of alphabetical ordering to sequences of objects of any type. Corresponding objects in two sequences are compared successively starting with the first, and the first two objects that differ determines the order of the sequences. Obviously, the objects in the sequence have to be comparable. The lexicographical_compare() algorithm compares two *ranges* that are defined by begin and end iterators. The first two arguments define the first range, and the third and fourth arguments are the begin and end iterators for the second range. The < operator is used by default for comparing elements but you can supply a function object that implements a less-than comparison as an optional fifth argument when necessary. The algorithm returns true if the first range is lexicographically less than the second range and false otherwise. Thus a false return implies that the first range is greater than or equal to the second. The ranges are compared element by element. The first pair of corresponding elements that are different determines the order of the ranges. If the ranges are of different lengths and the shorter range matches the initial sequence of elements from the longer range, the shorter range is less than the longer range. Two ranges that are of the same length with corresponding elements equal are equal. An empty range is always less than a non-empty range. Here is an example that uses lexicographical_compare():

```
std::vector<string> phrase1 {"the", "tigers", "of", "wrath"};
std::vector<string> phrase2 {"the", "horses", "of", "instruction"};
auto less = std::lexicographical_compare(std::begin(phrase1), std::end(phrase1),
                                         std::begin(phrase2), std::end(phrase2));
std::copy(std::begin(phrase1), std::end(phrase1), std::ostream_iterator<string>{std::cout, " "});
std::cout << (less ? "are" : "are not") << " less than ";
std::copy(std::begin(phrase2), std::end(phrase2), std::ostream_iterator<string>{std::cout, " "});
std::cout << std::endl;
```

Because the second elements in the ranges differ, and "tigers" is greater than "horses, this code will generate the following output:

```
the tigers of wrath are not less than the horses of instruction
```

You could add an argument to the lexicographical_compare() call and get the opposite result:

```
auto less = std::lexicographical_compare(std::begin(phrase1), std::end(phrase1),
                                         std::begin(phrase2), std::end(phrase2),
                        [](const string& s1, const string& s2){ return s1.length() < s2.length(); });
```

The algorithm uses the lambda expression that is the third argument to compare elements. This compares the lengths of strings in the ranges and because the length of the fourth element in phrase1 is less than the corresponding element in phrase2, phrase1 is less than phrase2.

Permutations of Ranges

In case you are unfamiliar with the term - a *permutation* is just one arrangement of a sequence of objects or values. For example, the possible permutations of the characters in "ABC" are:

"ABC", "ACB", "BAC", "BCA", "CAB", and "CBA"

There are six possible permutations of three different characters, the number being the result of $3 \times 2 \times 1$. In general, there are $n!$ possible permutations of n different objects, where $n!$ is $n \times (n-1) \times (n-2) \times \ldots \times 2 \times 1$. It's easy to see why this is so. With n objects you have n possible choices for the first object in a sequence. For each choice for the first object, there are n-1 objects left to choose from for the second in the sequence, so there are $n \times (n-1)$ possible choices for the first two. Having chosen the first two, there are n-2 left for the choice of the third, so there are $n \times (n-1) \times (n-2)$ possible sequences of the first three - and so on until for the last in the sequence it's Hobson's choice because there is just one left.

One range is a permutation of another if it contains the same elements but in a different order. The next_permutation() algorithm generates a rearrangement of a range in place that is the next permutation in lexicographic sequence of all those possible. It does this using the less-than operator by default. The arguments are iterators that define the range and the function returns a bool value that is true when the new permutation is greater than the previous arrangement of the elements and false if the previous arrangement was the greatest in the sequence, thus the lexicographically smallest permutation was created.

Here's how you could create permutations of a vector that contains four integers:

```
std::vector<int> range {1,2,3,4};
do
{
  std::copy(std::begin(range), std::end(range), std::ostream_iterator<int> {std::cout, " "});
  std::cout << std::endl;
} while(std::next_permutation(std::begin(range), std::end(range)));
```

The loop ends when next_permutation() returns false, indicating that the arrangement arrived at the minimum. This happens to create *all* permutations of the sequence in the range, but only because the initial arrangement, 1 2 3 4, is the first in the set of possible arrangements. One way to guarantee that you create all permutations is to use next_permutation() to get the minimum:

```
std::vector<string> words {"one","two", "three", "four", "five", "six", "seven", "eight"};
while(std::next_permutation(std::begin(words), std::end(words)))     // Change to minimum
;
do
{
  std::copy(std::begin(words), std::end(words), std::ostream_iterator<string> {std::cout, " "});
  std::cout << std::endl;
} while(std::next_permutation(std::begin(words), std::end(words)));
```

The initial sequence in words is not the minimum permutation sequence but the while loop continues until words does contain the minimum. The do-while loop then outputs the complete set. If you want to execute this fragment, bear in mind that it will produce $8!$, which is $40,320$ lines of output, so you might consider reducing the number of elements in words first.

The minimum permutation of a sequence of elements is when each element is less than or equal to the element that follows, so you could use the min_element() algorithm that returns an iterator pointing to the minimum element in a range, along with the iter_swap() algorithm that interchanges the elements that are pointed to by two iterators to create the permutation that is the minimum, like this:

```
std::vector<string> words {"one","two", "three", "four", "five", "six", "seven", "eight"};
for (auto iter = std::begin(words); iter != std::end(words)-1 ;++iter)
  std::iter_swap(iter, std::min_element(iter, std::end(words)));
```

The for loop iterates over iterators from the first in the range for the container to the second-to-last. The statement that is the body of the for loop swaps the element to which iter points with the element pointed to by the iterator that min_element() returns. This will ultimately produce the minimum permutation, which you could use as the starting point for next_permutation() to generate all permutations.

You could avoid all the overhead of arriving at the minimum permutation before you start creating all the permutations by creating a copy of the original container and changing the do-while loop:

```
std::vector<string> words {"one","two", "three", "four", "five", "six", "seven", "eight"};
auto words_copy = words;                          // Copy the original
do
{
  std::copy(std::begin(words), std::end(words), std::ostream_iterator<string> {std::cout, " "});
  std::cout << std::endl;
  std::next_permutation(std::begin(words), std::end(words));
} while(words != words_copy);                      // Continue until back to the original
```

The loop now continues to create new permutations until the original is arrived at.

Here's a working example that finds all permutations of the letters in a word:

```
// Ex7_03.cpp
// Finding rearrangements of the letters in a word
#include <iostream>                                // For standard streams
#include <iterator>                                // For iterators and begin() and end()
#include <string>                                  // For string class
#include <vector>                                  // For vector container
#include <algorithm>                               // For next_permutation()
using std::string;

int main()
{
  std::vector<string> words;
  string word;
  while(true)
  {
    std::cout << "\nEnter a word, or Ctrl+z to end: ";
    if((std::cin >> word).eof()) break;
    string word_copy {word};
    do
    {
      words.push_back(word);
      std::next_permutation(std::begin(word), std::end(word));
    } while(word != word_copy);
```

```
    size_t count{}, max{8};
    for(const auto& wrd : words)
      std::cout << wrd << ((++count % max == 0) ? '\n' : ' ');
    std::cout << std::endl;
    words.clear();                                    // Remove previous permutations
  }
}
```

This reads a word from the standard input stream into word, makes a copy in word_copy, then stores all permutations of the letters in word in the words container. The program continues to process words until you enter Ctrl+Z. The copy of word is used to decide when all permutations have been stored. The permutations are then written to the standard output stream, eight to a line. As I have said, the number of permutations increases rapidly with the number of elements being permuted, so don't try this with long words. The example is not very useful as it stands, but I'll revisit the program in Chapter 9, which introduces more details of using STL with files. There it will be possible to read a file that contains an extensive list of English words and search those to determine which permutations are valid words. Thus, the program finds anagrams of the original word and just outputs those.

You can supply a function object as a third argument to next_permutation() that defines a comparison function that is an alternative to the default. Here's how you could use this version to generate permutations of a sequence of words by comparing the last letters:

```
std::vector<string> words {"one", "two", "four", "eight"};
do
{
  std::copy(std::begin(words), std::end(words), std::ostream_iterator<string> {std::cout, " "});
  std::cout << std::endl;
} while(std::next_permutation(std::begin(words), std::end(words),
    [](const string& s1, const string& s2){return s1.back() < s2.back(); }));
```

This code generates all twenty-four permutations of the elements in words using the lambda expression that is passed as the last argument to next_permutation().

The next_permutation() algorithm generates permutations in ascending lexicographical sequence. When you want to produce permutations in descending sequence, you can use the prev_permutation() algorithm. This comes in the same two versions as next_permutation() and uses < to compare elements by default. Because the permutations are generated in descending sequence, the algorithm returns true most of the time, and returns false when the permutation that it creates is the maximum permutation. For example:

```
std::vector<double> data {44.5, 22.0, 15.6, 1.5};
do
{
  std::copy(std::begin(data), std::end(data), std::ostream_iterator<double> {std::cout, " "});
  std::cout << std::endl;
} while(std::prev_permutation(std::begin(data), std::end(data)));
```

This code outputs all twenty-four permutations of the four double values in data, because the initial sequence is the maximum and prev_permutation() only returns false when the input sequence is the minimum.

You can test whether one sequence is a permutation of another using the is_permutation() algorithm, which returns true when this is the case. Here's some code showing this algorithm applied in a lambda expression:

```
std::vector<double> data1 {44.5, 22.0, 15.6, 1.5};
std::vector<double> data2 {22.5, 44.5, 1.5, 15.6};
std::vector<double> data3 {1.5, 44.5, 15.6, 22.0};

auto test = [](const auto& d1, const auto& d2)
  {
    std::copy(std::begin(d1), std::end(d1), std::ostream_iterator<double> {std::cout, " "});
    std::cout << (is_permutation(std::begin(d1), std::end(d1), std::begin(d2), std::end(d2)) ?
                                                              "is": "is not")
             << " a permutation of ";
    std::copy(std::begin(d2), std::end(d2), std::ostream_iterator<double> {std::cout, " "});
    std::cout << std::endl;
  };

test(data1, data2);
test(data1, data3);
test(data3, data2);
```

The parameter types for the test lambda are specified using auto, which causes the actual types being deduced by the compiler as const std::vector<double>&. Lambda expressions that use auto to specify the parameter types are called *generic lambdas*. The test lambda expression uses is_permutation() to assess whether one argument is a permutation of another. The arguments to the algorithm are two pairs of iterators that define the ranges to be compared. The parameters to the bool value that is returned is used to select one of two possible strings to output. The output will be:

```
44.5 22 15.6 1.5 is not a permutation of 22.5 44.5 1.5 15.6
44.5 22 15.6 1.5 is a permutation of 1.5 44.5 15.6 22
1.5 44.5 15.6 22 is not a permutation of 22.5 44.5 1.5 15.6
```

There's another version of is_permutation() that allows the second range to be specified by just a begin iterator. In this case, the second range can contain a greater number of elements than the first, but only the number of elements that the first range contains will be considered. However, I recommend that you don't use it because it results in undefined behavior if the second range contains fewer elements than the first. I'll show some code that uses it anyway. You could add elements to data3 and the initial sequence of elements would still represent a permutation of data1. For example:

```
std::vector<double> data1 {44.5, 22.0, 15.6, 1.5};
std::vector<double> data3 {1.5, 44.5, 15.6, 22.0, 88.0, 999.0};
std::copy(std::begin(data1), std::end(data1), std::ostream_iterator<double> {std::cout, " "});
std::cout << (is_permutation(std::begin(data1), std::end(data1), std::begin(data3)) ?
                                                              "is": "is not")
         << " a permutation of ";
std::copy(std::begin(data3), std::end(data3), std::ostream_iterator<double> {std::cout, " "});
 std::cout << std::endl;
```

This will confirm that data1 is a permutation of data3 because only the first four elements in data3 are considered. You can add an additional argument to either version of is_permutation() to specify the comparison to be used.

You can use the shuffle() algorithm to create a random permutation of a range, but I'll defer discussion of this until Chapter 8 where I discuss the random number generating capabilities that the STL provides in detail.

Copying a Range

This section discusses algorithms for copying a range; but don't forget that when you want to move the entire contents of one container to another, you have other possibilities. The containers define the assignment operator that will copy the entire contents of one container to another container of the same type. There are constructors for containers that accept a range as the source of the initial contents, too. Most of the time, the algorithms in this section are used to copy subsets of the elements in a container.

You have already seen a number of applications of the copy() algorithm so you know how that works. It copies elements from a source range defined by the first two arguments that are input iterators to a destination range starting at the position specified by the third argument that must be an output iterator. You have three further algorithms that offer more than just a simple copying process.

Copying a Number of Elements

The copy_n() algorithm copies a specific number of elements from a source to a destination. The first argument is an input iterator pointing to the first source element, the second argument is the number of elements to be copied, and the third argument is an output iterator that points to the first position in the destination. The algorithm returns an iterator that points to one past the last element copied, or just the third argument - the output iterator - if the second argument is zero. Here's an example of using it:

```
std::vector<string> names {"Al",    "Beth",   "Carol", "Dan",  "Eve",
                            "Fred", "George", "Harry", "Iain", "Joe"};
std::unordered_set<string> more_names {"Janet", "John"};
std::copy_n(std::begin(names) + 1, 3, std::inserter(more_names, std::begin(more_names)));
```

The copy_n() operation copies three elements from the names container starting with the second name, to the associative container, more_names. The destination is specified by an insert_iterator object for the unordered_set container that is created by the inserter() function template. The insert_iterator object adds elements to the container by calling its insert() member.

Of course, the destination in a copy_n() operation can be a stream iterator:

```
std::copy_n(std::begin(more_names), more_names.size()-1,
                                    std::ostream_iterator<string> {std::cout, " "});
```

This outputs all the elements in more_names except for the last. Note that if the count of the number of elements to be copied exceeds the number available, your program will come to a sticky end. If the number of elements is zero or negative, the copy_n() algorithm does nothing.

Conditional Copying

The copy_if() algorithm copies elements from a source range for which a predicate returns true, so you can think of it as operating as a filter. The first two arguments are input iterators that define the source range, the third argument is an output iterator that points to the first position in the destination range, and the fourth argument is the predicate. An output iterator is returned that points to one past the last element copied. Here's an example of using copy_if():

```
std::vector<string> names {"Al",    "Beth",    "Carol", "Dan",   "Eve",
                           "Fred", "George", "Harry", "Iain", "Joe"};
std::unordered_set<string> more_names {"Jean", "John"};
size_t max_length{4};
std::copy_if(std::begin(names), std::end(names), std::inserter(more_names, std::begin(more_names)),
[max_length](const string& s){ return s.length() <= max_length; });
```

The copy_if() operation here only copies elements from names that are four characters or less because that is the condition imposed by the lambda expression that is the fourth argument. The destination is the unordered_set container, more_names, which already contains two four-letter names. As in the previous section, an insert_iterator adds the elements that qualify to the associative container. If you want to demonstrate that it worked, you can list the contents of more_names using the copy() algorithm:

```
std::copy(std::begin(more_names), std::end(more_names), std::ostream_iterator<string>
{std::cout, " "});
std::cout << std::endl;
```

Of course, the destination for copy_if() can also be a stream iterator:

```
std::vector<string> names {"Al",    "Beth",    "Carol", "Dan",   "Eve",
                           "Fred", "George", "Harry", "Iain", "Joe"};
size_t max_length{4};
std::copy_if(std::begin(names), std::end(names), std::ostream_iterator<string> {std::cout, " "},
                          [max_length](const string& s) { return s.length() > max_length; });
std::cout << std::endl;
```

This writes the names from the names container that have five or more characters to the standard output stream. This will output:

```
Carol George Harry
```

You can use an input stream iterator as the source for the copy_if() algorithm, as you can with other algorithms that require input iterators. Here's an example:

```
std::unordered_set<string> names;
size_t max_length {4};
std::cout << "Enter names of less than 5 letters. Enter Ctrl+Z on a separate line to end:\n";
std::copy_if(std::istream_iterator<string>{std::cin}, std::istream_iterator<string>{},
std::inserter(names, std::begin(names)),
  [max_length](const string& s) { return s.length() <= max_length; });
std::copy(std::begin(names), std::end(names), std::ostream_iterator<string> {std::cout, " "});
std::cout << std::endl;
```

The names container is an unordered_set that is empty initially. The copy_if() algorithm copies names read from the standard input stream, but only when they are four characters or less. Executing this code can produce the output:

```
Enter names of less than 5 letters. Enter Ctrl+Z on a separate line to end:
Jim Bethany Jean Al Algernon Bill Adwina Ella Frederick Don
^Z
Ella Jim Jean Al Bill Don
```

Names more than five letters are read from cin but discarded because the predicate specified by the fourth argument returns false in these instances. Thus, only six of the ten names that were entered are stored in the container.

Reverse Order Copying

Don't be misled by the name of the copy_backward() algorithm. It doesn't reverse the order of elements. It copies just like the copy() algorithm but starting from the last element and working back to the first. The copy_backward() algorithm copies the range specified by the first two iterator arguments. The third argument is the end iterator for the destination range and the source range is copied to the destination by copying the last element from the source range to the element preceding the end iterator for the destination as illustrated in Figure 7-1. All three arguments to copy_backward() must be bidirectional iterators, which are iterators that can be incremented or decremented. This implies that the algorithm can only be applied to ranges in the sequence containers.

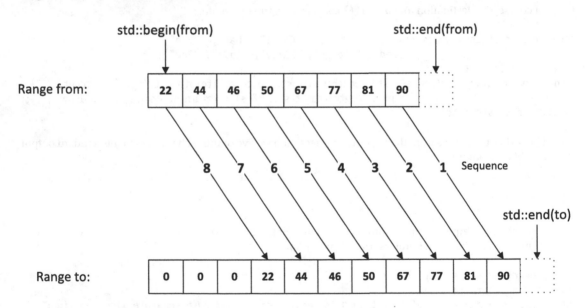

copy_backward(std::begin(from), std::end(from), std:end(to));

Figure 7-1. *How copy_backward() works*

Figure 7-1 shows how the last element from the source range, from, is copied first to the last element in the destination, to. Each successive element back through the source range from the source is copied to the destination at the position preceding the previous element. The elements in the destination must exist before the operation is carried out so the destination must have at least as many elements as the source, but it can have more. The copy_backward() algorithm returns an iterator that points to the last element copied, which will be the begin iterator for the range in its new position.

You may wonder what advantages copy_backward() offers over the regular copy() algorithm that copies elements starting with the first. One answer is when the ranges overlap. You can use copy() to copy elements into an overlapping destination range to the left - that is, to a position preceding the first element in the source range. If you attempt to use copy() to copy elements to the right in the same range, the operation won't work because elements that are still to be copied will be overwritten before they are copied. When you want to copy to the right you can use copy_backward() as long as the end of the destination range is to the right of the end of the source range. Figure 7-2 illustrates the difference between the two algorithms when copying to the right between overlapping ranges.

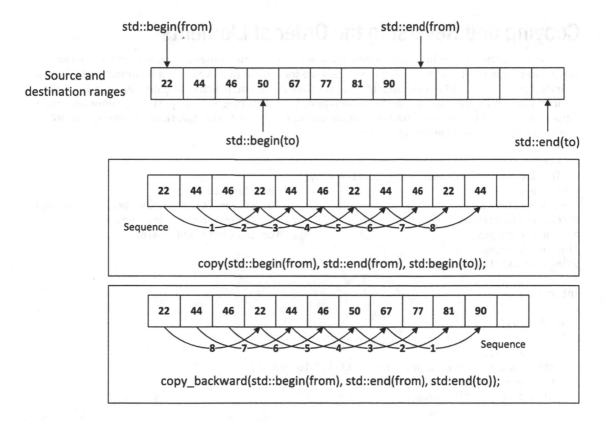

Figure 7-2. *Copying overlapping ranges to the right*

Figure 7-2 shows the result of applying the copy() and copy_backward() algorithm to the range at the top three positions to the right. It's evident that the copy() algorithm cannot do what you want when copying to the right because some elements get overwritten before they are copied. The copy_backward() algorithm does do what you want in this situation. The reverse is the case when copying to the left within a range - copy() works, but copy_backward() doesn't.

Here's some code to illustrate copy_backward() in action:

```
std::deque<string> song{"jingle", "bells", "jingle", "all", "the", "way"};
song.resize(song.size()+2);                    // Add 2 elements
std::copy_backward(std::begin(song), std::begin(song)+6, std::end(song));
std::copy(std::begin(song), std::end(song), std::ostream_iterator<string>{std::cout, " "});
std::cout << std::endl;
```

The number of elements in the deque container is increased by using its resize() member to create the extra elements needed for a reverse sequence copy operation to the right. The copy_backward() algorithm copies the original elements right by two positions, leaving the first two elements the same, so the output from this code will be:

```
jingle bells jingle bells jingle all the way
```

Copying and Reversing the Order of Elements

The reverse_copy() algorithm copies a source range to a destination range so that the elements in the destination are in reverse order. The source range is defined by the first two iterator arguments, which must be bidirectional. The destination is identified by the third argument, which is an output iterator that is the begin iterator for the destination. The behavior is undefined if the ranges overlap. The algorithm returns an output iterator that points to one past the last element in the destination range. Here's a working example that uses reverse_copy() and copy_if():

```
// Ex7_04.cpp
// Testing for palindromes using reverse_copy()
#include <iostream>                            // For standard streams
#include <iterator>                            // For stream iterators and begin() and end()
#include <algorithm>                           // For reverse_copy() and copy_if()
#include <cctype>                              // For toupper() and isalpha()
#include <string>
using std::string;

int main()
{
  while(true)
  {
    string sentence;
    std::cout << "Enter a sentence or Ctrl+Z to end: ";
    std::getline(std::cin, sentence);
    if(std::cin.eof()) break;

    // Copy as long as the characters are alphabetic & convert to upper case
    string only_letters;
    std::copy_if(std::begin(sentence), std::end(sentence), std::back_inserter(only_letters),
      [](char ch) { return std::isalpha(ch); });
    std::for_each(std::begin(only_letters), std::end(only_letters), [](char& ch)
    { ch = toupper(ch); });
```

```
  // Make a reversed copy
  string reversed;
  std::reverse_copy(std::begin(only_letters), std::end(only_letters),
  std::back_inserter(reversed));
  std::cout << '"' << sentence << '"'
    << (only_letters == reversed ? " is" : " is not") << " a palindrome." << std::endl;
  }
}
```

This program checks whether a sentence (or indeed many sentences) represents a *palindrome*; a palindrome is a sentence that reads the same backward or forward if you ignore little details such as spaces and punctuation. The while loop allows you to check as many sentences as you like. A sentence is read into sentence using getline(). If just Ctrl+Z is read, the EOF flag will be set for the input stream, which will terminate the loop. The letters in sentence are copied to only_letters using copy_if(). The lambda expression returns true only for letters, so any other characters will be ignored. Characters are appended to only_letters by the back_insert_iterator object that is created by back_inserter(). The for_each() algorithm applies the function specified by the third argument to the elements in the range defined by the first two arguments so here it converts the characters in only_letters to uppercase. A reversed copy of the contents of only_letters is created in reverse using the reverse_copy() algorithm. Comparing only_letters with reversed determines whether or not the input was a palindrome.

Here's some sample output:

```
Enter a sentence or Ctrl+Z to end: Lid off a daffodil.
"Lid off a daffodil." is a palindrome.
Enter a sentence or Ctrl+Z to end: Engage le jeu que je le gagne.
"Engage le jeu que je le gagne." is a palindrome.
Enter a sentence or Ctrl+Z to end: Sit on a potato pan Otis!
"Sit on a potato pan Otis!" is a palindrome.
Enter a sentence or Ctrl+Z to end: Madam, I am Adam.
"Madam, I am Adam." is not a palindrome.
Enter a sentence or Ctrl+Z to end: Madam, I'm Adam.
"Madam, I'm Adam." is a palindrome.
Enter a sentence or Ctrl+Z to end: ^Z
```

Palindromes are hard to create but a Frenchman, George Perec, managed to construct one containing more than a thousand words!

The reverse() algorithm reverses the elements in the range specified by its two bidirectional iterator arguments in place. You could use this in Ex7_04.cpp instead of reverse_copy() - like this:

```
string reversed {only_letters};
std::reverse(std::begin(reversed), std::end(reversed));
```

These two statements would replace the definition for reversed and the reverse_copy() call in Ex7_04.cpp. They create reversed as a duplicate of only_letters. Calling reverse() then reverses the sequence of characters in reversed in place.

Copying a Range Removing Adjacent Duplicates

The unique_copy() copies one range to another while removing successive duplicate elements. By default it uses the == operator to decide when elements are equal. The first two arguments are iterators specifying the source, and the third argument is an output iterator that points to the first element in the destination. An optional fourth argument accepts a function object that defines an alternative to the == operator. The algorithm returns an output iterator that points to one past the last element in the destination.

Copying a sequence such as 1, 1, 2, 2, 3 will result in the destination containing 1, 2, 3. Because only adjacent duplicates are eliminated, all elements in a sequence such as 1, 2, 1, 2, 3 will be copied. Of course, if the source range has been sorted, all duplicates will be removed, so the destination range will contain unique elements.

Here's some code showing unique_copy() applied to the characters in a string:

```
string text {"Have you seen how green the trees seem?"};
string result{};
std::unique_copy(std::begin(text), std::end(text), std::back_inserter(result));
std::cout << result << std::endl;
```

The source for the copy operation is the entire string, text, and the destination is a back_insert_iterator for result so each character that is copied will be appended to result. This outputs the almost useless sentence:

```
Have you sen how gren the tres sem?
```

The output does confirm that unique_copy() eliminates adjacent duplicates though.

When you supply your own comparison object, you are not limited to a simple equality - you can make it what you like. This allows the possibility of being selective about the duplicate elements that are not copied. Here's some code showing how you could remove duplicate spaces from a string:

```
string text {"There's   no air   in   spaaaaaace!"};
string result {};
std::unique_copy(std::begin(text), std::end(text), std::back_inserter(result),
                          [](char ch1, char ch2) { return ch1 == ' ' && ch1 == ch2; });
  std::cout << result << std::endl;
```

The fourth argument to unique_copy() is a lambda expression that returns true only when both arguments are a space. Executing this code results in the following output:

```
There's no air in spaaaaaace!
```

This shows that spaces have been eliminated but the a's in spaaaaaace have not.

Removing Adjacent Duplicates from a Range

You also have the unique() algorithm available that removes duplicates from a sequence in place. This requires forward iterators to specify the range to be processed. It returns a forward iterator that is the end iterator for the new range after removing duplicates. You can supply a function object as an optional third argument that defines an alternative to == for comparing elements. Here's an example:

```
std::vector<string> words {"one", "two", "two", "three", "two", "two", "two"};
auto end_iter = std::unique(std::begin(words), std::end(words));
std::copy(std::begin(words), end_iter, std::ostream_iterator<string>{std::cout, " "});
std::cout << std::endl;
```

This eliminates successive elements in words by overwriting them. The output will be:

```
one two three two
```

Of course, no elements are removed from the input range; the algorithm has no way to remove elements because it has no knowledge of their context. The entire range will still exist. However, there's no guarantees about the state of the elements beyond the new end If I use std::end(words) instead of end_iter to output the result in the code above, I get this output on my system:

```
one two three two  two two
```

The same number of elements still exists, but the element to which the new end iterator points is just the empty string; the last two elements are as before. The result may be different on your system. Because of this, it's a good idea to truncate the original range after executing unique(), like this:

```
auto end_iter = std::unique(std::begin(words), std::end(words));
words.erase(end_iter, std::end(words));
std::copy(std::begin(words), std::end(words), std::ostream_iterator<string> {std::cout, " "});
std::cout << std::endl;
```

The erase() member of the container removes elements from the new end iterator onward so end(words) will return end_iter.

Of course, you can apply unique() to characters in a string:

```
string text {"There's   no air   in   spaaaaaace!"};
text.erase(std::unique(std::begin(text), std::end(text),
                       [](char ch1, char ch2) { return ch1 == ' ' && ch1 == ch2; }),
           std::end(text));
std::cout << text << std::endl;                  // Outputs: There's no air in spaaaaaace!
```

This uses unique() to remove adjacent duplicate spaces from the text string. The code uses the iterator that unique() returns as the first argument to the erase() member of text, and this points to the first character to be erased. The second argument to erase() is the end iterator for text so all characters that follow the new string without duplicated spaces are removed.

Rotating Ranges

The rotate() algorithm rotates a sequence of elements left. This works as illustrated in Figure 7-3. To understand how rotating a range works, you can think of elements in a range as beads on a bracelet. The rotate() operation causes a new element to be the first element that the begin iterator will point. After the rotation the last element is the element preceding the new first element.

std::vector<int> ns {1, 2, 3, 4, 5, 6, 7, 8};

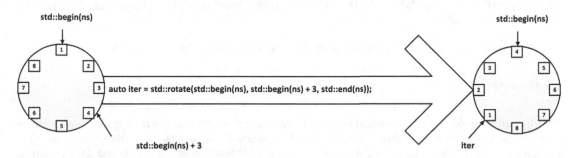

Figure 7-3. *How the rotate() algorithm works*

The first argument to rotate() is the begin iterator for the range; the second argument is an iterator that points to what should be the new first element, which must be within the range; the third argument is the end iterator for the range. The example in Figure 7-3 shows that the rotate() operation on the ns container makes the element with the value 4 the new first element and the last element will have the value 3. The circular sequence of the elements is maintained so it effectively just rotates the circle of elements until the new first element is the beginning of the range. The algorithm returns an iterator that points to the original first element in its new position. Here's an example:

```
std::vector<string> words {"one", "two", "three", "four", "five", "six", "seven", "eight"};
auto iter = std::rotate(std::begin(words), std::begin(words)+3, std::end(words));
std::copy(std::begin(words), std::end(words), std::ostream_iterator<string> {std::cout, " "});
std::cout << std::endl << "First element before rotation: " << *iter << std::endl;
```

This code applies a rotation to all the elements in words. Executing this code will produce the output:

```
four five six seven eight one two three
First element before rotation: one
```

The output demonstrates that "four" is the new first element, and the iterator that rotate() returns does indeed point to the previous first element, "one".

Of course, the range that you rotate does not have to be all the elements in a container. For example:

```
std::vector<string> words {"one", "two", "three", "four", "five",
                           "six", "seven", "eight", "nine", "ten"};
auto start = std::find(std::begin(words), std::end(words), "two");
auto end_iter = std::find(std::begin(words), std::end(words), "eight");
```

```
auto iter = std::rotate(start, std::find(std::begin(words), std::end(words), "five"), end_iter);
std::copy(std::begin(words), std::end(words), std::ostream_iterator<string> {std::cout, " "});
std::cout << std::endl << "First element before rotation: " << *iter << std::endl;
```

This uses the find() algorithm to obtain iterators pointing to elements in words that match "two" and "eight." These define the range to be rotated, which is a subset of the elements in the container. This range is rotated to make "five" the first element and the output shows that this works as expected:

```
one five six seven two three four eight nine ten
First element before rotation: two
```

The rotate_copy() algorithm generates a rotated copy of a range in a new range, leaving the original undisturbed. The first three arguments to rotate_copy() are the same as those for rotate(); the fourth argument is an output iterator that points to the first element of the destination range. The algorithm returns an output iterator for the destination that points to one past the last element copied. Here's an example:

```
std::vector<string> words {"one", "two", "three", "four", "five",
                           "six", "seven", "eight", "nine", "ten"};
auto start = std::find(std::begin(words), std::end(words), "two");
auto end_iter = std::find(std::begin(words), std::end(words), "eight");
std::vector<string> words_copy;
std::rotate_copy(start, std::find(std::begin(words), std::end(words), "five"), end_iter,
                                                std::back_inserter(words_copy));
std::copy(std::begin(words_copy), std::end(words_copy),
                                  std::ostream_iterator<string> {std::cout, " "});
std::cout << std::endl;
```

This produces a rotated copy of the elements from "two" to "seven" inclusive from words. The copied elements are appended to the words_copy container using a back_insert_iterator, which will call the push_back() member of words_copy to insert each element. The output that this code produces is:

```
five six seven two three four
```

The iterator that rotate_copy() returns here is the end iterator for the elements in words_copy. It is not recorded or used in this code, but it can be useful. For example:

```
std::vector<string> words {"one", "two", "three", "four", "five",
                           "six", "seven", "eight", "nine", "ten"};
auto start = std::find(std::begin(words), std::end(words), "two");
auto end_iter = std::find(std::begin(words), std::end(words), "eight");
std::vector<string> words_copy {20};                    // vector with 20 default elements
auto end_copy_iter = std::rotate_copy(start,
  std::find(std::begin(words), std::end(words), "five"), end_iter, std::begin(words_copy));
std::copy(std::begin(words_copy), end_copy_iter, std::ostream_iterator<string> {std::cout, " "});
std::cout << std::endl;
```

The words_copy container is created with twenty default elements. The rotate_copy() algorithm now stores the rotated range in existing elements in words_copy, starting at the beginning. The iterator that the algorithm returns is used to identify the end of the range in words_copy for output; without it, we would have to figure it out based on the number of elements in the source range.

Moving a Range

The move() algorithm moves the range specified by its first two input iterator arguments to a destination starting at the position defined by the third argument, which must be an output iterator. The algorithm returns an iterator to one past the last element that was moved in the destination. This is a *move* operation, so there is no guarantee that the input range of elements remains the same after the operation; the source elements will still exist, but may not have the same values so you should not use them after the move. You might use the move() algorithm if the source range is to be replaced, or is to be destroyed. If you need the source range to be undisturbed, use the copy() algorithm. Here's an example showing how you can use it:

```
std::vector<int> srce {1, 2, 3, 4};
std::deque<int> dest {5, 6, 7, 8};
std::move(std::begin(srce), std::end(srce), std::back_inserter(dest));
```

This appends all the elements from the vector container, srce, to the deque container, dest. To replace the existing elements in dest, you would use std::begin(dest) as the third argument to move(). You can use move() to move elements to a destination that overlaps the source range as long as the first element in the destination is outside the source range; this implies a move to the left within the range. Here's an example:

```
std::vector<int> data {1, 2, 3, 4, 5, 6, 7, 8};
std::move(std::begin(data) + 2, std::end(data), std::begin(data));
data.erase(std::end(data) - 2, std::end(data));        // Erase moved elements
std::copy(std::begin(data), std::end(data), std::ostream_iterator<int> {std::cout, " "});
std::cout << std::endl;                                // 3, 4, 5, 6, 7, 8
```

This moves the last six elements of data back to the beginning of the container. This works because the destination is outside the source range. The values of the last two elements cannot be guaranteed after the move. The elements are erased here but you could equally well reset them to a known value - such as zero. The result is shown in the comment in the last line. Of course, you could use the rotate() algorithm instead of move() to move the elements, in which case you would know the values of the last two elements for sure.

If the destination for a move operation lies within the source range, move() won't work correctly; this implies a move to the right within the range. The reason is that some elements will get overwritten before they are moved. The move_backward() algorithm will work though. The first two arguments specify the range to be moved and the third argument is the end iterator for the destination. Here's an example:

```
std::deque<int> data {1, 2, 3, 4, 5, 6, 7, 8};
std::move_backward(std::begin(data), std::end(data) - 2, std::end(data));
data[0] = data[1] = 0;                                 // Reset moved elements
std::copy(std::begin(data), std::end(data), std::ostream_iterator<int> {std::cout, " "});
std::cout << std::endl;                                // 0, 0, 1, 2, 3, 4, 5, 6
```

I used a deque container here, just for a change. This moves the first six elements two positions to the right. The elements whose values are not assured after the operation are reset to 0. The last line shows the result of the operation.

You can interchange two ranges using the swap_ranges() algorithm. The algorithm requires three arguments that are forward iterators. The first two are the begin and end iterators for one range, and the third argument is the begin iterator for the second range. Obviously, the ranges must be the same length. The algorithm returns an iterator for the second range that points to one past the last element swapped. Here's an example:

```
using Name = std::pair<string, string>;                // First and second name
std::vector<Name> people {Name{"Al", "Bedo"}, Name{"Ann", "Ounce"}, Name{"Jo", "King"}};
std::list<Name> folks {Name{"Stan", "Down"}, Name{"Dan", "Druff"}, Name{"Bea", "Gone"}};
std::swap_ranges(std::begin(people), std::begin(people) + 2, ++std::begin(folks));
std::for_each(std::begin(people), std::end(people),
                [](const Name& name)
                    {std::cout << '"' << name.first << " " << name.second << "\" ";});
std::cout << std::endl;                                 // "Dan Druff" "Bea Gone" "Jo King"
std::for_each(std::begin(folks), std::end(folks),
                [](const Name& name)
                    {std::cout << '"' << name.first << " " << name.second << "\" "; });
  std::cout << std::endl;                               // "Stan Down" "Al Bedo" "Ann Ounce"
```

The vector and list containers store elements of type pair<string,string> that represent names. The swap_ranges() algorithm is used to swap the first two elements in people with the last two elements in folks. There's no operator<<() function overload for writing pair objects to a stream so copy() can't be used with an output stream iterator listing the containers. I chose to use the for_each() algorithm to produce the output by applying a lambda expression to each element in the containers. The lambda expression just writes the members of the Name element that is passed to it to the standard output stream. The comments show the output from executing this code.

There's a function template that overloads the swap() algorithm that is defined in the utility header with the prototype:

```
template<typename T1, typename T2> void swap(std::pair<T1,T2> left, std::pair<T1,T2> right);
```

This swaps pair<T1,T2> objects and is used by swap_ranges() to interchange elements in the preceding code fragment.

The swap() template that swaps two objects of the same type T is also defined in the utility header. In addition to the overload for pair objects, there are template overloads in the utility header that will interchange two container objects of any given type. That is, it will swap two list<T> containers or two set<T> containers but not a list<T> with a vector<T> or a list<T1> with a list<T2>. Another swap() template overload can swap two arrays of the same type. There are also several other overloads of swap() to interchange objects of other types including tuple and smart pointer types. As you have seen earlier in this chapter, the iter_swap() algorithm is a little different; it swaps the elements pointed to by two forward iterators.

Removing Elements from a Range

It's impossible to remove elements from a range without knowing their context - the container in which the elements are stored. Thus the algorithms that 'remove' elements don't, they just overwrite selected elements or omit to copy elements. The number of elements in a range from which elements are 'removed' will not be altered by the remove operation. There are four remove algorithms:

- `remove()` removes elements from the range specified by the first two forward iterator arguments that equal the object that is the third argument. Essentially each matching element is removed by overwriting it by the element that follows. The algorithm returns an iterator that points to one past the new last element in the range.

- `remove_copy()` copies elements from the range specified by the first two forward iterator arguments to a destination range identified by the third argument, omitting elements that equal the fourth argument. The algorithm returns an iterator that points to one past the last element copied to the destination range. The ranges must not overlap.

- `remove_if()` removes elements from the range specified by the first two forward iterator arguments for which the predicate that is the third argument returns `true`.

- `remove_copy_if()` copies elements from the range specified by the first two forward iterator arguments to a destination range identified by the third argument, for which the predicate that is the fourth argument returns `true`. The algorithm returns an iterator that points to one past the last element copied to the destination. The ranges must not overlap.

Here's how you might use `remove()`:

```
std::deque<double> samples {1.5, 2.6, 0.0, 3.1, 0.0, 0.0, 4.1, 0.0, 6.7, 0.0};
samples.erase(std::remove(std::begin(samples), std::end(samples), 0.0), std::end(samples));
std::copy(std::begin(samples), std::end(samples), std::ostream_iterator<double> {std::cout, " "});
std::cout << std::endl;                              // 1.5 2.6 3.1 4.1 6.7
```

The `samples` contains physical measurements that should never be zero. The `remove()` algorithm eliminates the spurious zero values by moving the other elements left to overwrite them. The iterator that `remove()` returns is the new end for the range of elements that result from the operation so this is used as the begin iterator for the range to be erased by calling the `erase()` member of `samples`. The comment shows the elements that remain.

You use `remove_copy()` when you need to retain the original range and create a new range that is a copy with selected elements removed. For example:

```
std::deque<double> samples {1.5, 2.6, 0.0, 3.1, 0.0, 0.0, 4.1, 0.0, 6.7, 0.0};
std::vector<double> edited_samples;
std::remove_copy(std::begin(samples), std::end(samples), std::back_inserter(edited_samples), 0.0);
```

Non-zero elements are copied from the `samples` container to the `edited_samples` container, which happens to be different - it's a `vector`. The elements are added to `edited_samples` by a `back_insert_iterator` object so the container will contain just the elements copied from `samples`.

The remove_if() algorithm offers a much more powerful capability for removing elements from a range that just match a value. The predicate determines whether or not an element is removed; as long as it accepts an element from the range as an argument and returns a bool value, anything goes. Here's an example:

```
using Name = std::pair<string, string>;      // First and second name
std::set<Name> blacklist {Name {"Al", "Bedo"}, Name {"Ann", "Ounce"}, Name {"Jo", "King"}};
std::deque<Name> candidates {Name {"Stan", "Down"}, Name {"Al", "Bedo"}, Name {"Dan", "Druff"},
                       Name {"Di", "Gress"}, Name {"Ann", "Ounce"}, Name {"Bea", "Gone"}};
candidates.erase(std::remove_if(std::begin(candidates), std::end(candidates),
                            [&blacklist](const Name& name) { return blacklist.count(name); }),
                 std::end(candidates));
std::for_each(std::begin(candidates), std::end(candidates), [](const Name& name)
                       {std::cout << '"' << name.first << " " << name.second << "\" "; });
  std::cout << std::endl;                     // "Stan Down" "Dan Druff" "Di Gress" "Bea Gone"
```

This code models dealing with applicants for membership of a club that doesn't accept the hoi polloi. The names of people who are known troublemakers are stored in the blacklist container, which is a set. The current applicants for membership are stored in the candidates container, which is a deque. The remove_if() algorithm is used to make sure no names from the blacklist container make it through the selection process. The predicate is a lambda expression that captures the blacklist container by reference. The count() member of the set container will return 1 when the argument is present. The value that the predicate returns is implicitly converted to bool, so the predicate effectively returns true for every element in candidates that appears in blacklist so these will be removed from candidates. The candidates that make it through the selection process are shown in the comment.

The remove_copy_if() is to remove_copy() as remove_if() is to remove(). Here's how it works:

```
std::set<Name> blacklist {Name {"Al", "Bedo"}, Name {"Ann", "Ounce"}, Name {"Jo", "King"}};
std::deque<Name> candidates {Name {"Stan", "Down"}, Name {"Al", "Bedo"}, Name {"Dan", "Druff"},
                       Name {"Di", "Gress"}, Name {"Ann", "Ounce"}, Name {"Bea", "Gone"}};
std::deque<Name> validated;
std::remove_copy_if(std::begin(candidates), std::end(candidates), std::back_inserter(validated),
                          [&blacklist](const Name& name) { return blacklist.count(name); });
```

This code accomplishes the same as the previous fragment except the result is stored in the validated container and the candidates container is not modified.

Setting and Modifying Elements in a Range

The fill() and fill_n() algorithms offer an easy way to populate a range of elements with a given value. fill() populates an entire range; fill_n() sets a value for the number of elements you specify starting at the element pointed to by a given iterator. Here's how fill() might be used:

```
std::vector<string> data {12};                     // Container has 12 elements
std::fill(std::begin(data), std::end(data), "none"); // Set all elements to "none"
```

The first two arguments to fill() are forward iterators defining the range. The third argument is the value to be assigned to each element. Of course the range does not have to represent all the elements in a container. For example:

```
std::deque<int> values(13);                              // Container has 13 elements
int n{2};                                                // Initial element value
const int step {7};                                      // Element value increment
const size_t count{3};                                   // Number of elements with given value
auto iter = std::begin(values);
while(true)
{
  auto to_end = std::distance(iter, std::end(values));// Number of elements remaining
  if(to_end < count)                                     // In case no. of elements not a
                                                         // multiple of count
  {
    std::fill(iter, iter + to_end, n);                   // Just fill remaining elements...
    break;                                               // ...and end the loop
  }
  else
  {
    std::fill(iter, std::end(values), n);                // Fill next count elements
  }
    iter = std::next(iter, count);                       // Increment iter
    n += step;
}
```

The values container is created with 13 elements. This is a situation where you *must* use parentheses for the value to be passed to the constructor; using braces will create a container with a single element with the value 13. Within the loop, the fill() algorithm is used to assign a values to sequences of count elements. iter starts out as the begin iterator for the container, and if there are sufficient elements remaining, it is incremented by count on each loop iteration so it points to the first element in the next sequence. Executing this sets the elements in values to:

```
2 2 2 9 9 9 16 16 16 23 23 23 30
```

The arguments to fill_n() are a forward iterator pointing to the first element in the range to be modified, the number of elements to be modified, and the value to be set. The distance() and next() functions are defined in the iterator header. The former works with input iterators but the latter requires forward iterators.

Generating Element Values with a Function

You have already seen that you can use the for_each() algorithm to apply a function object to each element within a range. The function object has a parameter that references an element in the range defined by the first two arguments to the algorithm so it can change the value stored directly. The generate() algorithm is a little different. The first two arguments are forward iterators that specify a range, and the third argument is a function object defining a function of the form:

```
T fun();     // T is a type that can be assigned to an element in the range
```

There's no access to the values of elements within the range from within the function. The generate() algorithm simply stores the value returned by the function for each element in the range; and there's nothing returned by generate(). To make the algorithm useful, you need to be able to generate different values to be assigned to different elements within a function with no parameters. One possibility is to define the third argument to generate() as a function object that captures one or more external variables. Here's an example:

```
string chars (30, ' ');                    // 30 space characters
char ch {'a'};
int incr {};
std::generate(std::begin(chars), std::end(chars), [ch, &incr]
                                           {
                                             incr += 3;
                                             return ch + (incr % 26);
                                           });
  std::cout << chars << std::endl;         // chars is: dgjmpsvybehknqtwzcfiloruxadgjm
```

The chars variable is initialized with a string of 30 space characters. The values that the lambda expression that is the third argument to generate() returns will be stored in successive characters in chars. The lambda captures ch by value and incr by reference, so the latter can be modified in the body of the lambda. The lambda returns the character that results from adding incr to ch, the increment value is modulo 26 so the return value is always within the range 'a' to 'z', given the starting value is 'a'. The result of this operation is shown in the comment. It's possible to devise a lambda that will work for any upper- or lowercase letter and only generate letters of the type stored in ch, but I'll leave that as an exercise for you.

The generate_n() algorithm works in a similar way to generate(). The difference is that while the first argument is still the begin iterator for the range, the second argument is a count of the number of elements to be set by the third argument. The range must have at least the number of elements defined by the second argument to avoid a program crash. Here's an example:

```
string chars (30, ' ');                    // 30 space characters
char ch {'a'};
int incr {};
std::generate_n(std::begin(chars), chars.size()/2,[ch, &incr]
                                           {
                                             incr += 3;
                                             return ch + (incr % 26);
                                           });
```

Here, only half the characters in chars will have new value set by the algorithm. The second half will remain as space characters.

Transforming a Range

The transform() algorithm applies a function to elements in a range and stores the values returned by the function in another range. It returns an iterator that points to one past the last element stored in the output range. One version of the algorithm has similarities to for_each() in that you apply a unary function to a range of elements that can modify their values, but there are significant differences. The function applied using for_each() must have a void return type, and you alter values in the input range through a reference parameter to the function. With transform() the unary function must return a value, and you have the possibility to store the results of applying the function in another range, and the elements in the output range can be of a different type from the input range. There's another difference too: with for_each(), a function is always applied to elements in sequence, but with transform() this is not guaranteed.

A second version of transform() allows a binary function to be applied to corresponding elements from two ranges, but let's look at applying a unary function to a range first. In this version of the algorithm, the first two arguments are input iterators defining the input range, the third argument is an output iterator for the first element in the destination, and the fourth argument is the unary function. The function must accept an element from the input range as the argument and must return a value that can be stored in the output range. Here's an example:

```
std::vector<double> deg_C {21.0, 30.5, 0.0, 3.2, 100.0};
std::vector<double> deg_F(deg_C.size());
std::transform(std::begin(deg_C), std::end(deg_C), std::begin(deg_F),
            [](double temp){ return 32.0 + 9.0* temp/5.0; });  // Result 69.8 86.9 32 37.76 212
```

The transform() algorithm call converts the Centigrade temperature values in the deg_C container to Fahrenheit and stores the result in the deg_F container. The deg_F container is created with the number of elements needed to store all the results so the third argument is the begin iterator for deg_F. You could store the results in an empty container by using a back_insert_iterator as the third argument to transform():

```
std::vector<double> deg_F;                      // Empty container
std::transform(std::begin(deg_C), std::end(deg_C), std::back_inserter(deg_F),
            [](double temp){ return 32.0 + 9.0* temp/5.0; });  // Result 69.8 86.9 32 37.76 212
```

The elements storing the result of the operation are created in deg_F by the back_insert_iterator; the result is the same.

The third argument can be an iterator pointing to an element in the input container. For example:

```
std::vector<double> temps {21.0, 30.5, 0.0, 3.2, 100.0};              // In Centigrade
std::transform(std::begin(temps), std::end(temps), std::begin(temps),
            [](double temp)
                { return 32.0 + 9.0* temp / 5.0; });  // Result 69.8 86.9 32 37.76 212
```

This converts the values in the temps container from Centigrade to Fahrenheit. The third argument is the begin iterator for the input range, so the result of applying the function specified by the fourth argument is stored back in the element to which it is being applied.

Here's some code that illustrates a situation where the destination range is of a different type from the input range:

```
std::vector<string> words {"one", "two", "three", "four", "five"};
std::vector<size_t> hash_values;
std::transform(std::begin(words), std::end(words), std::back_inserter(hash_values),
                            std::hash<string>());   // string hashing function
std::copy(std::begin(hash_values), std::end(hash_values),
                            std::ostream_iterator<size_t> {std::cout, " "});
std::cout << std::endl;
```

The input range contains string objects, and the function that is applied to the elements is the standard hashing function object that is defined in the string header. The hashing function returns a hash value as type size_t, and these values are stored in the hash_values container using a back_insert_iterator object that is returned by the back_inserter() helper function from the iterator header. On my system, this code produces the output:

3123124719 3190065193 2290484163 795473317 2931049365

Your system may produce different output. Note that because the destination range is specified as a back_insert_iterator object, the transform() algorithm here would return an iterator of type back_insert_iterator<vector<size_T>> so you could not use this as the end iterator for the input range to the copy() algorithm. To make use of the iterator that transform() returns, the code would need to be:

```
std::vector<string> words {"one", "two", "three", "four", "five"};
std::vector<size_t> hash_values(words.size());
auto end_iter = std::transform(std::begin(words), std::end(words), std::begin(hash_values),
                        std::hash<string>());    // string hashing function
std::copy(std::begin(hash_values), end_iter, std::ostream_iterator<size_t> {std::cout, " "});
std::cout << std::endl;
```

Now transform() returns the end iterator for the range of elements in the hash_values container.

There's nothing to prevent you from calling an algorithm from within the function that is applied by the transform() function to a range of elements. Here's an illustration of the possibility:

```
std::deque<string> names {"Stan Laurel", "Oliver Hardy", "Harold Lloyd"};
std::transform(std::begin(names), std::end(names), std::begin(names),
    [](string& s) { std::transform(std::begin(s), std::end(s),std::begin(s), ::toupper);
                    return s;
                  });
  std::copy(std::begin(names), std::end(names), std::ostream_iterator<string> {std::cout, " "});
  std::cout << std::endl;
```

The transform() algorithm applies a function that is defined by a lambda expression to the elements in the names container. The lambda expression calls transform() to apply the toupper() function that is defined in the cctype header to each of the characters in the string that is passed to it. The net effect is to convert each of the elements in names to uppercase, so the output would be:

STAN LAUREL OLIVER HARDY HAROLD LLOYD

Of course, there are other, possibly simpler ways of achieving the same result.

The version of transform() that applies a binary function expects five arguments:

- The first two arguments are input iterators for the first input range.

- The third argument is the begin iterator for the second input range, and obviously, this range must contain at least as many elements as the first input range.

- The fourth argument is an output iterator that is the begin iterator for the range where the results of applying the function are to be stored.

- The fifth argument is a function object defining a function that has two parameters that will accept arguments that are elements from the two input ranges and return a value that can be stored in the output range.

Let's consider an example of some simple geometric calculations. A polyline is a succession of lines between points. A polyline could be represented by a vector of Point objects, and the segments in the polyline are the lines joining successive points. If the last point is identical to the first, the polyline will be closed - a polygon. Figure 7-4 shows an example with Point defined as a type alias like this:

```
using Point = std::pair<double, double>;        //  pair<x,y> defines a point
```

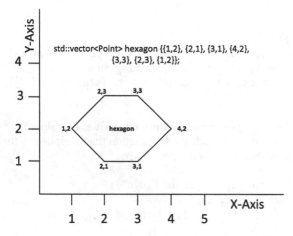

Length of segment between points x_1, y_1 and $x_2, y_2 = \sqrt{((x_1 - x_2)^2 + (y_1 - y_2)^2)}$

Figure 7-4. *A polyline that represents a hexagon*

There are seven points so the hexagon object in Figure 7-4 has six line segments. Since the first and last points are the same, the six line segments do indeed form a polygon - a hexagon. We can calculate the lengths of the line segments using the transform() algorithm:

```
std::vector<Point> hexagon {{1,2}, {2,1}, {3,1}, {4,2}, {3,3}, {2,3}, {1,2}};
std::vector<double> segments;                        // Stores lengths of segments
std::transform(std::begin(hexagon), std::end(hexagon) - 1, std::begin(hexagon) + 1,
               std::back_inserter(segments),
               [](const Point& p1, const Point& p2)
  { return std::sqrt(
               (p1.first-p2.first)*(p1.first - p2.first) +
               (p1.second - p2.second)*(p1.second - p2.second)); });
```

The first input range to transform() contains the Point objects in hexagon from the first to the second-to-last. The second input range starts with the second Point object so the arguments to successive calls of the binary function will be points 1 and 2, points 2 and 3, points 3 and 4, and so on, until the last two points from the input ranges, 6 and 7. Figure 7-4 shows the formula for the distance between two points, x_1, y_1 and $x_2, y_2,$ and the lambda expression that is the last argument to transform() implements this. Each segment length that is computed by the lambda expression is stored in the segments container. We could output the segments length and the total perimeter of the hexagon using two more algorithms such as this:

```
std::cout << "Segment lengths: ";
std::copy(std::begin(segments), std::end(segments),
                                    std::ostream_iterator<double> {std::cout, " "});
std::cout << std::endl;
std::cout << "Hexagon perimeter: "
         << std::accumulate(std::begin(segments), std::end(segments), 0.0) << std::endl;
```

The segment lengths are output using the copy() algorithm. The accumulate() function sums the values of the elements in segments to produce the total length of the perimeter.

Replacing Elements in a Range

The replace() algorithm replaces elements matching a given value with a new value. The first two arguments are forward iterators for the range to be processed, the third argument is the value to be replaced, and the fourth argument is the new value. Here's how it works:

```
std::deque<int> data {10, -5, 12, -6, 10, 8, -7, 10, 11};
std::replace(std::begin(data), std::end(data), 10, 99);    // Result: 99 -5 12 -6 99 8 -7 99 11
```

Here, all elements in the data container that match 10 are replaced by 99.

The replace_if() algorithm replaces elements with a new value when a predicate returns true. The third argument is the predicate and the fourth is the new value. The parameter type is typically a const reference to the element type; the const is not mandatory but the predicate should not modify the argument. Here's an example of using replace_if():

```
string password {"This is a good choice!"};
std::replace_if(std::begin(password), std::end(password),
            [](char ch){return std::isspace(ch);}, '_');   // Result: This_is_a_good_choice!
```

The predicate returns true for any element that is a space character so these will be replaced by underlines.

The replace_copy() algorithm does what replace() does but the result is stored in another range, leaving the original unchanged. The first two arguments are forward iterators for the input range, the third is the begin iterator for the output range, and the last two are the value to be replaced and the replacement. Here's an example:

```
std::vector<string> words {"one", "none", "two", "three", "none", "four"};
std::vector<string> new_words;
std::replace_copy(std::begin(words), std::end(words), std::back_inserter(new_words),
            string{"none"}, string{"0"});   // Result: "one", "0", "two", "three", "0", "four"
```

After executing this code, new_words will contain string elements as shown in the comment.

The last algorithm for selectively replacing elements in a range is replace_copy_if(), which does the same as replace_if() but with the result stored in another range. The first two arguments are the iterators for the input range, the third argument is the begin iterator for the output, and the last two are the predicate and the replacement value respectively. Here's an example:

```
std::deque<int> data {10, -5, 12, -6, 10, 8, -7, 10, 11};
std::vector<int> data_copy;
std::replace_copy_if(std::begin(data), std::end(data),
                     std::back_inserter(data_copy),
                  [](int value) {return value == 10;}, 99); // Result: 99 -5 12 -6 99 8 -7 99 11
```

The data_copy container is a vector, just to show that the output container can be different from the input container. It will end up containing the elements shown in the comment as a result of executing this code.

Applying Algorithms

I'll create a final working example in this chapter that applies some of the algorithms to plotting curves on the standard output stream. This will be a bit more realistic. A curve will be defined by a range of, pair<double,double> objects that represent x,y points. We can first define a plot() function template that will plot a curve on the standard output stream. The template type parameter will be the type of the iterators that define the range, so the points can originate in any sequence container, or possibly an array. Each point will be plotted as an asterisk, with the x axis across the page and the y axis down the page. Because this output is to a character stream, the aspect ratio of the font will affect the aspect ratio of the plot. Ideally the font should have the same width and height and I chose an 8×8 font on my system.

The parameters to the plot() function will be the iterators defining the range of points on the curve, a string specifying the name of the curve for output, and the number of characters in the width of the plot. The last two parameters will have default values to allow them to be omitted. The range of x values in the points will have to fit within the number of characters specified for the plot width. This will determine a step for x between one character and the next. To maintain the aspect ratio of the plot, the steps between y values between rows - down the page - will be the same as the step between x values. Here's the code for the plot() function template:

```
template<typename Iterator>
void plot(Iterator begin_iter, Iterator end_iter, string name = "Curve", size_t n_x = 100)
{ // n_x is plot width in characters, so it's the number of characters along the x axis

  // Comparison functions for x and for y
  auto x_comp = [](const Point& p1, const Point& p2) {return p1.first < p2.first; };
  auto y_comp = [](const Point& p1, const Point& p2) {return p1.second < p2.second; };

  // Minimum and maximum x values
  auto min_x = std::min_element(begin_iter, end_iter, x_comp)->first;
  auto max_x = std::max_element(begin_iter, end_iter, x_comp)->first;

  // Step length for output - same step applies to x and y
  double step {(max_x - min_x) / (n_x + 1)};

  // Minimum and maximum y values
  auto min_y = std::min_element(begin_iter, end_iter, y_comp)->second;
  auto max_y = std::max_element(begin_iter, end_iter, y_comp)->second;
```

```
size_t nrows {1 + static_cast<size_t>(1 + (max_y - min_y)/step)};
std::vector<string> rows(nrows, string(n_x + 1, ' '));

// Create x-axis at y=0 if this is within range of points
if(max_y > 0.0 && min_y <= 0.0)
  rows[static_cast<size_t>(max_y/step)] = string(n_x + 1, '-');

// Create y-axis at x=0 if this is within range of points
if(max_x > 0.0 && min_x <= 0.0)
{
 size_t x_axis {static_cast<size_t>(-min_x/step)};
 std::for_each(std::begin(rows), std::end(rows),
   [x_axis](string& row) { row[x_axis] = row[x_axis] == '-' ? '+' : '|'; });
}

std::cout << "\n\n      " << name << ":\n\n";
// Generate the rows for output
auto y {max_y};                              // Upper y for current output row
for(auto& row : rows)
{
  // Find points to be included in an output row
  std::vector<Point> row_pts;                // Stores points for this row
  std::copy_if(begin_iter, end_iter, std::back_inserter(row_pts),
  [&y, &step](const Point& p) { return p.second < y + step && p.second >= y; });

  std::for_each(std::begin(row_pts), std::end(row_pts),  // Set * for pts in the row
  [&row, min_x, step](const Point& p)
                    {row[static_cast<size_t>((p.first - min_x) / step)] = '*'; });
  y -= step;
}
// Output the plot - which is all the rows.
std::copy(std::begin(rows), std::end(rows), std::ostream_iterator<string>{std::cout, "\n"});
std::cout << std::endl;
}
```

Two lambda expressions, x_comp and y_comp, are defined for comparing x and y values. These are used in the max_element() and min_element() algorithm calls that find the upper and lower limits for x values and y values. The limits for x are used to determine the step length that will apply horizontally between characters in a row of the output, and vertically between one output row and the next. The number of rows in the output is determined from the range of y values and the step length. Each row in the output will be a string object so the complete plot will be created in the rows container, which is a vector of string objects.

To create the plot in rows, it's necessary to find the points with y values that belong in each row. These will be points with y values that are from some current y value up to y+step. The copy_if() algorithm copies points from the input range that meet this condition into the row_pts container for each row. The x values of the points in row_pts are then used in the function passed to for_each(). For each point the function determines the index of the character in the current row that corresponds to the x value of the point, and sets it to an asterisk.

The example includes two functions that create the points for a specific type of curve. One creates points on a sine curve, which is relatively simple to calculate; and the other for a cardioid, which is a little more complicated but is an interesting curve. Sine curves are interesting because they turn up in so many contexts. Audio signals can be regarded as combinations of sine waves of different frequencies and amplitudes for instance. The function in the example will just compute points for the curve defined by the

319

equation $y = \sin(x)$ but you could easily extend it to allow for different frequencies and amplitudes. Here's the code for the function:

```
// Generate x,y points on curve y = sin(x) for x values 0 to 4π
std::vector<Point> sine_curve(size_t n_pts = 100)
{ // n_pts is number of data points for the curve
  std::vector<double> x_values(n_pts);
  double value {};
  double step {4 * pi / (n_pts - 1)};
  std::generate(std::begin(x_values), std::end(x_values),
    [&value, &step]() { double v {value};
                        value += step;
                        return v; });
  std::vector<Point> curve_pts;
  std::transform(std::begin(x_values), std::end(x_values), std::back_inserter(curve_pts),
    [](double x) { return Point {x, sin(x)}; });
  return curve_pts;
}
```

The points are returned as Point elements in a vector container, where Point is an alias for type pair<double,double>. The code uses the generate() algorithm to produce x values from 0 to 4π. The transform() algorithm then creates the Point objects in the curve_pts container, which is returned.

The Cartesian equation for a cardioid based on a circle with radius r is $(x^2 + y^2 - r^2)^2 = 4r^2((x - r^2)^2 + y^2)$, which is not very useful for determining points on the curve. A much more useful representation is the parametric form, where x and y values are defined in terms of an independent parameter, t:

$$x = r(\cos(t) - \cos(2t)) \; y = r(\sin(t) - \sin(2t))$$

By varying t from 0 to 2π we can obtain points on a cardioid corresponding to rolling a circle radius r around another circle with the same radius. We can define a function to generate points using these equations very easily:

```
std::vector<Point> cardioid_curve(double r = 1.0, size_t n_pts = 100)
{ // n_pts is number of data points
  double step = 2 * pi / (n_pts - 1);                // Step length for x and y
  double t_value {};                                 // Curve parameter

  // Create parameter values that define the curve
  std::vector<double> t_values(n_pts);
  std::generate(std::begin(t_values), std::end(t_values),
                        [&t_value, step]() { auto value = t_value;
                                             t_value += step;
                                             return value; });

  // Function to define an x,y point on the cardioid for a given t
  auto cardioid = [r](double t)
                { return Point {r*(2*cos(t) + cos(2*t)), r*(2*sin(t) + sin(2*t))}; };

  // Create the points for the cardioid
  std::vector<Point> curve_pts;
  std::transform(std::begin(t_values), std::end(t_values), std::back_inserter(curve_pts),
                                             cardioid);
  return curve_pts;
}
```

320

This is essentially the same logic as for the sine curve. The generate() algorithm creates a range of values for the independent variable, which in this case is the equation parameter, t. The cardioid lambda expression is defined independently simply because it's easier to see this way. It creates a Point object for a given t from the parametric equations. The transform() algorithm applies cardioid to the vector of t values that is the input range to create a vector of Point objects on the curve.

The main() program to plot a sine curve and a cardioid is now very simple:

```cpp
// Ex7_05.cpp
// Apply some algorithms to plotting curves
// To get the output with the correct aspect ratio, set the characters
// in the standard output stream destination to a square font, such as 8 x 8 pixels
#include <iostream>                          // For standard streams
#include <iterator>                          // For iterators and begin() and end()
#include <string>                            // For string class
#include <vector>                            // For vector container
#include <algorithm>                         // For algorithms
#include <cmath>                             // For sin(), cos()
using std::string;
using Point = std::pair<double, double>;

static const double pi {3.1415926};

// Definition of plot() function template here...

// Definition of sine_curve() function here...

// Definition of cardioid_curve() function here...

int main()
{
  auto curve1 = sine_curve(50);
  plot(std::begin(curve1), std::end(curve1), "Sine curve", 90);
  auto curve2 = cardioid_curve(1.5, 120);
  plot(std::begin(curve2), std::end(curve2), "Cardioid", 60);
}
```

The static variable, pi, is defined at global scope to make it available to all the code in the program; it's used by both functions that generate curves. There's interaction between the number of points defining a curve, the range of x values, and the width of the plot. The discretization that's implicit in a character plot means that parts of a curve may look a little flat - or lumpy. The output that I got is shown in Figure 7-5.

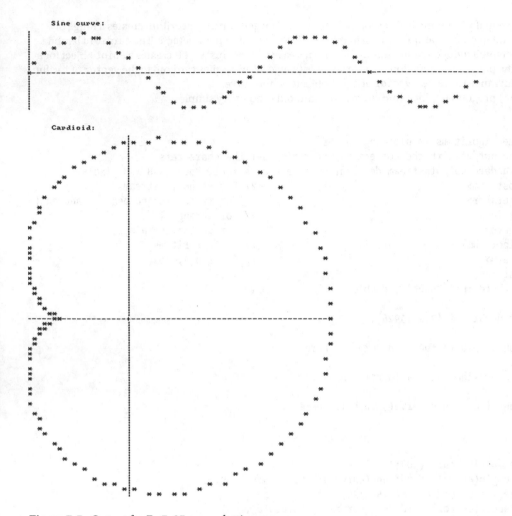

Figure 7-5. *Output for Ex 7_05.cpp - plotting curves*

Summary

This chapter has shown how rich the spectrum of algorithms offered by the STL is. You often have more than one option for an algorithm to carry out a given operation, and that's in addition to writing a loop yourself. The ultimate choice in any situation often comes down to personal preference. Generally, an algorithm will often be faster than programming a loop explicitly, but code that uses a loop is sometimes easier to understand. However, writing your own loop is more prone to error so using algorithms where you can is preferred.

For reference, here's a summary of the algorithms you have seen in this chapter:

Finding the number of elements in a range with a given property

- `all_of(Input_Iter beg, Input_Iter end, Unary_Predicate p)` returns true if p returns true for all elements in [beg,end).

- `any_of(Input_Iter beg, Input_Iter end, Unary_Predicate p)` returns true if p returns true for any element in [beg,end).

- `none_of(Input_Iter beg, Input_Iter end, Unary_Predicate p)` returns `true` if `p` returns `false` for all elements in [`beg`,`end`).

- `count(Input_Iter beg, Input_Iter end, const T& obj)` returns the number of elements in [`beg`,`end`) that are equal to `obj`.

- `count_if(Input_Iter beg, Input_Iter end, Unary_Predicate p)` returns the number of elements in [`beg`,`end`) for which `p` returns `true`.

Comparing ranges

- `equal(Input_Iter1 beg1, Input_Iter1 end1, Input_Iter2 beg2)` returns `true` if elements from the range [`beg1`,`end1`) are equal to corresponding elements from the range beginning `beg2`.

- `equal(Input_Iter1 beg1, Input_Iter1 end1, Input_Iter2 beg2, Input_Iter2 end2)` returns `true` if elements from the range [`beg1`,`end1`) are equal to corresponding elements from the range [`beg2`,`end2`).

- `equal(Input_Iter1 beg1, Input_Iter1 end1, Input_Iter2 beg2, Binary_Predicate p)` returns `true` if `p` returns `true` for corresponding elements in the range [`beg1`,`end1`) and the range beginning `beg2`.

- `equal(Input_Iter1 beg1, Input_Iter1 end1,`
  `        Input_Iter2 beg2, Input_Iter2 end2, Binary_Predicate p)`
  returns `true` if `p` returns `true` for corresponding elements in the ranges [`beg1`,`end1`) and [`beg2`,`end2`).

- `mismatch(Input_Iter1 beg1, Input_Iter1 end1, Input_Iter2 beg2)` returns a `pair<Input_Iter1, Input_Iter2>` object containing iterators that point to the first pair of elements that are unequal.

- `mismatch(Input_Iter1 beg1,Input_Iter1 end1,Input_Iter2 beg2,Input_Iter2 end2)` returns the same as the previous version.

- `mismatch(Input_Iter1 beg1, Input_Iter1 end1,`
  `        Input_Iter2 beg2, Binary_Predicate p)` returns a
  `pair<Input_Iter1,Input_Iter2>` object containing iterators that point to the first pair of elements for which `p` returns `false`.

- `mismatch(Input_Iter1 beg1, Input_Iter1 end1,`
  `        Input_Iter2 beg2, Input_Iter2 end2, Binary_Predicate p)`
  returns the same as the previous version.

- `lexicographical_compare(Input_Iter1 beg1, Input_Iter1 end1,`
  `                        Input_Iter2 beg2, Input_Iter2 end2)` returns
  `true` if the ranges contain the same number of elements and corresponding elements are equal; otherwise it returns `false`.

- `lexicographical_compare(Input_Iter1 beg1, Input_Iter1 end1,`
  `                        Input_Iter2 beg2, Input_Iter2 end2,`
  `                        Binary_Predicate p)` returns `true` if the ranges
  contain the same number of elements and `p` returns `true` for all corresponding pairs of elements; otherwise it returns `false`.

Permuting a Range of Elements

- next_permutation(Bi_Iter beg, Bi_Iter end) rearranges the elements into the next permutation in ascending lexicographical sequence if there is a next permutation, and returns true. Otherwise, the elements are rearranged into the first permutation in sequence and the algorithm returns false.

- next_permutation(Bi_Iter beg, Bi_Iter end, Compare compare) rearranges the elements into the next permutation in lexicographical sequence based on the element comparison function, compare, and returns true. If there is no next permutation, the elements are rearranged into the first permutation in the sequence based on compare and the algorithm returns false.

- prev_permutation(Bi_Iter beg, Bi_Iter end) rearranges the elements into the previous permutation in ascending lexicographical sequence if there is a previous permutation, and returns true. Otherwise, the elements are rearranged into the last permutation in sequence and the algorithm returns false.

- next_permutation(Bi_Iter beg, Bi_Iter end, Compare compare) rearranges the elements into the previous permutation in lexicographical sequence based on the element comparison function, compare, and returns true. If there is no next permutation, the elements are rearranged into the last permutation in the sequence based on compare and the algorithm returns false.

- is_permutation(Fwd_Iter1 beg1, Fwd_Iter1 end1, Fwd_Iter2 beg2) returns true if the (end1-beg1) elements in the range starting at beg2 are a permutation of the range [beg1,end1), and false otherwise. Elements are compared using ==.

- is_permutation(Fwd_Iter1 beg1, Fwd_Iter1 end1, Fwd_Iter2 beg2, Binary_Predicate p) does the same as the previous version except that elements are compared for equality using p.

- is_permutation(Fwd_Iter1 beg1, Fwd_Iter1 end1, Fwd_Iter2 beg2, Fwd_Iter2 end2) returns true if the range [beg2,end2)is a permutation of the range [beg1,end1), and false otherwise. Elements are compared using ==.

- is_permutation(Fwd_Iter1 beg1, Fwd_Iter1 end1, Fwd_Iter2 beg2, Fwd_Iter2 end2, Binary_Predicate p) does the same as the previous version except that elements are compared for equality using p.

Copying elements from a range

- copy(Input_Iter beg1, Input_Iter end1, Output_Iter beg2) copies the range [beg1, end1) to the range beginning at beg2. It returns an iterator that points to one past the last element copied in the destination.

- copy_n(Input_Iter beg1, Int_Type n, Output_Iter beg2) copies n elements from the range starting at beg1 to the range beginning at beg2. It returns an iterator that points to one past the last element copied in the destination.

- copy_if(Input_Iter beg1, Input_Iter end1, Output_Iter beg2, Unary_Predicate p) copies elements from the range [beg1, end1) for which p returns true to the range beginning at beg2. It returns an iterator that points to one past the last element copied in the destination.

- `copy_backward(Bi_Iter1 beg1, Bi_Iter1 end1, Bi_Iter2 end2)` copies the range [beg1, end1) to the range ending at end2. The operation copies elements in reverse sequence starting with the element pointed to by end1-1. The algorithm returns an iterator, iter, that points to the last element copied in the destination, so after the operation the destination range will be [iter, end2).

- `reverse_copy(Bi_Iter beg1, Bi_Iter end1, Output_Iter beg2)` copies the range [beg1, end1) to the range beginning at beg2 in reverse, and returns an iterator, iter, that points to one past the last element copied in the destination. Thus [beg2, iter) will contain the elements from [beg1, end1) in reverse order.

- `reverse(Bi_Iter beg, Bi_Iter end)` reverses the order of elements in the range [beg, end).

- `unique_copy(Input_Iter beg1, Input_Iter end1, Output_Iter beg2)` copies the range [beg1, end1) to the range beginning at beg2, omitting successive duplicates. Elements are compared using == and the algorithm returns an iterator that points to one past the last element copied in the destination.

- `unique_copy(Input_Iter beg1, Input_Iter end1, Output_Iter beg2, Binary_Predicate p)` does the same as the previous algorithm except that elements are compared using p.

- `unique(Fwd_Iter beg, Fwd_Iter end)` removes successive duplicates from the range [beg, end) by copying left to overwrite them. Elements are compared using == and the algorithm returns an end iterator for the range that results from the operation.

- `unique(Fwd_Iter beg, Fwd_Iter end, Binary_Predicate p)` does the same as the previous algorithm except that elements are compared using p.

Moving a range

- `move(Input_Iter beg1, Input_Iter end1, Output_Iter beg2)` moves the range [beg1, end1) to the range beginning at beg2. The algorithm returns an iterator that points to one past the last element moved in the destination. beg2 must not be within [beg1, end1).

- `move_backward(Bi_Iter1 beg1, Bi_Iter1 end1, Bi_Iter2 end2)` moves the range [beg1, end1) to the range ending at end2, and the elements are moved in reverse sequence. The algorithm returns an iterator that points to the last element moved to the destination. end2 must not be within [beg1, end1).

Rotating a range of elements

- `rotate(Fwd_Iter beg, Fwd_Iter new_beg, Fwd_Iter end)` rotates the elements in [beg, end) counter clockwise so that new_beg becomes the first element in the range. The algorithm returns an iterator that points to the elements that was originally first in the range.

- `rotate_copy(Fwd_Iter beg1, Fwd_Iter new_beg1, Fwd_Iter end1, Output_Iter beg2)` copies all the elements from [beg1, end1) to the range beginning at beg2, so that the element to which new_beg1 points is the first element in the destination. The algorithm returns an iterator that points to one past the last element in the destination.

Removing elements from a range

- `remove(Fwd_Iter beg, Fwd_Iter end, const T& obj)` removes elements from [`beg, end`) that are equal to `obj` and returns an iterator pointing to one past the last element in the range that results.

- `remove_if(Fwd_Iter beg, Fwd_Iter end, Unary_Predicate p)` removes elements from [`beg, end`) for which `p` returns true. The algorithm returns an iterator pointing to one past the last element in the range that results.

- `remove_copy(Input_Iter beg1, Input_Iter end1, Output_Iter beg2, const T& obj)` copies elements from [`beg1, end1`) to the range beginning at `beg2`, omitting elements that are equal to `obj`. The algorithm returns an iterator that points to one past the last element in the destination.

- `remove_copy_if(Input_Iter beg1, Input_Iter end1, Output_Iter beg2, Unary_Predicate p)` copies elements from [`beg1, end1`) to the range beginning at `beg2`, omitting elements for which `p` returns true. The algorithm returns an iterator that points to one past the last element in the destination.

Replacing elements in a range

- `replace(Fwd_Iter beg, Fwd_Iter end, const T& obj, const T& new_obj)` replaces elements in [`beg, end`) that are equal to `obj` by `new_obj`.

- `replace_if(Fwd_Iter beg, Fwd_Iter end, Unary_Predicate p, const T& new_obj)` replaces elements in [`beg, end`) for which `p` returns true by `new_obj`.

- `replace_copy(Input_Iter beg1, Input_Iter end1, Output_Iter beg2, const T& obj, const T& new_obj)` copies elements from [`beg1, end1`) to the range beginning at `beg2`, replacing elements that are equal to `obj` by `new_obj`. The algorithm returns an iterator that points to one past the last element in the destination. The ranges must not overlap.

- `replace_copy_if(Input_Iter beg1, Input_Iter end1, Output_Iter beg2, Unary_Predicate p, const T& new_obj)` copies elements from [`beg1, end1`) to the range beginning at `beg2`, replacing elements for which `p` returns true by `new_obj`. The algorithm returns an iterator that points to one past the last element in the destination. The ranges must not overlap.

Modifying elements in a range

- `fill(Fwd_Iter beg, Fwd_Iter end, const T& obj)` stores `obj` in each of the elements in the range [`beg, end`).

- `fill_n(Output_Iter beg, Int_Type n, const T& obj)` stores `obj` in the first n elements of the range starting at `beg`.

- `generate(Fwd_Iter beg, Fwd_Iter end, Fun_Object gen_fun)` stores value returned by `gen_fun` in each of the elements in [`beg, end`). `gen_fun` must have no parameters and return a value that can be stored in the range.

- `generate_n(Output_Iter beg, Int_Type n, Fun_Object gen_fun)` stores n values returned by `gen_fun` in the first n elements of the range beginning at `beg`. The algorithm returns an iterator that points to one past the last value stored.

- `transform(Input_Iter beg1, Input_Iter end1,`
  `Output_Iter beg2, Unary_Op op)` applies op to each element in the range [`beg1, end1`) and stores the value returned in the corresponding elements of the range beginning at beg2.

- `transform(Input_Iter1 beg1, Input_Iter1 end1,`
  `Input_Iter2 beg2, Output_Iter beg3, Binary_Op op)` applies op to corresponding pairs of element in the range [`beg1, end1`) and the range beginning at beg2 and stores the value returned in the corresponding elements of the range beginning at beg3.

Swap Algorithms

- `swap(T& obj1, T& obj2)` swaps the value obj1 and obj2. A second version of this algorithm swaps two arrays of the same type, which implies they are the same length.

- `iter_swap(Fwd_Iter iter1, Fwd_Iter iter2)` interchanges the values pointed to by iter1 and iter2.

- `swap_ranges(Fwd_Iter1 beg1, Fwd_Iter1 end1, Fwd_Iter2 beg2)` interchanges corresponding elements between the range [`beg1, end1`) and the range beginning at beg2. The algorithm returns an iterator that points to the last element in the range beginning at beg2.

I'm afraid you can't sit back and relax yet - even if you *are* feeling comfortable with the algorithms you have seen up to now. There are more to come in the chapters that follow. In particular, Chapter 10 will introduce algorithms that are specific to numerical computation

EXERCISES

Use algorithms as far as possible in all these exercises.

1. Write a program to read dates from the standard input stream as:

   `month(string) day(integer) year(4-digit integer)`

   Store the dates as `tuple` objects in a `deque` container. Find the number of different months that occur in the container and output it. Find the different month names and output them. Copy dates for each different month into separate containers. Output the dates for each month in descending order of days within years.

2. Read an arbitrary number of heights from the standard input stream as:

   `feet (integer) inches(floating point)`

   and store each height in a container as a `pair` object. Use the `transform()` algorithm to convert the heights to metric values stored as `tuple` objects (meters, centimetres, millimeters - all integer) in another container. Use the `transform()` algorithm to create pair objects in a third container that combine both corresponding height representations. Use an algorithm to output the elements from this container so that feet, inch and metric representations of each height are displayed.

3. Write a program that will:

    • read a paragraph that includes punctuation from the standard input stream and store the words as elements in a sequence container.

    • determine the number of word duplicates in the input.

    • assemble all words of less than five characters in a container and output them.

4. Write a program to read a phrase of an arbitrary number of words and use algorithms to assemble all different permutations in a container and output them. Test the program with phrases containing up to five words. (You can try more than five if you want but keep in mind that there are n! permutations of n words.)

5. Read an arbitrary number of names consisting of a first and a second name from the standard input stream. Store the names in a container of pair<string,string> elements. Extract the names that have a common initial letter for the second name into separate containers and output their contents. Reproduce the original set of names in another container of pair<char, string> objects where the first member of the pair is the initial, and the second member is the second name. Output the names in the new form in order of second name lengths.

CHAPTER 8

■ ■ ■

Generating Random Numbers

The need to generate random numbers arises very often. Most games programs, programs that simulate the real world, almost always need the ability to generate random numbers. Testing a complex program usually needs random input at some point to validate that the program works under diverse conditions, and it's often convenient to generate such input programmatically. Of course, random numbers can be used to generate random choices of objects, so you have the ability to create random selections of anything.

Unless noted otherwise, all the STL templates discussed in this chapter are defined in the random header. There's a lot in the random header, some of which is very specialized and certainly more than I can discuss in detail. The aim of this chapter is to get you started with using the random number generation facilities of the STL by explaining and demonstrating the capabilities that I think are most useful generally. In this chapter you will learn:

- What is meant by a random number.

- What a random number engine is and what are the engines provided by the STL.

- What is meant by entropy in the context of random number generation.

- What a random number generator is and how a generator relates to an engine.

- What a random number engine adapter is.

- How to generate nondeterministic random sequences.

- What a distribution is and what distributions are provided by the STL.

- How to create a random rearrangement of a range of elements.

There are a number of mathematical equations in this chapter that provide precise explanations of how some algorithms work. You can ignore these if math is not your forte, without limiting your ability to understand how to apply the capabilities that are described.

What Is a Random Number?

Randomness implies unpredictability. True randomness only exists in the natural world. Where lightning will strike is random; if there is a storm brewing you can be fairly sure there will be lightning strikes but you cannot predict exactly where – just don't stand under a tree. Weather in the UK is random. Every day there is a forecast for tomorrow, which is frequently wrong, in spite of the enormously powerful, hugely expensive computers used to produce the forecast.

To describe a number as random requires a context – a previous sequence of numbers. Two is not a random number by itself, it's just 2. However, if 2 arrives next in the sequence 46, 1011, 874, 34, 998871, then it's possible that it is a value in a random number sequence. A number is random when it appears in a sequence, and knowledge of previous numbers in the sequence does not enable you to predict the next number. Of course, this doesn't imply that successive numbers must be different. The sequence 4, 4, 4, 4 may – or may not be part of a random sequence; it certainly can occur for successive throws of a dice. This makes it very difficult to determine whether a given sequence is random, and there are special mathematical tests for randomness – which I won't be going into in this book.

Digital computers are deterministic, which means that a calculation will *always* produce exactly the same result for a given set of input values. Thus, unless there is something seriously wrong with the hardware, the results produced by *any* program code cannot be random. Thus a computer cannot compute a random number sequence; the next number is always determined by the values used in the algorithm producing it. However, a digital computer can produce *pseudo-random* sequences of numbers. They are sequences because the pseudo-random property only has meaning in the context of a sequence; the numbers are called *pseudo*-random because they are produced by a computer and therefore cannot be *genuinely* random. Having said that, I'll drop the *pseudo* – and just use random in the rest of this chapter.

Probability, Distributions, and Entropy

Generating random numbers implicitly involves some concepts from statistics, which I'll explain in outline here. This section is here just in case you are not familiar with these ideas. This section should be enough to enable you to understand the rest of this chapter, even though these concepts may be new to you. But for a complete understanding of these ideas, you should consult a tutorial on statistics.

What Is Probability?

Probability is a value between 0 and 1 inclusive that measures the likelihood of an event occurring. Zero (0) indicates that an event can never arise, and 1 indicates that it is certain. The probability of throwing a 6 with a die that's not loaded – or indeed throwing any of the possible values – is 1/6. The probability of throwing any of the numbers is 1.

In general, the probability of an event occurring is the number of times it does occur divided by the number of occasions when it could have occurred. If the probability of an event happening is p, then the probability that it won't happen is 1-p. This can provide valuable guidance on what to expect in life. For instance, the chances of winning the lottery in the UK where you choose 6 numbers from 49, is about 1 in 14,000,000; this implies the chances of *not* winning are about 13,999,999/14,000,000, which is about as close to certainty as you can get. To put this in perspective, you are more than 10 times more likely to be struck by lightning than you are to win the lottery.

What Is a Distribution?

A *distribution* describes the likelihood of a variable assuming a particular value within a range. Distributions can be *discrete* or continuous:

- A *discrete distribution* describe the probabilities of a variable assuming any of a fixed set of values. A distribution for integer values is a discrete distribution by definition. A variable that represents the result of throwing a die is a typical example of a discrete distribution; it can only have integer values from 1 to 6. The sum of the probabilities for the possible values in a discrete distribution is always 1.

- A *continuous distribution* represents the probability of a continuous variable assuming a particular value within a range. A continuous variable can assume any value within a range; the temperature at a given time of day is an example.

The curve representing the probabilities for values of a continuous random variable over a range is called a *probability density function* (PDF). The probability of a variable having a given value is the point on the PDF corresponding to the value. The probability of the variable assuming any of the values in a range from a to b, is the area under the PDF curve between a and b. This implies that the area under the PDF between a and b must be 1 because the variable always has to be one of the possible values in the range. If it's a sure thing, the probability is 1.

The equivalent of a PDF for discrete variables is called a *discrete probability function*. The probabilities for different values of a discrete variable are often indicated graphically by a set of points or vertical bars. As I said, the sum of the probabilities must add up to 1.

There are many different distributions that model how events occur or how measurements vary in the real world. These are mostly described by mathematical equations that are easiest to grasp when shown graphically. Examples of four distributions are shown in Figure 8-1.

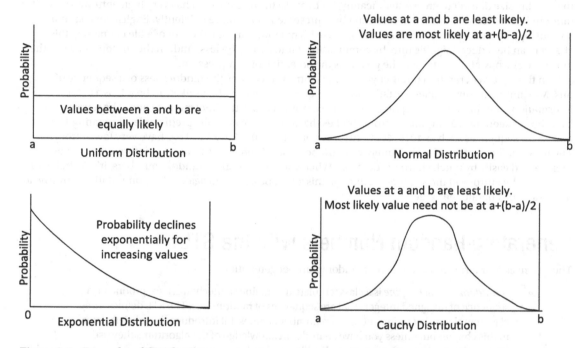

Figure 8-1. *Examples of distributions*

Each of the diagrams in Figure 8-1 shows the probability for a range of possible values occurring. The horizontal axis records the value of a variable; the vertical axis is the probability. Different kinds of variables in the real world can have vastly different distributions. With the *uniform distribution* shown in Figure 8-1, all possible values are equally likely; the results of throwing a die is represented by a uniform distribution. A *normal distribution* represents a value that varies either side of a mean value. The life of a light bulb is likely to be a normal distribution, because light bulbs will work for a time period that will typically vary either side of an average – typically 2000 hours for the old filament bulbs and supposedly more than 15,000 hours for the latest LED bulbs, although the latter is not always confirmed in practice. The *exponential distribution* typically relates to the way events occur over time: the time interval between particles being emitted by a radioactive material, for example. The fourth example in Figure 8-1 is the *Cauchy distribution*. In the illustration it looks vaguely similar to the normal distribution but it isn't the same – the shape of the curve can vary considerably. The Cauchy distribution turns up less frequently in real life than the others shown here; one context is energy distribution for an unstable state in quantum mechanics. Sometimes, a distribution is referred to by different names; the normal distribution is also called the *Gaussian distribution*, for example. There are even more distribution varieties supported by the STL, as you'll see.

What Is Entropy?

Entropy is a measure of disorder. The heat death of the universe will be when it reaches maximum entropy, which is inevitable according to the second law of thermodynamics. It won't be yet though – you still have time to finish this book. The meaning of *entropy* in the context of data was developed by an American mathematician named Claude Shannon. Entropy measures the efficiency with which information is represented; it's also a measure of the disorder in the data. Compressing a file using a lossless method, such as that used to generate a ZIP file, increases the entropy. If you compress a file into a ZIP archive and find that the file size doesn't decrease significantly, it's because the original data has very high entropy – it's quite random in other words – and therefore can't be represented much more efficiently. English text has quite low entropy because it's not very random. Because it's not random data, the size of a file containing this chapter can be reduced significantly by compressing it into a ZIP. The less random the contents of a file, the lower the entropy of the data, and the greater is the potential for compression.

In the context of random number generation, entropy measures the randomness of a sequence of bits. Maximum entropy implies a totally random sequence with each bit as likely to be a 1, as a 0; the information content of such a sequence is at a maximum because the information cannot be represented by a shorter sequence. Minimum entropy implies that a sequence is totally predictable; alternating 1's and 0's, or sequences such as 1010 1010 1010 ... or 1100 1101 1100 1101... have very low entropy. The information content of such sequences is low because it is predictable, and the information can be represented easily by much shorter sequences. When you are generating random numbers, it's desirable to maximize the entropy of the sequence, although this has to be balanced against the computational overhead necessary to generate the values.

Generating Random Numbers with the STL

The STL uses four terms in the context of random number generation:

- A *random number engine* is a class template that defines a mechanism for producing a sequence of unsigned integers that are sequences of random bits. The STL defines three class templates that represent random number engines. I'll introduce these briefly later in this chapter but unless you have an in-depth knowledge of the algorithms they use, you won't want to use them directly. You'll use a *random number generator*.

- A *random number generator* is a predefined instance of a random number engine class template. Each generator applies a specific set of template arguments to a random number engine class template – so it is a type alias. The STL provides several predefined random number generators that implement well-known algorithms for random number generation.

- A *random number engine adapter* is a class template for generating a sequence of random numbers by modifying a sequence generated by another random number engine.

- A *distribution* expresses the probability with which numbers in a random sequence occur across the range. The STL defines class templates that define function objects for a wide variety of different distributions, including those shown in Figure 8-1.

The reason for multiple distribution class templates for random number generation is because the sequences you will want to generate in a given context will depend on the nature of the data. The pattern of arrival of patients at a hospital is likely to be very different from the pattern of arrival of customers at a shop, so different distributions will apply. Further, the pattern for shop customers will vary depending on the kind of shop and its location among other things, so different distributions may be needed to model customer arrivals for different shops.

There are several random number engines and generators because there is no one algorithm for generating random numbers that suits all circumstances. Some algorithms can produce longer non-repeating sequences than others; some require less computational overhead than others. When you understand the characteristics of the data you want to model, you are in a position to decide which distribution and which random sequence generating capability to use.

Seeds in Random Number Generation

An algorithm for random number generation always starts with one or more *seeds*, which represent the initial input to the calculation that produces the random numbers. The seeds determine the *initial state* of a random number generator and determine the entire sequence. The *state* of a random number generator consists of all the data that is needed to compute the next value in a sequence. The algorithms are recursive, so the seed or seeds create the initial state that is used to produce the first value in the sequence; generating that value changes the state, which is then used to generate the next value, and so on. Thus a random number generator will always produce the same sequence for a given seed or seeds. This is obviously very helpful during testing of a program; determining whether or not a program is working correctly when the input data could change arbitrarily from one run to the next would not be easy to say the least. Of course, once a program is tested, you'll probably want a different sequence from a random number generator each time the program runs. Games programs that always do the same things will not be interesting. To produce difference sequences at different times, you must supply different seeds – ideally with random values. These are called *nondeterministic values* because they cannot be predicted.

All random number generation algorithms in the STL can be initiated with a single seed. If more seeds are required to define the initial state, they are created automatically. Clearly, the entropy of a random number sequence is going to depend on the seed. The number of bits in a seed is significant. With a 1-byte seed, you only have 255 possible values, so you can only produce a maximum of 255 different sequences. To maximize the entropy of a random sequence, you need two things: you need a seed value that is truly random – not pseudo-random, and you need the range of possible values for the seed to be large.

Obtaining Random Seeds

The random_device class defines function objects for generating random unsigned integer values that you can use as seeds. The class should use nondeterministic sources for the values, which are usually provided by the operating system. The C++ 14 standard does allow the possibility for a random number engine to be used when nondeterministic sources are not available, but in most implementations this won't be necessary. Nondeterministic sources can be such things as the times between successive keyboard keystrokes, or intervals between mouse clicks, or the current clock time, or by measuring some physical property.

You can create a random_device object like this:

```
std::random_device rd;              // Source of seeds!
```

The constructor has a parameter of type string& that has an implementation-defined default value. When you omit it, as here, you get the default random_device object for your environment. In theory the parameter allows you to supply a string that identifies a nondeterministic source to be used, but you need to check your documentation to discover whether this option is available with your C++ library. Here's how you can create a seed value from the random_device object:

```
auto my_1st_seed = rd();
```

This creates my_1st_seed with an initial value from the function object, rd. Here's a program that should succeed in generating a succession of seeds:

```
// Ex8_01.cpp
// Generating a succession of 8 seeds
#include <random>                              // For random_device class
#include <iostream>                            // For standard streams

int main()
{
  std::random_device rd;                       // A function object for generating seeds
  for(size_t n {}; n < 8; ++n)
    std::cout << rd() << " ";
    std::cout << std::endl;
}
```

This just calls the function that rd represents eight times and outputs the values it returns. I ran this twice and got the following two lines of output:

3638171046 3646201712 2185708196 587272045 1669986587 2512598564 1822700048 3845359386
360481879 3886461477 1775290740 2501731026 161066623 1931751494 751233357 3821236773

You'll notice that the values output from the two runs are completely different. Aside from operator()(), the random_device class only defines three other function members. The min() and max() members return the minimum and maximum possible values for the output respectively. The entropy() member returns an estimate for the entropy of the source as type double or 0 if the implementation is using a random number engine and not a nondeterministic source.

Seed Sequences

The seed_seq class is a helper for setting the initial state of a random number generator. As you'll see, you can create a random number generator and thus set its initial state by passing a single seed value to its constructor. The constructor argument can also be a seed_seq object that can generate several 32-bit unsigned values that provide the generator with more entropy than a single integer. You can also use the values generated by a seed_seq object to seed several random number generators.

The seed_seq class is not just a simple container for a set of values. A seed_seq object *generates* any number of unsigned integer values based on a set of integers you pass to the constructor. The generated values are produced by applying a predefined algorithm. You can specify one or more integers to the seed_seq constructor either as a range, or as an initializer list. The generated values will be distributed over the entire range of a 32-bit unsigned integer values, regardless of how your input values are distributed, or how many there are. For the same seed_seq constructor arguments, you always get the same sequence of generated values. Here are some statements that illustrate various ways for creating a seed_seq object:

```
std::seed_seq seeds1;                                  // Default object
std::seed_seq seeds2 {2, 3, 4, 5};                     // Create from simple integers

std::vector<unsigned int> data {25, 36, 47, 58};       // A vector of integers
std::seed_seq seeds3 {std::begin(data), std::end(data)}; // Create from a range of integers
```

Of course, you can also use values returned by a random_device object as arguments to the seed_seq constructor:

```
std::random_device rd {};
std::seed_seq seeds4 {rd(), rd()};                    // Create from non-deterministic integers
```

Each time this code executes, the seeds4 object will generate different values.

You can store a given number of values from a seed_seq object in a container by passing a range specified by two iterators to the generate() function member of the seed_seq object. For example:

```
std::vector<unsigned int> numbers (10);               // Stores 10 integers
seeds4.generate(std::begin(numbers), std::end(numbers));
```

Calling the generate() member of seeds4 stores the generated values in the numbers array. We can see the kind of values a seed_seq object generates under various conditions with a working example:

```
// Ex8_02
// Values generated by seed_seq objects
#include <random>                                      // For seed_seq, random_device
#include <iostream>                                    // For standard streams
#include <iterator>                                    // For iterators
#include <string>                                      // For string class
using std::string;

// Generates and list integers from a seed_seq object
void gen_and_list(const std::seed_seq& ss, const string title = "Values:", size_t count = 8)
{
  std::vector<unsigned int> values(count);
  ss.generate(std::begin(values), std::end(values));
  std::cout << title << std::endl;
  std::copy(std::begin(values), std::end(values),
                            std::ostream_iterator<unsigned int>{std::cout, " "});
  std::cout << std::endl;
}

int main()
{
  std::random_device rd {};                            // Non-deterministic source - we hope!
  std::seed_seq seeds1;                                // Default constructor
  std::seed_seq seeds2 {3, 4, 5};                      // From consecutive integers
  std::seed_seq seeds3 {rd(), rd()};

  std::vector<unsigned int> data {25, 36, 47, 58};
  std::seed_seq seeds4(std::begin(data), std::end(data));  // From a range
  gen_and_list(seeds1, "seeds1");
  gen_and_list(seeds1, "seeds1 again");
  gen_and_list(seeds1, "seeds1 again", 12);
  gen_and_list(seeds2, "seeds2");
  gen_and_list(seeds3, "seeds3");
  gen_and_list(seeds3, "seeds3 again");
  gen_and_list(seeds4, "seeds4");
```

```
  gen_and_list(seeds4, "seeds4 again");
  gen_and_list(seeds4, "seeds4 yet again", 12);
  gen_and_list(seeds4, "seeds4 for the last time", 6);
}
```

gen_and_list() is a helper function that generates a given number of values from a seed_seq object and outputs them following an identifying title. It's used in main() to show values generated from seed_seq objects that have been created in a variety of ways. I got the following output, but yours will certainly differ in at least some respects:

```
seeds1
3071959997 669715714 1197567577 671623915 1173633267 2920800313 1209690436 2235109613
seeds1 again
3071959997 669715714 1197567577 671623915 1173633267 2920800313 1209690436 2235109613
seeds1 again
3527767669 372316564 1386412362 441784 2145070594 2276674640 2205342996 1276311706
1119507491 75413245 2656280031 1908737279
seeds2
3388710944 2239790942 3836628790 2213304795 3411013659 2658117409 3275085354 3542843550
seeds3
3899021117 3310665364 4171568438 3922561248 250650243 1402466647 3483637440 3437969619
seeds3 again
3899021117 3310665364 4171568438 3922561248 250650243 1402466647 3483637440 3437969619
seeds4
2664408363 1749470183 3260020574 1632320446 534203587 2689329558 3154702548 1526239767
seeds4 again
2664408363 1749470183 3260020574 1632320446 534203587 2689329558 3154702548 1526239767
seeds4 yet again
2165145204 3274376652 3408995137 1909945219 3899048536 1143678586 807504975 3977354488
3428929103 552995692 24106733 509227013
seeds4 for the last time
1443036549 3195987434 1624705198 3337303804 479673966 3579734797
```

The output shows several things about the values that a seed_seq object generates:

- You get a wide range of 32-bit integers generated, regardless of how you create the seed_seq object. Even the object that the default constructor creates generates values across the range.

- The generate() member produces as many different values as are necessary to fill the range you specify.

- You can call generate() as many times as you like.

- The values in a sequence produced by the generate() member depends on the length of the sequence. Sequences of a given length will be the same. Sequences of different lengths will contain different values.

If you execute the program twice, you'll see that the values generated are the same for the same argument values to the seed_seq constructor. The sequences can only differ on different runs if different constructor arguments are supplied, as is the case with values returned by the rd function object.

There are two other function members of the seed_seq class. The size() member returns the number of seed values that were used to create the object. The param() member makes the original seed values available; it expects an output iterator that identifies the destination for the values as an argument and has no return value. The param() member stores the original seed values you supplied to the constructor in the range that begins with the iterator argument. Here's a code fragment that illustrates how these two function members work:

```
std::seed_seq seeds {3, 4, 5};
std::vector<unsigned int> data(seeds.size());        // Element for each seed value
seeds.param(std::begin(data));                        // Stores 3 4 5 in data
```

This creates a vector with the number of elements determined by the value returned by the size() member of the seeds object. The param() member of seeds then stores the three values passed to the constructor in data. You could also append the values to the container, like this:

```
seeds.param(std::back_inserter(data));                // Appends 3 4 5 to data
```

Of course, you don't need to store the values – you could pass an output stream iterator as the argument to param():

```
seeds.param(std::ostream_iterator<unsigned int>{std::cout, " "});  // 3 4 5 to cout
```

Distribution Classes

A *distribution* in the STL is a function object: an instance of a class that represents a particular distribution. To produce random numbers with a given distribution, you apply the distribution to the numbers produced by a random number generator. This is done by passing a random number generator object as the argument to the function object that is a distribution; the function object will return a random value that conforms to the distribution. It may seem odd that I'm introducing distributions before I have discussed the random number generators in detail. There's a couple of reasons for this:

- You should *always* use a distribution object to obtain random numbers. A distribution object limits and shapes the sequence that a random number generator produces into the form required by your application context. Choosing and using the appropriate distribution object guarantees that the random values will be within the distribution you want. Applying your own algorithm to values from a random number generator directly is unlikely to produce a distribution with the proper characteristics.

- To fully understand the differences between the random number generators, you require knowledge of the mathematics of the algorithms that they implement. Most programmers won't need or want to get into this. The STL provides a default random number generator that will suffice for many, if not most programmers, when combined with a suitable distribution object.

I'll introduce the default random number generator in this section so we can use it knowledgably with distribution objects and then discuss the distribution types that the STL provides. I'll explain the other random number generators after I have discussed the types of distributions the STL provides.

There are 21 class templates for distributions, many of which are quite specialized. I'll discuss in detail those that in my judgment are likely to be of most interest, and I'll show how you might use them. I'll just outline the rest and leave you to look into them in more depth if you need to. If you just want to generate random sequences without getting into all the possibilities, getting a grasp of this section in this chapter is maybe all you need. But first, to usefully work with a distribution, we need a random number generator, so that's the next topic.

The Default Random Number Generator

The default random number generator is a general-purpose source of random unsigned integers that is defined by the std::default_random_engine type alias. What this alias represents is implementation defined; you should look into the documentation for your library for the details of what it offers. It will typically be an instance of one of the three random number engine class templates that I'll introduce later in this chapter. The template-type arguments will have been chosen to provide satisfactory sequences for the occasional user. Here's the simplest way to create a generator of type default_random_engine:

```
std::default_random_engine rng1;          // Create random number generator with default seed
```

This calls the default constructor so the initial state will be set using a default seed value. The random number sequence will always be the same from the rng1 generator when it is executed on different occasions because the seed stays the same. You can supply your own seed of course:

```
std::default_random_engine rng2 {10};     // Create rng with 10 as seed
```

This creates rng2 with 10 as the seed, so the random sequence from this generator will be different from rng1 but still fixed. If you want to get a different sequence each time the code executes, you supply a nondeterministic seed:

```
std::random_device rd;                    // Non-determinstic seed source
std::default_random_engine rng3 {rd()};   // Create random number generator
```

The seed value is obtained using the function object, rd, which is of type random_device. Each rd() call will return a different value, and if your implementation of random_device is nondeterministic, the sequence produced by successive calls of rd() will be different for each execution of a program.

Another option is to supply a seed_seq object as the argument to the default_random_engine constructor:

```
std::seed_seq sd_seq {2, 4, 6, 8};
std::default_random_engine rng4 {sd_seq};  // Same random number sequence each time

std::random_device rd;                    // Non-determinstic seed source
std::default_random_engine rng5 {std::seed_seq{rd(), rd(), rd()}};
```

This first generates the rng4 generator using a seed_seq object created from fixed initial seeds; the sequence from rng4 will be the same on each execution of the code. rng5 is constructed from a seed_seq object that has values produced by a random_device function object so you'll never know what the sequence will be – a surprise every time. We are now in a position to look into creating and using distribution objects and start some serious random activities.

Creating Distribution Objects

As I said earlier, a distribution is represented by a function object that requires a random number generator object as the argument to produce values within the distribution. Each time you execute the distribution object, it returns a random number within the distribution it represents, which it generates from the values it obtains from the random number generator. Successive values after the first that a distribution returns depend on the preceding value. Creating a distribution object will require a set of parameter values that will depend on the type of distribution. For example, a uniform distribution requires upper and lower bounds for the values to be generated, whereas a normal distribution will require values for the mean and standard deviation. Although there are substantial differences between distributions of different type, they do have a lot in common. *All* distribution objects will have the following public members:

- result_type is a type alias defined within the class for the type of values generated.

- min() is a function member that returns the minimum value that a distribution object can generate.

- max() is a function member that returns the maximum value that a distribution object can generate.

- reset() is a function member that should reset a distribution object to its original state so the next value returned will not depend on the previous value. Whether or not this happens depends on your implementation. If the values returned by the distribution are independent, reset() does nothing.

- param_type is a type alias defined within the class for a struct. Different distributions will require different sets of parameter values, possibly of differing types, and these values are stored within a struct of type param_type that is specific to the distribution.

- param() is a function member that accepts an argument of type param_type to reset the parameters for the distribution object to new values.

- param() is an overload of the previous member that has no parameters and that returns the param_type object that the distribution object contains.

- A default constructor that has default values for the parameter(s) that define the distribution.

- A constructor that accepts an argument of type param_type to define the distribution.

I'll show how these members are used for some types of distribution. The stream insertion and extraction operators, << and >>, are overloaded for distribution types to transfer the internal state of a distribution object to a stream, or to read the state back from a stream. This offers the possibility of restoring the state for a distribution from a previous execution of a program.

Uniform Distributions

In a uniform distribution, all values in a range are equally likely. Uniform distributions can be discrete or continuous, as shown in Figure 8-2.

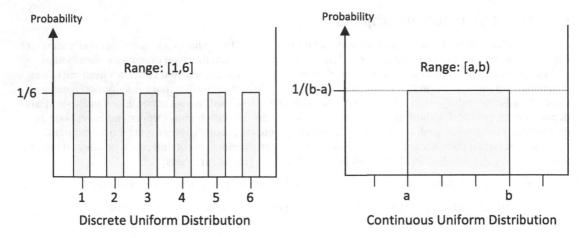

Figure 8-2. *Uniform distributions*

Note the specifications of the ranges in Figure 8-2. A discrete uniform distribution includes both the upper and lower bounds; a continuous uniform does not include the upper bound, so the variable can never be the value of the upper bound.

Discrete Uniform Distributions

The uniform_int_distribution class template defines distribution objects that will return random integers that are uniformly distributed over a closed range [a,b]. The template parameter is the type of integers to be generated and the default type is int: the type alias result_type that is defined within the class corresponds with the type of values generated by the distribution. Only integer types are acceptable as the template-type argument. One constructor has two parameters that identify the upper and lower limits for the range; the default value of the lower limit is 0, and the default for the upper limit is the maximum for the type of values generated. Here's an example:

```
std::uniform_int_distribution<> d;    // Distribution over 0 to  max for type int, inclusive
std::cout << "Range from 0 to "
         << std::numeric_limits<std::uniform_int_distribution<>::result_type>::max()
         << std::endl;                 // Range from 0 to 2147483647
```

The first statement calls the default constructor to create the distribution object, d. Everything is defaulted so the type of value generated will be int, and the range will be from 0 to the maximum for type int. The last comment shows the output that I get for the range limits; the upper limit is the maximum value of type int, which is produced by the numeric_limits() function template that is defined in the limits header. There's an easier way to get hold of the range limits. You can call the min() and max() members that all distribution objects have:

```
std::cout << "Range from " << d.min() << " to " << d.max() << std::endl;
```

There's another possibility in this case. The uniform_int_distribution class template also defines function members a() and b() that return the lower and upper limits of the range respectively so you could write the previous statement as:

```
std::cout << "Range from "<< d.a() << " to " << d.b() << std::endl;
```

The names of the a() and b() members indicate a little better than min() and max() how the values they return relate to a uniform distribution.

If you just want a distribution for a range of integers greater than or equal to a given value, you just supply the first constructor argument:

```
std::uniform_int_distribution<> d {500};
  std::cout << "Range from "<< d.a() << " to " << d.b()
          << std::endl;                          // Range from 500 to 2147483647
```

Of course, the constructor argument could be negative. Typically you will want to specify both range limits, so here's a more realistic example that does this:

```
std::uniform_int_distribution<long> dist {-5L, 5L};
std::random_device rd;                           // Non-deterministic seed source
std::default_random_engine rng {rd()};           // Create random number generator
for(size_t i {}; i < 8; ++i)
  std::cout << std::setw(2) << dist(rng) << " ";   // -3  0  5  1 -2 -4  0  4
```

The first statement defines a distribution object for random integers of type long. The range is from -5 to +5 inclusive, so there are 11 possible values that the distribution object can return. Consequently, the probability of each of the possible values occurring is 1/11. In general, for a uniform distribution of integers over the range [a,b], the probability of any particular value being returned is 1/(1+b-a). On my system, I got the output shown in the comment appended to the last statement from executing this code, but it's definitely going to be different on your system.

You can call the param() member of a uniform distribution to change the range of values it produces. The object that you pass to the param() member here Uniform distribution:uniform_int_distribution class specifies new range limits – and its type is specified by the param_type alias that is defined by the distribution class. You can also call param() without an argument to obtain an object encapsulating the current parameter set for the distribution. The following code illustrates both possibilities:

```
std::uniform_int_distribution<> dist {0, 6};
std::random_device rd;                           // Non-determinstic seed source
std::default_random_engine rng {rd()};           // Create random number generator
for(size_t i {}; i < 8; ++i)
  std::cout << std::setw(3) << dist(rng) << " ";   // first output line
std::cout << std::endl;

// Save old range and set new range
auto old_range = dist.param();                   // Get current params
dist.param(std::uniform_int_distribution<>::param_type {-10,20});
for(size_t i {}; i < 8; ++i)
  std::cout << std::setw(3) << dist(rng) << " ";   // Second output line
std::cout << std::endl;

// Restore old range...
dist.param(old_range);
for(size_t i {}; i < 8; ++i)
  std::cout << std::setw(3) << dist(rng) << " ";   // Third output line
std::cout << std::endl;
```

This code produces the following output on my system:

```
 6   1   5   6   1   3   6   2
19  16  15   5   0   7   6  -8
 0   0   0   3   2   6   6   5
```

You could simplify the type of the argument to param() by defining an alias:

```
using Range = std::uniform_int_distribution<>::param_type;
```

Now you can write the param() call to set a new range as:

```
dist.param(Range {-10,20});
```

There are various ways you can use the ability to change the range limits. One obvious application is when you need several uniform distributions of values of a given type in a program, each with a different set of parameters. You can use just one distribution object, and set the parameters as necessary anywhere in a program. Let's put together an example that does exactly that.

Applying Uniform Integer Distributions

This example, Ex8_03.cpp, will use a uniform_int_distribution object to deal cards. It's quite a lot of code, so I'll introduce it piecemeal. To allow a single distribution object to be used in various places in the code, we can define it as a static object in a function, like this:

```
std::uniform_int_distribution<size_t>& dist()
{
  static std::uniform_int_distribution<size_t> d;
  return d;
}
```

The distribution will return values of type size_t, which will be unsigned integers. The default limits apply initially, but we can set limits by calling param() for the object. To use the distribution object, you just call the dist() function to obtain a reference to it. We can package a single random number generator in the same way:

```
std::default_random_engine& rng()
{
  static std::default_random_engine engine {std::random_device()()};
  return engine;
}
```

The static engine object is initialized with the value returned by a random_device object so it will produce a different sequence each time it is created. The expression dist(rng()) will return a random number within the distribution.

I'll represent a card by a pair object that encapsulates the suit and the face value. I'll define the possible suit and face values by enum types:

```
enum class Suit : size_t { Clubs, Diamonds, Hearts, Spades };
enum class Face : size_t { Two, Three, Four, Five, Six, Seven,
                           Eight, Nine, Ten, Jack, Queen, King, Ace };
```

The default values for the enumerators start at 0, which is important because we will use the enumerator values to index a container to obtain a string that represents a name for the Suit or Face instance.

We can define aliases for the type of a card, a hand of cards, a deck of cards, and a collection of hands:

```
using Card = std::pair<Suit,Face>;                    // The type of a card
using Hand = std::list<Card>;                         // Type for a hand of cards
using Deck = std::list<Card>;                         // Type for a deck of cards
using Hands = std::vector<Hand>;                      // Type for a container of hands
using Range = std::uniform_int_distribution<size_t>::param_type;
```

Defining a deck and a hand as list containers will allow rapid removal of a random card. You could use a different sequence container such as a vector.

We will want to output Card objects so it will be useful to implement operator<<() to write Card objects to a stream. Here's the definition of the function to overload << for Card objects:

```
std::ostream& operator<<(std::ostream& out, const Card& card)
{
  static std::array<string, 4> suits {"C", "D", "H", "S"};           // Suit names
  static std::array<string, 13> values {"2", "3", "4", "5", "6", "7",  // Face value names
                                "8", "9", "10", "J", "Q", "K", "A"};
  string suit {suits[static_cast<size_t>(card.first)]};
  string value {values[static_cast<size_t>(card.second)]};
  return out << std::setw(2) << value << suit;
}
```

Here's the definition of a function to initialize a Deck container to the standard set of 52 cards:

```
Deck& init_deck(Deck& deck)
{
  static std::array<Suit,4> suits{Suit::Clubs, Suit::Diamonds, Suit::Hearts, Suit::Spades};
  static std::array<Face, 13> values {Face::Two, Face::Three, Face::Four, Face::Five, Face::Six,
                             Face::Seven, Face::Eight, Face::Nine, Face::Ten,
                             Face::Jack,  Face::Queen, Face::King, Face::Ace};
  deck.clear();
  for(const auto& suit : suits)
    for(const auto& value : values)
    deck.emplace_back(Card {suit, value});
  return deck;
}
```

All the objects that represent different suits are stored in the suits container. The objects that represent possible card face values are elements in the values container. Both containers are array types, which are almost as efficient as using a standard C++ array. The major advantage is that an array container always knows its size; it also provides checking for out of range index values when you use the at() member. The nested loops emplace elements in deck that are Card objects representing all values of each suit.

The cards are in sequence in an initialized Deck object. We need to deal cards to hands, but we want the hands to receive random cards. We could shuffle the cards in the deck before the deal, but in the interests of exercising a distribution with different limits, we will deal the cards by selecting at random from the deck. Here's a function that does that:

```
void deal(Hands& hands, Deck& deck)
{
  auto d = dist();
  while(!deck.empty())
  {
    for(auto&& hand : hands)
    {
      size_t max_index = deck.size() - 1;
      d.param(Range{0, max_index});
      auto iter = std::begin(deck);
      std::advance(iter, d(rng()));
      hand.push_back(*iter);
      deck.erase(iter);
    }
  }
}
```

This deals all the cards from the Deck object that is passed as the second argument. The cards are distributed between however many Hand objects there are in the Hands container that is the first argument. The outer loop continues until the deck is exhausted, which is indicated when its empty() member returns true. The inner loop deals one card to each hand in hands, so eventually, all the Card objects in deck will be distributed between the Hand objects in hands.

In the loop, max_index is initialized to the maximum legal index value for the elements in deck. The limits for values produced by the distribution object that dist() returns are set to 0 and max_index, which will cause the distribution object to generate values from a different range on each loop iteration. iter is initialized to the begin iterator for the range of elements in deck, and then advanced by the value of the expression d(rng()), which will be a random increment from 0 to max_index. After adding the element specified by *iter to the current hand, the element is erased from the deck container.

The cards in a hand will be in random order because they were chosen at random, but once it has been dealt, a hand is easier to assess if the cards are in ascending sequence. This function will sort each hand in a Hands container:

```
void sort_hands(Hands& hands)
{
  for(auto&& hand : hands)
    hand.sort([](const auto& crd1, const auto& crd2) { return crd1.first < crd2.first ||
                              (crd1.first == crd2.first && crd1.second < crd2.second); });
}
```

The loop iterates over the Hand objects in hands. The elements in each Hand container are sorted by calling the sort() member for the container object. The argument is a comparison function defined by a generic lambda expression that orders Card objects by face value within suit.

We will definitely want to output the hands when they have been dealt. The following function will take care of this:

```
void show_hands(const Hands& hands)
{
  for(auto&& hand : hands)
  {
    std::copy(std::begin(hand), std::end(hand), std::ostream_iterator<Card> {std::cout, " "});
    std::cout << std::endl;
  }
}
```

This uses the copy() algorithm to copy the hands from the hands container to an output stream iterator that writes to cout. The stream iterator will write each Card object in a hand to the output stream using the operator<<() function we defined earlier. Whenever we want a show of hands, we can just call show_hands().

We can now put these functions together in a complete example that will create a standard deck of cards, deal four hands, then output the hands that were dealt:

```
// Ex8_03.cpp
// Dealing cards at random with a distribution
#include <iostream>             // For standard streams
#include <ostream>             // For ostream stream
#include <iomanip>             // For stream manipulators
#include <iterator>           // For iterators and begin() and end()
#include <random>             // For random number generators & distributions
#include <utility>           // For pair<T1,T2> template
#include <vector>           // For vector<T> container
#include <list>             // For list<T> container
#include <array>           // For array<T,N> container
#include <string>         // For string class
#include <type_traits>   // For is_same predicate

using std::string;
enum class Suit : size_t {Clubs, Diamonds, Hearts, Spades};
enum class Face : size_t {Two, Three, Four, Five, Six, Seven,
                          Eight, Nine, Ten, Jack, Queen, King, Ace};
using Card = std::pair<Suit,Face>;         // The type of a card
using Hand = std::list<Card>;             // Type for a hand of cards
using Deck = std::list<Card>;             // Type for a deck of cards
using Hands = std::vector<Hand>;         // Type for a container of hands
using Range = std::uniform_int_distribution<size_t>::param_type;

// Definition of operator<<() for a Card object goes here...

// Definition of rng() to return a reference to a static default_random_engine object goes here...

// Definition of dist() for a reference to a static uniform_int_distribution<size_t> object here...
```

```
// Definition of init_deck() to initialize a deck to a full set of 52 cards here...

// Definition of deal() that deals a complete deck here...

// Definition of sort_hands() to sort cards in hands here...

// Definition of show_hands to output all hands here...

int main()
{
  // Create the deck
  Deck deck;
  init_deck(deck);

  // Create and deal the hands
  Hands hands(4);
  deal(hands, deck);

  // Sort and show the hands
  sort_hands(hands);
  show_hands(hands);
}
```

I got the following show of hands:

3C	9C	10C	QC	AC	2D	3D	9D	QD	2H	6H	JS	QS
2C	4C	6D	8D	JD	KD	3H	8H	9H	KH	9S	10S	KS
5C	6C	8C	5D	AD	5H	10H	JH	QH	3S	4S	7S	AS
7C	JC	KC	4D	7D	10D	4H	7H	AH	2S	5S	6S	8S

Of course, a further possibility for exercising a distribution with this example is for the players to now play, each playing one random card from their hand in a round. I'm not going to tell you how. It's Exercise 2 at the end of this chapter for you to implement!

Continuous Uniform Distributions

The uniform_real_distribution class template defines a continuous distribution that returns floating-point values that are type double by default. You can create a distribution object that will return values in the range [0, 10) like this:

```
std::uniform_real_distribution<> values {0.0, 10.0};
std::random_device rd;                          // Non-determinstic seed source
std::default_random_engine rng {rd()};          // Create random number generator
for(size_t i {}; i < 8; ++i)
  std::cout << std::fixed << std::setprecision(2)
            << values(rng) << " ";              // 8.37 6.72 6.41 6.08 6.89 6.10 9.75 4.07
```

The way in which you create and use `uniform_real_distribution` function objects closely parallels what you saw with `uniform_int_distribution` objects. You pass a random number generator object as the argument to the distribution function object to obtain a random value. You can get and set the range limits by calling the `param()` member of an object. A `uniform_real_distribution` object also has `a()` and `b()` members in addition to the `min()` and `max()` members that return the range limits for the distribution. Note that the range for a continuous distribution is semi-open with the upper limit excluded from the range of possible values that the distribution object can return.

Real-world situations where a uniform continuous distribution applies to a variable are rare. Measurements of parameters relating to the weather do not have equally likely values over a range for example. A possible real example is that the angular position of the second hand on your watch when you look at it is likely to be uniformly distributed - but it's not particularly useful. Uniform continuous distributions are used in Monte Carlo methods that have applications in the finance industry, as well as engineering and science. I'll put together a working example in another context - a program using a continuous uniform distribution to get a value for π.

Using a Continuous Uniform Distribution

Did you know that you can determine the value of π with a stick? This doesn't involve threatening a mathematician with the stick to persuade them to tell you the value. It just involves throwing the stick onto the floor. It doesn't even have to be a stick - you can throw any straight object - a pencil or even a frankfurter would do. It must be a bare floor though - with floorboards, and the object you throw, as well as being straight, must have a length that is less than the width of a floorboard. The process is simple - you just count how many times you throw the stick, and how many times the stick crosses the edge of a board when it lands.

You need to throw the stick a significant number of times to get a decent result. Of course, this could take some time and would be somewhat tedious, not to say tiring. With the help of a couple of uniform real distributions though, we can get a computer to do the throwing - and the counting. Figure 8-3 shows a stick on a floor in a random position and its relationship to the floorboards. To explain what happens requires a little math, but it's not difficult.

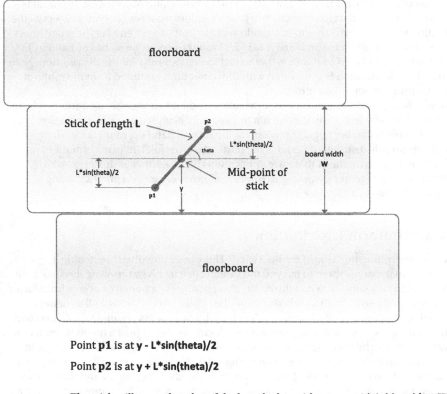

Point **p1** is at **y - L*sin(theta)/2**

Point **p2** is at **y + L*sin(theta)/2**

The stick will cross the edge of the board when either: **y + L*sin(theta)/2 ≥ W**

or: **y - L*sin(theta)/2 ≤ 0**

Figure 8-3. *A stick lying on the floor*

Figure 8-3 shows the stick in an arbitrary position that is at distance y from the bottom edge of a board and at an angle theta to the board. The stick will always land on one board or another, so we only need to consider one board. Figure 8-3 shows the conditions for the stick to intersect the edge of a board. This will be the case when either end of the stick, denoted by p1 and p2, is on or over the edge of the board. For the stick to cross a board edge, the distance from the center of the stick to the closest edge must be less than L*sin(theta)/2.

We throw the stick many, many, times, then count the total number of throws as throws, and the number of times the stick overlapped an edge of a board as, hits. So now we have these two counts, how can we get the value of π from them? Figure 8-4 should help.

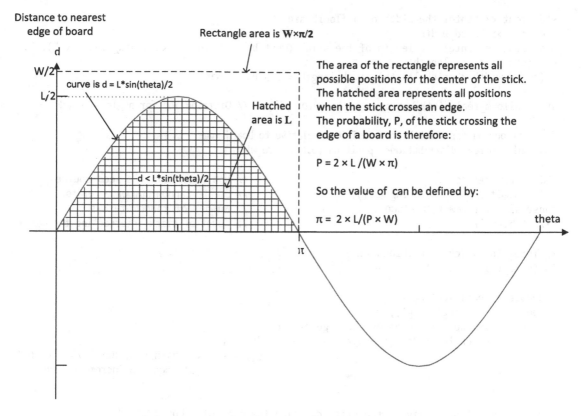

Figure 8-4. *Determining π from the probability of the stick crossing an edge of a floorboard*

The probability, P, of the stick crossing the edge of a floorboard will be the ratio of hits to throws. We can therefore get the value of π using P and the last equation in Figure 8-4. π is the result of the expression:

```
2*stick_length*throws/(board_width*hits)
```

Now we know how it all works, here's the code to implement it:

```cpp
// Ex8_04.cpp
// Finding pi by throwing a stick
#include <iostream>                      // For standard streams
#include <random>                        // For distributions, random number gen
#include <cmath>                         // For sin() function

int main()
{
  const double pi = 3.1415962;
  double stick_length{};                 // Stick length
  double board_width {};                  // Board width
```

```
  std::cout << "Enter the width of a floorboard: ";
  std::cin >> board_width;
  std::cout << "Enter the length of the stick (must be less than " << board_width << "): ";
  std::cin >> stick_length;
  if(board_width < stick_length) stick_length = 0.9*board_width;

  std::uniform_real_distribution<> angle {0.0, pi};    // Distribution for angle of stick

  // Distribution for stick center position, relative to board edge
  std::uniform_real_distribution<> position {0.0, board_width};

  std::random_device rd;                               // Non-deterministic seed source
  std::default_random_engine rng {rd()};               // Create random number generator
  const size_t throws{5'000'000};                      // Number of random throws
  size_t hits {};                                      // Count of stick intersecting the board

  // Throw the stick down throws times
  for(size_t i {}; i < throws; ++i)
  {
    double y {position(rng)};
    double theta {angle(rng)};
    // Check if the stick crosses the edge of a board
    if(((y + stick_length*sin(theta)/2) >= board_width) ||
                          ((y - stick_length*sin(theta) / 2) <= 0))
      ++hits;                                           // It does, so increment count
  }

  std::cout << "Probability of the stick crossing the edge of a board is: "
            << (static_cast<double>(hits)/ throws) << std::endl;
  std::cout << "Pi is: " << (2* stick_length*throws)/(board_width*hits) << std::endl;
}
```

You may have spotted a tiny weakness in this program - to determine a value for π, you need to know the value of π before you start. However, it's just a simulation - and an excuse to use uniform real distributions. The only alternative is to *really* throw a stick 5,000,000 times, which might be an option if you are very fit and have a very durable stick. If you can manage one throw every 3 seconds, you should be done in about 8 months - as long as you don't need to eat or sleep...

Random positions of the center of the stick relative to the edge of a floorboard are generated by the position distribution object and the angle of the stick for each position is produced by the angle distribution. The loop body implements the calculations in Figure 8-3, and the code after the loop just uses the equations from Figure 8-4. You can change the number of throws to whatever is reasonable on your system. I got the following output:

```
Enter the width of a floorboard: 12
Enter the length of the stick (must be less than 12): 5
Probability of the stick crossing the edge of a board is: 0.265281
Pi is: 3.14132
```

Of course, the output can vary between runs because the random sequences will be different each time the program executes. The length of the stick relative to the floorboard width also has an effect, as does the number of throws.

■ **Note**   For those who need to know, showing that the hatched area under the curve in Figure 8-4 is just the length of the stick requires a bit of calculus - the area will be:

$$area = \frac{L}{2}\int_0^\pi \sin\theta$$

The integral of $\sin\theta$ is $(-\cos\theta)$ so the area is $\frac{L}{2}((-\cos\pi)-(-\cos 0))$, which evaluate to $\frac{L}{2}(1+1)$, which is simply L!

Creating a Standard Uniform Distribution

A *standard uniform distribution* is a continuous distribution over the range [0,1). The generate_canonical() function template provides a standard uniform distribution of floating-point values over the range [0,1) with a given number of random bits. There are three template parameters: the floating-point type, the number of random bits in the mantissa, and the type of the random number generator used. The argument to the function is the random number generator so the last template argument is deduced. Here's how it might be used:

```
std::vector<double> data(8);                       // Container with 8 elements
std::random_device rd;                             // Non-determinstic seed source
std::default_random_engine rng {rd()};             // Create random number generator

std::generate(std::begin(data), std::end(data),
          [&rng] { return std::generate_canonical<double, 12>(rng); });

std::copy(std::begin(data), std::end(data), std::ostream_iterator<double>{std::cout, " "});
```

The generate_canonical() function is called in the lambda expression that is the third argument to the generate() algorithm. The lambda will return random values of type double with 12 random bits so generate() will populate the elements in data with such values.. Executing these statements on my system produce the following output:

0.766197 0.298056 0.409951 0.955263 0.419199 0.737496 0.547764 0.91622

The output above is showing perhaps more digits than we want, bearing in mind only 12 random bits are specified. You could limit the output like this:

```
std::copy(std::begin(data), std::end(data),
    std::ostream_iterator<double>{std::cout << std::fixed << std::setprecision(4) , " "});
```

The stream manipulators are applied to each output value so now the output is something like:

0.8514 0.5707 0.8322 0.6626 0.7026 0.8854 0.5427 0.8886

If you really want to get at the bits, you could use the hexfloat manipulator to output the values in hexadecimal format.

Obviously the fewer random bits, the more limited the range of possible random values. You can maximize the range by specifying the number of bits as the maximum for the type. Here's some code that shows how:

```
std::vector<long double> data;                      // Empty container
std::random_device rd;                              // Non-determinstic seed source
std::default_random_engine rng {rd()};              // Create random number generator

std::generate_n(std::back_inserter(data), 10, [&rng]
{ return std::generate_canonical<long double, std::numeric_limits<long double>::digits>(rng); });

std::copy(std::begin(data), std::end(data), std::ostream_iterator<long double>{std::cout, " "});
std::cout << std::endl;
```

Note the differences from the previous code. This time generate_n() is used with the first argument as a back_insert_iterator for the data container so the elements are added to data by calling its push_back() member. The second template argument for generate_canonical() is the value of the digits member of the numeric_limits object for the long double type. This is the number of bits in the mantissa for the type so we specify the maximum number of random bits that are possible with the type (only 53 on my system). I got this output, but yours will be different:

```
0.426365 0.0635646 0.208444 0.198286 0.338378 0.490884 0.841733 0.975676 0.193322 0.346017
```

Normal Distributions

A normal (or Gaussian) distribution is shown in Figure 8-5. It is a continuous bell-shaped curve with values equally divided either side of a *mean* - the mean being just the average value. It's a probability distribution so the area under the curve is 1. A normal distribution is completely defined by two parameters, the *mean*, and the *standard deviation* - which is a measure of how spread out the values are either side of the mean.

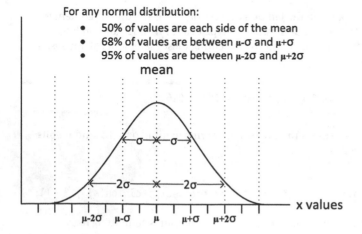

Figure 8-5. *The normal distribution*

The mean and standard deviation are represented by the Greek characters μ - mu, and σ - sigma, respectively, and for n samples of a variable x, these are defined by the following equations:

$$\mu = \frac{\sum\limits_{0}^{n} x_i}{n} \qquad \sigma = \sqrt{\frac{\sum\limits_{0}^{n}(x_i - \mu)^2}{n-1}}$$

Thus the mean is just the sum of the values divided by however many there are - the average value in other words. You obtain the standard deviation by summing the squares of the differences between each value and the mean, dividing that by n-1, then taking the square root of the result. The relative width and height of the normal distribution curve can vary considerable with different values for the mean and standard deviation. However, the distribution of values is always as indicated in Figure 8-5. This implies that if you know the mean and standard deviation for a variable that conforms to a normal distribution, such as the height of individuals in a large population for example, then you know that 95% of the people will have a height no more than 2σ different from the mean. A *standard normal distribution* has a mean of 0 and a standard deviation of 1.

The uniform_distribution template defines distribution object types that produce random floating-point values; by default these are type double. The default constructor creates a standard normal distribution - so the mean is 0 and the standard deviation is 1.0:

```
std::normal_distribution<> dist;                          // mu: 0 sigma: 1
```

Here's how you can create a normal distribution with a specific mean and standard deviation:

```
double mu {50.0}, sigma {10.0};
std::normal_distribution<> norm {mu, sigma};
```

This defines a distribution object to produce double values with a mean of 50.0 and a standard deviation of 10.0. To generate values, you pass a random number generator to the norm function object. For example:

```
std::random_device rd;
std::default_random_engine rng {rd()};
std::cout << "Normally distributed values: "
          << norm(rng) << " " << norm(rng) << std::endl;   // 39.6153 45.5608
```

You can obtain the values for the mean and standard deviation by calling the mean() and stddev() members of the object:

```
std::cout << "mu: " << norm.mean() << " sigma: " << norm.stddev()
          << std::endl;                                    // mu: 50 sigma: 10
```

You can get both values encapsulated in a param_type object by calling the param() member without an argument. To set the mean and or standard deviation, you pass a param_type object to the param() member. The param_type object will have function members with the same names as members of the distribution class to which it relates that make the mean and standard deviation available. Here's an example of using these:

```
using Params = std::normal_distribution<>::param_type;    // Type alias for readability
double mu {50.0}, sigma {10.0};
std::normal_distribution<> norm {mu, sigma};               // Create distribution
auto params = norm.param();                                // Get mean and standard deviation
norm.param(Params {params.mean(), params.stddev() + 5.0}); // Modify params
```

```
std::cout << "mu: " << norm.mean() << " sigma: " << norm.stddev()
          << std::endl;                            // mu: 50 sigma: 15
```

This calls param() without an argument to obtain the param_type object that contains the mean and standard deviation. A Params object is passed to a second call of param() to increase the standard deviation by 5.0.

You can set the mean and standard deviation temporarily by passing a param_type object as a second argument in a distribution object call:

```
using Params = std::normal_distribution<>::param_type; // Type alias for readability
std::random_device rd;
std::default_random_engine rng {rd()};
std::normal_distribution<> norm {50.0, 10.0};          // Create distribution
Params new_p {100.0, 30.0};                            // mu=100 sigma=30
std::cout << norm(rng, new_p) << std::endl;            // Generate value with new_p: 100.925
std::cout << norm.mean() << " " << norm.stddev()
          << std::endl;                                // 50 10
```

The mean and standard deviation defined by new_p only apply for the execution of norm where it is passed as the second argument. The original mean and standard deviation will apply to subsequent norm calls without a second argument.

The min() and max() members return the minimum and maximum values the distribution can produce. This is not particularly useful with a normal distribution because the values will be the smallest and largest values that can be represented by the type of the value that is returned:

```
std::cout << "min: " << norm.min() << " max: " << norm.max()
          << std::endl;                      // min: 4.94066e-324 max: 1.79769e+308
```

Using a Normal Distribution

This working example will allow normal distribution objects to be created with mean and standard deviation values entered from the keyboard. The program will generate a large number of random values using the distribution object then plot these as a histogram to show the shape of the curve. The probability will be across the page and the sample values down the page. Here's the code for a function template to plot a range of values:

```
template<typename Iter>
void dist_plot(Iter& beg_iter, Iter& end_iter, size_t width=90)
{
  // Create data for distribution plot
  std::map<int, size_t> plot_data;                     // Elements are pair<value, frequency>

  // Make sure all values are present in the plot
  auto pr = std::minmax_element(beg_iter, end_iter, [](const double v1, const double v2)
                                                    {return v1 < v2; });
  for(int n {static_cast<int>(*pr.first)}; n < static_cast<int>(*pr.second); ++n)
    plot_data.emplace(n,0);
```

```
  // Create the plot data
  std::for_each(beg_iter, end_iter,
    [&plot_data](double value) { ++plot_data[static_cast<int>(std::round(value))]; });

  // Find maximum frequency to be plotted - must fit within page width
  size_t max_f {std::max_element(std::begin(plot_data), std::end(plot_data),
    [](const std::pair<int,int>& v1, const std::pair<int,int>& v2)
                          { return v1.second < v2.second; })->second};

  // Draw distribution as histogram
  std::for_each(std::begin(plot_data), std::end(plot_data),
    [max_f, width](const std::pair<int, int>& v)
  {std::cout << std::setw(3) << v.first << " -| "
                          << string((width*v.second) / max_f, '*') << std::endl; });
}
```

The plot is created by first creating a map container that contains pair elements that each store an integer value and the frequency of its occurrence. With low numbers of values to be plotted, it is possible that values within a range may not be generated. These still should be present in the histogram though. To make sure all values within the range to be plotted are present, we find the minimum and maximum values using the minmax_element() algorithm, then create all elements within this range in the map with zero counts. The minmax_element() algorithm returns iterators that point to the minimum and maximum elements so these must be dereference to obtain the values. Because the values in the input range can be floating-point, they are converted to an integer before they are stored in the map. The lambda expression that is applied to each element by the for_each() algorithm rounds each value to the nearest integer using the round() function that is defined in the cmath header, before converting the value to type size_t. The result is then stored in the map. In the unlikely event that the integral value is not already in the map, it will be added as a new element with the second member - its frequency - incremented to 1; if it's already in the map, which will usually be the case, the second member of the pair will be incremented. The round() function rounds values that are midway between integers away from zero, thus avoiding a bias towards zero.

The maximum frequency value is obtained using the max_element() algorithm. In this case elements are compared by a lambda expression that just compares the second members of the elements. The max_f variable is initialized with the second member of the pair to which the iterator returned by max_element() points. The histogram is drawn as a series of string objects by the for_each() algorithm. Each string contains the number of asterisks that corresponds to the frequency count after scaling so that the maximum fits within width characters on a line.

Here's the program that makes use of dist_plot():

```
// Ex8_05.cpp
// Checking out normal distributions
#include <random>                    // For distributions and random
number generators
#include <algorithm>                 // For generate(), for_each(),
                                     //     max_element(), transform()
#include <numeric>                   // For accumulate()
#include <vector>                    // For vector container
#include <map>                       // For map container
#include <cmath>                     // For pow(), round() functions
#include <iostream>                  // For standard streams
#include <iomanip>                   // For stream manipulators
#include <string>                    // For string class
```

```
using std::string;
using Params = std::normal_distribution<>::param_type;

// Template for dist_plot() function goes here...

int main()
{
  std::random_device rd;
  std::default_random_engine rng {rd()};
  std::normal_distribution<> norm;
  double mu {}, sigma {};
  const size_t sample_count {20000};
  std::vector<double> values(sample_count);
  while(true)
  {
    std::cout << "\nEnter values for the mean and standard deviation, or Ctrl+Z to end: ";
    if((std::cin >> mu).eof()) break;
    std::cin >> sigma;
    norm.param(Params{mu, sigma});
    std::generate(std::begin(values), std::end(values), [&norm, &rng]{ return norm(rng); });

    // Create data to plot histogram and plot it
    dist_plot(std::begin(values), std::end(values));

    // Get the mean and standard deviation for the generated random values
    double mean {std::accumulate(std::begin(values), std::end(values), 0.0)/ values.size()};

    std::transform(std::begin(values), std::end(values), std::begin(values),
                   [&mean](double value) { return std::pow(value-mean,2); });
    double s_dev
    {std::sqrt(std::accumulate(std::begin(values), std::end(values), 0.0)/(values.size() - 1))};
    std::cout << "For generated values, mean = " << mean
              << " standard deviation = " << s_dev << std::endl;
  }
}
```

On each while loop iteration, you are prompted to enter the mean and standard deviation for a normal distribution. The loop continues until you enter Ctrl+Z instead of a value for the mean. The values you enter are used to create a param_type object that is passed to the param() member of the distribution object, norm, which sets the mean and standard deviation for the distribution. A vector containing sample_count elements of type double is created, and each element is set to a random value returned by the distribution object, norm, by the generate() algorithm. The distribution corresponding to these values is then produced by calling dist_plot(). To see how close the mean and standard deviation for the generated values are to the original specification, these are calculated using the accumulate() and transform() algorithms respectively.

I got this output for the input shown:

```
Enter values for the mean and standard deviation, or Ctrl+Z to end: 8 3
 -3 -|
 -2 -|
 -1 -| *
  0 -| **
  1 -| ******
  2 -| ***********
  3 -| *********************
  4 -| *******************************
  5 -| **************************************************
  6 -| *****************************************************************
  7 -| ****************************************************************************
  8 -| ********************************************************************************
  9 -| ******************************************************************************
 10 -| ***********************************************************************
 11 -| ****************************************************
 12 -| ******************************
 13 -| *********************
 14 -| ***********
 15 -| *****
 16 -| **
 17 -| *
 18 -|
 19 -|
 20 -|
 21 -|
For generated values, mean = 8.02975 standard deviation = 2.99916

Enter values for the mean and standard deviation, or Ctrl+Z to end: ^Z
```

The output shows that the distribution of the generated values has the right shape, and the mean and standard deviation computed from the random values correspond very closely with those specified for the distribution object. You can try different means and standard deviations to get an idea of how the shape changes.

Lognormal Distributions

A *lognormal distribution* is related to a normal distribution in that it represents the distribution for a random variable where the distribution for the *logarithm* of the value is a normal distribution. A lognormal distribution is defined by a mean and a standard deviation, but these parameters don't relate to the variable, they relate to the *logarithm* of the variable. To be specific, a lognormal distribution of a random variable x with a mean, μ, and a standard deviation, σ, implies that $\log x$ is a normal distribution with a mean of μ and a standard deviation of σ. Figure 8-6 illustrates a lognormal distribution curve, and the effect of varying the mean and standard deviation.

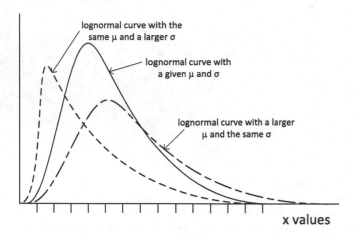

Figure 8-6. *Lognormal distributions*

For many random variables in nature, a lognormal distribution is a closer representation of the probabilities than a normal distribution. The infection rates for many illnesses follow a lognormal pattern.

An instance of the `lognormal_distribution` template defines a lognormal distribution object that returns floating-point values of type `double` by default. Here's a definition of a lognormal distribution object with a mean of `5.0` and a standard deviation of `0.5`:

```
double mu {5.0}, sigma {0.5};
std::lognormal_distribution<> norm {mu, sigma};
```

The constructor arguments have default values of 0 and 1 so omitting the arguments defines a *standard lognormal distribution*. There's another constructor that accepts a `param_type` object that encapsulates the mean and standard deviation as the argument.

As well as the function members that all distribution types have, a `lognormal_distribution` object has function members `m()` and `s()` that return the mean and standard deviation respectively. You use an object in the same way as you have seen with other distributions, so let's try it out in an example.

Using a Lognormal Distribution

This example will use the dist_plot() function template from Ex8_05 with a small change to suppress output lines in a plot that contain zero asterisks. This is because a lognormal curve can have a very long tail, which you don't need to see to appreciate the shape of the distribution. The last statement in plot_data() will be:

```
std::for_each(std::begin(plot_data), std::end(plot_data),
    [max_f, width](const std::pair<int, int>& v)
    { if((width*v.second)/max_f > 0)
      std::cout << std::setw(3) << v.first << " -| "
              << string((width*v.second)/max_f, '*') << std::endl;
    });
```

Here's the program:

```cpp
// Ex8_06.cpp
// Checking out lognormal distributions
#include <random>                    // For distributions and random number generators
#include <algorithm>                 // For generate(), for_each(), max_element(), transform()
#include <numeric>                   // For accumulate()
#include <iterator>                  // For back_inserter()
#include <vector>                    // For vector container
#include <map>                       // For map container
#include <cmath>                     // For pow(), round(), log() functions
#include <iostream>                  // For standard streams
#include <iomanip>                   // For stream manipulators
#include <string>
using std::string;
using Params = std::lognormal_distribution<>::param_type;

// Modified plot_data template goes here...

int main()
{
  std::random_device rd;
  std::default_random_engine rng {rd()};
  std::lognormal_distribution<> log_norm;
  double mu {}, sigma {};
  const size_t sample_count {20000};
  std::vector<double> values(sample_count);
  std::vector<double> log_values;
  while(true)
  {
    std::cout << "\nEnter values for the mean and standard deviation, or Ctrl+Z to end: ";
    if((std::cin >> mu).eof()) break;
    std::cin >> sigma;
    log_norm.param(Params {mu, sigma});
    std::generate(std::begin(values), std::end(values), [&log_norm, &rng] { return log_norm(rng); });

    // Create data to plot lognormal curve
    dist_plot(std::begin(values), std::end(values));

    // Create logarithms of values
    std::vector<double> log_values;
    std::transform(std::begin(values), std::end(values), std::back_inserter(log_values),
      [] (double v){ return log(v); });

    // Create data to plot curve for logarithms of values
    std::cout << "\nThe distribution for logarithms of the values:\n";
    dist_plot(std::begin(log_values), std::end(log_values));
```

```
    // Get the mean and standard deviation - for the logarithms of the values
    double mean {std::accumulate(std::begin(log_values), std::end(log_values), 0.0)/log_
    values.size()};

    std::transform(std::begin(log_values), std::end(log_values), std::begin(log_values),
                [&mean](double value) { return std::pow(value - mean, 2); });

    double s_dev {std::sqrt(std::accumulate(std::begin(log_values),
                            std::end(log_values), 0.0)/(log_values.size() - 1))};

    std::cout << "For generated values, mean = " << mean
            << " standard deviation = " << s_dev << std::endl;
  }
}
```

This code works in essentially the same way as Ex8_05, with an indefinite while loop that allows you to try a variety of parameters. The obvious difference is that it uses a lognormal_distribution object. There's an additional plot on each loop iteration showing the distribution for the logarithms of the generated values. The mean and standard deviation relate to the logarithms of the values, too.

Here's some sample output:

```
Enter values for the mean and standard deviation, or Ctrl+Z to end: 3 .3
  8 -| *
  9 -| ******
 10 -| **********
 11 -| ******************
 12 -| *****************************
 13 -| ******************************************
 14 -| ***********************************************************
 15 -| ***********************************************************************
 16 -| *********************************************************************************
 17 -| ***************************************************************************************
 18 -| ****************************************************************************************
 19 -| *****************************************************************************************
 20 -| *****************************************************************************************
 21 -| *************************************************************************************
 22 -| *****************************************************************************
 23 -| ***********************************************************************
 24 -| ************************************************************
 25 -| ***************************************************
 26 -| ********************************************
 27 -| ************************************
 28 -| *******************************
 29 -| ************************
 30 -| ********************
 31 -| ****************
 32 -| *************
 33 -| ***********
 34 -| *********
 35 -| *******
```

```
36 -| ******
37 -| ******
38 -| *****
39 -| ****
40 -| **
41 -| **
42 -| **
43 -| *
45 -| *
```

```
The distribution for logarithms of the values:
 2 -| ****
 3 -| ****************************************************************************************
 4 -| ****
For generated values, mean = 2.99837 standard deviation = 0.298659
```

```
Enter values for the mean and standard deviation, or Ctrl+Z to end: ^Z
```

You can see that the logarithms of the values are normally distributed; it's a very narrow plot with a very small standard deviation. I chose a small value for the standard deviation to avoid a very long tail in the lognormal plot, which would occupy too much space in the book, but I suggest that you try different values to see how the shape changes. With a larger σ, the first plot will be much longer, and the second plot will look more like a typical normal distribution. Values of 3 and 2.1 should work well.

Other Distributions Related to the Normal Distribution

The STL defines four further templates for distributions categorized with the normal distribution, and they all generate random values of type double by default. I'll just outline them here - they are created and used in a similar way to the distributions you have seen. If you need them, you'll know a lot about them already:

- The chi_squared_distribution template defines distribution types for objects that are defined from a floating-point parameter that is the number of degrees of freedom; the default is 1.0. An object has a function member, n(), that returns the number of degrees of freedom. This distribution is used widely in hypothesis testing - checking how well the real world matches a theory of how it is supposed to behave. In some disciplines, a mismatch between the real world and the theory is so disappointing that an adjustment of the real world measurements to fit the theory is deemed necessary.

- The cauchy_distribution template defines distribution types that are similar to the normal distribution but with heavier tails either side of the median. An instance is defined by two parameter values, the median, a, which defines the mid-point, and the spread, b, which determines how wide the curve is. These values can be obtained by calling the a() and b() function members for an object. Formally, a Cauchy distribution has no mean or standard deviation, although the median identifies the mid-point value.

- The `fisher_f_distribution` template defines distribution types that are used to determine when two variances are equal; it's the ratio of two chi-squared distributions. An instance is defined by two parameter values - the number of degrees of freedom in the numerator distribution and the number of degrees of freedom for the denominator; the default values are both 1.0.

- The `student_t_distribution` template defines distribution types that are used for small numbers of samples and/or when the standard deviation is not known. An instance is created using a single parameter value that specifies the number of degrees of freedom; the default value is 1.0.

Sampling Distributions

Sampling distributions are useful when you need to define a distribution based on a set of sample values, typically samples from the real world. These distributions don't have fixed probability curves - you define the likelihood for values across a range, or a set of ranges. The STL supports three sampling distributions - the discrete distribution, the piecewise constant distribution, and the piecewise linear distribution.

The Discrete Distribution

The `discrete_distribution` template defines distributions that return random integers in a range, [0, n), based on probability weights for each of the possible values from 0 to n-1. The weights enable you to decide on whatever distribution you want for the values returned. An obvious application of this distribution is to use the value returned to select random objects or values from a range that can be accessed using an index. The range can contain any type of object, including function objects, so this offers tremendous flexibility. If you want to implement a fruit machine simulator, this distribution will help.

You must supply a number of weights for the values to be generated; the number of weights will determine the number of possible values that can be generated and the values of the weights are used to determine the probabilities. Here's an example of how you could simulate throwing a loaded die with face values from 1 to 6:

```
std::discrete_distribution<size_t> d{1, 1, 1, 1, 1, 3};      // Six possible values
std::random_device rd;
std::default_random_engine rng {rd()};
std::map<size_t, size_t> results;                            // Store the results of throws
for(size_t go {}; go < 5000; ++go)                           // 5000 throws of the die
  ++results[d(rng)];

for(const auto& pr : results)
  std::cout << "A " << (pr.first+1) << " was thrown " << pr.second << " times\n";
```

The initializer list for the constructor contains 6 weights, so the distribution will only generate values from the range [0,6) - which implies values 0 through 5 inclusive. The weight for the last value is three times that of the other values so this will be three times as likely to come up as the others. Executing this produced:

```
A 1 was thrown 607 times
A 2 was thrown 645 times
A 3 was thrown 637 times
A 4 was thrown 635 times
A 5 was thrown 617 times
A 6 was thrown 1859 times
```

The six is definitely more likely. The weights are floating-point values that express the relative probabilities for the integer values to be generated. The probability for each value is its weight divided by the sum of all the weights, so the first five values each have a probability of 1/8 and the last value a probability of 3/8. The same distribution would be produced by this statement:

```
std::discrete_distribution<size_t> d{20, 20, 20, 20, 20, 60};
```

The probability for each value from 0 to 4 is 20/160, which is 1/8, and the probability for the last value is 60/160 or 3/8.

You can also specify the weights by a range. Here's a variation of the first code fragment using the same random number generator:

```
std::array<double,6> wts {10.0, 10.0, 10.0, 10.0, 10.0, 30.0};
std::discrete_distribution<size_t> d{std::begin(wts), std::end(wts)};
std::array<string, 6> die_value {"one", "two", "three", "four", "five", "six"};
std::map<size_t, size_t> results;                    // Store the results of throws
for(size_t go {}; go < 5000; ++go)                   // 5000 throws of the die
  ++results[d(rng)];

for(const auto& pr : results)
  std::cout << "A " << die_value[pr.first] << " was thrown " << pr.second << " times\n";
```

The weights here are from an array container. This time the values produced by the distribution object are used to index an array for output. Here's what I got:

```
A one was thrown 653 times
A two was thrown 601 times
A three was thrown 611 times
A four was thrown 670 times
A five was thrown 600 times
A six was thrown 1865 times
```

A further option for defining the weights for a discrete_distribution object is to supply the constructor with a unary function to create a given number of weights from two parameter values. The way this works is a little complicated so we'll examine it step by step.

There are four arguments to this constructor:

- The count of the number of weights, n,

- Two values of type double, xmin and xmax , which are used to calculate probabilities,

- The unary operator, op.

xmax must be greater than xmin, If n is zero, only one probability with a value of 1 will be generated, so in this case the distribution will always produce the same value - 0.

An increment, which I'll call step, is defined as (xmax - xmin)/n. The probabilities are calculated by executing op(xmin + (2*k+1)*step/2) with values of k from 0 to n-1.

Thus the weights will be:

op(xmin + step/2), op(xmin + 3*step/2), op(xmin + 5*step/2), ... op(xmin + (2*n-1)*step/2)

An example with numerical values will help clarify what is happening. Suppose n is 6, and xmin and xmax are 0 and 12, so the value of step is 2. If we assume that op is defined so that it doubles the argument value, the weights will be: 2, 6, 10, 14, 18, 22. The probabilities will therefore be 1/36, 1/12, 5/36, 7/36, 1/4, and 11/36. Here's the definition of the distribution object for that:

```
std::discrete_distribution<size_t> dist {6, 0, 12, [](double v) { return 2*v; }};
```

The unary operator is defined by a lambda expression that returns twice the argument value. You can retrieve the probabilities from a discrete_distribution object by calling its probabilities() member. You could obtain the probabilities for the dist object like this:

```
auto probs = dist.probabilities();               // Returns type vector<double>
std::copy(std::begin(probs), std::end(probs),
     std::ostream_iterator<double> { std::cout << std::fixed << std::setprecision(2), " " });
std::cout << std::endl;                           // Output:  0.03 0.08 0.14 0.19 0.25 0.31
```

In general, the number of probabilities is arbitrary, corresponding to however many weights you specify, so they are returned in a vector<double> container. The output that is shown in the comment corresponds with the values of the fractions I showed earlier.

You can set new probabilities for a discrete_distribution object by calling its param() member with a different set of weight values; the number of weights can be different too:

```
dist.param({2, 2, 2, 3, 3});                     // New set of weights
auto parm = dist.param().probabilities();
std::copy(std::begin(parm), std::end(parm),
     std::ostream_iterator<double> {std::cout << std::fixed << std::setprecision(2), " "});
std::cout << std::endl;                           // Output: 0.17 0.17 0.17 0.25 0.25
```

The argument to the first param() member call is a list of weights that are different in values and number than the original. Calling param() without an argument returns a param_type object, but you don't know exactly what type that alias represents. However, you do know that it supports the same function members for accessing parameters as the original distribution object. This means that in this case, you can get at the values in the param_type object by calling the probabilities() member of the param_type object. This returns a vector<double> container that you can then access. The comments show the probabilities that it contains, and you can see that they correspond with the new set of weights.

Using a Discrete Distribution

We can apply discrete_distribution objects to implement a simple game you play against the computer using four dice. The dice are unusual in that the numbers of the faces are non-standard and each die is different. The faces on the dice have the following values:

```
die 1: 3 3 3 3 3 3
die 2: 0 0 4 4 4 4
die 3: 1 1 1 5 5 5
die 4: 2 2 2 2 6 6
```

To play the game, you first choose any of the four dice. The computer then chooses a die from the remaining three. There are 15 throws of the two dice and for each throw, the die with the highest face value wins. Whoever wins the highest number of throws out of the 15 is the winner. Since no two dice have faces with a common value, one die or the other always wins a throw, and with an odd number of throws, a game cannot be drawn.

An easy way to implement this would be to define a Die class to represent a die, so that each Die object stored the values of its 6 faces. The class could define a function member to simulate throwing a die using a discrete_distribution object that you define like this:

```
std::discrete_distribution<size_t> throw_die{1, 1, 1, 1, 1, 1};
```

However, an object with all values having the same probability is not much of a demonstration of a discrete distribution, so I will take a different and somewhat more complicated approach. We can define the class to represent a die in the Die.h header like this:

```
#ifndef DIE_H
#define DIE_H
#include <random>                    // For discrete_distribution and random number generator
#include <vector>                    // For vector container
#include <algorithm>                 // For remove()
#include <iterator>                  // For iterators and begin() and end()

// Alias for param_type for discrete distribution
using Params = std::discrete_distribution<size_t>::param_type;

std::default_random_engine& rng();

// Class to represent a die with six faces with arbitrary values
// Face values do not need to be unique.
class Die
{
public:
  Die() { values.push_back(0); };

  // Constructor
  Die(std::initializer_list<size_t> init)
  {
    std::vector<size_t> faces {init}; // Stores die face values
    auto iter = std::begin(faces);
    auto end_iter = std::end(faces);
    std::vector<size_t> wts;          // Stores weights for face values
    while(iter != end_iter)
    {
      values.push_back(*iter);
      wts.push_back(std::count(iter, end_iter, *iter));
      end_iter = std::remove(iter, end_iter, *iter++);
    }
    dist.param(Params {std::begin(wts), std::end(wts)});
  }

  size_t throw_it() { return values[dist(rng())]; }
```

```
private:
  std::discrete_distribution<size_t> dist; // Probability distributtion for values
  std::vector<size_t> values;              // Face values
};
#endif
```

The class has two private members, a `discrete_distribution<size_t>` object, `dist`, which will be used to generate a random face value for the die, and a `vector` container, `values`, which stores unique face values. The default constructor creates an object with a default distribution object that will always return 0 and with the `values` member containing a single value of 0. The second constructor expects an initializer list that specifies the face values for a die. The initializer list is used to initialize the local `faces` container with the face values. Face values can be duplicated, and the weight for each face value - that determines its probability - will be just the number of times that face value occurs. The `while` loop in the constructor iterates over the current range of elements in `faces` and counts the number of times the face value that is the first element occurs. The count is stored in the `wts` container and the face value to which it applies is added to the `values` member. All occurrences of the current face value are then removed from `faces` and the new end iterator arising from the deletions is stored in `end_iter`. When the loop ends, `values` will contain all the unique face values for the die and `wts` will contain the corresponding weights. Calling `param()` for the `dist` member sets the parameters for the distribution to be the weights in the `wts` container.

The code for the program to use the `Die` class to implement the game looks like this:

```
// Ex8_07.cpp
// Implementing a dice throwing game using discrete distributions
#include <random>                    // For discrete_distribution and random number generator
#include <array>                     // For array container
#include <utility>                   // For pair type
#include <algorithm>                 // For count(), remove()
#include <iostream>                  // For standard streams
#include <iomanip>                   // For stream manipulators
#include "Die.h"                     // Class to define a die

// Random number generator available throughout the program code
std::default_random_engine& rng()
{
  static std::default_random_engine engine {std::random_device()()};
  return engine;
}

int main()
{
  size_t n_games {};               // Number of games played
  const size_t n_dice {4};         // Number of dice

  std::array<Die, n_dice> dice     // The dice
  {
    Die {3, 3, 3, 3, 3, 3},
    Die {0, 0, 4, 4, 4, 4},
    Die {1, 1, 1, 5, 5, 5},
    Die {2, 2, 2, 2, 6, 6}
  };
```

```
std::cout <<
    "For each game, select a die from the following by entering 1, 2, 3, or 4 (or Ctrl+Z to end):\n"
              << "die 1: 3 3 3 3 3 3\n"
              << "die 2: 0 0 4 4 4 4\n"
              << "die 3: 1 1 1 5 5 5\n"
              << "die 4: 2 2 2 2 6 6\n";

size_t you {}, me {};                                      // Stores index of my dice and your dice

while(true)
{
  std:: cout << "\nChoose a die: ";
  if((std::cin >> you).eof()) break;                      // For EOF - it's all over

  if(you == 0 || you > n_dice)                            // Only 1 to 4 allowed
  {
    std::cout << "Selection must be from 1 to 4, try again.\n";
    continue;
  }

  // Choose my die as next in sequence
  me = you-- % n_dice;                                     // you from 0 to 3, and me you+1 mod 4
  std::cout << "I'll choose:  " << (me+1) << std::endl;

  // Throw the dice
  const size_t n_throws {15};
  std::array<std::pair<size_t, size_t>, n_throws> goes; // Results of goes -
                                                  // pair<me_value, you_value>
  std::generate(std::begin(goes), std::end(goes),        // Make the throws
    [&dice, me, you] { return std::make_pair(dice[me].throw_it(), dice[you].throw_it()); });

  // Output result of game
  std::cout << "\nGame " << ++n_games << ":\n";

  // Output results of my throws...
  std::cout << "Me : ";
  std::for_each(std::begin(goes), std::end(goes),
    [](const std::pair<size_t, size_t>& pr)
  {  std::cout << std::setw(3) << pr.first; });
  auto my_wins = std::count_if(std::begin(goes), std::end(goes),
                                        [](const std::pair<size_t, size_t>& pr)
                                        { return pr.first > pr.second; });
  std::cout << " My wins:   " << std::setw(2) <<  std::right << my_wins
            << "    I " << ((my_wins > n_throws / 2) ? "win!!" : "lose {:-(")
            << std::endl;
```

```
    // Output results of your corresponding throws - aligned below mine...
    std::cout << "You: ";
    std::for_each(std::begin(goes), std::end(goes), [](const std::pair<size_t, size_t>& pr)
                                        { std::cout << std::setw(3) << pr.second; });
    std::cout << " Your wins: " << std::setw(2) << std:: right << n_throws - my_wins
            << "    You " << ((my_wins <= n_throws / 2) ? "win!!" : "lose!!!")
            << std::endl;
  }
}
```

The dice array container holds the Die objects for the four different die. After the prompt for input, the game is played in the while loop, one complete game per iteration. The player's die selection is stored in you and the computer's choice in me. A selection is from 1 to 4 so this is decremented to allow its use as an index to the dice array. The me variable is arbitrarily set to the next die in sequence, modulo 4, so if you selects the last die at index 3, me will select the first at index 0.

The n_throws variable specifies the number of throws for a game, 15 in this case; an odd number of games ensures that there is always a winner. The generate() algorithm carries out the 15 throws of the two dice for a game and stores the result of each throw in a pair object, where the first member stores the computer's die value and the second member the player's. A throw of the two dice is executed by the lambda expression that is the third argument to generate(). The results of throwing each die is produced by calling its throw_it() member.

The number of throws that the computer wins is calculated by the count_if() algorithm and stored in my_wins. The count is incremented if the first member of each pair object from the goes container is greater than the second. The player's win count is n_throws-my_wins.

I got the following output:

```
For each game, select a die  from the following by entering 1, 2, 3, or 4 (or Ctrl+Z to end):
die 1: 3 3 3 3 3 3
die 2: 0 0 4 4 4 4
die 3: 1 1 1 5 5 5
die 4: 2 2 2 2 6 6

Choose a die: 2
I'll choose:  3

Game 1:
Me :   5  1  5  1  5  5  1  1  5  5  5  5  1  5  5 My wins:   11   I win!!
You:   4  0  4  4  4  4  4  4  4  4  4  0  4  4  4 Your wins:  4   You lose!!!

Choose a die: 4
I'll choose:  1

Game 2:
Me :   3  3  3  3  3  3  3  3  3  3  3  3  3  3  3 My wins:    9   I win!!
You:   6  6  2  2  2  2  2  2  6  6  2  2  2  6  6 Your wins:  6   You lose!!!

Choose a die: 1
I'll choose:  2
```

```
Game 3:
Me :  0  0  0  0  4  4  4  4  4  0  4  4  4  4  4 My wins:   10   I win!!
You:  3  3  3  3  3  3  3  3  3  3  3  3  3  3  3 Your wins:  5   You lose!!!

Choose a die: 3
I'll choose:  4

Game 4:
Me :  6  2  2  2  2  6  2  2  2  2  6  2  2  2  2 My wins:    9   I win!!
You:  5  5  5  5  1  5  5  5  1  1  5  1  1  1  5 Your wins:  6   You lose!!!

Choose a die: 3
I'll choose:  4

Game 5:
Me :  2  2  6  2  2  2  6  2  2  2  2  6  2  6  6 My wins:   12   I win!!
You:  5  5  5  1  1  5  5  1  1  1  1  1  1  1  5 Your wins:  3   You lose!!!

Choose a die: 3
I'll choose:  4

Game 6:
Me :  6  2  2  2  2  2  6  2  2  2  2  6  6  2  2 My wins:    8   I win!!
You:  5  5  5  5  5  5  1  1  1  1  5  5  1  5  1 Your wins:  7   You lose!!!

Choose a die: 2
I'll choose:  3

Game 7:
Me :  5  5  1  1  5  5  5  5  5  5  5  1  1  1  1 My wins:   10   I win!!
You:  4  4  4  0  4  4  4  0  4  4  4  4  0  4 Your wins:  5   You lose!!!

Choose a die: ^Z
```

The computer is remarkably successful - it won every game. Its success is because the player chooses a die first. The four dice are an example of *non-transitive dice* that were invented by an American statistician called Bradley Efron. In general, numerical relationships are transitive, which means that if a>b and b>c, it's safe to say that a>c. It's not so with these dice. For the Die objects in the dice array, the following is the case for the game implemented by Ex8_07:

- dice[3] beats dice[2] beats dice[1] beats dice[0] beats dice[3] !

This is because of the probabilities for the face values that result from a throw:

- dice[3] beats dice[2] because a 6 from dice[3] (probability 1/3) always wins, and a 2 from dice[3] (probability 2/3) wins when dice[2] is 1 (probability 1/2). So the overall probability of a win by dice[3] is 1/3 + 2/3 × 1/2, which is 2/3.

- dice[2] beats dice[1] because a 5 from dice[2] (probability 1/2) always wins, and a 1 from dice[2] (probability 1/2) wins when dice[1] is 0 (probability 1/3). So the overall probability of a win by dice[2] is 1/2 + 1/2 × 1/3, which is 2/3.

- dice[1] beats dice[0] because a 4 from dice[1] (probability 2/3) always wins.

- dice[0] beats dice[3] because a 3 from dice[0] (probability 1) wins when dice[3] is 2 (probability 2/3). So the overall probability of a win by dice[0] is 1 × 2/3, which is 2/3.

This means that whichever die you choose, the computer can choose a die from the remaining three that has a 66% chance of beating you.

Piecewise Constant Distributions

The piecewise_constant_distribution template defines a distribution that generates floating-point values with a set of piecewise subintervals. The values from a given subinterval are uniformly distributed within it and each subinterval has its own weight. An object is defined by a set of n interval boundaries that define n-1 constant subintervals and a set of n-1 weights that apply to the subintervals. Figure 8-7 illustrates this.

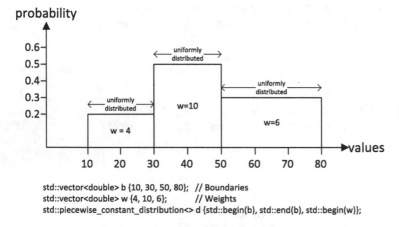

```
std::vector<double> b {10, 30, 50, 80};   // Boundaries
std::vector<double> w {4, 10, 6};          // Weights
std::piecewise_constant_distribution<> d {std::begin(b), std::end(b), std::begin(w)};
```

Figure 8-7. *The piecewise constant distribution*

The distribution in Figure 8-7 defines three intervals, each with its own weight. The three intervals are defined by four boundary values that are defined in the container b. Each interval has a weight that is defined by an element of the container w. The first two constructor arguments are iterators that specify the range of boundaries, and the third argument is an iterator pointing to the first element in the range of weights. Values within each interval will be uniformly distributed and the probability of a random value being within a particular interval is determined by the weight for the interval.

In addition to the function members that all distribution objects implement, a piecewise_constant_distribution has intervals() and densities() members that return the interval boundaries and the *probability densities* for the values in the intervals; both functions return the values in vector containers. We can apply these members and obtain some insight into the effect of the distribution by trying out a similar distribution to that shown in Figure 8-7, but with narrower intervals, so less space is needed for the output:

```
// Ex8_08.cpp
// Demonstrating the piecewise constant distribution
#include <random>                          // For distributions and random number generator
#include <vector>                          // For vector container
#include <map>                             // For map container
```

```cpp
#include <utility>                          // For pair type
#include <algorithm>                        // For copy(), count(), remove()
#include <iostream>                         // For standard streams
#include <iterator>                         // For stream iterators
#include <iomanip>                          // For stream manipulators
#include <string>                           // For string class
using std::string;

int main()
{
  std::vector<double> b {10, 20, 35, 55};   // Intervals: 10-20, 20-35, 35-55
  std::vector<double> w {4, 10, 6};         // Weights for the intervals
  std::piecewise_constant_distribution<> d {std::begin(b), std::end(b), std::begin(w)};

  // Output the interval boundaries and the interval probabilities
  auto intvls = d.intervals();
  std::cout << "intervals: ";
  std::copy(std::begin(intvls), std::end(intvls), std::ostream_iterator<double>{std::cout, " "});
  std::cout << "  probabilities: ";
  auto probs = d.densities();
  std::copy(std::begin(probs), std::end(probs), std::ostream_iterator<double>{std::cout, " "});
  std::cout << '\n' << std::endl;

  std::random_device rd;
  std::default_random_engine rng {rd()};
  std::map<int, size_t> results;            //Stores and counts random values as integers

  // Generate a lot of random values...
  for(size_t i {}; i < 20000; ++i)
    ++results[static_cast<int>(std::round(d(rng)))];

  // Plot the integer values
  auto max_count = std::max_element(std::begin(results), std::end(results),
                  [](const std::pair<int, size_t>& pr1, const std::pair<int, size_t>& pr2)
                    { return pr1.second < pr2.second; })->second;
  std::for_each(std::begin(results), std::end(results),
                            [max_count](const std::pair<int, size_t>& pr)
                          { if(!(pr.first % 10))  // Display value if multiple of  10
                              std::cout << std::setw(3) << pr.first << "-|";
                            else
                              std::cout << "    |";
                            std::cout << std::string(pr.second * 80 / max_count, '*')
                                  << '\n'; });
}
```

This creates a distribution with the intervals and weights that you see, generates a large number of values using the distribution, and then plots the frequency with which the values occur as a histogram, after converting them to integers. The values run down the page with the bars indicating the relative frequency from left to right. I got the following output:

```
intervals: 10 20 35 55    probability densities: 0.02 0.0333333 0.015

10-|************************
   |******************************************
   |*****************************************
   |*****************************************
   |*******************************************
   |*********************************************
   |***********************************************
   |***********************************************
   |*****************************************
   |******************************************
20-|*********************************************************
   |***********************************************************************
   |**********************************************************************
   |***********************************************************************
   |************************************************************************
   |**********************************************************************
   |*********************************************************************
   |****************************************************************************
   |*********************************************************************
   |****************************************************************************
30-|***************************************************************************
   |***************************************************************************
   |***********************************************************************
   |**********************************************************************
   |*****************************************************************************
   |*******************************************************
   |******************************
   |********************************
   |*****************************
   |*******************************
40-|************************************
   |*******************************
   |********************************
   |********************************
   |*********************************
   |********************************
   |********************************
   |********************************
   |*********************************
   |****************************
50-|*****************************
   |****************************
   |****************************
   |********************************
   |*******************************
   |***************
```

The interesting features of the output are the values for the *probability densities*, and the relative lengths of the bars in the first and last intervals. The intervals have weights 4 and 6 respectively so the probability of a value being in the first interval is 4/20, which is 0.2, the probability for a value being in the second interval is 10/20, which is 0.5, and the probability for a value being the last interval is 6/20, which is 0.3. However, the output bars are lower in the last interval than those in the first interval, which seems to conflict with these probabilities. Anyway, the *probability density values* in the output are different, so why is this?

The reason is that they are *not the same*. The probability densities are the probabilities that a *given value from an interval will occur*, not the probability that *a random value will be within an interval*. The probability density for a value corresponds to the probability that a value from the interval will occur, divided by the range of values in the interval. Thus the probability densities for values in each of the three ranges are therefore 0.2/10, 0.5/15, and 0.3/20, which fortunately is the same as the output. There will be approximately twice as many values generated in the last interval than in the first, but these are spread across a greater range, so the bars are shorter. Thus the bar lengths reflect the probability densities.

Piecewise Linear Distributions

The piecewise_linear_distribution template defines continuous distributions of floating-point values, where the probability density function results from joining the dots defined by a set of sample values; each sample value has a weight that determines its probability density value. Figure 8-8 shows an example.

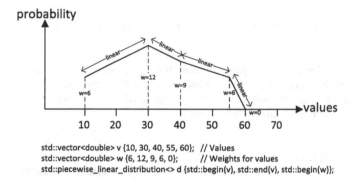

```
std::vector<double> v {10, 30, 40, 55, 60};  // Values
std::vector<double> w {6, 12, 9, 6, 0};      // Weights for values
std::piecewise_linear_distribution<> d {std::begin(v), std::end(v), std::begin(w)};
```

Figure 8-8. *A piecewise linear distribution*

Figure 8-8 shows a distribution determined by five sample values that are defined in the container v. Each value has a weight that is defined by a corresponding element of the container w, and each weight determines the probability density for the corresponding value. Probability densities for values between one sample and the next are linear between the probability densities for the two samples. The first two constructor arguments are iterators that specify the range of values, and the third argument is an iterator pointing to the first element in the range of weights. This distribution will generate random values from 10 to 60 with the probability densities represented by the piecewise linear curve. The sample values for a distribution can be obtained in a vector by calling its intervals() member. You can get the probability densities for these in a vector container by calling densities() for the distribution object.

Determining the probability densities for values in the entire range is a little complicated. The area under the entire probability curve represents the probability for *any* of the values from the entire range occurring so it has to be 1. To accommodate this, probabilities for values within the intervals are calculated as follows:

First s is calculated as the sum of the averages of the weights for the values that define the interval, each multiplied by the interval length. Thus in general, s is defined by the equation:

$$s = \sum_{0}^{n-1}(v_{i+1} - v_i)\frac{(w_{i+1} + w_i)}{2}$$

where v_i are the sample values and w_i are their corresponding weights.

The probability p for any value x in an interval between two sample values, $[v_i, v_{i+1})$ is determined by a linear combination of the probabilities for the sample values, where the probability contributions from each end of the interval are proportional to the distance of x from the sample values. In mathematical terms, the probability for x is:

$$p = \frac{w_i(v_{i+1} - x) + w_{i+1}(x - v_i)}{s(v_{i+1} - v_i)}$$

Thus for the example in Figure 8-8, s is:

(30 - 10)×(12 + 6)/2 + (40 - 30)×(9 + 12)/2 +(55 - 40)×(6 + 9)/2 + (60 - 55)×(0 + 6)/2

which amounts to 412.5.

The probability for the ith sample value will be w_i/s. so the probabilities for the values in Figure 8-8 are 6/412.5, 12/412.5, 9/412.5, 6/412.5, and 0/412.5. My trusty calculator indicates that these correspond to 0.0145, 0.029, 0.0218, 0.0145, and 0. A working example similar to Ex8_08 will show whether this is correct and also show the overall characteristics of the piecewise linear distribution:

```
// Ex8_09.cpp
// Demonstrating the piecewise linear distribution
#include <random>                    // For distributions and random number generator
#include <vector>                    // For vector container
#include <map>                       // For map container
#include <utility>                   // For pair type
#include <algorithm>                 // For copy(), count(), remove()
#include <iostream>                  // For standard streams
#include <iterator>                  // For stream iterators
#include <iomanip>                   // For stream manipulators
#include <string>                    // For string class
using std::string;

int main()
{
  std::vector<double> v {10, 30, 40, 55, 60};   // Sample values
  std::vector<double> w {6, 12, 9, 6, 0};       // Weights for the samples
  std::piecewise_linear_distribution<> d {std::begin(v), std::end(v), std::begin(w)};

  // Output the interval boundaries and the interval probabilities
```

```
auto values = d.intervals();
std::cout << "Sample values: ";
std::copy(std::begin(values), std::end(values), std::ostream_iterator<double>{std::cout, " "});
std::cout << "  probability densities: ";
auto probs = d.densities();
std::copy(std::begin(probs), std::end(probs), std::ostream_iterator<double>{std::cout, " "});
std::cout << '\n' << std::endl;

std::random_device rd;
std::default_random_engine rng {rd()};
std::map<int, size_t> results;                    // Stores and counts random values as integers

// Generate a lot of random values...
for(size_t i {}; i < 20000; ++i)
  ++results[static_cast<int>(std::round(d(rng)))];

// Plot the integer values
auto max_count = std::max_element(std::begin(results), std::end(results),
  [](const std::pair<int, size_t>& pr1, const std::pair<int, size_t>& pr2)
{ return pr1.second < pr2.second; })->second;
std::for_each(std::begin(results), std::end(results),
            [max_count](const std::pair<int, size_t>& pr)
            {
              if(!(pr.first % 10))  // Display value if multiple of  10
                std::cout << std::setw(3) << pr.first << "-|";
              else
                std::cout << "    |";
              std::cout << std::string(pr.second * 80 / max_count, '*')
                      << '\n';
            });
}
```

The only difference from Ex8_08 is the definition of the distribution object. With a piecewise linear distribution, there has to be the same number of weights as sample values. Here's my output from this program:

```
Sample values: 10 30 40 55 60    probability densities: 0.0145455 0.0290909 0.0218182
0.0145455 0

 10-|*****************
    |**********************************
    |*********************************
    |*****************************************
    |******************************************
    |*******************************************
    |*********************************************
    |**********************************************
    |***********************************************
    |************************************************
 20-|*****************************************************
```

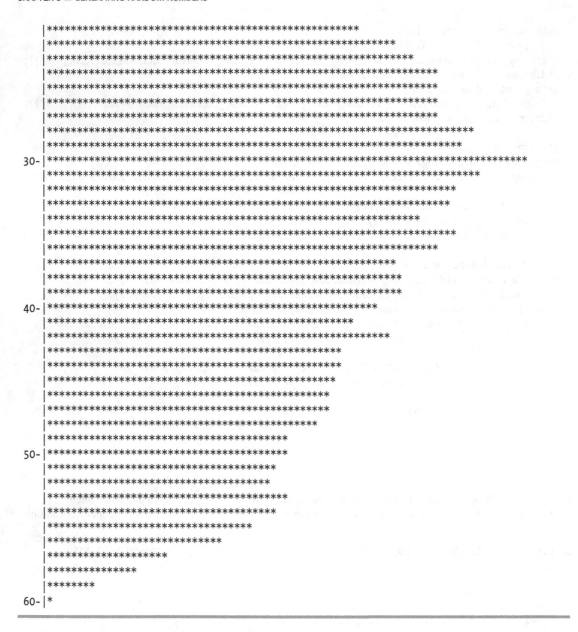

The probability densities are remarkably similar to the values my calculator produced, which is a relief. This distribution provides you with a powerful tool for defining probability density functions of any shape.

Other Distributions

The STL defines templates for a further nine types of distribution. I'll just outline them here for reference and show examples of plots of the random values produced by most of them. Keep in mind that the shape of a distribution curve can vary considerably with different sets of parameters, and the illustrations that are shown have been scaled to fit within a page width.

Poisson Distributions

A *Poisson distribution* defines a discrete PDF that represents the frequency of occurrence in a set of independent events, each with only two possible outcomes and where the probability of success can be different for different events. Events can be distributed over time or location. The distribution was originated by the famous French mathematician Simeon Poisson. One of its first applications was in modeling the probability of soldiers in the Prussian army being killed as result of being kicked by a horse. It can be used to model the likelihood of equipment failures over time or the incidence of traffic accidents.

The poisson_distribution template defines types of function objects that generate random non-negative integers that are of type int by default. An object is created from a double value for the mean for the distribution - for example

```
double mean {5.5};
std::poisson_distribution<> poisson_d {mean};
```

The default constructor assigns a default value for the mean of 1.0. An object has a mean() member that returns the value of the mean. The plot of the occurrences of random values produced by poisson_d defined above is shown in Figure 8-9.

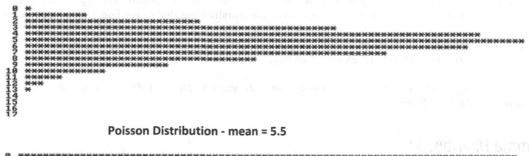

Poisson Distribution - mean = 5.5

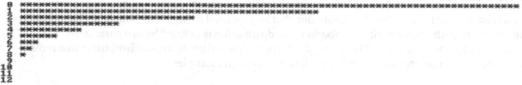

Geometric Distribution - p = 0.4

Exponential Distribution - lambda = 0.75

Figure 8-9. *Examples of Poisson, geometric, and exponential distributions*

Geometric Distributions

A geometric distribution is a discrete distribution that is used to model the number of trials necessary in order to achieve a success in something that has two possible outcomes. An example might be modeling how many randomly selected people you need to ask to find one that has bought this book. The geometric_distribution template defines discrete distribution types that return non-negative integer values that are of type int be default. The constructor argument is a double value specifying the probability of a trial resulting in success, so it must be between 0 and 1. Here's an example:

```
double p_success {0.4};
std::geometric_distribution<> geometric_d {p_success};
```

The object has a function member, p(), that returns the probability of success. The plot of the geometric_d distribution is shown in Figure 8-9.

Exponential Distributions

An *exponential distribution* models the time between the occurrences of events. You can think of it as the continuous equivalent of a geometric distribution. The exponential_distribution template defines distribution types that return floating-point values that are of type double by default. The argument to the constructor is a double value that represents an arrival rate, usually identified as *lambda*. Here's an example:

```
double lambda {0.75};
std::exponential_distribution<> exp_d {lambda};
```

The lambda() function member of the object returns the value for the arrival rate. A plot of this distribution is shown in Figure 8-9.

Gamma Distributions

A *Gamma distribution* is a continuous distribution that is often used to model waiting times for events but is more general than the exponential distribution. The distribution is defined by two parameters: a shape value, *alpha*, and a rate value, *beta*. The gamma_distribution template defines a distribution that returns floating-point values that are of type double by default. Here's an example:

```
double alpha {5.0}, beta {1.5};
std::gamma_distribution<> gamma_d {alpha, beta};
```

The alpha() and beta() function members return the parameters for a distribution object. A plot of values generated by gamma_d is shown in Figure 8-10.

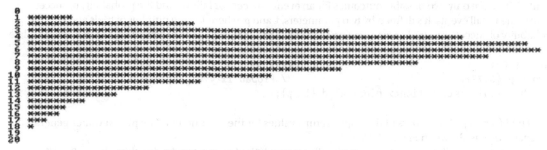

Gamma Distribution - alpha = 5.0 beta = 1.5

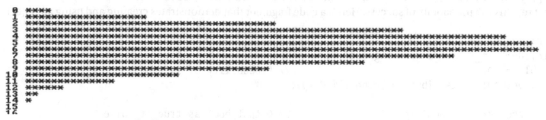

Weibull Distribution - a = 2.5 b = 7.0

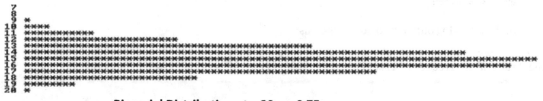

Binomial Distribution - t = 20 p = 0.75

Figure 8-10. *Examples of Gamma, Weibull, and binomial distributions*

Weibull Distributions

The *Weibull distribution* defines a continuous PDF that models failures rates as a function of time - usually of materials. It's defined by two parameters, the shape, a, and a scale, b. Here's an example of creating an instance of the weibull_distribution template:

```
double a {2.5};                          // Shape
double b {7.0};                          // Scale
std::weibull_distribution<> weibull_d {a, b};
```

The weibull_d object returns random values of type double by default. You can obtain the distribution parameters by calling it's a() and b() members. A plot of the values generated by weibull_d is shown in Figure 8-10.

Binomial Distributions

A *binomial distribution* is a discrete distribution that models the success rate in a set of independent binary events. There are only two possible outcomes for an event - success or failure, and the probability of success is the same for all events. It's defined by two parameters, t and p, where t is the number of trials and p is the probability of success in a trial. Here's how you can create an object using the binomial_distribution template:

```
int t {20};                              // Number of trials
double p {0.75};                         // Probability of success
std::binomial_distribution<> binomial_d {t, p};
```

The t() and p() members of the object return values for the parameters. The plot of values generated by binomial_d is shown in Figure 8-10.

A *Bernoulli distribution* is a binomial distribution with the t parameter having the value 1. The STL provides the bernoulli_distribution class to define this distribution. Since t is fixed as 1, you only need to supply a value for p to the constructor, and the object will return random bool values. There's a p() member that returns the probability of success. Here's a code fragment that demonstrates creating and using an object:

```
std::random_device rd;
std::default_random_engine rng {rd()};
double p {0.75};                         // Probability of success
std::bernoulli_distribution bernoulli_d {p};

std::cout << std::boolalpha;             // Output bool as true or false
for(size_t i {}; i < 15; ++i)
  std::cout << bernoulli_d(rng) << ' ';
std::cout << std::endl;
```

I got the following output from executing this:

```
true true false true true true true true false true false true true false true
```

Negative Binomial Distributions

A *negative binomial distribution* is a discrete distribution that models the number of failures in a sequence of trials that occur before a specified number of successes. The trials have only two possible results and are independent of one another. If the number of successes is 1, the distribution is the same as a geometric distribution. You can also visualize this distribution as modeling the number of failures before a given number of successes. The negative_binomial_distribution template defines types of objects that return integers that are of type int by default The constructor for the negative_binomial_distribution template requires two parameters, the number of failures, k, and the probability of success, p. Here's an example of creating an object:

```
int k {5};                               // Number of successes
double p {0.4};                          // Probability of success
std::negative_binomial_distribution<> neg_bi_d {k, p};
```

The k() and p() members of neg_bi_d return the values of the parameters. A plot of values generated by the neg_bi_d object is shown in Figure 8-11.

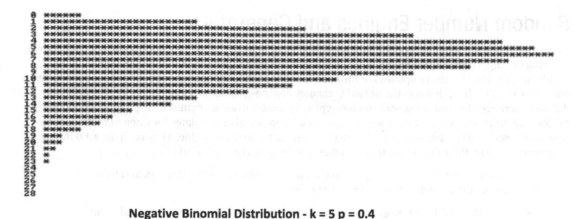

Negative Binomial Distribution - k = 5 p = 0.4

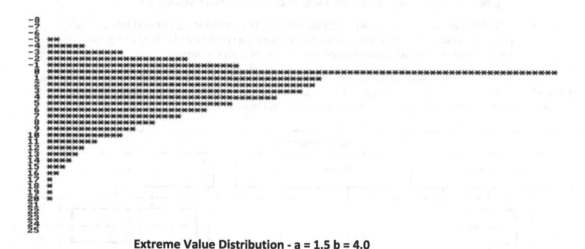

Extreme Value Distribution - a = 1.5 b = 4.0

Figure 8-11. *Examples of a negative binomial distribution and an extreme value distribution*

Extreme Value Distributions

An *extreme value distribution* is a continuous distribution that models the distribution of maxima or minima of sequences of independent variables that are distributed in the same way. One application is in modeling extremes of natural phenomena such as rainfall or earthquakes. The `extreme_value_distribution` template defines types of objects that return floating-point values that are type `double` by default. Two parameters are required by the constructor, the location parameter, a, and the scale parameter, b; both parameters are floating-point values. Here's an example:

```
double a {1.5};                         // location
double b {4.0};                         // Scale
std::extreme_value_distribution<> extreme_value_d {a, b};
```

The parameter values can be obtained for an object by calling it's a() and b() members. A plot of values produced by the extreme_value_d object is shown in Figure 8-11.

Random Number Engines and Generators

There are class templates for three *random number engines* in the STL. They each implement a well-known and effective algorithm for generating random number sequences, but with different advantages and disadvantages. These three templates are the basis for all ten standard *random number generator* class types offered by the STL. In addition to the `default_random_engine` generator type, which is implementation defined, there are nine further generator class types that customize the engines to implement known reliable algorithms for generating random sequences. There are also templates for three *random number engine adapters* that can customize a sequence from an instance of an engine. They each have a template parameter that identifies the engine to which they are applied. The engine adapter templates are:

- The `independent_bits_engine` adapter template modifies the values generated by an engine to have a specified number of bits.

- The `discard_block_engine` adapter template modifies the values generated by an engine to discard some values from a sequence of values of a given length.

- The `shuffle_order_engine` adapter template returns the values generated by an engine in a different sequence. It does this by storing a sequence of values of a given length from the engine, then returning these in a random sequence.

The generators classes either customize an engine template directly with a specific set of template parameter values, or customize another generator using a random number engine adaptor. The way in which generators are produced from engines is illustrated in Figure 8-12.

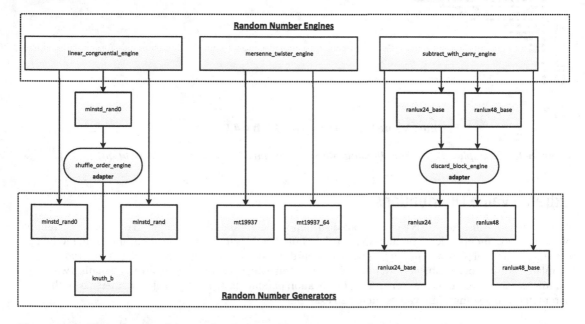

Figure 8-12. *The connection between random number generators and random number engines*

Each generator class type is created by applying a specific set of template parameters values to an engine template. I'll outline the random number engines here to give you an idea of what they do, but I strongly recommend that you use one of the random number generator class types that customize the engines, rather than try to customize the engine templates yourself. Let's examine the engines and the generator types that are defined from them in a little more detail.

The Linear Congruential Engine

The linear_congruential_engine class template implements one of the oldest and simplest algorithms for generating random sequences of integers called the *linear congruential method*. The algorithm involves three parameters, a multiplier, a, an increment, c, and a modulus, m. The choice of values for these is critical to producing a random sequence of reasonable quality. The process requires a single integer seed value and the first random value, x, is calculated conceptually like this:

```
unsigned int x = (a*seed + c) % m;
```

Each random number, x_n, is used to generate the next, x_{n+1}, using the formula:

$$x_{n+1} = (ax_n + c) \bmod m$$

Obviously, since the random value is a remainder, the maximum number of different values that can be generated is m, and for poor choices of a and c, it will be much less than that. While this algorithm is simple and fast, generators that are instances of one of the other engines such as the mersenne_twister_engine are preferable when a high quality random sequence is important to the application.

Generators Based on the Linear Congruential Engine

There are two random number generator types defined as aliases for instances of the linear_congruential_engine template, minstd_rand0 and minstd_rand, that generate 32-bit unsigned integers. The names come from "minimum standard random number generator". minstd_rand0 was proposed in 1988 by Stephen K. Park and Keith W. Miller as the minimum standard for generating random numbers because of the number of poor generators around at the time; it is defined with a as 16807, c as 0 and m as 2147483647. The value for m is the largest Mersenne prime less than 2^{32}. The minstd_rand generator is an improved version of minstd_rand0 with a as 48271.

The knuth_b random number generator implements an algorithm due to Donald Knuth by applying the shuffle_order_engine adapter to values produced by the minst_rand0 generator. It's described in his classic work, *The Art of Computer Programming Volume 2* along with a great deal more about methods for generating random numbers and tests for randomness. Applying the adapter increases the 'randomness' of the sequence by removing the dependency between successive values.

You use these generators - indeed *all* the generators - in exactly the same way as the default_random_engine you have seen For example:

```
std::random_device rd;
std::minstd_rand rng {rd()};
std::uniform_int_distribution<long> dist {-5L, 5L};
for(size_t i {}; i < 8; ++i)
  std::cout << std::setw(2) << dist(rng) << " ";      // 3 -5 -2  4 -5  4  1  0
```

The Mersenne Twister Engine

The mersenne_twister_engine class template implements the *Mersenne twister algorithm*, which is so-called because the period length is a *Mersenne prime*. A Mersenne prime is a prime of the form 2^n-1 so 7 and 127 are Mersenne primes; of course, the Mersenne prime used in the algorithm is *much much* larger. This engine is used very widely because it can generate very long high quality sequences but it has the disadvantage that it is relatively slow. The algorithm is complex and involves many parameters so I won't attempt to explain it here.

Generators that are Instances of the Mersenne Twister Engine

There are two type aliases for instances of mersenne_twister_engine that define specific generators. mt19937 generates random unsigned 32-bit integers and mt19937_64 generates unsigned 64-bit integers. The mt19937 random number generator has a period length of 219937-1, hence the name.

You use these in the same way as other generators:

```
std::random_device rd;
std::mt19937_64 rng {rd()};          // Generates random 64-bit integers
std::uniform_real_distribution<long double> dist {-5.0L, 5.0L};
for(size_t i {}; i < 8; ++i)
  std::cout << std::setw(5)
          << dist(rng)
          << " ";                    // -2.57481 3.0546 -1.6438 2.14798
                                      // -3.84095 0.973843 -2.98971 -2.1067
```

The Subtract with Carry Engine

The subtract_with_carry_engine template defines a random number engine that implements the *subtract with carry* algorithm that is an improvement over the linear congruential algorithm. Like the linear congruential method, the subtract with carry algorithm uses a recurrence relationship to define successive values in a sequence, but each value, x_i, is computed from *two* earlier values in the sequence, x_{i-r} and x_{i-s}, not just the predecessor. r and s are called the long and short lags respectively, and both must be positive and r must be greater than s. The equation for producing the sequence are:

$$\Delta_i = \left(x_{i-r} - x_{i-s} - c_{i-1} \right) \bmod m \text{ where } m \text{ is } 2^n \text{ and } n \text{ is the number of bits in a word.}$$

$$x_i = \Delta_i \text{ and } c_n = 0 \text{ if } \Delta_i\ 0$$

$$x_i = m + \Delta_i \text{ and } c_n = 1 \text{ if } \Delta_i < 0$$

c is a 'carry' that is either 0 or 1 depending on the previous state. The algorithm requires r seed values and an initial value for the carry, c. As with the linear congruential method, the subtract with carry algorithm is very sensitive to the choice of parameter values.

Generators that are Instances of the Subtract with Carry Engine

The ranlux24_base generator class produces random sequences of 24-bit integers with r as 24 and s as 10. The ranlux48_base class generates sequences of 48-bit integers with r as 12 and s as 5. As Figure 8-12 shows, there are two further classes for generators that use the subtract with carry engine, ranlux24 and ranlux48, which are produced by passing ranlux24_base and ranlux48_base to an instance of the discard_block_engine adapter. A ranlux24 instance discards 200 out of each block of 223 values that ranlux24_base produces; a ranlux48 instance discards 378 out of each block of 389 values produced by ranlux48_base so they are both picky about the values they will accept from the underlying source.

Both ranlux24 and ranlux48 are used extensively in Monte Carlo simulations. The ranlux name was originated by Fred James who first implemented the algorithm in Fortran; the name comes from *ran*dom and the *lux*ury of discarding so many values from the underlying sequence. Here's an example of using ranlux24:

```
std::random_device rd;
std::ranlux24 rng {rd()};
std::uniform_real_distribution<long double> d {-5.0L, 5.0L};
for(size_t i {}; i < 8; ++i)
  std::cout << std::setw(5) << d(rng)
            << " ";      // 2.02142 -0.920689 -0.277198 -1.33417 4.70217 -3.31706 -3.32692 4.36376
```

The code is essentially the same as for other generators. The generator object will produce the values it needs for the initial state based on the arguments to the constructor.

Shuffling a Range of Elements

The shuffle() algorithm rearranges the elements in a range into a random permutation. The function template for shuffle() is defined in the algorithm header but I'm including it here because it requires a random number generator. All possible arrangements of the elements are equally likely. The first two arguments to shuffle() are random access iterators that define the range, and the third argument is a function object that is a uniform random number generator that will be used to generate the random sequence. This code illustrates how it works:

```
std::random_device rd;
std::mt19937 rng {rd()};
std::vector<string> words {"one", "two", "three", "four", "five", "six", "seven", "eight"};
for(size_t i {}; i < 4 ; ++i)
{
  std::shuffle(std::begin(words), std::end(words), rng);
  std::for_each(std::begin(words), std::end(words),
                [](const string& word) {std::cout << std::setw(8) << std::left << word; });
  std::cout << std::endl;
}
```

The Mersenne twister engine `rng` is passed as the last argument to the `shuffle()` algorithm in the `for` loop. This rearranges the elements in the `words` container of each iteration. I got this output:

two	seven	three	five	six	eight	one	four
eight	five	seven	six	three	four	one	two
seven	one	five	six	eight	four	two	three
three	four	six	five	seven	one	two	eight

Summary

Generating random number sequences using the STL tools always involves three components:

- A *random number engine* that can generate random bit sequences. There are three class templates that define random number engines:

  - `mersenne_twister_engine` - capable of producing the highest quality sequences but it is the slowest of the three.

  - `linear_congruential_engine` - the simplest and the fastest but lesser quality sequences than the other two engines.

  - `subtract_with_carry_engine` - capable of generating better quality sequences than a `linear_congruential_engine` instance but the state occupies more memory and it's slightly slower.

- A *random number generator* that customizes an engine template to implement a specific algorithm for generating a uniform random sequence of non-negative integers. In addition to the `default_random_engine`, which is implementation defined, there are nine classes that define different generators:

  - `mt19937` and `mt19937_64` from the `mersenne_twister_engine` template.

  - `minstd_rand0`, `minstd_rand`, and `knuth_b` from the `linear_congruential_engine` template.

  - `ranlux24_base`, `ranlux48_base`, `ranlux24`, and `ranlux48` from the `subtract_with_carry_engine` template.

- A *distribution* function object that uses a sequence from a random number generator to generate sequences of integer or floating-point values with a given probability distribution. There are 21 templates that defines distributions - all but one are class templates:

  - Uniform distributions: `uniform_int_distribution`, `uniform_real_distribution`, and the `generate_canonical()` function template.

  - Normal distributions: `normal_distribution`, `lognormal_distribution`, `chi_squared_distribution`, `cauchy_distribution`, `fisher_f_distribution`, and `student_t_distribution`

  - Sampling distributions: `discrete_distribution`, `piecewise_constant_distribution`, and `piecewise_linear_distribution`

- Bernoulli distributions: bernoulli_distribution, geometric_distribution, binomial_distribution, and negative_binomial_distribution

- Poisson distributions: poisson_distribution, gamma_distribution, weibull_distribution, extreme_value_distribution, and exponential_distribution

Some of the random number generator types use a *random number engine adapter* to modify a random sequence from an engine. There are three class templates for engine adapters:

- shuffle_order_engine that is used to define knuth_b.

- discard_block_engine that is used to define ranlux24 and ranlux48.

- independent_bits_engine that is not otherwise applied in the STL.

A random number generator needs one or more seed values to initialize its state. The random_device class defines function objects that can return uniformly distributed sequences of non-negative integers that are nondeterministic in the majority of implementations. These can be used as seed values for a random number generator. To be sure that you will get good quality sequences, you should *not* use random number engines directly - *always* use a random number generator.

EXERCISES

1. Modify Ex8_03 to use the shuffle() algorithm to shuffle the cards before dealing.

2. Extend the solution to the previous exercise to play a game after dealing the four random hands. Each player will play a random card from their hand in turn. Output the cards played in each round and identify the player with the winning card - the winning card being the highest in the sort sequence.

3. Simulate throwing two standard dice using a single discrete distribution so the distribution object generates values for the sum of the two dice. Generate 5000 throws and plot them in a histogram.

4. Write a program to estimate the probability of all possible faces being shown together when throwing six standard dice simultaneously by simulating a large number of throws.

CHAPTER 9

■ ■ ■

Stream Operations

This chapter revisits the stream iterators that I introduced in Chapter 1 and discusses their capabilities in more detail. It also introduces stream buffer iterators and explains how you can use stream and stream buffer iterators in conjunction with other STL capabilities. In this chapter you will learn:

- What function members the stream iterator classes provide.

- How you can read and write individual data items with stream iterators.

- What stream buffer iterators are and how they differ from stream iterators.

- How you can read and write files using stream iterators.

- How you can read and write files using stream buffer iterators.

- What string streams are and the different types of string streams that the STL defines.

- How you can use stream iterators and stream buffer iterators with string streams.

Stream Iterators

As you know, a *stream iterator* is a single pass iterator that reads from a stream if it's an *input stream iterator* or writes to a stream if it's an *output stream iterator*. A stream iterator can only transfer data of one given type to or from a stream. If you want to use a stream iterator to transfer a series of data items of different types, you must arrange to package the data items into an object of a single type, and ensure that a stream insertion and/or extraction operator function for that type exists. Stream iterators are a little strange compared to other iterators. For instance, incrementing an input stream iterator doesn't just shift the iterator to point to the next data item - it reads a value from the stream. Let's get to the details.

Input Stream Iterators

An *input stream iterator* is an *input iterator* that can extract data from a stream in *text mode*, which implies that you cannot use it with binary streams. Two stream iterators are typically used to read all values from a stream: a *begin* iterator that points to the first value to be read and an end iterator that points to the end of the stream. The end iterator is identified when the end-of-file (EOF) stream state for an input stream is recognized. The `istream_iterator` template that is defined in the `iterator` header reads values of type T from a stream using the extraction operator, `>>`. For this to work, there must be an `operator>>()` function overload that reads values of type T from a `istream` object. Because it's an input iterator, an instance of `istream_iterator` is a single pass iterator; it can be used only once. By default the stream is assumed to contain characters of type `char`.

You create an `istream_iterator` object by passing an input stream object to the constructor. There's a copy constructor for duplicating `istream_iterator` objects. Here is an example of creating input stream iterators:

```
std::istream_iterator<string> in {std::cin};    // Reads strings from cin
std::istream_iterator<string> end_in;           // End-of-stream iterator
```

The default constructor creates an object that represents the end of a stream - which is when EOF is recognized.

While by default the stream is assumed to contain characters of type `char`, you can define input stream iterators to read a stream containing characters of another type. For example, here's how you could define stream iterators to read a stream that contains `wchar_t` characters:

```
std::basic_ifstream<wchar_t> file_in {"no_such_file.txt"};    // File stream of wchar_t
std::istream_iterator<std::wstring, wchar_t> in {file_in};    // Reads strings of wchar_t
std::istream_iterator<std::wstring, wchar_t> end_in;          // End-of-stream iterator
```

The first statement defines an input file stream of `wchar_t` characters. I'll remind you of some of the key details of file streams in the next section. The second statement defines a stream iterator for reading the file. The type of characters in the stream is specified by the second template type argument for `istream_iterator`, `wchar_t` in this instance. Of course, the first template type argument that specifies the type of object to be read from the stream now has to be `wstring`, which is the type for strings of `wchar_t` characters.

An `istream_iterator` object has the following function members:

- `operator*()` returns a reference to the current object in the stream. You can apply this operator more than once to reread the same value.

- `operator->()` returns the address of the current object in the stream.

- `operator++()` reads a value from the underlying input stream and stores it in the iterator object. A reference to the iterator object is returned. Thus the value of expression `*++in` will be the latest new value that was stored. This is not typical usage because it potentially skips the first value from the stream.

- `operator++(int)` reads a value from the underlying input stream and stores it in the iterator object, ready to be accessed using `operator*()` or `operator->()`. The function returns a *proxy* for the iterator object before the new value from the stream was stored. This means that the value of the expression `*in++` is the object stored in the iterator before the latest value from the underlying stream was read and stored.

There are also nonmember functions, `operator==()` and `operator!=()`, for comparing two iterator objects of the same type. Two input iterators are equal if they are both iterators for the same stream, or are both end-of-stream iterators; otherwise they are not equal.

Iterators and Stream Iterators

It's important to appreciate that input stream iterators are different from regular iterators in the way that they relate to the sequence of data items. A regular iterator points to an element in an array or a container. Incrementing a regular iterator changes what it points to; this has no effect on other iterators that point to elements in the same sequence. There can be several iterator objects each pointing to different elements in the same sequence. This is not the case with stream iterators.

This is evident when you consider what happens when you use stream iterators to read from the standard input stream; it may not be so obvious when the stream iterators are for files, but it still applies. If you create two input stream iterators that relate to the same stream, they both point to the first data item initially. If you read from the stream using one iterator, the other will no longer reference the first data value. When reading from the standard input stream, the value is *consumed* by the first iterator. This is because the iterator modifies the stream object when it reads a value. An input stream iterator not only changes what it points to - what you get when you dereference it - it also changes the position in the underlying stream that identifies where the next read operation will start. Thus two or more input stream iterators for a given stream *always* point to the next data item that is available from the stream. This implies that a range specified by two input stream iterators can *only* consist of a begin iterator and an end-of-stream iterator; you have no way to create two stream iterators that point to two different values in the same stream. That's not to say you can't use an input stream iterator to access data items one. at a time - as you'll see.

Reading Using Input Stream Function Members

Here's some code that illustrates how you might use the function members to read strings:

```
std::cout << "Enter one or more words. Enter ! to end:\n";
std::istream_iterator<string> in {std::cin};      // Reads strings from cin
std::vector<string> words;
while(true)
{
  string word = *in;
  if(word == "!") break;
  words.push_back(word);
  ++in;
}
std::cout << "You entered " << words.size() << " words." << std::endl;
```

The loop reads words from the standard input stream and adds them to a vector container until "!" is entered. The value of the expression *in is the current `string` object from the underlying stream. ++in causes the next string object to be read from the stream and stored in the iterator, in. Here's an example of the output from executing this code:

```
Enter one or more words. Enter ! to end:
Yes No Maybe !
You entered 3 words.
```

Here's a working example that illustrates how the function members *could* be used to read numerical data, but not necessarily how you *should* use them:

```
// Ex9_01.cpp
// Calling istream_iterator function members
#include <iostream>                                // For standard streams
#include <iterator>                                // For stream iterators

int main()
```

```
{
  std::cout << "Enter some integers - enter Ctrl+Z to end.\n";
  std::istream_iterator<int> iter {std::cin};        // Create begin input stream iterator...
  std::istream_iterator<int> copy_iter {iter};       // ...and a copy
  std::istream_iterator<int> end_iter;               // Create end input stream iterator
  // Read some integers to sum
  int sum {};
  while(iter != end_iter)                            // Continue until Ctrl+Z read
  {
    sum += *iter++;
  }
  std::cout << "Total is " << sum << std::endl;

  std::cin.clear();                                  // Clear EOF state
  std::cin.ignore();                                 // Skip characters

  // Read integers using the copy of the iterator
  std::cout << "Enter some more integers - enter Ctrl+Z to end.\n";
  int product {1};
  while(true)
  {
    if(copy_iter == end_iter) break;                 // Break if Ctrl+Z was read
    product *= *copy_iter++;
  }
  std::cout << "product is " << product << std::endl;

}
```

After displaying the prompt for input, we create an input stream iterator to read values of type int from cin; we then make a copy of the iterator object. We will be able to use the copy, copy_iter, to read input from cin after the original object, iter, has been used, We only need one end iterator object because this never changes. The first loop sums all the values read using the input stream iterator until the EOF stream state is recognized, which is set by reading Ctrl+Z flag from the stream. Dereferencing iter makes the value that it points to available, after which the post-increment operation moves iter to point to the next input. If this is Ctrl+Z, the loop will end.

Before we can read more data from cin, we must reset the EOF flag by calling clear() for the stream object; we also need to skip the '\n' character left in the input buffer, which is done by calling ignore() for the stream object. The second loop uses copy_iter to read values and computes their product. The principle difference from the first loop is that the loop is terminated by comparing copy_iter for equality with end_iter.

Here's an example of the output:

```
Enter some integers - enter Ctrl+Z to end.
1 2 3 4^Z
Total is 10
Enter some more integers - enter Ctrl+Z to end.
3 3 2 5 4^Z
product is 360
```

This is not how you would use an input stream iterator most of the time. Typically, you just use a stream begin and a stream end iterator as arguments to a function. You probably realized that the first loop and the output statement that follows it in Ex9_01 could be replaced by just one statement:

```
std::cout << "Total is " << std::accumulate(iter, end_iter, 0) << std::endl;
```

Here's some code that inserts floating-point values from cin into a container by using an input stream iterator:

```
std::vector<double> data;
std::cout << "Enter some numerical values - enter Ctrl+Z to end.\n";
std::copy(std::istream_iterator<double>{std::cin}, std::istream_iterator<double>{},
          std::back_inserter(data));
```

An arbitrary number of values will be appended to the vector container by the copy() algorithm until Ctrl+Z is read. There's a constructor for a vector container that accepts a range to initialize the elements, so you can read the values using the input stream iterator in the statement that creates the container:

```
std::cout << "Enter some numerical values - enter Ctrl+Z to end.\n";
std::vector<double> data {std::istream_iterator<double>{std::cin},
std::istream_iterator<double>{}};
```

This will read floating-point values from the standard input stream and use them as initial values for the elements in the container.

Output Stream Iterators

Output stream iterators are defined by the ostream_iterator template that has a first template parameter that is the type of value to be written and a second template parameter that is the type of characters in the stream; the second template parameter has a default value of char. An ostream_iterator object is an *output iterator* that can write objects of any type T to an output stream in text mode, as long as operator<<() has been implemented to write a T object to a stream. Because it's an output iterator, it supports pre- and post-increment operations and it is a single pass iterator. An output stream iterator defines its copy-assignment operator so that it writes a T object to a stream using the insertion operator. By default an output stream iterator writes values as sequences of char characters. You can write streams that will contain characters of a different type by specifying the type as the second template type argument An ostream_iterator type defines the following function members:

- *Constructors*: The first constructor creates a begin iterator for an output stream from an ostream object that is the first argument, and a delimiter string that is the second argument. The output stream object writes the delimiter string following each object that it writes to the stream. The second constructor omits the second argument, and it creates an iterator that just writes objects with no following delimiter.

- operator=(const T& obj) writes obj to the stream, then writes the delimiter string if one was specified to the constructor. The function returns a reference to the iterator.

- operator*() does nothing, apart from returning the iterator object. For an iterator to qualify as an output iterator, this operation must be defined.

- operator++() and operator++(int) are defined but do nothing, apart from returning the iterator object. For an iterator to qualify as an output iterator, the pre- and post-increment operations must be supported.

The operator functions that do nothing are essential because they are part of the specification of what you can do with an output iterator. If you write to a stream in text mode that you subsequently intend to read in text mode, you need delimiters between the values in the stream. For this reason, the constructor with two parameters is usually appropriate, although you can write delimiters explicitly.

Writing Using Function Members of an Output Stream Iterator

Here's an example showing various ways in which the function members can be used:

```cpp
// Ex9_02.cpp
// Using output stream iterator function members
#include <iostream>                              // For standard streams
#include <iterator>                              // For iterators and begin() and end()
#include <vector>                                // For vector container
#include <algorithm>                             // For copy() algorithm
#include <string>
using std::string;

int main()
{
  std::vector<string> words {"The", "quick", "brown", "fox", "jumped", "over", "the", "lazy", "dog"};

  // Write the words container using conventional iterator notation
  std::ostream_iterator<string> out_iter1 {std::cout};  // Iterator with no delimiter output
  for(const auto& word : words)
  {
    *out_iter1++ = word;                         // Write a word
    *out_iter1++ = " ";                          // Write a delimiter
  }
  *out_iter1++ = "\n";                           // Write newline

  // Write the words container again using the iterator
  for(const auto& word : words)
  {
    (out_iter1 = word) = " ";                    // Write the word and delimiter
  }
  out_iter1 = "\n";                              // Write newline

  // Write the words container using copy()
  std::ostream_iterator<string> out_iter2 {std::cout, " "};
  std::copy(std::begin(words), std::end(words), out_iter2);
  out_iter2 = "\n";
}
```

This writes the elements of the words container to the standard output stream in three different ways. The out_iter1 stream iterator is created by calling the constructor with just the output stream as the argument. The first loop uses conventional output iterator notation, incrementing the iterator after dereferencing it and copying the current value of word to the result of dereferencing out_iter1. A newline is written to the stream by the statement that follows the loop. Note that you cannot write this as:

```
out_iter1 = '\n';                                                  // Won't compile!
```

The iterator was defined to write string objects to a stream, so it cannot write any other type of data. The operator=() member will only accept an argument that is a string, so the statement will not compile.

As I described earlier, the operator*() member and the pre- and post-increment operators do nothing apart from returning a reference to the iterator. Thus you could dispense with these operations and produce the same output without them, as the statement in the second loop demonstrates. The parentheses in the statement are essential to ensure the second assignment operation that applies to the delimiter has the output iterator as its left operand.

The third line of output is produced by the copy() algorithm in the way you have seen in previous chapters. The values of the elements are copied to out_iter2, which is defined with a second constructor argument that specifies the delimiter string that is to follow each output value.

Overloading the Insertion and Extraction Operators

You must overload the insertion and extraction operators for any class type that you want to use with the stream iterators. This is easy for your own classes. You can provide get and set functions to access any private or public data members as necessary, or you can just specify the operator functions as friend functions. Here's a trivial example of a class that represents a name that illustrates this:

```
class Name
{
private:
  std::string first_name{};
  std::string second_name{};
public:
  Name() = default;
  Name(const std::string& first, const std::string& second) :
                                       first_name{first}, second_name {second} {}
  friend std::istream& operator>>(std::istream& in, Name& name);
  friend std::ostream& operator<<(std::ostream& out, const Name& name);
};

// Extraction operator for Name objects
inline std::istream& operator>>(std::istream& in, Name& name)
{ return in >> name.first_name >> name.second_name; }

// Insertion operator for Name objects
inline std::ostream& operator<<(std::ostream& out, const Name& name)
{ return out << name.first_name << ' ' << name.second_name; }
```

With the operator overloads defined here, you can read and write name objects using stream iterators, like this for example:

```
std::cout << "Enter names as first-name second-name. Enter Ctrl+Z on a separate line to end:\n";
std::vector<Name> names {std::istream_iterator<Name> {std::cin},
                         std::istream_iterator<Name>{}};
std::copy(std::begin(names), std::end(names), std::ostream_iterator<Name>{std::cout, " "});
```

The names container will be initialized with as many Name objects as you enter until Ctrl+Z is entered to end input. The copy() algorithm copies Name objects to the destination represented by the output stream iterator, which will write the objects to the standard output stream. Writing the first name and second names as we have here will prevent the alignment of names in columns by specifying a field width. For example, this won't work very well:

```
for(const auto& name: names)
  std::cout << std::setw(20) << name << std::endl;
```

The idea is to output the names aligned in a single column. This will not work because the width specification will only apply to the first_name member. You can allow this by changing the operator<<() function so that it concatenates the names before writing them out:

```
inline std::ostream& operator<<(std::ostream& out, const Name& name)
{ return out << name.first_name + ' ' + name.second_name; }
```

This is less efficient than the original because of the temporary string objects that are created along the way, but it does allow the previous loop to work as required.

Occasionally, you may want to treat output differently, depending on whether or not the destination is a file. For example, you might want to include additional information in output to the standard output stream that you don't want to include when you are writing to a file. You can accommodate this by testing the actual type of the ostream object:

```
inline std::ostream& operator<<(std::ostream& out, const Name& name)
{
  if(typeid(out) != typeid(std::ostream))
    return out << name.first_name << " " << name.second_name;
  else
    return out << "Name: " << name.first_name << ' ' << name.second_name;
}
```

Now a name is prefixed with "Name: " only when it is written to a stream that is an ostream object. For output to a file stream, or other type of stream derived from ostream, the prefix is omitted.

Using Stream Iterators with Files

The stream iterators have no knowledge of the nature of the underlying stream. Of course, they only work with streams in text mode, but otherwise they don't care what the data is. Any kind of stream can be read or written in text mode using stream iterators. This means that among other things you can use stream iterators to read and write *files* in text mode. Before I get into the specifics of using stream iterators with files, I'll remind you of some of the essential characteristics of file streams, and how you create stream objects that encapsulate files.

File Streams

A *file stream* encapsulates a physical file. A file stream has a *length*, which is the number of characters in the stream, so it's 0 for a new output file; it has a *beginning*, which is the index of the first character in the stream - index 0; and it has an *end*, which is the index one beyond the last character in the stream. It also has a *current position*, which is the index of where the next read or write operation will start. You can transfer data to and from a stream in *text mode* or in *binary mode*.

In *text mode*, the data is a sequence of characters. Data can be read or written using the extraction and insertion operators so for input at least, data items must be separated by one or more whitespace characters. Data is often written as a succession of lines terminated by '\n'. Some systems, such as Microsoft Windows, transform newline characters as they're read or written. Microsoft Windows writes a newline character as *two* characters: a carriage return and a line feed. When a carriage return and a line feed are read, they're mapped into a single character, '\n'. On other systems, the newline is written and read as a single character. Thus the length of a file input stream can depend on the system environment in which it originated.

In *binary mode*, bytes are transferred between memory and the stream without conversion. The stream iterators *only* work in text mode so you cannot use a stream iterator to read or write a binary file. *Stream buffer iterators*, which I'll explain later in this chapter, *can* read and write binary files.

Although binary mode operations transfer bytes to and from memory unchanged, there are still pitfalls when it comes to processing a binary file that was written on a different system. One consideration is the *endianness* of the system that wrote the file versus the endianness of the system reading the file. The endianness determine the order in which the bytes from a word in memory are written. In a *little-endian* processor, such as an x86 processor from Intel, the least significant bytes are in the lowest address, so bytes are written in the sequence from the least significant to the most significant. In a *big-endian* processor such as an IBM mainframe, bytes are in the opposite sequence with the most significant bytes in the low order address so they will appear in a file in the opposite sequence to a little-endian processor. Thus when you are reading a binary file from a big-endian system on a little-endian system, you need to account for the difference in byte order.

■ **Note**   *Big-endian byte order* is also known as *network byte order* because data is generally transmitted over the Internet in big-endian order.

File Stream Class Templates

There are three class templates that represent file streams: ifstream that represents a file input stream, ofstream that defines file streams for output, and fstream that defines file streams you can both read and write. The class hierarchy for these is shown in Figure 9-1.

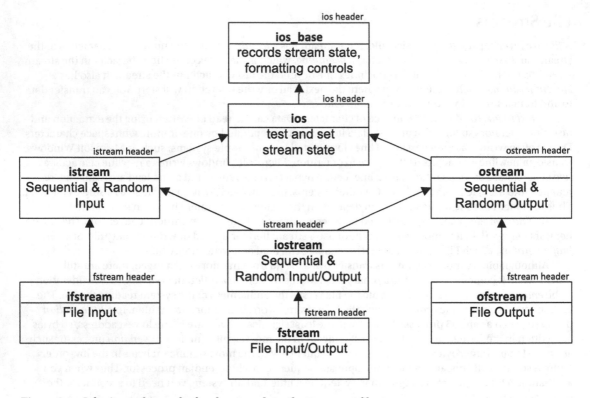

Figure 9-1. *Inheritance hierarchy for class templates that represent file streams*

The file stream templates inherit from istream and/or ostream so in text mode they work in the same way as the standard streams. What you can do with a file stream is determined by its open mode, which you specify by combinations of the following constants that are defined in the ios_base class:

- binary sets binary mode. If binary mode is not set - which is the default, the mode is text mode.

- app: moves to the end of the file before each write (***app***end operation).

- ate moves to the end of the file after opening it (***a***t ***t***he ***e***nd).

- in opens the file for reading. This is the default for an ifstream object and an fstream object.

- out opens the file for writing. This is the default for an ostream object and an fstream object.

- trunc truncates the existing file to zero length.

File stream objects are created in text mode by default; to get binary mode, you must specify the binary constant. Text mode operations use the >> and << operators to read and write data, and numerical values are converted to a character representation before they are written to a stream. In binary mode there's no data conversion; bytes in memory are written directly to the file. When you specify a name for a file that does not exist as an argument to the ofstream constructor, the file will be created. If you don't specify app or ate when you create or open a file output stream object, any existing file contents will be overwritten.

The dictionary.txt file that is read by some of the working examples in this chapter is included in the code download. This is a file written in text mode in the Microsoft Windows environment but the examples should still read it if you execute it in a different environment. The examples use Microsoft Windows paths on drive G:. I did this to make it more than likely you will need to change these to suit your system environment. This puts the onus on you to make sure you don't overwrite files that matter.

File Input Using a Stream Iterator

Once you have created a file stream object for reading a file, accessing the data using a stream iterator is essentially the same as reading from the standard input stream. We can write a program to find anagrams of a word by looking them up in a dictionary file that is in the code download. In this case we will read all the words from the dictionary file into a container using a stream iterator. Here's the code:

```cpp
// Ex9_03.cpp
// Finding anagrams of a word
#include <iostream>                    // For standard streams
#include <fstream>                     // For file streams
#include <iterator>                    // For iterators and begin() and end()
#include <string>                      // For string class
#include <set>                         // For set container
#include <vector>                      // For vector container
#include <algorithm>                   // For next_permutation()
using std::string;

int main()
{
  // Read words from the file into a set container
  string file_in {"G:/Beginning_STL/dictionary.txt"};
  std::ifstream in {file_in};
  if(!in)
  {
    std::cerr << file_in << " not open." << std::endl;
    exit(1);
  }
  std::set<string> dictionary {std::istream_iterator<string>(in),
                               std::istream_iterator<string>()};
  std::cout << dictionary.size() << " words in dictionary." << std::endl;

  std::vector<string> words;
  string word;
  while(true)
  {
    std::cout << "\nEnter a word, or Ctrl+z to end: ";
    if((std::cin >> word).eof()) break;
    string word_copy {word};
    do
```

```
  {
    if(dictionary.count(word))
      words.push_back(word);
    std::next_permutation(std::begin(word), std::end(word));
  } while(word != word_copy);

  std::copy(std::begin(words), std::end(words), std::ostream_iterator<string>{std::cout, " "});
  std::cout << std::endl;
  words.clear();                                          // Remove previous permutations
  }
  in.close();                                            // Close the file
}
```

There are over 100,000 words in the dictionary file so it may take a few seconds to read it. An ifstream object is created using the full path to the file, dictionary.txt. This is a text file containing a reasonable number of different words that can be searched to check for anagrams. The entire file contents are used as initial values for a set container. As you know, a set container will store the words in ascending sequence and each word in the container is its own key. The words container stores anagrams of a word entered from cin. Each word is read in the first if expression in the while loop. This calls eof() for the stream object, which will return true when Ctrl+Z is entered. Rearrangements of the letters in the input word are created by calling the next_permutation() algorithm in the inner do-while loop. Calling count() for each permutation, including the first, determines whether the word is in the dictionary container. If it is, the word is appended to the words container. The do-while loop ends when the permutation returns to the original word. When all the anagrams of a word have been found, the words are written to cout using the copy() algorithm with an output stream iterator as the destination. If you expected more than eight anagrams to occur, you could produce the output over multiple lines using a loop:

```
size_t count {}, max {8};
for(const auto& wrd : words)
  std::cout << wrd << ((++count % max == 0) ? '\n' : ' ');
```

Here's some sample output:

```
109582 words in dictionary.

Enter a word, or Ctrl+z to end: realist
realist retails saltier slatier tailers

Enter a word, or Ctrl+z to end: painter
painter pertain repaint

Enter a word, or Ctrl+z to end: dog
dog god

Enter a word, or Ctrl+z to end: ^Z
```

Repeated File Reads Using a Stream Iterator

Of course, if the dictionary file was very large, you might not want to read it all into memory. In this case you could use stream iterators to reread the file each time you want to look for an anagram. Here's a version that does that - although its performance is not exactly impressive:

```cpp
// Ex9_04.cpp
// Finding anagrams of a word by re-reading the dictionary file

// include directives & using directive as Ex9_03.cpp...

int main()
{
  string file_in {"G:/Beginning_STL/dictionary.txt"};
  std::ifstream in {file_in};
  if(!in)
  {
    std::cerr << file_in << " not open." << std::endl;
    exit(1);
  }
  auto end_iter = std::istream_iterator<string> {};

  std::vector<string> words;
  string word;
  while(true)
  {
    std::cout << "\nEnter a word, or Ctrl+z to end: ";
    if((std::cin >> word).eof()) break;
    string word_copy {word};
    do
    {
      in.seekg(0);                                      // File position at beginning

      // Use find() algorithm to read the file to check for an anagram
      if(std::find(std::istream_iterator<string>(in), end_iter, word) != end_iter)
        words.push_back(word);
      else
        in.clear();                                     // Reset EOF

      std::next_permutation(std::begin(word), std::end(word));
    } while(word != word_copy);

    std::copy(std::begin(words), std::end(words), std::ostream_iterator<string>{std::cout, " "});
    std::cout << std::endl;
    words.clear();                                      // Remove previous permutations
  }
  in.close();                                           // Close the file
}
```

The end stream iterator does not change, so it's defined as end_iter to allow it to be used more than once. The loop is basically the same except that the find() algorithm is used to discover whether a given permutation is in the file and therefore an anagram. The file position needs to be the first character position and calling seekg() for the file stream object ensures that this is the case. The first two arguments to find() are istream_iterator<string> objects that define a range that is from the current file position - which was set to the beginning - to the end of the file. The find() algorithm returns an iterator pointing to the element matching the third argument, or the end iterator if it is not present. Thus when find() returns the end stream iterator, word was not found; any other iterator returned means that it was found. It's essential to call clear() for the file stream object to clear the EOF flag when word is not found. If you don't subsequent attempts to read the file will fail because the EOF flag is set.

Here's some sample output that demonstrates that it works:

```
Enter a word, or Ctrl+z to end: rate
rate tare tear erat

Enter a word, or Ctrl+z to end: rat
rat tar art

Enter a word, or Ctrl+z to end: god
god dog

Enter a word, or Ctrl+z to end: ^Z
```

I chose to enter short words because the process of checking for an anagram is *painfully* slow. A word of n characters has n! permutations. Checking whether a permutation is in the file requires up to 100,000 or so read operations, depending on whether it's there. Therefore checking a word such as "retain" requires over 7 million read operations, so that's one reason why it's a slow process. An istream_iterator<T> object reads T objects from a stream one at a time so if there are a lot of objects, it's always going to be slow. Ex9_03.cpp is much faster that Ex9_04.cpp once the file has been read to initialize the set container because all subsequent operations are with the dictionary words in memory. A second reason why Ex9_03.cpp is faster is that accessing a set container involves a binary search, which is O(log n); accessing the file serially involves reading every word starting from the first until a match is found, which is O(n). If the data in a file is ordered (which the words in dictionary.txt are), you could use a binary search technique to find a data item. In this case using a stream iterator is superfluous because you will always be reading single words, which you can do more easily using the >> operator with the stream object. However, this is not easy to implement because the words are not the same size.

File Output Using a Stream Iterator

Writing to a file is no different from writing to the standard output stream. For example, you could use stream iterators to duplicate the contents of the dictionary.txt file, like this:

```
// Ex9_05.cpp
// Copying file contents using stream iterators
#include <iostream>                          // For standard streams
#include <fstream>                           // For file streams
#include <iterator>                          // For iterators and begin() and end()
#include <string>                            // For string class
using std::string;
```

```cpp
int main()
{
  string file_in {"G:/Beginning_STL/dictionary.txt"};
  std::ifstream in {file_in};
  if(!in)
  {
    std::cerr << file_in << " not open." << std::endl;
    exit(1);
  }
  string file_out {"G:/Beginning_STL/dictionary_copy.txt"};
  std::ofstream out {file_out, std::ios_base::out | std::ios_base::trunc };
  std::copy(std::istream_iterator<string> {in}, std::istream_iterator<string> {},
                                      std::ostream_iterator<string> {out, " "});
  in.clear();                                           // Clear EOF
  std::cout << "Original file length: " << in.tellg() << std::endl;
  std::cout << "File copy length: " << out.tellp() << std::endl;
  in.close();
  out.close();
}
```

This program copies the words from the input file to the output file, separating the words in the output with a space. This program always overwrites the contents of the output file. Here's the output that I got:

```
Original file length: 1154336
File copy length: 1154336
```

The output file stream has the open mode flag ios_base::trunc specified in addition to the ios_base::out flag, so the file will be truncated if it already exists. This prevents an ever-increasing file from being created if you run the example several times. If you inspect the contents of dictionary.txt with an editor, you'll see that the words are separated by a single space. We write the file copy with a single space between words, so the files are the same length. However, if the words in the original file were separated by two or more spaces, the file copy would be shorter. To be sure that you duplicate the original file exactly using stream iterators, you must read the file character by character, and prevent the >> operator from ignoring whitespace. Here's how you could do that:

```cpp
std::copy(std::istream_iterator<char>{in >> std::noskipws}, std::istream_iterator<char>{},
                                      std::ostream_iterator<char> {out});
```

This copies the in stream as characters, including whitespace. You could duplicate the file much faster with *stream buffer iterators*, which I'll explain later in this chapter.

Stream Iterators and Algorithms

You have already seen that you can use algorithms such as find() and copy()with stream iterators. You can use stream iterators to specify the data source for *any* algorithm that accepts input iterators to specify the data source. If an algorithm requires forward, bidirectional, or random access iterators to define the input, you can't use stream iterators. When an algorithm accepts an output iterator as a destination, it can be an output stream iterator. Here's an example that uses the count_if() algorithm with stream iterators to determine the frequency with which words with the same initial letter occur in dictionary.txt:

```cpp
// Ex9_06.cpp
// Using count_if() with stream iterators to count word frequencies
#include <iostream>                              // For standard streams
#include <iterator>                              // For iterators and begin() and end()
#include <iomanip>                               // For stream manipulators
#include <fstream>                               // For ifstream
#include <algorithm>                             // For count_if()
#include <string>
using std::string;

int main()
{
  string file_in {"G:/Beginning_STL/dictionary.txt"};
  std::ifstream in {file_in};
  if(!in)
  {
    std::cerr << file_in << " not open." << std::endl;
    exit(1);
  }
  string letters {"abcdefghijklmnopqrstuvwxyz"};
  const size_t perline {9};
  for(auto ch : letters)
  {
    std::cout << ch << ": "
      << std::setw(5)
      << std::count_if(std::istream_iterator<string>{in}, std::istream_iterator<string>{},
                                           [&ch](const string& s)
                                           { return s[0] == ch; })
      << (((ch - 'a' + 1) % perline) ? " " : "\n");
    in.clear();                                  // Clear EOF...
    in.seekg(0);                                 // ... and back to the beginning
  }
  std::cout << std::endl;
}
```

I got this output:

```
a:  6541 b:  6280 c: 10324 d:  6694 e:  4494 f:  4701 g:  3594 h:  3920 i:  4382
j:  1046 k:   964 l:  3363 m:  5806 n:  2475 o:  2966 p:  8448 q:   577 r:  6804
s: 12108 t:  5530 u:  3312 v:  1825 w:  2714 x:    79 y:   370 z:   265
```

This program demonstrate the count_if() algorithm using stream iterators, but it's very inefficient. The for loop iterates over the characters in letter and calls count_if() on each iteration to count the number of words beginning with the current letter by iterating over all the words in the file. Since the input file is ordered, there's no need to read the entire file each time. We could get the same result much faster using the for_each() algorithm:

```
std::map <char, size_t> word_counts;          // Stores word count for each initial letter
size_t perline {9};                           // Outputs per line

// Get the words counts for each initial letter
std::for_each(std::istream_iterator<string>{in}, std::istream_iterator<string>{},
                      [&word_counts](const string& s) {word_counts[s[0]]++;});

  std::for_each(std::begin(word_counts), std::end(word_counts),      // Write out the counts
                      [perline](const std::pair<char, size_t>& pr)
                      { std::cout << pr.first << ": "
                                      << std::setw(5) << pr.second
                                      << (((pr.first - 'a' + 1) % perline) ? " " : "\n");
                      });
  std::cout << std::endl;
```

The first call of the for_each() algorithm iterates over the words in the file and stores a new pair in the word_counts container the first time a word with a given initial letter is passed to the lambda expression. When a word is met with an initial letter that has been found previously, the value for the pair is incremented. The second for_each() call outputs the elements from the map. The file is processed only once, so it's around 26 times faster than the previous version.

The generate_n() algorithm works with a stream iterator. Here's how you could pass a stream iterator to an algorithm to create a file containing a series of numbers in Fibonacci sequence, then read the file to verify that it works:

```
// Ex9_07.cpp
// Using stream iterators to write Fibonacci numbers to a file
#include <iostream>              // For standard streams
#include <iterator>             // For iterators and begin() and end()
#include <iomanip>              // For stream manipulators
#include <fstream>              // For fstream
#include <algorithm>            // For generate_n() and for_each()
#include <string>
using std::string;

int main()
{
  string file_name {"G:/Beginning_STL/fibonacci.txt"};
  std::fstream fibonacci {file_name, std::ios_base::in | std::ios_base::out |
  std::ios_base::trunc};
  if(!fibonacci)
  {
    std::cerr << file_name << " not open." << std::endl;
    exit(1);
  }
  unsigned long long first {0ULL}, second {1ULL};
  auto iter = std::ostream_iterator<unsigned long long> {fibonacci, " "};
  (iter = first) = second;                             // Write the first two values
```

```
  const size_t n {50};
  std::generate_n(iter, n, [&first, &second]
  { auto result = first + second;
  first = second;
  second = result;
  return result; });
  fibonacci.seekg(0);                                          // Back to file beginning
  std::for_each(std::istream_iterator<unsigned long long> {fibonacci},
    std::istream_iterator<unsigned long long> {},
    [](unsigned long long k)
  { const size_t perline {6};
  static size_t count {};
  std::cout << std::setw(12) << k << ((++count % perline) ? " " : "\n");
  });
  std::cout << std::endl;
  fibonacci.close();                                           // Close the file
}
```

This uses an fstream object to encapsulate the file, and the file won't exist initially. An fstream object can both write and read the file and by default it will only open the file if it exists. Specifying ios_base::trunc as an open mode flag causes the file to be created if it does not already exist, and causes the contents to be truncated if it does. Fibonacci numbers grow quickly, so I use unsigned long long as the type for the values, and limited the number to 50, in addition to the first two. The first two numbers are defined in first and second and these are written to the file using iter, which is an output stream iterator. This leaves the file position at one past the value of second in the file so the 50 values written by the generate_n() algorithm will follow. After the values have been written, seekg() (*seek* for *g*etting data) is called to set the file back to the beginning, ready to be read. You would use seekp() (*seek* for *p*utting data) to reset the file position to write it.

The contents of the file are written to the standard output stream using the for_each() algorithm. The lambda expression writes six values to a line. You could use generate_n() to write a sequence of values of any type to a file that you can produce with a function object. Suppose that you needed a file of random temperature values with a normal distribution as a test data source. Here's how you could do that using stream iterators and generate_n():

```
// Ex9_08.cpp
// Using stream iterators to create a file of random temperatures
#include <iostream>                    // For standard streams
#include <iterator>                    // For iterators and begin() and end()
#include <iomanip>                     // For stream manipulators
#include <fstream>                     // For file streams
#include <algorithm>                   // For generate_n() and for_each()
#include <random>                      // For distributions and random number generator
#include <string>                      // For string class
using std::string;
```

```
int main()
{
  string file_name {"G:/Beginning_STL/temperatures.txt"};
  std::ofstream temps_out {file_name, std::ios_base::out | std::ios_base::trunc};
  const size_t n {50};                          // Number of temperatures required

  std::random_device rd;                        // Non-determistic source
  std::mt19937 rng {rd()};                       // Mersenne twister generator
  double mu {50.0}, sigma {15.0};                // Mean: 50 degrees SD: 15
  std::normal_distribution<> normal {mu, sigma}; // Create distribution

  // Write random temperatures to the file
  std::generate_n(std::ostream_iterator<double> { temps_out, " "}, n,
    [&rng, &normal]
  { return normal(rng); });
  temps_out.close();                             // Close the output file

  // List the contents of the file
  std::ifstream temps_in {file_name};            // Open the file to read it
  for_each(std::istream_iterator<double> {temps_in}, std::istream_iterator<double> {},
    [](double t)
      { const size_t perline {10};
        static size_t count {};
        std::cout << std::fixed << std::setprecision(2) << std::setw(5) << t
                  << ((++count % perline) ? " " : "\n");
    });
  std::cout << std::endl;
  temps_in.close();                              // Close the input file
}
```

I got the following output:

```
59.61 53.71 42.76 61.45 48.43 43.48 59.09 36.76 62.12 35.13
55.85 58.72 35.34 39.95 49.31 33.42 41.88 46.63 57.89 32.39
52.36 49.56 68.11 44.49 49.72 48.30 33.48 77.92 58.02 19.17
47.75 31.14 24.13 37.18 44.04 30.64 65.47 55.15 68.73 54.17
62.88 35.45 70.11  9.67 25.89 39.71 72.83 90.08 57.25 51.40
```

The way this works parallels the previous example, Ex9_07, except that the file is created using an ofstream object, then read using an ifstream object. The lambda expression that is the last argument to generate_n() produces the values that are written to the file; it returns random floating-point temperatures that are normally distributed with a mean of 50 and a standard deviation of 15. The normal object defines the distribution and the rng object is the random number generator. Although you can use stream iterators with generate_n(), you *can't* use them with the generate() algorithm because it requires forward iterators.

Stream Buffer Iterators

Stream buffer iterators are different from stream iterators in that they only transfer *characters* to or from a *stream buffer*. They access the buffer for a stream directly, so the insertion and extraction operators are not involved. There's no data conversion and there's no need for delimiters in the data, although if there are delimiters you can deal with them yourself. Because they read or write characters with no data conversion, stream buffer iterators can work with binary files. Stream buffer iterators are faster than stream iterators for reading or writing characters. The `istreambuf_iterator` template defines input iterators and the `ostreambuf_iterator` template defines output iterators. You can construct stream buffer iterators that read or write characters of any of the types `char`, `wchar_t`, `char16_t`, or `char32_t`.

Input Stream Buffer Iterators

To create an input stream buffer iterator to read characters of a given type from a stream, you pass the stream object to the constructor:

```
std::istreambuf_iterator<char> in {std::cin};
```

This object is an input stream buffer iterator that will read characters of type `char` from the standard input stream. An object that represents the end-of-stream iterator is produced by the default constructor:

```
std::istreambuf_iterator<char> end_in;
```

You could use these two iterators to read a sequence of characters from `cin` into a `string` until `Ctrl+Z` is entered on a separate line to signal the end of the stream - for example:

```
std::cout << "Enter something: ";
string rubbish {in, end_in};
std::cout << rubbish << std::endl;               // Whatever you enter will be output
```

The `string` object, `rubbish`, will be initialized with all the characters you enter from the keyboard until the end of stream is recognized.

An input stream buffer iterator has the following function members:

- `operator*()` returns a copy of the current character in the stream. The stream position is not advanced so you can obtain the current character repeatedly.

- `operator->()` accesses a member of the current character - if it has members.

- `operator++()` and `operator++(int)` both move the stream position to the next character. `operator++()` returns the stream iterator after moving the position and `operator++(int)` returns a *proxy* for the stream iterator as it was before moving the position. The prefix ++ operator is rarely used.

- `equal()` accepts an argument that is another input stream buffer iterator and returns `true` if neither the current iterator nor the argument are end-of-stream iterators, or both are end-of-stream iterators. If only one of them is an end-of-stream iterator, `false` is returned.

There are also nonmember functions, operator==() and operator!=(), which compare two iterators. You are not obliged to depend on the end of stream to terminate input. You can use the increment and dereference operators to read characters from a stream until a specific character is found. For example:

```
std::istreambuf_iterator<char> in {std::cin};
std::istreambuf_iterator<char> end_in;
char end_ch {'*'};
string rubbish;
while(in != end_in && *in != end_ch) rubbish += *in++;
std::cout << rubbish << std::endl;                    // Whatever you entered up to '*' or EOF
```

The while loop reads character from cin until either the end of stream is recognized, or until an asterisk is entered followed by the Enter key. The dereference operator applied to in in the loop body returns the current character in the stream, then the postfix increment operator moves the iterator to point to the next character. Note that dereferencing in in the loop expression demonstrates that it does not change the iterator; as long as it's not '*', the same character is read again in the loop body before the iterator is incremented.

Output Stream Buffer Iterators

You can create an ostreambuf_iterator object to write characters of a given type to a stream by passing a stream object to the constructor:

```
string file_name {"G:/Beginning_STL/junk.txt"};
std::ofstream junk_out {file_name};
std::ostreambuf_iterator<char> out {junk_out};
```

The out object can write characters of type char to the file output stream junk_out, which encapsulates the file with the name junk.txt. To write characters of a different type, such as char32_t for example, you just specify the template type argument as the character type. Of course, the stream must be created for the character type so you can't use ofstream because ofstream is an alias for type basic_ofstream<char>. Here's an example of how you could do it:

```
string file_name {"G:/Beginning_STL/words.txt"};
std::basic_ofstream<char32_t> words_out {file_name};
std::ostreambuf_iterator<char32_t> out {words_out};
```

This stream buffer iterator can write Unicode characters to the stream buffer. A file stream for characters of type wchar_t is defined by the alias wofstream.

You can also create an output stream buffer object by passing the address of a stream buffer to the constructor. You can produce object out above by writing:

```
std::ostreambuf_iterator<char> out {junk_out.rdbuf()};
```

The rdbuf() member of the ofstream object returns the address of the internal buffer for the stream. The rdbuf() member is inherited from ios_base, which is a base class for all stream objects.

An `ostreambuf_iterator` object has the following function members:

- `operator=()` writes the character that is the argument to the stream buffer. If EOF is recognized, which will be when the stream buffer is full, the write operation fails.

- `failed()` returns `true` when a previous write to the buffer failed. This will be when EOF is recognized because the output stream buffer was full.

- `operator*()` does nothing. This is defined because it is required for an `ostreambuf_iterator` object to be an output iterator.

- `operator++()` and `operator++(int)` do nothing. These are defined because they are required for an `ostreambuf_iterator` object to be an output iterator.

The only function member you are usually concerned with is the assignment operator. Here's one way to use it:

```
string ad {"Now is the discount of our winter tents!\n"};
std::ostreambuf_iterator<char> iter {std::cout};      // Iterator for output to cout
for(auto ch: ad)
  iter = ch;                                          // Write the character to the stream
```

Executing this code fragment writes the string to the standard output stream character by character. Of course, you can obtain the same result by using the `copy()` algorithm:

```
std::copy(std::begin(ad), std::end(ad), std::ostreambuf_iterator<char> {std::cout});
```

I'm sure you know that both examples are ludicrous ways of coding the equivalent of the following statement:

```
std::cout << ad;
```

It doesn't tell you much about output stream buffer iterators though...

Using Stream Buffer Iterators with File Streams

You can use stream buffer iterators to copy a file character by character with none of the overhead of formatted reads and writes. Here's a program that copies `dictionary.txt`:

```
// Ex9_09.cpp
// Copying a file using stream buffer iterators
#include <iostream>                                // For standard streams
#include <iterator>                                // For iterators and begin() and end()
#include <fstream>                                 // For file streams
#include <string>                                  // For string class
using std::string;

int main()
{
  string file_name {"G:/Beginning_STL/dictionary.txt"};
  std::ifstream file_in {file_name};
  if(!file_in)
```

```
{
  std::cerr << file_name << " not open." << std::endl;
  exit(1);
}
string file_copy {"G:/Beginning_STL/dictionary_copy.txt"};
std::ofstream file_out {file_copy, std::ios_base::out | std::ios_base::trunc};

std::istreambuf_iterator<char> in {file_in};           // Input stream buffer iterator
std::istreambuf_iterator<char> end_in;                 // End of stream buffer iterator
std::ostreambuf_iterator<char> out {file_out};         // Output stream buffer iterator
while(in != end_in)
  out = *in++;                                         // Copy character from in to out

std::cout << "File copy completed." << std::endl;

file_in.close();                                       // Close the file
file_out.close();                                      // Close the file
}
```

This copies the file encapsulated by the ifstream object, file_in, to the file encapsulated by the ofstream object, file_out. The input file is copied by copying the input file stream buffer to the output file stream buffer character by character. The while loop does the copying using stream buffer objects in and out. Dereferencing in returns the current character in the input buffer and the postfix ++ operator advances the iterator to the next character in the input buffer. The assignment operation for the output stream buffer object stores the character that is the right operand in the output stream buffer and advances the iterator to the next position in the output buffer.

This demonstrates using the function members of the stream buffer object directly but you could use the copy() algorithm. You could replace the while loop and the statements that define in, end_in, and out with a single statement:

```
std::copy(std::istreambuf_iterator<char> {file_in}, std::istreambuf_iterator<char> {},
                                    std::ostreambuf_iterator<char>{file_out});
```

This copies the range specified by the first two iterators to the destination that is the iterator specified by the third argument. The file buffers represent windows on the entire file streams and these are adjusted when necessary. Thus when an input buffer has been read it is replenished from the stream, and when an output buffer is full, it is written to the output stream.

The stream buffer iterators don't care how the original file was written. You could define the file streams as streams of wchar_t characters, which are two byte characters, like this:

```
std::wifstream file_in {file_name};
std::wofstream file_out {file_copy, std::ios_base::out | std::ios_base::trunc};
```

You can then copy the original file as wchar_t characters:

```
std::copy(std::istreambuf_iterator<wchar_t>{file_in}, std::istreambuf_iterator<wchar_t>{},
                                    std::ostreambuf_iterator<wchar_t> {file_out});
```

It's only necessary to change the template type parameter for the stream buffer iterators.

String Streams and Stream and Stream Buffer Iterators

You can use stream iterators and stream buffer iterators to transfer data to and from a *string stream*. String streams are objects that represent character buffers in memory for I/O and are instances of one of three templates that are defined in the sstream header:

- basic_istringstream that supports reading data from a character buffer in memory.

- basic_ostringstream that supports writing data to a character buffer in memory.

- basic_stringstream that supports both input and output operations on a character buffer.

The character data type is a template parameter and there are type aliases for string streams for type char: istringstream, ostringstream, and stringstream. The inheritance hierarchy for these are shown in Figure 9-2.

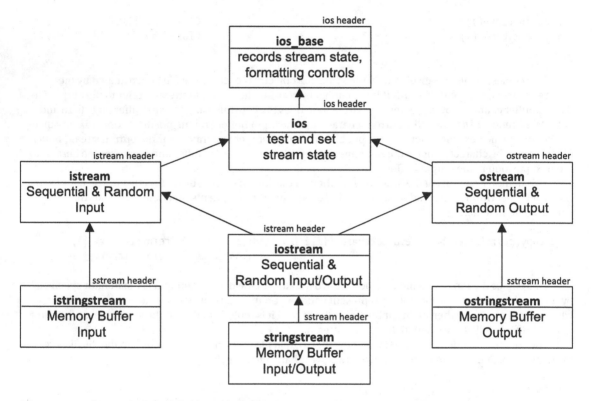

Figure 9-2. *Inheritance hierarchy for string stream types*

I'm sure you'll notice that the direct and indirect base classes are the same as those for the file stream types. This means that almost anything you can do with a file stream, you can also do with a string stream. You can perform formatted I/O with string streams using the insertion and extraction operators; this means you can read or write them using stream iterators. They also support the unformatted I/O operations that file streams support so you can read or write them using stream buffer iterators.

There are aliases for string stream types to store characters of type wchar_t; the names for these are the names of the char aliases prefixed by 'w'. I'll only use string streams for type char because they are most commonly required.

Being able to perform I/O operations on buffers in memory offers huge flexibility. When you need to read data many times, it's going to be much faster reading from a buffer in memory than from an external device. One circumstance where this arises is when the content of an input stream is variable, and you need to read it several times to figure out what the data is. I can demonstrate using a string stream with stream buffer iterators with a new version of Ex9_03.cpp:

```cpp
// Ex9_10.cpp
// Using a string stream as the dictionary source to anagrams of a word
#include <iostream>                              // For standard streams
#include <fstream>                               // For file streams
#include <iterator>                              // For iterators and begin() and end()
#include <string>                                // For string class
#include <set>                                   // For set container
#include <vector>                                // For vector container
#include <algorithm>                             // For next_permutation()
#include <sstream>                               // For string streams
using std::string;

int main()
{
  string file_in {"G:/Beginning_STL/dictionary.txt"};
  std::ifstream in {file_in};
  if(!in)
  {
    std::cerr << file_in << " not open." << std::endl;
    exit(1);
  }
  std::stringstream instr;                       // String stream for file contents
  std::copy(std::istreambuf_iterator<char>{in}, std::istreambuf_iterator<char>(),
                                std::ostreambuf_iterator<char>{instr});
  in.close();                                    // Close the file

  std::vector<string> words;
  string word;
  auto end_iter = std::istream_iterator<string> {};   // End-of-stream iterator
  while(true)
  {
    std::cout << "\nEnter a word, or Ctrl+z to end: ";
    if((std::cin >> word).eof()) break;

    string word_copy {word};
    do
    {
      instr.clear();                             // Reset string stream EOF
      instr.seekg(0);                            // String stream position at beginning

                                                 // Use find() to search instr for word
```

```
    if(std::find(std::istream_iterator<string>(instr), end_iter, word) != end_iter)
      words.push_back(word);                          // Store the word found

    std::next_permutation(std::begin(word), std::end(word));
  } while(word != word_copy);

  std::copy(std::begin(words), std::end(words), std::ostream_iterator<string>{std::cout, " "});
  std::cout << std::endl;
  words.clear();                                      // Remove previous anagrams
  }
}
```

The entire contents of dictionary.txt are copied to a stringstream object by the copy() algorithm. The copying process uses stream buffer iterators so there's no data conversion involved - the bytes from the file are copied to the instr object. Of course, you could use formatted I/O operations with stream iterators, in which case the copy operation would be:

```
std::copy(std::istream_iterator<string>{in}, std::istream_iterator<string>(),
                                    std::ostream_iterator<string>{instr, " "});
```

This certainly demonstrates that stream iterators work with string stream objects, but it will be a lot slower than the previous version. There's an even faster way to copy the contents of the file to the stringstream object:

```
instr << in.rdbuf();
```

The rdbuf() member of the ifstream object returns the address of a basic_filebuf object that encapsulates the file contents. basic_filebuf has basic_streambuf as a base class and operator<<() is overloaded to insert characters from a basic_streambuf object that is pointed to by the right operand into the basic_ostream object that is the left operand. This is a fast operation because no formatting or data conversion is involved.

Searching instr for anagrams is the same as for a file stream because it is a stream - it just happens to be in memory. Reading from the string stream moves the current position, so when you want to read the contents again, you must call its seekg() member to reset the position back to the start. Similarly, reading to the end of the data in instr sets the EOF flag and you must call the clear() member to reset the flag; subsequent read operations will fail if you don't.

Here's some sample output from Ex9_10.cpp:

```
Enter a word, or Ctrl+z to end: part
part prat rapt tarp trap

Enter a word, or Ctrl+z to end: painter
painter pertain repaint

Enter a word, or Ctrl+z to end: ^Z
```

This is faster on my system than Ex9_04.cpp, but it's still not impressive. It analyzes four-letter words fairly quickly but a seven-letter word takes much longer - and is slower than the Ex9_03.cpp version that read the file contents into a set container. Apart from the fact that a seven-letter word is going to take roughly 210 times as long as a four-letter word, this is in part an indication of how much overhead you have with formatted input using the extraction operator. Another reason that this is so much slower is that accessing the set container to find a word used a binary search, but here we are searching the words in the string stream sequentially from the start.

Summary

In this chapter I have explained various ways in which the STL helps you to work with streams. Stream iterators read and write formatted character streams and stream buffer iterators transfer bytes between memory and a stream with no conversion. Stream iterators are defined by class templates. istream_iterator defines single pass input iterators for reading a stream and ostream_iterator defines single pass output iterators for writing a stream. The type of data to be read or written is defined by the first template type argument. A second template type parameter identifies the character type for the stream and has a default value of type char. The istreambuf_iterator class template defines stream buffer iterators to read a stream and the ostreambuf_iterator template defines iterators to write a stream. The type of character in the stream is defined by the first template type parameter and has a default of type char.

You can read and write streams using the function members of the stream and steam buffer iterators, as some of the examples demonstrated, but this is rarely necessary or desirable. Using stream extraction or insertion operators for the stream directly is usually simpler and more efficient. The primary use of these iterators is with algorithms. Being able to transfer the contents of a file to an algorithm using input stream iterators, and writing the results to another file with an output stream iterator is a very powerful mechanism. The stream iterators and stream buffer iterators can often greatly simplify the code necessary to read and write files, but you pay a penalty in terms of increased execution time compared to using the I/O functionality provided by the stream classes. Where the data volumes are not large, the overhead is a reasonable price to pay for the simplicity of the code. However, when reading or writing large volumes of data, or reading or writing a stream repeatedly, the overhead may be unacceptable.

EXERCISES

1. Write a program that stores a first name and the age of a person as an object of type std::pair<string, size_t>. The program should read an arbitrary number of first name/age pairs and write them to an output file. The program should then close the file, open it as an input file, read the pair objects from the file, and write them to the standard output stream. All input and output should be carried out using stream iterators.

2. Write a program that will read the file produced by the solution to Exercise 1, and write a new file containing the pair objects in reverse order. All input and output should use stream iterators.

3. Write a program to read the contents of the file produced by the solution to Exercise 1 into a `stringstream` object using stream buffer iterators. Access the `string` and `size_t` values in the `stringstream` using an input stream iterator and write them as pair objects to a container; choose the container such that the pair objects are in ascending sequence of the names. Output the contents of the container to the standard output stream using stream iterators to demonstrate that everything works as it should.

4. Use stream iterators to write one hundred random integers to a file with values that are uniformly distributed between zero and one million. Use algorithms and stream iterators to determine the minimum and maximum values, and to calculate the average. Output the calculated values, then the values from the file, eight on each line. Use iterators for all input and output.

CHAPTER 10

■ ■ ■

Working with Numerical, Time, and Complex Data

This chapter is about three areas that the STL supports that are somewhat more specialized than the rest. The numeric header defines STL features that make numerical data processing easier or more efficient. The chrono header provides capabilities for working with time, both clock-on-the-wall time and time intervals. Finally, the complex header defines class templates that support operations with complex numbers.

In this chapter you will learn:

- How you create valarray objects for storing numerical data.

- What slice objects are and how you create and use them.

- What gslice objects are and how you use them.

- What the ratio class template is for and how you use it.

- How you access and use the clocks your hardware has.

- How you create objects that encapsulate complex numbers and the operations you can apply to them.

Numerical Calculations

The efficiency of numerical computation is of profound importance in many engineering, scientific, and mathematical contexts. While these contexts can be specialized, there are many relatively common application environments that can involve intensive numerical computations. Audio processing such as in voice recognition or in digital sound recording will involve digital filtering – a very processor-intensive process. Digital image processing is widespread in medical devices such as CT and MRI scanners, but is also in other applications that are common – if you have used an editing suite to improve your photos, you will have experience of how long some operations can take. The efficiency with which numerical calculations can be executed is critical in the majority of games programs. The next section is about the STL algorithms for numerical calculations, some of which you have already met. After that I'll introduce a class template that is designed to make numerical calculations with arrays of numbers as efficient as possible.

Numeric Algorithms

I'll occasionally use the terms *matrix* (plural *matrices*) and *vector* in this chapter. In mathematics and science, a *matrix* is a two-dimensional array of numbers. A *vector* is a one-dimensional array – a linear sequence of numbers. When I use the term *vector* in normal case in the text, I mean a one-dimensional array of numbers that is not necessarily in a `vector` container, but it could be. A matrix would typically be stored as a valarray object, which you'll learn about after I have explained the algorithms. You have already met some of the STL algorithms for processing numerical data but I'll include those in this chapter, along with those that are new. All these algorithms work with data sources that are ranges that you specify by input iterators.

Storing Incremental Values in a Range

The `iota()` function template that is defined in the `numeric` header fills a range with successive values of type T. The first two arguments are forward iterators that define the range and the third argument is the initial T value. The value you specify as the third argument is stored in the first element in the range. The values that are stored in elements after the first are obtained by applying the increment operator to the preceding element. Of course, this implies that type T must support `operator++()`. Here's how you could create a `vector` container of elements that are successive floating-point values:

```
std::vector<double> data(9);
double initial {-4};
std::iota(std::begin(data), std::end(data), initial);
std::copy(std::begin(data), std::end(data),
std::ostream_iterator<double>{std::cout << std::fixed << std::setprecision(1), " "});
std::cout << std::endl;              // -4.0 -3.0 -2.0 -1.0 0.0 1.0 2.0 3.0 4.0
```

Calling `iota()` with an initial value of `-4` sets the values of the elements in data to successive values from -4 to +4.

Of course, the initial value does not have to be integral:

```
std::iota(std::begin(data), std::end(data), -2.5);
                            // Values are -2.5 -1.5 -0.5 0.5 1.5 2.5 3.5 4.5 5.5
```

The increment is still 1 so the values will be as in the comment. You can apply the `iota()` algorithm to a range of any type as long as the increment operator works. Here's another example:

```
string text {"This is text"};
std::iota(std::begin(text), std::end(text), 'K');
std::cout << text << std::endl;      // Outputs: KLMNOPQRSTUV
```

It's easy to see what the output is as indicated in the comment – each character in the string is set to a sequence of characters with codes beginning with 'K'. What is happening in this example is not so obvious:

```
std::vector<string> words (8);
std::iota(std::begin(words), std::end(words), "mysterious");
std::copy(std::begin(words), std::end(words),std::ostream_iterator<string>{std::cout, " "});
std::cout << std::endl;              // mysterious ysterious sterious terious erious rious ious ous
```

The output is as in the comment. This is an interesting application of the algorithm but not very useful. This only works because the third argument to iota() is a string literal. If the argument was string{"mysterious"}, it would not compile because there is no operator++() defined for the string class. The argument value corresponding to the string literal is a pointer of type const char*, and the ++ operation is being applied to that. Thus for each element in words after the first, the pointer is incremented resulting in a letter being dropped from the front of the string literal. The result of applying ++ to the pointer is used to create a string object, which is then stored in the current element range. As long as ++ can be applied to the type of elements in a range, you can apply the iota() algorithm to them.

■ **Note**   It's interesting that the idea of the iota() algorithm originated from the iota operator, ι, in the IBM programming language APL. In APL, the expression ι10 created a vector of the integers from 1 to 10. APL was developed by Ken Iverson in the 1960s. It was a remarkably concise language with the implicit ability to handle vectors and arrays. A complete program in APL to read an arbitrary number of values from the keyboard, calculate their average, and then output the result could be expressed in 10 characters.

Summing a Range

The basic version of the accumulate() algorithm, which you have met, sums a range of elements using the + operator. The first two arguments are input iterators that define the range and the third argument is the initial value for the sum; the type of the third argument determines the type of value that is returned. There's a second version with a fourth parameter that is a binary function object to define the operation that is to be applied between the total and an element. This enables you to define your own addition operations when necessary. For example:

```
std::vector<int> values {2, 0, 12, 3, 5, 0, 2, 7, 0, 8};
int min {3};
auto sum = std::accumulate(std::begin(values), std::end(values), 0, [min](int sum, int v)
                                                                    {
                                                                      if(v < min) return sum;
                                                                      return sum + v;
                                                                    });
  std::cout << "The sum of the elements greater than " << min-1
            <<" is " << sum << std::endl;                        // 35
```

This ignores elements that have values less than 3. The condition could be as complex as you like, so you could sum elements within a given range, for example. The operation doesn't need to be addition. It can be any operation as long as it doesn't modify the operands or invalid the iterators that define the range. For instance, defining the function for numeric elements as a multiply operation would produce the product of the elements, as long as the initial value is 1. A function that implements the divide operation for floating-point elements would produce the reciprocal of the product of the elements if the initial value was 1. Here's how you could produce the product of elements:

```
std::vector<int> values {2, 3, 5, 7, 11, 13};
auto product = std::accumulate(std::begin(values), std::end(values), 1,
                                              std::multiplies<int>()); // 30030
```

This uses a function object from the functional header as the fourth argument. If there might be elements with zero values, you could ignore these with a lambda expression like that in the previous code fragment.

The string class supports addition so you can apply accumulate() to a range of string objects:

```
std::vector<string> numbers {"one", "two",    "three", "four", "five",
                        "six", "seven", "eight", "nine", "ten"};
auto s = std::accumulate(std::begin(numbers), std::end(numbers), string{},
                    [](string& str, string& element)
                        {
                            if(element[0] == 't') return str + ' ' + element;
                            return str;
                        });        // Result: " two three ten"
```

This code concatenates string objects beginning with 't' and separates them with a space. It is also possible that the result of executing the accumulate() algorithm can be a different type from the elements in the range to which it's applied:

```
std::vector<int> numbers {1, 2, 3, 10, 11, 12};
auto s = std::accumulate(std::begin(numbers), std::end(numbers), string {"The numbers are"},
                        [](string& str, int n)
                    {   return str + ": " + std::to_string(n);  });
std::cout << s << std::endl;        // Output: The numbers are: 1: 2: 3: 10: 11: 12
```

The to_string() function that the lambda expression uses returns a string representation of the numeric argument. Thus applying the accumulate() algorithm to the range of integers here returns the string shown in the comment.

Inner Product

The *inner product* of two vectors is the sum of the products of corresponding elements. For this to be possible, the vectors must be the same length. The inner product is a fundamental operation in matrix arithmetic. The product of two matrices is the matrix that results from the inner product of each row of the first matrix with each column of the second matrix. This is illustrated in Figure 10-1.

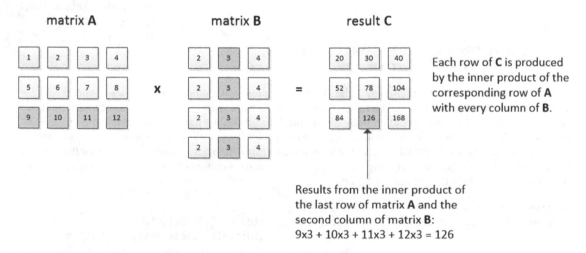

Figure 10-1. *Matrix multiplication and the inner product operation*

For a matrix product to be possible, the number of columns in the matrix that is the left operand must be the same as the number of rows in the matrix that is the right operand. If the left operand has m rows and n columns (an m×n matrix), and the right operand has n rows and k columns (an n×k matrix), the result is a matrix with m rows and k columns (an m×k matrix).

The inner_product() algorithm that is defined in the numeric header computes the inner product of two vectors. The function template has four parameters: the first two are input iterators defining the first vector, the third is a begin input iterator identifying the second vector, and the fourth parameter is the initial value for the sum. The algorithm returns the inner product of the vectors. Here's an example:

```
std::vector<int> v1(10);
std::vector<int> v2(10);
std::iota(std::begin(v1), std::end(v1), 2);       // 2 3 4 5 6 7 8 9 10 11
std::iota(std::begin(v2), std::end(v2), 3);       // 3 4 5 6 7 8 9 10 11 12
std::cout << std::inner_product(std::begin(v1), std::end(v1), std::begin(v2), 0)
          << std::endl;                            // Output: 570
```

For the standard definition of the inner product of two vectors, the initial value is 0, but you have the option of specifying a different initial value for the sum of the products of corresponding elements. It's important to use a literal of the correct type when using inner_product(). The following will show what I mean:

```
std::vector<double> data {0.5, 0.75, 0.85};
auto result1 = std::inner_product(std::begin(data), std::end(data), std::begin(data), 0);
double result2 = std::inner_product(std::begin(data), std::end(data), std::begin(data), 0);
auto result3 = std::inner_product(std::begin(data), std::end(data), std::begin(data), 0.0);
std::cout << result1 << " " << result2
          << " " << result3 << std::endl;         // Output: 0 0 1.535
```

The second and third statements apparently do the same thing, but the type of value returned is determined by the fourth argument. Even though the iterators point to floating-point arguments, the operation that combines the results of multiplying corresponding elements uses integer arithmetic when the initial value is of an integer type. The same applies to the accumulate() algorithm, so make sure literal initial values are of the appropriate type. Fortunately, most compilers will issue a warning when the literal for the initial value is of a different type from the elements involved in the operation. We can try out the inner_product() algorithm, and some others, in a working example.

Applying Inner Product

Least squares linear regression is a method for finding the coefficients, a and b of a line, $y = ax + b$, which is a best fit through a set of n x,y points, where the points are typically real-world data samples of some kind. The method, which is due to Gauss, finds the coefficients a and b such that the sum of the squares of the vertical distances of the sample points from the line is minimized. I'll show the equations that enable this without going into how they are developed, but if you don't want to bother with any of the maths, you can skip straight to the code.

Given n points, (x_i, y_i), the method involves solving the following equations:

$$nb + a\sum x_i = \sum y_i$$
$$b\sum x_i + a\sum x_i^2 = \sum x_i y_i$$

421

Solving these two equations for the coefficients a and b gives:

$$a = \frac{n\sum x_i y_i - \sum x_i \sum y_i}{n\sum x_i^2 - \left(\sum x_i\right)^2}$$

$$b = \mu_y - a\mu_x$$

If we can calculate the various summations along with the means of the x and y values, we can plug them into these equations to get the coefficients for the regression line. You saw in Chapter 8 that the equations for the mean, μ, for n values of a variable x are:

$$\mu_x = \frac{\sum x_i}{n}$$

Clearly, the `accumulate()` and `inner_product()` algorithms are going to be very helpful with this.

This example will fit a regression line to a set of data points from a file. The file is in the code download and records the cost of electricity per kilowatt hour and the installed watts of renewable power generating capacity per head of population for several European countries. The program output should show whether there may be a linear relationship between the installed renewable energy capacity and the cost to the consumer. Here's the code:

```
// Ex10_01.cpp
// Least squares regression
#include <numeric>                          // For accumulate(), inner_product()
#include <vector>                           // For vector container
#include <iostream>                         // For standard streams
#include <iomanip>                          // For stream manipulators
#include <fstream>                          // For file streams
#include <iterator>                         // For iterators and begin() and end()
#include <string>                           // For string class
using std::string;

int main()
{
  // File contains country_name renewables_per_person kwh_cost
  string file_in {"G:/Beginning_STL/renewables_vs_kwh_cost.txt"};
  std::ifstream in {file_in};

  if(!in)                                   // Verify  we have a file
  {
    std::cerr << file_in << " not open." << std::endl;
    exit(1);
  }

  std::vector<double> x;                    // Renewables per head
  std::vector<double> y;                    // Corresponding cost for a kilowatt hour
```

```
// Read the file and show the data
std::cout << "  Country   " << " Watts per Head " << " kwh cost(cents) " << std::endl;
while(true)
{
  string country;
  double renewables {};
  double kwh_cost {};

  if((in >> country).eof()) break;                          // EOF read - we are done
  in >> renewables >> kwh_cost;
  x.push_back(renewables);
  y.push_back(kwh_cost);
  std::cout << std::left << std::setw(12) << country        // Output the record
            << std::right
            << std::fixed << std::setprecision(2) << std::setw(12) << renewables
            << std::setw(16) << kwh_cost << std::endl;
}

auto n = x.size();                                          // Number of points
auto sx = std::accumulate(std::begin(x), std::end(x), 0.0); // Sum of x values
auto sy = std::accumulate(std::begin(y), std::end(y), 0.0); // Sum of y values
auto mean_x = sx/n;                                         // Mean of x values
auto mean_y = sy/n;                                         // Mean of y values

// Sum of x*y values and sum of x-squared
auto sxy = std::inner_product(std::begin(x), std::end(x), std::begin(y), 0.0);
auto sx_2 = std::inner_product(std::begin(x), std::end(x), std::begin(x), 0.0);

double a {}, b {};                                          // Line coefficients
auto num = n*sxy - sx*sy;                                   // Numerator for a
auto denom = n*sx_2 - sx*sx;                                // Denominator for a
a = num / denom;
b = mean_y - a*mean_x;
std::cout << std:: fixed << std::setprecision(3) << "\ny = "  // Output equation
          << a << "*x + " << b << std::endl;                // for regression line
}
```

The file is read in the while loop. Only the numerical values are stored and each complete record of a country name, watts of installed renewable capacity per head of population, and cost in cents per kilowatt hour are written to the standard output stream. The two numerical values are stored in vector containers; x stores the renewables capacity per head for each country and y stores the corresponding kilowatt hour cost.

The means for the x values and y values are calculated by using the accumulate() algorithm to sum the elements in each container, then dividing the result by the number of elements. The sum of squares of the x values and the sum of xy products are computed by the inner_product() algorithm. The results of these are used to calculate the a and b coefficients of the line by using the equations I showed earlier.

Note that we could simplify the equation for the coefficient a. If we divide the numerator and the denominator by n^2, the equation can be written like this:

$$a = \frac{\sum x_i y_i / n - \mu_x \mu_y}{\sum x_i^2 / n - \mu_x^2}$$

Now the sums of x values and y values are not needed explicitly. The code to compute the coefficients can be written as:

```
auto n = x.size();                                    // Number of points
// Calculate mean values for x, y, xy, and x-squared
auto mean_x = std::accumulate(std::begin(x), std::end(x), 0.0)/n;
auto mean_y = std::accumulate(std::begin(y), std::end(y), 0.0)/n;
auto mean_xy = std::inner_product(std::begin(x), std::end(x), std::begin(y), 0.0)/n;
auto mean_x2 = std::inner_product(std::begin(x), std::end(x), std::begin(x), 0.0)/n;

// Calculate coefficients
auto a = (mean_xy - mean_x*mean_y)/(mean_x2 - mean_x*mean_x);
auto b = mean_y - a*mean_x;
```

This achieves the same result with fewer statements. Figure 10-2 shows the output from the program on the right, and a plot of the regression line and the original data points on the left.

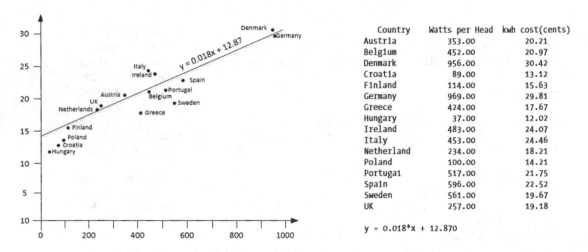

Figure 10-2. *Result of least squares linear regression*

The plot is fairly convincing – the original points are quite close to it. It looks as though every additional 100 watts of renewable energy generating capacity per head of population that gets installed is going to put almost 2 cents on the cost of every kilowatt hour that you use.

Defining Alternative Inner Product Operations

The version of inner_product() that you have seen multiplies corresponding elements in two input ranges, then sums the results. A second version has two more parameters that define function objects. The second function object defines the binary operation to be applied between pairs of corresponding elements in the two ranges and the first defines the binary operation to be used in place of addition to combine the results. The function objects you supply as arguments must not invalidate any iterators and must not modify the elements in either input range. Here's an example of how you could produce the product of sums, instead of the sum of products:

```
std::vector<int> v1(5);
std::vector<int> v2(5);
```

```
std::iota(std::begin(v1), std::end(v1), 2);        // 2 3 4 5 6
std::iota(std::begin(v2), std::end(v2), 3);        // 3 4 5 6 7
std::cout << std::inner_product(std::begin(v1), std::end(v1), std::begin(v2), 1,
                                        std::multiplies<>(), std::plus<>())
            << std::endl;                          // Output: 45045
```

The function objects used as argument in the inner_product() call are defined in the functional header. A plus<T> object computes the sum of two values of type T and the instance of the template here defines the operation to be applied to corresponding elements of type int from the input ranges. The instance of multiplies that is the fifth argument to inner_product() combines the results by multiplying them. Note that because the result is a product, the initial value must not be 0 if you want to avoid always getting a zero result. The functional header also defines the templates for other binary arithmetic operations that you could use with inner_product() - minus, divides and modulus. You could also use the templates for function objects that define bitwise operations; these are bit_and, bit_or, and bit_eor.

Adjacent Differences

The adjacent_difference() algorithm from the numeric header computes the difference between adjacent pairs of elements in an input range and stores the results in another range. The first element is copied unchanged to the new range, then the first element is subtracted from the second and stored as the second in the new range, the second is subtracted from the third and stored as the third in the new range, and so on. Here's an example:

```
std::vector<int> data {2, 3, 5, 7, 11, 13, 17, 19};
std::cout << "Differences: ";
std::adjacent_difference(std::begin(data), std::end(data),
                                        std::ostream_iterator<int>{std::cout, " "});
std::cout << std::endl;                        // Differences: 2 1 2 2 4 2 4 2
```

The differences between elements in the data container are output directly by the adjacent_difference() algorithm because the iterator for the output range is an output stream iterator that writes to cout. The output this produces is shown in the comment.

A second version of the algorithm allows you to specify an alternative to the subtraction operator that is applied to pairs of elements. Here's an example of that:

```
std::vector<int> data {2, 3, 5, 7, 11, 13, 17, 19};
std::cout << "Products: ";
std::adjacent_difference(std::begin(data), std::end(data),
                                        std::ostream_iterator<int>{std::cout, " "},
                                        std::multiplies<>());
std::cout << std::endl;                    // Products: 2 6 15 35 77 143 221 323
```

The fourth argument is a function object that specifies the operation between elements – an instance of multiplies from the functional header in this case. You can see that this produces products of successive elements in data. Any binary operation is acceptable as long as it does not change the input range or invalidate the iterators. Here's an example that computes Fibonacci numbers using the plus<T> function object as the operator between pairs of elements:

```
std::vector<size_t> fib(15, 1);                    // 15 elements initialized with 1
std::adjacent_difference(std::begin(fib), std::end(fib)-1, std::begin(fib)+1,
std::plus<size_t>());
```

```
std::copy(std::begin(fib), std::end(fib), std::ostream_iterator<size_t>{std::cout, " "});
std::cout << std::endl;              // Output: 1 1 2 3 5 8 13 21 34 55 89 144 233 377 610
```

The adjacent_difference() algorithm here adds pairs of elements in the fib container and writes the results back to the same container starting with the second element. The last element in fib is not included in the input range and the sum of the last two elements in the input range overwrites the values in the last element. After the operation, fib will contain a Fibonacci sequence beginning with 1. The comment shows the output that is produced by the copy() algorithm.

Partial Sums

The partial_sum() algorithm that is defined in the numeric header computes partial sums of elements within an input range and stores the results in an output range. It computes the sums of increasing length sequences from the input range starting with a sequence of length 1, so the first output value is just the first element, the next value is the sum of the first two elements, the next is the sum of the first three elements, and so on. This is the inverse of the adjacent_difference() algorithm so partial_sum() undoes what adjacent_difference() does. Here's an example:

```
std::vector<int> data {2, 3, 5, 7, 11, 13, 17, 19};
std::cout << "Partial sums: ";
std::partial_sum(std::begin(data), std::end(data), std::ostream_iterator<int>{std::cout, " "});
std::cout << std::endl;                    // Partial sums: 2 5 10 17 28 41 58 77
```

You can see that the output consists of sums of sequences of steadily increasing length. You can easily demonstrate that this is so by executing this:

```
std::vector<int> data {2, 3, 5, 7, 11, 13, 17, 19};
std::cout << "Original data: ";
std::copy(std::begin(data), std::end(data), std::ostream_iterator<int>{std::cout, " "});
std::adjacent_difference(std::begin(data), std::end(data), std::begin(data));
std::cout << "\nDifferences: ";
std::copy(std::begin(data), std::end(data), std::ostream_iterator<int>{std::cout, " "});
std::cout << "\nPartial sums: ";
std::partial_sum(std::begin(data), std::end(data), std::ostream_iterator<int>{std::cout, " "});
std::cout << std::endl;
```

Note that the output iterator here is the same as the begin iterator for the input range. This is legal. You might think that data could be overwritten but the algorithm is defined so as to prevent this. The output from executing this code is:

```
Original data: 2 3 5 7 11 13 17 19
Differences: 2 1 2 2 4 2 4 2
Partial sums: 2 3 5 7 11 13 17 19
```

The output shows that calculating the partial sums of the differences results in the original values, which is not really surprising.

Like the adjacent_difference() algorithm, you can provide a function object as an extra argument to partial_sum() that defines an operator to be used instead of addition. Here's how that might be applied:

```
std::vector<int> data {2, 3, 5, 7, 11, 13, 17, 19};
std::cout << "Partial sums: ";
std::partial_sum(std::begin(data), std::end(data),
std::ostream_iterator<int>{std::cout, " "}, std::minus<int>());
std::cout << std::endl;                      // Partial sums: 2 -1 -6 -13 -24 -37 -54 -73
```

The subtraction operator is used so the values are the results of, 2, 2-3, 2-3-5, 2-3-5-7, and so on.

Maxima and Minima

You have seen some of the algorithms for determining minima and maxima already but I'll include them all in this section anyway. There are three algorithms defined in the algorithm header that apply to ranges: min_element() returns an iterator that points to the minimum from an input range, max_element() returns an iterator that points to the maximum, and minmax_element() returns iterators for both as a pair object. The range must be specified by forward iterators; just input iterators are not sufficient. For all three algorithms you can optionally supply a third argument that defines the comparison function, in addition to the begin and end iterators for the range. Here's some code that shows the three algorithms applied to integers:

```
std::vector<int> data {2, 12, 3, 5, 17, -11, 113, 117, 19};

std::cout << "From values ";
std::copy(std::begin(data), std::end(data), std::ostream_iterator<int>{std::cout, " "});
std::cout << "\n     Min = " << *std::min_element(std::begin(data), std::end(data))
          << "  Max = " << *std::max_element(std::begin(data), std::end(data))
          << std::endl;

auto start_iter = std::begin(data) + 2;
auto end_iter = std::end(data) - 2;
auto pr = std::minmax_element(start_iter, end_iter);        // Get min and max

std::cout << "From values ";
std::copy(start_iter, end_iter, std::ostream_iterator<int>{std::cout, " "});
std::cout << "\n     Min = " << *pr.first << "  Max = " << *pr.second << std::endl;
```

The min_element() and max_element() are used to find the minimum and maximum from data. minmax_element() is applied to the same range, but omitting the first two and last two elements. Executing this will output the following:

```
From values 2 12 3 5 17 -11 113 117 19
    Min = -11  Max = 117
From values 3 5 17 -11 113
    Min = -11  Max = 113
```

The `algorithm` header also defines templates for `min()`, `max()`, and `minmax()` that return the minimum, maximum, or the minimum and maximum of two objects, or of an initializer list of objects. You have seen these used with two arguments to be compared. Here's an example of their use with an initializer list:

```
auto words = {string {"one"}, string {"two"}, string {"three"}, string {"four"},
    string {"five"}, string {"six"}, string {"seven"}, string {"eight"}};
std::cout << "Min = " << std::min(words)
        << std::endl;                      // Min = eight

auto pr = std::minmax(words, [] (const string& s1, const string& s2)
                                {return s1.back() < s2.back();});
std::cout << "Min = " << pr.first << "  Max = " << pr.second
        << std::endl;                      // Min = one  Max = six
```

`words` is an initializer list of `string` objects. It's important that the elements are `string` objects. If you use simply `char*` then the algorithms won't properly work because then you will be comparing addresses and not the string contents. The `min()` algorithm determines the minimum object in words using the default `operator<()` for `string` objects. The `minmax()` algorithm is then used to find the minimum and maximum object in the list using a custom comparison function that compares the last characters in the strings. The results are shown in the comments. There are versions of `min()` and `max()` that accept a function object as the last argument that defines the comparison.

Storing and Working with Numerical Values

The `valarray` class template that is defined in the `valarray` header defines types for objects that can store and manipulate sequences of numerical values. It's primarily intended for working with integer and floating-point values, but you can use it to store objects of a class type as long as the class meets certain conditions:

- The class *must not* be abstract.
- Public constructors *must* include a default constructor and a copy constructor.
- The destructor *must* be `public`.
- The class *must* define the assignment operator and it must be `public`.
- The class *must not* overload `operator&()`.
- The function members *must not* throw exceptions.

You cannot store references, or `const` or `volatile` qualified objects in a `valarray`. If your class meets all these constraints then you're in business.

The `valarray` template offers a great deal more for numerical data processing than any of the sequence containers such as a `vector`. First, and most important, it's designed to enable the compiler to optimize the performance of its operations in a way that does not apply to the sequence containers. However, whether or not your compiler *does* optimize `valarray` operations depends on the implementation. Second, there are a substantial number of unary and binary operations on `valarray` objects built in to the type. Third, there are also a huge number of built-in unary functions for applying many of the operations that are defined in the `cmath` header to every element. Fourth, a `valarray` type provides built-in capability to work with the data as an array of as many dimensions as you need.

Creating a `valarray` object is easy. Here are some examples:

```
std::valarray<int> numbers(15);              // 15 elements with default initial values 0
std::valarray<size_t> sizes {1, 2, 3};       // 3 elements with values 1 2 and 3
std::valarray<size_t> copy_sizes {sizes};    // 3 elements with values 1 2 and 3
std::valarray<double> values;                // Empty array
std::valarray<double> data(3.14, 10);        // 10 elements with values 3.14
```

Each constructor creates an object with a given number of elements. It's essential to use parentheses in the last statement that defines data; if you use braces, data will contain two elements with values 3.14 and 10.0. You can also create a `valarray` object initialized with a specified number of values from an ordinary array. For example:

```
int vals[] {2, 4, 6, 8, 10, 12, 14};
std::valarray<int> vals1 {vals, 5};          // 5 elements from vals: 2 4 6 8 10
std::valarray<int> vals2 {vals + 1, 4};      // 4 elements from vals: 4 6 8 10
```

There are other constructors that I'll introduce later because they have parameters of types that I have yet to explain.

Basic Operations on valarray Objects

A `valarray` object is like an array container in that you cannot add or delete elements. However, you can change the number of elements that a `valarray` object contains and assign a new value to them. For example:

```
data.resize(50, 1.5);                        // 50 elements with value 1.5
```

If there were elements stored in `data` prior to this operation, their values will be lost. When you need to obtain the number of elements, you can call the `size()` member.

The `swap()` member swaps the elements of the current object with those of a `valarray` object that you pass as the argument. For example:

```
std::valarray<size_t> sizes_3 {1, 2, 3};
std::valarray<size_t> sizes_4 {2, 3, 4, 5};
sizes_3.swap(sizes_4);                       // sizes_3 now has 4 elements and sizes_4 has 3
```

The number of elements contained in the `valarray` objects can be different, but obviously the elements in the two objects must be of the same type. The `swap()` member has no return value. There's a non-member `swap()` function template that does the same thing, so the last statement could be replaced by this:

```
std::swap(sizes_3, sizes_4);                 // Calls sizes_3.swap(sizes_4)
```

You can find the minimum and maximum values of the elements in a `valarray` by calling its `min()` and `max()` function members. For example:

```
std::cout << "The elements are from " << sizes_4.min() << " to " << sizes_4.max() << '\n';
```

For this to work, the elements must be of a type that supports `operator<()`.

The sum() member returns the sum of the elements, which it computes using += operator. Thus you could calculate the average value of the elements in a valarray like this:

```
std::cout << "The average of the elements " << sizes_4.sum()/sizes_4.size() << '\n';
```

This is much simpler than having to use the accumulate() algorithm.

There are no valarray members that return iterators for the elements but there are specialized non-member versions of begin() and end() that return random access iterators. This enables you to use the range-based for loop to access valarray elements and to apply algorithms to them; you'll see examples later. You can't use insert iterators with a valarray though because the members necessary to enable this are not there, which is because the size is fixed.

There are two function members for shifting the elements – that's shifting the sequence, not shifting bits in individual values. First, the shift() member shifts the entire sequence of elements by the number of elements specified by the argument. The function returns the result as a new valarray object, leaving the original unchanged. If the argument is positive, elements are shifted left, and a negative argument shifts the elements right. This works rather like a bit shift. Elements that are shifted in to the sequence from the left or the right will be 0, or its equivalent for the type. Of course, if you don't store the result of a shift operation back in the same valarray object, the original object is unchanged. Here's some code illustrating how this works:

```
std::valarray<int> d1 {1, 2, 3, 4, 5, 6, 7, 8, 9};
auto d2 = d1.shift(2);                           // Shift left 2 positions
for(int n : d2) std::cout << n << ' ';
std::cout << '\n';                               // Result: 3 4 5 6 7 8 9 0 0
auto d3 = d1.shift(-3);                          // Shift right 3 positions
std::copy(std::begin(d3), std::end(d3), std::ostream_iterator<int>{std::cout, " "});
std::cout << std::endl;                          // Result: 0 0 0 1 2 3 4 5 6
```

The comments explain what happens. I used different ways to output the results from the two cases just to show what is possible. d1 is not changed by any of these statements. The valarray template defines the assignment operator for objects so if you want to replace the original, you could just write:

```
d1 = d1.shift(2);                                // Shift d1 left 2 positions
```

The second possibility for shifting elements is to use the cshift() member. This shifts the sequence of elements *circularly* by the number of positions specified by the argument. The sequence of elements is rotated left or right, depending on whether the argument is positive or negative. This function member also returns a new object. Here's an example:

```
std::valarray<int> d1 {1, 2, 3, 4, 5, 6, 7, 8, 9};
auto d2 = d1.cshift(2);                          // Result d2 contains: 3 4 5 6 7 8 9 1 2
auto d3 = d1.cshift(-3);                         // Result d3 contains: 7 8 9 1 2 3 4 5 6
```

The apply() function is a very powerful member of valarray that applies a function to every element, and returns the results as a new valarray object. There are two apply() function members defined within the valarray class template as:

```
valarray<T> apply(T func(T)) const;
valarray<T> apply(T func(const T&)) const;
```

There are three things to note. First, both versions are const, so the original elements cannot be modified by the function. Second, the parameter is a function of a specific form with an argument of type T or const reference to T, and it returns a value of type T; if you try to use apply() with an argument that does not correspond to this, it won't compile. Third the return value is type valarray<T> so the result is always an array of elements of the same type and size as the original.

Here's an example of using the apply() member:

```
std::valarray<double> time {0.0, 1.0, 2.0, 3.0, 4.0, 5.0, 6.0, 7.0, 8.0, 9.0};  // Seconds
auto distances = time.apply([](double t)
                {
                    const static double g {32.0};  // Acceleration due to gravity ft/sec/sec
                      return 0.5*g*t*t;
                });                          // Result: 0 16 64 144 256 400 576 784 1024 1296
```

The distances object will contain how far a brick would fall after the corresponding number of seconds if you dropped it off a tall building; the building must be more than 1296 feet tall for the last result to be valid. Note that you can't use a lambda expression that captures variables from the enclosing scope as the argument because this would not match the specification for the parameter in the function template. For example, this won't compile:

```
const double g {32.0};
auto distances = times.apply([g](double t) { return 0.5*g*t*t; });    // Won't compile!
```

Capturing g by value in the lambda expression changes its type so that it does not conform to the apply template specification. For a lambda expression to be acceptable as the argument to apply(), the capture clause must be empty, it must have a parameter of the same type as the array, and it must return a value of that type.

The valarray header defines overloads for most of the functions from the cmath header so that they apply to all elements in a valarray object. The functions that accept a valarray object as an argument are:

```
abs(), pow() , sqrt(), exp(), log(), log10()
sin(), cos(), tan(), asin(), acos(), atan(), atan2()
sinh(), cosh(), tanh()
```

Here's an example that drags together code fragments from this section and provides an opportunity to use one of the cmath functions with a valarray object:

```
// Ex10_02.cpp
// Dropping bricks safely from a tall building using valarray objects
#include <numeric>                            // For iota()
#include <iostream>                           // For standard streams
#include <iomanip>                            // For stream manipulators
#include <algorithm>                          // For for_each()
#include <valarray>                           // For valarray
const static double g {32.0};                 // Acceleration due to gravity ft/sec/sec

int main()
{
  double height {};                           // Building height
  std::cout << "Enter the approximate height of the building in feet: ";
  std::cin >> height;
```

```
// Calculate brick flight time in seconds
double end_time {std::sqrt(2 * height / g)};
size_t max_time {1 + static_cast<size_t>(end_time + 0.5)};

std::valarray<double> times(max_time+1);           // Array to accommodate times
std::iota(std::begin(times), std::end(times), 0);   // Initialize: 0 to max_time
*(std::end(times) - 1) = end_time;                 // Set the last time value

// Calculate distances each second
auto distances = times.apply([](double t) { return 0.5*g*t*t; });

// Calculate speed each second
auto v_fps = sqrt(distances.apply([](double d) { return 2 * g*d;}));

// Lambda expression to output results
auto print = [](double v) { std::cout << std::setw(6) << static_cast<int>(std::round(v)); };

// Output the times - the last is a special case...
std::cout << "Time (seconds): ";
std::for_each(std::begin(times), std::end(times)-1, print);
std::cout << std::setw(6) << std::fixed << std::setprecision(2) << *(std::end(times)-1);

std::cout << "\nDistances(feet):";
std::for_each(std::begin(distances), std::end(distances), print);

std::cout << "\nVelocity(fps):  ";
std::for_each(std::begin(v_fps), std::end(v_fps), print);

// Get velocities in mph and output them
auto v_mph = v_fps.apply([](double v) { return v*60/88; });
std::cout << "\nVelocity(mph):  ";
std::for_each(std::begin(v_mph), std::end(v_mph), print);
std::cout << std::endl;
}
```

This determines what happens when you drop a brick from a high building. Here's some sample output for the *Burj Khalifa*, assuming you release the brick from a pole that is long enough to avoid the brick hitting the side of the building:

Enter the approximate height of the building in feet: 2722														
Time (seconds):	0	1	2	3	4	5	6	7	8	9	10	11	12	13 13.04
Distances(feet):	0	16	64	144	256	400	576	784	1024	1296	1600	1936	2304	2704 2722
Velocity(fps):	0	32	64	96	128	160	192	224	256	288	320	352	384	416 417
Velocity(mph):	0	22	44	65	87	109	131	153	175	196	218	240	262	284 285

First of all, what actually happens if you do this for real is that you end up in jail - or worse. Second of all, I *know* that the calculation ignores drag, but this book is about the STL, not physics. Third of all, I *know* you can get a velocity by multiplying the acceleration by the elapsed time, but then I wouldn't get to apply sqrt() to a valarray, would I?

432

All the code is quite straightforward. The constant g is defined at global scope because this is the easiest way to make it available in various places in the code, including the lambda expressions. The `times` array that stores elapsed times in seconds is populated with integral values start from 0 using the `iota()` algorithm, The last time value, which corresponds to when the brick hits the ground, is almost certainly not integral, so the specific value is stored. I used the `for_each()` to produce the output because it allows more control of the output values than using `copy()` and an output stream iterator. The last time value is unlikely to be a whole number of seconds, so this is treated as a special case for output. The `print` lambda is explicitly defined so it can be reused to output each set of values.

You can use the subscript operator, [ ], to get or set the value of an element at a given index in a valarray, but the subscript operator does much more than that, as you'll see later in this chapter.

Unary Operators

There are four unary operators that can be applied to a valarray object: +, -, ~, and !. The effect is to apply the operator to each element in the array and return the results in a new valarray object, leaving the original unchanged. You can only apply these to a valarray object if the element type supports the operator, and what they do – particularly with objects of class types – will depend on the type. The new elements that result from applying the ! operator to a valarray object are always of type bool, so the result of the operation is an object of type valarray<bool>. I'll discuss a context where this can be useful later in this chapter. The other operators must produce a result that is the same type as the original elements for the operation to be legal. For instance, the unary subtraction operator can only invert the sign of elements that are signed numerical values so it won't work with unsigned types. This shows the effect of the ! operator:

```
std::valarray<int> data {2, 0, -2, 4, -4};
auto result = !data;                       // result is of type valarray bool
std::copy(std::begin(result), std::end(result),
                          std::ostream_iterator<bool>{std::cout << std::boolalpha, " "});
std::cout << std::endl;                    // Output: false true false false false
```

When ! is applied to the values in data, the values are first implicitly converted to bool, and the operator applied to the result. If you were to output the values in data as bool values using the copy() algorithm, the result would be true false true true true, which explains why the output from the code above is as shown.

The ~ operator is bitwise *NOT* - or 1's complement. Here's an example:

```
std::valarray<int> data {2, 0, -2, 4, -4}; // 0x00000002 0 0xfffffffe 0x00000004 0xfffffffc
auto result = ~data;
std::copy(std::begin(result), std::end(result), std::ostream_iterator<int>{std::cout, " "});
std::cout << std::endl;                    // Output: -3 -1 1 -5 3
```

The result is produced by flipping the bits in the original integer values to produce the elements in result. For example, the second element in data has all bits 0, so applying ~ produces a value with all bits 1, which corresponds to -1 in decimal.

The + operator will have no effect on numerical values; the - operator will change the sign. For example:

```
std::valarray<int> data {2, 0, -2, 4, -4};
auto result = -data;
std::copy(std::begin(result), std::end(result), std::ostream_iterator<int>{std::cout, " "});
std::cout << std::endl;                    // Output: -2 0 2 -4 4
```

Of course, you can overwrite the original object if you want. In the interests of making the code less cluttered, from now on, I'll assume there is a using directive for std::valarray in effect and drop the std namespace qualifier for valarray types in code.

Compound Assignment Operators for valarray Objects

All the compound assignment operators have a left operand that is a `valarray` object. The right operand can be a value of the same type as the element stored, in which case the value is combined with the value of each element in the way determined by the operator. The right operand can also be a `valarray` object holding the same number and type of elements as the left operand. In this case the elements in the left operand are modified by combining corresponding elements from the right operand. The operators in this category are:

- Compound arithmetic assignment operators +=, -=, *=, /=, %=, for example:

```
valarray<int> v1 {1, 2, 3, 4};
valarray<int> v2 {3, 4, 3, 4};
v1+= 3;                              // v1 is: 4 5 6 7
v1 -= v2;                            // v1 is: 1 1 3 3
```

- Compound bitwise assignment operators &=, |=, ^=, for example:

```
valarray<int> v1 {1, 2, 4, 8};
valarray<int> v2 {4, 8, 16, 32};
v1 |= 4;                             // v1 is: 5 6 4 12
v1 &= v2;                            // v1 is: 4 0 0 0
v1 ^= v2;                            // v1 is: 0 8 16 32
```

- Compound shift assignment operators >>=, <<=, for example:

```
valarray<int> v1 {1, 2, 3, 4};
valarray<int> v2 {4, 8, 16, 32};
v2 <<= v1;                           // v2 is: 8 32 128 512
v2 >>= 2;                            // v1 is: 2 8 32 128
```

The compound bitwise and compound shift assignment operators typically apply to integer types.

Binary Operations on valarray Objects

You can apply any of the binary operators that apply to values of fundamental types to `valarray` objects, either to combine corresponding elements of two `valarray` objects, or to combine elements in a `valarray` with a value of the same type as the elements. Non-member operator functions for the following binary operations are defined in the `valarray` header:

- Arithmetic operators +, -, *, /, %

- Bitwise operators &, |, ^

- Shift operators >>, <<

- Logical operators &&, ||

There are versions of all these operators that allow the operation to be applied between a `valarray<T>` object and an object of type `T`, an object of type `T` and a `valarray` object, or between two `valarray` objects. An operation between two `valarray` objects required that they both have the same number of elements of the same type. The logical operators return a `valarray<bool>` object with the same number of elements as the `valarray` operand. The other operators return a `valarray` object with the same type and number of elements as the `valarray` operand.

It will be useful to be able to output the contents of a valarray object to cout to show what has happened. I'll use the following function template to do this:

```
// perline is the number output per line, width is the field width
template<typename T>
void print(const std::valarray<T> values,  size_t perline = 8, size_t width = 8)
{
  size_t n {};
  for(const auto& value : values)
  {
    std::cout << std::setw(width) << value << " ";
    if(++n % perline == 0) std::cout << std::endl;
  }
  if(n % perline != 0) std::cout << std::endl;
  std::cout << std::endl;
}
```

This will work for a valarray object containing elements of any type T that supports operator<<() for output streams.

I won't grind through examples of using all the binary operators – just an illustrative few. Here are some examples of binary arithmetic operations with valarray objects:

```
valarray<int> even {2, 4, 6, 8};
valarray<int> odd {3, 5, 7, 9};
auto r1 = even + 2;
print(r1, 4, 3);                        // r1 contains:    4   6   8  10
auto r2 = 2*r1 + odd;
print(r2, 4, 3);                        // r2 contains: 11  17  23  29
r1 += 2*odd - 4*(r2 - even);
print(r1, 4, 3);                        // r1 contains: -26 -36 -46 -56
```

The last statement uses the compound assignment operator that is a function member to add the result of the expression that is the right operand. This shows how you can combine operations involving valarray objects in essentially the same way as numerical values, including the use of parentheses. Here's a statement that uses a shift operation:

```
print(odd << 3, 4, 4);                  // Output is:  24   40   56   72
```

The first argument to print() is the valarray object that results from shifting the elements in odd left by three bit positions. The output is 4 values to a line in a field width of 4.

There are also non-member functions defined in the valarray header for comparing a valarray<T> object with another valarray<T> object, or comparing each element of a valarray<T> object with a value of type T. The comparison results in a valarray<bool> object with the same number of elements as the valarray involved. The operations supported are ==, !=, <. <=, >, and >=. Here are some examples of using these:

```
valarray<int> even {2, 4, 6, 8};
valarray<int> odd {3, 5, 7, 9};
std::cout << std::boolalpha;
print(even + 1 == odd, 4, 6);           // Output is:    true    true    true    true
  auto result = (odd < 5) && (even + 3 != odd);
  print(result);                        // Output is:    true    false   false   false
```

The second-to-last statement uses the binary && operator to combine the results of comparisons. The result indicates when odd elements are less than 5 and corresponding elements of even are not equal to the elements in odd after 3 has been added to the even elements; this is only true for the first elements in even and odd because odd < 5 is only true for the first element in odd and even + 3 != odd is always true.

There are helper classes that define objects for working with subsets of the elements in a valarray. The primary helper classes are std::slice and std::gslice. I'll drop the std namespace qualifier for these too in the code. Before getting deeper into what you can do with valarray objects, let's first explore how you work with a valarray using these helper classes.

Accessing Elements in valarray Objects

A valarray object stores its elements as a linear sequence. As I said earlier, you can obtain a reference to any element and get or set the value by using an index with the subscript operator. Here are some examples:

```
std::valarray<int> data {1,2,3,4,5,6,7,8,9};
data[1] = data[2] + data[3];                 // Data[1] is 7
data[3] *= 2;                                 // Data[3] is 8
data[4] = ++data[5] - data[2];                // data[4] is 4, data[5] is 7
```

It's just like accessing elements from a regular array. However, the subscript operator for a valarray object can do much more. You can use instances of helper classes with the subscript operator instead of an index. This enables you to specify and access subsets of the elements. The element selection mechanisms that the helper classes define enable you to work with the elements as though they are in arrays with two or more dimensions. It's important to understand how this works because this is one of the major advantages a valarray has over a sequence container.

There's a lot of detail to go through so let's look at the roadmap. We will first explore how the element selection mechanism works in general, then how you select particular rows or columns from a two-dimensional array. I'll explain how the helper classes work together with valarray objects in various ways to choose different subsets of elements and how the subsets are represented. After I have explained the various possibilities for generating a subset, I'll discuss what you can do with it. I'll get to how you apply these techniques in an application context after that.

Creating a Slice

The std::slice class is defined in the valarray header. A *slice* is defined by a slice object that you pass to the subscript operator for a valarray object like an index. Using a slice object as a subscript to a valarray object selects a subset of two or more elements. The elements that are selected are not necessarily contiguous in the array. The array elements that a slice selects are available as references, so you can access and/or change the values of these elements.

Essentially, a slice object encapsulates a series of index values for selecting elements from a valarray. You define a slice object by passing three values of type size_t to the slice constructor:

- The *start index* in the valarray object that identifies the first element in the subset.

- The *size*, which is the number of elements in the subset.

- The *stride*, which is the valarray index increment to get from one element in the subset to the next.

The arguments to the constructor are in the sequence I have described them so you could define a slice like this:

```
slice my_slice {3, 4, 2};                    // start index = 3, size = 4, stride = 2
```

This object identifies 4 elements starting at index 3, with succeeding index increments of 2. There's a copy constructor, so you can duplicate `slice` objects. The default constructor sets the start index, size, and stride to 0 and its only purpose is to allow the creation of arrays of `slice` objects.

You can obtain the start index from a `slice` object by calling its `start()` member. A `slice` object also has `size()` and `stride()` members that return the size and stride respectively. All three values are returned as type `size_t`.

In general, when you use a `slice{start, size, stride}` object as the subscript for a `valarray` object, you are selecting elements at index values:

```
start, start + stride, start + 2*stride,... start +(size - 1)*stride
```

Figure 10-3 illustrates an example of this with a `valarray` object that contains elements with values from 1 to 15.

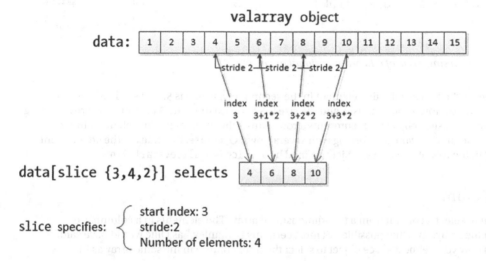

Figure 10-3. *Subset of elements in a valarray selected by a slice object*

The application of the subscript operator to `data` with a `slice` object as the argument in Figure 10-3 selects elements at index positions, 3, 5, 7, and 9, which are the fourth, sixth, eighth, and tenth elements in the array. The first argument to the `slice` constructor is the index of the first element, the second argument is the number of index values, and the third argument is the increment from one index value to the next. The result of using a `slice` object as an index to a `valarray<T>` object is another object – what else could it be? It's an object of type `slice_array<T>` that encapsulates references to the elements in the `valarray<T>` that are selected by the `slice`. I'll return to what you can do with a `slice_array` object after I have explained a bit more about how you use a slice.

Selecting a Row

Suppose that the values in the data object in Figure 10-3 represent a two-dimensional array with three rows of five elements – in row order. Figure 10-4 shows how you can select just the second row using a slice object.

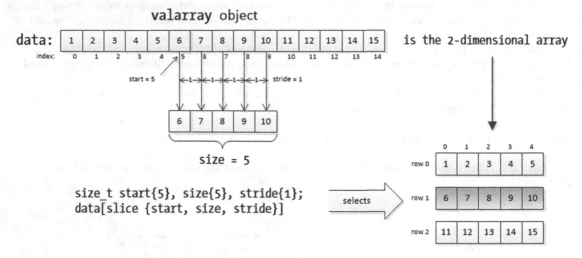

Figure 10-4. *Selecting a single row of a two-dimensional array*

The start index is the index of the first element in the second row, which is 5. The stride is 1 because the elements in each row are stored contiguously, and the size is 5 because there are 5 elements in a row. Calling the start() member of a slice object that represents a row returns the index of the first element in the row, which can be useful when you are working with several rows. Of course, the index of the nth element (indexing from 0) in the row of a valarray object defined by a_slice is a_slice.start()+n.

Selecting a Column

Suppose you want to select a column from a two-dimensional array. The elements in a column are not contiguous in the array, so is that possible? "It most certainly is, Stanley," as Ollie would have said. Figure 10-5 shows how you define a slice object to select the third column in the same array as in Figure 10-4.

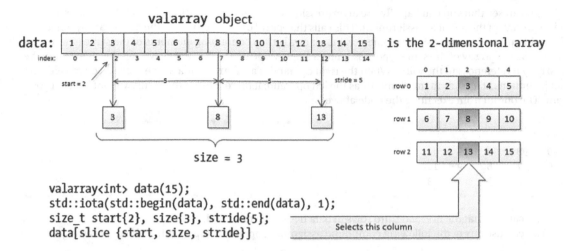

Figure 10-5. *Selecting a single column from a two-dimensional array*

As always, the start value is the index of the first element in the subsequence. The index increment from one element in a column to the next is 5, so this is the stride value. There are three elements in a column so size is 3.

Using a Slice

A slice_array<T> object is a proxy for the subset of elements that are selected from a valarray<T> object when you use a slice object as a subscript. This template defines a limited number of function members. The only public constructor available for slice_array is a copy constructor, so the only possibility for creating an object, beyond using a slice object as a subscript, is to create a duplicate slice_array object. For example:

```
valarray<int> data(15);
std::iota(std::begin(data), std::end(data), 1);
size_t start {2}, size {3}, stride {5};
auto d_slice = data[slice {start, size, stride}]; // References data[2], data[7], data[12]
slice_array<int> copy_slice {d_slice};              // Duplicate of d_slice
```

There's no default constructor so you cannot create arrays of slice_array objects. The only operations you can apply to a slice_array object are assignment, and compound assignments. The assignment operator sets all elements referenced by a slice_array object to a given value. You can also use it to set the elements referenced to the values of corresponding elements from another valarray, as long as the valarray has the same number of elements of the same type as the valarray to which the slice_array object relates. For example:

```
valarray<int> data {1, 2, 3, 4, 5, 6, 7, 8, 9, 10, 11, 12, 13, 14, 15};
valarray<int> more {2, 2, 3, 3, 3, 4, 4, 4, 4,  5,  5,  5,  5,  5,  6};
data[slice{0, 5, 1}] = 99;            // Set elements in 1st row to 99
data[slice{10, 5, 1}] = more;         // Set elements in last row to values from more
std::cout << "data:\n";
print(data, 5, 4);
```

You can see that you can happily use an expression such as data[slice{0, 5, 1}] that creates a slice_array on the left of an assignment. This calls the operator=() member of the slice_array object. The right operand can be a single element value, or a valarray containing elements of the same type, or another slice_array of the same type. Assigning a single value to a slice_array will set the elements in the valarray it references to the value. When the right operand is a valarray or a slice_array, you must ensure that it contains at least as many elements as the left operand; if there are less the result will not be what you want. The output from executing the code above is:

```
data:
  99   99   99   99   99
   6    7    8    9   10
   2    2    3    3    3
```

You can see that the first and third rows in data have been modified.

You can use any of the following compound assignment operators (op=) with a slice_array object:

- The arithmetic operations, +=, -=, *=, /-, and %=
- The bitwise operations &=, |=, and ^=,
- The shift operations >>= and <<=

In every case, the left operand must be a slice_array object and the right operand must be a valarray object containing the same type of elements as the slice_array. The op= operation will apply op between each element referenced the slice_array and the corresponding element in the valarray that is the right operand. Note that a right operand that is a single value *is not* supported; you always need a valarray object as the right operand, even if all the corresponding elements on the right have the same value.

The valarray that is the right operand typically contains the same number of elements as the right operand but it's not absolutely necessary. It must not contain fewer elements but it can contain more, in which case if the slice_array that is the left operand has n elements, the first n elements of the right operand are used for the operation. Here's an example that uses += to modify a slice of a valarray object:

```
valarray<int> data {1, 2, 3, 4, 5, 6, 7, 8, 9, 10, 11, 12, 13, 14, 15};
auto d_slice = data[slice {2, 3, 5}];   // References data[2], data[7], data[12]
d_slice += valarray<int>{10, 20, 30};   // Combines the slice with the new valarray
std::cout << "data:\n";
print(data, 5, 4);
```

The elements in data that are referenced by d_slice have the values of elements at corresponding index positions in the more object added to them. The output is:

```
data:
   1    2   13    4    5
   6    7   28    9   10
  11   12   43   14   15
```

After the operation, the elements in the column in the data array that the slice selects have values that result from 3+10, 8+20, and 13+30. Multiplying elements in a slice is just as easy:

```
valarray<int> factors {22, 17, 10};
data[slice{0, 3, 5}] *= factors;        // Values of the 1st column: 22 102 110
```

The slice object selects the first column from data and each element in this column is multiplied by the corresponding element in the factors object. If you just want to multiply the slice by a given value, you just create a suitable valarray object:

```
valarray<int> data {1, 2, 3, 4, 5, 6, 7, 8, 9, 10, 11, 12, 13, 14, 15};
slice row3 {10, 5, 1};
data[row3] *= valarray<int>(3, row3.size());          // Multiply 3rd row of data by 3
```

This multiplies the last 5 elements in data by 3. The number of elements in the valarray that is the right operand in the last statement is set by calling the size() member of the slice object. This ensures that the number of elements is the same as the number selected from data.

Suppose that you want to add the elements from one column in data to another column. You can't add a slice_array to a slice_array but you can still do what you want. One way is to use a valarray constructor that accepts a slice_array as an argument. With this constructor, the values referenced by the slice_array object are used to initialize the elements in the valarray object that is created. Then you can use this object as the right operand in a compound assignment with the slice_array. Here's how you could add the fifth column in data to the second and fourth columns:

```
valarray<int> data {1, 2, 3, 4, 5, 6, 7, 8, 9, 10, 11, 12, 13, 14, 15};
valarray<int> col5 {data[slice{4, 3, 5}]};            // Same as 5th column in data
data[slice{1, 3, 5}] += col5;                         // Add to 2nd column
data[slice{3, 3, 5}] += col5;                         // Add to 4th column
print(data, 5, 4);
```

The slice_array object that is produced by using a slice object as an index to data is passed as the argument to the valarray constructor to create the object col5. This valarray constructor is not defined as explicit, so it can be used for implicit conversions from a slice_array type to a valarray type. The col5 object could have been defined like this:

```
valarray<int> col5 = data[slice{4, 3, 5}];            // Convert slice_array to valarray
```

This calls the operator=() member of the col5 object, which expects the right operand to be a valarray object. The compiler will insert a call for the valarray constructor that accepts a slice_array object as the argument to convert the slice_array to a valarray. Note that this is not the same as the following statement:

```
auto col = data[slice{4, 3, 5}];                      // col will be type slice_array
```

There's no conversion here. This just defines col to be the slice_array object that results from indexing data with the slice object.

The output produced by the previous the block of code that calls print() will be:

```
 1   7   3   9   5
 6  17   8  19  10
11  27  13  29  15
```

Of course, it's also possible to do the same thing with a plain old loop:

```
size_t row_len {5}, n_rows {3};                      // Row length, number of rows
for(size_t i {}; i < n_rows*row_len; i += row_len)
{
  data[i+1] += data[i+4];                            // Increment 2nd column
  data[i+3] += data[i+4];                            // Increment 4th column
}
```

The loop index, i, steps through index values that select elements in the first column of data. Using an expression of the form i+n as a subscript for data in the loop body selects an element in the nth column. Let's see slice objects in action in a program that's more like a real application.

Applying Slices to Solve Equations

We can develop a program to use slice objects with valarray objects to solve a set of linear equations. Here's a typical set of linear equations:

$$2x_1 - 2x_2 - 3x_3 + x_4 = 23$$
$$5x_1 + 3x_2 + x_3 + 2x_4 = 77$$
$$x_1 + x_2 - 2x_3 - x_4 = 14$$
$$3x_1 + 4x_2 + 5x_3 + 6x_4 = 23$$

There are four linear equations involving four variables so it's possible to find the values for x_1, x_2, x_3, and x_4 that satisfy these equations as long as each equation is independent of the other three. Our program will use the well-known *Gaussian Elimination method* to solve a set of n linear equations in n unknowns and we will implement it using a valarray object to store the equations. The valarray object will store the coefficients for the variables and the value of the right-hand side for each equation. For example, you could store the equations above as the following valarray:

```
valarray<double> equations {2, -2, -3,  1, 23,
                            5,  3,  1,  2, 77,
                            1,  1, -2, -1, 14,
                            3,  4,  5,  6, 23 };
```

Note that the data in the equations object is a two-dimensional matrix with four rows and five columns. In general, n equations in n variables will be represented by n rows and n+1 columns. Before we can write any code, we need to understand the method.

Gaussian Elimination

The Gaussian Elimination method involves two basic steps. The first step is to transform the original set of equations into a different form that allows the values of the variables to be determined, and the second is to determine the values of the variables. Figure10-6 illustrates the concept.

$$a_{11}x_1 + a_{12}x_2 + a_{13}x_3 + a_{14}x_4 = c_1$$
$$a_{21}x_1 + a_{22}x_2 + a_{23}x_3 + a_{24}x_4 = c_2$$
$$a_{31}x_1 + a_{32}x_2 + a_{33}x_3 + a_{34}x_4 = c_3$$
$$a_{41}x_1 + a_{42}x_2 + a_{43}x_3 + a_{44}x_4 = c_4$$

Transformed into

$$b_{11}x_1 + b_{12}x_2 + b_{13}x_3 + b_{14}x_4 = d_1$$
$$b_{22}x_2 + b_{23}x_3 + b_{24}x_4 = d_2$$
$$b_{33}x_3 + b_{34}x_4 = d_3$$
$$b_{44}x_4 = d_4$$

a_{ij} is coefficient of variable x_j in equation i.

c_i is value of right hand side in equation i.

From the last equation we know that:
$x_4 = d_4/b_{44}$
Knowing x_4 we can determine x_3:
$x_3 = (d_3 - b_{34}x_4)/b_{33}$
We can continue in this way to obtain
the values of the other two variables

Figure 10-6. *What the Gaussian Elimination method does*

Figure 10-6 shows a general representation of four equations in four unknowns, where the a's are the coefficients, the x's are the variables, and the c's are the values on the right of the equations. The first step transforms the equations on the left into the form on the right, which is called *row echelon form*. Figure 10-6 describes the procedure for the second step, which obtains the values for all the variables from the equations in row echelon form. This process is called *back substitution*. So how do we transform the set of equations on the left into row echelon form?

The Elimination Process

I'm sure you know that you can add or subtract the same thing from both sides of an equation and you still have a valid equation. This means you can add or subtract a multiple of one equation from another, and you still have a valid equation. Figure 10-7 illustrates how you can apply this idea to convert a set of four linear equations represented as a matrix into row echelon form.

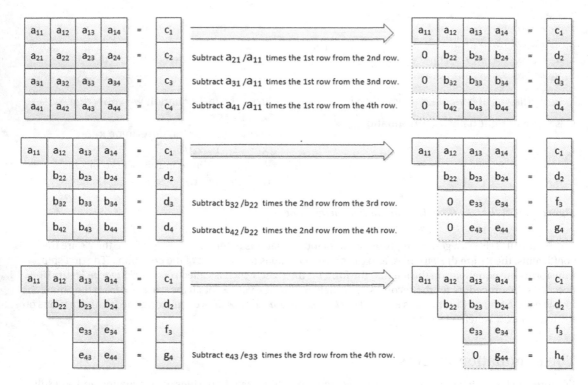

Figure 10-7. *Transforming linear equations into row echelon form*

Figure 10-7 shows how elements are set to zero in successive rows in the matrix in three steps. The first step is to subtract a specially chosen multiple of the first row from each of the subsequent rows. This process is repeated – subtracting multiples of the second and third rows, which results in the row echelon form. It's convenient to do it starting at the first row and working down but you could eliminate from rows in any sequence.

The element in the matrix that is chosen to eliminate corresponding elements from other rows is called a *pivot*. Each operation to subtract a multiple of one row from another changes the coefficient of the element corresponding to the pivot to 0, thus eliminating it. Of course, the operation also changes the values of the other coefficients so this is reflected in Figure 10-7 by the changes in the letters that represent them. This elimination process is possible as long as the equations are solvable. This will not be the case if any equation can result from a combination of one or more of the other equations.

Finding the Best Pivot

Of course, some coefficients may be zero, so you can't apply this elimination process arbitrarily. If a_{11} was 0 for instance, certain disaster would follow from subtracting the first row from the second. You need to be sure that the pivot element is not zero. It's also numerically advantageous if its absolute value is the largest in the column. The order of the equations represented by the rows in the matrix is arbitrary so the order of the rows can be changed at any time without affecting the problem. Thus if a given pivot is not the maximum, you can arrange for it to be the maximum by swapping the current pivot row with the row that contains the greatest absolute value. Figure 10-8 illustrates this process.

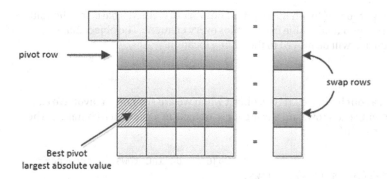

Figure 10-8. *Choosing the best pivot*

Figure10-8 shows a situation with five equations after the first elimination has been completed. The best value for the pivot is in the second-to-last row so this row is swapped with the second row before the next elimination step. Swapping all the elements in a row would be expensive on time when there are many variables, so it's better to avoid this. By using slice objects to identify rows, you can swap rows without moving any of the elements in the valarray that contains the matrix for the equations.

We know enough about how Gaussian Elimination works to develop the code. We'll store all the data for the equations in a valarray<double> object. There will be several functions in the program so I'll put definitions of all the functions other than main() in a separate source file, gaussian.cpp. I'll start with a function to read the data for the equations from the standard input stream.

Getting the Input Data

Each equation in n variables is of the form:

$$a_1x_1 + a_2x_2 + \ldots + a_nx_n = b$$

There will always be n equations and the n coefficients, a_i, for each equation and the value on the right will be stored as contiguous elements in the valarray object. Thus the input function must read n*(n+1) values and store them in a valarray. Here's the code to do that:

```
// Read the data for n equations in n unknowns
valarray<double> get_data(size_t n)
{
  valarray<double> equations(n*(n + 1));     // n rows of n+1 elements
  std::cout << "Enter " << n + 1
            << " values for each of "<< n << " equations.\n"
            << "(i.e. including coefficients that are zero and the rhs):\n";
  for(auto& coeff: equations) std::cin >> coeff;
  return equations;
}
```

The function expects the number of equations, which is the same as the number of variables, to be supplied as an argument, so the calling program, which will be main(), must supply this. This code would do it:

```
size_t n_rows {};
std::cout << "Enter the number of variables: ";
std::cin >> n_rows;
auto equations = get_data(n_rows);
```

445

The `valarray` object is created in `get_data()` with the required number of elements based on the value of the argument and the range-base `for` loop reads value from `cin` for every element. The object that is created locally in `get_data()` and returned will be moved to the calling location.

Rows as slice Objects

We want to avoid having to move data about in the `equations` object when we are selecting a pivot. We can do this by creating a `slice` object to define each row, and storing these objects in a sequence container. The `slice` objects can be created like this in `main()`:

```
std::vector<slice> row_slices;                          // Objects define rows in sequence
std::generate_n(std::back_inserter(row_slices), n_rows,
                                  [n_rows]()
                                  { static size_t index {};
                                    return slice {(n_rows+1)*index++, n_rows+1, 1};
                                  });
```

The `generate_n()` algorithm stores `n_rows` `slice` objects in the `row_slices` container using a lambda expression to create them. The lambda captures `n_rows` by value. The `slice` objects only differ in their start index values, which run from 0 in steps of `n_rows+1`, which is the length of a row. Each slice represents `n_rows+1` index values with a stride of 1. To interchange two rows, we just need to swap the `slice` objects for those rows in the `row_slices` container; the elements in the `valarray` can stay where they are.

You could store pointers to `slice` objects in the container, but since a `slice` object is very small, just 12 bytes on my system, it hardly seems worth the trouble. To work with the equations, we only need access to the `valarray` object that contains data for them and the `row_slices` container that defines the rows in the matrix. The size of the `row_slices` object is the number of rows, so while we have access to the `row_slices` container we know the number of rows and the length.

Finding the Best Pivot

You saw back in Figure10-7 how row echelon form of the equations can be produced by subtracting multiples of each row from the rows that follow. Each step eliminates a column of variables to the left of the diagonal so you end up with just one variable in the last row. Prior to each elimination step, it's necessary to find the best pivot from the rows involved in the step, and the overall loop that drives the elimination process will iterate over the rows from the first to the second-to-last. Finding the pivot always involves searching elements in a column that starts on a diagonal of the `equations` matrix and runs to the last row. You could identify and find the maximum element in a column by accessing elements in the `equations` object with two index values that you calculate. I'll use a `slice` object for the practice.

We need to be able to define a `slice` object that selects a column of elements that starts at the diagonal element in an arbitrary row. Figure10-9 shows how this is determined.

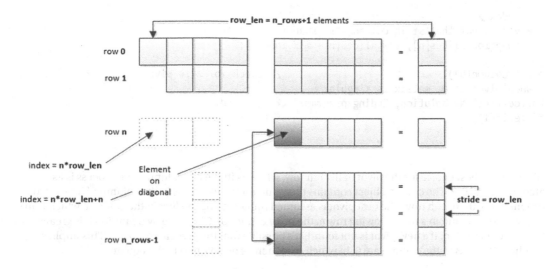

- Index values apply to the **valarray** containing the elements
- The valarray contains **n_rows*row_len** elements
- The slice object to select the shaded columns is:

$$\text{slice\{n*row\_len + n, n\_rows - n, row\_len\}}$$

Figure 10-9. *Determining the slice object for the column to search for a pivot*

There are n_rows rows representing equations in Figure10-9 with n_rows+1 elements in a row. The first row is row 0. The stride from any element to the element below is always the row length. The index of the first element in the nth row is n times the row length. The index for the diagonal element in the nth row will be the index of the first element in the nth row, plus n.

Here's the code for a function to set the best pivot for an arbitrary row:

```
// Selects the best pivot in row n (rows indexed from 0)
void set_pivot(const valarray<double>& equations, std::vector<slice>& row_slices, size_t n)
{
  size_t n_rows {row_slices.size()};          // Number of rows
  size_t row_len {n_rows + 1};                 // Row length = number of columns

  // Create an object containing the elements in column n, starting row n
  valarray<double> column {equations[slice {n*row_len + n, n_rows - n, row_len}]};
  column = std::abs(column);                   // Absolute values

  size_t max_index {};                         // Index to best pivot in column
  for(size_t i {1}; i < column.size(); ++i)    // Find index for max value
  {
    if(column[max_index] < column[i]) max_index = i;
  }
```

```
  if(max_index > 0)
  { // Pivot is not the 1st in column - so swap rows to make it so
    std::swap(row_slices[n], row_slices[n + max_index]);
  }
  else if(!column[0])                              // Check for zero pivot
  { // When pivot is 0, matrix is singular
    std::cerr << "No solution. Ending program." << std::endl;
    std::exit(1);
  }
}
```

This finds the best choice for the pivot in the nth row, which is in the nth column. The process is as illustrated in Figure10-9. The column object contains the values of the elements in the column of interest, the first element being in the nth row. The best pivot is assumed initially to be the first in the column, which is in row n. If the pivot is found in a row following row n, the pivot cannot be 0 because by definition it is greater than the element in row n. If a new pivot is not found, it's possible that the pivot in row n is 0. This implies that the other elements in the column are 0, in which case there is no solution to the equations.

Generating Row Echelon Form

The reduce_matrix() function will convert the matrix of values in equations to row echelon form using the set_pivot() function to choose the best pivot prior to reducing the elements in a column:

```
// Reduce the equations matrix to row echelon form
void reduce_matrix(valarray<double>& equations, std::vector<slice>& row_slices)
{
  size_t n_rows {row_slices.size()};              // Number of rows
  size_t row_len {n_rows + 1};                     // Row length
  for(size_t row {}; row < n_rows - 1; ++row)      // From 1st row to second-to-last
  {
    set_pivot(equations, row_slices, row);         // Find best pivot

    // Create an object containing element values for pivot row
    valarray<double> pivot_row {equations[row_slices[row]]};
    auto pivot = pivot_row[row];                    // The pivot element
    pivot_row /= pivot;                             // Divide pivot row by pivot

    // For each of the rows following the current row,
    // subtract the pivot row multiplied by the row element in the pivot column
    for(size_t next_row {row + 1}; next_row < n_rows; ++next_row)
    {
      equations[row_slices[next_row]] -=
                          equations[row_slices[next_row].start() + row] * pivot_row;
    }
  }
}
```

The function iterates over the rows in equations from the first to the second-to-last. For each row, the best pivot is chosen by calling set_pivot(). A valarray object is created containing copies of the elements from the current row – the pivot row. The operator/=() member of a valarray object divides each element of the left operand by the value of the right operand and this is applied to pivot_row with the value of the pivot element as the right operand to make the pivot coefficient 1. For each of the subsequent rows, the pivot row is multiplied by the value of the element in the pivot column, and the resultant `valarray` object is subtracted from the row. This will set the value of the element in the pivot column to 0.

Back Substitution

With the equations matrix in row echelon form, we can carry out back substitution to find values for the variables. The equation that is defined by the last row in the matrix has all variable coefficients zero except that for the last. The value of the last variable will therefore be the right-hand side divided by the value of the coefficient. If we divide the last row by the coefficient the last coefficient will be 1 and the value of the variable will be the value of the last element in the row. We can then multiply the last row by the coefficient for the variable from each of the previous rows and subtract it from each previous row in turn. This will eliminate the last variable from all the rows, and the second-to-last will now have just one nonzero coefficient. We can then repeat the process, which sound very much like a loop. Figure 10-10 shows the process with four equations.

The result of the process is that all coefficients are zero except for the diagonal, where they are 1. Thus the values in the last column represent the solution to the equations. Here's the code for the function to implement the process illustrated in Figure 10-10:

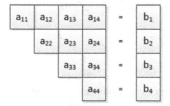

1. Start with row echelon form.

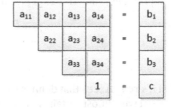

2. Divide the last row by a_{44}

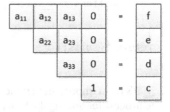

3. Subtract a multiple of the last row from each row above.

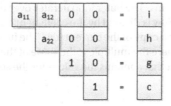

4. Divide the 3rd row by a_{33}

5. Subtract a multiple of the 3rd row from each row above

6. Divide the 2nd row by a_{22} then subtract a multiple of the 2nd from the 1st row.

Figure 10-10. *Back substitution*

```
// Perform back substitution and return the solution
valarray<double> back_substitution(valarray<double>& equations,
                                          const std::vector<slice>& row_slices)
{
  size_t n_rows{row_slices.size()};
  size_t row_len {n_rows + 1};

  // Divide the last row by the second to last element
  // Multiply the last row by the second to last element in each row and subtract it from the row.
  // Repeat for all the other rows
  valarray<double> results(n_rows);                     // Stores the solution
  for(int row {static_cast<int>(n_rows - 1)}; row >= 0; --row)
  {
    equations[row_slices[row]] /=
                    valarray<double>(equations[row_slices[row].start() + row], row_len);
    valarray<double> last_row {equations[row_slices[row]]};
    results[row] = last_row[n_rows];                     // Store value for x[row]
    for(int i {}; i < row; ++i)
    {
      equations[row_slices[i]] -= equations[row_slices[i].start() + row] * last_row;
    }
  }
  return results;
}
```

It's most important to remember that it's row_slices that defines the sequences of equations at this point. The process for finding the best pivot element will almost certainly change the order of the equations, which is done by interchanging elements in row_slices, not by moving elements in the equations array. The back substitution process therefore has to work with the rows in the order determined by row_slices, not with the rows in the order they appear in equations. Because of this, it's necessary to define the results object to store the values for the solution to the equations. The outer loop iterates over the rows in reverse order. On each iteration of the outer loop, the current row is divided by the coefficient on the diagonal. A valarray object, last_row, is then created that contains a copy of the current row. The inner loop then subtracts a multiple of last_row from each preceding row, where the multiple is the value of the diagonal element in the row. When the outer loop ends, the results object that contains the values for the solution is returned.

The Complete Program

The program consists of two files. The gaussian.cpp file contents will be:

```
// Gaussian.cpp
// Functions to implement Gaussian elimination
#include <valarray>                           // For valarray, slice, abs()
#include <vector>                             // For vector container
#include <iterator>                           // For ostream iterator
#include <algorithm>                          // For copy_n()
#include <utility>                            // For swap()
#include <iostream>                           // For standard streams
#include <iomanip>                            // For stream manipulators
using std::valarray;
using std::slice;
```

```
// Definition for get_data() ...

// Definition for set_pivot() ...

// Definition for reduce_matrix() ...

// Definition for back_substitution() ...
```

The main() program just has to read the data and call the functions from gaussian.cpp in the right order then output the result. The contents of Ex10_03.cpp will be:

```cpp
// Ex10_03.cpp
// Using the Gaussian Elimination method to solve a set of linear equations
#include <valarray>                              // For valarray, slice, abs()
#include <vector>                                // For vector container
#include <iterator>                              // For ostream iterator
#include <algorithm>                             // For generate_n()
#include <utility>                               // For swap()
#include <iostream>                              // For standard streams
#include <iomanip>                               // For stream manipulators
#include <string>                                // For string type
using std::string;
using std::valarray;
using std::slice;

// Function prototypes
valarray<double> get_data(size_t n);
void reduce_matrix(valarray<double>& equations, std::vector<slice>& row_slices);
valarray<double> back_substitution(valarray<double>& equations,
                                    const std::vector<slice>& row_slices);

int main()
{
  size_t n_rows {};
  std::cout << "Enter the number of variables: ";
  std::cin >> n_rows;
  auto equations = get_data(n_rows);

  // Generate slice objects for rows in row order
  std::vector<slice> row_slices;                          // Objects define rows in sequence
  size_t row_len {n_rows + 1};
  std::generate_n(std::back_inserter(row_slices), n_rows,
                                [row_len]()
                                { static size_t index {};
                                  return slice {row_len*index++, row_len, 1};
                                });

  reduce_matrix(equations, row_slices);                   // Reduce to row echelon form
  auto solution = back_substitution(equations, row_slices);
```

```
// Output the solution
size_t count {}, perline {8};
std::cout << "\nSolution:\n";
string x{"x"};
for(const auto& v : solution)
{
  std::cout << std::setw(3) << x + std::to_string(count+1) << " = "
            << std::fixed << std::setprecision(2) << std::setw(10)
            << v;
  if(++count % perline) std::cout << '\n';
}
std::cout << std::endl;
}
```

The first action in main() is to read the number of variables for the problem to be entered. Next, the data for the equations is read by calling get_data() and the resultant valarray object will be moved to equations. A vector of slice objects that select successive rows in equations is created. The start indexes begin at 0 and increase in increments of the row length. The size and stride for all slice object are the row length and 1 respectively. Calling reduce_matrix() followed by back_substitution() returns the solution, unless no solution is possible. The solution values are output in the last loop. You can use a range-based for loop to iterate through elements in a valarray object because iterators are available.

Here's an example of the output when solving six equations:

```
Enter the number of variables: 6
Enter 7 values for each of 6 equations.
(i.e. including coefficients that are zero and the rhs):
 1  1  1  1  1  1   8
 2  3 -5 -1  1  1 -18
-1  5  2  7  2  3  40
 3  1 10  2  1 11 -15
 3 17  5  1  3  2  41
 5  7  3 -4  2 -1   9

Solution:
 x1 =      -2.00
 x2 =       1.00
 x3 =       3.00
 x4 =       4.00
 x5 =       7.00
 x6 =      -5.00
```

You could usefully trace the progress of reducing the matrix by adding output for equations at appropriate points in reduce_matrix(). You could track the back substitution mechanism in a similar way. This would give you a good insight into the Gaussian Elimination method in action. You could use the print() function template you saw earlier in this chapter to do it. Using slice objects is simple stuff. It's time to look at something a bit more challenging.

Multiple Slices

The valarray header defines the gslice class, which is a generalization of the idea of a slice. A gslice object generates index values from a start index, just like a slice, but it produces two or more slices, and the way it does this is a little complicated. Essentially, a gslice presumes that elements are selected from a valarray object that represents a multidimensional array as a linear sequence of elements. A gslice object is defined by three parameter values. The first constructor argument is a *start index* and is a value of type size_t that identifies the first element in the first slice, as with a slice. The second argument is a valarray<size_t> object where each element specifies a *size*. For each size specified by the second constructor argument, there is a corresponding stride; these strides are defined by the third argument, which is a valarray<size_t> object with the same number of elements as the second argument. The stride for each size in the second argument is the corresponding element in the third argument.

Of course, each slice that a gslice represents has a start index, a size, and a stride. The start index for the first slice is the first argument to the gslice constructor. The size of the first slice is the first element in the valarray of sizes, and the stride is the first element in the valarray of strides. You should find that straightforward but now it gets a little tricky, but stay with it.

The index values generated by the first slice are *start indexes* for application of the *second slice*. In other words, the second slice defines a new set of indexes from *each* index that results from the first slice. This process continues.

Each slice after the first is applied to *every* index generated by the previous slice, and they each result in a set of index values. For example, if the first slice from a gslice object has a size of 3, it defines three index values; if the second slice has a size of 2, it generates 2 index values. The size and stride of the second slice are used three times – with each of the index values from the first slice as start indexes. Thus you get 6 index values in all from the two slices, which selects 6 elements from a valarray.

The result of using a gslice as a subscript for a valarray can include multiple references to a given element. This occurs when the sequences of indexes produced by the last slice from a gslice overlap. A simple example of the way a gslice selects elements from a valarray is illustrated in Figure 10-11.

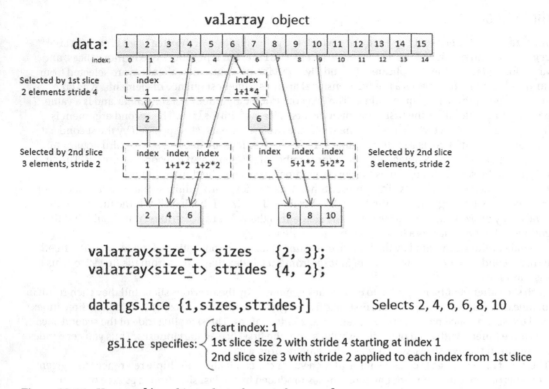

```
valarray<size_t> sizes   {2, 3};
valarray<size_t> strides {4, 2};

data[gslice {1,sizes,strides}]          Selects 2, 4, 6, 6, 8, 10
```

gslice specifies:
- start index: 1
- 1st slice size 2 with stride 4 starting at index 1
- 2nd slice size 3 with stride 2 applied to each index from 1st slice

Figure 10-11. *How a* gslice *object selects elements from a* valarray

The gslice object in Figure10-11 defines two slices. Figure10-11 shows how the first slice produces 2 index values that are the start indexes for repeated applications of the second slice with size 3. Because the final two index sequences overlap, the element at index 5 with the value 6 is duplicated in the result. In general, the number of elements that a gslice object selects is the product of the size values defined by the valarray object that is the second constructor argument - 2×3 in this case.

As with a slice object, using a gslice to index a valarray<T> results in an object that encapsulates references to elements in the valarray, but the object is of a different type – it's of type gslice_array<T>. I'll get to how you use this later. First, let's look at some of the things we can do with gslice objects.

Selecting Multiple Rows or Columns

You can select multiple rows or multiple columns from a valarray object using a gslice object as the argument to the subscript operator. The selected rows or columns have to be evenly spaced, by which I mean that the increment between the first elements in successive rows or columns is the same. Selecting two or more *rows* is relatively straightforward. The start index for the gslice will be the index of the first element in the first row to be selected. The first size will be the number of rows, and the corresponding stride will be the step between rows, which is a multiple of the length of a row. The second size and stride values select the elements in each row, so the second size is the row length and the second stride is 1.

Suppose you defines valarray objects, with names sizes and strides, like this:

```
valarray<size_t> sizes {2, 5};          // Two size values
valarray<size_t> strides {10, 1};       // Stride values corresponding to the size values
```

The expression to select the first and third rows from the array in Figure10-11 is:

```
data[gslice{0, sizes, strides}]
```

The two rows start at index values 0 and 10; these indexes are the result of the first slice that is defined by the start index 0 that is the first argument to the gslice constructor, and the first size and its corresponding stride value in the valarray objects that are the second and third arguments to the gslice constructor. Each row has 5 contiguous elements, and the rows are selected by the second size, 5, and its corresponding stride value, 1. Note that you are not obliged to define sizes and strides explicitly. You could write the expression to select the two rows as:

```
data[gslice{0, {2, 5}, {10, 1}}]
```

Now let's consider the more difficult task of selecting two or more *columns*. As an example, let's see how you could select the first, third, and last columns from the array in Figure10-11. Figure10-12 illustrates this with the columns that are selected grayed out in the two-dimensional representation of the elements.

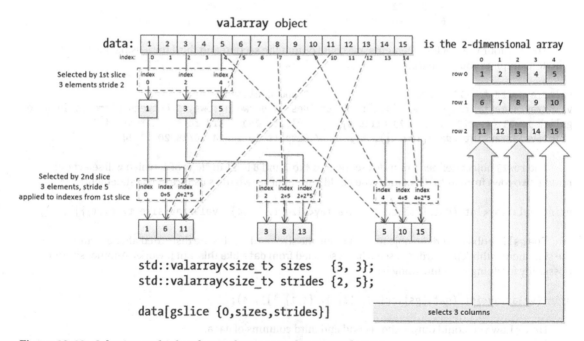

Figure 10-12. *Selecting multiple columns from a two-dimensional array*

The first size and stride determine the index values for the first elements in each of the columns to be selected. The second size and stride selects the elements in each column; the increment between elements in a column is the row length. Since the first stride is fixed, you can only select two or more columns that are equally space in this way; you could not select the first, second, and fifth columns for example.

It gets more complicated with gslice objects that define 3 or more slices that you could apply to arrays with three or more dimensions but it works in the same way. You need to take care that a gslice object does not create invalid index values; if it does, the results are undefined, and the effect is definitely not good. Most of the time, slice and gslice objects are applied to arrays with one or two dimensions, so I'll be concentrating on those.

Using gslice Objects

A gslice_array<T> object that you get when you index a valarray<T> object with a gslice object has a lot in common with a slice_array object. It has the same range of function members as a slice_array so the same range of operators can be applied to it. You have an assignment operator and the same range of op= operators. There's also a valarray constructor that accepts a gslice_array object as the argument and it can be used for implicit conversions from a gslice_array<T> type to valarray<T>.

Let's consider some things we can do with a gslice. Suppose we define the following valarray object:

```
valarray<int> data { 2,   4,   6,   8,      // 4 x 4 matrix
                    10, 12, 14, 16,
                    18, 20, 22, 24,
                    26, 28, 30, 32};
```

This has four rows of four elements. We could output the second and third rows using the print() function template you saw earlier:

```
valarray<size_t> r23_sizes {2,4};        // 2 and 4 elements
valarray<size_t> r23_strides {4,1}; // strides: 4 between rows, 1 between elements in a row
gslice row23 {4, r23_sizes, r23_strides}; // Selects 2nd + 3rd rows - 2 rows of 4
print(valarray<int>(data[row23]), 4);    // Outputs 10 12 14 16/18 20 22 24
```

The row23 object defines row index sequences 4 to 7 and 8 to 11 in steps of 1, which will select the middle two rows from data. Of course, you could output these two rows using a single statement:

```
print(valarray<int>(data[gslice{4, valarray<size_t> {2,4}, valarray<size_t> {4,1}}]), 4);
```

The gslice object and the objects containing the sizes and strides are discarded after executing the statement. I think it's harder to see what is selected from data like this, but it works. Another shorter possibility for doing the same thing is:

```
print(valarray<int>(data[gslice{ 4, {2,4}, {4,1} }]), 4);
```

Here's how you could output the second and third columns of data:

```
std::valarray<size_t> sizes2 {2,4};      // 2 and 4 elements

// strides: 1 between columns, 4 between elements in a column
std::valarray<size_t> strides2 {1,4};
gslice col23 {1, sizes2, strides2};      // Selects 2nd and 3rd columns - 2 columns of 4
print(valarray<int>(data[col23]), 4);  // Outputs 4 12 20 28/6 14 22 30
```

The start index for the gslice is the second element, which is the first element in the second column. It should be clear by now how this identifies the two columns from data.

We could now add the values of the second and third rows to the second and third columns, like this:

```
data[col23] += data[row23];
print(data, 4);
```

Executing these statements will produce the following output:

2	14	24	8
10	24	34	16
18	34	44	24
26	44	54	32

If you compare this with the original values used to initialize data, you'll see that we got the result desired. The second column is 4+10, 12+12, 20+14, 28+16; the third column is 6+18, 14+20, 22+22, 30+24.

Selecting Arbitrary Subsets of Elements

There may be time when you want more flexibility in accessing valarray elements than that provided by slice and gslice that offer inherently regular indexing of a valarray. In this case you can use a valarray<size_t> object that contains an arbitrary set of index values as the subscript for a valarray<T> object. The result is an object of type indirect_array<T> that encapsulates references to the elements at the index values. Note that the index values must be type size_t; a valarray<int> won't work.

An indirect_array object has the same function members as a slice_array object so you can do the same things with it. There's also a valarray constructor that enables implicit conversions from type indirect_array<T> to type valarray<T>.

Any combination of elements from the array can be selected using a valarray<size_t> object, but you should not duplicate index values. If an indirect_array object contains duplicate references, the result of operations with it are undefined; it may work some of the time, but not necessarily all of the time. Here's an example of selecting an arbitrary set of elements from a valarray:

```
valarray<double> data {2,  4,  6,  8, 10, 12, 14, 16, 18, 20, 22, 24, 26, 28, 30, 32};
std::valarray<size_t> choices {3, 5, 7, 11};      // Indexes to select arbitrary elements
print(valarray<double>(data[choices]));           // Values selected:  8  12 16    24
data[choices] *= data[choices];                   // Square the values
print(valarray<double>(data[choices]));           // Result:        64 144 256 576
```

The choices object contains index values that select four floating-point values from the data object. The second-to-last statement squares the values selected by choices and the result of executing these statements is shown in the comments. Because choices is a valarray, you can perform arithmetic operations on the set of index values to produce a new set. For example:

```
size_t incr{3};
data[choices+incr] += valarray<double>(incr+1, choices.size());  // Add 4 to selected elements
print(valarray<double>(data[choices+incr]));                     // 18 22 26 34
```

The expression choices+incr results in a new valarray<size_T> object containing index values from choices incremented by 3, so it contains 6, 8, 10, and 14. Using the new valarray object as the argument to the subscript operator for data returns an indirect_array<double> object containing references to the data elements with values 14, 18, 22, and 30. The += operation increments these values by the values of corresponding elements of the valarray<double> object that is the right operand, which are all 4.

Selecting Elements Conditionally

You saw earlier that you can use comparison operators to compare corresponding elements in a valarray<T> object with corresponding elements in another valarray<T> object, or with a value of type T. The result in either case is a valarray<bool> object that has element values that are the result of the elements comparisons. You can pass a valarray<bool> object to the subscript operator for a valarray that will select elements corresponding to true so you have a way to select elements based on any condition you can contrive. The result of using a valarray<bool> object as a subscript is a mask_array<T> object, where T is the type of value in the array being accessed. A mask_array object has the same functionality as a slice_array. Here's a very contrived example:

```
std::uniform_int_distribution<int> dist {0, 25};
std::random_device rd;                         // Non-deterministic seed source
std::default_random_engine rng {rd()};         // Create random number generator
std::valarray<char> letters (52);

for(auto& ch: letters)
  ch = 'a' + dist(rng);                        // Random letter 'a' to 'z'
print(letters,26, 2);

auto vowels = letters == 'a'||letters =='e'|| letters == 'i' ||
              letters == 'o' || letters == 'u';
valarray<char> chosen {letters[vowels]};       // Contains copies of the vowels in letters
size_t count {chosen.size()};                  // The number of vowels
std::cout << count << " vowels were generated:\n";
print(chosen, 26, 2);

letters[vowels] -= valarray<char>('a'-'A', count);
print(letters, 26, 2);
```

   This code is to demonstrate selecting elements conditionally – it's definitely not the best way of doing what it does. It incidentally draws on a couple of things you saw back in Chapter 8. The letters object stores elements of type char and it is populated with random lowercase letters in the range-based for loop using a uniform discrete distribution. The distribution, dist, generates values in the range 0 to 25 inclusive so in the loop we get letters from 'a' to 'z' inclusive. The vowels object is produced by ORing the result of comparing the elements in letters with each vowel. Each comparison produces a valarray<bool> object with the same number of elements as letters. The object will have elements that are true when the corresponding element is the vowel. ORing these together (using the non-member operator||() function) results in a valarray<bool> object that contains elements with the value true when the corresponding element of letters is any lowercase vowel. Using the valarray<bool> object, vowels, to subscript letters produces a mask_array<char> object that references the elements in letters that are vowels. Finally, the operator-=() member of the mask_array<char> is called to decrement the elements in letters that are vowels by the difference between 'a' and 'A', thus converting them to uppercase.

I got this output:

```
d a v i d h o t x v i v d o p i i n d q p g r q f s
 g i c e w o b r e t a b w l l q j h x f j h n p o y

13 vowels were generated.
 a i o i o i i i e o e a o

d A v I d h O t x v I v d O p I I n d q p g r q f s
 g I c E w O b r E t A b w l l q j h x f j h n p O y
```

I was encouraged by this output. The first eight random letters gives credence to the idea that with a large enough array, and executing the code enough times, you could generate the complete works of Shakespeare.

Rational Arithmetic

The ratio header defines the ratio template type, which is a strange beast in many ways, particularly because everything it does is done at compile time, not at runtime. You don't need to create objects – just instances of the ratio class template that define types. An understanding of the ratio class template is essential if you are going to use the clocks and timers that I'll discuss later in this chapter.

A *rational number* is just a fraction – a ratio of two integers. As you know, many decimal fractions cannot be represented exactly as binary numbers – or as decimal number come to that. For instance, you can't represent 2/3 exactly in either binary or decimal notation; both representations would require an infinite number of digits to be exact so floating-point representations of many rational numbers always deviate slightly from their exact values. The error is quite small, of course, with a 24-bit mantissa the error will usually be no greater than 2^{-24}. This is negligible – until you do some calculations with such values. Suppose a rational number has the exact value V, but in floating-point its value is V-e, where e is a very small error. Let's consider a simple example of multiplying the floating-point value by itself. The value is the result of (V-e)*(V-e), which evaluates to $V^2-2Ve+e^2$. The exact result we would like is V^2 so the rest is the deviation from the correct result. The e^2 part is of the order of 2^{-48}, which we can ignore, but the rest, 2Ve is not so negligible. The error in the result of the calculation is 2V times larger than the error in the original value and this error can increase further as a result of subsequent calculations. The ratio template and other template types that the ratio header defines offer a kind of a way to overcome this – at least at compile time.

The ratio template defines *types* that represent rational numbers defined by a numerator and a denominator that are both integral values of type intmax_t. intmax_t is defined in the cstdint header to be the integer type in your implementation with the maximum range. Note that it's *types* that represent rational numbers, not *objects*. Thus you can represent 2/3 by the following type:

```
using v2_3 = std::ratio<2, 3>;                    // A type to represent two thirds
```

The template parameters for the v2_3 type are the values of the numerator and the denominator for the rational number. These values are stored in static members of the class type, num and den respectively, which are constant static members so you cannot change them after you have defined a type. The den parameter has a default value of 1 so you can define types that represent integers by just specifying the first type argument. For example, ratio<99> is a type representing the value 99. I'll assume there's a using directive for std::ratio in effect for subsequent code and drop the std namespace name qualifier.

A ratio type always represents a number in its lowest terms. If you define the type ratio<4,8> for example, num and den will have the values 1 and 2 respectively. You could output the number that v2_3 represents at runtime with the following statement:

```
std::cout << "The v2_3 type represents " << v2_3::num << "/" << v2_3::den << std::endl;
```

Arithmetic operations between ratio types are defined by further template types, so the compiler does the work. Here's how you could add 2/3 and 3/7:

```
using v2_3 = ratio<2, 3>;                // A type to represent two thirds
using v3_7 = ratio<3, 7>;                // A type to represent three sevenths
using sum = std::ratio_add<v2_3, v3_7>;  // A type representing the sum of 2/3 and 3/7
std::cout << sum::num << "/" << sum::den << std::endl;    // Output: 23/21
```

An instance of ratio_add<T1,T2> is a specialization of the ratio template, ratio<T3,T4>. T3 and T4 will be values that correspond to the numerator and denominator for the result of the addition. Because it's a specialization of the ratio type, the sum type has static members, num and den, that represent the numerator and denominator for the rational number that results from the operation, so we are able to output these.

You don't have to define an alias for each ratio type. The compiler can deduce the type. You could define the addition as:

```
using sum = ratio_add< ratio<2, 3>, ratio<3, 7>>;  // A type for the sum of 2/3 and 3/7
```

This does the same as the previous definition of the sum alias. There are other template types that represent arithmetic operations between rational numbers:

- A ratio_subtract<T1, T2> type instance is a ratio type that represents the result of subtracting the value represented by type T2 from the value represented by type T1.

- A ratio_multiply<T1, T2> type instance is a ratio type that represents the product of the values represented by types T1 and T2.

- A ratio_divide<T1, T2> type instance is a ratio type that represents the result of dividing the value represented by type T1 by the value represented by type T2.

All of these work at compile time, result in a specialization of the ratio template, and you can apply them in any combination you like. The result is a ratio type so the result is always in its lowest terms. This minimizes the risk of either the numerator or the denominator exceeding the capacity of the integer type after multiple arithmetic operations. There are checks for a zero denominator too. Here's an example of arithmetic with ratio type instances:

```
using result = std::ratio_multiply<std::ratio_add<ratio<2, 3>, ratio<3, 7>>, ratio<15>>;
std::cout << result::num << "/" << result::den << std::endl; // Output: 115/7
```

The definition of result produces a ratio instance that results from (2/3+3/7)*15. The value it represents is shown in the comment.

There are templates for representing the result of comparing the values that two ratio types represent and the comparisons are evident from the template type names:

```
ratio_equal<RT1, RT2>          ratio_less<RT1, RT2>        ratio_less_equal<RT1, RT2>
ratio_not_equal<RT1, RT2>      ratio_greater<RT1, RT2>     ratio_greater_equal<RT1, RT2>
```

The template parameters are instances of the `ratio` template that represent rational numbers. Each comparison template type has a static `bool` member, `value`, which will be `true` if the comparison of the numbers the `ratio` types represent results in `true`. You can use this at runtime to check on relationships between `ratio` instances:

```
using div1 = std::ratio_divide<ratio<7, 10>, ratio<11, 7>>;
using div2 = std::ratio_divide<ratio<9, 5>, ratio<3, 7>>;
std::cout << "(7/10)/(11/7) "
          << (std::ratio_greater<div1, div2>::value ? "is" : "is_not")
          << " greater than (9/5)/(3/7)" << std::endl;
```

All the types for comparing `ratio` types define the operator `bool()` and the function call operator, `operator()()`. The former allows an object of a comparison type to be implicitly converted to type `bool`, so you could write:

```
std::ratio_greater<div1, div2> cmp;
std::cout << "(7/10)/(11/7) " << (cmp ? "is" : "is_not") << " greater than (9/5)/(3/7)"
                                                          << std::endl;
```

The first statement creates an object that represents the result of comparing the `ratio` types. The `cmp` object is implicitly converted to type `bool` in the output statement by calling it's `operator bool()` member.

You could also write the output statement as:

```
std::cout << "(7/10)/(11/7) " << (cmp() ? "is" : "is_not") << " greater than (9/5)/(3/7)"
                                                            << std::endl;
```

This calls `operator()()` for the `cmp` object, which returns the value member so the result is the same. Of course, the result of the comparison is `false`.

The `ratio` header also defines the following aliases for `ratio` type instances that represent useful SI ratios:

SI Prefix	Value	Type Alias	Value
deca	10	deci	10^{-1}
hecto	10^2	centi	10^{-2}
kilo	10^3	milli	10^{-3}
mega	10^6	micro	10^{-6}
giga	10^9	nano	10^{-9}
tera	10^{12}	pico	10^{-12}
peta	10^{15}	femto	10^{-15}
exa	10^{18}	atto	10^{-18}
zetta	10^{21}	zepto	10^{-21}
yotta	10^{24}	yocto	10^{-24}

The types that represent integral constants all have the second template parameter and thus the den member as the default value 1; for the others it's the first template parameter and thus the num member that is 1. The types yocto, zepto, zetta, and yotta won't be defined if the maximum value representable by type `intmax_t` on your system is not large enough. These constants are useful in minimizing the possibility of error, particularly when you need to use the very large or very small SI ratios. It's easy to put too many or too few zeroes by mistake.

The statements I have shown demonstrate how the `ratio` template type works, but what is it for? You are not going to be using it for doing vast amounts of computation at compile time. Its purpose is to allow rational numbers to be defined easily at compile time, specifically via template parameter values. Performing any necessary arithmetic operations with these at compile time helps avoid the possibility of overflow. You'll meet an STL template in the next section that requires you to supply a ratio template type instance as a template parameter value.

Temporal Templates

There's often a need to work with time intervals in a program. Game programs are an obvious context where this is likely to be necessary and there's a requirement to measure execution performance for many applications. Of course, measuring time does not just involve software. The underlying hardware provides the clocks and interval timing capabilities and the STL capabilities that your implementation provides is the interface to the hardware via the operating system. All the time functionality that the STL provides will ultimately connect with the timers in the hardware via the interfaces provided by your operating system.

The `chrono` header defines classes and class templates that relate to time intervals or durations, instants in time, and clocks. As you'll see later, you are likely to want to use the facilities of the `ctime` header with times from clocks. All names in the `chrono` header are defined within the `std::chrono` namespace. Time intervals, instants in time, and clocks are interrelated, and the relationships between these are as follows:

- A *duration* is a time interval defined as a number of time *ticks*, where you specify what a tick is in terms of seconds. Thus a tick is the base period for measuring a duration. Objects of types that are instances of the `duration` template define durations. The default time interval represented by a tick is one second but you can define it as some multiple or fraction of a second. For example, if you define a tick as 3600 seconds it implies that a duration of 10 is 10 hours; you could also define a tick as a tenth of second for instance, in which case a duration of 10 represents one second.

- A *clock* records the passage of time from a given fixed instant – called an *epoch*. An epoch is a fixed *time point*. There are three class types that encapsulate hardware clocks and I'll describe these later. Time is measured in ticks so a given *clock* will be defined by an *epoch* and a duration that determines the *tick* period.

- An instance in time is called a *time point*, which will be represented by an object of the `time_point` class template type. A time point is a *duration* relative to a time start point, where the time start point is an *epoch* that is defined by a *clock*. Thus a given time point will be defined by a *clock* that provides the epoch and a *duration* that defines the number of ticks relative to the epoch and the tick period.

We'll start by looking at how you define a duration and what you can do with it.

Defining Durations

The std::chrono::duration<T,P> template type in the chrono header represents *durations*. The template parameter T is the type for the value, which is typically one of the fundamental arithmetic types, and the value corresponding to the parameter P is the number of seconds that a *tick* represents, which is the number of seconds that will correspond to a value of 1. The value for P must be specified by a ratio type and it has a default of ratio<1>. Here are some examples of durations:

```
std::chrono::duration<int,
std::milli> IBM650_divide {15};              // A tick is 1 millisecond so 15 milliseconds
std::chrono::duration<int> minute {60};       // A tick is 1 second by default so 60 seconds
std::chrono::duration<double, ratio<60>> hour {60}; // A tick is 60 seconds so 60 minutes

// A tick is a microsecond so 1 millisecond
std::chrono::duration<long, std::micro> millisec {1000L};

// A tick is fifth of a second so 1.1 seconds
std::chrono::duration<double, ratio<1,5>> tiny {5.5};
```

The first statement uses the milli alias from the ratio header that corresponds to ratio<1, 1000>. The second statement omits the second template parameter value so it is ratio<1>, which means the duration is in units of 1 second. In the third statement the ratio<60> template parameter values specifies that a tick is 60 seconds thus the value of the hour object is measured in minutes and its initial value represents an hour. The fourth statement uses the micro type that the ratio header defines to be ratio<1, 1000000> so a tick is a microsecond and the millisec variable has an initial value that represents a millisecond. The last statement defines an object where a tick is one-fifth of a second and the initial value of tiny is 5.5 fifths, which is 1.1 seconds.

The chrono header defines aliases in the std::chrono namespace for commonly used duration types with values of an integer type. The standard aliases are:

```
nanoseconds<integer_type, std::nano>        microseconds<integer_type, std::micro>
milliseconds<integer_type, std::milli>      seconds<integer_type>
minutes<integer_type, std::ratio<60>>       hours<integer_type, std::ratio<3600>>
```

The integer type for the value of a duration with each of these aliases depends on your implementation but the C++ 14 standard requires that they allow a duration of at least 292 years, positive or negative. On my system the types hours and minutes store a duration as type int and the others store it as type long long. Thus you could define the millisec variable in the previous code fragment as:

```
std::chrono::microseconds millisec {1000};   // Duration is type long long on my system
```

This is *not* the exact equivalent of the previous definition for millisec on my system because the first type argument previously was long - here it's long long. You could also define millisec like this:

```
std::chrono::milliseconds millisec {1};      // Duration is also type long long on my system
```

Of course, this definition is even more different from the original. The initial value of the variable represents the same time interval - 1 millisecond - but the time unit for the duration here is one millisecond, whereas in the previous statement it's one microsecond. The former definition for millisec allows a much more accurate representation of a duration.

Arithmetic Operations between Durations

You can apply the prefix and postfix increment and decrement operators to a duration object and you can obtain the number of ticks an object represents by calling the count() member. Here's code that illustrates this:

```
std::chrono::duration<double, ratio<1,5>> tiny {5.5};      // Measured in 1/5 second
std::chrono::microseconds very_tiny {100};                 // Measured in microseconds
++tiny;
very_tiny--;
std::cout << "tiny = " << tiny.count()
          << " very_tiny = " << very_tiny.count()
          << std::endl;                                    // tiny = 6.5 very_tiny = 99
```

You can apply any of the binary arithmetic operators, +, -, *, /, and % to duration objects and obtain a duration object as the result. These are implemented as non-member operator functions. Here's an example:

```
std::chrono::duration<double, ratio<1,5>> tiny {5.5};
std::chrono::duration<double, ratio<1,5>> small {7.5};
auto total = tiny + small;
std::cout << "total = " << total.count() << std::endl;     // total = 13
```

The arithmetic operators also work with operands of types that can be different instances of the std::chrono::duration<T,P> template where both template arguments can be different. This is achieved by converting both operands to their common type using a specialization of the common_type<class... T> template that is defined in the type_traits header. For arguments of types duration<T1, P1> and duration <T2, P2>, the return value will be a duration type, duration<T3, P3>. T3 will be the common type between T1 and T2; this will be the type that would result from applying an arithmetic operation to values of these types. P3 will be the greatest common divisor for P1 and P2. An example will make this clearer:

```
std::chrono::milliseconds ten_minutes {600000};   // A tick is 1 millisecond so 10 minutes
std::chrono::minutes half_hour {30};              // A tick is 1 minute so 30 minutes
auto total = ten_minutes + half_hour;             // 40 minutes in common tick period
std::cout << "total = " << total.count()
          << std::endl;                           // total = 2400000
```

The result of the addition has to be 40 minutes so you can deduce that total is an object of type milliseconds. Here's another example:

```
std::chrono::minutes ten_minutes {10};                           // 10 minutes
std::chrono::duration<double, std::ratio<1,5>> interval {4500.0}; // 15 minutes
auto total_minutes = ten_minutes + interval;
std::cout << "total minutes = " << total_minutes.count()
          << std::endl;                                           // total minutes = 7500
```

The type for the value for total_minutes is double. We know that the result has to be 25 minutes, which is 1500 seconds; the value of the result is 7500 so its tick period is ratio<1,5> – a fifth of a second. I think it's better to avoid arithmetic with mixed duration types as far as possible because it's too easy to lose track of what a tick is.

All the arithmetic operators that you can apply to duration objects can be used in compound assignments where the left operation is a duration object. The right operand with these += and -= operations must be a duration object. With *= and /= the right operand must be a numerical value of the same type as the tick count for the left operand, or can be implicitly converted to it. The right operand for %= can be a duration object or a numerical value. They each produce the result you might expect. For example, here's code that uses +=:

```
std::chrono::minutes short_time {20};
std::chrono::minutes shorter_time {10};
short_time += shorter_time;                                    // 30 minutes
std::chrono::hours long_time {3};                              // 3hrs = 180 minutes
short_time += long_time;
std::cout << "short_time = " << short_time.count() << std::endl; // short_time = 210
```

The operands for the first += operation are both of the same type so the value stored in the object that is the right operand is added to the left operand. For the second += operation the operands are different types but the right operand is implicitly converted to the type of the left operand. This is possible because the conversion is to a duration type with a shorter tick period. It won't work in the opposite direction – so you cannot use += with long_time as the left operand and the right operand as short_time.

Conversions between Duration Types

In general, one duration type can always be implicitly converted to another duration type if they are both floating-point duration values. For integer values an implicit conversion is only possible when the tick period of the source type is an integral multiple of the tick period of the destination type. Here are some examples:

```
std::chrono::duration<int, std::ratio<1, 5>> d1 {50};    // 10 seconds
std::chrono::duration<int, std::ratio<1, 10>> d2 {50};   // 5 seconds
std::chrono::duration<int, std::ratio<1, 3>> d3 {45};    // 15 seconds
std::chrono::duration<int, std::ratio<1, 6>> d4 {60};    // 10 seconds
d2 += d1;                          // OK - implicit conversion of d1
d1 += d2;                          // Won't compile 1/10 not a multiple of 1/5
d1 += d3;                          // Won't compile 1/3 not a multiple of 1/5
d4 += d3;                          // OK - implicit conversion of d3
```

You can force a conversion by specifying it explicitly using the duration_cast template. Here's an example that assumes d1 and d2 have their initial values as defined in the code above:

```
d1 += std::chrono::duration_cast<std::chrono::duration<int, std::ratio<1, 5>>>(d2);
std::cout << d1.count() << std::endl;                    // 75 - i.e. 15 seconds
```

The first statement uses duration_cast to allow the operation to increment d1 by the duration d2 to proceed. The result is exact in this instance but this won't always be the case. For example:

```
std::chrono::duration<int, std::ratio<1, 5>> d1 {50};    // 10 seconds
std::chrono::duration<int, std::ratio<1, 10>> d2 {53};   // 5.3 seconds
d1 += std::chrono::duration_cast<std::chrono::duration<int, std::ratio<1, 5>>>(d2);
std::cout << d1.count() << std::endl;                    // 76 - i.e. 15.2 seconds
```

You cannot express the sum of the duration values d1 and d2 as an integral multiple of .2 seconds so the value of the result is slightly out. If the value for d2 was 54, the correct result of 77 would be obtained.

The duration type supports assignment so you can assign the value of one duration object to another. Implicit conversion will apply if the condition I described at the beginning of this section applies; otherwise you need to cast the right operand explicitly.

For example, you can write the following:

```
std::chrono::duration<int, std::ratio<1, 5>> d1 {50};        // 10 seconds
std::chrono::duration<int, std::ratio<1, 10>> d2 {53};       // 5.3 seconds
d2 = d1;                                                      // d2 is 100 = 10 seconds
```

Comparing Durations

You have a full complement of operators for comparing two duration objects. These are implemented as non-member functions and allow duration objects of different types to be compared. The process determines the tick period that is common to the operands and compares the duration values when represented in the common tick period. For example:

```
std::chrono::duration<int, std::ratio<1, 5>> d1 {50};        // 10 seconds
std::chrono::duration<int, std::ratio<1, 10>> d2 {50};       // 5 seconds
std::chrono::duration<int, std::ratio<1, 3>> d3 {45};        // 15 seconds
if((d1 - d2) == (d3 - d1))
  std::cout << "both durations are "
          << std::chrono::duration_cast<std::chrono::seconds>(d1 - d2).count()
          << " seconds" << std::endl;
```

This shows comparing duration objects that result from arithmetic operations. They are equal of course so the output will be produced. The cast to type seconds allows the integral number of seconds to be presented, regardless of the duration type of the result. If you wanted non-integral values for the number of seconds, you could cast to type duration<double>.

Duration Literals

The chrono header defines operators that enable you to specify literals that are duration object. These operators are defined in the std::literals::chrono_literals namespace where the namespaces literals and chrono_literals are inline. You can use the literal operators for duration literals with the declaration:

```
using namespace std::literals::chrono_literals;
```

However, this declaration is automatically included if you specify the declaration:

```
using namespace std::chrono;
```

466

You specify a duration literal as an integer or floating- point value and a suffix that specifies the tick period. There are six suffixes you can use:

- h is hours. 3h or 1.5h for example.

- min is minutes. 20min or 3.5min for example.

- s is seconds, 10s or 1.5s for example.

- ms is milliseconds. 500ms or 1.5ms for example.

- us is microseconds. 500us or 0.5us for example.

- ns is nanoseconds. 2ns or 3.5ns for example.

If a duration literal has an integral value, it will be the appropriate alias type from those defined in the chrono header so 24h will be a literal of type std::chrono::hours for example and 25ms will be of type std::chrono::milliseconds. If the value for a literal is not integral, the literal will be a duration type with a floating-point value type. The period for floating-point values will depend on the suffix; for suffixes h, min, s, ms, us, and ns, the tick periods will be ratio<3600>, ratio<60>, and ratio<1>, milli, micro, and nano respectively.

Here's an illustration of some of the ways they can be used:

```
using namespace std::literals::chrono_literals;
std::chrono::seconds elapsed {10};      // 10 seconds
elapsed += 2min;                        // Adding type minutes to type seconds: 130 seconds
elapsed -= 15s;                         // 115 seconds
```

The duration literals are very useful when you need to change intervals by amounts such as those illustrated. Keep in mind that for arithmetic to be possible, the tick period of the value that is the right operand must be an integral multiple of the tick period for the left operand. For instance:

```
elapsed += 100ns;          // Won't compile!
```

The elapsed variable has a tick period of 1 and you cannot add a duration with a period of less than 1 to it. You can use literals to define variables of the same type as the literal. For example:

```
auto some_time = 10s;        // Variable of type seconds, value 10
elapsed = 3min - some_time;  // Set to difference between literal and variable: result 170
some_time *= 2;              // Doubles the value - now 20s
const auto FIVE_SEC = 5s;    // Cannot be changed
elapsed = 2s + (elapsed - FIVE_SEC)/5; // Result 35
```

Here, some_time will be a variable of type seconds, which is type duration<long long, ratio<1>>, and a value of 10. The third statement illustrates that you can change the value of some_time. FIVE_SEC is of type const seconds, so you cannot change its value. The last statement shows an arithmetic expression involving a duration literal, a duration variable, a const seconds object, and an integer literal.

Clocks and Time Points

The clock types that the STL defines provide the interface to the hardware clock or clocks via the operating system. A clock has a tick period and time is measured by a clock as a number of ticks. You have three kinds of clocks defined in the std::chrono namespace:

- The system_clock class encapsulates the current real clock time. Although time generally increases with this clock, it may decrease at any time. Of course, wall clock time can decrease when it's adjusted seasonally between winter and summer. It will also change if it moves to a different time zone.

- The steady_clock class encapsulates a clock suitable for recording time intervals. This clock always increases – it cannot be decremented.

- An instance of the high_resolution_clock is a clock with the shortest tick period available on the current system. With some implementations, this may be just an alias for system_clock or steady_clock, in which case it provides no additional resolution.

Each clock type defines its own epoch and duration. The duration determines the tick period for the clock and the type for recording the number of ticks relative to the epoch. A clock is *steady* if the time it records always increases, and always increases in steps of the same length – the time between clock ticks is constant in other words. This is not true of all clocks. A system_clock is not usually a steady clock because it is not guaranteed to be always increasing and system activity can affect the time between registering ticks. This is why the steady_clock type is preferred for measuring time intervals.

Each clock type encapsulates a clock that is physical hardware – as part of your processor or a chip elsewhere – but having three clock class types does not mean that you necessarily have three distinct clocks. There's no need and little point to create clock objects. The clock types provide their interface to a hardware clock through static members.

All three clock types have a public static data member is_steady that is of type bool. The value of this member indicates whether or not the clock is a steady clock. is_steady is *always* true for a steady_clock, and can be true or false for the other clock types, depending on your implementation. Having said that, is_steady is usually false for a system_clock. If your code depends on having a steady clock, you should always check the state of the is_steady member - or just use steady_clock. It's easy to check for a steady clock:

```
std::cout << std::boolalpha << std::chrono::system_clock::is_steady << std::endl;
```

This statement outputs false on my system, and probably will on yours too. Of course, if the high_resolution_clock type is an alias for system_clock, you only have one steady clock. Every clock class defines the following type aliases as members:

- rep is an alias for the arithmetic type for recording a number of ticks

- period is an alias for a ratio template type that defines a tick in seconds

- duration is an alias for std::chrono::duration<rep, period>

- time_point is an alias for the time point type that represent an instant in time for the clock. This will be std::chrono::time_point<std::chrono::Clock_Type>.

So when you need to know the period for a clock of type system_clock, the expression system_clock::period provides it. This is a ratio type so the numerical value for the number of seconds a tick represents is system_clock::period::num divided by system_clock::period::den.

Creating Time Points

A `time_point` object represents an instant in time that is measured relative to an epoch, which is defined by a clock. Thus a `time_point` object is always defined based on an epoch, and a duration relative to that epoch. When you ask a clock for the time, you get a `time_point` object. The `std::chrono::time_point` class template defines `time_point` types. This template has two type parameters, a clock type, `Clock` – which will provide the epoch, and a duration type – which will be the `duration` type that the `Clock` type defines by default. Thus when you define a `time_point` object where the first template type parameter value is `std::chrono::system_clock`, the default value for the second type parameter will be `std::chrono::system_clock::duration`.

A `time_point` object always relates to a specific clock type so it's usually convenient to use the `time_point` type alias that is a member of a particular clock type when you create an object. However, you can specify the clock type as a template parameter value if you wish. For example:

```
std::chrono::system_clock::time_point tp_sys1;               // Default object - the epoch
std::chrono::time_point<std::chrono::system_clock> tp_sys2;  // Default object - the epoch
```

Both statements call the default `time_point<system_clock>` constructor. The default constructor creates an object that represents the epoch for the type of clock you specify so the duration is 0. The first statement is less verbose and is therefore preferable. You can make the code even less verbose by defining aliases for clock and time point types, and I'll do that in subsequent code.

You can create a `time_point` object that represents an instant relative to an epoch using a `duration` argument to the constructor. The `duration` object defines the time to be added to the epoch:

```
using Clock = std::chrono::steady_clock;
using TimePoint = std::chrono::time_point<Clock>;
TimePoint tp1 {std::chrono::duration<int> (20)};            // Epoch + 20 seconds
TimePoint tp2 {3min};                                       // Epoch + 180 seconds
TimePoint tp3 {2h};                                         // Epoch + 720 seconds
TimePoint tp4 {5500us};                                     // Epoch + 0.0055 seconds
```

These statements illustrate that the `duration` object you pass to the `time_point` constructor can have any tick period. The `TimePoint` alias could also be defined with this directive:

```
using TimePoint = Clock::time_point;
```

You can define a `time_point` object with a tick period that is different from that of the clock type defining the epoch. For example:

```
std::chrono::time_point<std::chrono::system_clock, std::chrono::minutes> tp {2h};
```

This is not something you would do unless you had a good reason. This defines a `time_point` object, `tp`, with the epoch defined by the `system_clock` type, the period as minutes with the initial value as the duration literal that represents two hours.

Durations of Time Points

You can obtain a duration object from a time_point object that represents the elapsed time since the epoch by calling its time_since_epoch() function member:

```
using Clock = std::chrono::steady_clock;
using TimePoint = Clock::time_point;
TimePoint tp1 {std::chrono::duration<int> (20)};        // Epoch + 20 seconds
auto elapsed = tp1.time_since_epoch();                  // Duration for the time interval
```

Now you have the duration object, you have the time it represents. You don't know the type for the elapsed object but you know it is a duration type and therefore you can cast it to a known duration type. For instance, you can obtain the number of nanoseconds that elapsed represents like this:

```
auto ticks_ns = std::chrono::duration_cast<std::chrono::nanoseconds>(elapsed).count();
```

The value of ticks_ns is the number of nanoseconds in the interval that elapsed represents. Of course, if you don't need the time to nanosecond resolution, you can cast it to one of the other duration type aliases such as milliseconds, seconds, or hours. You could use the time_since_epoch() function to define a function template that will display the interval that any time_point represents in seconds:

```
// Outputs the exact interval in seconds for a time_point<>
template<typename TimePoint>
void print_timepoint(const TimePoint& tp, size_t places = 0)
{
  auto elapsed = tp.time_since_epoch();            // duration object for the interval

  auto seconds = std::chrono::duration_cast<std::chrono::duration<double>>(elapsed).count();
  std::cout << std::fixed << std::setprecision(places) << seconds << " seconds\n";
}
```

Casting the elapsed object using duration_cast<double> produces a duration object that contains the tick count as a double value and the tick period as one second. Calling count() for this object returns the time in seconds as a value of type double. The value is written out with the number of places after the decimal point determined by the second argument. We'll use the print_timepoint() function template in a working example in the next section.

Arithmetic with Time Points

There's a copy assignment operator for time_point objects and you can add a duration object to a time_point or subtract a duration from it. The result of addition or subtraction is a new time_point object where the interval is that of the original time_point adjusted by the duration object. Addition and subtraction are implemented as non-member operator functions. You can also use += and -= operators with the right operand as a duration object to increment or decrement a time_point object. These are function members of the time_point object that is the left operand. Here's a complete program that demonstrates these operations:

```
// Ex10_04.cpp
// Arithmetic with time-point objects
#include <iostream>                              // For standard streams
#include <iomanip>                               // For stream manipulators
```

```
#include <chrono>                                    // For duration, time_point templates
#include <ratio>                                     // For ratio templates
using namespace std::chrono;

// Function template for print_timepoint() goes here...

int main()
{
  using TimePoint = time_point<steady_clock>;
  time_point<steady_clock> tp1 {duration<int>(20)};
  time_point<system_clock> tp2 {3min};
  time_point<high_resolution_clock> tp3 {2h};
  std::cout << "tp1 is ";
  print_timepoint(tp1);

  std::cout << "tp2 is ";
  print_timepoint(tp2);

  std::cout << "tp3 is ";
  print_timepoint(tp3);

  auto tp4 = tp2 + tp3.time_since_epoch();
  std::cout << "tp4 is tp2 with tp3 added: ";
  print_timepoint(tp4);

  std::cout << "tp1 + tp2 is ";
  print_timepoint(tp1 + tp2.time_since_epoch());

  tp2 += duration<time_point<system_clock>::rep, std::milli> {20'000};
  std::cout << "tp2 incremented by 20,000 milliseconds is ";
  print_timepoint(tp2);
}
```

The using directive for the std::chrono namespace makes the type names available without qualification and implicitly includes the namespace containing the operator functions for duration literals. This example shows various applications of arithmetic with time_point objects that relate to different types of clocks. The arithmetic always involves adding a duration to a time_point. The duration you obtain from a time_point object has no specific knowledge of the clock from which the interval originated, so you can add it to a time_point based on a different clock. The output makes it clear what happens:

```
tp1 is 20 seconds
tp2 is 180 seconds
tp3 is 7200 seconds
tp4 is tp2 with tp3 added: 7380 seconds
tp1 + tp2 is 200 seconds
tp2 incremented by 20,000 milliseconds is 200 seconds
```

You can cast a time_point object to an object of a time_point type with a different duration. The new object will have the epoch from the same clock as the source object. If the duration of the destination has a lower resolution tick than the source, data can be lost in the process. The time_point_cast template in the std::chrono namespace does the conversion; the template type parameter value is the new duration type. For example:

```
using TimePoint = std::chrono::time_point<std::chrono::system_clock, std::chrono::seconds>;
TimePoint tp_sec {75s};                            // 75 seconds
auto tp_min = std::chrono::time_point_cast<std::chrono::minutes>(tp_sec);
print_timepoint(tp_min);                           // 60 seconds
```

Because the cast converts to minutes, the extra 15 seconds in the original duration is lost.

Comparing Time Points

You can compare two time_point objects for a given clock using any of the operators ==, !=, <, <=, >=, and >. The result of a comparison is produced by comparing the result of calling time_since_epoch() for the operands. While the time_point objects must relate to the same clock, they can have different tick periods and the comparison will take account of that. Here is some code showing examples of their use:

```
using TimePoint1 = std::chrono::time_point<std::chrono::system_clock>;
using TimePoint2 = std::chrono::time_point<std::chrono::system_clock, std::chrono::minutes>;
TimePoint1 tp1 {120s};
TimePoint2 tp2 {2min};
std::cout << "tp1 ticks: "    << tp1.time_since_epoch().count()
        << "  tp2 ticks: " << tp2.time_since_epoch().count() << std::endl;
std::cout << "tp1 is " << ((tp1 == tp2) ? "equal":"not equal") << " to tp2" << std::endl;
```

The output produce by these statements is:

```
tp1 ticks: 1200000000   tp2 ticks: 2
tp1 is equal to tp2
```

From the output you can see the tick counts for tp1 and tp2 are not at all the same because the ticks represent different amounts of time, but tp1 and tp2 represent the same instant in time measured from the epoch of the system_clock so they return true when compared for equality. All the comparison operators compare time_point objects in terms of the time periods they represent, not their tick counts.

Operations with Clocks

Apart from the default constructor that each clock type has, all function members of the clock types are static. All clocks include an epoch that is a fixed time point, a duration, and a static member now() that returns a time_point object that represents the current time. All clock classes define the following type aliases as members:

- rep is the type used to record a number of ticks.

- period is a type that defines the tick period, and it will be an instance of the ratio template. The ratio of the static num and den members of this type define the time period for a clock tick in seconds.

- duration is the duration type that records the number of ticks since the epoch and will correspond to the type std::chrono::duration<rep, period>.

- time_point is the type for time point values that the now() function member of a clock returns. This will be the template type std::chrono::time_point<clock_type>.

In addition to the now() function that all three clock types implement, the system_clock type defines two further function members that are static. These provide conversions between objects of a time_point type, which will be std::chrono::time_point<std::chrono::system_clock>, and objects of type std::time_t, which is the type defined in the ctime header for representing time intervals. The to_time_t() member of system_clock accepts a time_point argument and returns it as type time_t, and the from_time_t() member does the reverse. The to_time_t() function is particularly useful because it enables you to convert a time_point object that the now() member of system_clock returns to a string that represents the calendar time – the time, day, and date – using the capabilities provided by the ctime header. The ctime header is the C++ version of the C header time.h. Some of the functions in the ctime header are deprecated because they are unsafe but there are no alternatives in the Standard Library at present for some of them. There are a variety of ways you can use the functions defined in the ctime header to obtain a string containing the time, day, and date. I'll just show how you could output this information and leave it to you to explore the ctime header further:

```
using Clock = std::chrono::system_clock;
auto instant = Clock::now();                      // Returns type std::chrono::time_point<Clock>
std::time_t the_time = Clock::to_time_t(instant);
std::cout << std::put_time(std::localtime(&the_time),
                "The time now is: %R.%nToday is %A %e %B %Y. The time zone is %Z.%n");
```

■ **Note** Using localtime() may result in in a compiler error because the function is unsafe. The alternatives are not standard C++ – localtime_s() with Microsoft Visual Studio 2015 or localtime_r() with Linux compilers, so I have used localtime() in the code. Use whichever is appropriate in your environment when you compile this.

The output from executing this on my system at this moment is:

```
The time now is: 13:27.
Today is Thursday  3 September 2015. The time zone is GMT Summer Time.
```

The localtime() function from the ctime header accepts a pointer to a time_t object and returns a pointer to an internal static object of type tm. This is passed to the put_time() manipulator that is defined in the iomanip header, which returns an object that is effectively a formatted output function for the tm object pointed to by its first argument. The second argument is a format string that determines how the data stored in the tm object is presented. There are a large number of conversion specifiers, each preceded by %, that specify how and in what sequence the various data members of a tm object are displayed.

A tm object is a struct containing the following members of type int:

- tm_sec (0 to 60), tm_min (0 to 59), and tm_hour (0 to 23) are the second, minute, and hour specifying the time.

- tm_mday (1 to 31), tm_mon (0 to 11), tm_year specify day, month and year for the date.

- tm_wday (0 to 6) and tm_yday (0 to 365) specify the day in the week and the day in the year.

- tm_isdst has a positive value if daylight saving time is in effect, is zero if it is not, and negative if the information is not available.

You can access any of these values through the pointer that the local_time() function returns – like this for example:

```cpp
std::time_t t = Clock::to_time_t(Clock::now());
auto p_tm = std::localtime(&t);
std::cout << "Time: " << p_tm->tm_hour << ':'
                      << std::setfill('0') << std::setw(2) << p_tm->tm_min
                      << std::endl;                    // Time: 15:06
```

There is a range of format specifiers in the put_time() format string that are specific to the members of the tm struct, and they are each preceded by the % character. Examples are %H to write tm_hour as a 24-hour clock value and %I to write it as a 12-hour clock value, %A to write tm_wkday as a full-day name, and %B to write tm_mon as full-month name. The format specifiers for members of a tm object can be in any sequence and you can include other text as necessary in the format string including %n to get a newline and %t for a tab. There are many other format specifier for tm data members that you'll find in the documentation for put_time() in your C++ Standard Library.

Timing Execution

It's often useful to be able to measure the elapsed time for execution in a program and you can do this easily using a clock. To illustrate this, we can add code to main() in Ex10_03 to determine how long it takes to solve a set of equations and to output the elapsed time. Here's the code for Ex10_05.cpp:

```cpp
// Ex10_05.cpp
// Determining the time to solve a set of linear equations
#include <valarray>                      // For valarray, slice, abs()
#include <vector>                        // For vector container
#include <iterator>                      // For ostream iterator
#include <algorithm>                     // For generate_n()
#include <utility>                       // For swap()
#include <iostream>                      // For standard streams
#include <iomanip>                       // For stream manipulators
#include <string>                        // For string type
#include <chrono>                        // For clocks, duration, and time_point
using std::string;
using std::valarray;
using std::slice;
using namespace std::chrono;

// Function prototypes
valarray<double> get_data(size_t n);
void reduce_matrix(valarray<double>& equations, std::vector<slice>& row_slices);
valarray<double> back_substitution(valarray<double>& equations,
                                   const std::vector<slice>& row_slices);

// Code for print_timepoint() template goes here...

int main()
{
// Code to read the data for the equations as in Ex10_03.cpp...
```

```
auto start_time = steady_clock::now();                    // time_point object

// Code to generate slice objects for rows as in Ex10_03.cpp...

// Code to solve equations as in Ex10_03.cpp...

auto end_time = steady_clock::now();                      // time_point object
auto elapsed = end_time - start_time.time_since_epoch();
std::cout << "Time to solve " << n_rows << " equations is ";
print_timepoint(elapsed);

// Code to output the solution as in Ex10_03.cpp...
}
```

This makes use of the print_timepoint() function template you saw earlier in this chapter and, of course, the gaussian.cpp file from Ex10_03 is also needed. The complete program is in the code download as Ex10_05. Timing the solution process only requires one statement preceding the solution code in main(), and four statements following it. Similar code could be used for timing a computation in any application. On my system I got this output for solving six equations:

```
Enter the number of variables: 6
Enter 7 values for each of 6 equations.
(i.e. including coefficients that are zero and the rhs):
 1  1  1  1  1  1   8
 2  3 -5 -1  1  1 -18
-1  5  2  7  2  3  40
 3  1 10  2  1 11 -15
 3 17  5  1  3  2  41
 5  7  3 -4  2 -1   9
Time to solve 6 equations is 0.000219379 seconds

Solution:
 x1 =      -2.00
 x2 =       1.00
 x3 =       3.00
 x4 =       4.00
 x5 =       7.00
 x6 =      -5.00
```

It took about 220 microseconds on my system to solve the six equations, which is not bad at all.

Complex Numbers

Complex number are numbers of the form a + bi, where a and b are real numbers – floating-point values in C++ code – and i is $\sqrt{-1}$. a is referred to as the *real* part of a complex number and b that multiplies i is referred to as the *imaginary* part. Applications that use complex numbers tend to be specialized; complex numbers are used in electrical and electromagnetic theory for example, in-digital signal processing, and in mathematics of course. Complex numbers are also used to generate the very pretty fractal images for Mandelbrot sets and Julia sets. Because complex numbers are of narrower interest than other facilities provided by the STL, I'll just introduce the basics in fairly concise form. If you know nothing about complex numbers, you can skip this section.

The complex header defines capabilities for working with complex numbers. Instances of the complex<T> template type represent complex number and there are three specializations of the type defined: complex<float>, complex<double>, and complex<long double>. I'll use complex<double> throughout this section but operations with the other specializations are essentially the same.

Creating Objects That Represent Complex Numbers

There's a constructor for the complex<double> type that accepts two arguments – the first argument is the value of the real part and the second is the value of the imaginary part. For example:

```
std::complex<double> z1 {2, 5};          // 2 + 5i
std::complex<double> z;                   // Default parameter values are 0 so 0 + 0i
```

There's also a copy constructor so you can duplicate z1 like this:

```
std::complex<double> z2 {z1};            // 2 + 5i
```

Clearly you are going to need complex literals as well as complex objects and there are three operator functions defined in the namespace std::literals::complex_literals where the literals and complex_literals namespaces are defined inline. You can access the operator functions for complex literals with a using directive for the std::literals::complex_literals namespace, a using directive for the std::literals namespace, or a using directive for the std::complex_literals namespace. I'll assume one or other of these directives and a using directive for std::complex is in effect for code in the rest of this section.

The operator""i() function defines literals of type complex<double> that have a real part of 0. Thus 3i is a literal that is the equivalent of complex<double>{0, 3}. Of course, you can express a complex number with a real and imaginary part – for example:

```
z = 5.0 + 3i;                            // z is now complex<double>{5, 3}
```

This shows how you define a complex number with both parts nonzero, and incidentally demonstrates that the assignment operator is implemented for complex objects. You use a suffix of if for complex<float> literals and il for complex<long double> literals, for example, 22if or 3.5il. These are defined by the functions operator""if() and operator""il(). Note that you cannot write 1.0+i or 2.0+il because i and il here will be interpreted as variable names; you must write 1.0 +1i and 2.0+1.0il.

All complex types define function members real() and imag(). These can be used to access the real or imaginary parts of an object, or to set those parts by supplying an argument. For example:

```
complex<double> z{1.5, -2.5};            // z:  1.5 - 2.5i
z.imag(99);                              // z:  1.5 + 99.0i
z.real(-4.5);                            // z: -4.5 + 99.0i
std::cout << "Real part: " << z.real()
        << " Imaginary part: " << z.imag()
        << std:: endl;                   // Real part: -4.5 Imaginary part: 99
```

The versions of real() and imag() that accept an argument return nothing.

There are non-member function templates that implement stream extraction and insertion operators for complex objects. When you are reading a complex number from a stream, it can be just the real part, 55 for example, just the real part between parentheses, (2.6), or the real and imaginary parts between braces and separated by a comma like this, (3, -2). If you only supply the real part, the imaginary part will be 0. Here's an example:

```
complex<double> z1, z2, z3;          // 3 default objects 0+0i
std::cout << "Enter 3 complex numbers: ";
std::cin >> z1 >> z2 >> z3;          // Read 3 complex numbers
std::cout << "z1 = " << z1 << " z2 = " << z2 << " z3 = " << z3 << std::endl;
```

Here's an example of the input and the output that results:

```
Enter 3 complex numbers: -4 (6) (-3, 7)
z1 = (-4,0) z2 = (6,0) z3 = (-3,7)
```

If there are no parentheses for the input of a complex number, there cannot be an imaginary part. However, with parentheses you can omit the imaginary part. The output of a complex number always has parentheses around it and the imaginary part is output even when it is 0.

Complex Arithmetic

The complex class template defines non-member functions for the binary operators +, -, *, and / with complex operands and for unary + and - operators. There are function members that define +=, -=, *=, and /=. Here are some examples of their use:

```
complex<double> z {1,2};             // 1+2i
auto z1 = z + 3.0;                   // 4+2i
auto z2 = z*z + (2.0 + 4i);         // -1+8i
auto z3 = z1 - z2;                   // 5-6i
z3 /= z2;                            // -.815385-0.523077i
```

Note that operations between a complex object and a numeric literal requires that the numeric literal is of the correct type. You cannot add an integer literal such as 2 to a complex<double> object; for this to work you must write 2.0.

Comparisons and Other Operations on Complex Numbers

There are non-member function templates for comparing two complex objects for equality or inequality. You also have the == and != operations to compare a complex object with a numeric value, where the numeric value is treated as a complex number with the imaginary part as 0. For equality, both parts must be equal. If the real or imaginary parts of the operands differ, they are not equal. For example:

```
complex<double> z1 {3,4};            // 3+4i
complex<double> z2 {4,-3};           // 4-3i
std::cout << std::boolalpha
        << (z1 == z2) << " "         // false
        << (z1 != (3.0 + 4i)) << " " // false
        << (z2 == 4.0 - 3i)   << '\n'; // true
```

The results in the comments should be clear. Note how the compiler treats 4.0 - 3i as a single complex number in the last comparison.

Another way to compare complex numbers is to compare their *magnitudes*. The magnitude of a complex number is the same as that of a vector with component values the same as the real and imaginary parts, so it's the square root of the sum of the squares of the two parts. The non-member function template abs() accepts an argument of type complex<T> and returns its magnitude as type T. Here's an example of applying the abs() function to z1 and z2 as defined in the previous code fragment:

```
std::cout << std::boolalpha
          << (std::abs(z1) == std::abs(z2))      // true
          << " " <<  std::abs(z2 + 4.0 + 9i);    // 10
```

The last output value is 10 because the expression that is the argument to abs() evaluates to (8.0+6i); 8^2 plus 6^2 is 100 and the square root of that is 10.

There are other non-member function templates that provide properties of a complex number:

- The norm() function template returns the square of the magnitude of a complex number.

- The arg() template returns the phase angle in radians, which for a complex number z corresponds to std::atan(z.imag()/z.real()).

- The conj() function template returns the complex conjugate, which for a number a+bi is a-bi.

- The polar() function template accepts a magnitude and a phase angle as arguments and returns the complex object corresponding to that.

- The proj() function template returns the complex number that is the projection of the complex argument on to the Riemann sphere.

There are non-member function templates that provide a complete set of trigonometric and hyperbolic functions for complex arguments. There are also versions of the cmath functions exp(), pow(), log(), log10(), and sqrt() for complex arguments. Here's an interesting example:

```
complex<double> zc {0.0, std::acos(-1)};
std::cout << (std::exp(zc) + 1.0) << '\n';        // (0, 1.22465e-16) or zero near enough
```

acos(-1) is π so this demonstrates the truth of Euler's astounding equation that shows how π and Euler's number e are related:

$$e^{i\pi} + 1 = 0$$

A Simple Example Using Complex Numbers

This example applies complex numbers to generating a fractal image of a Julia set from the infinite number that are possible. This won't be a brilliant image of a Julia set because it has to be a character-based presentation but it will give you an idea of how it looks. These are usually plotted as colored pixels, but this requires operating system functions. You create a quadratic Julia set by applying the following iterative equation to points, z, in the complex plane:

$z_{n+1} = z_n^2 + c$, where c is a complex constant. The value of c determines the shape of the Julia set.

Each new z is a different point in the complex plane. A Julia set is comprised of points in the complex plane for which the equation can be applied indefinitely without the magnitude of z tending to infinity. Of course, you need a strategy to decide whether or not z is tending to infinity. Within the program, the equation will be applied to the complex number z that represents each pixel a reasonably large number of times, and if the magnitude of z remains less than 2, the point is in the Julia set. If it is greater than 2, most likely it will tend to infinity and is therefore not in the Julia set. The program will use features of the chrono header to determine how long it takes to generate the image. The output looks best if the font is square —I used an 8x8 pixel font. Here's the program code:

```cpp
// Ex10_06.cpp
// Using complex objects to generate a fractal image of a Julia set
#include <iostream>                                    // For standard streams
#include <iomanip>                                     // For stream manipulators
#include <complex>                                     // For complex types
#include <chrono>                                      // For clocks, duration, and time_point
using std::complex;
using namespace std::chrono;
using namespace std::literals;

// Function template definition for print_timepoint() goes here...

int main()
{
  const int width {100}, height {100};                 // Image width and height
  size_t count {100};                                  // Iterate count for recursion
  char image[width][height];
  auto start_time = steady_clock::now();               // time_point object for start
  complex<double> c {-0.7, 0.27015};                   // Constant in z = z*z + c

  for(int i {}; i < width; ++i)                        // Iterate over pixels in the width
  {
    for(int j {}; j < height; ++j)                     // Iterate over pixels in the height
    {
      // Scale real and imaginary parts to be between -1 and +1
      auto re = 1.5*(i - width/2) / (0.5*width);
      auto im = (j - height/2) / (0.5*height);
      complex<double> z {re,im};                       // Point in the complex plane
      image[i][j] = ' ';                               // Point not in the Julia set
      // Iterate z=z*z+c count times
      for(size_t k {}; k < count; ++k)
      {
        z = z*z + c;
      }
      if(std::abs(z) < 2.0)                            // If point not escaping...
        image[i][j] = '*';                             // ...it's in the Julia set
    }
  }
  auto end_time = std::chrono::steady_clock::now();    // time_point object for end
  auto elapsed = end_time - start_time.time_since_epoch();
  std::cout << "Time to generate a Julia set with " << width << "x" << height << " pixels is ";
  print_timepoint(elapsed, 9);

  std::cout << "The Julia set looks like this:\n";
  for(size_t i {}; i < width; ++i)
  {
    for(size_t j {}; j < height; ++j)
      std::cout << image[i][j];
    std::cout << '\n';
  }
}
```

The program uses the print_timepoint() template that you met earlier to output the elapsed time. The complete program code is in the code download as Ex10_06.cpp. I got the following output – the plot of the Julia set is in Figure 10-13:

```
Time to generate a Julia set with 100x100 pixels is 0.286463017 seconds
The Julia set looks like this:
```

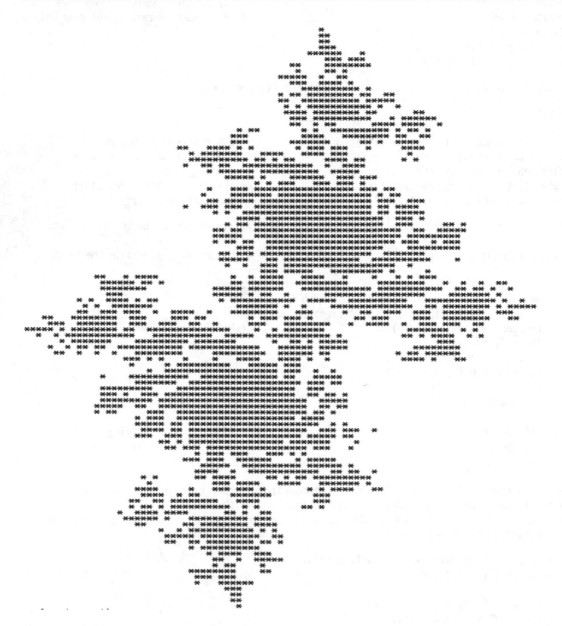

Figure 10-13. *The Julia set generated by Ex10-06*

There's quite a lot of computation involved. On my system it took about a third of a second to compute the points in the set.

Summary

The valarray class template that is defined in the valarray header is intended to enable the compiler to make numerical calculations more efficient than with other arrays or containers and has the potential to allow parallel operations. A valarray object provides a basis for large-scale compute-intensive numerical calculations in C++. Objects of type slice represent one-dimensional sequences of elements distributed at a given interval from the data stored in a valarray. A slice object allows you to express operations on an entire row or column of an array. A gslice object is a generalization of a slice, and represents a set of evenly spaced slice objects. A gslice enables you to express operations to be applied to all the rows or columns it defines.

The ratio header defines the ratio class template and each ratio *type* defines a rational number so there is no need or point to defining ratio objects. The ratio header also defines the following class templates for applying the binary add, subtract, multiply and divide operations to the rational numbers that two ratio types represent:

```
ratio_add<typename R1, typename R2>        ratio_subtract<typename R1, typename R2>
ratio_multiply<typename R1, typename R2>   ratio_divide<typename R1, typename R2>
```

Each of these templates defines a new ratio type that represents the result of the operation. There are also templates that generate a bool value that results from comparing ratio types.

The chrono header defines classes that are the interface to the hardware clocks. Three classes are defined for clocks:

- system_clock represents clock-on-the-wall time and can be used to determine the time and date.

- steady_clock is a monotonic clock that is typically used to measure time intervals.

- high_resolution_clock is the clock that provides the highest resolution for time measurements. This clock type may be an alias for one of the other two clock types.

The clock types only have static members, so there's no need to define clock objects. A clock measures time relative to a fixed instant, called an *epoch*. An instant in time is returned by the now() function member of a clock as an instance of a time_point type that contains a reference to the clock that defines the epoch and the time interval relative to the epoch. An interval of time is represented by an instance of the duration<typename Rep, typename Period=ratio<1>> template. A time interval is a number of *ticks* expressed as a value of type Rep. A tick is the number of seconds defined by the ratio type that is the second duration template type argument; the default value ratio<1> specifies that a tick is 1 second.

The complex<T> class template is defined in the complex header. Instances of the template are types that represent complex numbers with the real and imaginary parts stored as values of type T. There are specializations of the complex template for types float, double, and long double. There is a comprehensive range of functions defined that support operations with complex numbers.

EXERCISES

1. Write a program that generates 100,000 floating-point values that are normally distributed between 1 and 100 and stores them in a `valarray`. Consider the array to be 100 rows of 1000 elements. Calculate and output the mean for each row using `slice` objects.

2. Modify the program from Exercise 1 to calculate the standard deviation for the values in each row in addition to the mean, output the time to complete the calculations, then output the mean and standard deviation for each row. (The formula for the standard deviation is in Chapter 8.) The program should also output the date of execution.

3. Modify the solution for Exercise 2 to output the time in nanoseconds to calculate the standard deviation for each row.

4. Modify `Ex10_06` from this chapter to use a `valarray` to store the image.

5. This exercise is for you if you are a fan of algebra and complex number. Write a program to read the coefficients of an arbitrary quadratic equation:

$$ax^2 + bx + c = 0$$

Use complex objects to determine and output the roots of the equation using the standard formula:

$$x = \frac{-b \pm \sqrt{b^2 - 4ac}}{4ac}$$

Index

Get the eBook for only $5!

Why limit yourself?

Now you can take the weightless companion with you wherever you go and access your content on your PC, phone, tablet, or reader.

Since you've purchased this print book, we're happy to offer you the eBook in all 3 formats for just $5.

Convenient and fully searchable, the PDF version enables you to easily find and copy code—or perform examples by quickly toggling between instructions and applications. The MOBI format is ideal for your Kindle, while the ePUB can be utilized on a variety of mobile devices.

To learn more, go to www.apress.com/companion or contact support@apress.com.

Printed in the United States
By Bookmasters